The Penguin New Zealand Wine Guide

Vic Williams is a widely published wine and food writer. He is Cellar Director for The New Zealand Wine Society and New Zealand wine consultant for Cathay Pacific Airways. His columns and articles appear in newspapers and magazines all over the country, and for 14 years he has broadcast a regular wine and restaurant review on Auckland's top-rating radio station, NewstalkZB. He has appeared as a television presenter on several programmes, is a sought-after speaker for conferences and social functions and has delivered presentations on New Zealand wine and food in Melbourne, Sydney, Seattle, California, New York, Hong Kong and on board cruise liners.

2003

THE PENGUIN
NEW ZEALAND
WINE
GUIDE

Vic Williams

PENGUIN BOOKS

PENGUIN BOOKS

Penguin Books (NZ) Ltd, cnr Airborne and Rosedale Roads, Albany,
Auckland 1310, New Zealand
Penguin Books Ltd, 27 Wrights Lane, London W8 5TZ, England
Penguin Putnam Inc, 375 Hudson Street, New York, NY 10014, United States
Penguin Books Australia Ltd, 250 Camberwell Road,
Camberwell, Vic 3124, Australia
Penguin Books Canada Ltd, 10 Alcorn Avenue, Toronto,
Ontario, Canada M4V 3B2
Penguin Books (South Africa) (Pty) Ltd, 24 Sturdee Avenue,
Rosebank, Johannesburg 2196, South Africa
Penguin Books India (P) Ltd, 11, Community Centre, Panchsheel Park,
New Delhi 110 017, India
Penguin Books Ltd, Registered Offices: Harmondsworth, Middlesex, England

First published by Penguin Books (NZ) Ltd, 2003

1 3 5 7 9 10 8 6 4 2

Copyright © Vic Williams, 2003

Designed and typeset by Egan-Reid Ltd, Auckland
Printed in Australia by McPherson's Printing Group

ISBN 0 14 301816 7

Contents

Introduction

This is the eleventh edition of *The Penguin New Zealand Wine Guide*, and it reviews wines from large and small producers all over the country. New Zealand has nearly 400 wine companies, and almost every one has a range of labels. Even if you visit your local wine store every day, you will have trouble keeping up with the new bottles on the shelves. This *Guide* can't hope to review every bottle out there, but it should help you make the right choice.

Apart from a few that are sampled at trade shows or at the winery, the wines are tasted masked, to ensure impartial analysis. I use a Riedel tasting glass, designed specifically to emphasise the various nuances in any wine. The wines have been listed whether or not they rated well.

There is one overriding thing to remember as you browse through this book. A 'good' wine is one you enjoy – end of story. If you don't enjoy a wine that has won multiple gold medals and trophies, then it's not for you. Learn to trust your palate, and have the confidence to express your opinion. Anyone who says you are 'wrong' is a wine snob. Wine is made to be enjoyed, and if we lose sight of that simple fact, we've lost the whole point of the thing. The assessments in this book are solely mine, and I generally find that most people agree with them – but I am fully aware that taste is a highly individual matter.

The wine descriptions are designed to be as straightforward and user-friendly as I can make them. Occasionally, I have resorted to semi-technical terms to get a particular point across, but these are explained in the Glossary at the back of the book.

Most of the wines should be readily available, and I trust any that are hard to find will prove worth the search.

Wines made exclusively for sale through mail-order clubs and societies are not reviewed, although some that are sold both by mail-order and through retail outlets are listed. I act as a consultant to several of the clubs, and even though most of the labels were masked when I tried the wines for this book, I wanted to avoid any suggestion of conflict of interest. In any case, mail-order wines are invariably accompanied by their own comprehensive tasting notes.

For reasons of space, sparkling, rosé and dessert wines are rated for quality and value, but don't carry full descriptions. Cask wines are not reviewed.

A low and a high figure is listed for each wine because there can be wide variance between retail outlets. If you find a particular wine at a lower price, well done. If it is more expensive, I apologise – but I suggest you shop around.

Collecting details on so many wines each year is a logistical nightmare, and I couldn't manage it without the generous support of the industry. As always, I sincerely thank the winemakers and winery owners for their co-operation.

Wine is designed to be enjoyed in the relaxed company of fine food and good friends. If this *Guide* helps in that enjoyment, my labours have been well worthwhile.

Vic Williams

Vic Williams
February 2003

The Rating System

The rating system used in this book is designed to help you make a quick analysis. Quality is rated in glasses, from one to five, and value in stars. The value ratings are decided by computer, but in some cases they have been modified to take rarity into account.

QUALITY

ŸŸŸŸŸ   Magic in a bottle – a product that encapsulates everything that is good about the winemaker's art.

ŸŸŸŸ𝟋   Excellent wine that will taste every bit as good as a five-glass model in all but the most analytical of circumstances.

ŸŸŸŸ   Excellent wine, only a couple of shades away from a top rating.

ŸŸŸ𝟋   Good, fault-free, eminently drinkable wine with just a touch of class.

ŸŸŸ   It won't make the earth move, but it will be drinkable enough in most situations.

ŸŸ𝟋   Honestly made wine, possibly displaying one or two minor faults but still drinkable.

ŸŸ   An unremarkable wine that needs to be extremely well priced to merit consideration.

𝟋 and Ÿ   No matter how cheap it is, look for something else.

VALUE

☆ ☆ ☆ ☆ ☆ Grab as much as you can afford, quickly. The winemaker is a saint, or the accountant is on extended leave.

☆☆☆☆⯪ A bargain by anybody's standards, well worth buying by the case.

☆☆☆☆ Still great value, but the company isn't quite as generous as some of its competitors.

☆☆☆⯪ Good-value wine, selling for a fraction less than its quality merits.

☆☆☆ A fairly priced wine. You'll get what you pay for.

☆☆⯪ Either the company is being a bit hopeful or the wine is priced partly for its rarity.

☆☆ Cheekily priced wine. The company needs to be jolted back to commercial reality.

☆⯪ At this level, the asking price far exceeds the quality.

☆ Forget it. Keep your wallet or purse firmly shut.

CELLARING TIMES

We use a vertical bottle to indicate wines that should be enjoyed in their youth, but we're not suggesting you stand them up. All wines should be stored horizontally, to keep the corks moist and swollen.

Enjoy without delay. This wine is either so good right now there would be no advantage in cellaring it, or it's on the way downhill and won't benefit from being put away.

2 Good to drink now, but will keep, change a little and perhaps improve if cellared for up to the number of years indicated.

1–4 Should be cellared for the minimum and maximum number of years indicated.

5 Put it away in a quiet spot for the number of years suggested.

The cellaring estimations should be taken from September 2002.

Cellaring

WHY CELLAR WINE?

Not all wine benefits from being cellared. Unoaked Marlborough sauvignon blanc, for example, is nearly always at its impressive best when it is young, fresh and tasting primarily of the grapes from which it was made. But when a wine has been made using a number of winery techniques, it can take time for its various flavour characteristics to marry.

Cellared wine takes on new aromas and flavours, often summed up as 'bottle age' characters. Old chardonnay, for example, even if it has seen no oak, develops toasty, nutty, dried-fruit aromas, and red wines made from various grape varieties develop stewed-fruit, pencil-shaving and chocolate aromas, and often take on a leathery bouquet.

Good-quality wine, both red and white, loses its freshness and becomes mellow, soft and smooth.

STORING YOUR WINE

Wine must be stored on its side, so the cork remains moist and swollen. If the cork dries out it will eventually shrink, allowing air into the bottle and leading to oxidation. Current research indicates that sparkling wine is better stored standing up, allowing the gas to gather at the top, but it will certainly do it no harm to store it horizontally.

The maximum ideal cellar temperature is 18°C – less is good, more is bad. But if the choice is between a room that remains constantly at 18°C or a little above, and another that swings wildly from, say, 10°C to 18°C, choose the one with the more constant temperature. It is change of temperature that wine hates most.

Wine also hates vibration, which means it should be stored away from things like washing machines or constantly used stairs, and it's happiest in the dark.

THE END OF THE CORK?

Wine buyers this year and next will see increasing numbers of bottles secured not with a cork, but with a screwcap designed specifically for wine. Not everybody is keen on the trend, but it will solve one of the winery's biggest problems – corked wines.

A corked wine is not one that has bits of cork floating in it. It is a wine that smells musty, like mouldy cardboard or the interior of an old wardrobe, because of a substance called 2,4,6–trichloro anisole (TCA). It lives in the bark of the cork tree, but it doesn't become obvious until the cork comes into contact with the wine. It used to be rare, but current estimates are that it affects one wine in 30 to some degree, and is horrifyingly obvious in about one in 60.

So don't mourn the loss of the cork in your favourite bottle. You are almost certainly looking at the way of the future.

THE AGEING PROCESS

Most wine takes a long time to reach its peak, and then conveniently stays there for quite a while. Deterioration, once it starts, is rather more rapid.

A rough idea of how long a wine will last can be gained from how long it stays pleasant after the bottle has been opened. If it starts to fade after a few hours, it isn't a long-term cellaring prospect. If it rounds out and softens in a pleasant way, it should mature well.

THE BEST GRAPE TYPES FOR CELLARING

This is a very rough guide – some 'non-cellarers' will age well, while others that should cellar well will fall over.

Wines at the top of both columns cellar best, the wines at the bottom are best in their youth:

White wines

Chardonnay	Riesling
Chenin blanc	Oak-aged sauvignon blanc
Gewürztraminer	Sémillon
Müller-Thurgau	Unoaked sauvignon blanc

Red wines

Syrah	Cabernet sauvignon & blends
Malbec	Pinot noir
Merlot	Pinotage

Wine and Food

The huge recent interest in matching wine and food is pretty much a New World phenomenon.

In the traditional winemaking countries of Europe, local wine is enjoyed with the food of the region. Some of the matches may indeed be great, but it's unlikely the diners will even notice – it will simply be taken for granted. That's because people with a long history of enjoying food and wine don't see them as separate entities. They are both simply components of the meal.

We should adopt a similar attitude. Choosing wines to go with a particular dish should be the same as selecting the herbs and spices – just part of the planning.

In many European winemaking regions the law determines which grapes can be grown, and the resulting wine is what the locals drink. If you live in Burgundy, for example, you drink chardonnay if you want white, pinot noir if you want red. You wouldn't dream of drinking cabernet sauvignon – that comes from Bordeaux, which might as well be on another planet.

We are much better off in New Zealand. We can buy a wine of any style, made from any grape we choose. We can decide whether to go for a local bottle or give an import a whirl – we can even buy two very different styles to see which one we like best. There are no limits.

The same thing applies to food. If we're preparing a meal at home, we can prepare it in any way we please. We might take our inspiration from Italy, France or Mexico. We might decide to try a Japanese recipe, or one from Canton, Szechuan or Hunan in China. Maybe we'll think Korean, or Vietnamese, or Cambodian – whatever we decide, we can find the ingredients. The same choice is available to us when we dine out.

When it comes to choosing wine, that's quite a challenge. For a start, Asian countries don't have a wine culture, so there are no traditional wine and food matches – we're on our own.

The core principle in matching wine with ANY dish is not to look solely at the star ingredient. Every flavour on the plate should be taken into consideration, and the wine should either echo or complement at least some of them – and that's where the fun starts.

The important thing is not to be intimidated. Thousands of articles have been written about wine and food matching, and a lot of them try to set rules in concrete. Forget all that – the bottom line is . . . there ARE no rules.

There are guidelines, but finding the perfect combination of flavours is a personal thing. As with all aspects of wine appreciation, what works for you might not work for someone else. Matching wine and food should always be FUN, whether you're doing it at home or in a restaurant.

One of the rules that used to be unbreakable was that you had to serve white wine with white meat, and red wine with red meat.

That's okay as a very broad guide, but it is far more important to match the strength of the wine to the robustness of the flavours in the food.

Most people would serve a big-hearted red with steak or roast beef, but there are those among us who don't like red wine – so what do you do? A delicate riesling would get lost in the flavour rush, but you'd certainly get away with a big, chunky chardonnay, because then you're matching the food with wine that has a bit of grunt.

Red wine with fish? Why not! You wouldn't serve a big syrah with steamed flounder, but you can certainly serve a lighter red, say pinot noir, with rare-cooked tuna. Admittedly, tuna has red flesh, but it's still fish.

Remember to consider not just the flavour of the wine and food, but also the TEXTURE – and that will usually involve looking at the cooking method.

Pan-frying cooks in direct contact with the fat or oil, so pan-fried dishes often go well with oily wine, like a big chardonnay.

Dishes that have been char-grilled have a smoky character, so they might suit smoky wines like merlot, or oak-aged sauvignon blanc. They can also taste faintly charred, and that can be tied in with the charring on the inside of an oak barrel, so it's worth trying a barrel-fermented chardonnay, or an oak-aged red.

Even the leanest roast red meats have a faintly fatty character that coats the inside of your mouth, and that tends to soften big, alcoholic wines. If you roast the meat with herbs, try to choose some that will marry with the flavours of the wine you plan to serve.

Braising gives you the best opportunity for wine matching, because you can use some of the wine in the actual cooking process. It's a long, slow form of cooking, which gives the dish rich flavours, so look for a wine that echoes that richness.

There are some foods and wines that don't work together for purely technical reasons, but it's a pretty short list.

Big, chunky reds and some fish don't get on because the tannin in the wine reacts with the fish oil, and that causes a metallic taste – like drinking from one of those silver goblets that used to be obligatory wedding gifts. That's why pinot noir works with tuna, but cabernet is generally too tannic.

The tannins in red also react with some sweet dishes, so red wine with dessert isn't usually a good idea – but, once again, it can work. Try a bitter-sweet chocolate pudding with cabernet sauvignon or syrah – it can be a brilliant combination.

Eggs are difficult – although there's nothing wrong with a glass of dry white alongside an omelette – and artichoke hearts tend to give wine a metallic taste. Asparagus can also be a problem, but unoaked sauvignon blanc works pretty well.

I have suggested a dish with nearly every wine in this *Guide*. The ideas are mine and those of the friends who share our table. Many have been tried, others are combinations I believe should work well.

I hope you DO try some of them, but you will derive equal enjoyment from developing your own special combinations.

A few final tips about serving wine and food:

- Don't overchill your whites – it kills their flavour. Half an hour in the refrigerator for still whites and an hour for sparkling wines is about right.
- Conversely, don't serve your reds too warm. The term 'room temperature' was developed in Europe. Here, our rooms are warmer, so you might even need to refrigerate your reds briefly in summer. If you do find yourself having to warm a red (perhaps because it's come from a cool cellar), 20 minutes in the warming cupboard should suffice. Don't put it in hot water, or in front of the heater. Wine likes its flavours to be aroused gently, not kick-started.
- Plan the meal so you serve lighter and drier wines before heavier and sweeter ones, and if you are serving both dessert and cheese, serve the cheese first. It makes for a better-balanced meal.

Enjoy!

Best Wines

We're lucky in New Zealand. In many countries, wines at the bottom of the price heap are barely drinkable, but in New Zealand the standard is at least reasonable right across the board. Some brands might lack excitement, but they are seldom truly bad.

The top wines in each category are those I believe are benchmarks for the variety, but other factors are also considered. There's not much point in my recommending a wine that is impossible to buy, so reasonable availability is part of the equation, which automatically cuts out tiny producers who sell almost exclusively by mail order. Value is also taken into account. Some may be more expensive than average, but I believe the prices are justified by their exceptional quality.

BEST CHARDONNAY
Ngatarawa Alwyn Reserve Chardonnay 2000
It's smartly balanced, reasonably easy to find and priced better than many of its top-shelf competitors.

BEST CHENIN BLANC
Millton Gisborne Chenin Blanc Te Arai Vineyard 2000
Second year in a row for the Milltons, which shows it pays to take this underrated grape seriously.

BEST GEWÜRZTRAMINER
Te Whare Ra Duke of Marlborough Gewürztraminer 2001
It's won every other accolade going, and it deserves to. If you can't find it, try contacting the winery.

BEST PINOT GRIS
Herzog Marlborough Pinot Gris 2001
I suspect it's a 'love it or hate it' style, but I'm firmly in the former camp. It's not for wimps, but it's beautifully made.

BEST RIESLING
Felton Road Dry Riesling 2002
Another two-time winner. The company produces three great rieslings, but I prefer the beautifully focused flavours of this dry version.

BEST SAUVIGNON BLANC AND/OR SÉMILLON
Craggy Range Old Renwick Vineyard Sauvignon Blanc 2002
A new name, but one that is already getting a lot of publicity. The flavour profile is classic, but it's got more style than many of the genre.

BEST CABERNET SAUVIGNON, MERLOT OR BLEND
Vidal Estate Reserve Merlot/Cabernet Sauvignon 2000
It's expensive, but it offers a power of flavour for your dollar. Also worth tracking down is the $80-plus Vidal Estate Joseph Soler Cabernet. It was released too late for inclusion in the main text, but it's an absolute beauty.

BEST PINOT NOIR
Villa Maria Reserve Marlborough Pinot Noir 2001
I was dubious about this trophy winner's 15% alcohol level. 'Too much for pinot,' I thought. Then I tried the wine, and was won over.

BEST PINOTAGE
Muddy Water Waipara Pinotage 2000
It's not easy to find, but this smartly balanced rendition of the style deserves a wider audience.

BEST SYRAH
Mills Reef Elspeth Syrah 2001
The Prestons are doing more than most with their Gimblett Road-grown Shiraz grapes, using them in a range of reds.

BEST SPARKLING WINE
Deutz Marlborough Cuvée Blanc de Blancs
The 'standard' model is also pretty smart, but I lean towards this all-chardonnay version of Montana's big-selling bubbly.

BEST ROSÉ OR BLUSH
Unison Rosé 2002
It's dry, it's lovely to look at – and it's delicious to drink. Try it with poached salmon and you'll get the point.

BEST DESSERT WINE
Palliser Estate Martinborough Noble Chardonnay 2000
With so many sweeties hitting the $50 mark and beyond, I decided this delicious and well-priced interpretation of the style deserved the top spot.

White Wines

Chardonnay

We try to avoid technical expressions in the *Guide*, but you'll find more of them in this chapter than anywhere else. That's because winemakers love using various winery techniques to add complexity to chardonnay. They are likely to ferment and mature it in barrels, made of either French or American oak, or sometimes a combination of the two. They might choose to use the grapes' own indigenous yeasts, rather than laboratory-bred 'tame' models, and they will often stir them once they have expired, a technique known as 'lees stirring'. It is also common to allow chardonnay to undergo a natural process called malolactic fermentation. Strictly speaking, it's not a fermentation at all, but that's by the by. It converts the fledgling wine's malic acids (think unripe apples) to lactic acids (think milk), which gives it a creamy softness as a result. Balancing the various flavours that each of these techniques adds is part of the art of winemaking.

AD (Alpha Domus) Chardonnay

Evert Nijzink worked in Bordeaux, France, before heading for the Hawke's Bay. His European experience was mostly with reds, but he's no slouch with whites, as this top-shelf model shows.

Current Release 2000 The nose is distinctively perfumed, with a suggestion of super-ripe nectarines at the back. It's sweet on the front palate, boasts firmness and rich fruit through the middle and finishes with good grip and a further lick of sweetness. It's brilliant with braised rabbit, but you could treat chicken legs the same way – just make sure you use really good stock, plus a splash of this wine.

STYLE **dry**
QUALITY ♟ ♟ ♟ ♟ ♟
VALUE ☆ ☆ ☆
GRAPES **Chardonnay**
REGION **Hawke's Bay**
CELLAR 4
PRICE **$34–36**

Akarua Chardonnay

STYLE dry
QUALITY ▾ ▾ ▾ ▾ ▾
VALUE ☆ ☆ ☆
GRAPES Chardonnay
REGION Central Otago
CELLAR 🍾 3
PRICE $25–28

The 50-hectare Bannockburn Heights vineyard was established by well-known businessman Sir Clifford Skeggs in 1996. Nearly 70% of the vines are pinot noir, but this chardonnay shows that other varieties also perform well.

Current Release 2001 Mealy and spicy on the nose, with something like marmalade also part of the equation, this cool-climate chardonnay starts out well. It's a big wine on the palate, with chunky, mouth-filling flavours and a satisfyingly lingering finish. Match that rusticity with grunty dishes like casseroled pork and baby onions, served on polenta.

Alan McCorkindale Marlborough Chardonnay

STYLE dry
QUALITY ▾ ▾ ▾ ▾
VALUE ☆ ☆ ☆
GRAPES Chardonnay
REGION Marlborough
CELLAR 🍾 4
PRICE $24–27

Alan McCorkindale spent several years in charge of the well-appointed Corbans winery in Marlborough before taking up a position as winemaker at St Helena, in Canterbury. Now, he's producing wine under his own name.

Current Release 1999 After a year in French oak barrels, this wine has pleasant toasted hazelnut aromas behind the citrus impressions on the nose. It's smooth-centred, sweet-fruited and moderately rich on the palate, and has a fresh-faced finish. It makes a good partner for pan-fried blue cod.

Alana Estate Martinborough Chardonnay

STYLE dry
QUALITY ▾ ▾ ▾ ▾
VALUE ☆ ☆ ☆
GRAPES Chardonnay
REGION Martinborough
CELLAR 🍾 1–4
PRICE $29–32

This nicely made chardonnay has had all the drama. The grapes were pressed as whole bunches, and the juice was fermented in new and one-year-old French barrels, using both wild and laboratory-bred yeasts.

Current Release 2000 There was a fair whack of timber behind the ripe grapefruit aromas when I tried the wine soon after its release, but that should have settled down by now. It's broadly textured, with smooth-edged peach and lemon flavours and a reasonably long finish. It goes well with mussel and saffron chowder.

Alexandra Wine Company Feraud Chardonnay

STYLE dry
QUALITY ▾ ▾ ▾ ▾
VALUE ☆ ☆ ☆ ☆
GRAPES Chardonnay
REGION Central Otago
CELLAR 🍾 1–3
PRICE $20–22

The Alexandra Wine Company team named this chardonnay for Jean Desire Feraud, who pioneered grape growing in the Central Otago district way back in the 1860s. He'd be amazed at the number of vineyards there today.

Current Release 2000 Grapefruit and spice contribute all the right aromas to the bouquet. It's a nicely focused wine that starts quite gently, but builds to display understated power in the middle and on the finish. It's good with penne pasta tossed with discs of baked zucchini and bocconcini cheese.

Allan Scott Marlborough Chardonnay

Around 80% of the juice was fermented and aged for seven months in French oak barrels, 50% of which were new, and the same 80% was encouraged to go through an acid-softening malolactic fermentation.

Current Release 2001 There's only a touch of oak toast on the nose, and that's all to the good. Mostly, the aromas are of rock melon and freshly cut nectarines. It's creamy but well focused on the palate, and makes a good partner for fish cakes, pan-fried in olive oil and served with slightly spicy home-made mayonnaise.

STYLE **dry**
QUALITY ♟ ♟ ♟ ♟
VALUE ☆ ☆ ☆ ☆
GRAPES **Chardonnay**
REGION **Marlborough**
CELLAR ▤ 3
PRICE **$20–23**

Allan Scott Prestige Marlborough Chardonnay

Allan Scott's 'Prestige' wines are produced when he finds parcels of exceptional fruit. They're not usually made in large quantities, so might take a bit of a search. This is a worthy member of the portfolio.

Current Release 2000 Big and spicy on the nose, rich and smartly focused on the palate, albeit with a chunky edge, this is an immediately appealing wine that will appeal to chardonnay traditionalists. Partner it with a whole baked snapper and you will join the list of fans.

STYLE **dry**
QUALITY ♟ ♟ ♟ ♟ ♟
VALUE ☆ ☆ ☆
GRAPES **Chardonnay**
REGION **Marlborough**
CELLAR ▤ 4
PRICE **$30–33**

Alpha Domus Chardonnay

Alpha Domus winemaker Evert Nijzink has been in the habit of travelling to France each year to work in wineries in the south of the country, so he tends to combine New World and Old World philosophies.

Current Release 2002 The oak spice is in good balance with the grapefruit and peach aromas on the nose and adds a savoury edge to the smooth-textured flavour profile. It's an elegant wine, but it gives a feeling of suppressed power. I enjoyed a glass recently with freshly opened mussels served in a bowl with garlic and pulped tomatoes. Yum!

STYLE **dry**
QUALITY ♟ ♟ ♟ ♟ ♟
VALUE ☆ ☆ ☆ ☆ ☆
GRAPES **Chardonnay**
REGION **Hawke's Bay**
CELLAR ▤ 3
PRICE **$18–21**

Amor-Bendall Chardonnay

This new Gisborne establishment has no vines in production, but buys fruit from local growers. The winery is small but very well equipped. Noel Amor makes the wines while his partner, Alison Bendall, handles marketing.

Current Release 2000 Peaches and a trace of lemon juice sit nicely in the bouquet. Having no oak makes it a very clean-cut wine with good balance between ripe fruit and keen acids. It should sit well alongside a platter of freshly shucked oysters.

STYLE **dry**
QUALITY ♟ ♟ ♟ ♟
VALUE ☆ ☆ ☆ ☆ ☆
GRAPES **Chardonnay**
REGION **Gisborne**
CELLAR ▤ 2
PRICE **$17–19**

Amor-Bendall Chardonnay Reserve

STYLE **dry**
QUALITY ▽ ▽ ▽ ▽ ▽
VALUE ☆ ☆ ☆ ☆
GRAPES **Chardonnay**
REGION **Gisborne**
CELLAR **3**
PRICE **$23–26**

This upmarket member of the tiny A-B portfolio was part-fermented in a mixture of French and American oak barrels and stayed there for just over four months. It scored gold at the New Zealand Wine Society Royal Easter Wine Show.
Current Release 2000 Peaches and cream! That's the overriding impression on the nose and the front palate of this smooth-centred chardonnay. The flavours put me in mind of melons, and the oak stays where it should – in the background. Enjoy it with pork spareribs, ideally cooked on the barbecue.

Askerne Hawke's Bay Chardonnay

STYLE **dry**
QUALITY ▽ ▽ ▽
VALUE ☆ ☆ ☆
GRAPES **Chardonnay**
REGION **Hawke's Bay**
CELLAR **2**
PRICE **$25–27**

Fermentation in French oak barrels, 40% of them new, and a full malolactic fermentation have softened the texture of this chardonnay. Vineyard owner John Loughlin is also involved in the meat industry.
Current Release 2001 The oak influence is quite light in the bouquet – the dominant impression is of ripe citrus. It's not a big wine, but it has a good quota of savoury flavours and an easy-going, creamy texture. Try it alongside poached chicken breasts served on a 'jam' of reduced red onion.

Ata Rangi Craighall Chardonnay

STYLE **dry**
QUALITY ▽ ▽ ▽ ▽ ▽
VALUE ☆ ☆ ☆
GRAPES **Chardonnay**
REGION **Martinborough**
CELLAR **5**
PRICE **$38–42**

This is the top-of-the-heap chardonnay for the Ata Rangi crew. It was made entirely from Mendoza clone chardonnay grapes and fermented in French oak barrels. About 60% was encouraged to go through a malolactic fermentation.
Current Release 2001 Spicy oak sits happily behind the primary aromas of freshly cut nectarines. It's rich and creamy on the palate, with ripe fruit nicely balanced by keen but integrated acids. It would make a perfect partner for a free-range chicken, rubbed with lemon juice and olive oil before being roasted.

Ata Rangi Petrie Chardonnay

STYLE **dry**
QUALITY ▽ ▽ ▽ ▽
VALUE ☆ ☆ ☆ ☆
GRAPES **Chardonnay**
REGION **Martinborough**
CELLAR **4**
PRICE **$25–28**

The grapes for this second-tier chardonnay came from Neil Petrie's vineyard at East Taratahi, about 20 minutes from Martinborough township. It was fermented in French oak barrels, 25% of which were new.
Current Release 2001 Muesli, marmalade and freshly cut peaches make an appealing aromatic trio on the nose. The texture is creamy and the balance between fruit and oak pretty well spot-on. Overall, a moderately rich wine that goes well with scallops seared with mushrooms in good olive oil.

Babich East Coast Chardonnay

Including Auckland in the East Coast designation is stretching the point a wee bit, but it makes labelling simpler. Neill Culley fermented this wine in stainless steel, but it spent a few months maturing in French barrels.
Current Release 2000 Citric aromas are edged by just a suggestion of oaky spice. It's clean-cut and refreshing on the palate, with keen acids giving it plenty of zing in the middle. The finish is a little short, but it's certainly lively. I like it with a pile of grilled chicken wings.

STYLE **dry**
QUALITY ♟♟♟♟
VALUE ☆☆☆☆
GRAPES **Chardonnay**
REGION **Gisborne**
Hawke's Bay
Auckland
CELLAR 🍾 **3**
PRICE **$15–17**

Babich Irongate Chardonnay

This chardonnay is consistently one of the top wines to come from the highly regarded Gimblett Gravels region, famous for exceptional drainage and overnight heat retention. It was fermented and matured in French oak barrels.
Current Release 2000 The aromas are of grapefruit and dried peel, with oak providing an elegantly spicy backdrop. It's viscous on the palate, although it has had none of the malolactic fermentation that normally adds this texture, but the overall impressions are of superbly ripe, juicy grapes. Yum! Enjoy it with a free-range corn-fed chicken, simply roasted and served with your favourite vegetables.

STYLE **dry**
QUALITY ♟♟♟♟♟
VALUE ☆☆☆
GRAPES **Chardonnay**
REGION **Hawke's Bay**
CELLAR 🍾 **4**
PRICE **$35–38**

Babich The Patriarch Chardonnay

Named in honour of Josip Babich, who worked long hours in the gum-fields of the far north to save enough money to buy the land where the winery is still situated, this is the top-of-the-line chardonnay for the company.
Current Release 2000 You like your chardonnays in the 'big smoothie' category? Look no further. This big-hearted example of Adam Hazeldine's skills has loads of classy, citric fruit and perfectly balanced oak to set it off. It's great with braised rabbit on a bed of mashed kumara.

STYLE **dry**
QUALITY ♟♟♟♟♟
VALUE ☆☆⚘
GRAPES **Chardonnay**
REGION **Hawke's Bay**
CELLAR 🍾 **4**
PRICE **$40–43**

Babich Winemaker's Reserve Chardonnay

The fruit came from a vineyard in the Fernhill region, where strong vine growth makes it necessary to pluck leaves away to expose the ripening grapes to the sun. The wine was matured in a mixture of new and used French oak barrels.
Current Release 2000 Citrus characters dominate the bouquet, with no more than a suggestion of spicy oak. It's nicely focused on the palate, staying with the citrus theme but adding a few stonefruit flavours to the mix. It works well with Chinese-style prawn spring rolls.

STYLE **dry**
QUALITY ♟♟♟♟
VALUE ☆☆☆⚘
GRAPES **Chardonnay**
REGION **Hawke's Bay**
CELLAR 🍾 **3**
PRICE **$20–23**

Bilancia Chardonnay

STYLE **dry**
QUALITY ♟ ♟ ♟ ♟
VALUE ☆ ☆ ☆
GRAPES **Chardonnay**
REGION **Hawke's Bay**
CELLAR 🍾 3
PRICE **$27-29**

The fruit for this big-hearted chardonnay came from a new site for label owners, Warren Gibson and Lorraine Leheney. The juice was fermented and the fledgling wine matured in French oak barrels with a capacity of 225 litres – considered the optimum size.
Current Release 2000 The nose is big and peachy with accents of grainy toast from its time in oak. It's rich and creamy on the palate, with good weight and a savoury finish. Enjoy it alongside roasted turkey breasts served over grilled polenta.

Black Barn Vineyards Barrel Fermented Chardonnay

STYLE **dry**
QUALITY ♟ ♟ ♟ ♟
VALUE ☆ ☆ ☆ ☆
GRAPES **Chardonnay**
REGION **Hawke's Bay**
CELLAR 🍾 4
PRICE **$26-28**

Black Barn Vineyards is the new label for wines sourced from the Lombardi property in Hawke's Bay. This extraordinary spot boasts a 2000-seat amphitheatre, a restaurant, an underground cellar and stylish accommodation.
Current Release 2001 The nose is chunky and spicy, with suggestions of dried fruit and muesli. It's creamy and rich on the palate, and put me in mind of grilled peaches and cream. The finish is long and satisfying. Partner it with grilled pork chops served with mashed pumpkin and young green beans.

Black Barn Vineyards Unoaked Chardonnay

STYLE **dry**
QUALITY ♟ ♟ ♟ ♟
VALUE ☆ ☆ ☆ ☆
GRAPES **Chardonnay**
REGION **Hawke's Bay**
CELLAR 🍾 2
PRICE **$19-22**

Not only is it unoaked, but it contains a tiny bit of residual sugar – not enough to kick it out of the 'dry' category, but it certainly gives it a faintly sweet lift through the mid-palate.
Current Release 2002 With no oak to confuse the issue, the bouquet is predictably citric. It's thoroughly pleasant on the palate, boasting lifted stonefruit flavours in fresh-faced surroundings. That lick of sweetness makes its presence felt on the finish, and makes it a good partner for a roast pork sandwich with equally sweet-edged chutney.

Black Ridge Chardonnay

STYLE **dry**
QUALITY ♟ ♟ ♟ ♟
VALUE ☆ ☆ ☆
GRAPES **Chardonnay**
REGION **Central Otago**
CELLAR 🍷 1-4
PRICE **$25-27**

Verdun Burgess aged 50% of this wine in French oak barrels, half of which were new. It was allowed to go through a malolactic fermentation, a natural process that converts sharp malic acids to softer lactic acids.
Current Release 2001 The oak hasn't altered the fact that it is a fruit-led wine, and that's all to the good. It's citric, lean and focused with an elegantly clean-cut finish. Try it with pan-fried cod in a lemon-infused sauce and you'll get the point.

Borthwick Estate Chardonnay

Paddy Borthwick fermented this wine in French oak barrels, 40% of which were new. Unusually, the entire batch was allowed to go through an acid-softening malolactic fermentation. The lees left over from fermentation were stirred to add further complexity.

Current Release 1999 The nose is so perfumed it reminded me of riesling, but the whiff of spicy oak straightened me out. It's a nicely textured wine, presumably thanks to the malolactic, with smooth-edged peach-like flavours and a lingering finish. Partner it with chicken legs and thighs in a creamy sauce and drink a toast to Paddy.

STYLE **dry**
QUALITY ☼ ☼ ☼ ☼
VALUE ☆ ☆ ☆ ☆
GRAPES **Chardonnay**
REGION **Wairarapa**
CELLAR **3**
PRICE **$20–23**

Brajkovich Chardonnay

Kumeu River's Michael Brajkovich used both French oak barrels and stainless-steel tanks to ferment the juice for this second-tier chardonnay. About 70% of the juice was allowed to go through a malolactic fermentation.

Current Release 2002 Smoky oak sits behind the subtle aromas of grapefruit and lime juice. The malolactic fermentation has helped give it a pleasantly creamy texture through the middle and seemingly extended the finish. It goes well with seared broadbill steaks, now available from a few good fish shops around the country.

STYLE **dry**
QUALITY ☼ ☼ ☼ ☼
VALUE ☆ ☆ ☆ ☆ �½
GRAPES **Chardonnay**
REGION **West Auckland**
CELLAR **3**
PRICE **$19–22**

Brookfields Bergman Chardonnay

The name comes from the Ingrid Bergman roses in the winery garden – owner Peter Robertson is obviously a fan. This smart chardonnay is a popular buy at the winery restaurant, both by the bottle and the glass.

Current Release 2001 Oak spice from its time in a mixture of French and American barrels is quite gentle in the bouquet. It's appealingly sweet-fruited, with well-integrated acids making it very approachable. Enjoy it alongside parsnip and Parmesan risotto.

STYLE **dry**
QUALITY ☼ ☼ ☼ ☼
VALUE ☆ ☆ ☆ ☆ �½
GRAPES **Chardonnay**
REGION **Hawke's Bay**
CELLAR **3**
PRICE **$18–20**

Brookfields Marshall Bank Chardonnay

Unusually for the variety, all the French oak barrels in which this chardonnay was matured were brand-new. Equally unusually, Peter Robertson put it through a 100% malolactic fermentation – most producers settle for 20 or 30%.

Current Release 2001 Naturally enough, there's a fair whack of spicy oak on the nose, but there's enough peach and melon-like fruit character to balance it. It's very smooth and broad on the palate, with peach and nectarine flavours edged by smartly integrated acids. It makes a good partner for braised pork with mushrooms and sage.

STYLE **dry**
QUALITY ☼ ☼ ☼ ☼ ☼
VALUE ☆ ☆ ☆
GRAPES **Chardonnay**
REGION **Hawke's Bay**
CELLAR **1–4**
PRICE **$30–33**

Cairnbrae Clansman Marlborough Chardonnay

STYLE **dry**
QUALITY ▽ ▽ ▽ ▽
VALUE ☆ ☆ ☆
GRAPES **Chardonnay**
REGION **Marlborough**

CELLAR ▯ **3**
PRICE **$22–26**

With a name like that it should come from Dunedin, but this big-hearted chardonnay contains fruit from the heart of the Wairau Valley. The winemaking team fermented it in American oak barrels and left it there for nearly six months. **Current Release 2000** Weet-Bix and toast characters back up the aromas of ripe rock melons in the bouquet, and there's a dash of coconut in there as well. It's super-smooth on the palate, with peaches-and-cream flavours and a faintly oily finish. Enjoy it alongside rabbit in a cream and mustard-based sauce.

Canadoro Martinborough Chardonnay

STYLE **dry**
QUALITY ▽ ▽ ▽ ▽
VALUE ☆ ☆ ☆
GRAPES **Chardonnay**
REGION **Martinborough**

CELLAR ▯ **4**
PRICE **$28–30**

Greg Robins put this chardonnay through a complete malolactic fermentation, but he says because the natural malic acids were very low it didn't make a lot of difference. It spent 10 months in one-year-old French oak barrels. **Current Release 2000** There's just a touch of oaky spice behind the melon aromas. It's a pretty wine on the palate, with nicely focused flavours in smooth surroundings. The finish isn't long, but it's pleasant enough. It would go well with pumpkin and kumara gnocchi.

Canterbury House Waipara Chardonnay

STYLE **dry**
QUALITY ▽ ▽ ▽ ▽
VALUE ☆ ☆ ☆ ☆
GRAPES **Chardonnay**
REGION **Waipara**

CELLAR ▯ **3**
PRICE **$18–20**

In 1999, Mark Rattray made oaked and unoaked chardonnays and labelled them accordingly. This one splits the two styles – 40% was matured in French barrels, while the rest stayed in stainless steel. **Current Release 2000** There's a nice belt of toasted hazelnut on the nose to go with the grapefruit aromas. It's richly fruited, creamy and nicely balanced, with peach and nectarine flavours supported by gentle acids. It makes a good companion for delicate chicken-filled spring rolls.

Carrick Central Otago Chardonnay

STYLE **dry**
QUALITY ▽ ▽ ▽ ▽ ▽
VALUE ☆ ☆ ☆ ☆
GRAPES **Chardonnay**
REGION **Central Otago**

CELLAR ▯ **4**
PRICE **$24–26**

Only 20% of the French oak barrels in which this chardonnay spent its quiet time were new because winemaker Steve Davies didn't want to overpower the fruit. He encouraged it to go through a 100% malolactic fermentation. **Current Release 2001** The careful oak treatment has added gentle spice to the citrus and stonefruit aromas. It's sweet-edged and biscuit-like on the palate, with smartly integrated acids ensuring plenty of life through to the lingering finish. Try it with teriyaki salmon on Japanese udon noodles.

Chancellor Estates Waipara Mt Cass Road Chardonnay

The back label talks about 'hints' of oak, which probably means the wine spent only a brief time in barrels, and that most of them were used. That makes sense, because there's some good fruit in there.

Current Release 2000 The oak may have been minimal, but there's still a healthy belt of toast behind the orange-peel aromas. It's smooth and direct on the palate, with a creamy finish that makes it a good partner for chicken, cubed, pan-fried and stirred into a sour cream reduction sauce.

STYLE **dry**
QUALITY ♟ ♟ ♟ ♟
VALUE ☆ ☆ ☆ ☆
GRAPES **Chardonnay**
REGION **Waipara**
CELLAR 🍷 3
PRICE **$18–21**

Chard Farm Judge & Jury Chardonnay

The name comes from a rocky outcrop across the gorge from the winery. Part of it is shaped like the head of a judge, complete with wig, and a dozen or so other 'heads' are part of the group.

Current Release 1999 The bouquet is invitingly spicy, with chunky citric and nectarine aromas filling in the gaps. It's a big, creamy wine with nice balance between fruit and oak. Our bottle went down a treat with a bowl of kumara gnocchi, and I fancy it would also go well with a classic roast pork dinner.

STYLE **dry**
QUALITY ♟ ♟ ♟ ♟ ♟
VALUE ☆ ☆ ☆
GRAPES **Chardonnay**
REGION **Central Otago**
CELLAR ▭ 1–4
PRICE **$31–34**

Charles Wiffen Chardonnay

Charles and Sandi Wiffen live in Cheviot, Canterbury, but their vineyard is in Marlborough. To confuse the issue further, the wine is made by Anthony Ivecivich at West Brook, in Auckland. This chardonnay spent 10 months in French oak barrels, half of them new.

Current Release 2001 Maturation in French oak has added a gentle spiciness to the peaches-and-cream aromas. It's faintly citric, elegant and creamy on the palate, with a lingering finish. It makes a good partner for spaghetti tossed with prawns, baby mussels and thinly sliced fennel in sour cream.

STYLE **dry**
QUALITY ♟ ♟ ♟ ♟
VALUE ☆ ☆ ☆ ☆
GRAPES **Chardonnay**
REGION **Marlborough**
CELLAR 🍷 3
PRICE **$22–24**

Church Road Chardonnay

Church Road is in Hawke's Bay, but in 2001 frost decimated a large portion of the fruit destined for this popular chardonnay. Marlborough grapes made up the shortfall. Tony Prichard put both portions into French oak barrels for six months.

Current Release 2001 I get toasted almonds on the nose, and that suits me fine. It's a nicely focused wine with great balance between fruit and oak, a smooth texture and a long finish. Nice one, Tony! Enjoy it with seafood lasagne, or something with equally outspoken flavours.

STYLE **dry**
QUALITY ♟ ♟ ♟ ♟
VALUE ☆ ☆ ☆ ☆
GRAPES **Chardonnay**
REGION
Marlborough 56%
Hawke's Bay 44%
CELLAR 🍷 3
PRICE **$22–24**

Church Road Cuve Series Chardonnay

STYLE **dry**
QUALITY ♟♟♟♟
VALUE ☆ ☆ ☆
GRAPES **Chardonnay**
REGION **Hawke's Bay**

CELLAR **3**
PRICE **$33–36**

Relying less on oak than the other chardonnays in the Church Road range, this recent release was made from hand-harvested fruit, pressed quickly to remove the skins with the aim of achieving delicacy.
Current Release 1998 It worked! It's sweet-fruited and spicy on the nose, with a suggestion of honeycomb adding to the picture, but the overall impression is of delicacy and style. Broad on the palate, it has gentle citric flavours and fully integrated acids. It needs gentle food – try steamed flounder drizzled with sesame oil.

Church Road Reserve Chardonnay Hawke's Bay

STYLE **dry**
QUALITY ♟♟♟♟
VALUE ☆ ☆ ☆ ☆
GRAPES **Chardonnay**
REGION **Hawke's Bay**

CELLAR **4**
PRICE **$30–34**

Tony Prichard and Peter Hurlstone selected the best fruit from the company's Koropiko Estate vineyard for this chardonnay. The juice was fermented in new French barrels and left there for 10 months.
Current Release 1999 Toasted Vogel's and freshly cut grapefruit set the scene for a serious chardonnay. The creamy texture gives it a lot of elegance, but there's some pretty powerful fruit richness in there as well, and that's a clever balancing act. It's great with a salad based around bocconcini, puy lentils and rocket.

Clearview Estate Reserve Chardonnay

STYLE **dry**
QUALITY ♟♟♟♟
VALUE ☆ ☆ ☆
GRAPES **Chardonnay**
REGION **Hawke's Bay**

CELLAR **6**
PRICE **$35–38**

Tim Turvey makes some of the biggest chardonnays in the country, but they're hard to find. In 2001, the vines cropped low but the grapes had intense flavour. Around 60% were pressed as whole bunches, bypassing the crusher/destemmer.
Current Release 2001 Toast made from full-grain bread is the first impression on the bouquet, with grilled grapefruit halves coming in afterwards. It's big, rich and has flavours vaguely like spiced lemon honey through the middle, leading to a sweet-edged finish. It makes a good partner for osso buco made from genuine white veal shin pieces.

Clifford Bay Marlborough Single Vineyard Chardonnay

STYLE **dry**
QUALITY ♟♟♟♟
VALUE ☆ ☆ ☆ ☆ ☆
GRAPES **Chardonnay**
REGION **Marlborough**

CELLAR **3**
PRICE **$19–22**

Here's another good advertisement for Marlborough's Awatere Valley, rapidly shaping up as one of the most exciting winemaking regions in the country. It also boasts some of the most spectacular scenery.
Current Release 2000 It spent around 15 weeks in oak barrels, and they have added a touch of toasted hazelnuts to the marmalade-like aromas. It's richly fruited and full-on in its flavours, with an attractively spicy finish. To sum up, a smart wine that sits well with couscous-stuffed quail.

Cloudy Bay Chardonnay

The name is internationally famous for sauvignon blanc, but this chardonnay is every bit as good. The grapes were picked at night to capture all their flavour, then the juice was fermented in French oak barrels, 20% of them new.
Current Release 2000 Rock melon and dried apricots – that's what I get on the nose. The flavour profile boasts the full complement of rich stonefruit flavours, but with a lively edge provided by cleverly integrated acids. The finish is long and supremely satisfying. It deserves the best, so track down a pheasant and roast it as an accompaniment.

STYLE **dry**
QUALITY ♟ ♟ ♟ ♟ ♟
VALUE ☆ ☆ ☆
GRAPES **Chardonnay**
REGION **Marlborough**
CELLAR **4**
PRICE **$34–37**

Collards Blakes Mill Chardonnay

This is the Collard family's second-label chardonnay, but the fruit comes from the highly regarded Rothesay vineyard in West Auckland. It is a popular buy at the cellar door shop in Lincoln Road, Henderson.
Current Release 2000 The oak is in the form of gentle spice on the nose – mostly, the aromas are of ripe, citric fruit. It's creamy and light-hearted on the palate, with peach-like flavours in clean-cut surroundings. Try it with a simple fish burger, or something equally undemanding.

STYLE **dry**
QUALITY ♟ ♟ ♟ ♟
VALUE ☆ ☆ ☆ ☆ ☆
GRAPES **Chardonnay**
REGION **West Auckland**
CELLAR **2**
PRICE **$12–14**

Collards Rothesay Chardonnay

The Rothesay vineyard is situated in Waimauku, not far from the Matua Valley winery. In 2001, cropping levels were 20% less than average, giving Bruce Collard some highly concentrated fruit to work with.
Current Release 2001 A hint of spice sits behind the major aromas of ripe grapefruit and peaches. The texture is exceptionally smooth as a result of a full acid-softening malolactic fermentation, and the flavours broad and complex. It makes a fine partner for a chicken casserole, served with mashed potatoes enlivened with truffle oil.

STYLE **dry**
QUALITY ♟ ♟ ♟ ♟
VALUE ☆ ☆ ☆
GRAPES **Chardonnay**
REGION **West Auckland**
CELLAR **4**
PRICE **$30–33**

Coopers Creek Gisborne Chardonnay

Simon Nunns sourced grapes from three different vineyards for this chardonnay. Unusually, the barrels in which 45% of the fledgling wine spent six quiet months were all made from American oak.
Current Release 2000 Vanilla and coconut aromas give away the US contribution, but there's enough ripe, peachy fruit to keep things in balance. The flavours lean more to the citric end of the spectrum, giving it plenty of mid-palate liveliness. It's a natural partner for pan-fried snapper with a lemon/cream sauce.

STYLE **dry**
QUALITY ♟ ♟ ♟
VALUE ☆ ☆ ☆ ☆
GRAPES **Chardonnay**
REGION **Gisborne**
CELLAR **2**
PRICE **$16–18**

Coopers Creek Hawke's Bay Chardonnay

STYLE dry
QUALITY ??????
VALUE ☆☆☆☆☆
GRAPES Chardonnay
REGION Hawke's Bay

CELLAR 3
PRICE $19–21

The fruit came from two vineyards, and Simon Nunns put the baby wine into a mixture of French and American oak, new and used, for 10 months. It went through a total acid-softening malolactic fermentation.
Current Release 2000 Gentle spice backs the sweet, peach-like fruit aromas. It's nicely textured, with the stonefruit impressions carrying on through the middle and onto the lingering, spice-edged finish. Try it with pan-fried brains with browned butter.

Coopers Creek Swamp Reserve Chardonnay

STYLE dry
QUALITY ?????
VALUE ☆☆☆☆
GRAPES Chardonnay
REGION Hawke's Bay

CELLAR 3
PRICE $27–29

American visitors to the Creek's West Auckland tasting room are fascinated by this label. They can't believe anyone would really use the word 'swamp' as part of a wine name. Historically, it relates to Swamp Road, in Hawke's Bay.
Current Release 1999 Nectarine aromas are backed by gentle oak spice on the nose. It's rich, ripe-fruited and mouth-fillingly creamy, and boasts a big, spicy finish that lasts a very long time. The Coopers Creek team recommends it for crayfish, salmon or trout. I'll go along with that!

Corbans Chardonnay

STYLE dry
QUALITY ???
VALUE ☆☆☆☆
GRAPES Chardonnay
REGION Gisborne

CELLAR 2
PRICE $14–16

Corbans has a bewildering number of variations on the chardonnay theme. This one carries one of the simplest labels in the range. Winemaker Brent Laidlaw matured it in a mixture of French and American oak barrels.
Current Release 2002 Aromas like freshly cut peaches backed by gentle spice push all the right buttons in the bouquet. It's light, creamy and pleasant on the palate, with absolutely no sharp edges and nothing to take exception to. Enjoy it with chicken drumsticks, marinated in olive oil and chopped parsley before being grilled or pan-fried.

Corbans White Label Chardonnay

STYLE dry
QUALITY ??
VALUE ☆☆☆☆☆
GRAPES Chardonnay
REGION Various

CELLAR 1
PRICE $9–11

The fine print on the label tells us this cheap-and-cheerful chardonnay comes from 'New Zealand and Australia', but goes into no more detail. It's a big seller in supermarkets, where it is often specialled down to ludicrously low prices.
Current Release 2001 Spiced grapefruit and lemons are the major aromatic associations. It's simple, clean, faintly sweet on the finish but with absolutely no sharp edges. It would be fine with a pile of the Colonel's best, or a simple chicken sandwich.

Corbans Winemakers Cottage Block Hawke's Bay Chardonnay

The hand-picked fruit used for this top-shelf chardonnay came from the Brooklands vineyard in the Omarunui Valley. The fledgling wine spent a few quiet months in new and one-year-old French oak barrels.

Current Release 1999 Nutty, savoury oatmeal aromas suggest it's going to be a biggie, and it is. Sweet, super-ripe fruit flavours give it a mouth-filling texture and lead to a smartly focused, spicy finish. The back label suggests partnering it with chicken, with almonds and dried apricots in the stuffing.

STYLE **dry**
QUALITY ♟ ♟ ♟ ♟ ♟
VALUE ☆ ☆ ☆ ✰
GRAPES **Chardonnay**
REGION **Hawke's Bay**
CELLAR 3
PRICE **$29–32**

Corbans Winemakers Cottage Block Marlborough Chardonnay

With an alcohol level of 14%, this is a big chardonnay. The grapes were picked by hand and pressed as whole bunches, bypassing the crusher, and the juice was fermented and matured for 10 months in new and one-year-old French oak barrels.

Current Release 2001 Savoury, spicy oak sits happily behind the primary aromas of grapefruit and freshly cut nectarines. It's a big, broad wine with a creamy texture and loads of ripe fruit flavours. The finish is long and satisfying. It works well with mussel fritters, but I like it best with Spanish seafood paella.

STYLE **dry**
QUALITY ♟ ♟ ♟ ♟ ♟
VALUE ☆ ☆ ☆ ✰
GRAPES **Chardonnay**
REGION **Marlborough**
CELLAR 3
PRICE **$29–32**

Covell Estate Chardonnay

Both 1999 and 1998 versions of this chardonnay are currently on sale at the winery, but in my view this is the better of the two. Both were fermented in French oak barrels, 40% of them new, and left there to mature for a year.

Current Release 1999 There's a gentle backdrop of oak spice behind the ripe peach aromas on the nose. It's citric and well-focused on the palate, with a short, apple-like finish. Try it with thick slices of roast pork on sourdough bread, smeared with home-made mayonnaise.

STYLE **dry**
QUALITY ♟ ♟ ♟
VALUE ☆ ☆ ☆
GRAPES **Chardonnay**
REGION **Murupara**
CELLAR 1
PRICE **$20–23**

Covell Estate 'Estate' Chardonnay

Bob and Des (Desirée) Covell have the only vineyard in their region, and if that wasn't enough of a challenge, they grow their grapes according to strict Bio-Gro standards. This chardonnay carries no vintage, but I tried it soon after bottling.

Current Release (non-vintage) The bouquet is chunky, with a faintly oxidative note at the back. It is citric and quite lean on the palate, but with at least a suggestion of ripe peach flavours towards the finish. Try it with a chicken and mustard sandwich.

STYLE **dry**
QUALITY ♟ ♟
VALUE ☆ ☆ ☆
GRAPES **Chardonnay**
REGION **Murupara**
CELLAR
PRICE **$14–16**

Craggy Range Winery Chardonnay Apley Road Vineyard

STYLE **dry**

QUALITY ♟♟♟♟

VALUE ☆ ☆ ☆☆

GRAPES **Chardonnay**

REGION **Hawke's Bay**

CELLAR 🍾 **3**

PRICE **$23–26**

Steve Smith is the only viticulturist in the world to hold coveted Master of Wine status, which means he knows as much about wine in the bottle as grapes on the vine. That's quite an asset to this newly formed Hawke's Bay company.
Current Release 1999 Gentle oak and dried orange peel aromas join forces on the bouquet. It's so smooth on the palate it seems positively viscous, which should make it a good partner for pork cutlets in a mustard/cream sauce.

Craggy Range Winery Seven Poplars Vineyard Chardonnay

STYLE **dry**

QUALITY ♟♟♟♟♟

VALUE ☆ ☆ ☆☆

GRAPES **Chardonnay**

REGION **Hawke's Bay**

CELLAR 🍾 **3**

PRICE **$28–31**

The Craggy Range winemaking team makes extensive use of 'wild' yeasts, rather than laboratory-bred models. This chardonnay was fermented and matured in French oak barrels, 60% of them new, and underwent a full malolactic fermentation.
Current Release 2001 The nose is funky and spicy, and that is followed by a flavour profile that put me in mind of grilled grapefruit halves. It's super-smooth thanks to the malolactic, and has flavours on the finish akin to white chocolate. Sounds complex? It is. Try it with chicken breasts, but push a crushed garlic clove under the skin of each one before you grill them.

Crossroads Classic Chardonnay

STYLE **dry**

QUALITY ♟♟♟♟

VALUE ☆ ☆ ☆☆

GRAPES **Chardonnay**

REGION **Hawke's Bay
Gisborne**

CELLAR 🍾 **2**

PRICE **$20–23**

The Crossroads team has produced a range of differently styled chardonnays over the years. This lightly oak-aged model was sourced from vineyards in Hawke's Bay and Gisborne. It's a popular buy at the cellar door shop in Fernhill, Hawke's Bay.
Current Release 2000 It's no biggie, but it's got a lot of fresh-faced appeal. The aromas are of butterscotch and peaches, with a dash of marmalade for extra interest, and the same impressions drift onto the smooth-edged palate. It finishes cleanly with a suggestion of fresh limes. Try it with tabbouleh.

Daniel Schuster Petrie Vineyard Selection

Daniel Schuster is one of the Canterbury greats, yet his efforts are probably better known overseas than they are here. He consults to big names around the world but is enthusiastic about his own country, particularly the Waipara region.

Current Release 2000 There's an interesting feral edge behind the grapefruit aromas in the bouquet. It's deliciously smooth on the palate with stonefruit flavours in the middle but a suggestion of lemon right on the finish. Right now, it would work with pan-fried snapper drizzled with lemon juice, but in a couple of years it will be happier with roasted quail.

STYLE **dry**
QUALITY ♟ ♟ ♟ ♟
VALUE ☆ ☆ ☆
GRAPES **Chardonnay**
REGION **Waipara**
CELLAR 4
PRICE **$30–34**

Dashwood Marlborough Chardonnay

Dashwood is a second label for Vavasour, the company that pioneered the Awatere Valley as prime winemaking territory. Glenn Thomas sourced fruit from the Wairau Valley for this one, saving his own grapes for the top label.

Current Release 2000 It's pretty hard to pick up oak on the nose, and that's just what Glenn intended. The lemon and grapefruit aromas lead to a nicely balanced collection of peach-like flavours, smartly balanced by integrated acids. I like it with grilled chicken thighs, rubbed with a thin film of grainy mustard.

STYLE **dry**
QUALITY ♟ ♟ ♟ ♟
VALUE ☆ ☆ ☆ ☆ ☆
GRAPES **Chardonnay**
REGION **Marlborough**
CELLAR 2
PRICE **$17–19**

De Redcliffe Estates Chardonnay

Made from grapes grown on the home vineyard at Mangatawhiri and down south in Marlborough, this simple but pleasant chardonnay was partly fermented in barrels. It has won a couple of bronze medals.

Current Release 1999 I get toast and grapefruit on the nose. It's quite citric on the palate, with impressions of limes and lemons in a smooth-edged framework. The finish is a bit short, but pleasant enough. We enjoyed ours with a rocket, blue cheese and walnut salad.

STYLE **dry**
QUALITY ♟ ♟ ♟ ♟
VALUE ☆ ☆ ☆ ☆
GRAPES **Chardonnay**
REGION **Waikato**
         Marlborough
CELLAR 2
PRICE **$15–17**

Delegat's Hawke's Bay Chardonnay

The grapes for this well-priced chardonnay came from several sites around Hawke's Bay. The juice was fermented in French oak barrels, but none of them were new because Michael Ivicevich didn't want to overpower the fruit.

Current Release 2001 The bouquet is citric and spicy, with grapefruit aromas discernible at the back. It's grainy on the front palate but creamy in the middle, and boasts a lick of sweet spice on the finish. I like it with couscous topped with mussels, steamed just until they open.

STYLE **dry**
QUALITY ♟ ♟ ♟ ♟
VALUE ☆ ☆ ☆ ☆
GRAPES **Chardonnay**
REGION **Hawke's Bay**
CELLAR 3
PRICE **$15–17**

Delegat's Reserve Chardonnay Barrique Fermented

STYLE dry
QUALITY ▽ ▽ ▽ ▽ ▽
VALUE ☆ ☆ ☆ ☆ ☆
GRAPES Chardonnay
REGION Hawke's Bay
CELLAR ▭▭▷ 1–4
PRICE $20–23

Grapes for this top-shelf chardonnay came from just one vineyard, known as The Vicarage. It spent a year in French oak barrels, and the lees left over from fermentation were stirred regularly.

Current Release 2001 Savoury oak and ripe nectarines get together on the nose, and I fancy I also detect a wee touch of butterscotch. It's a powerful wine, but it retains an overall impression of elegance, and that's an impressive balancing act. Partner it with pieces of corn-fed free-range chicken, baked with chopped garlic.

Denton Chardonnay

STYLE dry
QUALITY ▽ ▽ ▽ ▽
VALUE ☆ ☆ ☆
GRAPES Chardonnay
REGION Nelson
CELLAR ▯ 3
PRICE $24–26

Richard and Alexandra Denton had a great year in 2002. They won awards for Best Tourism Experience at the Nelson Tourism Awards, then took the Supreme Award as overall winner. They capped that with a prize for Best Winery Café at the Taste Nelson celebrations.

Current Release 2000 Big, spicy oak sits alongside the grapefruit peel aromas of ripe chardonnay. It's smooth on the front palate, quite citric in the middle but finishes with decidedly peachy characters. It would make a splendid partner for one of Alex's chicken salad creations.

Domaine Georges Michel Golden Mile Marlborough Chardonnay

STYLE dry
QUALITY ▽ ▽ ▽ ▽
VALUE ☆ ☆ ☆
GRAPES Chardonnay
REGION Marlborough
CELLAR ▯ 1
PRICE $23–24

Most producers worried about cork taint are switching to screwcaps, but this chardonnay uses the alternative, a plastic stopper. Earlier versions looked and acted quite differently from corks, but this one bears a reasonably close resemblance.

Current Release 2000 Light toast and melon aromas form an inviting bouquet. It's nicely focused on the palate and enjoys an appealingly creamy texture through to the moderately long finish. Pay tribute to its French heritage by partnering it with coq au vin blanc (chicken casseroled in white wine).

Dry River Amaranth Chardonnay

STYLE dry
QUALITY ▽ ▽ ▽ ▽ ▽
VALUE ☆ ☆ ☆
GRAPES Chardonnay
REGION Martinborough
CELLAR ▯ 5
PRICE $36–38

Dry River wines are exceedingly rare and seldom make it to retail shelves, but they're included because the label is one of the country's best. Neil and Dawn McCallum simply never make a dud wine.

Current Release 2001 The oak is stylish and gentle, and sits behind aromas suggestive of freshly squeezed grapefruit juice. It's immaculately focused, yet enjoys a creamy texture. Flavours? Nectarines come to mind, but suffice it to say they are perfectly balanced and delicious. Serve it with the best – crayfish, halved and grilled.

Drylands Marlborough Winemakers Reserve Chardonnay

French oak got the nod from winemaker Darryl Woolley for fermentation of most of this chardonnay, but a small amount did its thing in American barrels and another bit stayed in tanks. The barrel-fermented portion stayed there for six months.
Current Release 2001 Butterscotch and All-Bran get it together in the bouquet, with suggestions of dried figs to keep things interesting. The sweet-edged flavour profile is all about ripe peaches and nectarines, with the variety's usual citric notes pushed to the back. Enjoy it with a wedge of really oozy brie, served with thin slices of grainy toast.

STYLE **dry**
QUALITY ♟♟♟♟
VALUE ☆ ☆ ☆ ☆
GRAPES **Chardonnay**
REGION **Marlborough**
CELLAR 3
PRICE **$19–22**

Equinox Hawke's Bay Chardonnay

Equinox is a new Hawke's Bay company with a small portfolio of well-made wines. The small print on the label tells us this one was 'barrel fermented', and apparently the barrels used were new and one-year-old French models.
Current Release 2001 There's no more than a touch of oak spice on the nose – gentle timber seems to be an Equionox trademark. I like the creamy texture and richly fruited, ripe flavours through the middle. Citric characters cut in to ensure a refreshing finish. Enjoy it alongside a platter of room-temperature grilled prawns on rocket leaves.

STYLE **dry**
QUALITY ♟♟♟♟
VALUE ☆ ☆ ☆ ☆
GRAPES **Chardonnay**
REGION **Hawke's Bay**
CELLAR 3
PRICE **$20–23**

Esk Valley Chardonnay (Black Label)

Blending is almost always a part of winemaking, but Gordon Russell took the concept to extremes to craft this approachable chardonnay – the fruit came from 28 different spots in Bay View, Dartmoor and around Gimblett Road.
Current Release 2001 There's just a touch of gentle oak spice on the nose, backing aromas that put me in mind of baked peaches. The texture is creamy and the flavours ripe and moreish through the middle and onto the keen-edged finish. Try it with crumbed pork schnitzels and you should be perfectly satisfied.

STYLE **dry**
QUALITY ♟♟♟
VALUE ☆ ☆ ☆
GRAPES **Chardonnay**
REGION **Hawke's Bay**
CELLAR 3
PRICE **$20–22**

Esk Valley Reserve Chardonnay

Gordon gives his top-of-the-heap chardonnay nearly a year in oak, and puts some of it through a malolactic fermentation. The fruit in '99 came from three different sites, and each parcel was treated separately.
Current Release 1999 There's some nicely tuned, savoury oak backing the grapefruit characters on the nose. It's fresh on the front palate, smooths out in the middle and finishes with a dash of zing. That's a nice combination, and makes it a good partner for kumara and smoked fish cakes with dill-flavoured hollandaise.

STYLE **dry**
QUALITY ♟♟♟♟
VALUE ☆ ☆ ☆
GRAPES **Chardonnay**
REGION **Hawke's Bay**
CELLAR 1–4
PRICE **$30–33**

Fairhall Downs Marlborough Chardonnay

STYLE **dry**
QUALITY ▽ ▽ ▽ ▽
VALUE ☆ ☆ ☆ ☆
GRAPES **Chardonnay**
REGION **Marlborough**

CELLAR 🍾 **3**
PRICE **$18–21**

The Fairhall Downs team believes its fruit reacts best to quite modest oak treatment. The vines are some of the area's oldest, and the fruit was sold to various companies before the label was launched.
Current Release 2001 Light toast sits behind the aromas of freshly cut nectarines and peaches. It's a soft-textured middleweight on the palate, with gentle acids and a sweet-fruited finish. It goes well with chicken pieces and capsicum tossed with penne pasta in a light cream sauce.

Felton Road Barrel Fermented Chardonnay

STYLE **dry**
QUALITY ▽ ▽ ▽ ▽ ▽
VALUE ☆ ☆ ☆ ☆
GRAPES **Chardonnay**
REGION **Central Otago**

CELLAR 🍾 **4**
PRICE **$30–34**

Blair Walter used the grapes' own natural yeasts to ferment this wine. It spent 11 months in oak barrels sourced in Burgundy, home to some of the world's most famous – and most expensive – chardonnays.
Current Release 2001 The nose is decidedly toasty, with citric aromas pushed to the back. It's ripe-fruited and creamy on the palate, big but focused. It's a great match for braised rabbit and baby onions.

Felton Road Chardonnay

STYLE **dry**
QUALITY ▽ ▽ ▽ ▽
VALUE ☆ ☆ ☆ ☆
GRAPES **Chardonnay**
REGION **Central Otago**

CELLAR 🍾 **3**
PRICE **$22–24**

The back label tells us this chardonnay is 'not oak dominant'. That's hardly surprising – it has never seen the inside of a barrel, but was entirely fermented and matured in stainless-steel tanks.
Current Release 2002 No oak? It's still a bit spicy on the nose, but ripe stonefruit aromas dominate. The flavour profile is clean and direct, and reminiscent of baked peaches. It works well with Thai-flavoured chicken pieces.

Fiddler's Green Waipara Chardonnay

STYLE **dry**
QUALITY ▽ ▽ ▽ ▽
VALUE ☆ ☆ ☆
GRAPES **Chardonnay**
REGION **Waipara**

CELLAR 🍾 **3**
PRICE **$30–33**

The Fiddler's Green winemaking team fermented this chardonnay in one-year-old French oak barrels and left it there for 10 months. Because the oak wasn't new it doesn't dominate the fruit.
Current Release 2001 Spice from the barrels is quite subdued on the nose, just as the producers intended. There's a bit of the same character on the front palate to go with the citric flavours. It's nicely textured, quite generous through the middle and finishes cleanly and without fanfare. It should work well alongside a brace of fritters based on corn and chopped prosciutto.

Firstland Reserve Chardonnay

You need good eyesight if you want much detail about this wine – the front label is in the form of a badly typed 'cellar note', and it's pretty well illegible. It looks pretty, but is a clear case of fancy design winning over common sense.

Current Release 2000 There's a healthy dash of toasted nuts behind the citric characters on the nose. It's equally citric on the palate, which gives it a direct flavour profile, although the finish is smooth and moderately long. Try it with chicken in a creamy sauce, served on couscous.

STYLE **dry**
QUALITY ▽▽▽▽
VALUE ☆☆☆☆
GRAPES **Chardonnay**
REGION
  Hawke's Bay
  Mangatawhiri
CELLAR 2
PRICE **$22–24**

Floating Mountain Chardonnay

Mark Rattray has been around the Canterbury wine scene for more years than he probably cares to remember, making wine for a range of producers. Now, he's got his own Floating Mountain portfolio.

Current Release 2001 Mark says he doesn't make 'Sunday afternoon swillers', and suggests enjoying this seriously big wine (14% alcohol) with appropriate food. It's got toast and marmalade on the nose and loads of chunky, full-on stonefruit flavours. Barbecued skin-on chicken thighs and drumsticks would work well.

STYLE **dry**
QUALITY ▽▽▽▽▽
VALUE ☆☆☆☆
GRAPES **Chardonnay**
REGION **Waipara**
CELLAR 4
PRICE **$31–34**

Forrest Vineyard Selection Chardonnay

This small-production wine is the result of a visit to the Forrest winery by a touring Spanish winemaker. He got chatting to John and Brigid Forrest about chardonnay styles, so John decided to let him make one.

Current Release 2001 Muesli and comb honey are the impressions I get on the nose. It's smartly balanced, with impressive smoothness through the middle but enough acid zing to lift the peach-like fruit, particularly on the finish. Partner it with the Spanish fish stew named zarzuela (pronounced tharthuella) and toast its maker.

STYLE **dry**
QUALITY ▽▽▽▽▽
VALUE ☆☆☆
GRAPES **Chardonnay**
REGION **Marlborough**
CELLAR 3
PRICE **$30–33**

Foxes Island Chardonnay

John Belsham believes in holding his wines back until he feels they are ready. Many producers have released 2001 and even 2002 chardonnays onto the market, but this one didn't hit the shelves until the latter part of 2002. It was worth the wait.

Current Release 2000 Sweet oak sits behind aromas reminiscent of super-ripe lemons. It's impeccably focused, with clean fruit in straighforward surroundings. If you like chardonnay with grunt it's not for you, but if you appreciate elegance, seek out a bottle. Enjoy it with a whole snapper, baked with lemon slices in the cavity.

STYLE **dry**
QUALITY ▽▽▽▽
VALUE ☆☆☆
GRAPES **Chardonnay**
REGION **Marlborough**
CELLAR 3
PRICE **$34–36**

Framingham Marlborough Chardonnay

STYLE **dry**
QUALITY ▼▼▼▼
VALUE ☆☆☆☆
GRAPES **Chardonnay**
REGION **Marlborough**
CELLAR **3**
PRICE **$23–25**

Antony Mackenzie, known to his mates as Ant, fermented this chardonnay in French oak barrels, 20% of them new. About 60% was encouraged to go through a malolactic fermentation.
Current Release 2001 Spice from the oak is quite gentle on the nose – the major aromas are of citric fruit and peaches. It's smooth-centred, but the integrated acids add about the right amount of crispness to the finish. Try it with Chinese-style casseroled pork and eggplant and you should be well pleased.

Gibbston Valley Greenstone Chardonnay

STYLE **dry**
QUALITY ▼▼▼▼
VALUE ☆☆☆
GRAPES **Chardonnay**
REGION **Central Otago**
CELLAR **2**
PRICE **$23–25**

In past years, this clean-cut chardonnay has contained a small percentage of Marlborough fruit, but in 2001 it was 100% Central Otago. Grant Taylor calls it his 'savvie-style chardonnay' because it sees no oak.
Current Release 2001 With no timber to get in the way, the bouquet is cheerfully citric and very upfront. It's fresh and peachy on the palate, with well-tuned acids in straightforward surroundings. Enjoy it alongside pan-fried gurnard drizzled with lemon juice and good olive oil.

Gibbston Valley Reserve Chardonnay

STYLE **dry**
QUALITY ▼▼▼▼▼
VALUE ☆☆☆
GRAPES **Chardonnay**
REGION **Central Otago**
CELLAR **4**
PRICE **$30–33**

Winemakers vary in their interpretation of how long a maturing wine should be left in contact with the yeast lees left over from fermentation. Grant Taylor doesn't muck about – this one spent a full 11 months.
Current Release 2000 Gentle toast backs the aromas of fresh-cut peaches and nectarines. It's more melon-like on the palate, with creamy, well-focused flavours nicely edged by smartly integrated acids. There's no better partner for casseroled chicken, preferably of the corn-fed variety.

Gillan Marlborough Chardonnay

STYLE **dry**
QUALITY ▼▼▼▼▼
VALUE ☆☆☆☆
GRAPES **Chardonnay**
REGION **Marlborough**
CELLAR **3**
PRICE **$21–23**

Toni and Terry Gillan are Marlborough personalities whose local business interests over the years have included ownership of a shopping centre and a hotel, as well as the wine company and tasting facility.
Current Release 2000 Sweet-edged melon and citrus fruit aromas are in good balance with the lightly spiced oak. It's quite an elegant wine on the palate, with stonefruit flavours and gentle acids working to one another's advantage. Enjoy it with prawn risotto.

Gladstone Chardonnay

Christine Kernohan fermented only half of this wine in oak barrels, leaving the rest to do its thing in a stainless-steel tank. It's a very approachable wine that is a popular choice in the growing number of restaurants and cafés around the Wairarapa region.
Current Release 2001 Impressions of apples and pears are in good shape in the bouquet and drift onto the front palate. It's a nicely balanced wine with attractive ripe fruit characters and a sensible level of oak. We enjoyed ours alongside a pile of grilled polenta 'sticks' dipped into home-made mayonnaise.

STYLE **dry**
QUALITY ♟♟♟♟
VALUE ☆☆☆☆
GRAPES **Chardonnay**
REGION **Wairarapa**
CELLAR 3
PRICE **$23–26**

Glover's Richmond Chardonnay

This expression of Dave Glover's chardonnay style is made without oak. He crops the fruit at extremely low levels to give greater concentration and makes it quite simply, with only minimal contact with the yeast lees left over from fermentation.
Current Release 1997 With no timber to get in the way, the bouquet screams of melons and lime juice. It's fresh and lively on the palate, with citric flavors edged by the trademark Glover acids and is just starting to hit its straps after five years in the bottle. Partner it with freshly shucked rock oysters and you'll see where Dave was coming from.

STYLE **dry**
QUALITY ♟♟♟♟
VALUE ☆☆☆
GRAPES **Chardonnay**
REGION **Nelson**
CELLAR 2
PRICE **$24–26**

Glover's Richmond Rebecca Chardonnay

Dave Glover's whites often have pretty fierce acids when they're young, so holding this one back for a few years was a good idea. It's all but sold out at the cellar door, but you might find the odd bottle at serious wine shops around the country.
Current Release 1998 The bouquet is decidedly citric, with dried lemon peel the overriding aromatic association. It's lively, clean and fresh on the front palate, develops savoury notes through the middle and finishes by returning to the citrics again. Splash a little into the pan after you've sealed some chicken thighs in olive oil, added a squeeze of lemon juice and cook them until they're just done. Enjoy a glass or two as an accompaniment.

STYLE **dry**
QUALITY ♟♟♟♟
VALUE ☆☆☆☆
GRAPES **Chardonnay**
REGION **Nelson**
CELLAR 3
PRICE **$22–24**

Goldridge Estate Premium Reserve Chardonnay

Goldridge Estate is a second range of wines within the Matakana Estate portfolio. The fruit for this chardonnay was pressed as whole bunches, and the fledgling wine spent 11 months in French oak barrels.
Current Release 2000 The oak has added a grainy, biscuity edge to the melon and nectarine aromas. It's big, rich and smartly balanced on the palate with a crisp edge guaranteeing a refreshing finish. The back label suggests partnering it with 'decadent' dishes like scallop and prawn cannelloni. Fair enough!

STYLE **dry**
QUALITY ♟♟♟♟
VALUE ☆☆☆☆
GRAPES **Chardonnay**
REGION **Matakana**
CELLAR 2
PRICE **$19–22**

Goldridge Estate Premium Reserve Marlborough Chardonnay

STYLE **dry**
QUALITY ♟♟♟
VALUE ☆☆☆
GRAPES **Chardonnay**
REGION **Marlborough**
CELLAR 🍾 2
PRICE **$20–23**

A bit of careful label watching is necessary when buying Goldridge chardonnays. Both Matakana and Marlborough versions are produced, and both are labelled as Premium Reserve. This one usually commands a slight price premium. **Current Release 2000** Comb honey and grilled grapefruit halves – yep, that's chardonnay alright! The flavours are sweet-edged, peach-like and smartly balanced, with the oak playing a supporting role to the ripe fruit. It's a pleasant wine that sits well with savoury dishes like seafood lasagne.

Goldwater Roseland Marlborough Chardonnay

STYLE **dry**
QUALITY ♟♟♟♟
VALUE ☆☆☆☆
GRAPES **Chardonnay**
REGION **Marlborough**
CELLAR 🍾 2
PRICE **$21–24**

Kim and Jeanette Goldwater were Waiheke pioneers, but have expanded their 'mini-empire' to include production bases in other parts of the country. This chardonnay was sourced from a stone-covered site near Blenheim. **Current Release 2001** Gentle oak spice sits behind the rock melon aromas on the nose. It's a nicely focused wine, with flavours reminiscent of ripe citrus fruit and melon, all in a smooth package. It makes a splendid partner for a salad based around just-seared Marlborough Sounds salmon.

Goldwater Zell Waiheke Island Chardonnay

STYLE **dry**
QUALITY ♟♟♟♟
VALUE ☆☆☆
GRAPES **Chardonnay**
REGION
   Waiheke Island
CELLAR 🍾 4
PRICE **$39–43**

This is only the third vintage of the Goldwater family's home-grown chardonnay, but it has established a reputation for excellence right around the world. The grapes were picked by hand and pressed as whole bunches, bypassing the crusher/destemmer. **Current Release 2001** Savoury oak and aromas that put me in mind of grilled peach halves start things off well. It's smooth, ripe-fruited and smartly balanced on the palate, and would make a fine partner for a brace of barbecued or grilled scampi with home-made mayonnaise for dipping.

Greenhough Chardonnay

STYLE **dry**
QUALITY ♟♟♟
VALUE ☆☆☆
GRAPES **Chardonnay**
REGION **Nelson**
CELLAR 🍾 2
PRICE **$21–24**

Most local producers favour French oak for maturation of chardonnay, but Andrew Greenhough used half French, half American barrels. Some were brand-new, others were seasoned by a year's use. **Current Release 2001** The cracked wheat and baked peach bouquet on this chardonnay leads to a melon-like, smooth-as-cream flavour profile. It's nicely made wine that works well with pan-fried pork chops – with crackling, of course!

Grove Mill Marlborough Chardonnay

David Pearce kept parcels of his chardonnay juice separate when he crafted this wine. The various parts spent between nine and 12 months in French oak barrels, around 15 to 20% of which were new.
Current Release 2001 Ripe rock melon, spicy oak and a suggestion of grainy toast form a pleasant and inviting bouquet. It's ripe-fruited on the palate, but with clean-cut acids to keep things nicely focused. We enjoyed ours with a bowl of penne pasta tossed with pine nuts, chopped smoky bacon, garlic and olive oil.

STYLE **dry**
QUALITY ♟ ♟ ♟ ♟
VALUE ★ ★ ★ ☆
GRAPES **Chardonnay**
REGION **Marlborough**
CELLAR 🍾 3
PRICE **$24–26**

Gunn Estate Chardonnay

Gunn Estate was established in the Otihi Valley, Hawke's Bay, in 1994. The label has become particularly well-known for unoaked styles, both white and red, although nowadays barrels are used more than they used to be.
Current Release 2000 With no timber to confuse the issue this chardonnay smells of lemons and grapefruit skin. The flavours are more reminiscent of ripe peaches and the texture is quite creamy – usually the prerogative of oaked styles. It's good with directly flavoured food like pan-fried snapper fillets, drizzled with a little lemon juice just before they're served.

STYLE **dry**
QUALITY ♟ ♟ ♟ ♟
VALUE ★ ★ ★ ★ ★
GRAPES **Chardonnay**
REGION **Hawke's Bay**
CELLAR 🍾 2
PRICE **$15–17**

Gunn Estate Skeetfield Chardonnay

This wine is named in memory of Colin Francis Gunn, father of winery founder, Denis Gunn. Colin was a world-class clay target shooter, and the skeet field where he used to practise is now a chardonnay vineyard.
Current Release 2000 A nine-month spell in oak barrels, 60% of them new, has added a fair whack of sweet spice to the stonefruit aromas. It's creamy on the palate, partly from the oak and partly from a 35% malolactic fermentation. It's nice wine that goes well with pumpkin risotto, laced with a little fresh sage.

STYLE **dry**
QUALITY ♟ ♟ ♟ ♟
VALUE ★ ★ ★ ★
GRAPES **Chardonnay**
REGION **Hawke's Bay**
CELLAR 🍾 3
PRICE **$20–23**

Hawkesbridge Sophie's Vineyard Chardonnay

Mike and Judy Veal got into winemaking because they liked the look of the lifestyle. It has proved hard work, but a silver medal for this nicely made chardonnay helped make it all worthwhile.
Current Release 1998 Attractive melon-like notes in the bouquet start things off well. It's direct but quite stylish, with ripe fruit, a keen edge and a reasonably long finish. It works well with tuatua fritters dabbed with aioli (garlic mayonnaise).

STYLE **dry**
QUALITY ♟ ♟ ♟ ♟
VALUE ★ ★ ★ ★
GRAPES **Chardonnay**
REGION **Marlborough**
CELLAR 🍾 3
PRICE **$19–21**

Hawkesbridge Sophie's Vineyard Chardonnay Reserve

STYLE **dry**
QUALITY 🍷 🍷 🍷 🍷
VALUE ★ ★ ★ ☆
GRAPES **Chardonnay**
REGION **Marlborough**
CELLAR 🍾 **3**
PRICE **$25–28**

The Veals made only 100 cases of this top-shelf chardonnay, but the odd bottle can still be found in country wine shops. It was made from grapes laboriously picked by hand to give more control.
Current Release 1997 Mineral notes on the nose are typical of Marlborough. It's a big, solid wine with waves of fruit flavour supported by spicy oak. Enjoy it with greenshell mussels, steamed open in a splash of the wine diluted with water and spiked with fresh herbs.

Hawkesbridge Sophie's Vineyard Premium Chardonnay

STYLE **dry**
QUALITY 🍷 🍷 🍷 🍷 🍷
VALUE ★ ★ ★ ★
GRAPES **Chardonnay**
REGION **Marlborough**
CELLAR 🍾 **3**
PRICE **$22–25**

The gold medal '99 was matured solely in French oak, but this later model spent some of its quiet time in American barrels. Hawkesbridge wines are becoming rare as the company puts more emphasis on exports.
Current Release 2000 The oak spice is subtle and controlled, providing just enough backing for the melon and citrus fruit aromas. It's richly textured, nicely balanced and boasts a sweet finish. It makes a good partner for roast chicken, and works even better if the bird is rubbed with lemon juice before it hits the oven.

Hay's Lake Chardonnay

STYLE **dry**
QUALITY 🍷 🍷 🍷 🍷 🍷
VALUE ★ ★ ★ ★ ☆
GRAPES **Chardonnay**
REGION **Central Otago**
CELLAR 🍾 **3**
PRICE **$22–24**

Rudi Bauer put this wine into oak barrels, 20% of them new. The yeast lees left over from fermentation were left in to allow them to contribute to the flavour, and a full acid-softening malolactic fermentation was encouraged.
Current Release 2001 The wine is sweet-edged, ripe-fruited and spicy, and that applies pretty well equally to both the bouquet and the flavour profile. It's very direct in its appeal, and has an attractive savoury note towards the finish. It's good with braised pork and mushrooms.

Herzog Marlborough Chardonnay

STYLE **dry**
QUALITY 🍷 🍷 🍷 🍷 🍷
VALUE ★ ★ ☆
GRAPES **Chardonnay**
REGION **Marlborough**
CELLAR 🍾 **4**
PRICE **$39–43**

Hans Herzog does nothing by halves. This chardonnay spent a year in all-new French oak barrels, and was encouraged to undergo a full malolactic fermentation. It's a popular buy in the plush winery restaurant.
Current Release 2001 Naturally enough, it's a BIG wine, with lashings of spicy oak on the otherwise citric nose and rich, ripe full-on flavours through the middle. The finish is long and reminiscent of a freshly cut Golden Queen peach. If you visit the restaurant, try it with the white veal and pesto.

Highfield Marlborough Chardonnay

Alistair Soper fermented this wine in French oak, 30% of which was new, and left it there for 11 months. Wild yeasts were used for 20% of the juice, and a mixture of laboratory-bred models for the remainder.

Current Release 2000 The savoury bouquet has shades of honey on Vogel's toast — obviously a real Kiwi wine! It's smooth enough to qualify as 'creamy', but smartly integrated acids ensure things don't get too loose. Enjoy it with lemonfish, known as rig in the deep south, simply pan-fried and drizzled with serious olive oil.

STYLE **dry**
QUALITY ♟ ♟ ♟ ♟
VALUE ☆ ☆
GRAPES **Chardonnay**
REGION **Marlborough**
CELLAR **3**
PRICE **$32–35**

Huia Marlborough Chardonnay

Claire and Mike Allen aged this ripe-fruited chardonnay in barrels for a few months, but they were all between one and three years old. Obviously, they had far less influence on the fruit than new models would have done.

Current Release 2000 With no new oak to dominate proceedings the spice on the nose is gentle and understated. The clean, ripe stonefruit flavours sit in smooth surroundings, making this a very approachable wine that goes well with straightforward dishes like chicken pieces in a creamy sauce, served with young green beans.

STYLE **dry**
QUALITY ♟ ♟ ♟ ♟
VALUE ☆ ☆ ☆
GRAPES **Chardonnay**
REGION **Marlborough**
CELLAR **3**
PRICE **$28–32**

Huntaway Reserve Gisborne Chardonnay

The Huntaway Chardonnay label is worn by wines from various parts of the country, but Gisborne always seems to play a part. This one uses fruit solely from there, but its blended predecessors are still on a few shelves.

Current Release 2000 Marmalade on toast! That's what I get on the nose of this friendly wine. The flavours are creamy and citric, and remain stylishly focused from start to finish. It makes a smart companion for a pile of Parmesan-dusted grilled chicken drumsticks.

STYLE **dry**
QUALITY ♟ ♟ ♟ ♟ ♟
VALUE ☆ ☆ ☆ ☆ ☆
GRAPES **Chardonnay**
REGION **Gisborne**
CELLAR **3**
PRICE **$20–23**

Hunter's Chardonnay

Jane Hunter and Gary Duke have established a huge international reputation with a series of award-winning sauvignons, but they're equally good with chardonnay. Most of the juice for this one was fermented and matured in French oak.

Current Release 2000 Aromas of toasted nuts give away the time in timber. They sit behind suggestions of freshly cut nectarines. That stonefruit impression continues on the palate, where it is joined by flavours vaguely suggestive of dried figs. The texture is creamy and the finish moderately long. Enjoy it with mushrooms in a creamy sauce, served on grainy toast.

STYLE **dry**
QUALITY ♟ ♟ ♟ ♟
VALUE ☆ ☆ ☆
GRAPES **Chardonnay**
REGION **Marlborough**
CELLAR **2**
PRICE **$21–23**

Hyperion Helios Chardonnay

STYLE **dry**
QUALITY ♟ ♟ ♟ ♟
VALUE ☆ ☆ ☆ ⸜
GRAPES **Chardonnay**
REGION **Matakana**
CELLAR ▭ **1–3**
PRICE **$25–28**

The back label attributes Helios, who 'climbed the vault of heaven and cast sunrays on the earth', with creating this wine's intensity. Can't argue with that! John Crone put it in oak barrels, mostly French and 50% new, for eight months.
Current Release 2000 There's some nice oak spice behind the butterscotch characters on the nose. It's creamy and elegant on the palate, with smartly balanced citrusy acids cutting in on the finish. It's good with an oven-baked snapper fillet with potato wedges and braised fennel.

Johanneshof Marlborough Chardonnay

STYLE **dry**
QUALITY ♟ ♟ ♟
VALUE ☆ ☆ ☆
GRAPES **Chardonnay**
REGION **Marlborough**
CELLAR ▯ **2**
PRICE **$21–23**

Warwick Foley and Edel Everling hold their wines back until they feel they're ready. Other people are releasing 2001 and even 2002 chardonnays, but this is their current model. It won a bronze medal at the New Zealand Wine Society Royal Easter Wine Show.
Current Release 1998 The oak is still surprisingly dominant in the bouquet given that this is a five-year-old wine, but there is some good stonefruit character behind all that spice. It's a smooth-centred middleweight on the palate, and goes well with veal schnitzels, crumbed, fried in olive oil and served with lemon wedges.

Kahurangi Estate Chardonnay

STYLE **dry**
QUALITY ♟ ♟ ♟ ⸜
VALUE ☆ ☆ ☆ ⸜
GRAPES **Chardonnay**
REGION **Nelson**
CELLAR ▯ **3**
PRICE **$20–23**

Kahurangi Estate operates a pleasant café through the day from September 1 until the end of April, and the olives and olive oil offered in some dishes are from trees grown alongside the vines.
Current Release 2000 American oak barrels, used for maturation but not fermentation, have added a toasted nut character to the nectarine and grapefruit aromas. It's smooth-centred, reasonably mouth-filling and finishes cleanly. It's good with Indonesian mee goreng.

Kahurangi Estate Unwooded Chardonnay

STYLE **dry**
QUALITY ♟ ♟ ♟ ⸜
VALUE ☆ ☆ ☆ ☆ ⸜
GRAPES **Chardonnay**
REGION **Nelson**
CELLAR ▯ **2**
PRICE **$17–19**

The grapes for this unoaked member of the Kahurangi Estate portfolio were grown on north-facing slopes, in typically heavy Moutere clay. The back label tells us it is the owners' favourite style.
Current Release 2000 Grapefruit and lime juice characters are in good nick on the nose. The citric flavours are quite direct in their appeal, but the creamy texture smooths out the mid-palate. It works well with pan-fried gurnard fillets in a light creamy sauce.

Kaimira Estate Golden Bay Chardonnay

Only part of this wine was matured in oak barrels, while the rest did its thing in stainless steel. It's a sensible approach that prevents the timber from dominating the flavour. It worked well here, and has made the wine a popular restaurant buy.

Current Release 2001 Keeping the oak to a minimum means the toastiness on the nose is quite subdued, allowing the citric fruit to take charge. It's nicely balanced on the palate with no sharp edges and a pleasing texture. Enjoy it with poached chicken breasts on couscous.

STYLE **dry**
QUALITY ♟ ♟ ♟ ♟
VALUE ☆ ☆ ☆ ☆ ☆
GRAPES **Chardonnay**
REGION **Nelson**
CELLAR **2**
PRICE **$16–18**

Kaimira Estate Nelson Chardonnay

This member of the Kaimira Estate portfolio has benefited from an extra 12 months' bottle-age. It was held back from release, but even so it's getting pretty hard to find. If you spot a bottle, grab it – it's good.

Current Release 2000 Just the right amount of toasty oak sits behind the ripe peach and melon aromas. It's a generous wine on the palate, with sweet citrus and stonefruit flavours sitting in appealingly smooth surrounds. It would make a good partner for salmon hash cakes with home-made mayonnaise.

STYLE **dry**
QUALITY ♟ ♟ ♟ ♟ ♟
VALUE ☆ ☆ ☆ ☆ ☆
GRAPES **Chardonnay**
REGION **Nelson**
CELLAR **3**
PRICE **$19–22**

Kawarau Estate Chardonnay

The back label tells us that just 20% of this wine was fermented and briefly aged in oak casks from Burgundy, while the rest stayed in stainless-steel tanks. It is sent to both the UK and the US.

Current Release 2000 The oak has given it a faint touch of spice on the nose to go with the aromas of freshly cut peaches. It's equally fruit-led on the palate, with the peach and nectarine flavours sitting in clean, smooth-edged surrounds. It goes well with braised rabbit – revenge on a plate for bunny-ravaged Otago residents.

STYLE **dry**
QUALITY ♟ ♟ ♟ ♟
VALUE ☆ ☆ ☆ ☆
GRAPES **Chardonnay**
REGION **Central Otago**
CELLAR **2**
PRICE **$18–21**

Kawarau Estate Reserve Chardonnay

Grapes for this clean-cut chardonnay all came from Kawarau's own vineyard in the foothills of the Pisa Range. The property has full Bio-Gro certification, which means no herbicides, fungicides or pesticides are used.

Current Release 2000 Lemon, grapefruit and a subtle suggestion of spicy oak make for a pleasant introduction. The citric theme continues on the palate, which boasts nicely tuned acids surrounding the middleweight ripe-fruit flavours. It's a straightforward wine that goes well with grilled chicken breasts over couscous.

STYLE **dry**
QUALITY ♟ ♟ ♟ ♟
VALUE ☆ ☆ ☆
GRAPES **Chardonnay**
REGION **Central Otago**
CELLAR **3**
PRICE **$25–27**

Kemblefield Hawke's Bay Chardonnay (Signature)

STYLE **dry**
QUALITY ♟ ♟ ♟ ♟
VALUE ☆ ☆ ☆ ☆⸱
GRAPES **Chardonnay**
REGION **Hawke's Bay**

CELLAR 🍶 **3**
PRICE **$17–19**

Careful label reading is necessary with the Kemblefield range of chardonnays. This one carries the signature of the owner and winemaker, John Kemble. The winery now features an impressive tasting room, incorporating a versatile function centre.
Current Release 2002 There's just a touch of mealiness behind the citric aromas on the nose. The flavour profile is sweet-edged on the front, clean and fresh in the middle and spicy on the finish. It goes particularly well with a batch of corn cakes, served with baked potato wedges and green beans.

Kemblefield The Distinction Hawke's Bay Chardonnay

STYLE **dry**
QUALITY ♟ ♟ ♟ ♟
VALUE ☆ ☆⸱
GRAPES **Chardonnay**
REGION **Hawke's Bay**

CELLAR 🍶 **3**
PRICE **$27–30**

The 77-hectare Kemblefield vineyard was established in 1992 at Mangatangi, Hawke's Bay. John Kemble fermented this member of his portfolio in French oak barrels, 25% of which were new. It sat on the yeast lees for nine months before being bottled.
Current Release 2000 Freshly cut nectarines, grainy toast and a dash of butterscotch form a pleasant aromatic introduction. It's ripe-fruited and rich on the palate, with suggestions of mandarin and peach. It works well alongside a wedge or two of red capsicum and zucchini frittata, served at room temperature.

Kemblefield The Reserve Hawke's Bay Chardonnay

STYLE **dry**
QUALITY ♟ ♟ ♟ ♟ ♟
VALUE ☆ ☆ ☆
GRAPES **Chardonnay**
REGION **Hawke's Bay**

CELLAR 🍶 **4**
PRICE **$36–38**

John Kemble used 50% new oak for this chard. It sat on the yeast lees for a full year. The selection of which fruit belongs where begins in the vineyard, but the final decision isn't made until the juice has done its thing for a few months.
Current Release 2000 There's an attractive savoury note behind the predominant aromas of toast and dried figs. The flavour profile is rich and the texture creamy, and the finish sweet-fruited and long. It's very smart wine that goes splendidly with roast chicken – but be sure to use a corn-fed, free-range bird.

Kim Crawford Te Awanga Vineyard Chardonnay

STYLE **dry**
QUALITY ♟ ♟ ♟
VALUE ☆ ☆⸱
GRAPES **Chardonnay**
REGION **Hawke's Bay**

CELLAR 🍶 **1**
PRICE **$27–29**

Kim Crawford now makes the wines that used to be labelled Te Awanga. The vineyard is near the Hawke's Bay coast, so maritime breezes cool the air and extend the growing season.
Current Release 2000 Oak spice dominates the citrus fruit on the nose. It's broad and quite nicely fruited, with good balance and a moderately long finish. Partner it with gentle food, like steamed tarakihi fillets.

Kim Crawford Tietjen Gisborne Chardonnay

Gisborne viticulturist Paul Tietjen has grown grapes for countless award-winning wines over the years. The fact that his name is featured on many labels is a measure of the respect held for him by the industry.
Current Release 2000 Peach, Prince melon and oatmeal biscuits both contribute to the bouquet. It's superbly smooth on the palate, with fully integrated acids putting just enough of an edge on the ripe fruit flavours. It makes a splendid partner for a brace of char-grilled scampi.

STYLE **dry**
QUALITY ♟♟♟♟♟
VALUE ☆☆☆☆
GRAPES **Chardonnay**
REGION **Gisborne**
CELLAR 3
PRICE **$27–29**

Kim Crawford Unoaked Marlborough Chardonnay

This nicely made chardonnay has become a cult wine in wine bars and cafés around the country. As the label tells us, it is made without oak – but Kim lavishes other techniques on it, including a full acid-softening malolactic fermentation.
Current Release 2001 I get aromas that remind me of peaches and rock melon rather than the citrus fruits often associated with the unoaked style. It's impressively smooth thanks to the malolactic, with great approachability through the middle and a clean-cut finish. Kim suggests enjoying it with 'fusion' food, so try it with chicken strips and noodles in an Asian-flavoured broth.

STYLE **dry**
QUALITY ♟♟♟♟
VALUE ☆☆☆☆☆
GRAPES **Chardonnay**
REGION **Marlborough**
CELLAR 1
PRICE **$17–20**

Koura Bay Mount Fyffe Marlborough Chardonnay

Only 50% or so of the barrels used for fermentation and maturation of this wine were new, so as not to overpower the fruit. Some of the juice was encouraged to go through a malolactic fermentation.
Current Release 2001 That spicy oak is in pretty good shape on the nose. It's quite savoury in its flavours, and has nicely controlled acids. A pleasant middleweight that goes well with fish and chips from a shop that takes such things seriously.

STYLE **dry**
QUALITY ♟♟♟
VALUE ☆☆☆☆
GRAPES **Chardonnay**
REGION **Marlborough**
CELLAR 2
PRICE **$20–23**

Kumeu River Chardonnay

Even though this and the Mate's Vineyard chardonnays are regarded as two of the best wines of their style in the country, the Brajkovich family makes subtle changes from vintage to vintage. Unusually, this one saw no new oak.
Current Release 2001 Marmamade on hot buttered toast – that's the bouquet. This is a big, rich wine with a creamy texture but an edge of smartly integrated acids that cut in to enliven the lingering finish. There's no better match for a simple pasta dish like good Italian spaghetti tossed with pan-fried zucchini discs, chopped garlic and freshly grated Parmesan.

STYLE **dry**
QUALITY ♟♟♟♟♟
VALUE ☆☆☆
GRAPES **Chardonnay**
REGION **West Auckland**
CELLAR 6
PRICE **$36–38**

Kumeu River Mate's Vineyard Chardonnay

STYLE **dry**
QUALITY ▽▽▽▽▽
VALUE ☆☆☆
GRAPES **Chardonnay**
REGION **West Auckland**

CELLAR 🍾 **6**
PRICE **$46–49**

Named for the late patriarch of the Brajkovich family, this is one of the country's classiest chardonnays. The fruit comes from a small vineyard directly over the road from the winery, and in 2001 only 300 cases were produced.
Current Release 2001 There's a definite family resemblance to the 'straight' version above, but this beautifully modulated chardonnay seems more elegant. The oak spice is gentle on the nose and the sweet fruit is nicely balanced by subtle acids. The overall impression is of immaculate balance. Don't overpower it with strong-flavoured food – try it with flounder, pan-fried to crisp the skin and served whole.

La Strada Chardonnay

STYLE **dry**
QUALITY ▽▽▽▽▽
VALUE ☆☆☆
GRAPES **Chardonnay**
REGION **Marlborough**

CELLAR 🍾 **4**
PRICE **$43–45**

Unusually for Marlborough, Fromm has made a name for itself with a range of big-hearted reds, many made from varieties that supposedly don't do well in the province. They are invariably impressive, as is this chard.
Current Release 2001 Great balance makes this wine a success – it's got ample oak spice and a good quota of marmalade-like fruit, but neither stands out. The texture is elegantly smooth and the finish goes on for a very long time. It's good with pork loin braised with lots of garlic and onion.

La Strada Reserve Chardonnay

STYLE **dry**
QUALITY ▽▽▽▽▽
VALUE ☆☆☆
GRAPES **Chardonnay**
REGION **Marlborough**

CELLAR 🍾 **3**
PRICE **$45–48**

It's from the 1998 vintage, but Hatsch Kalberer didn't bottle this until October 1999. That would generally be considered a long time in oak for a red, let alone a chardonnay.
Current Release 1998 It's certainly different. The bouquet is reminiscent of marmalade, with a touch of nutty oak at the back. It's super-smooth, richly fruited but with acids that add life without making their presence obvious. It makes a fabulous partner for grilled crayfish, but pan-fried cod would do.

Lake Chalice Marlborough Chardonnay

STYLE **dry**
QUALITY ▽▽▽▽
VALUE ☆☆☆☆
GRAPES **Chardonnay**
REGION **Marlborough**

CELLAR 🍾 **3**
PRICE **$18–21**

The Lake Chalice team used fruit from three different chardonnay clones for this wine. The grapes were picked by hand and the juice sat on the yeast lees left over from fermentation for several weeks.
Current Release 2001 There's a savoury note behind the grapefruit-like primary aromas on the nose. It's been made with little winery artifice, with the result that the finished wine is fresh, clean and appealingly direct. Corn and red onion fritters would make a good match.

Lake Chalice Platinum Chardonnay

Platinum is the top label in the Lake Chalice firmament. The fruit for this latest model came entirely from five different clones of the chardonnay vine, all grown on the company's own Falcon vineyard.
Current Release 2001 Savoury notes back the fig and grapefruit aromas in the bouquet. The texture's the thing on the palate – it's smooth enough to qualify as 'creamy', but ripe peach flavours and smartly integrated acids keep the balance spot-on. Pull the cork next time you're planning a traditional roast pork dinner with all the trimmings.

STYLE **dry**
QUALITY ♟♟♟♟♟
VALUE ☆☆☆
GRAPES **Chardonnay**
REGION **Marlborough**
CELLAR 4
PRICE **$25–28**

Lake Chalice Unoaked Chardonnay

Unoaked chardonnays aren't nearly as common as they were a few years ago, so this one screams out the door of those retailers lucky enough to score a few cases. This latest model is sealed with a screwcap.
Current Release 2002 With nothing to get in the way, the wine gives us loads of lemon and lime juice characters on the nose and a fresh, very direct flavour profile. It's clean and uncomplicated, which makes it a good match for similarly direct food. Try freshly shucked oysters, served with a pile of lightly buttered grainy bread.

STYLE **dry**
QUALITY ♟♟♟
VALUE ☆☆☆
GRAPES **Chardonnay**
REGION **Marlborough**
CELLAR 2
PRICE **$18–21**

Lake Hayes Central Otago Chardonnay

Central Otago has a reputation for producing expensive wines, so this nicely tuned chardonnay is considered a bargain. The grapes used were mostly from the Mendoza clone, which is the traditional one in this country. It spent very little time in oak.
Current Release 1999 The brief time in barrels means the spice is gentle on the nose, and is dominated by the primary aromas of ripe peaches and lemon rind. It's clean, fresh and very appealing on the palate – not a big chardonnay, but all the better for it. Enjoy it with pork schnitzels, crumbed and pan-fried.

STYLE **dry**
QUALITY ♟♟♟♟♟
VALUE ☆☆☆☆
GRAPES **Chardonnay**
REGION **Central Otago**
CELLAR 3
PRICE **$20–23**

Langdale of Canterbury Reserve Chardonnay

It says Langdale of Canterbury on the front label, but the back label tells us the fruit for this bronze medal-winning chardonnay came from the Wickham vineyard in Grovetown, near Blenheim. It was matured in French oak barrels for a year.
Current Release 2000 Think lemons and grilled peaches – that's the bouquet. The texture is approachably creamy at first, but comes into sharper focus through the middle. The finish is decidedly citric and moderately long. Just lightly chilled so the temperature difference isn't too great, it works well with a hearty Tuscan-style bean and cabbage soup.

STYLE **dry**
QUALITY ♟♟♟♟
VALUE ☆☆
GRAPES **Chardonnay**
REGION **Marlborough**
CELLAR 3
PRICE **$27–31**

Lawson's Dry Hills Marlborough Chardonnay

STYLE **dry**
QUALITY ♟ ♟ ♟ ♟
VALUE ☆ ☆ ☆ ☌
GRAPES **Chardonnay**
REGION **Marlborough**
CELLAR 🍾 **3**
PRICE **$22–25**

Made from the harvest of four Wairau Valley vineyards, this chardonnay was mostly fermented in French oak barrels with ages from one to four years. A small amount stayed in stainless-steel tanks, presumably to add focus.
Current Release 2000 Spicy but faintly melon-like on the nose, broad and creamy on the palate, this is archetypal Marlborough chardonnay. The oak is in good balance with the ripe fruit, and the acids know their place. Enjoy it with a brace of Chinese-style crab spring rolls.

Le Grys Marlborough Unwooded Chardonnay

STYLE **dry**
QUALITY ♟ ♟ ♟ ♟
VALUE ☆ ☆ ☆ ☆ ☌
GRAPES **Chardonnay**
REGION **Marlborough**
CELLAR 🍾 **3**
PRICE **$19–21**

Unwooded chardonnays looked as if they were going to become commonplace a couple of years ago, but only a few producers persisted with the style. This one is finished with a screwcap closure.
Current Release 2002 The bouquet is quite savoury despite the lack of oak, but peach and grapefruit aromas predominate. It's creamy on the palate, impressively ripe-fruited and smooth right through to the finish. It would make a good partner for Malay-style prawn laksa.

Lincoln Heritage Collection Patricia Barrique Fermented Chardonnay

STYLE **dry**
QUALITY ♟ ♟ ♟ ♗
VALUE ☆ ☆ ☆ ☆ ☌
GRAPES **Chardonnay**
REGION **Gisborne**
CELLAR 🍾 **2**
PRICE **$17–19**

Most producers favour French oak barrels to ferment their chardonnay juice, but Justin Papesch used American timber for this well-priced chardonnay. A small portion was put through a malolactic fermentation.
Current Release 2000 Vogel's bread and toasted nuts back the melon-like primary aromas. The flavours are distinctly citric, and the clean-cut finish even drifts to the apple end of the spectrum. It makes a good partner for a pie filled with Greenshell mussels.

Lincoln President's Selection Gisborne Chardonnay

STYLE **dry**
QUALITY ♟ ♟ ♟ ♟
VALUE ☆ ☆ ☆ ☌
GRAPES **Chardonnay**
REGION **Gisborne**
CELLAR 🍾 **2**
PRICE **$24–26**

Chris and Anne Parker provided the fruit for this nicely focused chardonnay. Fermentation took place in French oak barrels, and the infant wine stayed in them for 10 months, in contact with the yeast lees.
Current Release 2000 Gentle, nutty oak sits happily behind the aromas of spiced peaches and grapefruit. It's quite big on the palate, but crisp acids ensure things stay lively and refreshing. It makes a good partner for a vegetable terrine based around capsicums and eggplant.

Lincoln Winemaker's Series Gisborne Chardonnay

'Winemaker's Series' sounds pretty flash, but in fact this is the entry-level chardonnay in the Lincoln portfolio. It has been, the back label tells us, 'lightly oaked', which means the grapes call the shots on the palate.
Current Release 2001 The bouquet doesn't give a lot of anything away, but there are some pleasant grapefruit characters in there once you get your nostrils working. Sweet-fruited and direct, it will offend nobody and goes well enough with simple dishes like crumbed gurnard and fries, served with tartare sauce or home-made mayonnaise for dipping.

STYLE **dry**
QUALITY ♟ ♟ ♟
VALUE ☆ ☆ ☆ ☆ ☆
GRAPES **Chardonnay**
REGION **Gisborne**
CELLAR **2**
PRICE **$14–16**

Lincoln Winemaker's Series Parklands Estate Chardonnay

Justin Papesch fermented 40% of the juice for this well-priced chardonnay in two year-old American oak barrels, and put it through an acid-softening malolactic fermentation. The rest stayed in stainless steel.
Current Release 2000 Grapefruit and coconutty oak set the scene. It's not a big wine, but it has attractive middleweight grapefruit flavours in smooth surroundings. Open it to accompany a platter of wok-fried chicken pieces, tossed with a little oyster sauce just before they are served.

STYLE **dry**
QUALITY ♟ ♟ ♟
VALUE ☆ ☆ ☆ ☆
GRAPES **Chardonnay**
REGION **Gisborne**
CELLAR **2**
PRICE **$15–17**

Linden Estate Chardonnay

Winemaker Nick Chan describes this as 'New World wine made with a tradition firmly placed in the old'. It was fermented with wild yeasts in oak barrels, only a few of which were new, and given a full malolactic fermentation.
Current Release 2001 Clean and citric on the nose, creamy and full-bodied on the palate, this is classy chardonnay. If you're into blockbuster flavours it's not for you, but I like its straightforward elegance. It goes well with a fillet of super-fresh snapper or tarakihi, simply fried and sprinkled with chopped parsley.

STYLE **dry**
QUALITY ♟ ♟ ♟ ♟
VALUE ☆ ☆ ☆ ☆
GRAPES **Chardonnay**
REGION **Hawke's Bay**
CELLAR **3**
PRICE **$22–24**

Lombardi Barrel Fermented Chardonnay

The nicely situated Lombardi property is well-known as a concert venue, but its wines are also popular around the country. In 1999, the chardonnay contained a percentage of Gisborne fruit, but this one is all from the home region.
Current Release 2000 The perfumed nose reminded me of dried oranges – unusual for chardonnay, but pleasant enough. It's rich and creamy on the palate, with good weight and a lingering finish. I enjoyed a glass recently alongside an absolutely traditional pork pie, and was well pleased.

STYLE **dry**
QUALITY ♟ ♟ ♟ ♟
VALUE ☆ ☆ ☆ ☆
GRAPES **Chardonnay**
REGION **Hawke's Bay**
CELLAR **3**
PRICE **$22–24**

Longbush Gisborne Chardonnay

STYLE dry
QUALITY ▽ ▽ ▽ ▽
VALUE ☆ ☆ ☆ ☆ ☆
GRAPES Chardonnay
REGION Gisborne

CELLAR 3
PRICE $17–19

This mid-range chardonnay from Gisborne's Thorpe brothers was made from grapes that were pressed as whole bunches, rather than being put through a crusher/destemmer. It was matured in a mixture of French and American oak barrels, 26% of them new.

Current Release 1999 Peachy aromas mingle with faint spice from the oak. The flavours are citric and well-focused, there's good weight through the middle and the finish is clean and direct. Enjoy it alongside a brace of barbecued prawns.

Longbush Woodlands Reserve Chardonnay

STYLE dry
QUALITY ▽ ▽ ▽ ▽
VALUE ☆ ☆ ☆ ☆
GRAPES Chardonnay
REGION Gisborne

CELLAR 3
PRICE $20–23

Made from hand-picked fruit, this top-shelf chardonnay was split into two parcels after fermentation, with 43% spending a year in French oak while the rest relaxed for 10 months in two-year-old French and American barrels.

Current Release 1999 The bouquet carries little evidence of that complex oak treatment – rather, the aromas are of ripe peaches and nectarines. It's smooth and creamy on the palate with citric and stonefruit flavours through the middle and a nicely lifted finish. It's good with crumbed pork schnitzels and young green beans.

Longridge Hawke's Bay Chardonnay

STYLE dry
QUALITY ▽ ▽ ▽ ▽
VALUE ☆ ☆ ☆ ☆ ☆
GRAPES Chardonnay
REGION Hawke's Bay

CELLAR 3
PRICE $15–17

Speculation was rife that Montana would drop the Longridge range once it took over the Corbans portfolio, but instead the labels have been simplified to give them a cleaner look. Matt Mitchell makes the wines.

Current Release 2000 I get Weet-Bix and grapefruit on the nose and pleasantly spice-edged fruit on the palate. It's bigger than some previous examples have been, and boasts a refreshing, grapefruity finish. It goes well with braised pork shoulder and parsnips.

Longview Estate Unwooded Chardonnay

STYLE dry
QUALITY ▽ ▽ ▽ ▽
VALUE ☆ ☆ ☆ ☆ ☆
GRAPES Chardonnay
REGION Northland

CELLAR 3
PRICE $18–20

This nicely maintained Northland winery has developed a keen local following for its timber-free chardonnays. Head for Whangarei's recently revitalised port area and you'll spot this one on a few café and restaurant wine lists.

Current Release 2001 The bouquet is citric, like grapefruit juice, but I also get something that reminds me of a freshly cut Pacific Rose apple. With no oak to confuse things it is direct and sweet-fruited on the palate, with a delightfully refreshing finish. It works particularly well with a plate of paua fritters, served with thick slices of buttered grainy bread and lemon wedges.

Main Divide Chardonnay

Main Divide is a Pegasus Bay label, and denotes that the fruit may not all come from Canterbury. The oak barrels in which this chardonnay spent 12 months were all a couple of years old, so they had a minimal effect on the flavour.

Current Release 2001 Despite the careful use of older oak, there's still a spicy edge on the peach-like aromas. It's not a big wine, but it has a good quota of pleasant citrus and stonefruit flavours in an easy-going package. It's good with pan-fried baby octopus – or should that be octokittens?

STYLE **dry**
QUALITY ♟ ♟ ♟ ♟
VALUE ☆ ☆ ☆ ☆
GRAPES **Chardonnay**
REGION
  Canterbury 50%
  Marlborough 50%
CELLAR 🍾 2
PRICE **$19–21**

Margrain Chardonnay

Strat Canning used a full malolactic fermentation to craft this chardonnay – a departure from his normal style. Only a few of the oak barrels in which it was matured were new. The 2000 vintage is also available in some stores, and it's just as good.

Current Release 2001 The oak has added quite gentle spice to the bouquet to go with the peach and melon aromas. It's sweet-fruited and nicely balanced on the palate, with a smooth texture and a clean-cut finish. It goes well with pan-fried gurnard drizzled with a little lemon juice and olive oil.

STYLE **dry**
QUALITY ♟ ♟ ♟ ♟
VALUE ☆ ☆ ☆
GRAPES **Chardonnay**
REGION **Martinborough**
CELLAR 🍾 3
PRICE **$30–32**

Marsden Estate Chardonnay

The four-hectare Marsden Estate vineyard produces about 3000 cases a year, most of which are sold through the company's own winery restaurant. Grapes are also crushed under contract for other tiny local vineyards.

Current Release 2000 Having seen no oak, this is a fresh-faced and lively wine with very direct citric aromas on the nose. That suggests it will be a lightweight, but at 14% alcohol, it most definitely is not! Chunky but smooth-edged flavours work well with Hong Kong-style lemon chicken, or an Italian fish salad.

STYLE **dry**
QUALITY ♟ ♟ ♟ ♟
VALUE ☆ ☆ ☆ ☆
GRAPES **Chardonnay**
REGION **Northland**
CELLAR 🍾 2
PRICE **$19–21**

Martinborough Vineyard Chardonnay

Some producers like the Mendoza clone of chardonnay, which has been around for several years, while others lean to more recent arrivals. The Martinborough Vineyard team hedged their bets by combining six clones from three sites.

Current Release 2001 Toasty oak combines with aromas reminiscent of ripe mangoes and marmalade. It's a very generous wine on the palate, featuring flavours that suggest just-cut nectarines and freshly baked bread. The finish is long and memorable. It makes a great partner for thick slices of eggplant, crumbed and shallow-fried in olive oil.

STYLE **dry**
QUALITY ♟ ♟ ♟ ♟ ♟
VALUE ☆ ☆ ☆
GRAPES **Chardonnay**
REGION **Martinborough**
CELLAR 🍾 4
PRICE **$35–38**

Matariki Reserve Chardonnay

STYLE **dry**
QUALITY ▽ ▽ ▽ ▽ ▽
VALUE ☆ ☆ ☆
GRAPES **Chardonnay**
REGION **Hawke's Bay**
CELLAR 3
PRICE **$35–38**

John and Rosemary O'Connor have made their name with a line-up of big, weighty reds, but this nicely tuned chardonnay shows that they know a thing or two about white grapes as well. It's not always easy to find, but it's worth a search.

Current Release 2000 Fruity rather than oaky on the nose and rich, smooth and nicely weighted on the palate, this is an immediately appealing wine that should find favour even with those who profess not to like the variety. Pour a glass to accompany a sandwich of good bread, poached chicken breast and home-made mayonnaise and you will soon convert them.

Matawhero Estate Chardonnay

STYLE **dry**
QUALITY ▽ ▽ ▽ ▽
VALUE ☆ ☆ ☆ ☆ ☆
GRAPES **Chardonnay**
REGION **Gisborne**
CELLAR 3
PRICE **$17–19**

This is Denis Irwin's 'standard' chardonnay, made in a more commercial style than I suspect he prefers. The 1997 model was released AFTER this one, so you might find both on the shelves.

Current Release 1998 The touch of spice on the nose backgrounds aromas that are surprisingly pear-like. It's citric and quite lean on the palate, yet it couldn't be described as austere – rather, it simply seems well focused. Partner it with freshly shucked rock oysters some hot summer afternoon.

Matawhero Reserve Chardonnay

STYLE **dry**
QUALITY ▽ ▽ ▽
VALUE ☆ ☆
GRAPES **Chardonnay**
REGION **Gisborne**
CELLAR 3
PRICE **$29–33**

Most people use barriques, which hold 225 litres of wine, to mature their chardonnay. Denis Irwin broke with tradition by putting this one into 500-litre puncheons for around 18 months.

Current Release 1999 Using bigger barrels has lessened the oak influence on the nose, so the spice is quite gentle. It's clean on the palate and carries the sort of citric flavours usually associated with younger wine. Its focus suggests it could do with more time yet in the bottle. It works well next to a risotto flavoured with grilled capsicums.

Matua Valley Chardonnay

STYLE **dry**
QUALITY ▽ ▽ ▽ ▽
VALUE ☆ ☆ ☆ ☆ ☆
GRAPES **Chardonnay**
REGION **Various**
CELLAR 2
PRICE **$12–14**

Matua Valley produces several chardonnays. Some carry regional identification, others are named for the vineyard that supplies the grapes. This one has neither – it's labelled simply as chardonnay, and the grapes come from all over the country.

Current Release 2000 I get suggestions of grapefruit and dried orange peel on the nose. It's smooth on the palate, moderately rich through the middle and has a short but lively finish. Winemaker Mark Robertson says he likes it with pan-fried scallops, and as it carries a whisper of residual sweetness he's probably spot-on.

Matua Valley Eastern Bays Chardonnay

Any oak this big-selling chardonnay gets is hardly worth talking about. Mark Robertson aims at making a fruit-led wine that is at home in casual circumstances, not one to be discussed in hushed tones.

Current Release 2002 I get dried orange rind and a suggestion of comb honey on the nose, and I'm perfectly happy to do so. It's lean, clean and sharply focused on the palate, with citric flavours and lively acids, particularly on the finish. Szechuan-style noodles with chunks of fresh tarakihi would be the way to go.

STYLE **dry**
QUALITY ♗ ♗ ♗
VALUE ☆ ☆ ☆ ☆
GRAPES **Chardonnay**
REGION **Clevedon**
         Hawke's Bay
CELLAR **2**
PRICE **$16–18**

Matua Valley Judd Estate Chardonnay

Grapes from the Judd Estate vineyard have won many awards for Matua over the years. Mark Robertson matured this member of the portfolio in a mixture of French and American oak barrels, 30% of which were new.

Current Release 2000 Grainy toast and dried orange peel kick things off in fine style. It's richly fruited but with good focus guaranteed by the keen but integrated acids that drift through the middle and onto the lingering finish. Enjoy it alongside a platter of tempura-battered prawns.

STYLE **dry**
QUALITY ♗ ♗ ♗ ♗ ♗
VALUE ☆ ☆ ☆ ☆
GRAPES **Chardonnay**
REGION **Gisborne**
CELLAR **4**
PRICE **$27–29**

Matua Valley Matheson Vineyard Hawke's Bay Chardonnay

Mark Robertson allowed 50% of the juice for this chardonnay to go through an acid-softening malolactic fermentation. It was fermented and matured in French oak, sitting on the yeast lees. Matheson wines are popular at restaurants around the country.

Current Release 2001 The oak has added spice to the bouquet, but its influence is quite gentle behind the primary aromas of figs and freshly cut peaches. It's rich and ripe on the palate, but remains well focused through to the refreshingly lively finish. Enjoy it with pork chops braised over slivered red cabbage cooked long enough for it to almost melt.

STYLE **dry**
QUALITY ♗ ♗ ♗ ♗
VALUE ☆ ☆ ☆ ☆
GRAPES **Chardonnay**
REGION **Hawke's Bay**
CELLAR **4**
PRICE **$20–23**

Matua Valley Settler Chardonnay

The Matua team says the fruit for this well-priced chard came from 'various vineyards in New Zealand's major wine producing regions', which we presume translates as Hawke's Bay, Gisborne and Marlborough. It is topped with a screwcap closure.

Current Release 2002 The nose is like spiced marmalade, but the flavours lean more to the apple end of the spectrum. It's nicely focused and very citric on the palate – not particularly complex, but enjoyable enough with simple fare like a chicken and avocado filled roll.

STYLE **dry**
QUALITY ♗ ♗ ♗
VALUE ☆ ☆ ☆ ☆ ☆
GRAPES **Chardonnay**
REGION **Various**
CELLAR **2**
PRICE **$12–14**

Melness Chardonnay

STYLE **dry**
QUALITY �
VALUE ☆ ☆ ☆
GRAPES **Chardonnay**
REGION **Canterbury**
CELLAR ▭ **1–3**
PRICE **$24–26**

Previous Melness chardonnays have contained a percentage of Marlborough fruit, but this latest model is 100% Canterbury. It spent nine months in American oak barrels. The big-hearted '99 is also available at the cellar door.
Current Release 2000 The nose is chock-full of the yeast-edged, toasty characters of outspoken American oak, but citric fruit wins through on the palate. It's smooth and direct, with an impression of ripe lemons on the reasonably sustained finish. Try it with a potato and red onion frittata.

Mill Road Hawke's Bay Chardonnay

STYLE **dry**
QUALITY �
VALUE ☆ ☆ ☆ ☆
GRAPES **Chardonnay**
REGION **Hawke's Bay**
CELLAR ▯ **1**
PRICE **$13–15**

Made in a style described in the official tasting note as 'lightly oaked', this simply structured chardonnay offers a fair bit of flavour for your buck. The name comes from a flour mill that used to sit on the banks of the Ngaruroro River in Hawke's Bay.
Current Release 2000 The savoury, toasty notes behind the citric aromas are a surprise in a chardonnay in this price category, but I'm not complaining. Things settle down in the flavour department. It's simple and undemanding, and as such deserves to accompany a pile of chicken and cress sandwiches, or something equally straightforward.

Mills Reef Elspeth Chardonnay

STYLE **dry**
QUALITY �
VALUE ☆ ☆ ☆ ☆
GRAPES **Chardonnay**
REGION **Hawke's Bay**
CELLAR ▯ **3**
PRICE **$27–31**

Paddy and Tim Preston arranged for the fruit for his top-shelf chardonnay to be picked by hand, and back at their Bay of Plenty winery they matured the fledgling wine in French oak barrels for 18 months, sitting on the yeast lees left over from fermentation.
Current Release 2000 Grainy toast and grilled grapefruit halves form a pleasant introduction. It's nicely weighted on the palate, smooth but with lashings of ripe fruit. Partner it with firm-fleshed fish like lemonfish or tuna, brushed with olive oil and baked.

Mills Reef Hawke's Bay Chardonnay

STYLE **dry**
QUALITY �
VALUE ☆ ☆ ☆ ☆
GRAPES **Chardonnay**
REGION **Hawke's Bay**
CELLAR ▯ **2**
PRICE **$14–16**

This is number three in the line-up of Mills Reef chardonnays, but it still scores highly with me. Above it comes the Reserve version, then the top-shelf Elspeth model. That's an impressive line-up – there's something for everyone!
Current Release 2001 Lightly charred oak, grilled grapefruit and freshly cut peaches form an attractive trio on the nose. It's creamy and biscuity on the palate, not a 'biggie' but thoroughly enjoyable alongside simple dishes like grilled or barbecued chicken drumsticks served with a chunky home-made tomato and basil dip.

Mills Reef Reserve Hawke's Bay Chardonnay

It gets only half the time in oak of the pricier Elspeth version, but this classy chardonnay still rates up the top with me. Once again, the barrels were all French, because the Prestons believe they suit the grape better than their American equivalents.

Current Release 2000 More citric than the Elspeth but with the same toasty aromas part of the picture, this is really another side of the same coin. It's creamy on the palate, with rich stonefruit flavours through the middle and a suggestion of lemon on the finish. It's great with shallow-fried gurnard, drizzled with olive oil and lemon juice just before it leaves the pan.

STYLE **dry**
QUALITY ♛ ♛ ♛ ♛
VALUE ☆ ☆ ☆ ☆
GRAPES **Chardonnay**
REGION **Hawke's Bay**
CELLAR 🍾 **4**
PRICE **$19–23**

Millton Gisborne Chardonnay Opou Vineyard

The fine print under the vintage on the label simply tells us this wine was barrel fermented. In fact, the oak treatment was quite complex – it was fermented in small barrels, then transferred to larger models for ageing.

Current Release 1999 I get oatmeal biscuits on the nose, with ripe peach and grapefruit aromas in the background. It's nicely fruited, soft-centred and very classy on the palate, and makes a fine companion for a traditional Italian osso buco, using white veal if at all possible.

STYLE **dry**
QUALITY ♛ ♛ ♛ ♛ ♛
VALUE ☆ ☆ ☆
GRAPES **Chardonnay**
REGION **Gisborne**
CELLAR 🍾 **3**
PRICE **$30–33**

Mission Hawke's Bay Jewelstone Chardonnay

Paul Mooney pressed the grapes for this chardonnay as whole bunches, bypassing the crusher/destemmer that is usually the first machine they see. The process is believed to retain every last nuance of flavour, but it can leave sediment.

Current Release 2001 Grilled lemons and peach halves – that's the bouquet. It's a nicely textured wine, with stonefruit flavours edged by gentle acids through the middle and a return to the citric impressions on the finish. Prawns pan-fried with a little preserved lemon would be the way to go.

STYLE **dry**
QUALITY ♛ ♛ ♛ ♛
VALUE ☆ ☆ ☆
GRAPES **Chardonnay**
REGION **Hawke's Bay**
CELLAR 🍾 **3**
PRICE **$28–32**

Mission Hawke's Bay Moteo Reserve Chardonnay

Paul Mooney encouraged this chard to go through a full acid-softening malolactic fermentation, then fermented and matured it in French oak barrels, 30% of them new, for around nine months. It's a popular buy in the nicely situated restaurant.

Current Release 2001 I get a suggestion of butterscotch behind the primary aromas of ripe grapefruit and spicy oak. It's nicely textured, boasting a smooth edge on the citrus and stonefruit flavours. The finish is touched with sweetness and spice. It's good with chicken pieces in Japanese-style noodle broth.

STYLE **dry**
QUALITY ♛ ♛ ♛ ♛
VALUE ☆ ☆ ☆ ☆
GRAPES **Chardonnay**
REGION **Hawke's Bay**
CELLAR 🍾 **3**
PRICE **$21–23**

Mission Hawke's Bay Reserve Chardonnay

STYLE **dry**
QUALITY ♟ ♟ ♟ ♟
VALUE ☆ ☆ ☆ ☆
GRAPES **Chardonnay**
REGION **Hawke's Bay**

CELLAR ▯ **3**
PRICE **$21–23**

A bit of careful label watching is necessary when buying Mission chardonnay. This is one of two Reserve wines in the portfolio, and there are others that look pretty similar at a quick glance. It's a popular restaurant wine around the country.

Current Release 2001 The butterscotch aroma that seems to be a trademark of Mission chards is again in evidence on the nose, along with lightly toasted oak and a suggestion of lemon. It's smooth on the palate, but clean-cut acids give it plenty of life, especially on the finish. Enjoy it with fish and chips from a dedicated 'chippie'.

Moana Park Chardonnay

STYLE **dry**
QUALITY ♟ ♟ ♟
VALUE ☆ ☆ ☆ ☆
GRAPES **Chardonnay**
REGION **Hawke's Bay**

CELLAR ▯ **2**
PRICE **$16–18**

Although its 2001-vintage cellarmate is labelled 'lightly oaked', this earlier model didn't see a lot more timber. The grapes for both wines came from the same Dartmoor Valley site.

Current Release 2000 Despite the apparent lack of barrel ageing, there's a fair bit of oak spice on the nose, with grapefruit and peach aromas pushed to the back. It's nicely fruited on the palate, with the oak now acting as a smoothing agent. The finish is creamy and moderately long. Enjoy it with triangles of split pita bread, topped with Parmigiano and grilled.

Moana Park Lightly Oaked Chardonnay

STYLE **dry**
QUALITY ♟ ♟ ♟ ♟
VALUE ☆ ☆ ☆ ☆
GRAPES **Chardonnay**
REGION **Hawke's Bay**

CELLAR ▯ **2**
PRICE **$20–23**

Only a small percentage of this wine was matured in oak barrels, so it should satisfy the 'unoaked chardonnay' brigade. Moana Park is a new label operating from a vineyard in the picturesque Dartmoor Valley in Hawke's Bay.

Current Release 2001 The bouquet is citric, with gentle spice filling in the background. There's some pretty big fruit in there, edged by smartly integrated acids that lift the middle and add extra life to the finish. It makes a good companion for a whole baked snapper, especially if it's stuffed with breadcrumbs flavoured with lemon rind.

Montana Estates '0' Ormond Estate Gisborne Chardonnay

STYLE **dry**
QUALITY ♟ ♟ ♟ ♟ ♟
VALUE ☆ ☆ ☆ ☆
GRAPES **Chardonnay**
REGION **Gisborne**

CELLAR ▯ **3**
PRICE **$29–32**

Montana's initial-series wines, especially this big-hearted chardonnay, are popular on restaurant wine lists right around the country. Steve Voysey used a mixture of hand-picked and machine-harvested grapes for this latest model.

Current Release 1999 Gentle spice behind the marmalade and peach aromas shows the oak treatment was finely tuned. It's rich and full-flavoured on the palate, but seems more elegant than some previous examples. That makes it a good companion for pan-fried pork chops.

Montana Gisborne Chardonnay

Winemakers Steve Voysey and Peter Bristow fermented a portion of this wine in oak barrels, but the major part was left to do its thing in stainless steel because they wanted plenty of mid-palate vibrancy. It worked.

Current Release 2002 There's a gentle touch of spice on the nose, but mostly it speaks of dried lemon rind and other citrus associations. It's light on the front palate, faintly creamy through the middle and lean on the finish. It needs food with an acid component – try poached chicken strips tossed in vinaigrette with a squeeze of lemon juice.

STYLE **dry**
QUALITY ♟ ♟ ♟
VALUE ☆ ☆ ☆ ☆⯨
GRAPES **Chardonnay**
REGION **Gisborne**
CELLAR **1**
PRICE **$14–16**

Montana 'R' Renwick Estate Chardonnay

The label concept for Montana's 'initial' series came from an Italian designer, and the bottles certainly stand out on the shelves. Given that they represent the best of each region, they are pretty well priced. This one is a classic of the local style.

Current Release 1999 The bouquet is toasty, rich and full and the flavours on the front palate give the same impression. It's appealingly creamy through the middle and boasts nicely focused citrus and stonefruit flavours right through to the lingering finish. Partner it with a bowl of lightly spiced cubes of firm-fleshed fish with noodles in broth.

STYLE **dry**
QUALITY ♟ ♟ ♟ ♟ ♟
VALUE ☆ ☆ ☆⯨
GRAPES **Chardonnay**
REGION **Marlborough**
CELLAR **4**
PRICE **$26–29**

Montana Reserve Marlborough Barrique Fermented Chardonnay

The barrique referred to in the name is a 225-litre barrel, considered the optimum size for maturing wine. Both French and American models were used – the latter are considered more outspoken, so have a greater influence on the flavour.

Current Release 2001 There's certainly plenty of toasty, savoury oak on the nose, but the fruit is also in good nick. It's smooth centred, impressively textured and nicely balanced, which adds up to a highly drinkable package. If you can get hold of some real veal shanks on the bone, make tomato-free osso buco, splash a bit in the pot and finish the bottle as an accompaniment.

STYLE **dry**
QUALITY ♟ ♟ ♟ ♟ ♟
VALUE ☆ ☆ ☆ ☆⯨
GRAPES **Chardonnay**
REGION **Marlborough**
CELLAR **3**
PRICE **$21–24**

Morton Estate Boar's Leap Unoaked Chardonnay

Boar's Leap is a limestone cliff near Morton's Riverview vineyard, and it got its name from the Maori legend of a wild pig that leaped from there to an adjacent cliff, thus eluding its pursuers.

Current Release 2000 With no timber to get in the way, the nose is shyly citric and very direct. There's nothing missing on the palate – it's nicely fruited and surprisingly full-bodied, and goes well with a pile of pure pork chipolata sausages, served as finger food with buttered bread and a selection of mustards.

STYLE **dry**
QUALITY ♟ ♟ ♟ ♟
VALUE ☆ ☆ ☆ ☆ ☆
GRAPES **Chardonnay**
REGION **Hawke's Bay**
CELLAR **1**
PRICE **$14–16**

Morton Estate Hawke's Bay Chardonnay (White Label)

STYLE **dry**
QUALITY 🍷 🍷 🍷
VALUE ★ ★ ★ ☆
GRAPES **Chardonnay**
REGION **Hawke's Bay**

CELLAR 📖 **3**
PRICE **$17–19**

Three vineyards contributed fruit for this well-priced chardonnay. The juice was fermented in French oak barrels with ages varying between one and five years. Around 15% was encouraged to undergo an acid-softening malolactic fermentation.

Current Release 2000 The aromas are of peach skins and grapefruit rind, with no more than a suggestion of oak spice. It's citric, clean and very direct in its flavours, which should make it a good partner for chicken and capsicum kebabs.

Morton Estate Riverview Hawke's Bay Chardonnay

STYLE **dry**
QUALITY 🍷 🍷 🍷 🍷
VALUE ★ ★ ★ ★
GRAPES **Chardonnay**
REGION **Hawke's Bay**

CELLAR 📖 **1**
PRICE **$19–21**

Yes, that is the right vintage – this four-year-old wine was re-released in 2002 after winning a handful of silver medals earlier in its career. Evan Ward fermented it in 225-litre French oak barrels and left it there for 11 months.

Current Release 1998 The nose is complex with spice, toast and grilled peach characters all vying for attention. The flavours lean more to the citric end of the spectrum – think cream on grilled grapefruit and you'll be close. I don't suggest that as a food match, however. It's much better with grilled or barbecued prawns.

Mount Riley Marlborough Chardonnay

STYLE **dry**
QUALITY 🍷 🍷 🍷 🍷
VALUE ★ ★ ★ ★ ★
GRAPES **Chardonnay**
REGION **Marlborough**

CELLAR 📖 **3**
PRICE **$16–18**

With an alcohol level of 14%, this is serious stuff. Top chardonnay label for Mount Riley is the multi award-winning Seventeen Valley model, but this 'little brother' is also impressive. Only some of the juice was fermented in oak.

Current Release 2001 Think of dried orange peel with a touch of vanilla and you've got a handle on the bouquet. It's sweet-fruited and mouth-filling on the palate, with oak acting as little more than seasoning – as it should. The finish is long and smartly balanced. Partner it with veal schnitzels scattered with pan-fried mushrooms.

Mount Riley Seventeen Valley Marlborough Chardonnay

STYLE **dry**
QUALITY 🍷 🍷 🍷 🍷 🍷
VALUE ★ ★ ★ ☆
GRAPES **Chardonnay**
REGION **Marlborough**

CELLAR 📖 **4**
PRICE **$32–34**

Mount Riley's Seventeen Valley vineyard is situated five minutes south of Blenheim, and it has done exceptionally well for the company. This chardonnay has won several awards, including a trophy and a fistful of gold medals here and overseas.

Current Release 2000 Comb honey, toasted nuts and grilled peach halves – I get suggestions of all three on the nose. It's sweet-edged, ripe and opulent on the palate, but with an underlay of counterbalancing acids to keep things from getting out of hand. It's a good match for grilled prawns served on Parmesan risotto fritters.

Mountford Chardonnay

C.P. Lin is the only blind winemaker I've ever met, and he certainly doesn't treat his lack of sight as a disability. In fact, he is confident that it means his other senses are heightened, and with winemaking, that's an attribute.
Current Release 2001 Gentle spice and subtle citrus characters form an elegant bouquet. It's clean and youthful on the front palate, beautifully focused through the middle and boasts a long, satisfying finish. It makes a great partner for braised or char-grilled vegetables like eggplant, capsicums and zucchini.

STYLE **dry**
QUALITY ♜♜♜♜♜
VALUE ☆ ☆
GRAPES **Chardonnay**
REGION **Waipara**
CELLAR **6**
PRICE **$49–53**

Moutere Hills Nelson Chardonnay

Simon Thomas was chuffed to win a silver medal with the '99 version of this wine at the 2000 Air New Zealand Wine Awards, and there's still a wee bit for sale around Nelson.
Current Release 2000 Spicy oak and ripe peaches share the honours on the nose, but the flavours lean more to the melon and citrus end of the spectrum. It's nicely balanced and boasts a super-refreshing finish. Enjoy it with a boil-up of paddle crabs – from Nelson, of course.

STYLE **dry**
QUALITY ♜♜♜♜
VALUE ☆ ☆ ☆ ☆
GRAPES **Chardonnay**
REGION **Nelson**
CELLAR **3**
PRICE **$21–23**

Mud House Wines Marlborough Chardonnay

John and Jennifer Joslin have two labels, Mud House and Le Grys. This member of their portfolio was matured in French oak, and 45% was put through a malolactic fermentation.
Current Release 2000 Toast and grapefruit are in pretty equal balance on the nose. It's creamy, richly fruited and very smartly balanced, which makes it an ideal companion for a classic corn-fed chicken, wiped with olive oil, roasted and served with all the trimmings.

STYLE **dry**
QUALITY ♜♜♜♜♜
VALUE ☆ ☆ ☆ ☆ ☆
GRAPES **Chardonnay**
REGION **Marlborough**
CELLAR **3**
PRICE **$23–25**

Mudbrick Vineyard Church Bay Chardonnay

Waiheke Island is known as red wine country, but Nick Jones has a big following for this chardonnay, made from the hand-picked fruit of low-yielding vines. It is available only from the winery and its attached restaurant.
Current Release 2001 The bouquet is gently citric, with a backing of spicy oak. A smooth-textured middleweight on the palate, it has pleasant, peach-like fruit and subdued acids. That makes it a good match for pan-fried chicken breasts, particularly if the chef favours a creamy sauce spiked with a dash of lemon juice.

STYLE **dry**
QUALITY ♜♜♜♜
VALUE ☆ ☆ ☆
GRAPES **Chardonnay**
REGION
Waiheke Island
CELLAR **2**
PRICE **$29–32**

Mudbrick Vineyard Hawke's Bay Chardonnay

STYLE dry
QUALITY ▢ ▢ ▢
VALUE ☆ ☆ ☆
GRAPES Chardonnay
REGION Hawke's Bay

CELLAR 2
PRICE $22–24

Mudbrick is one of several Waiheke wineries to source fruit from other parts of the country. This chardonnay was a popular buy at the cellar door and in the restaurant, but it's become pretty hard to find.

Current Release 2000 The minerally note on the nose is more reminiscent of Marlborough than Hawke's Bay, but it's pleasant enough. It's a smooth-centred middleweight on the palate, and sits nicely next to a platter of Japanese-style tempura-battered vegetables.

Muddy Water Waipara Chardonnay

STYLE dry
QUALITY ▢ ▢ ▢ ▢
VALUE ☆ ☆ ☆
GRAPES Chardonnay
REGION Waipara

CELLAR 3
PRICE $28–31

This wine was fermented in French oak barrels, but only 10% of them were new so as not to intimidate the fruit. Only wild yeasts were used, and the bubbling juice was encouraged to go through a complete malolactic fermentation.

Current Release 2001 The oak has added a gentle touch of toast to the primary aromas reminiscent of grilled grapefruit halves. It's sweet-fruited and smartly balanced on the palate, and would make a good partner for subtle dishes like cubes of firm-fleshed fish in a creamy sauce studded with diced celery, served on rice.

Murdoch James Unoaked Chardonnay

STYLE dry
QUALITY ▢ ▢ ▢ ▢
VALUE ☆ ☆ ☆
GRAPES Chardonnay
REGION Martinborough

CELLAR 2
PRICE $23–25

Unoaked chardonnay was once touted as a cult wine for the future, but it didn't happen. The style still has a small but loyal following, but most producers have gone back to the barrel. This one has beaten its oaked cellarmate in competitions.

Current Release 2002 With no timber to get in the way the bouquet is pure grapefruit, with a touch of something akin to pears. It's rich, sweet-fruited and surprisingly big on the palate, with lasting citrus flavours and a clean-cut finish. Pan-fried chicken breasts with braised witloof would be good.

Mystery Creek Chardonnay

STYLE dry
QUALITY ▢ ▢ ▢ ▢
VALUE ☆ ☆ ☆ ☆
GRAPES Chardonnay
REGION Waikato

CELLAR 2
PRICE $20–23

Mystery Creek Wines was launched by a couple of ex-Villa Maria employees. Fermented in one-year-old oak barrels and allowed to go through a complete malolacic fermentation, this member of their range has had all the drama.

Current Release 2001 Because the barrels weren't new, they have added only subtle spice to the bouquet – the primary aromas are of grapefruit juice and freshly cut peaches. Toasted nut and ripe stonefruit characters on the palate sit in fairly rustic surroundings, making the wine a good match for the likes of pork and fennel sausages with grainy mustard.

Mystery Creek Reserve Chardonnay

Both French and American barrels were used for the fermentation and maturation of this big-hearted chardonnay, and every one of them was brand-new. That's unusual for the variety, but it has worked well.

Current Release 2001 All that oak has added some pretty serious toastiness to the peach and grapefruit characters on the nose. It's creamy on the front palate, but gets big and chunky through the middle. It sits well with roast pork, sliced and draped over a pile of mashed kumara spiked with ginger.

STYLE **dry**
QUALITY ♟ ♟ ♟ ♟
VALUE ☆ ☆ ☆ ☆
GRAPES **Chardonnay**
REGION **Waikato**
CELLAR **3**
PRICE **$25–27**

Nautilus Marlborough Chardonnay

Clive Jones gets his chardonnay fruit from several vineyards in Marlborough's Wairau Valley. This latest model spent 10 months in oak barrels, 25% of which were new. Around 40% was encouraged to go through a malolactic fermentation.

Current Release 1999 The oak is quite subtle on the nose, acting as a backdrop to typical Marlborough melon aromas. It has developed a creamy texture in the last few months, but carries enough acid freshness to stay in good balance. It works well with a whole salmon, drizzled with lemon juice and baked.

STYLE **dry**
QUALITY ♟ ♟ ♟ ♟
VALUE ☆ ☆ ☆ ☆
GRAPES **Chardonnay**
REGION **Marlborough**
CELLAR **3**
PRICE **$23–26**

Neudorf Moutere Chardonnay

Most producers switching to screwcap closures have done so for only part of their production, using them for the 'drink now' styles or offering their distributors a choice. Not Tim and Judy Finn – everything they make has the new top.

Current Release 2001 The oak spice is subtle on the nose, sitting happily behind the predominant aromas of ripe peaches and oatmeal biscuits. It's immaculately focused on the palate, with melon and citrus fruit characters edged by integrated acids and that ever-present but understated oak. Crab cakes, made from Mapua crabs, are the way to go.

STYLE **dry**
QUALITY ♟ ♟ ♟ ♟ ♟
VALUE ☆ ☆ ☆
GRAPES **Chardonnay**
REGION **Nelson**
CELLAR **6**
PRICE **$42–44**

Neudorf Nelson Chardonnay

The grapes for this member of Tim and Judy Finn's small portfolio came from vineyards in Brightwater, Motueka and the Moutere Hills. The juice was fermented with wild yeasts in French oak barrels, 30% of which were new.

Current Release 2001 The oak is quite gentle on the nose, backing aromas suggestive of a freshly cut peach muffin. It's got loads of sweet fruit on the palate and a texture that fills the mouth in most satisfactory fashion. Partner it with mussel fritters, ideally made from Nelson mussels.

STYLE **dry**
QUALITY ♟ ♟ ♟ ♟ ♟
VALUE ☆ ☆ ☆ ☆
GRAPES **Chardonnay**
REGION **Nelson**
CELLAR **4**
PRICE **$27–29**

Nga Waka Martinborough Chardonnay

STYLE dry
QUALITY 🍷🍷🍷🍷
VALUE ★★½
GRAPES Chardonnay
REGION Martinborough
CELLAR 3
PRICE $34–36

Roger Parkinson used French oak barrels for the maturation of this wine. Around 30% were new, others varied in age from one to four years. He also put 20% of the juice through an acid-softening malolactic fermentation.

Current Release 2000 Spicy peach aromas make a good start. It's nicely textured, with well-focused peach and grapefruit flavours in smooth surroundings. It needs gentle food to bring out its attributes – try it with steamed tarakihi fillets, drizzled with lemon juice and olive oil.

Ngatarawa Alwyn Reserve Chardonnay

STYLE dry
QUALITY 🍷🍷🍷🍷🍷
VALUE ★★★
GRAPES Chardonnay
REGION Hawke's Bay
CELLAR 4
PRICE $34–36

This is the top-of-the-heap chardonnay in the Ngatarawa collection. That means it is made from the best fruit Alwyn Corban can find and matured in the best barrels in his collection. The oak is all French.

Current Release 2000 Honeycomb and a dash of bran form an inviting bouquet. It's deliciously creamy on the palate, with complex flavours suggesting nectarines, grapefruit and even guavas. Its ideal partner would be roast pheasant, but failing that a corn-fed free-range chicken would work pretty well.

Ngatarawa Glazebrook Chardonnay

STYLE dry
QUALITY 🍷🍷🍷🍷
VALUE ★★★½
GRAPES Chardonnay
REGION Hawke's Bay
CELLAR 3
PRICE $23–25

Gary Glazebrook, after whose family this wine is named, was a founding partner with winemaker Alwyn Corban of the Ngatarawa enterprise. In October, Alwyn's family marked a century of involvement with wine in New Zealand.

Current Release 2000 The bouquet is very stylish, with subtle oak spice sitting happily behind the aromas of a freshly cut peach. It's creamy and rich on the palate, but sensibly tuned acids ensure it stays refreshing through to the gentle finish. It's good with crumbed chicken thighs, served as finger food with home-made mayonnaise for dipping.

Ngatarawa Stables Hawke's Bay Chardonnay

STYLE dry
QUALITY 🍷🍷🍷½
VALUE ★★★★½
GRAPES Chardonnay
REGION Hawke's Bay
CELLAR 2
PRICE $16–18

Alwyn Corban has made a nice job of this second-tier chardonnay. A portion was put through an acid-softening malolactic fermentation, and oak was involved in the maturation. It's a popular restaurant wine around the country.

Current Release 2001 The savoury notes of dried orange peel and spicy oak form a pleasant introduction. It's very focused on the palate, with direct citric flavours and a clean-cut finish. Partner it with a platter of raw and parboiled vegetable sticks with seriously good olive oil for dipping.

Nikau Point Hawke's Bay Chardonnay Reserve

With an alcohol level of 14%, this is a biggie. The company is new, based in Auckland but dedicated to 'showing off the best of the Pacific', according to the publicity material that arrived with the wine. The label wears a stylised palm.
Current Release 2000 The bouquet is understated, but there's some gentle oak spice and a suggestion of stonefruit if you search. It's a different story on the palate, where the ripe fruit flavours sit in creamy surrounds. The finish is lively and refreshing. It's a good match for corn and red capsicum fritters.

STYLE **dry**
QUALITY ♟♟♟♟
VALUE ☆☆☆☆☆
GRAPES **Chardonnay**
REGION **Hawke's Bay**
CELLAR **3**
PRICE **$17–19**

Nikau Point Hawke's Bay Unoaked Chardonnay

We tend to think of unoaked chardonnays as being a little lighter, but this one has the same massive 14% alcohol level as its Reserve-labelled big brother. The company is aiming at supermarket sales, and the wines are certainly priced right.
Current Release 2000 I get pineapple and rock melon on the nose, with the variety's more usual citric characters pushed to the back. It's ripe-fruited and quite rich on the palate, and boasts considerably more depth than most members of the 'no timber' club. Pull the cork next time you're planning a chicken-topped fettucine dish with a cream-based sauce.

STYLE **dry**
QUALITY ♟♟♟♟
VALUE ☆☆☆☆☆
GRAPES **Chardonnay**
REGION **Hawke's Bay**
CELLAR **3**
PRICE **$14–16**

Nobilo Fall Harvest Chardonnay

It's cheap and cheerful, and the back label tells us it is 'best enjoyed young', but this chardonnay still gets a bit of fuss made over it at the winery. Darryl Woolley fermented a portion in French oaks and left it sitting on the yeast lees for 11 months.
Current Release 2000 The nose is like savoury All-Bran, which bodes well. The flavour profile is simple and direct, but there's nothing wrong with that – especially at this price! Partner it with crumbed and shallow-fried pork schnitzels and you will have spent more on the meal than the wine.

STYLE **dry**
QUALITY ♟♟♟
VALUE ☆☆☆☆☆
GRAPES **Chardonnay**
REGION **Gisborne**
CELLAR **1**
PRICE **$12–14**

Nobilo Icon Series Chardonnay East Coast Selection

Combining fruit from different regions is anathema to Europeans, but it makes perfect sense in the New World because it gives the winemaker more options when it comes to defining the final flavour.
Current Release 2001 A spell in French oak barrels has added a touch of toast to the grapefruit and lemon bouquet. The flavour profile is more peaches and cream – soft, reasonably rich and clean on the finish. It makes a good partner for chicken chow mein with crispy noodles.

STYLE **dry**
QUALITY ♟♟♟♟
VALUE ☆☆☆
GRAPES **Chardonnay**
REGION **Marlborough**
CELLAR **2**
PRICE **$20–23**

Nobilo Poverty Bay Chardonnay

STYLE dry
QUALITY ♟♟♟
VALUE ☆☆☆☆
GRAPES Chardonnay
REGION Gisborne

CELLAR 1
PRICE $15–17

Fermentation of this well-priced chardonnay took place in stainless-steel tanks and oak barrels. The wooded component was left in place for 11 months, during which time it was stirred regularly to shake up the yeast lees left over from fermentation.
Current Release 2000 I get lemon rind and peaches on the nose, a combination that gives the wine instant appeal. The oaked component makes its presence felt with a nut-like edge on the stonefruit flavours. It's no 'biggie', but it sits quite happily alongside a brace of barbecued chicken wings.

Odyssey Gisborne Chardonnay

STYLE dry
QUALITY ♟♟♟♟
VALUE ☆☆☆☆
GRAPES Chardonnay
REGION Gisborne

CELLAR 1–4
PRICE $19–21

Rebecca Salmond fermented and matured this chardonnay in used oak because she didn't want to overpower the fruit. About 20% was put through an acid-softening malolactic fermentation.
Current Release 2000 Stonefruit aromas dominate the bouquet – think peaches and nectarines. It's smooth, ripe-fruited and pleasant, with a moderately long finish. It makes a good partner for an open sandwich based around poached chicken breasts and rocket leaves on good, grainy bread.

Okahu Estate Clifton Northland Chardonnay

STYLE dry
QUALITY ♟♟♟♟
VALUE ☆☆☆☆
GRAPES Chardonnay
REGION Northland

CELLAR 3
PRICE $20–23

This is one of two Clifton chardonnays in the Okahu Estate collection – the other has 'Reserve' printed quite boldly on the label. Don't confuse them – they've both done well, but the Reserve has picked up several top awards.
Current Release 2000 Subtle spice and a suggestion of marmalade start things rolling on the nose. It's smooth enough on the palate to qualify as creamy, but the integrated acids ensure a reasonably vivacious finish. Chicken breasts in a cream-based sauce judiciously laced with lemon juice (stir it vigorously to prevent curdling) would work well.

Okahu Estate Clifton Reserve Chardonnay

STYLE dry
QUALITY ♟♟♟♟
VALUE ☆☆☆☆
GRAPES Chardonnay
REGION Northland
        Hawke's Bay

CELLAR 4
PRICE $28–32

This big-hearted two-region blend was aged in French and American oak barrels for 15 months, sitting on the yeast lees left over from fermentation. Around 60% was encouraged to undergo a malolactic fermentation.
Current Release 2000 There's some lovely spice to go with the grapefruit aromas on the nose, leading to a flavour profile that screams of ripe fruit, tempered by the vanilla characters of oak. The finish is long and satisfying. Partner it with chicken legs, brushed with olive oil and rubbed with Cajun spices before being grilled.

Okahu Estate Shipwreck Bay Northland Chardonnay

Shipwreck Bay sits to the west of the Okahu Estate vineyard and winery in the far north. It's on a windswept section of coastline, so it's pretty obvious how it got its evocative name. **Current Release 2001** The nose is decidedly bready, but there's a hint of lemon juice at the back. A creamy texture makes an exciting introduction on the front palate. It's got good focus and a refreshingly citric finish. It makes a good partner for mussels, steamed open, topped with garlicky crumbs and quickly grilled.

STYLE **dry**
QUALITY ▽ ▽ ▽ ▽
VALUE ☆ ☆ ☆ ☆
GRAPES **Chardonnay**
REGION **Northland**
CELLAR 2
PRICE **$19–23**

Old Coach Road Nelson Unoaked Chardonnay

Old Coach Road is a second label for Seifried Estate. The wines are exceptionally well priced and have won a few awards in national competitions. You'll spot plenty of them in Nelson restaurants.
Current Release 2000 With no oak to get in the way the bouquet is openly lemony, with a suggestion of dried orange peel at the back. The flavours are equally citric, but with an apple-like edge, and the finish is super-lively. It's good alongside Nelson oysters, served raw with cracked pepper.

STYLE **dry**
QUALITY ▽ ▽ ▽ ▽
VALUE ☆ ☆ ☆ ☆ ☆
GRAPES **Chardonnay**
REGION **Nelson**
CELLAR 1
PRICE **$11–13**

Omaka Springs Marlborough Chardonnay

Ian Marchant is the winemaker for this 60-hectare Marlborough property. The owners' background is in growing olives and making oil, so introducing wine was a logical move. If they add a bakery they'll have the summer dining market cornered!
Current Release 2001 I get the aromas of Prince melons on the nose, and that suits me fine. It's a nicely focused wine with direct flavours, smartly integrated oak and a clean-cut finish. The ideal partner? Obviously, crusty bread with good, green-tinged olive oil for dipping.

STYLE **dry**
QUALITY ▽ ▽ ▽ ▽
VALUE ☆ ☆ ☆ ☆
GRAPES **Chardonnay**
REGION **Marlborough**
CELLAR 2
PRICE **$17–19**

Omaka Springs Marlborough Reserve Chardonnay

Vineyard owners Geoff and Robina Jensen were thrilled to pick up a gold medal for this stylish chardonnay at the New Zealand Wine Society Royal Easter Wine Show. Ian Marchant fermented and matured it in French oak barrels, all of them brand-new.
Current Release 2000 The bouquet is savoury as a result of all that new timber, but the fruit is big enough not to be intimidated. It's creamy and rich on the palate, with loads of ripe-fruit flavours and a full-on finish. It goes splendidly with a plate of pappardelle pasta tossed with whole blanched beans and freshly made pesto.

STYLE **dry**
QUALITY ▽ ▽ ▽ ▽ ▽
VALUE ☆ ☆ ☆ ☆
GRAPES **Chardonnay**
REGION **Marlborough**
CELLAR 3
PRICE **$25–27**

Oyster Bay Marlborough Chardonnay

STYLE **dry**
QUALITY ♟ ♟ ♟ ♟ ♟
VALUE ☆ ☆ ☆ ☆ ½
GRAPES **Chardonnay**
REGION **Marlborough**

CELLAR 🍾 **3**
PRICE **$20–23**

The Oyster Bay range has been a huge export success for Jim and Rosemari Delegat and their team, but they make sure there's enough at home to feature on restaurant wine lists right around the country.
Current Release 2000 Fermenting 75% of the juice in oak has added gentle spice to the peach-like bouquet. It's sweet-fruited and smooth on the palate, not a big chardonnay but nicely tuned and very approachable. It works really well with an oyster and fennel pie.

Palliser Estate Chardonnay

STYLE **dry**
QUALITY ♟ ♟ ♟ ♟ ♟
VALUE ☆ ☆ ☆ ½
GRAPES **Chardonnay**
REGION **Martinborough**

CELLAR 🍾 **4**
PRICE **$30–34**

Making this wine was a percentage game for Allan Johnson. It was fermented in French oak barrels using 50% wild yeasts. At the same time, 20% was encouraged to go through a malolactic fermentation.
Current Release 2001 Gentle toast, grapefruit juice and freshly cut peaches form an invitingly aromatic trio. The spicy edge on the impressively rich flavours gives it a hugely appealing texture. The finish is long and very pleasurable. It goes well with most shellfish dishes, but is a standout with mussel risotto.

C.J. Pask Gimblett Road Chardonnay

STYLE **dry**
QUALITY ♟ ♟ ♟ ♟
VALUE ☆ ☆ ☆ ☆
GRAPES **Chardonnay**
REGION **Hawke's Bay**

CELLAR 🍾 **3**
PRICE **$22–24**

Frost badly clobbered the Pask vineyards in 2001, so this chardonnay was the last produced until the 2002 version hit the shelves – which hadn't happened as this *Guide* went to print.
Current Release 2000 Subtly spicy on the nose, sweet-fruited and smartly balanced on the palate, this wine is beginning its journey to smooth maturity. Because only 20% was aged in barrels, all a year old, it is fruit that calls the shots. That makes it a good partner for simple dishes like pan-fried chicken breasts, sliced thickly and draped over mashed kumara.

C.J. Pask Reserve Chardonnay

STYLE **dry**
QUALITY ♟ ♟ ♟ ♟
VALUE ☆ ☆ ☆ ½
GRAPES **Chardonnay**
REGION **Hawke's Bay**

CELLAR 🍾 **4**
PRICE **$26–28**

Kate Radburnd's top chardonnay is a big seller throughout the country, particularly in restaurants. This latest version is on sale alongside the equally good gold medal-winning '99 in some wine shops.
Current Release 2000 The nose is toasty and faintly nutty, with chardonnay's grapefruit aromas content to take a back seat. The fresh-faced flavours sit in creamy surrounds on the palate, ensuring richness and length. Enjoy it with a line-up of crumbed prawns, shallow-fried in olive oil.

C.J. Pask Roy's Hill Chardonnay

Roy's Hill is a second label for Chris Pask and winemaker Kate Radburnd, but some of the wines are pretty smart. This one uses fruit from the recently designated Gimblett Gravels region, where river shingle litters the ground.

Current Release 2000 Lemons, apples and a dash of oaky spice get together on the nose. It's smooth and smartly balanced, not a heavyweight by any means but all the more pleasant because of it. It makes an excellent partner for chicken breasts, poached in good stock with a little of the wine and served on couscous.

STYLE **dry**
QUALITY ♟ ♟ ♟ ♟
VALUE ☆ ☆ ☆ ☆
GRAPES **Chardonnay**
REGION **Hawke's Bay**
CELLAR 3
PRICE **$17–19**

Pegasus Bay Chardonnay

This classy chardonay has had all the treatment money can buy. The French barrels in which it was matured came from three different coopers, and 25% of them were new. It was put through a 50% malolactic fermentation.

Current Release 2001 The bouquet is nutty, with aromas of fresh bread and grapefruit juice adding to the mix. It's deliciously ripe-fruited, and has a texture that fills the mouth with flavour – think peaches and nectarines and you'll be on the right track. It deserves to sit next to crumbed scallopini made with real white veal.

STYLE **dry**
QUALITY ♟ ♟ ♟ ♟ ♟
VALUE ☆ ☆ ☆
GRAPES **Chardonnay**
REGION **Waipara**
CELLAR 4
PRICE **$31–33**

Pencarrow Martinborough Chardonnay

Pencarrow is a second label for Martinborough's Palliser Estate vineyard, but wines in the portfolio have sometimes oupointed their more expensive cellarmates in competitions. This one was fermented in French and American oak.

Current Release 2001 Melons and limes are the twin aromatic sensations. It's focused, sweet-fruited and refreshing with a spicy finish. It could be accused of being a little obvious, but it's certainly approachable. Enjoy it with fish and chips from a serious shop and you'll get the point.

STYLE **dry**
QUALITY ♟ ♟ ♟ ♟
VALUE ☆ ☆ ☆ ☆
GRAPES **Chardonnay**
REGION **Martinborough**
CELLAR 2
PRICE **$18–22**

Peninsula Estate Anchorage Chardonnay

Anchorage is the new name for the wine previously named Christopher, for winemaker Christopher Lush. It is made from the oldest chardonnay vines on the island, and is mostly sold at the cellar door and in a few local restaurants.

Current Release 2001 The nose is like sweet, toasted muesli, a legacy of its time in oak barrels. Citric fruit is pushed to the back. It's a nicely balanced wine with a smooth texture, integrated acids and a clean finish. Pan-fried tarakihi drizzled with browned butter and sprinkled with chopped parsley works well as a partner.

STYLE **dry**
QUALITY ♟ ♟ ♟ ♟
VALUE ☆ ☆
GRAPES **Chardonnay**
REGION
  Waiheke Island
CELLAR 3
PRICE **$28–32**

Ponder Estate Artist's Reserve Marlborough Chardonnay

STYLE **dry**
QUALITY ♛ ♛ ♛ ♛
VALUE ☆ ☆ ☆
GRAPES **Chardonnay**
REGION **Marlborough**
CELLAR 🍾 **4**
PRICE **$35–38**

There's not a lot of Mike Ponder's top-shelf chardonnay about, but it's well worth a search. The fruit was picked by hand, and the fledgling wine was put into new French oak barrels for three months.

Current Release 2000 Spicy oak and a touch of butterscotch add to the aromas of ripe rock melons and peaches. It's creamy on the palate, with big fruit filling the mouth and ensuring a refreshing finish. It makes a good companion for seafood-topped risotto.

Quarry Road Chardonnay

STYLE **dry**
QUALITY ♛ ♛ ♛
VALUE ☆ ☆ ☆ ☆
GRAPES **Chardonnay**
REGION **Waikato**
CELLAR 🍾 **3**
PRICE **$16–18**

Winemaker Toby Cooper put this chardonnay into American oak barrels for five months and encouraged 50% of the juice to go through an acid-softening malolactic fermentation. The 2001 model can also be spotted on a few shelves.

Current Release 2002 Spicy, toast-like aromas from the barrels are easy to find, but there's a good whack of citrus fruit in there as well. The same lemon/lime notes carry through onto the palate and add life and zing to the finish. It's not a biggie, but its faintly lean characters quite suit pan-fried gurnard drizzled with olive oil and lemon juice.

Ransom Barrique Chardonnay

STYLE **dry**
QUALITY ♛ ♛ ♛ ♛
VALUE ☆ ☆ ☆❧
GRAPES **Chardonnay**
REGION **Matakana**
CELLAR 🍾 **3**
PRICE **$23–27**

The Ransom vineyard tasting room is the first one visitors to the Matakana region spot on their drive up north. Robin Ransom recently supplied wine to the makers of the television drama *Mercy Peak*, and got an on-screen credit for his trouble.

Current Release 2000 Concentrated fruit is one reason why the oak doesn't dominate this pleasantly balanced wine. The aromas and flavours all fit into the 'peaches and cream' mould, but there's a nice citric edge to the finish. Enjoy it with a bowl of greenshell mussels, ideally from the Matakana region.

Ransom Gumfield Chardonnay

STYLE **dry**
QUALITY ♛ ♛ ♛ ❧
VALUE ☆ ☆ ☆ ☆
GRAPES **Chardonnay**
REGION **Matakana**
CELLAR 🍾 **3**
PRICE **$19–22**

Robin Ransom didn't want to overpower the fruit that went into this mid-range chardonnay, so around half the barrels in which it was matured were two or three years old. That means they had very little oak character left to give.

Current Release 2000 Holding back on the oak means there is only a suggestion of spice on the nose to back the peach and grapefruit primary aromas. It's rich through the middle and finishes with a citric flourish. Partner it with chicken cooked with Moroccan-style preserved lemon, served over couscous.

Revington Vineyard Chardonnay

In 1998, loads of sunshine meant Ross Revington could pick his grapes before April – the first time he'd been able to do so since 1991. That meant there was no chance they'd be affected by early rain.

Current Release 1998 Sweet oak and nectarine aromas start things off well. It's powerful but elegant on the palate, with nicely integrated acids ensuring a smooth texture. The finish is long and sweet-fruited – smart stuff! It's good with a tart based around pumpkin and blue cheese.

STYLE **dry**
QUALITY ♟♟♟♟♟
VALUE ☆ ☆ ☆ ☆
GRAPES **Chardonnay**
REGION **Gisborne**
CELLAR **2**
PRICE **$26–30**

Rimu Grove Nelson Chardonnay

Winemaker Patrick Stowe's great-great-great-great-grandfather had a vineyard in the Napa Valley, California, so planting vines in Nelson was following a family tradition – albeit a few generations late.

Current Release 2001 Apples are as important a crop as grapes in Nelson, and there's a suggestion of them on the nose of this well-focused chardonnay. It's direct, clean and lively on the palate with a zingy, refreshing finish. Partner it with a salad of flaked fish and chopped fennel in mayonnaise.

STYLE **dry**
QUALITY ♟♟♟
VALUE ☆ ☆ ☆
GRAPES **Chardonnay**
REGION **Nelson**
CELLAR **2**
PRICE **$22–24**

Rimu Grove Reserve Chardonnay

Fruit for this top-shelf chard came from two vineyards – the home site in the Moutere Hills, and another property in nearby Brightwater. Around 60% of the juice was fermented in French oak barrels, but only 10% of them were new.

Current Release 2001 Think toasted nuts and grilled grapefruit halves – that's the bouquet. It seems quite direct at first, but there's a lot of citrus fruit complexity through the middle. The finish is clean and faintly spicy. It makes a good partner for rissoles made from chopped chicken and mashed kumara.

STYLE **dry**
QUALITY ♟♟♟♟
VALUE ☆ ☆☆
GRAPES **Chardonnay**
REGION **Nelson**
CELLAR
PRICE **$32–34**

Rippon Chardonnay

Russell Lake matured this chardonnay in French oak barrels, 20% of which were new. Chardonnay has a tough time getting ripe in Central Otago, so wines made from it tend to have higher acids than they do in other parts of the country.

Current Release 1999 The oak isn't particularly obvious in the bouquet, adding no more than a suggestion of spice to the citric aromas. That impression of lemons and grapefruit continues on the palate, putting an edge on the otherwise creamy texture. The finish is lively and refreshing. Partner it with a chicken pie, served with South Island potatoes and Brussels sprouts.

STYLE **dry**
QUALITY ♟♟♟♟
VALUE ☆ ☆ ☆
GRAPES **Chardonnay**
REGION **Central Otago**
CELLAR **3**
PRICE **$29–33**

Riverside Dartmoor Chardonnay

STYLE dry
QUALITY 🍷🍷🍷½
VALUE ★★★★½
GRAPES Chardonnay
REGION Hawke's Bay
CELLAR 2
PRICE $16–18

Rachel and Ian Cadwallader's Riverside vineyard and winery has been in business since 1989. Just 25% of this member of their range spent two months in used oak barrels, while the rest stayed in tanks.

Current Release 2000 Ripe melon and sliced peaches get it together on the nose. It's direct in its flavours, citric in the middle and clean-cut on the finish. That makes it a good partner for snapper fillets, pan-fried with a little chopped fennel and drizzled with good olive oil.

Riverside Stirling Chardonnay

STYLE dry
QUALITY 🍷🍷🍷
VALUE ★★
GRAPES Chardonnay
REGION Hawke's Bay
CELLAR 3
PRICE $31–34

This is the top chardonnay for the Riverside team, and it's still reasonably easy to find even six years after the grapes were picked. The fruit came from the same region as the Dartmoor model, but more new oak was used for maturation.

Current Release 1999 Think ripe, freshly cut apples and a squeeze of lemon juice plus a touch of spicy oak and you'll be close to the bouquet. It's a little lean on the palate, but it certainly has good focus. The finish is very refreshing. It needs food with a bit of acid zing – chicken in a lemony sauce would be perfect.

Robard & Butler Chardonnay

STYLE dry
QUALITY 🍷🍷
VALUE ★★½
GRAPES Chardonnay
REGION Gisborne, Hawke's Bay, Marlborough
CELLAR
PRICE $12–14

Fruit from three regions was fermented in stainless-steel tanks, but did see the inside of a few French barrels later in its development. Robard & Butler used to be a Corbans label, but is now promoted as a separate entity.

Current Release 2000 The bouquet has some pleasant grapefruit characters, but the flavour profile is thin and reedy, albeit with some citric characters drifting through towards the finish. One to lose at the back of the cellar.

Robard & Butler Gisborne Mendoza Chardonnay

STYLE dry
QUALITY 🍷🍷🍷
VALUE ★★★★
GRAPES Chardonnay
REGION Gisborne
CELLAR 1
PRICE $12–14

Mendoza refers to the clone of chardonnay used to make this wine. It is being phased out in some parts of the country, but it formed the original backbone of our chardonnay industry.

Current Release 2000 It wasn't fermented in oak, but a spell in barrels has added toasted nut aromas to the usual citrics. It's gentle, light and pleasant in an undemanding sort of way, and works just fine with a brace of grilled chicken wings and drumsticks, sprinkled with sea salt and cracked pepper.

Robard & Butler Hawke's Bay Chardonnay

Robard & Butler wines are part of the Montana/Corbans portfolio. Many of them are made from imported juice, but this one is pure Hawke's Bay. It's no show-stopper, but it's very good value.
Current Release 2000 Lemons and grapefruit have got the gig on the nose. The citrus associations continue on the oak-free palate, giving it a squeaky-clean flavour profile. All that straight-up fruit makes it a good partner for pan-fried fish fillets drizzled with a little olive oil and lemon juice.

STYLE **dry**
QUALITY ♟ ♟ ♟
VALUE ☆ ☆ ☆ ☆
GRAPES **Chardonnay**
REGION **Hawke's Bay**
CELLAR **2**
PRICE **$12–14**

Rongopai Vintage Reserve Chardonnay

This was one of the last wines made by Rongopai founder Tom van Dam before he retired. It was fermented in oak and encouraged to undergo a partial malolactic fermentation.
Current Release 2000 The bouquet is like freshly sliced grainy bread, the result of a lot of stirring of the yeast lees. It's creamy on the palate, with satisfyingly ripe flavours and a clean-cut finish. We enjoyed ours with Japanese soba noodles in miso and chicken broth.

STYLE **dry**
QUALITY ♟ ♟ ♟ ♟
VALUE ☆ ☆ ☆ ☆
GRAPES **Chardonnay**
REGION **Waikato**
CELLAR **2**
PRICE **$21–23**

Rossendale Marlborough Chardonnay

It's labelled Marlborough, but 20% of the juice for this well-priced chardonnay came from the winery's home region of Canterbury. Around 60% was aged in oak for nine months, and a little went through malolactic fermentation.
Current Release 2000 Spicy oak and ripe nectarines join hands on the nose. It's a smooth-centred middleweight with impressions of peaches and cream though the centre but enough acid to ensure a moderately zingy finish. Enjoy it with a salad of penne pasta tossed with chopped red capsicum, torn mint leaves and olive oil.

STYLE **dry**
QUALITY ♟ ♟ ♟ ♟
VALUE ☆ ☆ ☆ ☆
GRAPES **Chardonnay**
REGION
Marlborough 80%
Canterbury 20%
CELLAR **2**
PRICE **$18–20**

Ruben Hall Chardonnay

This cheap-and-cheerful chard from Villa Maria is better than the packaging suggests. There's no vintage, but the strip across the bottom of the label says the fruit was sourced in Chile, Australia and New Zealand. That's certainly covering the field!
Current Release (non-vintage) Grapefruit characters are often associated with far more expensive wine, but there they are in the bouquet. It's simple and obvious, but there's certainly nothing that will cause any upset from the punters – and look at the price! Try it with chicken wings, barbecued in summer or pan-fried in winter.

STYLE **dry**
QUALITY ♟ ♟ ♟
VALUE ☆ ☆ ☆ ☆ ☆
GRAPES **Chardonnay**
REGION **Various**
CELLAR **2**
PRICE **$9–11**

Sacred Hill Barrel Fermented Chardonnay

STYLE **dry**
QUALITY ☆☆☆☆☆
VALUE ★★★★☆
GRAPES **Chardonnay**
REGION **Hawke's Bay**
CELLAR **3**
PRICE **$20–23**

This nicely made chardonnay can often be found for less than $20, which is very good buying. Tony Bish pressed whole bunches of grapes, then fermented the juice in a mixture of new and used French and American barrels. It stayed in oak for 10 months.
Current Release 2001 The bouquet is mealy, with suggestions of cracked wheat. The flavours are rich and creamy, and put me in mind of peaches and rock melon. Partner it with a pile of pan-fried squid, served with aioli dipping sauce, and you'll be a happy wee wine lover.

Sacred Hill Whitecliff Vineyards Chardonnay

STYLE **dry**
QUALITY ☆☆☆☆
VALUE ★★★★★
GRAPES **Chardonnay**
REGION **Hawke's Bay**
CELLAR **3**
PRICE **$15–17**

Whitecliff Vineyards is Sacred Hill's second-tier range of wines, but Tony Bish still lavishes plenty of care and attention on them. This member of the portfolio was allowed to undergo a partial malolactic fermentation.
Current Release 2000 Marmalade, beeswax and a touch of mealiness make for a tempting bouquet. It's a nicely balanced wine, with an approachably creamy texture and a good proportion of citrus and peach flavours. Try it with a serious chicken sandwich made with honest, grainy bread.

Saint Clair Marlborough Chardonnay

STYLE **dry**
QUALITY ☆☆☆☆
VALUE ★★★★☆
GRAPES **Chardonnay**
REGION **Marlborough**
CELLAR **3**
PRICE **$19–21**

The fruit came partly from the Wairau Valley and partly from the Awatere Valley, and in both cases it was picked in the cool of the evening to maximise the flavours. Unusually for a Marlborough chard, it was matured in American barrels, rather than French.
Current Release 2001 Spicy, toasty and reminiscent of muesli — that's the bouquet summed up. It's rich and creamy on the palate, with suggestioins of ripe stonefruit taking the honours. Match it with a classic roast chicken dinner, ideally using a free-range, corn-fed bird.

Saint Clair Marlborough Unoaked Chardonnay

STYLE **dry**
QUALITY ☆☆☆☆
VALUE ★★★★☆
GRAPES **Chardonnay**
REGION **Marlborough**
CELLAR **2**
PRICE **$17–19**

Made from fruit picked in the company's own Awatere Valley vineyard, this non-wooded chardonnay joined its oaked cellarmate in the silver medal lists at the New Zealand Wine Society Royal Easter Wine Show. That's quite an achievement for winemakers Kim Crawford and Matt Thomson.
Current Release 2001 The savoury note on the nose partners the aromas of dried orange peel. It's sweet-fruited on the palate, and put me in mind of figs and butterscotch. The finish is rich and long. It goes well with green pea and bacon risotto.

Saint Clair Omaka Reserve Chardonnay

Kim Crawford used two different chardonnay clones to craft this beauty. The Clone 6 fruit came from the Awatere Valley, while the more common Mendoza clone component was grown in the Omaka Valley. It was aged in American oak barrels for 10 months.

Current Release 2001 That big, nutty American oak is so much in evidence on the nose that it reminded me of All-Bran. The flavour profile is rich and complex, with thoughts of cut peach, cream and toasted hazelnuts all coming to mind. It makes a splendid partner for an Italian dish that combines penne pasta, cream and chopped walnuts.

STYLE **dry**
QUALITY ♇♇♇♇
VALUE ☆☆☆
GRAPES **Chardonnay**
REGION **Marlborough**
CELLAR **4**
PRICE **$28–32**

Saints Vineyard Selection Chardonnay

The Saints range has done exceptionally well for Montana, and is particularly popular in restaurants right around the country. The inter-regional blend would probably confuse the rule-bound French, but who cares? It works, and that's all that matters.

Current Release 2001 Spiced figs – that's what I get on the nose, and since figs are my favourite fruit, that's just fine and dandy. It's rich, smartly balanced and smooth-textured on the palate, which helps make it a perfect partner for whole fish baked in oven paper with cream and herbs.

STYLE **dry**
QUALITY ♇♇♇♇
VALUE ☆☆☆☆☆
GRAPES **Chardonnay**
REGION **Gisborne**
　　　　Marlborough
CELLAR **3**
PRICE **$17–19**

Sanctuary Marlborough Chardonnay

Sanctuary is a second label for Marlborough's Grove Mill wine company. The name refers to a corner of the home vineyard that acts as a haven for wading birds, including pukekos and an occasional grey heron.

Current Release 2002 Maturing the wine in mostly used French barrels has added just a whisper of spice to the citric aromas. It's light, smooth and clean on the palate, with a crisp-edged finish. It would make a good accompaniment for grilled chicken wings sprinkled with sea salt and plenty of cracked black pepper.

STYLE **dry**
QUALITY ♇♇♇
VALUE ☆☆☆☆
GRAPES **Chardonnay**
REGION **Marlborough**
CELLAR **2**
PRICE **$15–17**

Seifried Barrique Fermented Winemaker's Collection Chardonnay

The barrels in which this wine spent a quiet 10 months were American, but they were put together by a French firm named Demptos. Hermann Seifried encouraged 70% to go through a malolactic fermentation.

Current Release 2000 Rock melon on the nose is backed by a suggestion of coconut, a typical character of American oak. It's chunkier on the palate than it was when I first tried it some months ago, but remains smartly balanced and rich with a refreshingly citric finish. It is perfect alongside a pile of mixed shellfish with grainy bread.

STYLE **dry**
QUALITY ♇♇♇♇♇
VALUE ☆☆☆☆
GRAPES **Chardonnay**
REGION **Nelson**
CELLAR **4**
PRICE **$23–25**

Seifried Nelson Chardonnay

STYLE **dry**
QUALITY ▼ ▼ ▼ ▽
VALUE ★ ★ ★ ★ ☆
GRAPES **Chardonnay**
REGION **Nelson**

CELLAR 🍾 **4**
PRICE **$16–19**

Hermann and Agnes Seifried must be feeling pretty good about their chardonnay skills. Two of the three gold medals awarded to New Zealand examples of the variety at the 2000 International Wine Challenge in London went to their wines.
Current Release 2000 Spicy oak and marmalade make up the bouquet. It's smooth and creamy with peach and lime flavours, medium weight and a clean, controlled finish. It makes a good partner for chunks of lemonfish, pan-fried or cooked on the flat plate of the barbecue.

Selaks Founder's Reserve North Island Chardonnay

STYLE **dry**
QUALITY ▼ ▼ ▼ ▼ ▼
VALUE ★ ★ ★ ★ ☆
GRAPES **Chardonnay**
REGION **Hawke's Bay
Gisborne**

CELLAR 🍾 **3**
PRICE **$23–25**

This two-region chardonnay had all the right treatment at the winery. The grapes were pressed as whole bunches, bypassing the crusher-destemmer, and the juice was fermented in new French barrels and left there to mature.
Current Release 2000 The nose is immediately appealing, with its toasty, nutty aromas. It's richly fruited, creamy and smartly balanced on the palate, and would make an ideal partner for a pile of greenshell mussels, steamed open, taken out of their shells, lightly battered and deep-fried.

Selaks Founder's Reserve Gisborne Chardonnay

STYLE **dry**
QUALITY ▼ ▼ ▼ ▼ ▼
VALUE ★ ★ ★ ★ ★
GRAPES **Chardonnay**
REGION **Gisborne**

CELLAR 🍾 **3**
PRICE **$22–24**

After taking the Champion Chardonnay trophy at the Liquorland Top 100 awards in 2000, the Selaks team must have been disappointed with this white's bronze medal at the 2001 New Zealand Wine Society Royal Easter Wine Show.
Current Release 1999 Toasty oak and grapefruit share the honours in the bouquet. It's richly fruited and positively creamy in the flavour department and boasts one of the longest finishes in the business. There's nothing better with a corn-fed chicken, roasted whole in a kettle barbecue.

Selaks Premium Selection Marlborough Chardonnay

STYLE **dry**
QUALITY ▼ ▼ ▼ ▽
VALUE ★ ★ ★ ★ ★
GRAPES **Chardonnay**
REGION **Marlborough**

CELLAR 🍾 **2**
PRICE **$15–17**

The official tasting note for this wine talks about 'oak contact' rather than barrels, so it's odds-on it was fermented in stainless steel, but with a 'tea bag' of oak chips suspended in the tank. Cheating? Not at all – it's a perfectly sensible way to keep the price down.
Current Release 2001 I get honeycomb on toast in the bouquet and it makes an appealing introduction. It's a well-focused middleweight on the palate, with peachy fruit edged by smooth-faced acids. Partner it with chicken pieces pan-fried with strips of red and yellow capsicum and you'll be well satisfied.

Sherwood Estate Reserve Canterbury Chardonnay

The fruit came from the Canterbury Plains, and the bunches were pressed whole to retain every last nuance of flavour. After fermentation and a full malolactic, the fledgling wine spent 13 months in oak barrels.

Current Release 2000 Sweet, peachy fruit aromas make an appealing introduction. It's a nicely focused wine, with a lush texture, smartly balanced oak and acid and a lingering finish. Enjoy it alongside Chinese-style fried rice with prawns and peas, fresh if possible.

STYLE **dry**
QUALITY ♆ ♆ ♆ ♆
VALUE ☆ ☆ ☆
GRAPES **Chardonnay**
REGION **Canterbury**
CELLAR 🍾 **3**
PRICE **$28–30**

Shingle Peak Marlborough Chardonnay

Mark Robertson used fruit from both the Wairau and Awatere Valleys for this wine, and said it was 'an interesting one to put together'. He left in a wee touch of residual sugar, but it simply lifts the fruit without upsetting the balance.

Current Release 2002 Light oak spice sits at the back of the Golden Queen peach aromas. It's tinged with sweetness on the front palate but keen acids keep things in proportion. The finish is fresh and lingering. Enjoy it alongside a plate of corn fritters, ideally made from fresh corn.

STYLE **dry**
QUALITY ♆ ♆ ♆ ♆
VALUE ☆ ☆ ☆ ☆
GRAPES **Chardonnay**
REGION **Marlborough**
CELLAR 🍾 **3**
PRICE **$20–23**

Sileni Cellar Selection Chardonnay

The 2001 vintage was a tough one for Sileni Estates – an unseasonal frost knocked out 90% of the home vineyards. As a result, this latest model is a blend of fruit from Marlborough, Gisborne and Hawke's Bay. Grant Edmonds fermented only part of the juice in French oak barrels, leaving the rest in stainless steel.

Current Release 2002 Lemon rind and peaches are the major aromatic associations. It's creamy and direct on the palate and finishes cleanly. Try it alongside crumbed and shallow-fried strips of chicken breast topped with mushrooms in a light creamy sauce.

STYLE **dry**
QUALITY ♆ ♆ ♆
VALUE ☆ ☆ ☆
GRAPES **Chardonnay**
REGION **Hawke's Bay**
CELLAR 🍾 **2**
PRICE **$22–25**

Sileni Estates Chardonnay

This is the first time the Sileni winemaking team has been able to get fruit from the company's Plateau vineyard at Maraekakako. The juice was fermented in French oak barrels, 60% of them new.

Current Release 2000 Spicy oak is certainly in evidence, but it's stylishly subtle on the nose. There's nothing subtle about the flavours. This is a big, mouth-filling chardonnay with suggestions of peaches and nectarines lasting right through to the finish. It's a monty alongside crab cakes with lemon hollandaise.

STYLE **dry**
QUALITY ♆ ♆ ♆ ♆ ♆
VALUE ☆ ☆ ☆
GRAPES **Chardonnay**
REGION **Hawke's Bay**
CELLAR 🍾 **4**
PRICE **$35–37**

Soljans Barrique Reserve Hawke's Bay Chardonnay

STYLE **dry**
QUALITY ♀♀♀♀
VALUE ☆☆☆☆
GRAPES **Chardonnay**
REGION **Hawke's Bay**

CELLAR ▓ **3**
PRICE **$20–23**

This is the top chardonnay in the Soljan collection, and was matured for 10 months in a mixture of new and used French oak barrels. Tony Soljan doesn't like too much timber in his chards, but there's a reasaonable whack in this one.
Current Release 2000 A year ago I described the oak as restrained, but it has come to the fore with bottle age. It's smooth enough to qualify as creamy on the palate, with ripe-fruit flavours and a long, spicy finish. It makes a good partner for grilled chicken sausages from a serious butcher.

Soljans Estate Hawke's Bay Chardonnay

STYLE **dry**
QUALITY ♀♀♀♀
VALUE ☆☆☆☆☆
GRAPES **Chardonnay**
REGION **Hawke's Bay**

CELLAR ▓ **2**
PRICE **$15–17**

In past years this has been made as an unoaked style, but for the first vintage of the new millennium Tony Soljan admits to using 'just a touch'. It has certainly done it no harm, and the wine is selling as well as ever at the winery shop.
Current Release 2000 I get grapefruit on the nose and front palate, and the citric theme continues on the palate. It's direct in its appeal, with the oak serving only to soften the finish. It makes a good partner for an Italian style 'stew' of borlotti beans with chopped onion and sage.

Solstone Chardonnay Wairarapa Valley

STYLE **dry**
QUALITY ♀♀♀♀
VALUE ☆☆☆
GRAPES **Chardonnay**
REGION **Wairarapa**

CELLAR ▓ **3**
PRICE **$23–25**

The Solstone vineyard and winery, near Masterton, is planted in the traditional Bordeaux style. That means the vines are close together and the grapes hang quite close to the stone-covered soil, taking advantage of the sun's reflected warmth.
Current Release 2001 Fermentation and maturation for 50% of the juice in new French barrels has added gentle spice to the aromas of freshly cut nectarines. It's an elegant wine with no sharp edges, understated stonefruit and citrus flavours and a faintly savoury finish. Enjoy it with a wedge of oozy brie.

Spencer Hill Evans Vineyard Moutere Chardonnay

STYLE **dry**
QUALITY ♀♀♀♀♀
VALUE ☆☆☆
GRAPES **Chardonnay**
REGION **Nelson**

CELLAR ▓ **4**
PRICE **$34–37**

Philip Jones makes chardonnay under his top-shelf Spencer Hill label only when he considers the fruit is exceptional, so this is the first since 1998. It is matured in French oak barrels and underwent a 100% malolactic.
Current Release 2000 Light toast, marmalade and frsshly cut nectarines – put them together and you've got the bouquet sussed. It's rich and creamy on the palate with great focus through to the lingering finish. I like it with pan-fried chicken breasts drizzled with a lightly citric sauce made by reducing a splash of the wine and a tiny bit of lemon juice with the pan juices.

Spy Valley Chardonnay

Spy Valley is the local nickname for the Waihopai Valley, where two giant 'golf balls' hide communications equipment rumoured to beam information about New Zealanders to security boffins in Wellington and the US.
Current Release 2001 Toasty oak and aromas that reminded me of grilled peach halves start things off. The flavours are of marmalade, the texture is creamy and the finish has a suggestion of dry-fried nuts. It's a nicely balanced wine that goes well with a brace of cheese-topped grilled zucchini.

STYLE **dry**
QUALITY ♟♟♟⸮
VALUE ☆ ☆ ☆
GRAPES **Chardonnay**
REGION **Marlborough**
CELLAR 🍾 **2**
PRICE **$20–23**

St Francis Golf Links Hawke's Bay Chardonnay

It's hard to avoid the golf course as you drive around the Hawke's Bay vineyards. It has been suggested that the land would be great for grapes, but any change of use seems unlikely, at least in the foreseeable future.
Current Release 2000 Smart stuff! The oak provides just enough spice to back the ripe melon and fig aromas, and the flavours are rich, nicely textured and properly citric, especially on the finish. Open it next time you're roasting a whole corn-fed chicken and you should be very pleased indeed.

STYLE **dry**
QUALITY ♟♟♟♟
VALUE ☆ ☆ ☆⸮
GRAPES **Chardonnay**
REGION **Hawke's Bay**
CELLAR 🍾 **3**
PRICE **$23–26**

Staete Landt Chardonnay

Fourteen months in French barrels, 25% of them new, was the oak regime for this ripe-fruited Marlborough chardonnay. That's an unusually long time for white wine, but it has certainly done no harm.
Current Release 2001 The oak is gentle and stylish on the nose, and sits happily behind the grapefruit aromas. It's complex, sweet-fruited and classy on the palate, with flavours in the 'peaches and cream' category. It makes a good partner for chicken legs finished with a mustard and cream sauce.

STYLE **dry**
QUALITY ♟♟♟♟
VALUE ☆ ☆ ☆
GRAPES **Chardonnay**
REGION **Marlborough**
CELLAR 🍾 **3**
PRICE **$28–32**

Stonecroft Chardonnay

Alan and Glen Limmer are so well-known for syrah, regularly heralded as the best in the country, that the other wines in their portolio are often forgotten. This chardonnay was matured in French oak barrels, 50% of them new.
Current Release 2000 The nose combines suggestions of toasted nuts and marmalade, and that's all to the good. It's a weighty, smooth wine on the palate, with acids that are totally integrated and so act as a support to the rich fruit flavours. Penne pasta with cockles and pipis would make an ideal partner.

STYLE **dry**
QUALITY ♟♟♟⸮
VALUE ☆ ☆ ☆
GRAPES **Chardonnay**
REGION **Hawke's Bay**
CELLAR 🍾 **3**
PRICE **$31–33**

Stoneleigh Marlborough Chardonnay

STYLE **dry**
QUALITY ☆☆☆☆☆
VALUE ☆☆☆☆☆
GRAPES **Chardonnay**
REGION **Marlborough**

CELLAR **3**
PRICE **$17–19**

This stylish chardonnay was fermented in French oak barrels and put through a 60% malolactic fermentation, while the rest stayed in tanks. I like it just as much as the pricier 'Rapaura Series' version.
Current Release 2001 The oak spice is wonderfully gentle on the nose and forms a pleasant backdrop to the aromas of just-cut peaches. Sweet fruit flavours fill the palate, but they are balanced against well-tuned acids. It's a very smart wine that works spectacularly well with a simple roast chicken.

Stoneleigh Marlborough Chardonnay Rapaura Series

STYLE **dry**
QUALITY ☆☆☆☆☆
VALUE ☆☆☆☆☆
GRAPES **Chardonnay**
REGION **Marlborough**

CELLAR **3**
PRICE **$22–24**

This 1999-vintage Rapaura Series chardonnay differs from the 'standard' model because it spent a full year in French oak barrels, and most of the juice went through a malolactic fermentation.
Current Release 1999 It was worth the effort! The melon and citrus notes in the bouquet are backed by deliciously spicy oak, and the same characters drift onto the front palate. It's rich, creamy and nicely balanced, and goes perfectly with penne pasta tossed just before serving with Parmigiano cheese and a raw egg yolk.

Stonyridge Row 10 Chardonnay

STYLE **dry**
QUALITY ☆☆☆☆☆
VALUE ☆☆
GRAPES **Chardonnay**
REGION **Waiheke Island**

CELLAR **3**
PRICE **$48–50**

You'll have to visit the Stonyridge winery or eat at the adjacent café to try this rare white. Stephen White made just enough to accompany his popular vineyard meals, and to have a white alternative to his legendary and spectacularly priced Larose red.
Current Release 2000 Melons and grapefruit set the scene, with gentle oak adding a spicy edge. It's a well-tuned chardonnay with a pleasantly smooth texture and a long, citric finish. It works well alongside chicken breasts smeared with a good stock reduction sauce and drizzled with just a dash of lemon juice.

Tasman Bay Marlborough Chardonnay

STYLE **dry**
QUALITY ☆☆☆☆
VALUE ☆☆☆☆☆
GRAPES **Chardonnay**
REGION **Marlborough Nelson**

CELLAR **3**
PRICE **$18–21**

Tasman Bay is a Spencer Hill Estate label, mostly used for wines made from grapes grown on vineyards away from the home base at Nelson. Philip Jones put this one into new French and American barrels for seven months.
Current Release 2000 I get a dash of lemon rind on the nose, enhancing the impression of marmalade. It's smooth-textured and sweet-edged, with an attractive dash of spice from the oak on the finish. It sits happily alongside a pile of grilled Cajun-dusted chicken drumsticks.

Te Awa Farm Frontier Hawke's Bay Chardonnay

It's all chardonnay, but Jenny Dobson used grapes of three different clones grown on five separate sites. The fruit was fermented in new, one and two-year-old French barrels and left there for 11 months. Just 10% was allowed to go through a malolactic fermentation.

Current Release 2000 The nose reminds me of All-Bran, with maybe a touch of Corn Flakes for good measure. Breakfast! It's deliciously ripe-fruited on the palate with good weight and a creamy texture. The finish is smooth and long. Partner it with gnocchi tossed in a cream-based sauce with chunks of pork sausage that you've bought from a serious butcher.

STYLE **dry**
QUALITY ♟ ♟ ♟ ♟ ♟
VALUE ☆ ☆ ☆
GRAPES **Chardonnay**
REGION **Hawke's Bay**
CELLAR
PRICE **$35–37**

Te Awa Farm Longlands Hawke's Bay Chardonnay

This is Te Awa's 'second label' chardonnay, but some people prefer it to the top-shelf Frontier version. Jenny Dobson fermented it in a mixture of French and American oak barrels and left it there for nine months.

Current Release 2002 Spicy oak sits behind the predominant aromas of peaches and lemon rind. It's clean and nicely focused, and works well with a hearty seafood chowder, served only lightly chilled.

STYLE **dry**
QUALITY ♟ ♟ ♟ ♟
VALUE ☆ ☆ ☆ ☆
GRAPES **Chardonnay**
REGION **Hawke's Bay**
CELLAR 🍾 **3**
PRICE **$20–23**

Te Kairanga Martinborough Chardonnay

This is the 'standard' Te Kairanga chardonnay, but it still gets all the treatment. The alcohol level is 14%, indicating that the fruit was very ripe, and the juice was fermented in French oak barrels, 30% of them new. It spent 12 months sitting on the yeast lees.

Current Release 2001 Gentle oak backs the peach-like aromas on the nose. It's citric and focused on the palate and smooth through the middle, and boasts a sweet-edged, spicy finish. Pull the cork next time you're having pork chops, splash a little into the pan to make a sauce and you should be well pleased.

STYLE **dry**
QUALITY ♟ ♟ ♟ ♟
VALUE ☆ ☆ ☆
GRAPES **Chardonnay**
REGION **Martinborough**
CELLAR 🍾 **3**
PRICE **$25–27**

Te Kairanga Martinborough Reserve Chardonnay

The decision as to which fruit goes into the Reserve wine is made primarily in the vineyard. This latest model got the same oak treatment as the 'standard' chardonnay, with the addition of a 10% malolactic fermentation, but the grapes came from low-cropping vines.

Current Release 2001 Butterscotch and figs do it for me on the nose. The same butterscotch character makes it through to the finish, and in between there are heaps of ripe stonefruit flavours in a weighty but nicely balanced package. The Te Kairanga gang reckons it's a blinder alongside saffron risotto topped with slivers of paua. I don't know where they tried the dish, but it sounds excellent.

STYLE **dry**
QUALITY ♟ ♟ ♟ ♟
VALUE ☆ ☆ ☆
GRAPES **Chardonnay**
REGION **Martinborough**
CELLAR 🍾 **4**
PRICE **$30–33**

Te Mania Nelson Chardonnay

STYLE **dry**
QUALITY ☐☐☐☐
VALUE ☆☆☆☆☆
GRAPES **Chardonnay**
REGION **Nelson**
CELLAR **3**
PRICE **$18–21**

This classy chardonnay is made from three different grape clones, one of which is said to give peach-like flavours, while the others lean more to the citric end of the spectrum.
Current Release 2000 A wee bit of toasty oak mingles with the ripe nectarine and grapefruit aromas on the nose. Lively acids make for a super-refreshing flavour profile, and put a keen edge on the fruit-led finish. Partner it with crumbed, shallow-fried mussels and you should be well satisfied.

Te Mania Nelson Chardonnay Reserve

STYLE **dry**
QUALITY ☐☐☐☐☐
VALUE ☆☆☆☆
GRAPES **Chardonnay**
REGION **Nelson**
CELLAR **3**
PRICE **$28–31**

This chardonnay was made from hand-picked grapes and fermented in French oak barrels, but only around half of them were new because winemaker Jane Cooper didn't want the wood to dominate the fruit.
Current Release 2001 There's a shipload of toasty oak on the nose despite Jane's caution, but the fruit is big and chunky enough to take it. After that big introduction the flavour profile is surprisingly citric and direct, with an impression of freshly cut peaches right on the finish. It's great with crab fritters – made, of course, from Nelson crabs.

Te Mata Elston Chardonnay

STYLE **dry**
QUALITY ☐☐☐☐☐
VALUE ☆☆☆
GRAPES **Chardonnay**
REGION **Hawke's Bay**
CELLAR **5**
PRICE **$38–41**

Peter Cowley got around half his average crop in 2001, but this splendid chard is worth a search. The grapes, all from old vines, spent a year in oak barrels, 40% of them new, and underwent a full malolactic fermentation.
Current Release 2001 Oh boy! Spicy butter, freshly baked bread and a suggestion of something like Asian five-spice powder make for a tempting bouquet. It's deliciously sweet-fruited with rich, ripe flavours in a smooth framework. The finish is long and very, very satisying. A food match? Go for broke and enjoy it with roast pheasant.

Te Whare Ra Duke of Marlborough Chardonnay

STYLE **dry**
QUALITY ☐☐☐☐
VALUE ☆☆☆☆
GRAPES **Chardonnay**
REGION **Marlborough**
CELLAR **3**
PRICE **$25–27**

Te Whare Ra chardonnays start out as blockbusters, but some earlier vintages have fallen over after a couple of years. The mail-order brochure suggests this one could be cellared for eight years, but I've been rather more cautious.
Current Release 2000 There's a whack of toasty oak on the nose behind the peachy fruit aromas. It's rich, big and spicy on the palate, with a creamy texture that should make it good with pan-fried chicken pieces in a cream-based sauce.

Te Whau Chardonnay

Not a lot of this big-hearted chardonnay makes it to the mainland, such is its popularity at Te Whau's well-regarded vineyard restaurant. Never mind – a trip across the harbour is an enjoyable experience in summer.
Current Release 2001 Toasty oak, Weet-Bix and grapefruit – sounds like breakfast! That pleasant aromatic trio leads to a flavour profile that puts ripe stonefruit characters in deliciously creamy surroundings. Slow-cooked pork and fennel makes an excellent companion.

STYLE **dry**
QUALITY ♟ ♟ ♟ ♟
VALUE ☆ ☆ ☆
GRAPES **Chardonnay**
REGION **Waiheke Island**
CELLAR **3**
PRICE **$37–41**

Terrace Road Marlborough Chardonnay

Terrace Road wines are produced by sparkling wine specialist Cellier Le Brun. They used to be at the bottom end of the cheap-and-cheerful category, but quality seems to be increasing with each vintage.
Current Release 2000 Gentle toastiness and a splash of coconut give the oak away, but there's enough citric fruit in there to be going along with. The same citric impressions dominate the flavour profile and the finish is sweet-fruited and clean. Try it with sardines on toast.

STYLE **dry**
QUALITY ♟ ♟ ♟
VALUE ☆ ☆ ☆
GRAPES **Chardonnay**
REGION **Marlborough**
CELLAR **2**
PRICE **$19–22**

Thornbury Marlborough Chardonnay

Steve Bird sources his fruit from top sites in various regions. This member of his small collection spent 10 months in French oak barrels, 25% of them new. It also underwent a 30% malolactic fermentation.
Current Release 2001 Sweet fruit is much in evidence on the nose and the front palate. It's richly flavoured, but smartly integrated acids lift it nicely through the middle. The finish is clean-cut and refreshing. Enjoy it alongside a steaming bowl of Chinese noodles with sliced chicken.

STYLE **dry**
QUALITY ♟ ♟ ♟ ♟ ♟
VALUE ☆ ☆ ☆ ☆ ☆
GRAPES **Chardonnay**
REGION **Marlborough**
CELLAR **3**
PRICE **$20–23**

Timara Oak Aged Chardonnay

This wine is made from fruit picked in various parts of New Zealand and Australia, but the components are put together in this country. It's as good as many chards costing several dollars more, and that makes it a real bargain.
Current Release 2002 Spicy oak and an impression of marmalade give it a surprisingly classy bouquet. It's smooth and broadly textured on the palate, suffers from a touch of bitterness on the finish but still makes a pleasant, undemanding drop. It's good with battered tarakihi or cod and fries.

STYLE **dry**
QUALITY ♟ ♟ ♟
VALUE ☆ ☆ ☆ ☆ ☆
GRAPES **Chardonnay**
REGION **New Zealand Australia**
CELLAR **1**
PRICE **$11–13**

Tiritiri Reserve Gisborne Chardonnay

STYLE **dry**
QUALITY ▼ ▼ ▼ ▼
VALUE ☆ ☆ ☆
GRAPES **Chardonnay**
REGION **Gisborne**
CELLAR 🍾 **3**
PRICE **$28–31**

With just 0.27 hectares planted in grapes, Duncan and Judy Smith's fully organic Tiritiri vineyard in Gisborne is one of the smallest in the country. This chardonnay spent 10 months in new French oak barrels – two of them, to be precise.

Current Release 2001 Toast, melon and grilled grapefruit form the aromatic trio on the nose. It's citric and direct in its appeal, with keen but integrated acids adding life to the middle. The citric impression returns on the finish, making it a good match for tarakihi or cod fillets drizzled with lemon-spiked butter just before they're served.

Tohu Gisborne Chardonnay

STYLE **dry**
QUALITY ▼ ▼ ▼ ▼
VALUE ☆ ☆ ☆ ☆ ☆
GRAPES **Chardonnay**
REGION **Gisborne**
CELLAR 🍾 **3**
PRICE **$17–19**

This is the 'standard' Tohu chardonnay, but it's very smart wine. The back label tells us it has had 'light oak', but doesn't specify the type of barrels used or the amount of time the wine spent maturing in them.

Current Release 2001 Honeycomb and gentle oak spice form a pleasant aromatic duo. The texture is pleasantly creamy and the stonefruit flavours have quite good weight through the middle. It makes a good partner for most pan-fried fish – gurnard, with the skin left on, works particularly well.

Tohu Gisborne Reserve Chardonnay

STYLE **dry**
QUALITY ▼ ▼ ▼ ▼ ▼
VALUE ☆ ☆ ☆
GRAPES **Chardonnay**
REGION **Gisborne**
CELLAR 🍾 **3**
PRICE **$30–35**

Tohu wines are sold mostly by mail order in this country, although some can be found at Foodtown supermarkets. A large percentage of each year's production is exported to the UK and Europe.

Current Release 2000 Sweet 'n' spicy – that's the overriding impression on the nose. It's smooth-textured, smartly balanced and instantly appealing on the palate, with plenty of stonefruit flavours and a long finish. It's good with a prawn and scallop risotto, finished with a little cream and Parmesan.

Torlesse Chardonnay

STYLE **dry**
QUALITY ▼ ▼ ▼
VALUE ☆ ☆ ☆ ☆
GRAPES **Chardonnay**
REGION **Waipara**
CELLAR 🍾 **2**
PRICE **$15–18**

Torlesse always enjoyed a good following for its lightly oaked chardonnay. This time, the 'lightly oaked' designation has been moved to the back label. Marlborough fruit has been used in the past, but not in 2000.

Current Release 2000 The oak treatment may have been light, but it has still added a touch of spice to the citric aromas. It's clean, focused and straightforward on the palate and pleasant enough alongside simple fare like a chicken and mayonnaise sandwich.

Torlesse Waipara Chardonnay

Long-time Canterbury winemaker Kym Rayner is in charge of the tanks and barrels at Torlesse. The label has been around for a while, but the wines are sometimes hard to find in the North Island.

Current Release 2001 Kym has crafted a wine that fits the 'powerful but elegant' category. It's got decidedly pleasant savoury notes on the nose, and a good proportion of ripe peach and melon flavours in smooth surrounds. Enjoy it with chicken and pumpkin risotto, or something equally smooth-textured and flavoursome.

STYLE **dry**
QUALITY ♙ ♙ ♙ ♙
VALUE ☆ ☆ ☆ ☆
GRAPES **Chardonnay**
REGION **Waipara**
CELLAR **3**
PRICE **$20–23**

Trinity Hill Gimblett Road Chardonnay

Trinity Hill has built up a solid reputation for big reds, but the team also produces some very smart whites. This one has had all the drama – the grapes were picked by hand, pressed as whole bunches and matured in oak for 11 months.

Current Release 1999 There's plenty of oak on the nose, but the peachy fruit manages to fight its way through the timber. Creamy, ripe-fruited and hugely appealing on the palate, it's smart wine that makes a great partner for a whole roasted chicken, preferably free-range and corn-fed.

STYLE **dry**
QUALITY ♙ ♙ ♙ ♙ ♙
VALUE ☆ ☆ ☆
GRAPES **Chardonnay**
REGION **Hawke's Bay**
CELLAR **4**
PRICE **$35–37**

Trinity Hill Shepherds Croft Hawke's Bay Chardonnay

The grapes came from a couple of different sites. Warren Gibson fermented 50% of the juice in French oak barrels and left it there for eight months, then blended it with the batch that had been in stainless steel.

Current Release 2000 Spicy oak, lemon rind and a suggestion of fresh melon form a pleasant introduction. It's lively on the palate, with the citric notes continuing through to the clean-cut, refreshing finish. Not a 'biggie', but certainly enjoyable with the likes of pan-fried tarakihi fillets.

STYLE **dry**
QUALITY ♙ ♙ ♙ ♙
VALUE ☆ ☆ ☆ ☆
GRAPES **Chardonnay**
REGION **Hawke's Bay**
CELLAR **3**
PRICE **$21–23**

TW (Tietjen Witters) Chardonnay

The names Tietjen and Witters refer to the two long-time Gisborne grape growers who share label honours. The wine isn't easy to find, but it's well worth a search. It spent nine months in French oak barrels, a third of them new.

Current Release 2000 The bouquet is toasty and smart and there's some delightfully sweet-edged fruit on the palate. It's rich, but sensible acids ensure good balance. It goes well with a chicken and leek pie, served hot or at room temperature with a simple salad.

STYLE **dry**
QUALITY ♙ ♙ ♙ ♙ ♙
VALUE ☆ ☆ ☆ ☆
GRAPES **Chardonnay**
REGION **Gisborne**
CELLAR **4**
PRICE **$28–32**

Twin Islands Marlborough Chardonnay

STYLE **dry**
QUALITY ▽▽▽▽
VALUE ★★★★☆
GRAPES **Chardonnay**
REGION **Marlborough**

CELLAR **2**
PRICE **$16–18**

Twin Islands is a second label for Marlborough-based Nautilus Estate, but the wines in the range have their own enthusiastic bunch of fans. Clive Jones is the winemaker.
Current Release 2001 Lightly spiced on the nose, peachy with a citric edge on the palate, this is an immediately enjoyable, straightforward white that makes a perfect aperitif but also works pretty well with a line-up of chicken wings, lightly marinated in olive oil and chopped coriander before being grilled.

Vavasour Awatere Valley Marlborough Chardonnay

STYLE **dry**
QUALITY ▽▽▽▽
VALUE ★★★☆
GRAPES **Chardonnay**
REGION **Marlborough**

CELLAR **4**
PRICE **$25–28**

The fruit was harvested by hand in the company's own Awatere Valley vineyards, then put straight into the press without having to suffer the indignity of being crushed and destemmed first. Glenn Thomas believes that gives extra depth of flavour.
Current Release 2001 Well-focused citric aromas dominate the bouquet, with spicy oak pushed to the back. It's smooth and classy on the palate and has a sweet-edged finish. It would be wonderful alongside a prawn risotto.

Vidal Estate Chardonnay

STYLE **dry**
QUALITY ▽▽▽▽
VALUE ★★★★★
GRAPES **Chardonnay**
REGION **Hawke's Bay**

CELLAR **2**
PRICE **$16–18**

Rod McDonald must have been rapt, if a little surprised, when this 'standard' chardonnay beat its Reserve cellarmate to take a gold medal at the 2001 New Zealand Wine Society Royal Easter Wine Show. Its big brother, admittedly from the '99 vintage, managed only a bronze.
Current Release 2001 Nutty oak and grilled peaches are the aromatic associations I get on the nose. There's some seriously rich fruit in there, pulled together by sensitive oak and smartly integrated acids. It makes a good partner for a salad built around grilled squid.

Vidal Estate Reserve Chardonnay

STYLE **dry**
QUALITY ▽▽▽▽
VALUE ★★★☆
GRAPES **Chardonnay**
REGION **Hawke's Bay**

CELLAR **3**
PRICE **$30–34**

Rod McDonald sourced fruit from two vineyards for this top-shelf chardonnay, and organised for the grapes to be picked by hand. It spent 11 months in French oak barrels. He picked up a silver medal at the New Zealand Wine Society Royal Easter Wine Show for his trouble – but the cheaper 'Estate' version got a gold.
Current Release 2000 Spicy oak and cracked wheat dominate the bouquet. It's citric, lively and clean on the palate, with good weight and a crisp, refreshing finish. It works splendidly with squid rings, pan-fried with a little chopped garlic or crumbed and deep-fried.

Villa Maria Cellar Selection Hawke's Bay Chardonnay

This mid-range Villa chardonnay has performed above its status by picking up a stack of gold medals, including one at the Liquorland Top 100, the only one that matches local wines against imports from all over the world.

Current Release 2001 Spicy grapefruit and a suggestion of toasted nuts make a pleasant introduction. It's sweet-fruited on the front palate, shows off the citric side of its nature in the middle and finishes with a dash of oaky spice. It's good alongside a messy pile of Chinese-style grilled pork spareribs.

STYLE **dry**
QUALITY ♟♟♟♟♟
VALUE ☆☆☆☆☆
GRAPES **Chardonnay**
REGION **Hawke's Bay**
CELLAR **2**
PRICE **$20–23**

Villa Maria Private Bin East Coast Chardonnay

East Coast translates as Gisborne and Hawke's Bay, but the wine was made in Auckland. The winery team fermented the juice in oak barrels and allowed a portion to go through an acid-softening malolactic fermentation.

Current Release 2001 Toast and a suggestion of dried orange peel form a pleasant introduction. It's lean, clean and direct in its appeal, with acids that sit nicely on the ripe citrus flavours. Chinese-style stir-fried pork and bok choy suits it well.

STYLE **dry**
QUALITY ♟♟♟
VALUE ☆☆☆☆
GRAPES **Chardonnay**
REGION **Gisborne**
　　　Hawke's Bay
CELLAR **1**
PRICE **$16–18**

Villa Maria Private Bin Gisborne Chardonnay

Buying Villa wines sometimes requires careful label watching. This one is all Gisborne fruit, but there's another PB chardonnay that combines grapes from Gisborne and Hawke's Bay.

Current Release 2000 Faint oak spice, marmalade and a dash of muesli get it together on the nose. It's quite fat on the palate, with citric flavours in a broad frame. Integrated acids add about the right amount of edginess, particularly on the finish. Enjoy it with chicken pieces, braised and served on Puy lentils.

STYLE **dry**
QUALITY ♟♟♟♟
VALUE ☆☆☆☆☆
GRAPES **Chardonnay**
REGION **Gisborne**
CELLAR **2**
PRICE **$16–18**

Villa Maria Reserve Barrique Fermented Chardonnay

Only a small amount of this top-shelf chardonnay was made in 2000, so its many fans had to hunt for it. The grapes came from two sites, and most of them were fermented using their own natural yeasts. They're slow, but they give chunky flavours.

Current Release 2000 Spicy oak is in good shape on the nose, but it's not over the top. Citrus fruit still wins the day. It's more citric and less grunty than some previous versions, and I like it better for that. The texture is creamy and the finish fresh-faced and long. It goes well with a corn, pumpkin and goat cheese tart.

STYLE **dry**
QUALITY ♟♟♟♟♟
VALUE ☆☆☆
GRAPES **Chardonnay**
REGION **Gisborne**
CELLAR **4**
PRICE **$35–37**

Villa Maria Reserve Hawke's Bay Chardonnay

STYLE **dry**
QUALITY ♚ ♚ ♚ ♚ ♚
VALUE ☆ ☆ ☆
GRAPES **Chardonnay**
REGION **Hawke's Bay**
CELLAR 🍾 **4**
PRICE **$30—33**

Fruit for this member of Villa's Reserve portfolio comes from three sites in the Bay, and it is all harvested by hand. Pickers are told to discard any bunches that aren't up to scratch. You can't do that with a machine!
Current Release 2000 The citric characters on the nose – grapefruit, preserved lemon, dried orange peel – are more reminiscent of a Marlborough wine than one from the Bay. It's richly fruited, smartly balanced and clean-finishing, and makes a good partner for an onion and broccoli frittata, served with freshly shaved Parmesan.

Villa Maria Reserve Marlborough Chardonnay

STYLE **dry**
QUALITY ♚ ♚ ♚ ♚ ♚
VALUE ☆ ☆ ☆
GRAPES **Chardonnay**
REGION **Marlborough**
CELLAR 🍾 **3**
PRICE **$33—36**

Three gold medals in the first weeks after its release is the proud record of this nicely balanced chardonnay. The grapes were picked by hand and 15% of them were fermented using their own wild yeasts rather than laboratory-bred models.
Current Release 2000 Aromas reminiscent of figs, grapefruit and rock melon make an interesting introduction. It's richly flavoured and boasts a creamy texture, but smartly integrated acids ensure there's plenty of zing right through to the finish. A just-seared steak cut from a Marlborough Sounds salmon would be great with it.

Villa Maria Single Vineyard Fletcher Chardonnay

STYLE **dry**
QUALITY ♚ ♚ ♚ ♚ ♚
VALUE ☆ ☆☆
GRAPES **Chardonnay**
REGION **Marlborough**
CELLAR 🍾 **3**
PRICE **$40—43**

Villa launched its 'Single Vineyard' series to pay tribute to the growers who play such an important part in the New Zealand wine industry. The Fletcher family's Rocenvin Estate vineyard is on the Old Renwick Road, just out of Blenheim.
Current Release 2000 Stonefruit and lemon aromas kick things off in style. It's creamy and rich on the palate, with smartly integrated acids and a sweet-edged finish. It goes well with an asparagus frittata topped with shavings of the best Parmesan you can find.

Villa Maria Single Vineyard King Chardonnay

STYLE **dry**
QUALITY ♚ ♚ ♚ ♚ ♚
VALUE ☆ ☆ ☆ ☆☆
GRAPES **Chardonnay**
REGION **Marlborough**
CELLAR 🍾 **3**
PRICE **$22—24**

Villa Maria has made a speciality of blending wines from various sites, so there were a few raised eyebrows when the 'Single Vineyard' concept was unveiled. The wines are unlikely to be made every year – if the team thinks the fruit would be better suited to a blend, that's where it will end up.
Current Release 2000 The bouquet is spicy and mealy, although the wine received only minimal oak. The flavour profile tells a different story – it's citric and direct through the middle and finishes cleanly. We enjoyed ours alongside a seafood risotto that starred an indecent number of tuatua.

Waimarie Gimblett Road Chardonnay

Waimarie was launched by two Nobilo family members, Steve and Nick, with the aim of sourcing fruit from top sites. This member of the range spent 10 months in French oak and was put through an acid-softening malolactic fermentation.

Current Release 2000 Sweet citrussy fruit, a dash of butterscotch and a suggestion of spicy oak all contribute to the bouquet. There's some big fruit on the palate, but a crisp finish keeps things in perspective. It would be good alongside a classic dinner based around stuffed and roasted chicken.

STYLE **dry**
QUALITY ▯ ▯ ▯ ▯ ▯
VALUE ☆ ☆ ☆ ☆
GRAPES **Chardonnay**
REGION **Hawke's Bay**
CELLAR **3**
PRICE **$25–27**

Waimea Estates Bolitho Chardonnay

The Bolitho title is used for Waimea's top wines. This one was fermented in a mixture of French and American oak barrels, and allowed to go through a full malolactic fermentation. A word of warning: the alcohol level is 14.5%!

Current Release 2000 The time in barrels has given it a pleasantly nutty, spicy bouquet. It's a big, solid wine with oak ensuring mid-palate smoothness and adding a creamy edge to the lingering finish. It would make a great partner for chicken pieces in a creamy sauce, served on couscous.

STYLE **dry**
QUALITY ▯ ▯ ▯ ▯ ▯
VALUE ☆ ☆ ☆
GRAPES **Chardonnay**
REGION **Nelson**
CELLAR **4**
PRICE **$32–34**

Waimea Estates Chardonnay

Trevor Bolitho didn't want to overpower the fruit he picked from the 2000 vintage, so he fermented just over half the juice in oak barrels, leaving the rest to do its thing in stainless-steel tanks.

Current Release 2000 There's a mealy touch behind the grapefruit aromas on the bouquet. It's a decidedly fruit-led style, with rich flavours reminiscent of dried figs and preserved lemons. It's good with chicken breasts, dusted with dukkah (a spiced nut mix).

STYLE **dry**
QUALITY ▯ ▯ ▯ ▯
VALUE ☆ ☆ ☆ ☆☆
GRAPES **Chardonnay**
REGION **Nelson**
CELLAR **3**
PRICE **$19–21**

Waipara Hills Reserve Chardonnay

Waipara Hills draws much of its fruit from Marlborough, so watch the labels carefully if you're trying to identify regional characteristics. This one spent a full year in new French oak barrels.

Current Release 2001 The nose is smoky from all that brand-new timber, but there are some pleasant citrus aromas fighting to get out. It's sweet-edged, smooth and very clean on the palate, with peach-like flavours and a moderately long finish. Pork schnitzels should suit it well.

STYLE **dry**
QUALITY ▯ ▯ ▯ ▯
VALUE ☆ ☆
GRAPES **Chardonnay**
REGION **Marlborough**
CELLAR **3**
PRICE **$37–39**

Waipara Springs Barrique Chardonnay

STYLE dry
QUALITY 🍷🍷🍷🍷🍷
VALUE ★★★★★
GRAPES Chardonnay
REGION Waipara

CELLAR 🍶 4
PRICE $22–24

Waipara Springs was one of the region's first wineries. This member of the portfolio spent 11 months in oak barrels, 30% of them new. About 25% was encouraged to go through a malolactic fermentation.

Current Release 2001 Aromas like spiced pears and freshly cut peach wedges form a pleasant introduction. It's richly fruited, smooth-centred and chock-full of flavour – a class act. Partner it with Italian-style tuna – not seared, but cooked right through and served with a tomato-based sauce.

Waipara Springs Lightly Oaked Chardonnay

STYLE dry
QUALITY 🍷🍷🍷🍷
VALUE ★★★★☆
GRAPES Chardonnay
REGION Waipara

CELLAR 🍶 2
PRICE $18–20

'Lightly oaked' translates as putting a small portion of the fledgling wine into oak for three months. That seems about right for the style, and it has made the wine popular even among those who profess not to like the variety.

Current Release 2002 The oak is certainly hard to find – just as the winemaking team intended. It's citric on the nose and sweet-fruited on the front palate. Smartly balanced acids lift proceedings through the middle and give it a zingy finish. Partner it with a salad featuring goat cheese or feta and you'll get the point.

West Brook Barrique Fermented Chardonnay

STYLE dry
QUALITY 🍷🍷🍷🍷
VALUE ★★★★
GRAPES Chardonnay
REGION Hawke's Bay
     West Auckland

CELLAR 🍶 3
PRICE $18–20

Previous vintages of this wine have won gold and silver medals, but this one has managed only a bronze and a few four-star ratings from wine publications. No matter – it's a big seller at the cellar door.

Current Release 1999 The distinctive aroma of toasted nuts gives away the barrel fermentation and stirring of the yeast lees. It's broad, fat and quite rich, with integrated acids providing lift on the finish. Try it with a salad based around grilled fennel bulbs and olives.

West Brook Blue Ridge Vintage Reserve Marlborough Chardonnay

STYLE dry
QUALITY 🍷🍷🍷🍷
VALUE ★★★★
GRAPES Chardonnay
REGION Marlborough
CELLAR 🍷 1–4
PRICE $22–24

The small print on the label tells us this wine was barrique fermented. It spent 10 months in French oak, and 80% of the juice was put through an acid-softening malolactic fermentation.

Current Release 1999 There's some nice oak spice on the nose, backing citric and stonefruit aromas. The peach-like flavours are broadly focused, the texture creamy and the finish long and satisfying. It's good with a frittata made with cubed kumara, red onion and sage.

White Cloud Chardonnay

The House of Nobilo launched the White Cloud label a little over a decade ago, and it has been a huge world-wide success, particularly in Scandinavia.
Current Release (non-vintage) The nose is distinctly grainy, but there's a little ripe fruit lurking at the back. It's sweet-fruited on the palate, but leaving enough residual sugar to kick it out of the 'dry' category has thrown it a little off balance, at least to my palate. It's best on its own.

STYLE **off-dry**
QUALITY ▼ ▼ ▽
VALUE ☆ ☆ ☆
GRAPES **Chardonnay**
REGION **Marlborough**
CELLAR 1
PRICE **$9–11**

Whitehaven Chardonnay

Simon Waghorn matured just 30% of this wine in oak barrels for three months, leaving the rest in stainless steel. It was a good move – the wine won a silver medal at the 2001 New Zealand Wine Society Royal Easter Wine Show.
Current Release 2000 Light oak spice backs the grapefruit aromas on the nose. It's citric, creamy and smartly balanced, and would make a good partner for firm-fleshed fish, cubed, dusted with flour and shallow-fried, then served with a sauce based on coconut cream and just a touch of curry powder.

STYLE **dry**
QUALITY ▼ ▼ ▼ ▼
VALUE ☆ ☆ ☆ ☆ ☆
GRAPES **Chardonnay**
REGION **Marlborough**
CELLAR 3
PRICE **$17–19**

William Hill Alexandra Chardonnay

Winemaker David Grant fermented the juice for this chardonnay in French barrels, some new, some up to three years old. The fledgling wine stayed in them for a further six months.
Current Release 2001 Toasty oak is in good nick behind the cut peach aromas on the nose. It's sweet-edged and rich on the palate, with smart balance between fruit, oak and acid. Enjoy it with battered and deep-fried mussels.

STYLE **dry**
QUALITY ▼ ▼ ▼ ▼ ▽
VALUE ☆ ☆ ☆ ☆
GRAPES **Chardonnay**
REGION **Central Otago**
CELLAR 3
PRICE **$20–23**

Winslow White-rock Chardonnay

This member of the Winslow portfolio was matured in American barrels. That's unusual for this variety – most producers favour the subtler tones of French oak. Around 20% was put through a malolactic fermentation.
Current Release 2001 The spice behind the minerally notes on the nose is quite gentle, so maybe giving American timber a go was a good idea. It's ripe-fruited, creamy and with flavours reminiscent of a freshly cut peach. The finish is a bit short, but it's a pleasant drop that goes well with a serious chicken and celery sandwich.

STYLE **dry**
QUALITY ▼ ▼ ▼ ▽
VALUE ☆ ☆ ☆
GRAPES **Chardonnay**
REGION **Martinborough**
CELLAR 2
PRICE **$27–29**

Winslow White-rock Unoaked Chardonnay

STYLE **dry**
QUALITY ▯▯▯▯
VALUE ☆ ☆ ☆
GRAPES **Chardonnay**
REGION **Martinborough**

CELLAR ▯ **2**
PRICE **$25–27**

It's seen no oak, but winemaker Elise Montgomery did put 70% of the juice through an acid-softening malolactic fermentation. It's hard to find – Winslow wines have been in particularly short supply over the last couple of years.
Current Release 2002 Okay, it's not oak – but I still get a suggestion of Weet-Bix on the nose. The flavours are citric but gently so, and the texture is suitably smooth through the middle. Keen acids cut in to enliven the finish. Winery owners Steve and Jennifer Tarring suggest enjoying it with freshly opened rock oysters. Add a pile of lightly buttered grainy bread and you're in business.

Wishart Estate Barrique Fermented Chardonnay

STYLE **dry**
QUALITY ▯▯▯▯
VALUE ☆ ☆ ☆ ☆
GRAPES **Chardonnay**
REGION **Hawke's Bay**

CELLAR ▯ **3**
PRICE **$22–24**

The 'barrique' referred to in the title is a 225-litre barrel, considered the ideal size to add just enough oak character to the wine. It is also said to be the largest barrel that can be easily handled by one person, at least when it's empty.
Current Release 2001 There's a pleasant suggestion of preserved lemons behind the aromas of freshly cut nectarine, along with a dash of oak spice at the back. It's smooth enough to be called creamy on the palate, but integrated acids give it good lift on the moderately long finish. It's good with Moroccan-style chicken – with preserved lemon.

Wishart Estate Reserve Chardonnay

STYLE **dry**
QUALITY ▯▯▯▯
VALUE ☆ ☆ ☆
GRAPES **Chardonnay**
REGION **Hawke's Bay**

CELLAR ▯ **3**
PRICE **$26–29**

This upmarket chardonnay from Don Bird and his team spent 10 months in French oak barrels, and was encouraged to undergo an acid-softening partial malolactic fermentation. There's not a lot of it, so it's hard to find outside Hawke's Bay.
Current Release 2000 The spicy, toasted nut aromas give this wine a lot of appeal in the bouquet. It's nicely balanced on the palate, with smartly integrated acids adding just the right amount of zing to the ripe stonefruit flavours. It works well with a roasted capsicum risotto.

Wither Hills Chardonnay

STYLE **dry**
QUALITY ▯▯▯▯▯
VALUE ☆ ☆ ☆ ☆
GRAPES **Chardonnay**
REGION **Marlborough**

CELLAR ▯ **4**
PRICE **$29–33**

Big news for Wither Hills last year was the purchase of the company by Lion Nathan. Father and son founders John and Brent Marris are still involved, so nothing is expected to change, at least as far as quality is concerned.
Current Release 2001 Focus is what this classy chardonnay is all about. The oak is discernible in the form of gentle spice, and the rich fruit characters push all the right buttons – but nothing dominates. The finish is long and satisfying. It'great with a platter of Japanese-style seafood tempura.

Woodthorpe Chardonnay

The Woodthorpe vineyard, owned by members of the Te Mata Estate team, is situated on north-facing river terraces in the Tutaekuri Valley, Hawke's Bay. It has produced wines only in the last couple of vintages, but we will be hearing more of it.

Current Release 2002 Butterscotch and cracked wheat share the honours on the bouquet. There's some great fruit on the palate, giving it instant appeal. Enjoy it alongside directly flavoured dishes like couscous with roasted root vegetables.

STYLE **dry**
QUALITY ♟ ♟ ♟ ♟ ♟
VALUE ☆ ☆ ☆ ☆ ☆
GRAPES **Chardonnay**
REGION **Hawke's Bay**
CELLAR 🍾 **3**
PRICE **$19–21**

Yelas Winemaker's Reserve Hawke's Bay Chardonnay

Yelas is the premium label of Stephan Yelas' Pleasant Valley winery, in West Auckland. This member of the small portfolio spent nine months in French oak barrels, all of them new.

Current Release 1999 Toasty oak backs the ripe grapefruit aromas. It has been made in a broad style, with a creamy texture and very restrained acids. It's good with penne pasta tossed with cauliflower, good olive oil and freshly shaved Parmesan.

STYLE **dry**
QUALITY ♟ ♟ ♟ ♟
VALUE ☆ ☆ ☆ ☆
GRAPES **Chardonnay**
REGION **Hawke's Bay**
CELLAR 🍾 **2**
PRICE **$21–23**

Chenin Blanc and Blends

Chenin blanc is a variety we don't hear a great deal about, although it is an anonymous part of quite a few blends. It is popular because it has the ability to retain crisp acids even in exceptionally hot years, which means it can add zing to wines that might otherwise lean to blandness. The few producers who treat it as more than simply a useful tool are rewarded with wines that, at their best, can be compared to good chardonnay. Like its more famous cellarmate, chenin reacts well to techniques like oak fermentation and ageing, malolactic fermentation and lees stirring. Given this sort of care and attention, it is capable of turning from an outspoken, inelegant simpleton to a confident and stylish star.

Collards Hawke's Bay Chenin Blanc

STYLE **dry**
QUALITY 🍷 🍷 🍷 🍷 🍷
VALUE ★ ★ ★ ★ ☆
GRAPES **Chenin Blanc**
REGION **Hawke's Bay**

CELLAR 🍾 3
PRICE **$13–15**

To give it its full title it's now labelled 'Province of Hawke's Bay', but this is the same inexpensive wine that has been one of the great bargains of the local scene for several vintages. It gets some oak, but ripe fruit rules.

Current Release 2001 The bouquet is like pears and freshly cut apples, and the same characters can be found on the front palate. The balance between fruit and acid is spot-on, giving it a refreshing lift through the middle and on the zingy finish. It's good with oysters, topped with a little grated cheese and grilled.

Collards Summerfields Chenin/Sauvignon/Chardonnay

STYLE **off-dry**
QUALITY 🍷 🍷 🍷
VALUE ★ ★ ★ ★
GRAPES
  Chenin Blanc
  Sauvignon Blanc
  Chardonnay
REGION **West Auckland**
  Hawke's Bay

CELLAR 🍾 1
PRICE **$8–9**

This is possibly the only blend of these three varieties in the country, but that doesn't stop it being a popular buy at the friendly Collards cellar shop in Lincoln Road, in the Auckland suburb of Henderson.

Current Release 2000 Typical sauvignon herbaceousness is the dominant factor in the savoury bouquet. It's grassy and clean-cut in the middle, lean and frisky on the finish. It needs food to bring out its best, so try it alongside a heaping bowl of fried rice with ham and broccoli.

Esk Valley Chenin Blanc (Black Label)

Gordon Russell has always enjoyed working with the chenin grape, and takes it more seriously than many of his compatriots. This one was partly fermented in French and American oak barrels and matured on the yeast lees.
Current Release 1999 There's a savoury edge to the variety's more usual pear aromas. The palate structure is smooth, thanks to well-integrated acids, with reasonably rich flavours and a satisfying finish. It works well with hot-smoked trout – ask Gordon.

STYLE **off-dry**
QUALITY ♟♟♟♟
VALUE ☆ ☆ ☆
GRAPES **Chenin Blanc**
REGION **Hawke's Bay**
CELLAR 🍾 **3**
PRICE **$16–18**

Esk Valley Reserve Chenin Blanc

Gordon got the fruit for this top-shelf chenin from the stoniest corner of the vineyard. It was fermented in French oak barrels and stayed there for a further seven months. This was the last Reserve model he made, so it's very rare.
Current Release 1998 Spiced apples and pears get together in the bouquet. It's richly flavoured, big and quite weighty, but with a stylish finish lending an air of elegance. It makes a good partner for hot roast ham, so save it for one of the next few Christmases.

STYLE **dry**
QUALITY ♟♟♟♟♟
VALUE ☆ ☆ ☆
GRAPES **Chenin Blanc**
REGION **Hawke's Bay**
CELLAR 🍾 **5**
PRICE **$19–21**

Forrest Marlborough Chenin Blanc

And now for something completely different! John and Brigid Forrest left this chenin pretty sweet, matured it in old oak barrels and allowed a proportion of the juice to go through a malolactic fermentation.
Current Release 2001 The bouquet put me in mind of gently spiced pears. It's a very sensual wine on the palate, undeniably sweet but perfectly balanced – and that's quite a trick. It makes a lovely aperitif, but it also works pretty well with duck livers, pan-fried with olive oil and mirin (sweet Japanese cooking sake), then smeared onto thick slices of grainy toast.

STYLE **medium-sweet**
QUALITY ♟♟♟♟♟
VALUE ☆ ☆
GRAPES **Chenin Blanc**
REGION **Marlborough**
CELLAR 🍾 **8**
PRICE **$30–33**

Margrain Chenin Blanc Late Harvest

Martinborough pioneer, the late Stan Chifney, was a great fan of chenin, and some of his vineyards have been taken over by the Margrain team. This member of their range came from vines that were 32 years old – an extraordinary age by local standards.
Current Release 2002 Stan made most of his chenin on the sweet side, and Strat Canning has followed his example – the late-picked grapes were becoming raisined. The bouquet is like spiced pears, but the flavours are more like a fresh Pacific Rose apple. The finish is clean and bright. It's probably best on its own, but you could try it with mild blue cheese.

STYLE **medium-sweet**
QUALITY ♟♟♟♟
VALUE ☆ ☆
GRAPES **Chenin Blanc**
REGION **Martinborough**
CELLAR 🍾
PRICE **$27–29**

Mills Reef Hawke's Bay Chenin/Chardonnay

STYLE off-dry

QUALITY ▢▢▢

VALUE ★★★☆

GRAPES
  Chenin Blanc 60%
  Chardonnay 40%

REGION Hawke's Bay

CELLAR ▯

PRICE $11–13

It used to carry the Moffat Road designation, but now this cheap-and-cheerful blend goes out under the plain Mills Reef title. Whatever it's called, it's good value and has a keen following.

Current Release 2000 Pear and apple aromas kick things off nicely. It's got plenty of ripe fruit flavours, with the chenin component contributing a steely edge. The finish is sweet-fruited and clean. It makes a good partner for wedges of cheese-topped polenta, grilled and served as finger food.

Millton Gisborne Chenin Blanc Te Arai Vineyard

STYLE off-dry

QUALITY ▢▢▢▢▢

VALUE ★★☆

GRAPES Chenin Blanc

REGION Gisborne

CELLAR ▭ 1–5

PRICE $25–27

Chenin blanc isn't overly popular, but this splendid wine from Gisborne's James and Annie Millton shows just what can be done with it when it is given the status it deserves. Barrel ageing is just one of the techniques used to give it complexity.

Current Release 2000 Pears and mineral notes create an encouraging introduction. It's quite closed on the palate, but there's a feeling of restrained power. On its own, it seems austere despite the slight sweetness, but it comes alive with food. Enjoy it alongside a home-made pie filled with smoked fish and thinly sliced fennel.

Quarry Road Chenin Blanc

STYLE off-dry

QUALITY ▢▢▢▢

VALUE ★★★★

GRAPES Chenin Blanc

REGION Waikato

CELLAR ▯ 3

PRICE $13–15

I've listed it as off-dry, but it is on the drier side of that designation. Toby Cooper made it simply, without resorting to the oak maturation or other techniques favoured by some chenin blanc producers.

Current Release 2002 Chunky characters reminiscent of muesli and dried apples set the scene in the bouquet. It's rich on the palate, but the variety's typically vibrant acids keep things in check. The finish is pleasantly oily. It would make a great partner for a chicken and mushroom stew.

Terrace Road Chenin Blanc

STYLE dry

QUALITY ▢▢▢▢

VALUE ★★☆

GRAPES Chenin Blanc

REGION Marlborough

CELLAR ▯ 2

PRICE $18–20

Chenin blanc is a pretty rare commodity in Marlborough, which is one reason why this one has a keen following at the pleasant Cellier Le Brun café. Like many of the region's whites, it is sealed with a screwcap.

Current Release (non-vintage) It's freshly citric in the bouquet and has flavours reminiscent of Gala apples and freshly cut pears, edged by the keen acids that typify the variety. It's good with pork, particularly if it's topped with a not-too-sweet apple sauce.

Villa Maria Private Bin East Coast Chenin Blanc/ Chardonnay

The East Coast designation means this wine is a blend not only of two varieties, but of two regions. Chenin blanc used to be blended with chardonnay more than it is nowadays, albeit usually anonymously. This cheap-and-cheerful interpretation of the style has won many friends.

Current Release 2001 The nose put me in mind of dried pears. It's frisky and clean-cut on the palate, with citric flavours and an appealing directness. Only a trace of bitter apple on the finish mars the good impression. Still, it works just fine with good, old-fashioned fish and chips.

STYLE **off-dry**

QUALITY ♟ ♟ ♟

VALUE ★ ★ ★

GRAPES **Chenin Blanc Chardonnay**

REGION **Gisborne Hawke's Bay**

CELLAR 🍾 **1**

PRICE **$11–13**

West Brook Hawke's Bay Chenin Blanc

West Brook has been producing a chenin blanc for many years, and it has won a fistful of awards. Adding a smidgen of sauvignon blanc is a clever idea – it lifts the fruit and adds extra character.

Current Release 1999 Pears and tangelos are the aromatic associations for me, and I'm perfectly happy with that. It's a nicely weighted wine, crisp and lively, but with good depth of sweet fruit flavours. It should be good with a slightly sweet Vietnamese salad based around chicken and thinly sliced cucumber.

STYLE **off-dry**

QUALITY ♟ ♟ ♟ ♟

VALUE ★ ★ ★ ★

GRAPES
**Chenin Blanc 85%
Sauvignon Blanc 15%**

REGION **Hawke's Bay**

CELLAR 🍾 **3**

PRICE **$12–14**

Gewürztraminer

Gewürztraminer is the world's most distinctive grape variety. Its spicy, exuberant aromas are often compared to fresh ginger, cloves and lychees, and its flavours can be equally outspoken. Traditionally, it has been a difficult variety to place with food, and was often suggested for curry simply because it refused to be intimidated. In recent vintages, winemakers have learned to leave the skins in contact with the juice for a shorter time, lessening the variety's brashness but retaining all of its liveliness. This new style of gewürz still likes to star, but it will sit happily next to a pork roast or even lightly spiced seafood dishes. One warning: gewürz comes in all styles, from bone-dry to super-sweet, so you will need to seek advice before committing yourself to a particular bottle.

Alan McCorkindale Marlborough Gewürztraminer

STYLE **off-dry**
QUALITY ♈♈♈♈♈
VALUE ☆☆☆
GRAPES
  Gewürztraminer
REGION **Marlborough**

CELLAR 4
PRICE **$25–28**

You'll have to hunt for this nicely balanced gewürz – it sold like hot cakes after it took a good medal and the trophy for top in its class at the 2000 Air New Zealand Wine Awards.
Current Release 2000 This is classic gewürz, with gentle spice on the nose and a texture that leans towards smoothness. That all adds up to a thoroughly attractive package. It goes well with a gentle Malaysian curry built around chicken and coconut cream.

Allan Scott Marlborough Gewürztraminer

STYLE **off-dry**
QUALITY ♈♈♈♈♈
VALUE ☆☆☆☆⯪
GRAPES
  Gewürztraminer
REGION **Marlborough**

CELLAR 4
PRICE **$16–18**

This is one of the lesser-known members of the Allan Scott portfolio, but it is well worth searching out. It sells well whenever Asian-influenced dishes are featured on the menu of the company's pleasant winery restaurant.
Current Release 2002 Spicy on the nose, with all the right ginger and lychee associations, and deliciously ripe-fruited on the palate, this is an opulent mouthful. The sweetness level is perfect for the style, and the acids ensure it stays evenly balanced. It's great with the Indian/Malay dish called mee goreng.

Amor-Bendall Gewürztraminer

Noel and Alison Amor are gewürz fans, and they source fruit for this one from one of the best sites in the region. It's just dry enough to sneak into that category at competitions, but it does carry a whisper of residual sweetness.
Current Release 2001 This is a very open wine, with the usual spicy notes in good form in the bouquet and a good whack of sweet, clean fruit on the palate. It's nicely balanced and instantly approachable, and makes a good partner for spicy sausages like Spanish chorizo or French merguez, served with creamy mashed potatoes.

STYLE **off-dry**
QUALITY ♛ ♛ ♛ ♛ ʔ
VALUE ☆ ☆ ☆
GRAPES **Gewürztraminer**
REGION **Gisborne**
CELLAR 🍾 **4**
PRICE **$21–23**

Artisan Sunvale Estate Gisborne Gewürztraminer

Artisan front man, viticulturist Rex Sunde, believes the Sunvale vineyard in Tolaga Bay, north of Gisborne, is the oldest in the area. The vines were planted 30 years ago, and now give small crops of intensely concentrated fruit.
Current Release 2002 This latest gewürz is a little sweeter than its predecessor, but it tastes drier. That's a sign that the fruit and acid are in perfect balance. It boasts all the variety's classic spice on the nose and a broad, rich flavour profile. The finish is chunky but clean. We opened ours to go with a mild Goa-style prawn curry, and were well pleased.

STYLE **off-dry**
QUALITY ♛ ♛ ♛ ♛ ʔ
VALUE ☆ ☆ ☆ ☆
GRAPES **Gewürztraminer**
REGION **Gisborne**
CELLAR 🍾 **3**
PRICE **$17–19**

Askerne Hawke's Bay Gewürztraminer

Vineyard owner John Loughlin is a firm believer that the proper place of wine is alongside honest food – ideally using Hawke's Bay ingredients. Having spent time as head of Richmond Meats, he knows what he's talking about.
Current Release 2002 The nose is spicy and savoury in all the right places. It's richly fruited with a typically oily texture, but smartly tuned acids keep the balance about right. Enjoy it with a spiced carrot soup, served with thick slices of grainy toast.

STYLE **off-dry**
QUALITY ♛ ♛ ♛ ʔ
VALUE ☆ ☆ ☆
GRAPES **Gewürztraminer**
REGION **Hawke's Bay**
CELLAR 🍾 **3**
PRICE **$18–20**

Babich Winemaker's Reserve Gewürztraminer

The fruit came from the sought-after Gimblett Road area, better known for chardonnay. This was only its second crop, but it has formed the basis for a pretty smart wine.
Current Release 2000 The typical spice is subdued on the nose, but it's there if you search. It's quite riesling-like in its flavours, more floral than rich but with a good quota of well-focused fruit. It works well alongside a pile of chicken nibbles with a chilli mayonnaise dipping sauce.

STYLE **off-dry**
QUALITY ♛ ♛ ♛ ♛
VALUE ☆ ☆ ⅟
GRAPES **Gewürztraminer**
REGION **Hawke's Bay**
CELLAR 🍾 **4**
PRICE **$25–27**

Black Ridge Gewürztraminer

STYLE off-dry
QUALITY ▽ ▽ ▽ ▽ ▽
VALUE ☆ ☆ ☆ ☆
GRAPES Gewürztraminer
REGION Central Otago
CELLAR 🍾 6
PRICE $22–24

Verdun Burgess and Sue Edwards have a big following for this off-dry gewürz, made from grapes grown on their spectacularly sited rock-strewn vineyard. Some of the vines that gave up their fruit are 19 years old.

Current Release 2001 Now this is a classic gewürz nose. Spice, lychees, freshly cut ginger – they're all there. It's oily on the front palate, but clean-cut acids keep things on an even keel through the middle and on to the sweet-fruited finish. Braised pork chops would be the go here, served over a pile of mashed potatoes enriched with truffle oil. That's an expensive ingredient, but the wine deserves it.

Bladen Marlborough Gewürztraminer

STYLE off-dry
QUALITY ▽ ▽ ▽ ▽
VALUE ☆ ☆ ☆
GRAPES Gewürztraminer
REGION Marlborough
CELLAR 🍾 4
PRICE $23–26

Past examples of this wine have mostly headed toward the 'medium' category, but this one was made with no more than a whisper of residual sugar. That suits me just fine.

Current Release 2002 There's certainly classic gewürz spice on the nose, but it stays quite subtle. The oily texture is typical of the variety, and accentuates the richness of the fruit. It finishes with a trace of bitterness that won't be to everyone's taste, but is part of the style. It's great alongside hot-smoked salmon with a light chilli dressing.

Brookfields Gewürztraminer

STYLE off-dry
QUALITY ▽ ▽ ▽ ▽ ▽
VALUE ☆ ☆ ☆ ☆
GRAPES Gewürztraminer
REGION Hawke's Bay
CELLAR 🍾 3
PRICE $20–23

Gewürz is a popular line for Peter Robertson and the team. The style varies slightly from year to year, but it is usually pretty dry. This one carries just a whisper of sweetness.

Current Release 2000 The nose is spicy in the classic manner, but it's also quite elegant. All the right lychee and ginger flavours are there on the palate, and they're in perfect balance with the fresh but integrated acids. It's smart wine that sits well with roast pork.

Cloudy Bay Gewürztraminer

STYLE off-dry
QUALITY ▽ ▽ ▽ ▽ ▽
VALUE ☆ ☆ ☆
GRAPES Gewürztraminer
REGION Marlborough
CELLAR 🍾 5
PRICE $29–33

Didn't know Cloudy Bay made a gewürz? Not many people do. It's been produced for at least three vintages, but it's been available only from the cellar door. This is the first one to make it onto a few retail shelves.

Current Release 2000 Now this is classy! The spice is evident in the bouquet, but quite subtle, and it's much the same story on the palate. It is broad and complete, with perfect balance between rich fruit and integrated acids. In Alsace, where the grape comes from, they would probably enjoy it with goose, but it works pretty well with a brace of serious pork sausages.

Collards Hawke's Bay Gewürztraminer

The Collards produced one of New Zealand's first gewürztraminers, and have made some excellent examples over the years. This one was made from fruit sourced on a stone-covered site in Hawke's Bay.
Current Release 2002 Classic ginger-edged spice on the nose means there's no mistaking the variety. It's broadly flavoured and appealingly smooth on the palate, with straightforward flavours and a moderately long finish. Pull the cork next time you're cooking a mild chicken curry.

STYLE **off-dry**
QUALITY ♟♟♟♟
VALUE ☆☆☆
GRAPES **Gewürztraminer**
REGION **Hawke's Bay**
CELLAR ▤ 3
PRICE **$17–19**

Crab Farm Late Harvest Gewürztraminer

Most wines labelled 'Late Harvest' are super-sweet, but this one from the Jardines carries only 10g/l of residual sugar. That's good – as long as any restaurateurs stocking it realise it's not a 'stickie'.
Current Release 1996 The broadly spicy nose and oily texture put me in mind of similar wines from Alsace, in France. It's a chunky, rustic wine that is beginning to show its age, but it's certainly different! Try it with pure pork sausages with a slightly sweet apple-based sauce.

STYLE **medium-dry**
QUALITY ♟♟♟
VALUE ☆☆☆
GRAPES **Gewürztraminer**
REGION **Hawke's Bay**
CELLAR ▤ 1
PRICE **$15–17**

Dry River Estate Gewürztraminer

It's on the sweet side of medium, but this legendary gewürz is so beautifully balanced that it is suitable for a wide range of foods. Label owners Neil and Dawn McCallum like to sip it as a pre-dinner aperitif.
Current Release 2002 The spice is subdued on the nose, but crystallised ginger, honey and cloves all come to mind. It's broad and smooth on the palate, with rich fruit and a suggestion of honey, particularly on the finish. Enjoy it with duck liver pâté or a not-too-pungent blue cheese.

STYLE **medium**
QUALITY ♟♟♟♟♟
VALUE ☆☆⛇
GRAPES **Gewürztraminer**
REGION **Martinborough**
CELLAR ▤ 6
PRICE **$40–43**

Eskdale Gewürztraminer

Most restaurants serve their whites, particularly aromatic varieties like gewürz, far too cold. That annoys Eskdale's Kim Salonius. He believes his wines should be enjoyed at room temperature.
Current Release 1997 The bouquet has gewürz's classic spice, but it is in a chunky framework. It's a big, solid wine with layers of flavour and a lingering finish – quite different from anything else on the market. I like it with pork belly, braised in the Chinese way with soy, star anise and ginger.

STYLE **dry**
QUALITY ♟♟♟♟
VALUE ☆☆
GRAPES **Gewürztraminer**
REGION **Hawke's Bay**
CELLAR ▤ 3
PRICE **$26–29**

Forrest Estate Marlborough Gewürztraminer

STYLE **medium-dry**

QUALITY ♟ ♟ ♟ ♟

VALUE ☆ ☆ ☆ ☆

GRAPES
Gewürztraminer

REGION **Marlborough**

CELLAR **4**

PRICE **$19–21**

John and Brigid Forrest enjoy a good reputation for sauvignon blanc, sémillon and riesling, but this hard-to-find gewürz is not so well known. That's a shame, because it's a ripper! Track it down and enjoy.
Current Release 2001 Talk about rich! There's so much ripe fruit on the nose of this big-hearted beauty that it brings to mind a field full of flowers with a dash of cloves thrown in for good measure. It's big, oily and mouth-filling on the palate, and would be great with a haunch of wild pork, if you should be so lucky.

Framingham Marlborough Gewürztraminer

STYLE **medium**

QUALITY ♟ ♟ ♟

VALUE ☆ ☆

GRAPES
Gewürztraminer

REGION **Marlborough**

CELLAR **3**

PRICE **$22–24**

The sweetness level of this Marlborough-grown gewürz seems to vary quite dramatically from year to year. In 2001, the residual sugar level is 22 g/l, which places it firmly in the 'medium' category.
Current Release 2001 I get an impression of sugar-glazed grilled pears on the nose, suggesting the flavours will be pretty rich. In fact, it is relatively subdued after that big introduction, with broad flavours that focus themselves for a moderately lively finish. Enjoy it with a Malay-style prawn and coconut curry.

Huia Marlborough Gewürztraminer

STYLE **dry**

QUALITY ♟ ♟ ♟ ♟

VALUE ☆ ☆ ☆

GRAPES
Gewürztraminer

REGION **Hawke's Bay**

CELLAR **3**

PRICE **$25–27**

Claire Allen seems to have an affinity with this variety, and has made some excellent wines from it over the years. She once worked as a chef, which explains why her wines are invariably good with food.
Current Release 2002 It was a little shy on the nose when I tried it, but it may have come out of its shell by now. The flavour is ripe, with nicely controlled spice for extra interest. The finish put me in mind of freshly cut pears. It would be perfect with a serious sandwich made from thick slices of smoked ham with sweet-edged mustard.

Huntaway Reserve Marlborough Gewürztraminer

STYLE **dry**

QUALITY ♟ ♟ ♟ ♟

VALUE ☆ ☆ ☆

GRAPES
Gewürztraminer

REGION **Marlborough**

CELLAR **2**

PRICE **$20–23**

With an alcohol level of 14.5%, this is a serious mouthful of gewürz. High alcohol means the grapes were exceptionally ripe, for which they can thank the long, dry summer.
Current Release 1999 Spiced pineapple and crystallised ginger – that's what I get on the nose. The alcohol has given it a creamy, richly fruited flavour profile, but smart acids make sure the finish is refreshing and reasonably lively. Try it with a roast pork sandwich.

Hunter's Marlborough Gewürztraminer

It's not one of the better-known members of Jane Hunter's portfolio, but this classy gewürz is consistently good. Gary Duke has made a good job of this latest version, from a year he says suited the variety.

Current Release 2000 Many people find lychees in gewürz, and there's certainly an impression of them on the nose of this one. It's nicely focused, smooth through the middle but with just enough acid to lift the finish. Be old-fashioned and enjoy it with a grilled ham steak – but hold the pineapple!

STYLE **off-dry**
QUALITY ▽ ▽ ▽ ▽ ▽
VALUE ☆ ☆ ☆
GRAPES **Gewürztraminer**
REGION **Marlborough**
CELLAR 3
PRICE **$20–23**

Kaikoura Marlborough Gewürztraminer

I've listed it as 'off-dry', but with a residual sweetness level of 9.5g/l this nicely balanced gewürz is just under my 'medium-dry' limit of 10g/l. The fruit came from a site on the southern side of Marlborough's Wairau Valley.

Current Release 2002 The term 'rose petals' is often used to describe gewürz's distinctive aromas, and it certainly fits here. It's sweet-fruited on the palate, with no sign of the bitterness this variety can sometimes develop. Smartly integrated acids keep things refreshing on the finish. Try it with Moroccan-flavoured chicken on couscous.

STYLE **off-dry**
QUALITY ▽ ▽ ▽ ▽
VALUE ☆ ☆ ☆
GRAPES **Gewürztraminer**
REGION **Marlborough**
CELLAR 3
PRICE **$18–21**

Kemblefield Hawke's Bay Gewürztraminer

John Kemble sourced the fruit for this wine from a vineyard near the Tutaekuri River. Kuri is Maori for dog, and tutae means, to put it politely, 'droppings' – but don't let that put you off!

Current Release 2000 Classic ginger and spice paints a pleasant picture on the nose. I like the smooth texture and laid-back fruit character. It's not as charactersome as some earlier vintages from this producer, but it has its own softly spoken appeal. It's good with Chinese stir-fried pork and bok choy.

STYLE **dry**
QUALITY ▽ ▽ ▽ ▽
VALUE ☆ ☆ ☆ ☆
GRAPES **Gewürztraminer**
REGION **Hawke's Bay**
CELLAR 2
PRICE **$16–18**

Lawson's Dry Hills Marlborough Gewürztraminer

You might have to beg, borrow or steal to score a bottle of this gewürz – it's as rare as a Christian Heritage-voting atheist. It sells well because it has been raved about in publications right around the country.

Current Release 2002 The bouquet is absolutely classic – all ginger, lychees and spice. It's faintly oily on the palate, as are many Alsace interpretations of this grape, but has lashings of rich flavours bordered by integrated acids. Scallop and leek risotto spiked with just a little chopped ginger would make a good match.

STYLE **dry**
QUALITY ▽ ▽ ▽ ▽ ▽
VALUE ☆ ☆ ☆ ☆
GRAPES **Gewürztraminer**
REGION **Marlborough**
CELLAR 3
PRICE **$19–22**

Longbush Gisborne Gewürztraminer

STYLE dry
QUALITY 🍷 🍷 🍷 🍷
VALUE ★ ★ ★ ☆
GRAPES
Gewürztraminer
REGION Gisborne
CELLAR 🍾 3
PRICE $16–18

Dry gewürz is hard to find because the grape has a tendency to turn bitter on the finish, so most producers leave a compensatory dash of sweetness in the mix. Not the Thorpes – this one is as close to bone-dry as they come.
Current Release 2000 The characteristic spiciness is quite gentle in the bouquet, but there's enough to add extra interest to the ripe fruit on the front palate. It's rich and faintly oily on the palate and boasts a long finish. It makes a good partner for braised pork, spooned with its juices over a pile of mashed kumara.

Longridge Vineyards Gewürztraminer

STYLE off-dry
QUALITY 🍷 🍷 🍷 🍷
VALUE ★ ★ ★
GRAPES
Gewürztraminer
REGION
Hawke's Bay 46%
Gisborne 38%
Marlborough 16%
CELLAR 🍾 2
PRICE $15–18

Longridge was once used solely for Hawke's Bay wines, but now that Montana has absorbed the brand the fruit can come from anywhere in the country. This one had its fermentation stopped early to retain a little natural sweetness.
Current Release 2002 Aromas of ripe apples and pears are edged by a dash of typical spice on the nose. It's direct on the palate, with well-controlled acids lifting the fruit through the middle. The lick of sweetness cuts in on the finish. It's good with bacon, lettuce and tomato on warm focaccia.

Lynskeys Wairau Peaks Marlborough Gewürztraminer

STYLE off-dry
QUALITY 🍷 🍷 🍷 🍷
VALUE ★ ★ ★
GRAPES
Gewürztraminer
REGION Marlborough
CELLAR 🍾 3
PRICE $20–23

I've listed it as off-dry because it contains a smidgen of residual sweetness, but it qualifies as dry for competitive purposes. Unusually for this variety, Ray and Kathy Lynskey fermented a third of the juice in French oak barrels, but because they were older they haven't had a discernible effect on the flavour.
Current Release 2001 An impression of freshly cut ginger gives it a pretty classic gewürz bouquet. It's spicy and nicely focused on the palate, with smartly integrated acids adding life to the ripe fruit flavours. The finish is clean and refreshing. It works well with Singapore-style chicken and rice, but be cautious with the chillies.

Margrain Gewürztraminer

STYLE medium
QUALITY 🍷 🍷 🍷 🍷
VALUE ★ ★ ★ ☆
GRAPES
Gewürztraminer
REGION Martinborough
CELLAR 🍾 3
PRICE $27–29

The Margrain vineyard enjoys a good reputation, but not many people know about this gewürztraminer. It deserves a larger audience – it's good. Strat Canning left about 20g/l of residual sugar in it to lift the fruit.
Current Release 2002 There's a ton of classic spice on the nose. It's rich and sweet-fruited, and strongly reminiscent of crystallised ginger. The sweetness makes it a difficult match for food, so enjoy it on its own some hot summer's day.

Matawhero Estate Gewürztraminer

In 1968, Bill Irwin was ahead of his time in planting classical European grape varieties. His winemaking philosophies are largely shared by his son, Denis, who refuses to follow established flavour trails.

Current Release 1999 It doesn't seem particularly varietal on the nose, with Gewürz's typical spiciness pushed to the back. It's nicely balanced and clean-cut on the palate, gently spicy and with nicely integrated acids. It makes a good partner for a pork and mild chutney open sandwich.

STYLE **off-dry**
QUALITY ▽ ▽ ▽ ▽
VALUE ☆ ☆ ☆
GRAPES **Gewürztraminer**
REGION **Gisborne**
CELLAR 🍾 2
PRICE **$16–18**

Matawhero Reserve Gewürztraminer

Gewürztraminer is the variety that originally put Denis Irwin's Matawhero label on the map. Even the Queen has tried it – and is said to have enjoyed it. The style has varied over the years, but it has never been less than interesting.

Current Release 1999 The bouquet is certainly classic gewürz, with lychees and green ginger to the fore. It's oily on the palate, but smartly integrated acids give it excellent balance. It works well with the dishes of Alsace, home of the variety, so try it with pure pork sausages, braised and served with cabbage and mashed potatoes.

STYLE **dry**
QUALITY ▽ ▽ ▽ ▽
VALUE ☆ ☆ ☆
GRAPES **Gewürztraminer**
REGION **Gisborne**
CELLAR 🍾 4
PRICE **$26–29**

Mills Reef Reserve Hawke's Bay Gewürztraminer

Deciding how long to leave the skins in touch with the juice is a vexed question for gewürz producers. Too long, and the wine's finish will be bitter. Too short, and the famous spiciness will be subdued. The Prestons have got it down to a fine art.

Current Release 2002 The generous belt of perfume on the nose means there's no mistaking the variety. It's sweet-fruited on the front palate, faintly oily through the middle (typical of this grape) and smartly balanced on the finish. It's good on its own, but it would also work with a serious ham and mustard sandwich.

STYLE **off-dry**
QUALITY ▽ ▽ ▽ ▽
VALUE ☆ ☆ ☆
GRAPES **Gewürztraminer**
REGION **Hawke's Bay**
CELLAR 🍾 4
PRICE **$18–21**

Millton Gisborne Gewürztraminer

The fine print on the label tells us this is from James and Annie Millton's Growers Series, and that the fruit came from the McIldowie vineyard. The grapes were harvested over a three-week period to get a range of flavours.

Current Release 2001 The bouquet is splendidly clean, and carries hints of crystallised ginger. It leans more to ripe apples on the palate, but the overriding impression is of superbly rich fruit edged by cleverly integrated acids. I can think of nothing better to partner hot baked ham accompanied by Italian-style mustard fruits.

STYLE **off-dry**
QUALITY ▽ ▽ ▽ ▽
VALUE ☆ ☆ ☆
GRAPES **Gewürztraminer**
REGION **Gisborne**
CELLAR 🍾 3
PRICE **$23–26**

Mission Hawke's Bay Gewürztraminer

STYLE dry
QUALITY ♟ ♟ ♟
VALUE ★ ★☆
GRAPES
  Gewürztraminer
REGION Hawke's Bay

CELLAR 3
PRICE $17–19

Paul Mooney has made dry, medium and sweet versions of gewürz over the years, but in '99 he opted for total dryness – this wine has absolutely no residual sugar. The fruit came from the Church Road vineyard.

Current Release 1999 The nose is classic, with loads of lychee and green ginger aromas, but making it bone-dry means the flavour profile is very straightforward. It's pleasant, but if you like your gewürz with loads of upfront fruit flavours, look elsewhere. The rest of us will enjoy this one with simple fare like ham and mustard sandwiches.

Montana 'P' Patutahi Estate Gewürztraminer

STYLE off-dry
QUALITY ♟ ♟ ♟ ♟
VALUE ★ ★ ★
GRAPES
  Gewürztraminer
REGION Gisborne

CELLAR 5
PRICE $24–26

It's a little pricier than most of its competitors, but this big-hearted wine with the bold 'P' on the label is consistently top-notch. It's a popular restaurant wine, but plenty of it is also sold to take home.

Current Release 2000 Now this is what gewürz is all about. The spice seems quite subdued at first, but slowly builds on the bouquet. Fresh ginger and five-spice powder get it together to give it an intriguing, richly fruited flavour profile. Enjoy it with roast pork, complete with crackling and slices of roasted apple.

Mt Difficulty Gewürztraminer

STYLE medium
QUALITY ♟ ♟ ♟ ♟
VALUE ★ ★ ★
GRAPES
  Gewürztraminer
REGION Central Otago

CELLAR 2
PRICE $19–22

This is the first gewürztraminer from the team at Mt Difficulty, and apparently it will be the last. That's a shame – it's smart wine, so future vintages would have been keenly sought-after.

Current Release 2000 The bouquet is so perfumed it put me in mind of aftershave lotion, but it certainly doesn't taste like it! Sweet fruit gives it a luscious flavour profile, but it remains nicely balanced thanks to integrated acids that add life to the finish. It makes a good partner for Asian-style fish in a coconut-based sauce.

Peregrine Central Otago Gewürztraminer

STYLE off-dry
QUALITY ♟ ♟ ♟ ♟
VALUE ★ ★ ★☆
GRAPES
  Gewürztraminer
REGION Central Otago

CELLAR 5
PRICE $20–23

This is a real 'love it or hate it' gewürz – I've found audience reaction to be roughly 50 – 50 at the tastings where I've presented it. It's fractionally bitter on the finish, but that's a character I really like.

Current Release 2001 The aromas are strongly suggestive of dried apricots, which is appropriate enough given its geographic origins. It's a big, grunty wine on the palate, with loads of character through the middle and that distinctive gewürz bitterness cutting in right on the finish. Partner it with a brace of spicy all-pork sausages and you'll see the point.

Saints Vineyard Selection Gewürztraminer

Made from grapes grown on the same Patutahi vineyard as Montana's highly praised 'P' version of the same grape, this gewürz offers good value. It's a big seller in supermarkets as a match for pre-packaged Indian curries.

Current Release 2002 The bouquet is certainly classic – all lychees and ginger. It's oily on the palate, which is a good sign with this variety, with rich fruit kept in check by smartly tuned acids. Curry's the thing, but don't make it too hot or you'll kill the wine.

STYLE **off-dry**
QUALITY ▼▼▼▽
VALUE ☆☆☆
GRAPES **Gewürztraminer**
REGION **Gisborne**
CELLAR **3**
PRICE **$17–19**

Seifried Gewürztraminer

With around 11 g/l of residual sweetness, this is the most popular of the Seifried gewürz duo. The extra sweetness makes it a little more difficult to place with food, but it well deserves its success.

Current Release 2002 The bouquet was surprisingly shy when I tried this wine, but it hadn't been in the bottle long. It certainly has some classic spicy aromas and the flavours are well-focused and nicely balanced by sensible acids. Prawns with a sauce built around chopped ginger and light coconut cream would be the way to go.

STYLE **medium-dry**
QUALITY ▼▼▼▼
VALUE ☆☆☆
GRAPES **Gewürztraminer**
REGION **Nelson**
CELLAR **3**
PRICE **$19–21**

Seifried Winemaker's Collection Gewürztraminer Dry

Truly dry gewürz is a rare commodity. With no residual sugar the variety tends to be bitter on the finish, so most producers make it slightly sweet to compensate. Hermann Seifried accepts the bitterness as part of the style.

Current Release 2001 The bouquet is fiercely aromatic, with suggestions of crystallised ginger and tinned lychees. It's nicely focused on the palate, with that characteristic touch of bitterness simply adding complexity, at least to my palate. Try it with mussels cooked with Asian ingredients like galangal, lemongrass and – especially – tamarind.

STYLE **dry**
QUALITY ▼▼▼▼▽
VALUE ☆☆☆
GRAPES **Gewürztraminer**
REGION **Marlborough**
CELLAR **3**
PRICE **$23–25**

Soljans Estate Gisborne Gewürztraminer

Tony Soljan and his team have long enjoyed a good reputation with gewürz, but have been unable to source the fruit they wanted since 1998. Now, the wine is back, sporting a brand-new riesling-style bottle, and it is making its many fans very happy.

Current Release 2001 The nose has all the right gingerbread and lychee characteristics, and they also drift on to the front palate. It's richly textured, faintly oily but with crisp, clean acids keeping everything in good order. Tony suggests enjoying it alongside a light chicken curry, and it would work equally well with prawn laksa.

STYLE **off-dry**
QUALITY ▼▼▼▽
VALUE ☆☆☆
GRAPES **Gewürztraminer**
REGION **Gisborne**
CELLAR **3**
PRICE **$18–20**

Spy Valley Gewürztraminer

STYLE **off-dry**
QUALITY 🍷🍷🍷🍷🍷
VALUE ☆ ☆ ☆ ☆
GRAPES
  Gewürztraminer
REGION **Marlborough**
CELLAR 🍾 **4**
PRICE **$17–19**

All the whites in the Spy Valley range are pretty full-on, and this big-hearted gewürz is no exception. At nine grammes per litre, the sweetness level is just enough to kick it out of the 'dry' category.
Current Release 2002 There's ginger in the bouquet and on the finish. In between, the flavours are rich and mouthfilling, but good balance is assured by the smartly tuned acids. It's a well-proportioned wine that we enjoyed with a Moroccan-flavoured pumpkin soup cooked by a friend and neighbour.

Stonecroft Gewürztraminer

STYLE **medium**
QUALITY 🍷🍷🍷🍷🍷
VALUE ☆ ☆ ☆
GRAPES
  Gewürztraminer
REGION **Hawke's Bay**
CELLAR 🍾 **6**
PRICE **$28–32**

Stonecroft has a huge reputation for gewürztraminer, and has beaten high-fliers from around the world on a couple of occasions. The grapes were picked very ripe in '99, and some of their sweetness has been retained.
Current Release 1999 The bouquet is absolutely classic – flowers, lychees, ginger and guavas queue up to be noticed. That richness carries through to the palate, but integrated acids stop things from getting out of hand. It's too sweet for food, although a super-ripe pear just might stand up to the flavour rush.

Te Whare Ra Duke of Marlborough Gewürztraminer

STYLE **medium**
QUALITY 🍷🍷🍷🍷🍷
VALUE ☆ ☆ ☆
GRAPES
  Gewürztraminer
REGION **Marlborough**
CELLAR 🍾 **4**
PRICE **$25–28**

After winning a handful of gongs, including the trophy for top gewürz at the 2001 Air New Zealand Wine Awards, this luscious white is getting pretty hard to find. Even the mailorder brochure encourages buyers to 'hurry up', so if you want some, be quick.
Current Release 2001 Wow! Lashings of spice, gorgeously sweet fruit and perfect balance between fruit and varietal grapiness make this wine a standout. It's too sweet for most food, so enjoy it on its own. Mind you, it would be worth trying alongside creamy blue cheese smeared onto wheaty biscuits.

Villa Maria Private Bin East Coast Gewürztraminer

STYLE **off-dry**
QUALITY 🍷🍷🍷
VALUE ☆ ☆ ☆
GRAPES
  Gewürztraminer
REGION **Marlborough**
CELLAR 🍾 **3**
PRICE **$18–21**

The fruit for this mid-range gewürz came from a single site in Marlborough's Wairau Valley, and it was grown in near-drought conditions. Less than 40mm of rain was recorded on the vineyard from January until April.
Current Release 2002 The spice characters are quite subdued on the nose, but come to the fore on the front palate. Good fruit and smartly balanced acids keep things lively through to the finish. It makes a good partner for a line-up of spicy chicken sausages with parsnip mash.

Villa Maria Reserve Gewürztraminer

Back labels often tell us with pride that the grapes were picked by hand, but this is the first one I've seen to extol the virtues of machine harvesting. The major advantage is speed in getting the fruit to the winery.

Current Release 1999 The bouquet is spicy but elegant, and the flavours are clean and well-focused, which is unusual for this exuberant variety. It's beautifully balanced, with just enough residual sugar to lift the fruit on the finish. Enjoy it with Japanese yakitori chicken.

STYLE **dry**
QUALITY ▽▽▽▽
VALUE ☆ ☆ ☆
GRAPES
 Gewürztraminer
REGION **Marlborough**
CELLAR 4
PRICE **$20–23**

Whitehaven Single Vineyard Reserve Marlborough Gewürztraminer

Simon Waghorn bought the fruit for this stylish gewürz from Prue Wisheart, who owns the Two Ponds vineyard in Grovetown, Marlborough. The grapes were pressed as whole clusters, bypassing the usual crushing process.

Current Release 2000 Dried ginger on the nose mixes with pleasant floral notes. The super-smooth texture provides a rich framework for the faintly sweet fruit flavours, but there's enough zing through the middle to ensure things stay refreshing. It works brilliantly with prawn ravioli in a watercress cream sauce.

STYLE **off-dry**
QUALITY ▽▽▽▽▽
VALUE ☆ ☆ ☆☆
GRAPES
 Gewürztraminer
REGION **Marlborough**
CELLAR 4
PRICE **$19–21**

William Hill Alexandra Gewürztraminer

David Grant tells me the grapes for this pleasant gewürz were grown on free-draining alluvial soils. The grapes were picked by hand and the fermentation tank was cooled to help retain their flavours.

Current Release 2002 The classic spice is restrained on the nose, but it's there if you search. It's a stylish wine, smoother than most of the genre but with a reasonably lively finish. It's good with a simple ham salad.

STYLE **off-dry**
QUALITY ▽▽▽▽
VALUE ☆ ☆ ☆
GRAPES
 Gewürztraminer
REGION **Central Otago**
CELLAR 3
PRICE **$20–23**

Pinot Gris

Pinot gris, occasionally labelled pinot grigio, has been around for many years, but in the last three or so vintages it has suddenly become an exciting 'new' variety. Partly, this is because it is related to pinot noir, and with the world now singing the praises of local wines made from this softly spoken red, grape growers and winemakers figured its white cousin should perform equally well in our relatively cool climate. As it is for riesling, some caution is called for when buying a bottle. Both varieties are produced in a bewildering number of styles, from bone-dry to super-sweet, and pinot gris has the added complication of sometimes being fermented and/or matured in oak barrels. Check the following pages for dryness levels and production details, or seek a reliable wine shop and ask which bottle will best suit your needs.

Amor-Bendall Gisborne Pinot Gris

STYLE **dry**
QUALITY ▽ ▽ ▽ ▽
VALUE ☆ ☆ ☆ ☆ ✩
GRAPES **Pinot Gris**
REGION **Gisborne**

CELLAR 📖 **4**
PRICE **$18–21**

This is one of the few bone-dry examples of pinot gris on the market – most contain at least a wee bit of residual sugar. It's smart wine that suggests this variety has a big future in the region.

Current Release 2001 The grainy nose is a varietal giveaway. Lively acids give a refreshing edge to the pear-like primary flavours and a spicy finish keeps the interest up right to the end. It's a good wine for Chinese food – try it with wok-fried gingered fish and broccoli.

Ata Rangi Lismore Pinot Gris

STYLE **medium**
QUALITY ▽ ▽ ▽ ▽ ▽
VALUE ☆ ☆ ☆ ✩
GRAPES **Pinot Gris**
REGION **Martinborough**

CELLAR 📖 **4**
PRICE **$28–32**

The Lismore vineyard, about 500 metres from Ata Rangi's own plot, is owned by Ro and Lyle Griffiths. Oliver Masters fermented just 15% of their 2002 juice in new French oak barrels, leaving the rest in tanks.

Current Release 2002 Muesli, with the emphasis on dried pears and pineapple – that's what I get on the nose. It's sweet through the middle, but lively acids keep things in perfect balance. The sweetness makes it a tough call for food, so open a bottle to enjoy on its own some sunny afternoon.

Babich Marlborough Pinot Gris

The Babich winemaking team fermented 10% of the juice for this wine in two-year-old oak barrels, leaving the rest to do its thing in stainless steel. A portion also sat on the yeast lees left over from fermentation for four months.
Current Release 2002 The bouquet is deliciously savoury and the flavour profile rich, ripe-fruited and immaculately clean, particularly on the lingering finish. It's a nicely balanced wine that makes a good partner for salmon hash cakes drizzled with home-made mayonnaise.

STYLE **dry**
QUALITY ♀♀♀♀♀
VALUE ☆☆☆☆☆
GRAPES **Pinot Gris**
REGION **Marlborough**
CELLAR **3**
PRICE **$18–21**

Bilancia Pinot Grigio

Lorraine Leheney and Warren Gibson have carved out a big reputation with this grape, which they prefer to call by its Italian name. They are based in Hawke's Bay, but the fruit for this member of their portfolio came from Marlborough.
Current Release 2002 The bouquet is mealy, with a strong suggestion of dried pears. It's a nicely focused wine, ripe-fruited and smartly balanced, and boasts a fresh-faced, lively finish. It works particularly well with pan-fried gurnard fillets served on polenta cakes.

STYLE **dry**
QUALITY ♀♀♀♀♀
VALUE ☆☆☆☆
GRAPES **Pinot Gris**
REGION **Marlborough**
CELLAR **4**
PRICE **$28–31**

Bilancia Pinot Grigio Reserve

Lorraine fermented this top-shelf model in seasoned oak barrels, and put around 20% of the juice through an acid-softening malolactic fermentation. It has a big following, particularly in restaurants.
Current Release 2000 Aromas reminiscent of spiced pears are backed by the savoury characters of the oak. It's sweet-fruited, rich and creamy on the palate – pure class. It goes splendidly with fettucine pasta, tossed in a cream-based sauce flavoured with fresh sage.

STYLE **dry**
QUALITY ♀♀♀♀♀
VALUE ☆☆☆☆
GRAPES **Pinot Gris**
REGION **Hawke's Bay**
CELLAR **1–4**
PRICE **$30–33**

Bladen Marlborough Pinot Gris

The team at Bladen believes pinot gris suits a touch of oak, so this one spent a brief time in barrels. At 13 years of age, the vines are among the oldest of this variety in the region.
Current Release 2002 I get the aroma of a freshly cut Gala apple on the nose, with an attractive touch of spice adding extra interest. It's sweet-fruited on the front palate, boasts good balance through the middle courtesy of well-tuned acids, and finishes cleanly. Pork cutlets with a not-too-sweet apple sauce would make a good accompaniment.

STYLE **dry**
QUALITY ♀♀♀♀♀
VALUE ☆☆☆☆
GRAPES **Pinot Gris**
REGION **Marlborough**
CELLAR **3**
PRICE **$23–26**

Brookfields Pinot Gris

STYLE **off-dry**
QUALITY ♟♟♟♟
VALUE ☆☆☆☆
GRAPES **Pinot Gris**
REGION **Hawke's Bay**
CELLAR 🍾 **3**
PRICE **$20–23**

Peter Robertson was producing a pinot gris long before it became the fashionable 'new' variety, and it has always been a big seller for his talented team. The fruit comes from the Ohiti Estate vineyard, which he describes as 'arid'.
Current Release 2000 The bouquet is grainy and mealy – just the way I like it – with an echo of pears and figs at the back. There's some lovely fruit in there, sweet-edged, but with restrained acids to keep things in check. There's nothing better with Malaysian chicken satay.

Cairnbrae Marlborough Pinot Gris

STYLE **dry**
QUALITY ♟♟♟♟
VALUE ☆☆☆⟨
GRAPES **Pinot Gris**
REGION **Marlborough**
CELLAR 🍾 **3**
PRICE **$23–26**

Pinot gris is a new variety for Murray and Daphne Brown, and they've got high hopes for it. This one retains a whisper of sweetness, but not quite enough to kick it out of the 'dry' category.
Current Release 2000 The mealy, Weet-Bix and nashi pear bouquet promises good things to come. It's broadly textured, with a creamy mid-palate but enough acid zing to keep things refreshing through to the moderately long finish. It makes a great partner for a plate of lightly spiced sausages and Puy lentils.

Canterbury House Waipara Pinot Gris

STYLE **dry**
QUALITY ♟♟♟⟨
VALUE ☆☆☆☆
GRAPES **Pinot Gris**
REGION **Waipara**
CELLAR 🍾 **3**
PRICE **$18–20**

Winemakers are split on the right sweetness level for pinot gris and whether or not to put it in oak. Mark Rattray made this one bone-dry and matured it in used French barrels.
Current Release 2000 I like the grainy impression behind the primary aromas of dried pears. It's smooth on the front palate, gets a little lean in the middle but finishes with a ripe-fruited flourish. Try it alongside fettucine pasta with a creamy sauce spiked with chopped walnuts.

Carrick Central Otago Pinot Gris

STYLE **dry**
QUALITY ♟♟♟♟⟨
VALUE ☆☆☆☆
GRAPES **Pinot Gris**
REGION **Central Otago**
CELLAR 🍾 **4**
PRICE **$22–25**

I've listed it as dry, but this Central Otago pinot gris does carry a wee bit of residual sugar. Winemaker Steve Davies matured around 20% of the juice in oak, but because none of the barrels were new they have had minimal effect.
Current Release 2002 The aromas are of muesli, liberally laced with dried fruit. It tastes sweeter than it is thanks to the ripe fruit flavours, with pears to the fore. Crisp acids keep everything clean and fresh through to the lingering finish. Tuatua risotto should suit it well, especially if a pinch of saffron is stirred into the rice.

Corbans Pinot Gris

It's one of the best-priced examples of pinot gris on the market, and it's selling like hot cakes in supermarkets around the country. Winemaker Alex Kahl says he got fruit in great condition from the 2002 vintage.
Current Release 2002 Remember lemon sherbert? That's what this cheap-and-cheerful white smells like. It's clean and simple on the palate, with nothing that could offend anybody. Pull the cork next time you're slobbing out with takeaway fish and chips.

STYLE **dry**
QUALITY ▽ ▽ ▽
VALUE ☆ ☆ ☆
GRAPES **Pinot Gris**
REGION **Gisborne**
CELLAR 🍾
PRICE **$14–16**

Dry River Pinot Gris

I tasted this example of Dry River's most famous wine with a group of winemakers and fellow critics, and we all picked the sweetness at about twice its actual level. Neil McCallum says it's pure fruit extract.
Current Release 1999 Neil talks about quince and guavas on the nose – I get honey, pears and a touch of perfume. It's incredibly rich on the palate, but tightness on the finish suggests the winery's recommended cellaring time of at least two years from now is about right. Then, try it with honey-glazed hot baked ham.

STYLE **medium-dry**
QUALITY ▽ ▽ ▽ ▽ ▽
VALUE ☆ ☆ ☆
GRAPES **Pinot Gris**
REGION **Martinborough**
CELLAR ▭▭ **2–6**
PRICE **$31–33**

Escarpment Martinborough Pinot Gris

The wait is over! When Larry McKenna, the man they call 'The Prince of Pinot', left Martinborough Vineyards there was much wailing and gnashing of teeth among the cognoscenti. Now, he has resurfaced with his own label.
Current Release 2001 Perfumed and faintly grainy on the nose, rich, full-on and pear-like in its flavours, this is an extremely impressive debut. Larry fermented it in oak, but because none of the barrels were new they have rounded it out without affecting the flavour. In an ideal world, it would be enjoyed with roast pheasant.

STYLE **dry**
QUALITY ▽ ▽ ▽ ▽ ▽
VALUE ☆ ☆ ☆ ☆
GRAPES **Pinot Gris**
REGION **Martinborough**
CELLAR 🍾 **5**
PRICE **$28–32**

Esk Valley Hawke's Bay Pinot Gris

Gordon Russell sourced the fruit for this nicely tuned pinot gris from Margaret and Laurie Kaye's vineyard, right in the heart of the Esk Valley. He put 17% of the juice into oak barrels for fermentation, leaving the rest in tanks.
Current Release 2001 The aromas are broad and chunky and the flavour profile big and oily, much like some Alsace examples. It's a nicely balanced wine with suggestions of ripe pears bordered by integrated acids, and would go well with a traditional roast turkey dinner with all the trimmings.

STYLE **off-dry**
QUALITY ▽ ▽ ▽ ▽
VALUE ☆ ☆ ☆
GRAPES **Pinot Gris**
REGION **Hawke's Bay**
CELLAR 🍾 **3**
PRICE **$23–26**

Fairhall Downs Marlborough Brancott Valley Pinot Gris

STYLE **dry**
QUALITY 🍷 🍷 🍷 🍷 🍷
VALUE ☆ ☆ ☆ ☆
GRAPES **Pinot Gris**
REGION **Marlborough**
CELLAR 🍾 **4**
PRICE **$28–30**

Fairhall Downs doesn't have a high profile, but its wines have achieved impressive medal success. This pinot gris, 20% fermented in American oak, won gold at the 2000 Air New Zealand Wine Awards.
Current Release 2000 Pears and lightly toasted hazelnuts get it together on the nose. Ripe fruit gives it a luscious flavour profile, but it remains nicely tuned and lively through to the fresh-faced finish. Enjoy it alongside pan-fried pork schnitzels with a light lemony sauce.

Framingham Marlborough Pinot Gris

STYLE **medium**
QUALITY 🍷 🍷 🍷 🍷
VALUE ☆ ☆ ☆ ☆
GRAPES **Pinot Gris**
REGION **Marlborough**
CELLAR 🍾 **3**
PRICE **$22–24**

Winemaker Antony Mackenzie spent time in the original home of pinot gris, Alsace in France, and decided the secret of the wonderful local wines was low cropping in the vineyard. He employed the technique in 2001.
Current Release 2001 The nose is grainy and faintly rustic, in the nicest possible way. It's a very pretty wine on the palate, with fresh flavours, plenty of sweet fruit and nicely integrated acids. It's too sweet for many dishes, but you could try it with Moroccan-style spicy chicken.

Gibbston Valley Pinot Gris

STYLE **off-dry**
QUALITY 🍷 🍷 🍷
VALUE ☆ ☆ ☆
GRAPES **Pinot Gris**
REGION **Central Otago**
CELLAR ⬛ **1–4**
PRICE **$24–26**

Grant Taylor is pretty excited about the future of pinot gris in Central Otago. I've listed this as off-dry, but it carries only the merest suggestion of residual sweetness, which means it's a versatile wine with food.
Current Release 2002 I get dried pears on the nose, with perhaps a suggestion of muesli for extra interest. Typically dominant acids give it a lot of vibrancy on the palate, but when they settle down it should make a good partner for smoked chicken, tossed in chilli-spiked mayonnaise with a little diced pear.

Gladstone Pinot Gris

STYLE **dry**
QUALITY 🍷 🍷 🍷 🍷
VALUE ☆ ☆ ☆ ☆
GRAPES **Pinot Gris**
REGION **Wairarapa**
CELLAR 🍾 **3**
PRICE **$25–27**

'Gladstone is a state of mind', is the somewhat enigmatic statement on the back label. There's nothing enigmatic about this pinot gris, unless you count the four months spent by 10% of the juice in oak barrels in contact with the yeast lees left over from fermentation.
Current Release 2001 Spiced pears are the overriding aromatic impression in the bouquet. It's close to bone-dry but the intensely sweet fruit gives a different impression. The flavours are rich and ripe and the finish is crisp and clean. It would make an excellent partner for a salad of turkey breast and thinly sliced mango.

Grove Mill Marlborough Pinot Gris

After initially dabbling with various styles, most pinot gris producers have settled on dry versions. Not David Pearce – his is determinedly sweet-edged, and is likely to stay that way in future vintages.
Current Release 2002 It even SMELLS sweet – David reckons it's like sweet apricot jam on hot buttered scones, and that's pretty close. The flavours put me more in mind of pears and freshly cut Pacific Rose apples. That all sounds a bit over the top, but in fact it remains nicely balanced right through to the moderately long finish. It's best on its own, but you could try it with hot roast ham.

STYLE **medium**
QUALITY ♟♟♟♟
VALUE ★★★⯪
GRAPES **Pinot Gris**
REGION **Marlborough**
CELLAR 🍾 **5**
PRICE **$25–27**

Hawkesbridge Marlborough Pinot Gris

This well-priced pinot gris was made for Mike and Judy Veal by Hans Herzog, a Swiss-trained winemaker who with his wife, Therese, runs a winery and restaurant down the road from the Hawkesbridge vineyard.
Current Release 2000 Spiced pears and toasted muesli. Sound good? That's what I get in the bouquet, and it makes me very happy. It's a big wine, richly fruited and smartly balanced. The finish is long and super-satisfying. I like it! Open it to go with roast turkey and you'll see why.

STYLE **dry**
QUALITY ♟♟♟♟♟
VALUE ★★★★★
GRAPES **Pinot Gris**
REGION **Marlborough**
CELLAR 🍾 **3**
PRICE **$18–22**

Hay's Lake Pinot Gris

You won't see any more of this label. The name has been changed to Rockburn from the 2002 vintage.
Current Release 2001 Think muesli with an emphasis on dried pears and you'll be close to the bouquet. It's sweet-fruited and appealingly oily on the palate, and boasts a long, clean finish. It makes a good match for Louisiana-style seafood gumbo.

STYLE **dry**
QUALITY ♟♟♟♟
VALUE ★★★★
GRAPES **Pinot Gris**
REGION **Central Otago**
CELLAR 🍾 **3**
PRICE **$22–24**

Herzog Marlborough Pinot Gris

It's not easy to find, partly because it's a popular buy at the Herzog's Marlborough restaurant, but it's well worth a search. Hans Herzog makes it bone-dry and uses as little winery artifice as possible.
Current Release 2001 Spiced pears and muesli form a classic bouquet. Super-sweet fruit gives it a rich, ripe flavour profile, yet it remains delightfully refreshing – smart stuff! Enjoy it with Marlborough Sounds salmon, cooked medium-rare.

STYLE **dry**
QUALITY ♟♟♟♟♟
VALUE ★★★
GRAPES **Pinot Gris**
REGION **Marlborough**
CELLAR 🍾 **4**
PRICE **$34–36**

Huia Marlborough Pinot Gris

STYLE dry
QUALITY 🍷🍷🍷🍷🍷
VALUE ★★★★
GRAPES Pinot Gris
REGION Marlborough
CELLAR 3
PRICE $26–28

Claire and Mike Allen are good with gewürztraminer, so it is logical that they should also know how to handle the other great grape of France's Alsace region. They've certainly proved the point in the last couple of vintages.

Current Release 2002 Leaving just over three grammes per litre of residual sugar has lifted the pear-like fruit aromas on the nose. It's got an absolutely delightful texture – faintly oily, as are many Alsaçe versions, and with a long finish. It's great with a chunky duck liver terrine smeared onto thick slices of grainy toast.

Huthlee Estate Pinot Gris

STYLE dry
QUALITY 🍷🍷🍷
VALUE ★★★½
GRAPES Pinot Gris
REGION Hawke's Bay
CELLAR 3
PRICE $18–20

Huthlee has a keen following for this clean-cut white. This one is drier than previous versions, and has seen no oak. There's not a lot of it about, but it should still be available at the cellar door.

Current Release 2000 The nose is pear-like and clean, and the flavours are broad and nicely fruited. The finish is a bit austere, but that makes it a good partner for the direct flavours of food like raw rock oysters.

Hyperion Phoebe Pinot Gris

STYLE off-dry
QUALITY 🍷🍷🍷½
VALUE ★★★★
GRAPES Pinot Gris
REGION Matakana
CELLAR 3
PRICE $19–21

John Crone is a serious fan of pinot gris and has made a few different styles from it over the last few vintages. This one carries a little bit of sweetness, but the balance is pretty good.

Current Release 2000 Pear and citrus aromas start things off well. It's sweet-fruited and smooth on the palate, and manages a degree of elegance on the reasonably long finish. It's good with prawns, dusted with rice flour, pan-fried and served on a bed of creamed spinach.

Johanneshof Marlborough Pinot Gris

STYLE off-dry
QUALITY 🍷🍷🍷🍷🍷
VALUE ★★★★½
GRAPES Pinot Gris
REGION Marlborough
CELLAR 4
PRICE $24–26

Edel Everling and Warwick Foley say they made this wine in an Alsaçe style, with a little residual sugar left in at fermentation to lift the fruit. It certainly worked – it's very smart wine.

Current Release 2002 Pears and dried pineapple chunks – that's what I get on the nose. It's vibrant on the palate, with focused flavours but an underlying creamy feeling. That adds up to great drinkability. Stay with the Alsaçe ethos and partner it with serious pork and veal sausages, grainy mustard and sauerkraut – or at least cabbage.

Koura Bay Shark's Tooth Pinot Gris

Shark's Tooth? I'm not sure where the name comes from, but no doubt there's a good story behind it. The wine has had what the makers describe as a 'touch' of oak, but ripe fruit leads the way.

Current Release 2001 The nose has the grainy edge that this variety seems to have whether or not it has seen the inside of a barrel. It's ripe-fruited and smooth on the palate, with rich flavours through the middle and smartly integrated acids. It would go well with salmon steaks, cooked medium-rare and drizzled with lime-flavoured olive oil.

STYLE **off-dry**
QUALITY ♟♟♟♟
VALUE ☆☆☆☆
GRAPES **Pinot Gris**
REGION **Marlborough**
CELLAR 3
PRICE **$20–23**

Kumeu River Pinot Gris

Michael Brajkovich says slow pressing is important for the aromatic pinot gris grape, so that's exactly what this one got. I've listed it as off-dry, but it's on the drier side of that designation.

Current Release 2002 Spiced pears and peaty smoke form an appealing introduction. It's creamy and sweet-fruited on the palate with a squeaky-clean, faintly spicy finish. It works well with noodles with sliced pork and a few chopped Chinese pickles.

STYLE **off-dry**
QUALITY ♟♟♟♟♟
VALUE ☆☆☆☆
GRAPES **Pinot Gris**
REGION **West Auckland**
CELLAR 5
PRICE **$27–30**

Langdale of Canterbury Limited Release Pinot Gris

Only 72 cases were produced of this chunky white, partly because the crop was restricted to increase flavour in the grapes. New French barrels were used to ferment 20% of the juice, while the rest stayed in tanks.

Current Release 2000 I like the savoury edge on the dried pear aromas. It's richly fruited, but typically zingy South Island acids ensure it's got loads of life right through to the refreshing finish. The oak has added a toasty note that makes it a good partner for char-grilled eggplant and fennel bulb.

STYLE **dry**
QUALITY ♟♟♟♟
VALUE ☆☆☆☆
GRAPES **Pinot Gris**
REGION **Canterbury**
CELLAR 3
PRICE **$18–20**

Langdale of Canterbury Pinot Gris

Made from the fruit of low-yielding vines grown on three sites, this wine was left sitting on the yeast lees left over from fermentation to add extra complexity. It has scored a bronze medal and some good reviews.

Current Release 2001 Pears and muesli share the honours on the nose, along with a touch of dried pineapple. It's broadly textured, mealy through the middle and clean on the finish. It makes a good partner for thick slices of roast pork on grainy bread.

STYLE **dry**
QUALITY ♟♟♟
VALUE ☆☆☆
GRAPES **Pinot Gris**
REGION **Canterbury**
CELLAR 2
PRICE **$19–23**

Lawson's Dry Hills Marlborough Pinot Gris

STYLE **off-dry**
QUALITY ♟♟♟♟♟
VALUE ☆☆☆☆☆
GRAPES **Pinot Gris**
REGION **Marlborough**
CELLAR 🍾 3
PRICE **$19–23**

The back label says dry, but this stylish white has enough residual sweetness to place it right on the cusp of that category. The grapes came from the Hutchison vineyard, and a portion of the juice was fermented in French oak barrels, using wild yeasts.
Current Release 2001 It certainly tastes dry. The bouquet is like junior gewürz, with an impression of dried pears following the spicy, savoury aromas. Sweet fruit in chunky surrounds give it a very appealing palate structure, and that distinctive spiciness returns on the finish. We enjoyed ours with a friend's mild chicken curry and were well pleased.

Margrain Pinot Gris

STYLE **dry**
QUALITY ♟♟♟♟
VALUE ☆☆☆
GRAPES **Pinot Gris**
REGION **Martinborough**
CELLAR 🍾 3
PRICE **$28–30**

Pinot gris often carries a touch of sweetness in this country, but not this one – it's bone-dry. Strat Canning matured it in stainless-steel tanks, but because he regularly stirred the yeast lees left over from fermentation it has echoes of an oak-aged model.
Current Release 2001 Think freshly cut Pacific Rose apples and you'll have an idea of the bouquet. I like the grainy edge on the muesli-like flavours and the vivacious finish. It's a very refreshing wine that goes well with chicken pieces pan-fried in olive oil with sage leaves, sea salt and cracked pepper.

Martinborough Vineyard Pinot Gris

STYLE **dry**
QUALITY ♟♟♟♟♟
VALUE ☆☆☆
GRAPES **Pinot Gris**
REGION **Martinborough**
CELLAR 🍾 3
PRICE **$40–44**

This wine was made in two separate lots. Around half of the juice was fermented in used oak barrels, while the remainder did its thing in stainless-steel tanks. Unusually for the variety, 10% underwent a malolactic fermentation.
Current Release 2001 Aromas akin to savoury pears make a big impression on the nose. It's richly fruited with a superbly smooth texture on the palate, and finishes with a suggestion of comb honey. It works well with crumbed foods – try it with schnitzels of genuine white veal.

Matakana Estate Pinot Gris

STYLE **dry**
QUALITY ♟♟♟♟♟
VALUE ☆☆☆☆☆
GRAPES **Pinot Gris**
REGION **Matakana**
CELLAR 🍾 4
PRICE **$24–26**

The owners of picturesque Matakana Estate admire the pinot gris style of Alsace, in France, but they realise their own soil and weather will produce wines that reflect local conditions.
Current Release 2000 Oak spice, peaches, pears and something like toasted muesli add up to an interesting bouquet. This is a big, broad wine with rich flavours, a smooth texture and a full-on finish. The team recommends partnering it with prosciutto-wrapped scallops on lime-scented couscous. Yum!

McCashin's Marlborough Pinot Gris

Craig Gass left in just a touch of residual sugar to lift the fruit, and aged the wine in old barrels for nine months, sitting on the yeast lees left over from fermentation. He believes the oak has added just enough complexity.

Current Release 2000 I get Weet-Bix on the nose, which is fairly typical of the variety. It's broadly textured, with sweet fruit, gentle acids and a smooth but refreshing finish. It makes a good partner for pan-fried pork chops served with a pile of peppered parsnip, mashed with good olive oil.

STYLE **off-dry**
QUALITY ♟ ♟ ♟ ♟
VALUE ☆ ☆ ☆ ⸙
GRAPES **Pinot Gris**
REGION **Marlborough**
CELLAR **3**
PRICE **$23–25**

Mission Hawke's Bay Barrel Fermented Pinot Gris

The grapes for this classy pinot gris came from the Church Road vineyard, just along from the winery. They were picked by hand, and pressed as whole bunches without going through a crusher-destemmer.

Current Release 1999 I like the spicy edge the oak has added to the variety's usual ripe pear aromas. Like the unoaked version, now sold out, it's creamy on the palate but with nicely integrated acids adding just the right amount of crispness. It's smart wine that deserves to sit next to grilled crayfish.

STYLE **dry**
QUALITY ♟ ♟ ♟ ♟ ♟
VALUE ☆ ☆ ☆ ☆ ☆
GRAPES **Pinot Gris**
REGION **Hawke's Bay**
CELLAR **5**
PRICE **$14–16**

Morton Estate Hawke's Bay Pinot Gris (White Label)

This is the third vintage of this fresh and approachable pinot gris. Winemaker Evan Ward arranged for the grapes to be picked by hand in the company's Colefield and Riverview vineyards and got a small crop of excellent grapes.

Current Release 2001 If you think of savoury shortbread you'll have a good idea of the bouquet. It's sweet-fruited on the front palate and has a lot of refreshing vibrancy through the middle. Zingy acids on the finish complete the picture. It makes a good partner for firm-fleshed fish cooked in olive oil with a little lemon juice.

STYLE **dry**
QUALITY ♟ ♟ ♟ ♟
VALUE ☆ ☆ ☆ ☆ ☆
GRAPES **Pinot Gris**
REGION **Hawke's Bay**
CELLAR **3**
PRICE **$15–18**

Nautilus Marlborough Pinot Gris

Made with a dash of residual sugar and what the winemaking team describes as 'a little bit' of oak, this popular pinot gris is different from most. Nautilus wines are sold in 25 countries.

Current Release 2002 The nose is certainly grainy in the approved manner, and it's possible to find some pear aromas in there as well. It's smooth and broadly textured on the palate but there's enough acid to add the requisite amount of zing to the finish. Partner it with chicken on couscous and you should be perfectly happy.

STYLE **dry**
QUALITY ♟ ♟ ♟ ♟
VALUE ☆ ☆ ☆
GRAPES **Pinot Gris**
REGION **Marlborough**
CELLAR **3**
PRICE **$25–27**

Neudorf Marlborough Pinot Gris

STYLE **medium-dry**
QUALITY ♟ ♟ ♟
VALUE ☆ ☆ ☆ ☆
GRAPES **Pinot Gris**
REGION **Marlborough**
CELLAR 🍾 **3**
PRICE **$24–26**

This is the second release of the Finns' Marlborough pinot gris, and it will be the last because the vineyard where they sourced the fruit has been sold. Around 30% of the juice was fermented in French oak, and stopped to retain natural sweetness.

Current Release 2002 The bouquet is chunky and savoury, with sweet fruit to the fore. The texture is smooth, the flavours rich and the focus impeccable through to the lingering finish. Partner it with chicken cooked in the Vietnamese style with chopped ginger, soy and a touch of sugar.

Neudorf Moutere Pinot Gris

STYLE **off-dry**
QUALITY ♟ ♟ ♟ ♟ ♟
VALUE ☆ ☆ ☆ ☆
GRAPES **Pinot Gris**
REGION **Nelson**
CELLAR 🍾 **3**
PRICE **$28–30**

This is the first pinot gris Tim and Judy Finn have made from their own Moutere-grown fruit. It was fermented in French oak barrels using feral yeasts, and the ferment was stopped when Tim felt the sweetness level was balanced. It is sold only by mail order and from the winery.

Current Release 2001 The nose is like a freshly cut doyenné de comice pear, but with a touch of mealiness to round things out. It's sweet-fruited, rich and chock-full of flavour, and with a 14% alcohol level it certainly fills the mouth. Try it with tarakihi fillets wrapped in cooking paper with Asian spices before being baked.

Palliser Estate Pinot Gris

STYLE **off-dry**
QUALITY ♟ ♟ ♟ ♟ ♟
VALUE ☆ ☆ ☆ ☆
GRAPES **Pinot Gris**
REGION **Martinborough**
CELLAR 🍾 **3**
PRICE **$24–26**

Allan Johnson made this pinot gris just off-dry, but it's still good with food. It's a popular choice at the cellar door, which is a pleasant spot to visit and one of the first ports of call for weekending Wellingtonians.

Current Release 2001 The nose is grainy, with a strong suggestion of grilled pears. It's rich and mouth-filling on the palate, with the same savoury impression returning on the finish. We enjoyed ours with a plate of home-made pumpkin ravioli drizzled with sage butter. Yum!

Peregrine Central Otago Pinot Gris

STYLE **dry**
QUALITY ♟ ♟ ♟
VALUE ☆ ☆ ☆
GRAPES **Pinot Gris**
REGION **Central Otago**
CELLAR 🍾 **3**
PRICE **$23–26**

The Peregrine team has spent a lot of time on pinot gris, and has earned a good reputation with the variety as a result. This one was sourced from vineyards in the Gibbston area and underwent extensive stirring of the yeast lees.

Current Release 2001 There are some appealingly savoury notes on the nose, along with the usual varietal pear aromas. It's sweet-edged, oily and super-smooth on the palate, with straightforward flavours that suit simple dishes like pan-fried chicken breasts with a lemon-spiked cream sauce.

Quarry Road Pinot Gris

Pinot gris is being made in a number of different ways around the country. Some producers believe it suits oak maturation, others feel it needs a fair whack of sweetness. Not Toby Cooper. This one is dry and timber-free.

Current Release 2002 Think dried pears and you'll have an idea of the bouquet. It's a rich wine on the palate, with a creamy texture and good balance between the fruit and acids. The finish is a little short, but that may well change in time. Whenever you choose to enjoy it, try it with chicken drumsticks dusted with freshly grated Parmesan and grilled.

STYLE **dry**
QUALITY ▽ ▽ ▽ ▽
VALUE ☆ ☆ ☆ ☆☆
GRAPES **Pinot Gris**
REGION **Waikato**
CELLAR **3**
PRICE **$17–19**

Quartz Reef Pinot Gris

Rudi Bauer is listed as winemaker for a number of Central Otago properties, but Quartz Reef is his own label. This member of the portfolio is a popular restaurant choice in the deep south.

Current Release 2002 I get pears and apples on the nose, with a wee touch of graininess. It's sweet-fruited, rich and ripe on the palate and boasts nicely balanced acids that add life to the middle and length to the finish. It works well with seafood-topped pizza, particularly when prawns are featured.

STYLE **dry**
QUALITY ▽ ▽ ▽ ▽ ▽
VALUE ☆ ☆ ☆ ☆
GRAPES **Pinot Gris**
REGION **Central Otago**
CELLAR **3**
PRICE **$23–26**

Ransom Clos de Valerie Pinot Gris

Valerie Close is the road where the Ransom vineyard is planted, so Clos de Valerie was a logical name for this wine. Robin Ransom has established a good reputation with this newly fashionable variety.

Current Release 2000 The bouquet has some interesting chunky, mealy characters behind the variety's typical ripe pear aromas. The sweet edge gives it instantly appealing flavours, reminiscent of ripe Pacific Rose apples, but keen acids keep things under control. It's good with Chinese stir-fried pork and green beans.

STYLE **off-dry**
QUALITY ▽ ▽ ▽ ▽
VALUE ☆ ☆ ☆ ☆
GRAPES **Pinot Gris**
REGION **Matakana**
CELLAR **4**
PRICE **$20–24**

Rongopai Vintage Reserve Clevedon Pinot Gris

Clevedon, south of Auckland, is already well-known for food, and it is on the verge of establishing itself as a premium wine-producing region. Rongopai founder Tom van Dam went looking, and found a nice crop of pinot gris.

Current Release 2000 Chunky, spiced pear aromas provide instant appeal. It's a big, savoury wine with rich flavours, well-integrated acids and a full-on finish. Partner it with a pile of Kato roasted red and yellow capsicums – they come from the same area as the grapes.

STYLE **dry**
QUALITY ▽ ▽ ▽ ▽
VALUE ☆ ☆ ☆ ☆☆
GRAPES **Pinot Gris**
REGION **Clevedon**
CELLAR **2**
PRICE **$18–21**

Saint Clair Marlborough Pinot Gris

STYLE **dry**
QUALITY ♦ ♦ ♦ ♦
VALUE ☆ ☆ ☆ ☆ ⟡
GRAPES **Pinot Gris**
REGION **Marlborough**
CELLAR **3**
PRICE **$18–20**

This stylish white just squeezes into the 'dry' category, but ripe fruit makes it taste sweeter than it is. Some of the juice spent a little time in oak, but not long enough to have a major effect on the flavour. Some also went through an acid-softening malolactic fermentation.

Current Release 2002 Think muesli with an emphasis on dried pineapple and you'll have an idea of the bouquet. The texture is the thing on the palate – it's decidedly creamy, giving it great smoothness through the middle and on the lingering finish. It's good with chicken breasts rubbed with dukkah, a mix of roasted nuts and spices, before being pan-fried.

Seresin Pinot Gris

STYLE **dry**
QUALITY ♦ ♦ ♦ ♦ ♦
VALUE ☆ ☆ ☆ ☆
GRAPES **Pinot Gris**
REGION **Marlborough**
CELLAR **3**
PRICE **$25–27**

Brian Bicknell enjoys working with the pinot gris grape, and he has made a splendid job of crafting this wine from his 2001 harvest. The hand featured on the Seresin label was duplicated a dozen times by workers while the concrete was wet in the winery.

Current Release 2001 Ripe pears, rock melon and oak spice combine forces on the bouquet. It's a smartly balanced wine on the palate, with much the same characters in smooth surroundings. The finish is clean and long. It's good as a partner for wok-seared fish with Japanese soba noodles in broth.

Shingle Peak Marlborough Pinot Gris

STYLE **dry**
QUALITY ♦ ♦ ♦
VALUE ☆ ☆ ☆ ⟡
GRAPES **Pinot Gris**
REGION **Marlborough**
CELLAR **3**
PRICE **$17–19**

Shingle Peak wines do well for their owner, Matua Valley. They stand out on retail shelves and are a popular 'by the glass' choice in a number of wine bars and casual restaurants around the country.

Current Release 2001 Think baked pears – that's the nearest thing to the bouquet. It's smooth and clean on the palate, but with a crisp edge imparted by the lively but integrated acids. It's good with most Asian pork dishes – try stir-fried strips with garlic, ginger and broccoli.

Spencer Hill Evans Vineyard Moutere Pinot Gris

STYLE **dry**
QUALITY ♦ ♦ ♦ ♦ ♦
VALUE ☆ ☆ ☆ ☆ ☆
GRAPES **Pinot Gris**
REGION **Nelson**
CELLAR **3**
PRICE **$21–23**

Philip Jones and Mathew Rutherford believe in building complexity into their pinot gris. Half of the juice was fermented in older oak barrels and left there for five months, while the unoaked portion went through a malolactic fermentation.

Current Release 1999 The nose is grainy, with aromas of ripe pears filling in the gaps. It's big, rich and smart, with an oily texture to keep things running smoothly. I like it with a French-style fish stew, spiced with an indecent amount of saffron.

Spy Valley Marlborough Pinot Gris

Pinot noir grows well in Marlborough, so quite a few local producers are pinning their faith on its white cousin, pinot gris. The Spy Valley team obviously had no trouble getting the grapes ripe for this one – the alcohol level is 14.5%.

Current Release 2002 There's a rustic note on the nose that I rather like, along with a suggestion of spiced pears. It's ripe-fruited and clean on the palate with richness that seems to build towards the finish. A sandwich made from seriously good bread and filled with roast turkey and rocket would suit it nicely.

STYLE **off-dry**
QUALITY ♟ ♟ ♟ ♟
VALUE ☆ ☆ ☆ ☆
GRAPES **Pinot Gris**
REGION **Marlborough**
CELLAR 🍾 2
PRICE **$19–21**

Staete Landt Pinot Gris

Staete Landt was the name given to New Zealand by explorer Abel Tasman when he stumbled across us in the 1600s. Abel was from the Netherlands, as are the owners of this new property.

Current Release 2000 Oak fermentation usually makes pinot gris chunky and fat, but this one has retained a bit of delicacy. It's nicely balanced, with faintly pear-like flavours sitting in smooth surroundings. Enjoy it with prosciutto-wrapped quail, served on a bed of polenta.

STYLE **dry**
QUALITY ♟ ♟ ♟ ♟
VALUE ☆ ☆ ☆
GRAPES **Pinot Gris**
REGION **Marlborough**
CELLAR 🍾 3
PRICE **$34–36**

Stonecutter Martinborough Pinot Gris

Roger Pemberton worked for Martinborough high-flier Ata Rangi before launching his own label. Most of the wines are sold locally, but a few cases make it out to retail shelves further afield.

Current Release 2000 Spiced pears and a hint of dried ginger form a pleasant introduction. It's bone-dry, but the flavours still manage a sweet edge. It's clean-cut through the middle and boasts a big, rich finish. I like it with a classic roast of pork, with crackling and all the trimmings.

STYLE **dry**
QUALITY ♟ ♟ ♟ ♟
VALUE ☆ ☆ ☆
GRAPES **Pinot Gris**
REGION **Martinborough**
CELLAR 🍾 3
PRICE **$23–25**

Tasman Bay Marlborough Pinot Gris

Philip Jones is keen on pinot gris, but has made only a handful of wines from it. He believes low cropping is the best way to get concentrated fruit flavours, so the vines that gave him these grapes were forced to forfeit some of their bunches.

Current Release 2000 All-Bran and pears start things off in a most satisfactory fashion. It's a nicely controlled wine, with rich flavours, just the right amount of spicy oak and a clean-cut finish. There is nothing better with serious pork sausages and mashed kumara.

STYLE **dry**
QUALITY ♟ ♟ ♟ ♟
VALUE ☆ ☆ ☆ ☆ ☆
GRAPES **Pinot Gris**
REGION
 Marlborough 85%
 Nelson 15%
CELLAR 🍾 2
PRICE **$17–19**

Tasman Bay Nelson Pinot Gris

STYLE **off-dry**
QUALITY ♟ ♟ ♟ ♟ ♟
VALUE ☆ ☆ ☆ ☆ ☆
GRAPES **Pinot Gris**
REGION **Nelson**
CELLAR 🍾 **3**
PRICE **$17–19**

Phil Jones used Marlborough fruit for past versions of this wine, but in 2001 he found enough at home. It has been given a wee bit of oak – around 15% saw the inside of a barrel – but it remains fruit-led, exactly as he intended.
Current Release 2001 The aromas of lemon rind and Gala apples are backed by an appealing savoury note. It's smooth on the palate, with the sort of oiliness found in good Alsace pinot gris, and the finish is sweet-edged and satisfying. It makes a great partner for serious pork sausages with mashed potatoes, drizzled with a mild mustard sauce.

Torlesse Pinot Gris

STYLE **dry**
QUALITY ♟ ♟ ♟
VALUE ☆ ☆ ☆
GRAPES **Pinot Gris**
REGION **Waipara**
CELLAR 🍾
PRICE **$21–23**

Waipara's stony soils and dry climate seem well suited to the pinot gris grape, but so far local versions don't have the popularity of other varieties. That's bound to change as more producers make it part of their portfolio.
Current Release 2002 It's got all the right apple and pear aromas on the nose, but the structure is light and rather thin through the middle. It will round out slightly in time, but will never be an earth-mover. Take it to a party and forget it was yours.

Trinity Hill Pinot Gris

STYLE **off-dry**
QUALITY ♟ ♟ ♟ ♟
VALUE ☆ ☆ ☆ ☆
GRAPES **Pinot Gris**
REGION **Hawke's Bay**
CELLAR 🍾 **3**
PRICE **$22–24**

Fruit for this nicely focused wine came from a stony site right in the middle of the newly designated Gimblett Gravels region, where river shingle provides excellent drainage as well as reflective warmth for the grapes.
Current Release 2000 The bouquet is grainy, with a smoky edge. It's got lots of clean, savoury fruit sitting in a smooth-edged framework, and should make an excellent partner for crumbed and shallow-fried gurnard 'fingers', served with home-made mayonnaise.

Villa Maria Private Bin Hawke's Bay Pinot Gris

STYLE **dry**
QUALITY ♟ ♟ ♟ ♟
VALUE ☆ ☆ ☆ ☆ ☆
GRAPES **Pinot Gris**
REGION **Hawke's Bay**
CELLAR 🍾 **3**
PRICE **$15–17**

Pinot gris is a tight-bunched variety, and that makes it susceptible to rot. Keeping the fruit for this one clean involved many hours of leaf-plucking and crop-reduction in the vineyard.
Current Release 2000 The bouquet is chunky and mealy, the latter the legacy of its brief time in oak. It has a smooth, creamy texture, with flavours suggesting pears and muesli. It makes a nice partner for a salad based around prosciutto, Parmesan shavings and thin slices of pear.

Vin Alto Pinot Grigio

This wine is produced by Swiss-born, Italian-speaking Enzo Bettio and his wife, Margaret. Enzo was the first person to introduce New Zealanders to a great number of once-exotic foods through his Delmaine company, now sold.

Current Release 2000 The style is determinedly Italian, which is to say it doesn't come alive until it is enjoyed with food. The bouquet is citric with a hint of pears and the flavours are gentle and broad. Place it alongside a platter of roasted capsicums, olives, marinated carrot sticks and the like and you'll get the point.

STYLE **dry**

QUALITY 🍷 🍷 🍷 🍷

VALUE ☆ ☆ ☆

GRAPES **Pinot Gris**

REGION **Clevedon**

CELLAR 🍾 **3**

PRICE **$26–29**

Riesling

With increasing numbers of people looking for different wines to try, riesling is at last beginning to enjoy the sort of popularity it has long deserved. Its problem is not its fault; despite years of nagging from the wine press, few producers specify the sweetness level on the front label, and even if they do, 'dry' can sometimes still mean slightly sweet. That makes it difficult to order a bottle in a restaurant or to take home if you have a particular food match in mind. Check out the sweetness levels of wines in this chapter, or ask the wine salesperson's or waiter's advice. A well-made riesling is more elegant than any other white, so it's worth taking a little extra effort over its enjoyment.

Alan McCorkindale Waipara Valley Dry Riesling

STYLE **dry**
QUALITY ♟ ♟ ♟ ♟ ♟
VALUE ★ ★ ★ ☆
GRAPES **Riesling**
REGION **Waipara**

CELLAR 🍾 3
PRICE **$25–27**

Alan McCorkindale is based in Waipara, but in the past he has bought most of his fruit from Marlborough. This is the first riesling he's produced from his home region.
Current Release 2000 It contains no more than a whisper of residual sugar, but it manages to smell sweet and taste even more so. Well-tuned acids make sure things don't get out of control, and make it a good match for pan-fried chicken breasts drizzled with olive oil and a little lemon juice.

Alana Estate Martinborough Riesling

STYLE **off-dry**
QUALITY ♟ ♟ ♟ ♟
VALUE ★ ★ ★ ★
GRAPES **Riesling**
REGION **Martinborough**

CELLAR 🍾 3
PRICE **$17–19**

Martinborough isn't well-known for riesling, but John Kavanagh has made some attractive wines from the variety. He leaves the juice just a wee bit sweet by chilling the tank, sending the yeasts to sleep before they eat all the sugar.
Current Release 2000 It's probably a physiological impossibility, but I reckon this wine SMELLS crisp. It's got a touch of the florals, but lime juice is the major impression. It is just off-dry, with a wealth of delightfully ripe fruit balanced by clean-cut acids. Enjoy it with pan-fried gurnard, drizzled with lime juice.

Alexandra Wine Company Crag an Oir Riesling

This riesling, packaged in the tall, stylish Central Otago bottle, is hard to find away from the area, but it has a keen local following. Crag an Oir is one of two vineyards operated by the company.

Current Release 2000 The nose is distinctively perfumed and the flavours are citric and well focused. It has been made in quite a gentle style, but although it doesn't shout about its attributes it has a lot of appeal. It's dry enough to partner a range of foods, and goes particularly well with pan-fried chicken and ginger.

STYLE off-dry
QUALITY 3½ glasses
VALUE 3½ stars
GRAPES Riesling
REGION Central Otago
CELLAR 4
PRICE $17–19

Allan Scott Marlborough Riesling

Allan Scott enjoys a good reputation for riesling, a grape with which he has had quite a lot to do during his long career. This one carries 7.4 grammes per litre of residual sugar – just enough to kick it out of the dry category.

Current Release 2002 Grapefruit and dried orange peel get it together on the nose. It's rich, ripe and immaculately clean on the palate, with citric and pear flavours and smartly balanced acids. An old-fashioned pork roast with lots of vegetables would partner it well.

STYLE off-dry
QUALITY 4½ glasses
VALUE 4½ stars
GRAPES Riesling
REGION Marlborough
CELLAR 5
PRICE $16–18

Askerne Hawke's Bay Dry Riesling

With a sweetness level of just 4 g/l, this riesling really is dry, as described. Some versions carrying twice as much residual sugar still claim to be dry, which is a trap when you're trying to match them with food.

Current Release 2001 The bouquet is all about citrus fruit with a major emphasis on grapefruit. It's clean-cut, minerally and smartly balanced, with a vibrant finish. Partner it with grilled tarakihi with a relish made from chopped fennel and ginger.

STYLE dry
QUALITY 4 glasses
VALUE 4 stars
GRAPES Riesling
REGION Hawke's Bay
CELLAR 3
PRICE $16–18

Babich Marlborough Riesling

The Babich team has done well with riesling over the years, winning high awards and an occasional trophy with both Hawke's Bay and Marlborough versions. This one carries just a whisper of residual sweetness.

Current Release 2002 The perfumed nose carries suggestions of flowers and dried orange peel. It's richly fruited and carries its gentle sweetness well. The finish is clean and crisp. It works well alongside prawns tossed with home-made mayonnaise.

STYLE off-dry
QUALITY 4½ glasses
VALUE 4 stars
GRAPES Riesling
REGION Marlborough
CELLAR 4
PRICE $18–20

Bilancia Hawke's Bay Riesling

STYLE **medium**
QUALITY 🍷 🍷 🍷 🍷
VALUE ☆ ☆ ☆
GRAPES **Riesling**
REGION **Hawke's Bay**

CELLAR 🍾 3
PRICE **$25–27**

The Bilancia label is best-known for classy pinot gris, but Aussie-trained winemakers Warren Gibson and Lorraine Leheney are equally skilled with other varieties. Their own site is planted in syrah. Other varieties are bought from local growers.
Current Release 2001 There's a grainy edge to the pear and citrus aromas. The flavours reminded me of ripe apples drizzled with lemon juice. The sweetness cuts in towards the finish, adding richness and depth. It's too sweet for food, so try it on its own some sunny afternoon.

Black Ridge Riesling

STYLE **dry**
QUALITY 🍷 🍷 🍷 🍷
VALUE ☆ ☆ ☆
GRAPES **Riesling**
REGION **Central Otago**
CELLAR ▭▭▭ 1–5
PRICE **$20–23**

Verdun Burgess and Sue Edwards used to have the southernmost vineyard in the country, but in the last couple of years quite a few hardy souls have planted grapes even closer to the bottom of the island.
Current Release 2001 The floral nose is classic riesling, but it suggests the taste will be somewhat sweeter than it is. There's plenty of ripe fruit in there, but the flavour profile is clean, crisp and decidedly racy. It should blossom in the next year or so, after which it will sit happily next to a plate of braised rabbit.

Bladen Marlborough Riesling

STYLE **medium-dry**
QUALITY 🍷 🍷 🍷 🍷
VALUE ☆ ☆ ☆
GRAPES **Riesling**
REGION **Marlborough**

CELLAR 🍾 2
PRICE **$18–21**

The Bladen stand attracted a lot of interest at the second annual Marlborough Sauvignon Blanc celebration, held on both the Wellington and Auckland waterfronts. Despite the name, most companies presented several varieties.
Current Release 2002 Floral on the nose, citric and sweet on the front palate, this is a pretty typical example of the Marlborough riesling style. It's nicely balanced through the middle and finishes with a suggestion of freshly cut Pacific Rose apple. Enjoy it alongside similarly sweet-edged food, like prosciutto-wrapped melon.

Borthwick Estate Riesling

STYLE **dry**
QUALITY 🍷 🍷 🍷 🍷
VALUE ☆ ☆ ☆ ☆
GRAPES **Riesling**
REGION **Wairarapa**

CELLAR 🍾 3
PRICE **$17–19**

Paddy Borthwick has certainly paid his vinous dues. After training in South Australia he made wine in France, Switzerland, the US and Australia, then worked for Allan Scott Wines for five years before launching his own label.
Current Release 2000 Citric and minerally on the nose, sweet-centred and limey on the palate, this is a smart riesling that needs food to be at its best. Enjoy it with a platter of prawns, shelled then steamed with chopped lemon rind, and you will be well pleased.

Brightwater Vineyards Nelson Riesling

Riesling grows well in Nelson, but most local producers make it slightly sweet. This one carries a whisper of residual sugar, but to all intents and purposes it is dry. That makes it easier to place with food.

Current Release 2000 The floral nose has a touch of Aussie-style minerals in the background, which adds to the character. It's got a range of pretty flavours nicely edged by fresh-faced acids. It would make a good partner for veal sausages on Alsaçe-style choucroute.

STYLE **dry**
QUALITY ♟ ♟ ♟ ♟
VALUE ☆ ☆ ☆
GRAPES **Riesling**
REGION **Nelson**
CELLAR **3**
PRICE **$16–18**

Brookfields Riesling Dry

The grapes were grown on the Otihi Estate, which is adjacent to the Ngaruroro River, and they were picked by hand. Congratulations to the Brookfields team for specifying the dryness on the front label.

Current Release 2000 The bouquet is citric and minerally, and the flavour profile is light, clean and gentle – 'pretty' sums it up nicely. The dryness makes it a good partner for the gentle flavours of steamed or poached tarakihi fillets, simply drizzled with a little lemon juice and the best olive oil you can find.

STYLE **dry**
QUALITY ♟ ♟ ♟
VALUE ☆ ☆ ☆
GRAPES **Riesling**
REGION **Hawke's Bay**
CELLAR **2**
PRICE **$16–18**

Cairnbrae Old River Riesling

The grapes for this nicely balanced riesling came from the home 'Old River' vineyard, plus the Ellin site a few kilometres away. The term 'old river' alludes to the meandering water that once covered the Wairau Plains.

Current Release 2000 I get muesli on the nose, with an emphasis on dried pawpaw. It's nicely balanced, thanks to the clean-cut acids that put a keen edge on the rich flavours of tropical fruit. It makes a good partner for a salad of mesclun leaves, topped with warm pan-fried scallops.

STYLE **off-dry**
QUALITY ♟ ♟ ♟ ♟
VALUE ☆ ☆ ☆ ☆
GRAPES **Riesling**
REGION **Marlborough**
CELLAR **4**
PRICE **$17–19**

Canterbury House Waipara Riesling

The riesling grape seems eminently happy on Waipara's limestone soils. Mark Rattray made this one just off-dry because he wanted to emphasise the natural sweetness of the fruit.

Current Release 2000 Citrus blossom and dried orange peel get things going nicely on the nose. It's smooth-centred and smartly focused, with the citric impression returning on the finish. Try it with a seafood salad dressed with home-made mayonnaise.

STYLE **off-dry**
QUALITY ♟ ♟ ♟ ♟
VALUE ☆ ☆ ☆ ☆
GRAPES **Riesling**
REGION **Waipara**
CELLAR **1–5**
PRICE **$14–16**

Carrick Central Otago Riesling

STYLE medium-dry
QUALITY ♟♟♟♟♟
VALUE ☆☆☆☆
GRAPES Riesling
REGION Central Otago
CELLAR 🍾 5
PRICE $19–22

Carrick winemaker Steve Davies has plied his trade in California, Oregon and Marlborough, but is happy to be back in Central Otago. The company is a partnership between the owners of three adjoining Bannockburn vineyards.
Current Release 2002 Lemon juice and dried orange peel – that's what I get on the nose. It's clean and very lively on the palate, with fresh citrus characters edged by the keen acids that typify the region. Match the citric characters by serving it with a piece of pan-fried cod, drizzled with lemon juice and the best olive oil you can find.

Chancellor Estates Waipara Mt Cass Road Riesling

STYLE off-dry
QUALITY ♟♟♟♟
VALUE ☆☆☆☆
GRAPES Riesling
REGION Waipara
CELLAR 🍾 4
PRICE $16–18

Riesling is well-suited to the limestone soils of Waipara, and Chancellor's Chris Parker aims to produce some of the region's best examples. This one is just a shade off a dry rating.
Current Release 2000 The nose has all the correct floral and citric characters and they're in good balance with one another. It's a smartly focused wine, quite broad in the middle but with the citrics cutting back in to enliven the finish. Enjoy it with a mild blue cheese, served with bread rather than crackers.

Chard Farm Central Otago Riesling

STYLE off-dry
QUALITY ♟♟♟♟♟
VALUE ☆☆☆☆
GRAPES Riesling
REGION Central Otago
CELLAR 🍾 5
PRICE $19–22

Chard Farm was one of the first Central Otago wineries to establish a nationwide reputation. The vineyard site, alongside the Kawarau Gorge, is spectacular, but the clifftop road to the winery freaks out cautious visitors.
Current Release 1999 Big, floral and voluptuous on the nose, citric and focused on the palate, this is a splendidly made riesling. It's not bone-dry, but there are enough crisp acids to make it good alongside a range of foods. Try it with a gentle Malaysian prawn curry and you should be very happy indeed.

Charles Wiffen Riesling

STYLE off-dry
QUALITY ♟♟♟♟♟
VALUE ☆☆☆☆☆
GRAPES Riesling
REGION Marlborough
CELLAR 🍾 4
PRICE $17–19

The Charles Wiffen portfolio isn't big, but it commands a loyal following. The Wiffens, Charles and Sandi, grew grapes for other companies for many years, and they're enjoying having their own label.
Current Release 2002 It's just off-dry, but this well-tuned riesling is quite lush. The floral edge around the citric aromas is classic stuff, and the same sensations carry through to the palate. A suggestion of comb honey on the finish gives it an extra belt of richness. It's good with spicy chicken over couscous, served with a simple green salad.

Clifford Bay Marlborough Single Vineyard Riesling

The 'single vineyard' in the title refers to a sun-drenched site in the Awatere Valley, over the hills from Blenheim. The wine has won a stack of bronze medals and equivalent ratings from magazine tasting panels.
Current Release 2000 Classic lime juice and honey aromas give away the variety. It's broad, smooth and stylish, perhaps a little lacking in focus but still eminently drinkable. It would make an excellent partner for a piece of salmon, marinated with Asian spices and pan-roasted medium-rare.

STYLE **off-dry**
QUALITY ⚭ ⚭ ⚭ ⚭
VALUE ☆ ☆ ☆☆
GRAPES **Riesling**
REGION **Marlborough**
CELLAR **3**
PRICE **$16–18**

Collards Late Harvest Riesling

'Late Harvest' is often used on the labels of super-sweet dessert wine, but this one is just on the sweet side of medium. The grapes came partly from the home town of Henderson, and partly from the South Island.
Current Release 1999 Honeysuckle and other floral aromas start things off nicely. It's rich but quite citric, and therefore smartly balanced – thoroughly pleasant. Even though it's not as sweet as the label suggests, I believe it's still best enjoyed on its own.

STYLE **medium**
QUALITY ⚭ ⚭ ⚭ ⚭ ⚭
VALUE ☆ ☆ ☆ ☆ ☆
GRAPES **Riesling**
REGION **West Auckland Marlborough**
CELLAR **3**
PRICE **$14–16**

Collards Queen Charlotte Riesling

This classy and well-priced riesling is sold out at the tiny Collard's shop in Lincoln Road, West Auckland, but the odd bottle can still be found around the country. It's not quite as intense as the splendid '98, but it's pretty smart.
Current Release 2000 Floral and citric characters are typical of the variety, and they're present in equal strength on the nose. The citric theme continues on the palate, but the overall impression is of ripe, superbly clean fruit. It makes a great aperitif, or you could try it with a rich chicken or duck liver pâté.

STYLE **medium**
QUALITY ⚭ ⚭ ⚭ ⚭
VALUE ☆ ☆ ☆ ☆ ☆
GRAPES **Riesling**
REGION **Marlborough**
CELLAR **4**
PRICE **$15–17**

Coney Ragtime Riesling

This is the (slightly) sweeter of the two Coney rieslings, and it has picked up a couple of awards. Tim and Margaret Coney's vineyard is in Dry River Road, right in the heart of Martinborough's best grape-growing country.
Current Release 2001 The bouquet is floral and citric, just as it should be. The flavours are fruity but smartly focused and the acids just right for the style. A thoroughly pleasant wine that works well with prawns and new potatoes tossed in mayonnaise, ideally home-made.

STYLE **medium-dry**
QUALITY ⚭ ⚭ ⚭ ⚭
VALUE ☆ ☆ ☆ ☆
GRAPES **Riesling**
REGION **Martinborough**
CELLAR **4**
PRICE **$17–19**

Coney Rallentando Riesling

STYLE **dry**
QUALITY 🍷 🍷 🍷 🍷 🍷
VALUE ☆ ☆ ☆ ☆
GRAPES **Riesling**
REGION **Martinborough**
CELLAR ▭▭▷ **1–4**
PRICE **$19–23**

Almost bone-dry, this classy riesling tastes as if it should age for a good while. It's already drinking well, but there's an austere edge that suggests it will take a year or two to really begin to blossom.

Current Release 2000 The bouquet is solidly citric with lemons, limes and grapefruit all coming to mind. The natural sweetness of the fruit belies the palatory dryness, giving it a certain amount of richness through the middle and a refreshing finish. It should be good with a classic Caesar salad.

Coopers Creek Hawke's Bay Riesling

STYLE **off-dry**
QUALITY 🍷 🍷 🍷 🍷
VALUE ☆ ☆ ☆ ☆ ☆
GRAPES **Riesling**
REGION **Hawke's Bay**
CELLAR 🍶 **3**
PRICE **$15–17**

Marlborough is currently dominating the riesling scene in New Zealand, but some very good examples are made from grapes grown in other parts of the country. Simon Nunns has made a nice job of this one.

Current Release 2001 Grapefruit and lemon characters combine well on the nose. It's richly fruited and boasts nicely balanced acids through the middle, and the whisper of sweetness helps lift the finish without getting at all cloying. Try it with an Indonesian seafood curry.

Corbans Marlborough Riesling

STYLE **off-dry**
QUALITY 🍷 🍷 🍷
VALUE ☆ ☆ ☆
GRAPES **Riesling**
REGION **Marlborough**
CELLAR 🍶 **1**
PRICE **$13–15**

There's a new label for the wine formerly known as Corbans Estate Marlborough Riesling, but the off-dry style and drink-young philosophy remains the same. The fruit came into the winery in good condition, and was treated simply.

Current Release 2002 Citrus fruit and pears dominate the bouquet, which is quite inviting. It's soft-centred and a little thin through the middle, but pleasant enough with a bit of chilling. The winemaking team recommends trying it with emmental cheese. Fair enough!

Corbans White Label Johannisberg Riesling

STYLE **medium-dry**
QUALITY 🍷 🍷 🍷
VALUE ☆ ☆ ☆ ☆
GRAPES **Riesling**
REGION **Gisborne Marlborough**
CELLAR 🍶 **1**
PRICE **$7–9**

This inexpensive white is a big seller for Corbans, and has been known to beat higher-priced rivals in competitions. Johannisberg Riesling is apparently a specific sub-variety, but I doubt that much of it is used in this one nowadays.

Current Release 2001 Think lemon honey and dried orange peel and you've got the bouquet sussed. It's sweet-edged, light and simple on the palate – nothing to object to, but nothing to get excited about . . . apart from the price. It works okay with a platter of nibbles that emphasises shellfish.

Covell Estate Riesling

The 1998 version sold out in weeks, so local fans of the style had to wait a few months for this one. The Covells use the sort of botrytis-affected fruit that is normally reserved for dessert wines, but they ferment them to total dryness.
Current Release 1999 There's a funky bottle-aged character on the nose, and also a musty note from the botrytis. It's citric enough on the palate to invite a comparison with lime juice, which certainly gives it crispness on the finish. The tasting note suggests trying it on its own, but I think I'd prefer it with fish in a lemony sauce.

STYLE **dry**
QUALITY ▼ ▼ ▽
VALUE ☆ ☆
GRAPES **Riesling**
REGION **Murupara**
CELLAR 𝄃
PRICE **$18–20**

Crossroads Riesling

The Crossroads team has a soft spot for riesling. Like a lot of us, they particularly like the way it can change character quite dramatically after a couple of years in the bottle. The trick is to keep it that long!
Current Release 2000 I get orange blossoms on the nose, and I'm perfectly happy with that. It's simply structured, but it has good weight and a ripe-fruited, pleasant flavour profile. It's pretty sweet, so save it to enjoy on its own, in the company of a few good friends.

STYLE **medium**
QUALITY ▼ ▼ ▼ ▽
VALUE ☆ ☆ ☆ ☆⋆
GRAPES **Riesling**
REGION **Hawke's Bay**
CELLAR 𝄃 2
PRICE **$12–14**

De Redcliffe Marlborough Estates Riesling

Mark Compton makes his rieslings with lower alcohol levels than many. They're lean in their youth, but they often improve with age. The '99 model took a bronze medal, but silver some months later, and this one has also started out with a bronze.
Current Release 2000 Apples, limes and a touch of the florals at the back give it an inviting bouquet. That apple-like character is also much in evidence on the palate, where it adds a lot of zing to the ripe fruit flavours. It's good with a Thai-style beef and lemongrass salad.

STYLE **medium**
QUALITY ▼ ▼ ▼ ▽
VALUE ☆ ☆ ☆⋆
GRAPES **Riesling**
REGION **Marlborough**
CELLAR 𝄃 3
PRICE **$15–17**

Denton Nelson Dry Riesling

It contains a whisper of residual sweetness, but labelling it 'dry' is accurate – it certainly tastes that way. It's a popular buy at Richard and Alex Denton's winery shop, nicely situated on the seaward side of Nelson's Moutere Hills.
Current Release 2001 Aromas suggestive of oatmeal and dried apricots make a good impression on the nose. It's citric, clean and refreshing on the palate. The keen, high-acid finish gives notice that it will be worth cellaring for a few years. Then, enjoy it with a chicken salad in summer, or a crab and fennel pie in winter.

STYLE **off-dry**
QUALITY ▼ ▼ ▼ ▽
VALUE ☆ ☆ ☆
GRAPES **Riesling**
REGION **Nelson**
CELLAR ▭ 2–5
PRICE **$18–21**

Dry River Craighall Late Harvest Riesling

STYLE **sweet**
QUALITY ♟ ♟ ♟ ♟ ♟
VALUE ☆ ☆
GRAPES **Riesling**
REGION **Martinborough**

CELLAR **10**
PRICE **$41–44**

With a residual sugar level of around 60g/l, this wine is seriously sweet. So why isn't it in the dessert wine section? Because it has such impeccable balance that it doesn't taste like a dessert wine, and would suit quite a range of foods.
Current Release 2002 Lemon rind, perfume, apple blossoms – they're all there in the bouquet. The flavours are gently citric, but there's also a stonefruit character . . . perhaps a freshly cut Otago apricot. The finish is clean and lasts until next week. It's great on its own, but is astonishing with duck liver parfait.

Drylands Marlborough Winemakers Reserve Dry Riesling

STYLE **dry**
QUALITY ♟ ♟ ♟ ♟
VALUE ☆ ☆ ☆ ☆
GRAPES **Riesling**
REGION **Marlborough**

CELLAR **4**
PRICE **$17–19**

The fruit for this stylish riesling came from vines trellised in a system called Scott-Henry, which is designed to maximise the amount of sun that falls on the ripening bunches.
Current Release 2000 The variety's classic floral aromas are in good nick, and I was also reminded of freshly cut mandarins. It's rich but decidedly lemony in the middle and boasts refreshingly lively acids on the clean-cut finish. Try it with spring rolls and a dip made from lime juice, fish sauce, sugar and chopped chillies.

Esk Valley Riesling (Black Label)

STYLE **medium**
QUALITY ♟ ♟ ♟ ♟
VALUE ☆ ☆ ☆
GRAPES **Riesling**
REGION **Hawke's Bay**

CELLAR **6**
PRICE **$20–23**

Gordon Russell used fruit from 20 year-old vines to craft this riesling, and he ended up with something that's quite different from the norm. It's sweeter than his earlier versions, and carries an extraordinarily low alcohol level of just 9.5%.
Current Release 2001 I find suggestions of preserved lemon and dried orange peel on the nose. It's sweet-edged on the palate, and boasts considerable depth. It's drinking well now, but I believe it will age splendidly. Food? Perhaps pan-fried scallops with ginger, but I think its best use is as a refreshing pre-dinner aperitif.

Fairmont Estate Riesling

STYLE **off-dry**
QUALITY ♟ ♟ ♟ ♟
VALUE ☆ ☆ ☆ ☆
GRAPES **Riesling**
REGION **Wairarapa**

CELLAR **4**
PRICE **$15–18**

Right next to Gladstone Vineyards, Fairmont Estate has carved out a good name for itself in its short time in business. The region is well worth adding to any planned Martinborough itinerary.
Current Release 2000 The minerally bouquet reminded me of something from Australia's Clare Valley, but there's also a suggestion of more Kiwi lemon honey. It's sweet-edged, lively and nicely focused on the palate, and goes well with mussels, steamed open and drizzled with lime-laced mayonnaise.

Felton Road Block 1 Riesling

You'll have to hunt high and low for this wine, but you'll be trying something unique. Blair Walter's aim was to produce a white in the mould of the great Auslese styles of the Mosel, in Germany. It's super-sweet, but low in alcohol.

Current Release 2002 The bouquet put me in mind of baked lemons. It's deliciously balanced, rich but clean-cut and therefore very refreshing. The finish is vaguely apple-like. It would work with a creamy duck liver pâté, but it's best on its own, as an aperitif.

STYLE **sweet**
QUALITY �
VALUE ★ ★ ★☆
GRAPES **Riesling**
REGION **Central Otago**
CELLAR **10**
PRICE **$25–27**

Felton Road Dry Riesling

Few names have made as much of a splash in as short a time as Felton Road. This member of the portfolio was made using wild yeasts, and it was hard to find as soon as it was released. Want some? Talk nicely to your wine shop proprietor.

Current Release 2002 Remember lemon honey? That's the character on the nose. The fruit flavours are so full-on it's hard to believe it's virtually bone-dry, yet there is an underlying citric austerity that suggests it will continue to change for close to a decade. Whenever you pull the cork, try it with really good bratwürst sausages.

STYLE **dry**
QUALITY ♦
VALUE ★ ★ ★ ★☆
GRAPES **Riesling**
REGION **Central Otago**
CELLAR **1–9**
PRICE **$19–21**

Felton Road Riesling

Winning a gold medal, plus the trophy for Champion Riesling at the 2000 New Zealand Wine Society Royal Easter Wine Show really put this tiny Central Otago winery on the map.

Current Release 2002 The floral characters are quite subtle on the bouquet. It's sweet-fruited, but clever acid balance makes sure everything stays refreshing right through to the long finish. Try it with pan-fried chicken livers smeared onto hot buttered toast, or enjoy it on its own.

STYLE **off-dry**
QUALITY ♦
VALUE ★ ★ ★ ★☆
GRAPES **Riesling**
REGION **Central Otago**
CELLAR **8**
PRICE **$19–21**

Fiddler's Green Waipara Riesling

Fiddler's Green has a big following for riesling. The 2000 version is also on sale around the country. It's good, but almost completely dry. This one contains a whisper of sweetness.

Current Release 2001 The nose is minerally, reflecting the limestone soils of the Waipara region, but there's a touch of honeycomb in there as well. It's sweet-fruited and smartly balanced on the palate, with flavours reminiscent of pears, grapefruit and apples. Enjoy it with pork chops pan-fried with chopped fresh sage, sea salt and cracked pepper.

STYLE **off-dry**
QUALITY ♦
VALUE ★ ★ ★☆
GRAPES **Riesling**
REGION **Waipara**
CELLAR **3**
PRICE **$17–19**

Firstland Marlborough Riesling

STYLE **off-dry**
QUALITY ♛♛♛♛
VALUE ☆☆☆⛬
GRAPES **Riesling**
REGION **Marlborough**
CELLAR 🍾 **4**
PRICE **$18–20**

Dr John Forrest, from Forrest Estate, looked after this wine for Firstland's supervising winemaker, Mark Compton, whose major role is at the winery formerly known as De Redcliffe Estate in Mangatawhiri, 40 minutes or so south of Auckland.

Current Release 2000 A gentle floral edge on the lemon and lime juice nose identifies the variety, and invites you to take a sip. It's a crisp, apple-like riesling that is drinking well now, but should reward cellaring for at least a couple of years. Whenever you choose to pull the cork, try it with a pile of tuatua fritters.

Forrest Estate Dry Riesling

STYLE **dry**
QUALITY ♛♛♛
VALUE ☆☆☆
GRAPES **Riesling**
REGION **Marlborough**
CELLAR 🍾 **8**
PRICE **$20–23**

Many winemakers label their riesling dry, but include quite a bit of residual sugar. Not John Forrest – this one really is bone-dry. John is so confident in its ageing ability that he plans to release it in batches over the next decade.

Current Release 2001 Bone-dry it may be, but it still smells of sweet citrus fruit. On the palate, it has a delightful character that John describes as ocean spray, which is pretty well spot-on. The acids are in good balance with the fruit and the finish is long and minerally. Use the ocean analogy and partner it with mussel fritters.

Framingham Marlborough Classic Riesling

STYLE **medium**
QUALITY ♛♛♛♛
VALUE ☆☆☆
GRAPES **Riesling**
REGION **Marlborough**
CELLAR 🍾 **5**
PRICE **$20–23**

This is one of two rieslings in the Framingham portfolio, but you need to know that the 'classic' designation identifies it as the sweeter of the two. It sells in serious quantities overseas.

Current Release 2001 Floral and clean-cut on the nose, sweet-edged but nicely balanced on the palate, this is a class act. It gets away with its sweetness because of the lively acids, which means it is still a good partner for dishes like a salad of baby leaves and seared scallops.

Framingham Marlborough Dry Riesling

STYLE **dry**
QUALITY ♛♛♛♛
VALUE ☆☆⛬
GRAPES **Riesling**
REGION **Marlborough**
CELLAR 🍾 **6**
PRICE **$26–28**

Ant Mackenzie and the Framingham team like to hold their dry riesling back for a while to allow it to gain complexity. It's worth the wait. In 2001, it was made from particularly low-cropping vines, increasing the fruit intensity.

Current Release 2001 Cracked wheat and dried apricots get it together in the stylish bouquet. It's seriously citric, with suggestions of lemons and limes and a touch of dried orange peel. The finish is clean, faintly sweet-edged and impressively long. Enjoy it alongside a lightly spiced salad based on poached chicken breast and young rocket leaves.

Gibbston Valley Riesling

The sweetness level of Gibbston Valley rieslings has varied over the years. This one comes in at around 11g/l, which makes it pleasant on its own but not impossible to place with food.

Current Release 2002 The bouquet is floral, with light citrus aromas adding to the mix. It's clean and fresh on the palate thanks to some particularly strident acids, but they should quieten down in a year or two. Then, try it with hot-smoked salmon drizzled with vinaigrette that has been slightly sweetened with mirin (Japanese cooking sake).

STYLE **medium**
QUALITY ♟♟♟♟
VALUE ☆☆☆
GRAPES **Riesling**
REGION **Central Otago**
CELLAR ▭ **1–4**
PRICE **$24–26**

Giesen Canterbury Riesling Reserve Selection

The grapes came from several different vineyards in the Canterbury region. Most of the juice was fermented to total dryness, then blended with the remainder that had been left sweet.

Current Release 2001 Lemon rind and flowers fill the bouquet. It boasts a smooth texture on the palate, with obviously ripe fruit ensuring richness and a reasonable amount of depth. It's a medium-sweet, pretty wine that works best on its own.

STYLE **medium**
QUALITY ♟♟♟♟
VALUE ☆☆☆☆
GRAPES **Riesling**
REGION **Canterbury**
CELLAR 🍾 **4**
PRICE **$13–16**

Gladstone Wairarapa Riesling

Christine Kernohan sourced fruit from the Bunny vineyard at Waipipi to bolster her own home-grown grapes. The Gladstone vineyard is a pleasant place to visit, and holds various functions through the year, usually allied to new wine releases.

Current Release 2001 The nose is chunky and citric with a dried-flower background. It starts sweet, cuts back to more citric flavours through the middle and finishes cleanly. It makes a good partner for chicken breasts, marinated in a little lemon juice and olive oil before being grilled.

STYLE **off-dry**
QUALITY ♟♟♟♟
VALUE ☆☆☆☆
GRAPES **Riesling**
REGION **Wairarapa**
CELLAR 🍾 **3**
PRICE **$17–19**

Glenmark Proprietor's Reserve Riesling Dry

The price listed here is a bit of a guess. Winery owner John McCaskey hadn't decided when we spoke to him, because he said the wine was changing as it gained a bit of bottle age.

Current Release 1999 Lemons and grapefruit kick things off. It's a big, serious sort of riesling, focused and firm in the middle and quite dry on the finish. It should make a good partner for stir-fried chicken with Vietnamese mint and chilli.

STYLE **dry**
QUALITY ♟♟♟♟
VALUE ☆☆☆
GRAPES **Riesling**
REGION **Waipara**
CELLAR 🍾 **4**
PRICE **$18–20**

Glover's Richmond Riesling

STYLE **medium-dry**
QUALITY ♟ ♟ ♟ ♟
VALUE ☆ ☆ ☆ ⚡
GRAPES **Riesling**
REGION **Nelson**
CELLAR ▥ **1–4**
PRICE **$18–21**

Dave Glover has built his reputation with a series of muscular reds, but he also has a gentle hand with aromatic whites, as shown by this lively riesling. It wears a pretty pink capsule, and sells well at the winery shop.

Current Release 1998 The aromas of lemons and apples make an interesting combination in the bouquet. It's nicely fruited, with keen acids (something of a Glover trademark) making sure you don't nod off. Put it away somewhere quiet for a while, then check it out with chicken satay and a coconut-based dip.

Goldridge Estate Hawke's Bay Riesling

STYLE **medium-dry**
QUALITY ♟ ♟ ♟
VALUE ☆ ☆ ☆
GRAPES **Riesling**
REGION **Hawke's Bay**
CELLAR ▯ **3**
PRICE **$15–17**

Goldridge Estate is an alternative label for Matakana Estate, whose winery and tasting room is about a 40-minute drive north of Auckland. The non-geographic name gives the owners the opportunity to use grapes from anywhere in the country.

Current Release 2001 Slightly sweetened grapefruit juice is the overriding impression on the nose. It's a pleasantly fruited middleweight on the palate, with integrated acids giving it about the right amount of lift for the style. Take a bottle next time you're planning to visit a Thai restaurant – it suits the flavours.

Greenhough Riesling

STYLE **dry**
QUALITY ♟ ♟ ♟ ⚡
VALUE ☆ ☆ ☆ ⚡
GRAPES **Riesling**
REGION **Nelson**
CELLAR ▥ **1–4**
PRICE **$15–17**

Andrew Greenhough used fruit from the nearby Hope vineyard to bolster his own riesling crop for this wine. It won a bronze medal at the 1999 Air New Zealand Wine Awards, and has developed well since then.

Current Release 1999 Lime and grapefruit aromas form a tempting introduction. It's clean-cut on the palate, with flavours that put me in mind of lemon curd. It makes a good partner for chicken-topped couscous, especially if a little lemon rind is stirred through the grains.

Grove Mill Marlborough Riesling

STYLE **medium**
QUALITY ♟ ♟ ♟ ♟ ⚡
VALUE ☆ ☆ ☆ ☆
GRAPES **Riesling**
REGION **Marlborough**
CELLAR ▯ **4**
PRICE **$19–21**

David Pearce has won a series of awards and rave reviews with riesling, going right back to an impressive 90-point rating from the highly regarded American publication, *Wine Spectator*, for his 1997 version.

Current Release 2002 The bouquet evokes grapefruit juice, but there's a dash of honey in there as well. It's very sweet-fruited, but lively acids prevent it from becoming cloying. The finish is refreshing and very open. It's best on its own, but might work alongside roast pork with a fruit-based sauce.

Hay's Lake Riesling

The Hay's Lake and Lake Hayes labels are easily confused, especially as both hail from Central Otago. Rudi Bauer makes the wines in this portfolio, under contract to the doctor who owns the vineyard.

Current Release 2002 Lemons and limes put me in mind of riesling from Clare Valley, Australia, but the rich fruit flavours are pure Central Otago. Well-tuned acids provide the right amount of zing and ensure a refreshing finish. It's good with pan-fried gurnard fillets, drizzled with a little lemon juice just before they're served.

STYLE **off-dry**
QUALITY �
VALUE ☆☆☆⯨
GRAPES **Riesling**
REGION **Central Otago**
CELLAR 5
PRICE **$23–26**

Herzog Riesling

It's rare to find an absolutely bone-dry riesling, but this one fills the bill. Hans Herzog restricted his crop and it shows in the intensity of fruit. It's hard to find, but you'll definitely get it at the restaurant that carries the family name.

Current Release 2000 This is classic stuff! Pears and mineral notes kick things off in fine style. Perfect balance is the secret to its success – the acids are there, but they never threaten to dominate. It works really well alongside Alsace-style casseroled chicken on choucroute.

STYLE **dry**
QUALITY ooooo
VALUE ☆☆☆
GRAPES **Riesling**
REGION **Marlborough**
CELLAR 2–6
PRICE **$26–28**

Huia Marlborough Riesling

Husband and wife Claire and Mike Allen both learned their winemaking skills at Australia's Roseworthy College, near Adelaide. They established Huia in 1996, although they had already owned a vineyard for around five years.

Current Release 2001 The usual floral notes are quite understated on the nose, suggesting this will be a gentle sort of riesling. In fact, it's quite rich in the flavour department, with the sweet fruit sensibly balanced by keen-edged acids. Open a bottle next time you've got scallops on the menu. Their natural sweetness is perfect with the wine.

STYLE **off-dry**
QUALITY ooooo
VALUE ☆☆☆
GRAPES **Riesling**
REGION **Marlborough**
CELLAR 4
PRICE **$25–28**

Hunter's Marlborough Riesling

Gary Duke and his team have made some splendid wines from the riesling grape over the years, and this is one of the best. It carries a wee bit of residual sugar, but it's basically dry.

Current Release 1999 Elegance is what this wine is all about. The usual floral and citric aromas are there, but they're in particularly stylish form. It's rich but not over the top on the palate, with clean-cut acids ensuring the overall impression is simply refreshing. It works well with a Vietnamese prawn salad.

STYLE **dry**
QUALITY ooooⱺ
VALUE ☆☆☆☆⯨
GRAPES **Riesling**
REGION **Marlborough**
CELLAR 4
PRICE **$17–19**

Isabel Marlborough Riesling

STYLE **dry**
QUALITY ☐☐☐☐
VALUE ☆☆☆
GRAPES **Riesling**
REGION **Marlborough**
CELLAR **4**
PRICE **$20–23**

Jeff Sinnott arranged to have the grapes for this riesling picked by hand, then put the whole bunches into the press, bypassing the crusher-destemmer. He believes this technique intensifies the flavour.

Current Release 2000 I like the mineral edge on the honeysuckle and lime aromas. It's a very well focused wine, direct in its appeal and boasting a squeaky-clean, lingering finish. It's good with chicken breasts, grilled, cut into strips and draped over a mesclun salad.

Jackson Estate Marlborough Riesling Dry

STYLE **dry**
QUALITY ☐☐☐☐☐
VALUE ☆☆☆☆☆
GRAPES **Riesling**
REGION **Marlborough**
CELLAR **5**
PRICE **$16–18**

John Stichbury has always specified on the label that this wine is dry. That's to be applauded – too many riesling producers leave it to the consumer to guess, which can make for some disastrous wine and food matches.

Current Release 2000 The bouquet is limey and minerally – classic stuff. It's deliciously fresh on the palate, with keen acids edging the ripe citrus flavours. The finish is clean and nicely balanced. It's good with Chinese-style stir-fried pork and broccoli.

Johanneshof Marlborough Riesling

STYLE **off-dry**
QUALITY ☐☐☐☐
VALUE ☆☆☆☆
GRAPES **Riesling**
REGION **Marlborough**
CELLAR **4**
PRICE **$18–22**

Warwick Foley and Edel Everling learned some of their winemaking skills in Germany, so they are particularly good with the riesling grape. Some are made in a sweet dessert style, but this one has just enough residual sugar to kick it out of the 'dry' category.

Current Release 2000 Floral on the nose, with a touch of Aussie-style minerals, this is an appealing wine from the first sniff. It's quite citric on the palate, but that drop of sweetness means it retains plenty of richness through the middle and on the lingering finish. Try it with braised pork chops, served with baked pumpkin and young green beans.

Kahurangi Estate Riesling

STYLE **off-dry**
QUALITY ☐☐☐☐
VALUE ☆☆☆☆
GRAPES **Riesling**
REGION **Nelson**
CELLAR **3**
PRICE **$18–20**

Made from Redwood Valley grapes, this stylish riesling is a popular buy at Kahurangi's nicely laid-out cellar shop, and at a few restaurants around the Nelson and Richmond areas.

Current Release 2000 There's an edge of honeycomb on the more usual floral and citric aromas. The flavour profile continues the citric theme, and nicely integrated acids add about the right amount of an edge to the sweet-centred fruit. It makes a good partner for seared scallops, served just warm with baby salad greens.

Kaikoura Wine Company Marlborough Riesling

Kaikoura Wine Company's winery is closer to the sea than any other in the country. Grapes have been planted nearby, but in the meantime they are bought from contract growers in respected areas.

Current Release 2000 The nose boasts nectarine, tangerine and lemon aromas. It's nicely balanced on the palate, with gentle acids putting just enough of an edge on the floral, sweet-fruited flavours. Try it with a Thai prawn curry and you should be very happy indeed.

STYLE **medium-dry**
QUALITY ♟♟♟♟
VALUE ☆☆☆☆
GRAPES **Riesling**
REGION **Marlborough**
CELLAR 3
PRICE **$17–19**

Kaimira Estate Brightwater Dry Riesling

Kaimira Estate makes a trio of rieslings, and all three are popular at the cellar door. This one, as the label specifies, is the driest of the three, and that makes it easier to place with food.

Current Release 2001 The nose is citric and clean and the flavours are sweet-edged, despite the dryness, and reminiscent of marmalade. It's a very pretty wine that sits well with prawns, shelled and brushed with olive oil and a little lemon or lime juice before being grilled.

STYLE **dry**
QUALITY ♟♟♟♟
VALUE ☆☆☆☆
GRAPES **Riesling**
REGION **Nelson**
CELLAR 4
PRICE **$17–19**

Kaimira Estate Nelson Riesling

With a residual sugar level of just eight grammes per litre, this approachable riesling fails to qualify as 'dry' by only a whisker. It makes pleasant drinking on its own, but suits quite a number of different dishes.

Current Release 2001 Classic varietal floral characters waft out of the glass and form a good introduction. It's richly fruited and immaculately clean on the palate, with well-focused citrus flavours and a refreshing finish. Enjoy it with corn fritters dabbed with a faintly sweet chilli sauce.

STYLE **off-dry**
QUALITY ♟♟♟♟
VALUE ☆☆☆☆
GRAPES **Riesling**
REGION **Nelson**
CELLAR 3
PRICE **$17–19**

Kaimira Estate Nelson/Marlborough Riesling

The Kaimira Estate team draws most of its fruit from the family-run vineyard and a few sites nearby, but took a trip across the hills to buy a parcel of grapes to complete the riesling trio. This is the sweetest of the three, with 12g/l residual sugar.

Current Release 2001 Floral and faintly honeyed, this wine manages to SMELL sweet. That initial impression is backed up on the palate, which is full, rich and mouth-filling. You could try it with a Thai-style chicken curry, but it's best on its own.

STYLE **medium-dry**
QUALITY ♟♟♟♟
VALUE ☆☆☆☆
GRAPES **Riesling**
REGION **Nelson**
CELLAR 3
PRICE **$15–17**

Kim Crawford Marlborough Dry Riesling

STYLE off-dry
QUALITY 🍷🍷🍷🍷
VALUE ☆☆☆☆
GRAPES Riesling
REGION Marlborough
CELLAR 🍾 3
PRICE $18–21

Most riesling producers who want to make a slightly sweet style stop the fermentation before all the sugar has been eaten. Kim Crawford did things differently – he waited until fermentation was complete, then added a dash of late-harvest riesling.

Current Release 2001 It might contain a dash of sweet wine, but it's still close to bone-dry. The bouquet is citric and quite complex, and the flavour profile is direct, crisp-edged and very clean, particularly on the finish. It makes an excellent partner for salmon, marinated in lemon juice and grilled.

Konrad & Conrad Marlborough Riesling

STYLE off-dry
QUALITY 🍷🍷🍷
VALUE ☆☆
GRAPES Riesling
REGION Marlborough
CELLAR 🍾 4
PRICE $23–25

Marlborough is internationally famous for sauvignon blanc, but Konrad Hengstler is one of many locals to pin his faith on riesling. Incidentally, the alternatively spelled Conrad in the company name is Konrad's young son.

Current Release 2000 It's almost dry, but a wee bit of residual sugar was left intact to help lift the fruit. It's faintly honeyed on the nose and has flavours reminiscent of ripe apples and pears. Nicely balanced acids keep things refreshing. It would work well with chicken thigh pieces braised in good stock that has been enlivened with a squeeze of lemon juice.

Koura Bay Barney's Rock Riesling

STYLE off-dry
QUALITY 🍷🍷🍷
VALUE ☆☆☆
GRAPES Riesling
REGION Marlborough
CELLAR 🍾 3
PRICE $15–17

Koura Bay is in Marlborough's Awatere Valley, where the average temperatures are a few degrees warmer than in the better-known Wairau Valley, across the hills. It used to be farmland – now it's wall-to-wall vineyards.

Current Release 2001 There are some attractive perfumed notes in the bouquet and impressively sweet fruit on the front palate. It's rich and mouth-filling, but suffers from a little coarseness on the finish. Let it settle for a while, then try it with a serious pork and celery sandwich.

La Strada Riesling

STYLE off-dry
QUALITY 🍷🍷🍷🍷🍷
VALUE ☆☆☆☆
GRAPES Riesling
REGION Marlborough
CELLAR 🍾 1–6
PRICE $24–27

A bit of careful label-watching is necessary when you buy a Fromm La Strada riesling. This one's dry, but there are a couple of super-sweet versions in the range.

Current Release 2000 'Pretty' seems the right word to sum up the bouquet, with its charming floral-edged scents. There's some great fruit on the palate – clean, fresh and decidedly delicious. It's drinking well now, but should age superbly. Whenever you choose to pull the cork, try it with grilled squid or octopus.

Lake Chalice Marlborough Riesling

This riesling is a blend of fruit from the company's own Falcon vineyard and another site in the Lower Waihopai Valley, a few kilometres out of Blenheim. Fermentation was stopped before the yeasts had eaten all the sugar.

Current Release 2001 The nose is minerally and citric in the style of rieslings from Australia's Clare Valley. There's no mistaking the place of origin when you taste it – it's richly fruited with integrated acids that work well to keep the texture lively and fresh. It works brilliantly alongside a plate of pan-fried fresh scallops.

STYLE **medium-dry**
QUALITY ▽▽▽▽
VALUE ☆☆☆☆
GRAPES **Riesling**
REGION **Marlborough**
CELLAR 🍾 **4**
PRICE **$16–19**

Langdale of Canterbury Riesling

The unusual Langdale label certainly stands out on the shelves, with the name in script running vertically up the side. The winery complex boasts a pleasant restaurant that does good business, particularly in the summer months.

Current Release 2001 The bouquet is spicy and complex, but there is less excitement on the palate. It's pleasant, but quite straightforward with rich, sweet fruit, particularly on the finish. It's too sweet for most food, so chill it down and enjoy it as a summer sipper.

STYLE **medium**
QUALITY ▽▽▽
VALUE ☆☆☆
GRAPES **Riesling**
REGION **Canterbury**
CELLAR 🍾 **2**
PRICE **$18–21**

Lawson's Dry Hills Marlborough Riesling

Ross and Barbara Lawson are great supporters of screwcap closures, and recently sent the media a compilation of overseas comments on wines tainted by bad corks. The grapes for this riesling came from the heart of the Wairau Valley.

Current Release 2001 Marmalade – that's what I get on the nose. It's very direct in its appeal, with clean, fresh flavours leaning towards the citric end of the spectrum. It makes a good partner for tarakihi or gurnard, wrapped in cooking paper with a few lemon slices and a splash of olive oil before being baked.

STYLE **dry**
QUALITY ▽▽▽
VALUE ☆☆☆
GRAPES **Riesling**
REGION **Marlborough**
CELLAR 🍾 **4**
PRICE **$17–19**

Lincoln Winemaker's Series Marlborough Riesling

Listed on the back label as 'medium-dry', this nicely fruited white actually carries enough residual sugar to place it firmly in the 'medium' category. The winery suggests pulling the cork within 18 months, but I think it will go on longer.

Current Release 2000 Grapefruit and lime juice aromas promise good things to come. The citrus theme continues on the palate, but a floral edge gives it good varietal focus. Crisp acids balance the sweetness, which means it could realistically accompany food like Malay-style seafood satay.

STYLE **medium**
QUALITY ▽▽▽▽
VALUE ☆☆☆☆
GRAPES **Riesling**
REGION **Marlborough**
CELLAR 🍾 **3**
PRICE **$14–16**

Linden Estate Hawke's Bay Dry Riesling

STYLE **dry**
QUALITY ▽▽▽▽
VALUE ☆ ☆ ☆
GRAPES **Riesling**
REGION **Hawke's Bay**

CELLAR **3**
PRICE **$19–22**

This riesling is probably the least-known member of the Linden Estate portfolio. Winemaker Nick Chan has made it in a German style, with low alcohol (10.5%) and low acidity. The grapes came from 21-year-old vines.
Current Release 2002 The nose put me in mind of dried orange peel and lime juice. The low alcohol hasn't affected the fruit richness – it's decidedly sweet-edged, despite the dryness, and finishes cleanly. Partner it with the best pork sausages you can find and you'll see what Nick had in mind.

Loopline Vineyard Wairarapa Dry Riesling

STYLE **dry**
QUALITY ▽▽▽
VALUE ☆ ☆ ☆
GRAPES **Riesling**
REGION **Wairarapa**

CELLAR **3**
PRICE **$18–20**

Some rieslings are labelled dry even though they carry a bit of residual sugar, but this one has next to none. People who don't like the style can always opt for the 'standard' version, which is still only just off-dry.
Current Release 2000 I get apples and pears on the nose, along with a touch of the citrics, and the same sensations carry through to the palate. It's a very focused wine with direct flavours and a short but refreshing finish. It goes well with mussel tempura with a wasabi mayonnaise dipping sauce.

Loopline Vineyard Wairarapa Riesling

STYLE **medium-dry**
QUALITY ▽▽▽▽
VALUE ☆ ☆ ☆ ☆
GRAPES **Riesling**
REGION **Wairarapa**

CELLAR **4**
PRICE **$18–20**

One sip sells this stylish riesling – nearly everybody who tries it at the cellar door buys at least a bottle, and many walk out with a case. It also features on the wine lists of several local restaurants.
Current Release 2000 There's an attractive belt of honeysuckle on the nose, and something of the same character on the front palate. It's richly fruited, but smartly integrated acids keep things on an even keel. Enjoy it with scallops, steamed and served with a Thai dressing spiked with a little lime juice.

Main Divide Canterbury Riesling

STYLE **medium**
QUALITY ▽▽▽▽
VALUE ☆ ☆ ☆ ☆
GRAPES **Riesling**
REGION **Canterbury**

CELLAR **4**
PRICE **$17–19**

Made in a German style, this wine has an exceptionally low alcohol level of just 9%. In theory, that should affect its ability to age, but the Donaldsons are confident it won't – and German wines certainly age well.
Current Release 2001 The bouquet has loads of citric notes, but there's a wee suggestion of blossoming flowers in there if you search. The low alcohol would suggest that the grapes weren't very ripe, yet the flavours are rich and mouth-filling – clever stuff! It's best on its own, but you could try it with pink-cooked chicken livers squashed onto grainy toast.

Margrain Proprietor's Selection Riesling

The Margrain vineyard and winery complex include a row of pleasant villas that are popular with the corporate crowd. **Current Release 2002** Lemons, limes and orange blossoms get it together on the nose. There are loads of sweet fruit flavours in unusually savoury surroundings, but clean-cut acids keep things nicely in proportion. It's a nice drink on its own, but it also goes well with a creamy chicken or duck liver pâté.

STYLE **off-dry**
QUALITY 🍷🍷🍷🍷
VALUE ☆☆☆
GRAPES **Riesling**
REGION **Martinborough**
CELLAR 5
PRICE **$22–24**

Margrain Riesling

Strat Canning has made riesling in most styles over the years, but this one is absolutely bone-dry – a rarity for the variety. That might lessen its appeal, but it makes it easier to place with food. **Current Release 2001** The nose is citric and minerally enough to please fans of the Aussie Clare Valley style. It's refreshingly clean-cut on the palate, with crisp acids and a long, focused finish. It goes well with citric sauces – sacrifice a little to poach some chicken breasts and add a squeeze of lemon juice halfway the cooking time.

STYLE **medium**
QUALITY 🍷🍷🍷🍷
VALUE ☆☆☆
GRAPES **Riesling**
REGION **Martinborough**
CELLAR 3
PRICE **$24–26**

Martinborough Vineyard Jackson Block Riesling

The Jackson Block vineyard is owned by Bernie and Jane Jackson, and they picked the grapes for this classy riesling by hand, enabling them to select the very best bunches. It takes time, but they're convinced that it's worth it. **Current Release 2002** Pears and lemon juice form a stylish introduction. It's sweet-fruited, but with crisp acids to ensure the flavour is in no danger of becoming cloying. The citric character returns to add extra life to the finish. Pan-fried scallops with chopped ginger and garlic would make an excellent match.

STYLE **dry**
QUALITY 🍷🍷🍷🍷🍷
VALUE ☆☆☆☆
GRAPES **Riesling**
REGION **Martinborough**
CELLAR 5
PRICE **$22–24**

Martinborough Vineyard Riesling

Martinborough Vineyards has such a huge reputation for pinot noir that other members of the portfolio are seldom talked about. This riesling was made from fruit left to hang on the vine to concentrate the sugars. It came from two separate vineyards. **Current Release 2001** Lemons, dried orange peel and ripe pears get it together on the nose. Sweet fruit flavours make it immensely appealing on the palate, while sensibly integrated acids add just the right amount of life to the lingering finish. Partner it with braised pork and mashed potatoes and you will be well pleased.

STYLE **off-dry**
QUALITY 🍷🍷🍷🍷
VALUE ☆☆☆☆
GRAPES **Riesling**
REGION **Martinborough**
CELLAR 4
PRICE **$20–23**

Matua Valley Innovator Petrie Riesling

STYLE **dry**
QUALITY ♛ ♛ ♛ ♛ ♛
VALUE ☆ ☆ ☆ ☆
GRAPES **Riesling**
REGION **Wairarapa**

CELLAR **3**
PRICE **$20–23**

Mark Robertson sourced fruit from a site he loves for this bone-dry riesling. Lovers of the more common slightly sweet style might find it too austere, but it's a taste worth acquiring – and as a bonus its dryness makes it easier to place with food.

Current Release 2001 The nose is perfumed and quite floral, which usually indicates sweetness but in this case simply shows that the grapes were very ripe. It's smooth and well focused on the palate, with suggestions of citrus fruits and melon. It makes a good partner for a brace of tuatua fritters served at room temperature over a rocket salad.

McCashin's Waipara Riesling

STYLE **medium-dry**
QUALITY ♛ ♛ ♛ ♛ ♛
VALUE ☆ ☆ ☆ ☆ ☆
GRAPES **Riesling**
REGION **Waipara**

CELLAR **4**
PRICE **$14–16**

McCashin's is based in Nelson, but winemaker Craig Gass buys fruit from any part of the country that takes his fancy. He decided Waipara was the place to go looking for riesling grapes, and obviously got some beauties.

Current Release 2000 Imagine tangelos and old roses together and you'll have a handle on the bouquet. Sweet fruit is nicely balanced by lively but integrated acids, giving it a very refreshing structure. It's good on its own, or alongside chicken liver pâté on toasted triangles of pita bread.

Melness Riesling

STYLE **medium**
QUALITY ♛ ♛ ♛ ♛ ♛
VALUE ☆ ☆ ☆ ☆
GRAPES **Riesling**
REGION
  Waipara 50%
  Canterbury 50%

CELLAR **4**
PRICE **$19–21**

Melness wines are sold almost exclusively by mail order and at the cellar door, and they have a keen following. This riesling is on the sweet side of medium, but good balance keeps things in proportion.

Current Release 2000 Flowers and a touch of honeycomb start things off in style. Sweet fruit gives it a rich, full-on flavour profile, but apple-like acids cut in towards the finish to keep things nicely refreshing. It's best on its own, but you could try it with a super-smooth duck liver pâté.

Mills Reef Moffat Road Hawke's Bay Riesling

STYLE **off-dry**
QUALITY ♛ ♛ ♛ ♛
VALUE ☆ ☆ ☆ ☆
GRAPES **Riesling**
REGION **Hawke's Bay**

CELLAR **3**
PRICE **$14–16**

Tim and Paddy Preston are phasing out their Moffat Road designation for some varieties, but there's still plenty of this light-hearted riesling to be found on retail shelves. Surprisingly for a light white, the alcohol level is 12%.

Current Release 2000 Rose petals normally identify gewürztraminer, but they're definitely there on the nose of this riesling, along with the more usual lemon rind characters. It's sweet-edged, with flavours that reminded me of ripe papaya, and faintly spicy on the finish. Enjoy it on its own or with simple nibbles.

Mills Reef Reserve Hawke's Bay Riesling

Paddy Preston recommends cellaring this classy riesling for a year or two, but I'd like to try it after four. Mind you, it's good now. It won a silver medal at the 2000 Air New Zealand Awards and has matured nicely since.

Current Release 2000 The nose is the classic combination of lemon, dried orange peel and honeysuckle. It's a smartly focused wine, with great balance between ripe, sweet-edged fruit and keen but integrated acids. It would be good alongside a spinach and prosciutto frittata.

STYLE **off-dry**
QUALITY ♛ ♛ ♛ ♛ ♛
VALUE ☆ ☆ ☆ ☆ ☆
GRAPES **Riesling**
REGION **Hawke's Bay**
CELLAR **4**
PRICE **$14–17**

Millton Gisborne Riesling Opou Vineyard

The Opou vineyard at Manutuke is close to where the first vines were planted in Poverty Bay, way back in 1890. In line with the Millton's bio-dynamic philosophies, hyssop and other companion herbs are planted around the vines.

Current Release 2000 I get lemon honey (remember it?) on the nose, along with a minerally note. It tastes of freshly quartered sweet oranges and mandarins, but crisp acids prevent it from falling into the 'fruit juice' trap. It makes a good aperitif, and is pleasant with pâté on toast.

STYLE **medium**
QUALITY ♛ ♛ ♛ ♛ ♛
VALUE ☆ ☆ ☆ ☆
GRAPES **Riesling**
REGION **Gisborne**
CELLAR **4**
PRICE **$25–27**

Montana Marlborough Riesling

Made a little drier than some previous examples, this stylish wine has a huge following – in fact, it's probably the biggest-selling riesling in the country. It's also exported, and is a good advertisement for Marlborough's ample sunshine.

Current Release 2002 Lightly citric on the nose with a dash of honey for extra interest, this wine has immediate appeal. It's clean and smartly balanced on the palate, with ripe fruit and sensibly tuned acids both in fine shape. It's good on its own, but sits well with summer nibbles – grilled chicken wings, eggplant fritters and the like.

STYLE **off-dry**
QUALITY ♛ ♛ ♛ ♛
VALUE ☆ ☆ ☆ ☆ ☆
GRAPES **Riesling**
REGION **Marlborough**
CELLAR **4**
PRICE **$14–16**

Montana Reserve Vintage Release Riesling

Montana has got into the commendable habit of holding back one parcel of top-notch riesling until the winemaking team feels it's drinking at close to its best. This one came from a couple of classic stone-covered sites, and sells well.

Current Release 2000 Lime juice and dried orange peel form a handy alliance on the nose. It's a broad style of riesling, with gentle acids adding life to the sweet-edged fruit flavours. It makes a good partner for scallops, wok-fried in the Chinese way with chopped ginger and garlic.

STYLE **off-dry**
QUALITY ♛ ♛ ♛ ♛
VALUE ☆ ☆ ☆
GRAPES **Riesling**
REGION **Marlborough**
CELLAR **3**
PRICE **$20–23**

Morton Estate Marlborough Riesling (White Label)

STYLE **off-dry**
QUALITY ♟ ♟ ♟ ♟
VALUE ☆ ☆ ☆ ☆
GRAPES **Riesling**
REGION **Marlborough**
CELLAR 🍷 **3**
PRICE **$13–16**

Winemaker Chris Archer reckons this is his favourite wine style. He's happy at the Katikati winery because a lot of money has been spent recently on new equipment, including an impressive 90-tank 'farm' designed for easy access.

Current Release 2001 The bouquet is chunky and savoury, giving it more interest than many of the genre. Things are more traditional on the palate, where it's ripe-fruited, clean and smooth through to the finish. All in all, a pleasant drop that goes well with mussels tossed with rocket leaves and a little chopped celery in home-made mayonnaise.

Mt Difficulty Riesling

STYLE **dry**
QUALITY ♟ ♟ ♟ ♟ ♟
VALUE ☆ ☆ ☆ ☆
GRAPES **Riesling**
REGION **Central Otago**
CELLAR ▭ **1–4**
PRICE **$19–21**

Mt Difficulty has gained a cult following in the big cities for a smartly focused pinot noir, but the wines are good right through the portfolio. This riesling isn't seen on many wine lists. It should be.

Current Release 2000 It's quite lean at the moment, but I've marked this wine for its potential – the restrained power on the palate is palpable. It's limey and direct, with fruit richness saving itself for the finish, and will eventually make a good partner for pan-fried gurnard fillets with a lemon-grass sauce.

Mount Edward Central Otago Riesling

STYLE **medium-dry**
QUALITY ♟ ♟ ♟ ♟ ♟
VALUE ☆ ☆ ☆ ☆ ☆
GRAPES **Riesling**
REGION **Central Otago**
CELLAR 🍷 **5**
PRICE **$18–20**

Alan Brady says his aim is to produce a German style of riesling from the stony site behind his tiny winery, rather than what he sees as the fat, alcoholic wines produced by many New World companies.

Current Release 2000 I get grapefruit and limes on the nose, with a dash of the florals drifting onto the front palate. In fact it manages to TASTE floral – try it and you'll see what I mean. The acid balance is spot-on, and the finish clean and refreshing. It makes a good partner for grilled scampi with rice pilaf.

Mount Riley Marlborough Riesling

STYLE **off-dry**
QUALITY ♟ ♟ ♟
VALUE ☆ ☆ ☆
GRAPES **Riesling**
REGION **Marlborough**
CELLAR 🍷 **3**
PRICE **$14–16**

With just enough sweetness left in to kick it out of the 'dry' category, this is a wine that is good on its own, but sits happily alongside a range of foods, particularly if they're just a wee bit spicy.

Current Release 2002 Floral and appealingly savoury, this wine begs you to take a sip. The flavours echo the same characters, and the balance of sweet fruit and gentle acids is about right. It's a straightforward wine that sits well with a fillet of poached or steamed fish, dressed with a little chopped ginger and lemongrass.

Moutere Hills Nelson Riesling

Simon and Alison Thomas have a picturesque vineyard in poetically named Sunrise Valley. They don't make a lot of wine, but both this latest model and the '99 version are still on sale around Nelson.

Current Release 2000 There are suggestions of lemons and limes on the nose, suggesting the wine will be drier than it is. In fact, the flavours are rich and reminiscent of dried apricots and sweet ruby grapefruit. It works well with Malaysian-style chicken satay.

STYLE **medium-dry**
QUALITY ♟ ♟ ♟ ♟
VALUE ☆ ☆ ☆ ☆
GRAPES **Riesling**
REGION **Nelson**
CELLAR 3
PRICE **$16–18**

Mudbrick Nelson Riesling

The Mudbrick vineyard and winery complex is on Waiheke Island, in Auckland's Hauraki Gulf, but the grapes for this member of the portfolio came from the green hills of Nelson. It goes well with many of the dishes served at the winery restaurant.

Current Release 2002 There are a few Aussie-style lime juice and mineral notes in the bouquet, but the flavour profile is pure New Zealand, with suggestions of grapefruit through the middle and a clean, crisp finish. It's good with snapper fillets pan-fried with olive oil and a little chopped preserved lemon.

STYLE **off-dry**
QUALITY ♟ ♟ ♟ ♟
VALUE ☆ ☆ ☆ ☆
GRAPES **Riesling**
REGION **Nelson**
CELLAR 3
PRICE **$17–19**

Muddy Water Riesling Dry

The words 'no compromise' appear in much of the Muddy Water publicity material, and on the back labels. In this case, that translates as picking through the bunches so that only perfect grapes are selected, and fermenting the juice to dryness.

Current Release 2001 Citrus fruit and pears form an inviting bouquet. The same lemon/lime characters make it through pretty well unscathed onto the front palate, leading to a fresh-faced, squeaky-clean flavour profile. It needs time, but will eventually go brilliantly with a simple fillet of pan-fried cod, drizzled with lemon juice and the best olive oil you can find.

STYLE **dry**
QUALITY ♟ ♟ ♟ ♟
VALUE ☆ ☆ ☆
GRAPES **Riesling**
REGION **Waipara**
CELLAR 2–6
PRICE **$22–24**

Muddy Water Waipara Riesling James Hardwick

The sweeter of the two Muddy Water rieslings recently scored a Top 10 rating from the *Cuisine* magazine tasting team. I've rated it medium, but it's still dry enough to enjoy with food.

Current Release 2000 Orange peel and rock melon characters are backed by the distinctive Waipara minerally edge. It's got lashings of sweet fruit, but keen acids keep things on an even keel without threatening to dominate. It works well with Thai-style fish in a coconut and lemongrass broth.

STYLE **medium**
QUALITY ♟ ♟ ♟ ♟
VALUE ☆ ☆ ☆ ☆
GRAPES **Riesling**
REGION **Waipara**
CELLAR 5
PRICE **$18–21**

Murdoch James Reserve Riesling

STYLE **dry**
QUALITY ♟♟♟♟
VALUE ☆☆☆
GRAPES **Riesling**
REGION **Martinborough**

CELLAR 🍾 **5**
PRICE **$25–27**

Unusually for a dry riesling, this wine is sold in a 500ml bottle. The grapes came from the Coney vineyard, and they must have been very ripe – the alcohol level is 14%.
Current Release 2001 Lemon and lime impressions dominate the bouquet. There's some lovely fruit on the palate balanced by fresh but integrated acids. It's smart wine that goes well with a Chinese-style stir-fry of pork and beans.

Murdoch James Estate Riesling

STYLE **off-dry**
QUALITY ♟♟♟♟
VALUE ☆☆☆
GRAPES **Riesling**
REGION **Martinborough**

CELLAR 🍾 **4**
PRICE **$18–21**

Few people associate Martinborough with riesling, but in fact the variety grows very well there and has produced some marvellous wines in the last few years. This is one of the lesser-known examples, but it's worth a serious search.
Current Release 2002 Flowers and lemon peel make the variety easy to pick. Zesty, refreshing flavours make sipping it rather like biting into a chilled Gala apple. It boasts good balance between fruit and acid, and finishes cleanly and with authority. It would work well with pork and fennel sausages dressed with a lemon-spiked sauce.

Neudorf Brightwater Riesling

STYLE **off-dry**
QUALITY ♟♟♟♟♟
VALUE ☆☆☆☆
GRAPES **Riesling**
REGION **Nelson**

CELLAR 🍾 **4**
PRICE **$20–23**

This is the second riesling the Finns have made from Brightwater fruit. 'I'm a fan of riesling,' Tim writes, 'and the alcohol on this one is low enough to let you do some useful work after lunch.' I'm not so sure – the level is actually 12%.
Current Release 2002 Alcohol aside, it's lovely wine. The bouquet smells of lime juice and lemon rind and the flavour profile is remarkably sweet-fruited for an off-dry wine. It's rich and luscious, but with impeccably balanced acids. It's wonderful with fresh crab, if you don't mind the mess.

Neudorf Moutere Riesling

STYLE **medium**
QUALITY ♟♟♟♟♟
VALUE ☆☆☆
GRAPES **Riesling**
REGION **Nelson**

CELLAR 🍾 **6**
PRICE **$28–32**

The Finns picked less than half a tonne per acre from their home vineyard in 2002, giving them intensely flavoured fruit. They have made a deliciously concentrated wine from it. And you CAN work after this one – the alcohol level is 10%.
Current Release 2002 Savoury limes are the impression I get on the nose. It's sweet-fruited, rich and impressively smooth on the palate, but the label's trademark immaculately balanced acids keep things in great shape through to the finish. Food? Perhaps a rich chicken liver pâté, but it's best on its own.

Nga Waka Martinborough Riesling

This concentrated, bone-dry riesling is getting better each year – I upped its mark half a point a year after I tried it for the first time. I recently tasted a 1993 version, and it was drinking splendidly.

Current Release 2000 I get grapefruit and tangelos on the nose, which is absolutely fine. It's equally citric on the palate, where zesty acids pair up with the sweet fruit flavours to make an appealingly refreshing overall impression. It's good with pan-fried John Dory, drizzled with just a little lime juice.

STYLE **dry**
QUALITY ♟♟♟♟♟
VALUE ☆☆☆☆
GRAPES **Riesling**
REGION **Martinborough**
CELLAR 🍶 **6**
PRICE **$25–27**

Nobilo Icon Series Marlborough Selection Riesling

This wine was made in both islands. The grapes were harvested and crushed in Marlborough, then the juice was loaded into pressurised containers and shipped to the West Auckland winery for fermentation.

Current Release 1999 The citric notes in the bouquet have a steely edge. It's so smooth it seems almost slippery on the palate, but there's a reasonable quota of acids to balance the ripe fruit flavours. Try it with a platter of Japanese-style tempura vegetables.

STYLE **off-dry**
QUALITY ♟♟♟♟
VALUE ☆☆☆
GRAPES **Riesling**
REGION **Marlborough**
CELLAR 🍶 **4**
PRICE **$18–20**

Olssen's of Bannockburn Riesling

It's hard to find, particularly after a good write-up and rating in a recent *Cuisine* magazine, but this smart riesling from the deep South is worth a search. I've suggested cellaring for up to four years, but I suspect it will go on for much longer.

Current Release 2000 There's a steely edge to the primary aromas of lemon juice and rose petals. It's crisp and clean on the front palate, but then sweet fruit kicks in and drifts onto the lively finish. It's the perfect wine for Italian fritto misto (a selection of deep-fried seafood).

STYLE **dry**
QUALITY ♟♟♟♟♟
VALUE ☆☆☆☆
GRAPES **Riesling**
REGION **Central Otago**
CELLAR ▭ **1–4**
PRICE **$18–21**

Omaka Springs Marlborough Riesling

Omaka Springs doesn't have as high a profile as other, longer-established Marlborough companies, but steady success on the show circuit is changing that. This nicely tuned riesling won a bronze medal at the 2002 New Zealand Wine Society Royal Easter Wine Show.

Current Release 2001 I get a combination of corn flakes and lemon rind on the nose, which makes for an interesting introduction. It's fresh, clean and quite viscous on the palate, with the whisper of residual sweetness saving itself for the finish. Enjoy it with salmon dabbed with sesame oil before being grilled.

STYLE **off-dry**
QUALITY ♟♟♟♟
VALUE ☆☆☆☆
GRAPES **Riesling**
REGION **Marlborough**
CELLAR 🍶 **4**
PRICE **$14–16**

Palliser Estate Riesling

STYLE off-dry
QUALITY 🍷🍷🍷🍷
VALUE ★★★
GRAPES Riesling
REGION Martinborough
CELLAR 5
PRICE $20–23

This stylish riesling qualifies as dry for competition purposes, but only just. The touch of sweetness is not obvious, and it should help it age with grace and poise. The Stelvin screwcap closure hasn't affected sales one iota.

Current Release 2002 It's citric on the nose, clean and crisp through the middle and sweet-edged on the finish. That adds up to a refreshing drop with good balance between fruit richness and acid. It goes splendidly with thickly sliced ham on the bone smeared with a faintly sweet mustard.

Pegasus Bay Aria Late Picked Riesling

STYLE sweet
QUALITY 🍷🍷🍷🍷🍷
VALUE ★★½
GRAPES Riesling
REGION Waipara
CELLAR 8
PRICE $29–33

It's unashamedly sweet, but the Donaldsons insist it's not a dessert wine – they enjoy it with nuts and cheese. Its inspiration was the similarly styled wines from Alsace, the French region right on the German border.

Current Release 2001 The nose is lightly citric, and doesn't give away the amount of sweetness to come. In fact, it is beautifully balanced because the acids counteract the sugar without becoming a dominant force themselves – clever stuff! Take the Donaldsons' advice and try it with hazelnuts and a mild blue cheese.

Pegasus Bay Riesling

STYLE off-dry
QUALITY 🍷🍷🍷🍷🍷
VALUE ★★★½
GRAPES Riesling
REGION Waipara
CELLAR 6
PRICE $22–24

The Donaldsons thank an 'Indian summer' in Waipara for giving them riesling grapes in superlative condition. They were left on the vine until May, enabling them to get super-ripe. The wine has a remarkably low alcohol level of 10.5% – the sort of figure often seen on German labels.

Current Release 2001 Limes and dried orange peel are the predominant impression in the bouquet. It is sweet-edged, fresh and superbly clean on the palate, with flavours suggestive of citrus fruit and freshly cut melon leading to a lingering finish. It makes a good partner for braised rabbit.

Peregrine Central Otago Riesling

STYLE off-dry
QUALITY 🍷🍷🍷
VALUE ★★½
GRAPES Riesling
REGION Central Otago
CELLAR 3
PRICE $20–23

The grapes came from various sites around Central Otago's Cromwell basin, and they were cooled down during fermentation to give the winemaking team greater control. Peregrine often favours sweetness in its aromatics, but this one is just off bone-dry.

Current Release 2001 The nose is savoury and complex, with suggestions of honey on toast. It's very direct on the palate, with clean-cut flavours reminiscent of grapefruit juice and freshly squeezed lemons. All that citric character makes it good with Moroccan-style chicken with preserved lemon.

Ponder Estate Classic Riesling

The '99 version won a gold medal and trophy, and may be still available in limited quantities at the cellar door. This later model hasn't done as well, having scored only a bronze medal by the time this *Guide* was finalised.

Current Release 2000 Lime juice and a wee touch of honeysuckle get together on the nose. Sweet fruit flavours sit in straightforward surroundings on the palate. It's attractive, but doesn't reach the splendid heights of the earlier model. Try it with chicken liver pâté on toast triangles.

STYLE **medium**
QUALITY ♟ ♟ ♟
VALUE ☆ ☆ ☆
GRAPES **Riesling**
REGION
  Marlborough 70%
  Canterbury 30%
CELLAR 4
PRICE **$15–17**

Quarry Road Riesling

This riesling makes an excellent food wine because at 4g/l residual sweetness it truly is dry. The Waikato doesn't seem the obvious place to grow this cool climate-loving variety, but Toby Cooper has made a good job of it.

Current Release 2002 Lime juice and dried orange peel get it together on the nose. It's fresh, ripe-fruited and immaculately clean in the middle, then broadens out to form a pleasantly smooth finish. Partner it with a simple white risotto, tossed through with nothing more distracting than the best Parmesan you can find.

STYLE **dry**
QUALITY ♟ ♟ ♟ ♟
VALUE ☆ ☆ ☆ ☆
GRAPES **Riesling**
REGION **Waikato**
CELLAR 4
PRICE **$17–19**

Rippon Riesling

Russell Lake has made a crusade of producing Germanic rieslings from Central Otago grapes. They are often austere in their youth, but blossom beautifully after a few years in the bottle. Rippon fans have to be patient!

Current Release 2001 The current model seems less austere than some of its predecessors, but it will still repay cellaring. It's got suggestions of comb honey and orange blossom on the nose and a smooth, surprisingly creamy texture. The usual citric characters save themselves for the finish. It's good with steamed Chinese-style chicken in a faintly sweet broth.

STYLE **dry**
QUALITY ♟ ♟ ♟ ♟ ♟
VALUE ☆ ☆ ☆
GRAPES **Riesling**
REGION **Central Otago**
CELLAR 1–8
PRICE **$29–33**

Rongopai Vintage Reserve Te Kauwhata Riesling

The Rongopai team rushed this riesling onto the market and got a couple of bad reviews as a result. I left my sample for a couple of months, more by good luck than good management, but I'm very pleased that I did.

Current Release 2000 Grapefruit aromas are often associated with chardonnay, but I get them on the nose of this riesling, along with a dash of honey. It's got loads of ripe fruit and nicely tuned acids on the palate, and that makes it a great match for scallops, tossed quickly in a searingly hot pan.

STYLE **dry**
QUALITY ♟ ♟ ♟ ♟
VALUE ☆ ☆ ☆ ☆
GRAPES **Riesling**
REGION **Te Kauwhata**
CELLAR 5
PRICE **$17–19**

Rossendale Canterbury Riesling

STYLE **medium**
QUALITY ♟ ♟ ♟ ♟
VALUE ☆ ☆ ☆ ☆
GRAPES **Riesling**
REGION **Canterbury**

CELLAR **3**
PRICE **$15–17**

Half of the juice that went into this wine was fermented out to full dryness, while the rest was chilled down to prevent the yeasts from eating all the sugar. It was worth the trouble – it scored bronze at the Air New Zealand awards.

Current Release 2000 The company tasting note talks about limes, lemon zest and summer flowers, but I get something closer to grapefruit. It's richly fruited, with a sweet start but well-tuned acids to keep things on an even keel. It's good on its own, but also works well alongside a ham and grainy mustard sandwich.

Saint Clair Fairhall Reserve Riesling

STYLE **dry**
QUALITY ♟ ♟ ♟ ♟
VALUE ☆ ☆ ☆ ☆
GRAPES **Riesling**
REGION **Marlborough**

CELLAR **6**
PRICE **$19–21**

A silver medal at the Liquorland Top 100 boosted sales of this smartly made wine, and by association that of all riesling. It just tweaks into the dry category, but does carry a whisper of residual sweetness. The makers reckon it will age for a decade.

Current Release 2002 Dried lemon rind and grapefruit juice combine with a touch of the florals to create an appealing bouquet. That floral impression continues on the front palate, but then ripe fruit takes over. The acid balance is spot-on and the finish focused and fresh. It's good on its own, but you might like to try it with a serious ham and mustard sandwich.

Saint Clair Marlborough Riesling

STYLE **medium-dry**
QUALITY ♟ ♟ ♟ ♟ ♟
VALUE ☆ ☆ ☆ ☆ ☆
GRAPES **Riesling**
REGION **Marlborough**

CELLAR **4**
PRICE **$16–18**

Saint Clair has enjoyed medal success with almost every wine in its portfolio, so it's not surprising that its products move quickly off the shelves and are seen on the wine lists of good restaurants. This riesling is a popular member of the portfolio.

Current Release 2002 Gentle citric aromas set the scene on the nose, leading the way to a flavour profile that is sweet-centred, but boasts excellent acid balance. The overall impression is delightfully refreshing. It's good on its own, but sits nicely with Vietnamese-style prawn-filled rice paper rolls served with a slightly sweet dipping sauce.

Sanctuary Marlborough Riesling

STYLE **medium**
QUALITY ♟ ♟ ♟
VALUE ☆ ☆ ☆
GRAPES **Riesling**
REGION **Marlborough**

CELLAR **2**
PRICE **$15–17**

I've seen it described as 'off-dry', but this nicely fruited white has a residual sugar level of 17g/l, which translates as medium bordering on sweet. Never mind – it's nicely made and very popular.

Current Release 2002 Lemon rind on the nose suggests the flavours will be drier than they are. The sweetness is nicely offset by lively acids, so although it's good on its own, it could easily sit next to faintly sweet dishes like a Malaysian or Indonesian chicken and coconut curry.

Seifried Riesling

Hermann and Agnes Seifried have produced rieslings in every conceivable style over the years – they've even tried maturing it in oak barrels. This one carries 16 g/l of residual sweetness, which makes it a pleasant hot-day sipper.
Current Release 2001 The bouquet is minerally with a lemon edge, rather like some styles from Australia's Clare Valley. It's sweet-fruited in the flavour department, but lively acids keep things nicely in balance. It is great on its own, but you could try it with a lightish Malaysian or Indonesian curry.

STYLE **medium**
QUALITY ☖☖☖☖☖
VALUE ★★★★☆
GRAPES **Riesling**
REGION **Nelson**
CELLAR **4**
PRICE **$19–21**

Seifried Winemaker's Collection Riesling

Hermann and Agnes Seifried arranged for the grapes to be picked by hand for this top-shelf member of their extensive portfolio. They came from vines at the home vineyard in the Redwood Valley.
Current Release 2000 Citrus fruit and apple blossom notes start things off well. It's a smartly balanced wine, with apple and pear flavours in a lively framework and a satisfyingly lingering finish. It's good on its own, but also works well with Goa-style prawns, curried with coconut milk.

STYLE **medium**
QUALITY ☖☖☖☖
VALUE ★★★☆
GRAPES **Riesling**
REGION **Nelson**
CELLAR **3**
PRICE **$18–20**

Selaks Premium Selection Marlborough Riesling

The fine print on the label tells us the grapes for this riesling came from the company's Matador Estate vineyard, which is nicely situated in the heart of the province's best land.
Current Release 2000 Spice and honeysuckle aromas are backed by a dash of Aussie-style minerals. It's nicely fruited and moderately rich on the palate, and finishes cleanly. Enjoy it alongside a salad of radishes and sliced fennel, tossed with verjuice and extra-virgin olive oil.

STYLE **medium-dry**
QUALITY ☖☖☖
VALUE ★★★
GRAPES **Riesling**
REGION **Marlborough**
CELLAR **2**
PRICE **$15–17**

Seresin Riesling

Brian Bicknell arranged for the fruit for this delicious bone-dry riesling to be picked by hand to give him total control over the quality. Inferior bunches were left to rot on the vine or simply discarded.
Current Release 2000 There's a faint suggestion of honey behind the typical floral aromas in the bouquet. It's richly fruited, immaculately clean and nicely balanced – a delicious package! It would make a splendid partner for pan-fried duck livers squashed onto grainy toast.

STYLE **dry**
QUALITY ☖☖☖☖☖
VALUE ★★★★
GRAPES **Riesling**
REGION **Marlborough**
CELLAR **4**
PRICE **$21–23**

Sherwood Estate Canterbury Riesling

STYLE **medium**
QUALITY ♟ ♟ ♟
VALUE ☆ ☆ ☆ ⊱
GRAPES **Riesling**
REGION
  Canterbury 50%
  Waipara 50%
CELLAR ▤ **3**
PRICE **$14–16**

Grapes from Waipara and Canterbury – but isn't Waipara part of Canterbury? Strictly speaking, yes – but locals insist the climate and soil differences are sufficient for them to be considered separate regions.
Current Release 2001 It's clean-cut, sweet-edged, floral and light. That adds up to simple, undemanding drinkability, and there's nothing wrong with that. It's probably best on its own, but you could try it with a light Indonesian or Malaysian chicken curry.

Shingle Peak Marlborough Riesling

STYLE **dry**
QUALITY ♟ ♟ ♟ ♟
VALUE ☆ ☆ ☆ ☆
GRAPES **Riesling**
REGION **Marlborough**
CELLAR ▤ **4**
PRICE **$16–18**

Mark Robertson was excited about the quality of the riesling grapes he sourced from the 2002 vintage. He made sure the crop levels were kept low to ensure good flavour concentration, and fermented the juice at a very low temperature for the same reason.
Current Release 2002 The nose is spicy, with suggestions of lime juice and grapefruit. It's quite steely on the front palate, but impressions of freshly cut lemons and rock melon swing in through the middle. The finish is refreshing and clean. Mark suggests enjoying it with raw oysters – an unusual match for riesling, but it would most certainly work.

Soljans Marlborough Riesling

STYLE **off-dry**
QUALITY ♟ ♟ ♟ ♟
VALUE ☆ ☆ ☆ ☆ ⊱
GRAPES **Riesling**
REGION **Marlborough**
CELLAR ▤ **2**
PRICE **$15–17**

This riesling carries just enough residual sugar to kick it out of the 'dry' category. Riesling is sometimes hard to sell, but this one is a big seller at the many weddings and other functions hosted by the new winery.
Current Release 2000 The bouquet is citric and floral in equal measure, just the way it should be. It's a pretty wine in the flavour department, with good depth of fruit and clean-cut acids. Enjoy it with summer nibbles, with an emphasis on sweeter seafood like scallops and prawns.

Spy Valley Marlborough Riesling

STYLE **dry**
QUALITY ♟ ♟ ♟ ⊓
VALUE ☆ ☆ ☆ ⊱
GRAPES **Riesling**
REGION **Marlborough**
CELLAR ▤ **3**
PRICE **$15–17**

This was the first vintage at Spy Valley for winemaker Ant McKenzie. The fruit came from two different parts of the home vineyard and it was treated with as little winery artifice as possible to retain its freshness.
Current Release 2002 Grainy and minerally on the nose, well-focused, clean and lively on the palate, this is an attractive riesling that will develop more complexity over the next year or two. It goes well with mussels, steamed open, taken from their shells and tossed with chopped celery in home-made wasabi mayonnaise.

St Francis Marlborough Riesling

To date, St Francis wines have been made at the Ransom winery from grapes bought from contract growers in Marlborough and Hawke's Bay, but label owners Simon Lampen and Penny Reekie have big plans for the future.

Current Release 1999 I like the upfront, pear-like bouquet, and the same characters find their way to the front palate. It's sweet-fruited, perhaps a little obvious, but a pleasant drop nonetheless. It makes a good summer aperitif.

STYLE medium
QUALITY 🍷🍷🍷
VALUE ☆☆½
GRAPES Riesling
REGION Marlborough
CELLAR 3
PRICE $18–20

Stoneleigh Marlborough Riesling

This nicely focused white is one of the biggest-selling rieslings in the country, and must have done a great deal to introduce, or perhaps reintroduce, people to a variety that deserves greater public acclaim.

Current Release 2001 Gently floral, stylishly citric and just plain inviting on the nose, this is a very appealing wine. The flavours are clean and vibrant and the finish sweet-edged and moreish. Partner it with prawns, marinated in mirin and olive oil before being skewered and grilled.

STYLE off-dry
QUALITY 🍷🍷🍷🍷
VALUE ☆☆☆☆
GRAPES Riesling
REGION Marlborough
CELLAR 5
PRICE $17–19

Stratford Martinborough Riesling

Strat Canning is a riesling fan, and has great faith in the region's future in the Wairarapa. His wines aren't easy to find on restaurant lists out of Wellington, but they're worth ordering if you do find one.

Current Release 2000 Lemon juice and a touch of beeswax are in good shape on the nose. It's lively on the palate, with the citric theme joined by a wee trace of Aussie-style kero (yes, that is a good thing) towards the finish. It makes a good partner for risotto topped with shellfish and grated lemon rind.

STYLE off-dry
QUALITY 🍷🍷🍷🍷🍷
VALUE ☆☆☆☆½
GRAPES Riesling
REGION Martinborough
CELLAR 5
PRICE $18–20

Te Mania Nelson Riesling

Riesling grows well in Nelson, and local producers make the most of it. This one scored silver at the Bragato awards, and went on to take a gold medal at the 2002 New Zealand Wine Society Royal Easter Wine Show.

Current Release 2001 The nose is floral and faintly honeyed in the approved manner, leading to a nicely fruited flavour profile. It's a smartly balanced wine with richness and depth. The vaguely apple-like finish would make it a good match for a classic roast pork dinner.

STYLE off-dry
QUALITY 🍷🍷🍷🍷½
VALUE ☆☆☆☆½
GRAPES Riesling
REGION Nelson
CELLAR 3
PRICE $17–19

Te Whare Ra Duke of Marlborough Riesling

STYLE medium
QUALITY 🍷🍷🍷🍷🍷
VALUE ★★★★☆
GRAPES Riesling
REGION Marlborough

CELLAR 🍾 3
PRICE $16–18

Te Whare Ra wines are seldom seen in retail stores, but the company has a big mail-order following. It is most famous for a multi-award-winning gewürztraminer, but riesling also obviously suits the site.
Current Release 2000 Apricots, lime juice and a dash of honeycomb contribute to the appealing bouquet. It's unquestionably sweet, but nicely focused acids succeed pretty well in keeping things on the straight and narrow. You could try it with chicken liver pâté, but it's probably best on its own.

Torlesse Canterbury Riesling

STYLE off-dry
QUALITY 🍷🍷🍷🍷
VALUE ★★★☆
GRAPES Riesling
REGION Canterbury

CELLAR 🍾 3
PRICE $15–17

Torlesse produces two rieslings – this one, made from grapes grown in the broad Canterbury region, and another sourced solely from Waipara. They both sell well at the cellar door and on the wine lists of Christchurch restaurants.
Current Release 2001 The bouquet is floral and decidedly pretty – a good start. It's smartly balanced on the palate, with crisp acids adding just the right amount of zing to the rich fruit flavours. Enjoy it alongside a platter of prawns, marinated in lemon juice and Asian spices before being grilled.

Torlesse Waipara Riesling

STYLE off-dry
QUALITY 🍷🍷🍷🍷🍷
VALUE ★★★★☆
GRAPES Riesling
REGION Waipara

CELLAR 🍾 4
PRICE $16–18

Torlesse manager and winemaker, Kym Rayner, has a long history in the Canterbury and, particularly, Waipara districts. He has produced wine for several companies under contract, and has made a splendid job of this one.
Current Release 2001 The floral characters are quite gentle on the nose, but there's a good quota of ripe fruit on the front palate. It's refreshingly lively through the middle and carries just enough sweetness to lift the finish without going over the top. It would go well with a Thai-style dish featuring chicken and lemongrass, cooked with a very light shaving of rock sugar to match the touch of sweetness in the wine.

Vavasour Awatere Valley Riesling

STYLE off-dry
QUALITY 🍷🍷🍷🍷🍷
VALUE ★★★★
GRAPES Riesling
REGION Marlborough

CELLAR 🍾 5
PRICE $20–23

Glenn Thomas organised for the grapes for this riesling to be picked by hand, then pressed the whole bunches without putting them through a crusher-destemmer. He used the grapes' own natural yeasts, rather than laboratory-bred 'tame' models.
Current Release 2000 I get pure honeysuckle on the nose, which suggests the wine will be sweeter than it is. It's richly fruited on the palate with an edge of honey, and finishes with an attractive belt of citric fruit. Glenn recommends it for pan-fried fresh salmon, seared so it is just warmed through in the middle.

Vidal Estate Marlborough Riesling

The Vidal winery is in Hastings, Hawke's Bay, but Rod McDonald sourced the fruit for this pleasant riesling from a stone-covered site in Marlborough. I've listed it as off-dry, but it only just makes it – it's closer to the dry side of that definition.

Current Release 2002 Lime juice and lemons kick things off nicely. It's a focused, straightforward wine with citrus flavours through the middle and a pleasantly sweet-edged finish. It's good on its own or with chicken kebabs with a peanut and coconut sauce.

STYLE **off-dry**
QUALITY ▼ ▼ ▼ ▼
VALUE ★ ★ ★ ★
GRAPES **Riesling**
REGION **Marlborough**
CELLAR **3**
PRICE **$15–17**

Villa Maria Cellar Selection Marlborough Riesling

Slightly drier than the Private Bin version reviewed below, this Marlborough wine from the Villa team was made from grapes picked in the same two vineyards in the Wairau and Awatere Valleys. The fruit was picked in stages to ensure a good cross-section of flavours.

Current Release 2001 Orange rind and dried lemons – that's what I find on the bouquet. It's richly fruited, quite full through the middle and smartly balanced on the finish, which makes it good with well-flavoured dishes like Mediterranean-style seafood stew, served with thick slices of crusty bread.

STYLE **dry**
QUALITY ▼ ▼ ▼ ▼
VALUE ★ ★ ★
GRAPES **Riesling**
REGION **Marlborough**
CELLAR **4**
PRICE **$20–23**

Villa Maria Private Bin Marlborough Riesling

The Villa Maria winemaking team sourced fruit from sea-level vineyards in Marlborough's Wairau Valley and high-altitude sites in the Awatere Valley for this riesling. The object was to find grapes with a wide range of different flavours.

Current Release 2002 The bouquet is citric and spicy and the flavour profile sweet-fruited, and refreshing. That adds up to a pleasant drop that should suit a wide range of palates – the sort of wine that converts people to the wonders of the grape. Enjoy it on its own or with a chicken and radish sandwich.

STYLE **off-dry**
QUALITY ▼ ▼ ▼
VALUE ★ ★ ★
GRAPES **Riesling**
REGION **Marlborough**
CELLAR **3**
PRICE **$17–19**

Villa Maria Reserve Marlborough Riesling

Villa doesn't make a Reserve-labelled riesling every year, but in 2001 former winemaker Michelle Richardson (she has since left) was excited about the quality of fruit from the company's Marlborough vineyards. She did as little to it as possible.

Current Release 2001 Think apples and lemon peel and you've got an idea of the bouquet. It's ripe-fruited, boasts a pleasantly smooth texture and finishes with a refreshing dash of zing courtesy of the well-tuned acids. Partner it with a chunky pork terrine – but first, pour a glass to toast Michelle's future.

STYLE **off-dry**
QUALITY ▼ ▼ ▼ ▼
VALUE ★ ★ ★
GRAPES **Riesling**
REGION **Marlborough**
CELLAR **5**
PRICE **$23–26**

Voss Estate Riesling

STYLE off-dry
QUALITY ♟ ♟ ♟ ♟ ♟
VALUE ☆ ☆ ☆ ☆☆
GRAPES Riesling
REGION Martinborough

CELLAR 🍾 6
PRICE $16–19

There's not a lot of Gary Voss and Annette Atkins' classy riesling about, but it's worth a search. Gary reports that a small percentage of the fruit was infected by the so-called 'noble rot', botrytis. For riesling, that's okay.
Current Release 2000 Dried lemon peel and a touch of the florals set the scene. It's quite a complex wine, with rich flavours edged by zingy, faintly apple-like acids. The finish is long and refreshing. It's good on its own, but should also suit a terrine based on duck liver and pears.

Waimea Estates Classic Riesling

STYLE medium
QUALITY ♟ ♟ ♟ ♟
VALUE ☆ ☆ ☆ ☆☆
GRAPES Riesling
REGION Nelson

CELLAR 🍾 4
PRICE $15–17

Labelled 'Classic' to differentiate it from the dry version, this riesling carries 18 g/l of residual sugar. It had won no medals as we went to print, but I'm not the first commentator to give it a four-star rating.
Current Release 2000 Wow – talk about floral! Once you get past that perfumed bouquet, you are rewarded with a flavour profile heavy with rich, ripe fruit, nicely offset by fresh but integrated acids. It's good on its own, but you could try it with a salad based around pears and blue cheese.

Waimea Estates Riesling

STYLE dry
QUALITY ♟ ♟ ♟ ♟
VALUE ☆ ☆ ☆ ☆
GRAPES Riesling
REGION Nelson

CELLAR 🍾 4
PRICE $17–19

This stylish riesling, which just squeezes in to the dry category, won a silver medal at the 2000 Air New Zealand Wine Awards. It is sold in Australia and Japan, but there's apparently plenty left for us.
Current Release 2000 Honeysuckle and preserved lemons form a pleasant, if unlikely, union on the nose. It's lively, nicely focused and thoroughly pleasant, with well-tuned acids ensuring freshness on the finish. Try it with pan-fried pork chops and cabbage, served with grainy mustard.

Waipara Hills Dry Riesling

STYLE off-dry
QUALITY ♟ ♟ ♟ ♟
VALUE ☆ ☆ ☆
GRAPES Riesling
REGION Canterbury
       Marlborough
CELLAR ▥ 1–5
PRICE $18–20

The grapes were all hand-picked and came from eight different growers in Canterbury and Marlborough. The wine was made under contract by Alan McCorkindale. It's austere now, but it should age beautifully.
Current Release 2002 The bouquet is stongly citric – think lime juice and lemon rind and you'll be close. The same characters can be found on the palate, along with suggestions of freshly cut apple. The finish is squeaky-clean. Put it away for a while, then try it with a room temperature 'salad' of char-grilled root vegetables.

Waipara Hills Riesling

Like the dry version reviewed above, this wine came from eight sites in two regions and was made by Alan McCorkindale. Both wines are sold with Stelvin screwcap closures – no cork taint here!

Current Release 2002 The nose is quite minerally, with suggestions of grapefruit and dried lemon rind. It's richly fruited, smartly balanced and boasts flavours at the marmalade end of the spectrum. Partner it with Singapore-style chicken on coconut-flavoured rice and you should be very happy.

STYLE **medium**
QUALITY ▽▽▽▽
VALUE ★★★⯪
GRAPES **Riesling**
REGION **Canterbury**
Marlborough
CELLAR **4**
PRICE **$18—21**

Waipara Springs Riesling

The team at Waipara Springs is keen to make wines that go well with food, which is one of the reasons this riesling is just off-dry. A medium version is also made, but is usually sold only at the cellar door.

Current Release 2000 I get apple blossoms on the nose, and that suits me fine. It's direct, clean-cut and citric, with smartly integrated acids keeping things well under control. It's pleasant drinking on its own, but sits well with scallops, pan-fried with parsley and a little chopped ginger.

STYLE **dry**
QUALITY ▽▽▽▽
VALUE ★★★★
GRAPES **Riesling**
REGION **Waipara**
CELLAR **1—4**
PRICE **$17—19**

Whitehaven Riesling

Kenneth Coles, Caroline Coles and Steve Hammond grew the grapes, and Simon Waghorn did no more than he needed to in the interests of preserving as much of their natural freshness as possible. It was a good philosophy.

Current Release 2000 The nose is lightly and elegantly floral, and there's a dash of orange peel at the back. It's deliciously sweet-fruited on the front palate, but the richness is tempered by the keen-edged texture. A touch of spice provides a super finish, and makes it a good partner for lightly curried chicken.

STYLE **medium-dry**
QUALITY ▽▽▽▽▽
VALUE ★★★★★
GRAPES **Riesling**
REGION **Marlborough**
CELLAR **4**
PRICE **$14—16**

Whitehaven Single Vineyard Reserve Marlborough Riesling

Simon Waghorn arranged to have the grapes for this top-shelf riesling picked by hand, then pressed the whole bunches without putting them through a crusher-destemmer first.

Current Release 1999 The bouquet is citric, with a dash of honeycomb at the back. It's smooth-centred but with good clarity on the finish, and makes a good companion for a platter of tarakihi, cut into fingers, lightly crumbed and shallow-fried in peanut oil.

STYLE **off-dry**
QUALITY ▽▽▽▽
VALUE ★★★⯪
GRAPES **Riesling**
REGION **Marlborough**
CELLAR **4**
PRICE **$18—20**

William Hill Alexandra Riesling

STYLE **medium-dry**
QUALITY ▽ ▽ ▽ ▽
VALUE ☆ ☆ ☆
GRAPES **Riesling**
REGION **Central Otago**
CELLAR 🍾 4
PRICE **$18–21**

Winemaker David Grant arranged for the grapes to be picked by hand for this nicely fruited riesling. William Hill is currently promoting its wines extensively in the UK.

Current Release 2002 The bouquet makes me think of orange blossoms, and there is something of the same character on the front palate. It's ripe-fruited and nicely focused with acids that are about right for the degree of sweetness. Best on its own.

Winslow St Vincent Riesling

STYLE **medium-dry**
QUALITY ▽ ▽ ▽ ▽
VALUE ☆ ☆ ☆
GRAPES **Riesling**
REGION **Martinborough**
CELLAR 🍾 3
PRICE **$25–27**

The fruit came from the Long Bush Station vineyard, not far from Martinborough township, and it was pressed as whole bunches, bypassing the usual process of crushing and destemming. The technique is believed to keep in every nuance of flavour.

Current Release 2002 Pears, peaches and freshly cut apples – that's the aromatics sorted out. It's ripe and vibrant on the palate, with richness through the middle and a sweet apple-like finish. Roast pork with apple sauce would seem a logical way to go.

Sauvignon Blanc and Sémillon

It is sauvignon blanc, largely from Marlborough, that has put New Zealand firmly on the international wine map. Overseas commentators have been lavish in their praise, with several describing the local reading of the grape as the only truly new wine style of the past 100 years. Such adulation carries risks. When drought conditions in 1998 forced a change of style on local producers, British and American critics accused us of losing our way. In 1999 and 2000, things got back to normal, and since then growers have learned that to retain the sort of 'jump out of the glass' aromatic intensity that wins medals and wows the commentators, some of the grapes are best picked slightly unripe. Of course, not everyone agrees, and I'm certainly not alone in favouring the riper styles. I don't care too much if they don't win medals overseas – they're more pleasant to drink and easier to place with food and that, after all, is what it's all about. Sémillon bears some similarities to sauvignon blanc, and although this is changing as local vines mature, it shares this chapter because the two grapes are often blended together.

Allan Scott Marlborough Sauvignon Blanc

Allan and Catherine Scott were Marlborough pioneers, and now their children are following in their footsteps. Daughter Victoria handles marketing and son Josh is studying for a degree in oenology.
Current Release 2002 The bouquet is stylish and the fruit sweet-edged and rich on the front palate. Fresh-faced acids ensure there's plenty of lift through the middle and on the moderately long finish. Spaghetti tossed with nothing more distracting than parsley, garlic and top-quality olive oil would make a great match.

STYLE **dry**
QUALITY ♥ ♥ ♥ ♥
VALUE ☆ ☆ ☆ ☆
GRAPES
  Sauvignon Blanc
REGION **Marlborough**
CELLAR 1
PRICE **$18–20**

Alpha Domus Sauvignon Blanc

Evert Nijzink is a fan of big reds, and his wines have a solid following around the country. But Alpha Domus is no one-style wonder – this fresh-faced savvie isn't well known, but it has its own collection of fans.
Current Release 2002 The grassy edge is a bit of a blast from the past, but the cape gooseberry aromas are more up-to-date. It's clean and well-focused on the palate, with direct flavours and an edge of enthusiastic acids. It works well alongside a seafood platter with the emphasis on shellfish.

STYLE **dry**
QUALITY ♥ ♥ ♥ ♥
VALUE ☆ ☆ ☆
GRAPES
  Sauvignon Blanc 90%
  Sémillon 10%
REGION **Hawke's Bay**
CELLAR 1
PRICE **$18–20**

Alpha Domus Sémillon

STYLE **dry**
QUALITY ♈♈♈♈
VALUE ☆☆☆☆
GRAPES **Sémillon**
REGION **Hawke's Bay**
CELLAR 🍾 **4**
PRICE **$16–18**

Evert Nijzink gave this stylish sémillon just a smidgen of oak, but not enough to take away from the excellent fruit. Alpha Domus is best known for a series of big, strapping reds, but the whites are well worth checking out.

Current Release 2000 From its clean-cut, minerally bouquet to the spice-edged, smooth-textured profile this is a highly attractive wine. There's an impression of nashi pears on the front palate and something like rock melon in the middle, but that's searching for associations – mostly, it simply speaks of sensitively handled grapes. I like it with an oozy brie or camembert.

Alpha Domus Sémillon/Sauvignon Blanc

STYLE **dry**
QUALITY ♈♈♈♈
VALUE ☆☆☆☆
GRAPES
Sémillon 65%
Sauvignon Blanc 35%
REGION **Hawke's Bay**
CELLAR 🍾 **3**
PRICE **$17–19**

Most people who blend these two varieties make sauvignon blanc the major player. Evert Nijzink reverses the proportions, and the wine's popularity proves the public likes the result.

Current Release 1999 Think roasted red capsicums on grainy toast and you'll approximate the bouquet. It's quite complex on the palate, with rich fruit, a smooth texture and a spicy finish. It's an excellent food wine, and goes well with semi-soft cheese served with thin slices of lightly toasted bread.

Artisan Valley East Estate Single Vineyard Marlborough Sauvignon Blanc

STYLE **dry**
QUALITY ♈♈♈♈
VALUE ☆☆☆☆
GRAPES
Sauvignon Blanc
REGION **Marlborough**
CELLAR 🍾 **2**
PRICE **$17–19**

Artisan Wines was set up to represent the best growing regions in the country. The company draws its fruit from vineyards in Gisborne, Marlborough, Auckland and Hawke's Bay, and other areas may well be added to the collection in the future.

Current Release 2002 Pungent and perfumed on the nose, sweet-fruited and lush on the palate, this is pretty typical Marlborough savvie from a hot year. It's nicely balanced and very refreshing, which makes it good on its own, but if you want to try it with food, a chicken and fennel bulb salad would work well.

Askerne Hawke's Bay Barrel Fermented Sémillon

STYLE **dry**
QUALITY ♈♈♈♈
VALUE ☆☆☆
GRAPES **Sémillon**
REGION **Hawke's Bay**
CELLAR 🍾 **4**
PRICE **$18–20**

Sorrelle Pearson fermented this sémillon in French oak barrels, 80% a year old, 20% five years old. It stayed in the oak for 10 months before both components were tasted, blended and bottled.

Current Release 1999 The nose is still classically herbaceous, despite all that oak. The time in barrels has smoothed out the texture, so now it is quite creamy. Integrated acids leave it to the last to lift the fruit. Enjoy it alongside triangles of grilled pita bread with hummus dip.

Askerne Hawke's Bay Sauvignon Blanc

John Loughlin fermented 20% of this fresh-faced savvie in oak barrels while the rest did its thing in stainless steel. That wasn't enough to change the flavour, but it probably evened things out a little.
Current Release 2002 The sémillon has added a grassy edge to the aromas of straw and ripe cape gooseberries. It's fresh and lively on the palate, a little lean through the middle but enjoys a pleasantly sweet-fruited finish. Thai-style fish cakes would make a good accompaniment.

STYLE **dry**
QUALITY ♟♟♟♟
VALUE ☆ ☆ ☆
GRAPES
Sauvignon Blanc 88%
Sémillon 12%
REGION **Hawke's Bay**

CELLAR **1**
PRICE **$18—20**

Askerne Hawke's Bay Sémillon/Sauvignon Blanc

About 30% of this two-grape blend saw the inside of a barrel. Most producers who put these two varieties together make sauvignon the major player, but this one reverses the trend.
Current Release 1999 If you like old-style grassy sauvignon, this sémillon-dominant white will suit you fine. It's got some good hay-like aromas, but the flavour profile is lean and green, and seems to have become more so in the year or so since I last tried it. Lemon juice drizzled over a poached chicken breast would go some way towards balancing the acid.

STYLE **dry**
QUALITY ♟♟♟
VALUE ☆ ☆☆
GRAPES
Sémillon 80%
Sauvignon Blanc 20%
REGION **Hawke's Bay**

CELLAR ▯
PRICE **$16—18**

Ata Rangi Sauvignon Blanc

Oliver Masters reckons this is the best sauvignon he's ever made. Cropping the vineyard at three tonnes to the acre – way below the national average – gave him very intense fruit.
Current Release 2002 Lively aromas reminiscent of melon skin, cape gooseberries and kiwifruit start things off nicely. It's fresh-faced on the front palate, builds in richness through the middle and finishes clean. Enjoy it alongside a plate of hot-smoked salmon with warm toast.

STYLE **dry**
QUALITY ♟♟♟♟
VALUE ☆ ☆ ☆
GRAPES
Sauvignon Blanc
REGION **Martinborough**

CELLAR **2**
PRICE **$20—23**

Babich Fumé Vert

The name sounds like a grape variety, but it's not – it means 'smoky green' in French, and aims to describe the flavour profile. The blend and the regions change from year to year.
Current Release 2000 The nose has some pleasant spicy, savoury characters and the flavours are lively and quite rich, with a sweet edge. It's remarkably smart wine for this low price, and deserves its success. Enjoy it with a salad of cubed firm-fleshed fish and potatoes, served at room temperature with mayonnaise.

STYLE **dry**
QUALITY ♟♟♟
VALUE ☆ ☆ ☆ ☆ ☆
GRAPES
Sémillon 75%
Chardonnay 25%
REGION **Gisborne**
Auckland

CELLAR **2**
PRICE **$11—13**

Babich Marlborough Sauvignon Blanc

STYLE **dry**
QUALITY ⚱⚱⚱⚱
VALUE ☆ ☆ ☆
GRAPES
  Sauvignon Blanc
REGION **Marlborough**
CELLAR 🍾 1
PRICE **$18–20**

The Babich family recently purchased a vineyard in the sun-drenched Awatere Valley, and that's where some of the fruit for this nicely balanced sauvignon came from. The rest came from the Wairau Valley.
Current Release 2002 There's a touch of hot-year pungency on the nose, but it doesn't get carried away – sweet fruit is the major impression. The flavour profile is clean and crisp-edged and the finish reasonably lengthy. To sum up, a straightforward wine that suits simple fare like a smoked salmon sandwich.

Babich Winemaker's Reserve Sauvignon Blanc

STYLE **dry**
QUALITY ⚱⚱⚱⚱⚱
VALUE ☆ ☆ ☆
GRAPES
  Sauvignon Blanc
REGION **Marlborough**
CELLAR 🍾 3
PRICE **$24–27**

Just 10% of the fruit for this classy sauvignon was fermented and matured in one-year-old oak barrels, while the rest did its thing in stainless-steel tanks. That seems hardly enough to make a difference, but it is easy to pick.
Current Release 2001 The savoury notes on the nose signal that this is a far more complex wine than most of its regional mates. The flavour profile is smooth, nicely fruited and broad on the finish, which adds up to great drinkability. Enjoy it with a leek and sun-dried tomato frittata.

Black Barn Vineyards Hawke's Bay Sauvignon Blanc

STYLE **dry**
QUALITY ⚱⚱⚱⚱⚱
VALUE ☆ ☆ ☆ ☆
GRAPES
  Sauvignon Blanc
REGION **Hawke's Bay**
CELLAR 🍾 2
PRICE **$19–22**

Black Barn Vineyards is a new name on the Hawke's Bay wine scene, but the actual vines have been there for many years. The grapes are all picked by hand and pressed as whole bunches without going through a crusher-destemmer.
Current Release 2002 Gentle is a term that's not often associated with exuberant sauvignon blanc, but it seems to fit the bouquet of this one. It's smooth and classy on the palate, with nicely integrated acids lifting the fruit without trying to dominate proceedings. Not the usual savvie, but thoroughly enjoyable with the likes of poached oysters in a creamy sauce.

Bladen Marlborough Sauvignon Blanc

STYLE **dry**
QUALITY ⚱⚱⚱⚱
VALUE ☆ ☆ ☆
GRAPES
  Sauvignon Blanc
REGION **Marlborough**
CELLAR 🍾 2
PRICE **$19–21**

Grapes have been grown on the Bladen vineyard since 1989, but the crops were sold to major companies for nearly a decade. Wine has been produced under the property's own label only since 1997.
Current Release 2002 'Sweaty' doesn't sound like much of an attribute, but it is very much part of the bouquet of hot-year Marlborough savvies, and this one has loads of it behind the ripe passionfruit aromas. It's sweet-fruited and nicely balanced on the palate, and goes well with a roast pork and radish sandwich, made with really good grainy bread.

Cairnbrae The Stones Marlborough Sauvignon Blanc

Tony Bish wanted to keep the grapes cool when he planned this wine, so he arranged for them to be harvested at night, and later chilled the vat in which the juice was fermented. Slowing the process down makes it easier to control.

Current Release 2002 It's pretty classic stuff – clean and fresh on the nose and sweet-edged but refreshingly lively on the palate. The label has been around for a while, but this is the first one made by Tony. Partner it with a seared tuna steak on thinly sliced pan-fried potatoes and raise your glass to a job well done.

STYLE **dry**
QUALITY ♟♟♟♟♟
VALUE ☆☆☆☆
GRAPES
  Sauvignon Blanc
REGION **Marlborough**
CELLAR 🍾 **2**
PRICE **$19–21**

Carrick Central Otago Cairnmuir Road Sauvignon Blanc

Central Otago has made its name with pinot noir, but the partners in Cairnmuir Road Winery, which produces the Carrick range, believe it is equally suited to several other varieties. I'm not arguing.

Current Release 2002 Clean and crisp with no more than a suggestion of the pungency that characterises many Marlborough versions, this Central Otago savvie has immediate appeal. The fruit is sweet-edged, the flavours are clean and direct and the finish zingy and refreshing. It goes well with salmon-based fish cakes served with a simple green salad.

STYLE **dry**
QUALITY ♟♟♟♟
VALUE ☆☆☆⟨
GRAPES
  Sauvignon Blanc
REGION **Central Otago**
CELLAR 🍾 **2**
PRICE **$19–22**

Charles Wiffen Sauvignon Blanc

Long-time grape growers Charles and Sandi Wiffen live in Canterbury, but their vineyard is in Marlborough. They say it works well, and the wines certainly haven't suffered, as their award collection shows.

Current Release 2002 Pungent and fresh-faced on the nose, lively and clean on the palate, this is classic Marlborough savvie. It goes well with quite a wide range of foods, from freshly shucked rock oysters to smoked salmon on thin slices of buttered grainy toast. Enjoy!

STYLE **dry**
QUALITY ♟♟♟♟♟
VALUE ☆☆☆☆
GRAPES
  Sauvignon Blanc
REGION **Marlborough**
CELLAR 🍾 **1**
PRICE **$18–20**

Church Road Sauvignon Blanc

Don't expect the usual Kiwi style of savvie when you try this wine. The winemaking team likes to achieve something different, taking inspiration from the great sauvignon-based wines of the Graves region in Bordeaux, France.

Current Release 2002 There is a bit of Marlborough-style pungency on the nose, but it's unusually gentle. The flavour profile is smooth, broadly focused and very appealing. It's hard to identify particular fruit associations, but that's not the point. It goes well with chicken fricassee – remember that?

STYLE **dry**
QUALITY ♟♟♟♟
VALUE ☆☆☆⟨
GRAPES
  Sauvignon Blanc
REGION
  Marlborough 57%
  Hawke's Bay 43%
CELLAR 🍾 **3**
PRICE **$19–22**

Clearview Estate Reserve Te Awanga Sauvignon Blanc

STYLE **dry**

QUALITY ♟ ♟ ♟ ♟

VALUE ☆ ☆ ☆

GRAPES
**Sauvignon Blanc 97%
Sémillon 3%**

REGION **Hawke's Bay**

CELLAR 🍾 **2**

PRICE **$21–23**

Tim Turvey believes in getting some serious oak character into his sauvignon blanc. In 2001, that translated as fermenting the juice in mostly-new French barrels and leaving the fledgling wine in them for a further 10 months. He also added a dash of sémillon.

Current Release 2001 Despite all that new oak the spice characters are quite subdued on the nose – the major aromas are of cape gooseberries and pineapple. It's full-flavoured, ripe and rich on the palate, and would make an excellent partner for one of the Clearview Estate's tasting platters, featuring roasted vegetables, salami and the property's own olives.

Clifford Bay Estate Marlborough Single Vineyard Sauvignon Blanc

STYLE **dry**

QUALITY ♟ ♟ ♟ ♟ ♟

VALUE ☆ ☆ ☆ ☆ ☆

GRAPES
Sauvignon Blanc

REGION **Marlborough**

CELLAR 🍾 **2**

PRICE **$18–21**

Wines designated 'Single Vineyard' are top of the heap for Clifford Bay, and this nicely tuned savvie is a worthy member of the portfolio. The fruit came from a warm, stone-covered site.

Current Release 2002 Passionfruit has certainly got the gig on the nose, although it's possible to conjure up a freshly cut peach as well. It's rich but lively on the palate, with perfect balance between fruit and acid right through to the lingering finish. A crayfish salad would be a perfect partner, but tuatua fritters would do at a pinch.

Clifford Bay Marlborough Sauvignon Blanc

STYLE **dry**

QUALITY ♟ ♟ ♟ ♟ ♟

VALUE ☆ ☆ ☆ ☆ ☆

GRAPES
Sauvignon Blanc

REGION **Marlborough**

CELLAR 🍾 **2**

PRICE **$17–19**

Clifford Bay was one of the first Marlborough wineries to draw fruit exclusively from the sun-baked Awatere Valley. Impressive competition success with the first vintage gave the label the sort of publicity money can't buy.

Current Release 2001 That classic savvie pungency jumps out of the glass. It's deliciously sweet-fruited on the front palate, with plenty of the tropical fruit notes that seem to typify wines from the Awatere. It's got good weight, a healthy amount of richness and a lively finish. It's the ideal wine for chicken breasts, stuffed with blue cheese before being crumbed and pan-fried.

Cloudy Bay Sauvignon Blanc

Mention New Zealand wine almost anywhere in the world and someone will ask about Cloudy Bay. This classic Marlborough 'savvie' has played a huge part in putting the province of Marlborough on the map.

Current Release 2002 What can I say? As always, this latest release is lively, smartly focused and immaculately clean. It seems to avoid the pungency associated with so many of the region's savvies, relying instead on the satisfying flavours of fully ripe grapes for its appeal. There's nothing better with a piece of Marlborough Sounds salmon, just seared and warmed through.

STYLE **dry**
QUALITY ♟♟♟♟♟
VALUE ☆☆☆
GRAPES
  Sauvignon Blanc
  Sémillon
REGION **Marlborough**
CELLAR 2
PRICE **$26–28**

Cloudy Bay Te Koko

This alternative style to the classic Cloudy Bay 'savvie' is made quite differently. It spends 18 months in used oak barrels, and some of it is put through an acid-softening malolactic fermentation.

Current Release 1999 There's just a suggestion of spice on the nose and hints of passionfruit and lemon, but everything is subtle. The full, complex flavour profile is like no other Marlborough reading of this grape. If you're into outspokenness it's not for you. This is sav blanc for people who like to meditate. Enjoy it with kingfish steaks braised in chicken stock.

STYLE **dry**
QUALITY ♟♟♟♟♟
VALUE ☆☆☆
GRAPES
  Sauvignon Blanc
  Sémillon
REGION **Marlborough**
CELLAR 5
PRICE **$34–36**

Collards Old Vines Sémillon

Despite the vintage, this is a relatively new release for the Collard family, but it's proving a difficult one to sell. It shouldn't – it's very smart. The 'old vines' are on the home block, and they've been growing for about 20 years.

Current Release 1999 There's an attractive grainy, spicy edge to the melon-like aromas, and something of the same grainy character on the palate. It's nicely weighted, with a lively texture and a clean, crisp finish. It makes a great partner for Chinese lemon chicken.

STYLE **dry**
QUALITY ♟♟♟♟♟
VALUE ☆☆☆☆☆
GRAPES **Sémillon**
REGION **West Auckland**
CELLAR 4
PRICE **$16–18**

Collards Rothesay Sauvignon Blanc

This wine has long been a favourite with Collards fans. It receives a little oak, but not enough to bury the fruit. The Collards say they prefer this style to the super-young, pungent examples coming out of Marlborough.

Current Release 2001 It's certainly rounder and gentler on the nose than the average Marlborough savvie, and the same broadness carries over to the palate. The oak has softened the grape's natural exuberance and added faint spice to the finish. It's good with a salad based on smoked kahawai and rocket leaves.

STYLE **dry**
QUALITY ♟♟♟♟
VALUE ☆☆☆
GRAPES
  Sauvignon Blanc
REGION **West Auckland**
CELLAR 2
PRICE **$16–18**

Corbans Cottage Block Marlborough Sauvignon Blanc

STYLE dry
QUALITY ⍟ ⍟ ⍟ ⍟ ⍟
VALUE ☆ ☆ ☆
GRAPES
  Sauvignon Blanc
REGION Marlborough
CELLAR 3
PRICE $29–32

Only fruit from low-yielding vines was used to craft this stylish savvie. The team pulled leaves off to expose the ripening grapes to the sun, and harvested in the cool of the early morning to maximise flavours.

Current Release 2000 I get kiwifruit and passionfruit on the nose, an appealing combination that leads to a wealth of big, rich, sweet-fruited flavours. The oak spice shows itself on the finish, but it's very subdued. It's a smart wine that suits simple pasta dishes – try penne with bocconcini and chopped parsley.

Corbans Sauvignon Blanc

STYLE dry
QUALITY ⍟ ⍟ ⍟ ⍟
VALUE ☆ ☆ ☆ ☆
GRAPES
  Sauvignon Blanc
REGION Hawke's Bay
CELLAR 1
PRICE $14–16

It doesn't say so on the label, but this clean-cut savvie is made entirely from Hawke's Bay fruit. It presumably replaces the old 'Corbans Estate' wine which often blended grapes from Hawke's Bay and Gisborne.

Current Release 2002 It's fresh-faced, reedy and clean on the nose, sweet-edged and fruity on the palate. There's a faintly green edge towards the finish, but it's no big deal – in fact, it's quite refreshing. Pull the cork and pour a glass or two to go with a shellfish salad that puts a major emphasis on Marlborough Sounds mussels, the smaller the better.

Corbans White Label Sauvignon Blanc

STYLE off-dry
QUALITY ⍟ ⍟ ⍟
VALUE ☆ ☆ ☆ ☆ ⍟
GRAPES
  Sauvignon Blanc
REGION New Zealand
  Chile
CELLAR
PRICE $9–11

The label doesn't go into detail, but we presume a fair bit of the New Zealand juice came from Gisborne. Some companies have been criticised for importing savvie juice from Chile, but it certainly helps to keep the price down!

Current Release 2002 The bouquet is pretty classical – cape gooseberries, feijoas and freshly cut grass are all in there. So far, so good – but it seems disjointed on the palate, with overtly sweet fruit not quite in kilter. It's okay on its own if you chill it right down, but I'd be cautious about serving it with anything apart from olives and other simple nibbles.

Craggy Range Winery Old Renwick Vineyard Sauvignon Blanc

STYLE dry
QUALITY ⍟ ⍟ ⍟ ⍟ ⍟
VALUE ☆ ☆ ☆
GRAPES
  Sauvignon Blanc
REGION Marlborough
CELLAR 2
PRICE $20–23

Viticulturist Steve Smith's plans to make a series of wines from top sites around the country is going well. The Craggy Range label is quite new on the scene, but it enjoys an excellent reputation.

Current Release 2002 You want to taste classic Marlborough savvie? This is your wine. It has a savoury note on the bouquet and is deliciously sweet-fruited on the palate. The well-focused flavours lean toward the tropical fruit end of the spectrum, making it a good partner for a Polynesian-style fish salad.

Crossroads Sauvignon Blanc

The winemaking team sourced the grapes for this new millennium savvie from two vineyards, one in Maraekakaho, and one near the coast at Te Awanga. They say the different regional characters gave them more blending flexibility.

Current Release 2000 There's a faintly grainy edge to the pineapple and mango aromas. It's sweet-fruited and rich on the palate, but with nicely tuned acids providing a zesty finish. The slight amount of residual sugar makes it a good partner for Chinese sweet-and-sour pork.

STYLE **off-dry**
QUALITY ▽▽▽▽
VALUE ☆☆☆☆☆
GRAPES
  Sauvignon Blanc
REGION **Hawke's Bay**
CELLAR 2
PRICE **$15–17**

Dashwood Marlborough Sauvignon Blanc

Dashwood takes its name from an area on the seaward end of Marlborough's Awatere Valley. That's where 65% of the juice for this savvie came from. The rest was picked in the Wairau Valley, on the other side of the hills.

Current Release 2002 The bouquet is chunky and spice-edged, and the same characters can be found on the front palate. It's a very focused wine, clean and lively through the middle and refreshingly crisp on the finish. It would make a splendid partner for a whitebait fritter or two, so start counting down to the season.

STYLE **dry**
QUALITY ▽▽▽▽▽
VALUE ☆☆☆☆☆
GRAPES
  Sauvignon Blanc
REGION **Marlborough**
CELLAR 2
PRICE **$17–19**

Delegat's Hawke's Bay Sauvignon Blanc

If you want a textbook demonstration of the difference between Hawke's Bay and Marlborough sauvignon blanc, try a bottle of this alongside winemaker Michael Ivicevich's Oyster Bay version. Each is a classic of its regional style.

Current Release 2002 It's fresh, clean and lively in the bouquet, richly fruited and melon-like on the palate. That's what good Hawke's Bay savvie is all about, and it explains why this wine is such a big seller here and overseas. Try it alongside a platter of root vegetables brushed with olive oil, sprinkled with sea salt and baked.

STYLE **dry**
QUALITY ▽▽▽▽
VALUE ☆☆☆☆☆
GRAPES
  Sauvignon Blanc
REGION **Hawke's Bay**
CELLAR 2
PRICE **$13–15**

Domaine Georges Michel Marlborough Golden Mile Sauvignon Blanc

Georges Michel, along with fellow French expatriate Daniel Le Brun, was recently given a high honour from his government for expanding the reputation of his homeland world-wide. Formidable!

Current Release 2002 There's a dash of spice adding extra interest to the classic passionfruit aromas, and a suggestion of lime juice as well. It's richly fruited, smartly balanced and superbly refreshing – Marlborough sunshine in a glass. Pay homage to Georges' heritage by partnering it with the famous French dish, chicken with 40 cloves of garlic.

STYLE **dry**
QUALITY ▽▽▽▽▽
VALUE ☆☆☆☆☆
GRAPES
  Sauvignon Blanc
REGION **Marlborough**
CELLAR 2
PRICE **$17–19**

Dry River Sauvignon Blanc

STYLE **dry**
QUALITY � � � �
VALUE ★ ★ ★ ☆
GRAPES
  Sauvignon Blanc
REGION **Martinborough**

CELLAR ▤ 5
PRICE $23–26

I've often said that sauvignon blanc is best in its first year when it's full of youthful brashness, but Neil McCallum reckons this one will age for a decade or more. I've split the difference with my recommendation.

Current Release 2002 The bouquet is delicate – not a character often associated with this variety – and gently perfumed. It's minerally on the front palate, becomes creamy through the middle and finishes with a belt of immaculately clean, sweet-edged fruit. It goes well with salmon gravlax, but watch the vinegar and onions.

Drylands Marlborough Winemakers Reserve Sauvignon Blanc

STYLE **dry**
QUALITY � � � � ☜
VALUE ★ ★ ★ ★ ☆
GRAPES
  Sauvignon Blanc
REGION **Marlborough**

CELLAR ▤ 2
PRICE $19–21

Darryl Woolley left this savvie sitting on the yeast lees left over from fermentation for three months to give it extra complexity. His efforts have been rewarded with some enthusiastic commendations.

Current Release 2002 Pungent and savoury on the nose, sweet-fruited and rich on the palate, this is smart wine. It's more mouth-filling than most and boasts a suggestion of honeycomb on the finish. It makes a good partner for roast pork, complete with crackling (of course!) and all the trimmings.

Equinox Hawke's Bay Sauvignon Blanc

STYLE **dry**
QUALITY � � � � ☜
VALUE ★ ★ ★ ★ ★
GRAPES
  Sauvignon Blanc
REGION **Hawke's Bay**

CELLAR ▤ 2
PRICE $15–17

Made from a mixture of hand and machine-picked fruit, this classy savvie was partly oak-aged, but not enough to interfere with the vivid fruit characters that have made the New Zealand style an international hit.

Current Release 2002 The oak has added no more than a suggestion of spice to the ripe passionfruit and pineapple aromas. It's a nicely balanced wine, with sweet fruit flavours in front, plenty of zing through the middle and a memorable finish. I like it with Chinese-style salt and pepper squid.

Esk Valley Sauvignon Blanc (Black Label)

STYLE **dry**
QUALITY � � �
VALUE ★ ☆ ☜
GRAPES
  Sauvignon Blanc
REGION **Hawke's Bay**

CELLAR ▤ 2
PRICE $20–23

Who ever said making wine was easy? Gordon Russell sent out his cellar blending sheet with the tasting sample of this wine. It showed that even though the grapes came from only two sites, the finished wine is made up of 13 different components.

Current Release 2001 There's an earthy note behind the ripe citrus and melon aromas in the bouquet. It's smooth and quite broad on the palate, with fully integrated acids and a tiny suggestion of oak spice towards the finish. Use a little to steam open some greenshell mussels and serve the rest alongside.

Fairhall Downs Marlborough Sauvignon Blanc

One of the many Marlborough vineyards that supplied other companies with grapes before establishing its own label, Fairhall Downs has enjoyed major medal success in this country and overseas.

Current Release 2002 Pungent on the nose but impeccably clean, this is a nicely focused example of the local style. It's fresh-faced and appealing on the palate, with smartly integrated acids lifting the fruit nicely through the middle and on the reasonably long finish. Enjoy it with pasta, ideally home-made, tossed with baby mussels and a little cream.

STYLE **dry**
QUALITY ♟♟♟♟
VALUE ★★★★☆
GRAPES **Sauvignon Blanc**
REGION **Marlborough**
CELLAR 2
PRICE **$15–17**

Fiddler's Green Waipara Sauvignon Blanc

Barry Johns, winemaker and Christchurch lawyer, and his wife, Jennie, launched this Waipara label a couple of years ago. The name is actually that of the 30-hectare property, and is recognised on maps of the region.

Current Release 2001 It's pungent in the current style, but there's a measure of elegance not always found with this exuberant variety. The flavours are clean, sweet-edged and instantly appealing and the finish a good deal longer than most. It would make a fine companion for mussel fritters dabbed with home-made mayonnaise.

STYLE **dry**
QUALITY ♟♟♟♟♟
VALUE ★★★★☆
GRAPES **Sauvignon Blanc**
REGION **Waipara**
CELLAR 2
PRICE **$19–21**

Forrest Sauvignon Blanc

Dr John Forrest is a great fan of screwcapped wines, and uses the first lines of the rock classic 'Twist & Shout' on his promotional brochure. The fruit for this latest example of his style came from six different vineyards.

Current Release 2002 The fruit is sweet-edged, clean and fresh on the nose – there's very little evidence of typical Marlborough 'sweat'. It's a delightful wine on the palate, with flavours suggesting sliced mango and golden kiwifruit smartly edged by well-tuned acids. Go for broke and enjoy it with grilled crayfish.

STYLE **dry**
QUALITY ♟♟♟♟♟
VALUE ★★★★☆
GRAPES **Sauvignon Blanc**
REGION **Marlborough**
CELLAR 2
PRICE **$17–19**

Framingham Marlborough Sauvignon Blanc

Rex and P. J. Brooke-Taylor have come a long way from the days when all their grapes were sold to other companies. Now, they run a 1000-tonne winery and send a good percentage of their portfolio to various parts of the world.

Current Release 2002 The bouquet is certainly pungent, but it has more elegance than most. Sweet fruit and smartly balanced acids make it a lively but satisfying mouthful. It goes brilliantly with oyster pie accompanied by really small green beans.

STYLE **dry**
QUALITY ♟♟♟♟♟
VALUE ★★★☆
GRAPES **Sauvignon Blanc**
REGION **Marlborough**
CELLAR 2
PRICE **$20–23**

Gibbston Valley Sauvignon Blanc

STYLE **dry**

QUALITY ♟♟♟

VALUE ☆ ☆

GRAPES
Sauvignon Blanc

REGION **Central Otago**

CELLAR 🍾 1

PRICE **$23–25**

I've listed it as dry, but Grant Taylor did leave a wee bit of residual sweetness in this wine to lift the fruit. It's not at all obvious, and certainly doesn't interfere with its ability to accompany food.

Current Release 2001 The nose is fiercely pungent – this is like Marlborough savvie on steroids! The flavours are richly reminiscent of a range of tropical fruits and the finish is super-lively. It's not what could be called subtle, which makes it a good partner for fettucine pasta tossed with a healthy amount of pesto, preferably home-made.

Giesen Marlborough Sauvignon Blanc

STYLE **dry**

QUALITY ♟♟♟♟♟

VALUE ☆ ☆ ☆ ☆ ☆

GRAPES
Sauvignon Blanc

REGION **Marlborough**

CELLAR 🍾 2

PRICE **$17–19**

The winery is in Canterbury, but the Giesen brothers are astute enough to realise that Marlborough is the region overseas buyers want to see on their sauvignon blanc. The wine sells well, and they've made a nice job of this latest version.

Current Release 2002 Cape gooseberries, tamarillos and maybe even kiwifruit aromas can be found on the nose. It's richer than most examples on the palate, with sweet-edged flavours nicely balanced by fresh, lively acids. Forget food – it makes a startlingly refreshing aperitif.

Gladstone Wairarapa Sauvignon Blanc

STYLE **dry**

QUALITY ♟♟♟♟

VALUE ☆ ☆ ☆

GRAPES
Sauvignon Blanc

REGION **Wairarapa**

CELLAR 🍾 1

PRICE **$20–23**

Christine Kernohan fermented just 10% of this wine in French oak barrels and left it there for a few weeks, while the rest did its thing in a stainless-steel tank. She believes it has added a worthwhile amount of complexity.

Current Release 2001 Suggestions of ripe pineapple and rock melon dominate the bouquet, and that adds up to an enticing introduction. It's frisky on the palate, with a grassy edge that has barely been softened by the oak. The finish is clean-cut and direct. It goes well with Chinese-style stir-fried eggplant and pork.

Glover's Moutere Sauvignon Blanc

STYLE **dry**

QUALITY ♟♟♟♟

VALUE ☆ ☆ ☆

GRAPES
Sauvignon Blanc

REGION **Nelson**

CELLAR 🍾 2

PRICE **$16–18**

Sauvignon blanc shouldn't be aged? Don't tell Dave Glover – this is the current release of his tangy, bone-dry savvie, and it's tasting just fine. Don't expect classic varietal characters. This one is distinctively different.

Current Release 1997 The savoury note behind the ripe apple and pear aromas and the crisp, refreshing flavour profile give no indication whatever that this is a six-year-old wine. Austere in its youth, it has blossomed into a little beauty that would be right at home with a chicken and baby carrot casserole.

Goldridge Estate Premium Reserve Marlborough Sauvignon Blanc

Goldridge wines are part of the Matakana Estate portfolio. The grapes for this one came from two sites in Marlborough, both under the control of the same grower. The yield per hectare was kept low to increase intensity in the grapes.

Current Release 2001 There's a savoury edge that's a little different from the norm – the usual Marlborough pungency is relatively subdued. It's lively and fresh-faced on the palate, but a little creaminess through the middle adds depth. The company's tasting note suggests partnering it with Marlborough Sounds mussels, cooled and served with a tomato and basil salsa.

STYLE **dry**
QUALITY ♟ ♟ ♟ ♟
VALUE ☆ ☆ ☆
GRAPES
 Sauvignon Blanc 97.5%
 Sémillon 2.5%
REGION **Marlborough**
CELLAR 📖 1
PRICE **$20–23**

Goldwater Dog Point Marlborough Sauvignon Blanc

Kim and Jeanette Goldwater's vineyard and winery is on Waiheke Island, in Auckland's Hauraki Gulf, but they make more of this Marlborough wine than anything else in their portfolio.

Current Release 2002 The bouquet is pungent, clean and fresh, the flavours push all the right buttons and the finish is delightfully lingering. In other words, it's classy stuff! Pull the cork next time you're planning to enjoy a pile of just-opened mussels, butter a pile of good bread and relax.

STYLE **dry**
QUALITY ♟ ♟ ♟ ♟ ♟
VALUE ☆ ☆ ☆ ☆
GRAPES
 Sauvignon Blanc
REGION **Marlborough**
CELLAR 📖 2
PRICE **$19–22**

Greenhough Nelson Sauvignon Blanc

Nelson Sauvignon Blanc has similarities to the more famous Marlborough models over the hills, but many local examples seem to have a touch more elegance. This is one of them, and it sells well in restaurants around the country.

Current Release 2002 Rich fruit aromas reminiscent of kiwifruit and tamarillos start things rolling. It's fresh, clean-cut and lively, but with a considerable amount of depth – not a common attribute with this outspoken grape. Pour a glass to accompany the best hot-smoked salmon you can find.

STYLE **dry**
QUALITY ♟ ♟ ♟ ♟
VALUE ☆ ☆ ☆ ☆
GRAPES
 Sauvignon Blanc 91%
 Sémillon 9%
REGION **Nelson**
CELLAR 📖 1
PRICE **$17–21**

Grove Mill Marlborough Sauvignon Blanc

This clean-cut savvie is an immensely popular by-the-glass restaurant choice. David Pearce says he aimed to make a 'dry but fruity' wine with a considerable measure of elegance. He has succeeded well.

Current Release 2001 It's pungent in the modern style, but gently so. The flavour profile is classic stuff – clean, fresh and stimulating thanks to the lively acids that cut in towards the finish. It's good on its own, but goes well with Marlborough mussels, steamed open and served 'as is'.

STYLE **dry**
QUALITY ♟ ♟ ♟ ♟
VALUE ☆ ☆ ☆ ☆
GRAPES
 Sauvignon Blanc
REGION **Marlborough**
CELLAR 📖 2
PRICE **$20–23**

Gunn Estate Sauvignon Blanc

STYLE dry
QUALITY ♟♟♟♟
VALUE ★★★★⯪

GRAPES
Sauvignon Blanc

REGION
Marlborough 55%
Hawke's Bay 45%

CELLAR 🍾 2
PRICE $15–17

This is one of only a handful of wines to combine sauvignon blanc fruit from Marlborough and Hawke's Bay. It makes a lot of sense – fruit from each region has its own attributes, and they go together very well indeed.

Current Release 2002 It's seen no oak, but I still fancy I detect a touch of spice behind the cape gooseberry and passionfruit aromas. It's ripe-fruited and classy in the flavour department, with clean-cut acids providing freshness through the middle and lift on the finish. Mozzarella and fully ripe tomatoes on lightly grilled baguette slices would be perfect with it.

Hawkesbridge Willowbank Vineyard Sauvignon Blanc

STYLE dry
QUALITY ♟♟♟♟⯪
VALUE ★★★★

GRAPES
Sauvignon Blanc

REGION Marlborough

CELLAR 🍾 2
PRICE $18–20

Mike and Judy Veal have done well with sauvignon blanc, winning awards in this country and loads of orders from overseas. Mike is involved in Marlborough industry politics, and is highly respected for his contribution.

Current Release 2000 The nose is grassy in the classic manner, but there's plenty of rich fruit both in the bouquet and on the palate. It has a pleasant acid balance and a very refreshing finish. It's good with a rustic terrine based around roasted eggplant and capsicums.

Hay's Lake Sauvignon Blanc

STYLE dry
QUALITY ♟♟♟♟
VALUE ★★★

GRAPES
Sauvignon Blanc

REGION Central Otago

CELLAR 🍾 2
PRICE $22–24

Marlborough has got the front running for fiercely aromatic sauvignon blanc, but there are some very good examples coming from forther south – notably Central Otago.

Current Release 2002 It's grassy and faintly sweaty on the nose in the best Marlborough style, but the texture is a little smoother than that of many of its northern cousins. Overall, a fresh-faced savvie with a welcome point of difference. Enjoy it with a prawn and fennel-topped pizza.

Huia Marlborough Sauvignon Blanc

STYLE dry
QUALITY ♟♟♟♟⯪
VALUE ★★★⯪

GRAPES
Sauvignon Blanc

REGION Marlborough

CELLAR 🍾 2
PRICE $20–23

Claire and Mike Allen left some of the fermentation of this white up to the grapes' own natural yeasts, but most of it was the responsibility of laboratory-bred 'tame' models. It was obviously a good combination.

Current Release 2002 It's not as pungent as most Marlborough savvies from the 2002 vintage, and that means it has a touch of elegance about the bouquet. The flavour profile is sweet-fruited and attractive, and the acids add just the right amount of lift through the middle and on the finish. Match it with a prawn and braised fennel salad.

Huntaway Reserve Marlborough Sauvignon Blanc

Just 10% of this wine was fermented in oak barrels and stayed there for two months in contact with the yeast lees left over from fermentation. Those are both techniques usually reserved for chardonnay.
Current Release 2000 The bouquet reminds me of dried mango, a snack to which my wife is seriously addicted. It's rich and sweet-fruited on the palate with the oak making its presence felt in the form of a savoury note right on the finish. The winemaking team suggests enjoying it with seafood paella. Yes!

STYLE **dry**
QUALITY ♆ ♆ ♆ ♆ ♆
VALUE ☆ ☆ ☆
GRAPES
  Sauvignon Blanc
REGION **Marlborough**
CELLAR 🍾 3
PRICE **$20–23**

Huntaway Reserve Marlborough Sémillon

The Huntaway range has been good news for Corbans/ Montana. The wines sell well at retail level, are popular in restaurants, and have picked up quite a few competition awards both here and overseas.
Current Release 1999 I get spicy, savoury notes on the nose, and there's a minerally edge in there as well. It's got good weight and an appealing texture – smooth, but with lots of life around the edge. Overall, it's smart wine that combines well with most shellfish dishes – mussel risotto would be good.

STYLE **dry**
QUALITY ♆ ♆ ♆ ♆ ♆
VALUE ☆ ☆ ☆ ☆
GRAPES **Sémillon**
REGION **Marlborough**
CELLAR 🍾 4
PRICE **$18–20**

Hunter's Sauvignon Blanc

Jane Hunter and her team have played a major part in placing New Zealand wines on the international wine map. This savvie has had tremendous success overseas in its various vintages, going right back to the 1980s.
Current Release 2002 The bouquet is spicy and fresh in the classic Marlborough style. The lively start on the palate had me thinking of apples and lemons, but the fruit sweetness that kicks in toward the finish levels things out nicely. It makes a great partner for butterflied and grilled fresh sardines, sold locally as pilchards.

STYLE **dry**
QUALITY ♆ ♆ ♆
VALUE ☆ ☆ ☆
GRAPES
  Sauvignon Blanc
REGION **Marlborough**
CELLAR 🍾 2
PRICE **$18–20**

Hunter's Winemaker's Selection Sauvignon Blanc

A spell in French oak barrels differentiates this wine from the 'plain' Hunter's savvie. Gary Duke reckons it could be cellared for four or five years. He may well be right, but I've been a bit more conservative.
Current Release 2000 Spicy oak on the nose fits well with the passionfruit-like aromas – in other words, it doesn't dominate. It's quite richly flavoured, full and clean, with acids that are just right for the style. Enjoy it with home-made or Italian imported spaghetti tossed with pipis or tuatua.

STYLE **dry**
QUALITY ♆ ♆ ♆
VALUE ☆ ☆
GRAPES
  Sauvignon Blanc
REGION **Marlborough**
CELLAR 🍾 3
PRICE **$21–23**

Isabel Marlborough Sauvignon Blanc

STYLE **dry**
QUALITY ♟♟♟♟
VALUE ☆☆☆
GRAPES
  Sauvignon Blanc
REGION **Marlborough**

CELLAR ▯ 1
PRICE **$23–25**

This wine has done exceptionally well in overseas taste-offs. A high-powered panel recently voted it the top New Zealand sauvignon in a tasting of 80 examples for the UK's prestigious *Wine* magazine, and awarded it a score of 91 out of 100.

Current Release 2001 The nose is sweaty in the currently approved Marlborough style, with cape gooseberry aromas filling in the gaps. It's smooth-centred on the palate thanks to the smartly integrated acids, and finishes with a pleasant belt of sweet fruit. Enjoy it alongside a brace of barbecued scampi, served drizzled with a little olive oil.

Jackson Estate Sauvignon Blanc

STYLE **dry**
QUALITY ♟♟♟♟♟
VALUE ☆☆☆☆⟨
GRAPES
  Sauvignon Blanc
REGION **Marlborough**

CELLAR ▯ 2
PRICE **$18–21**

John Stichbury is a huge fan of screwcap closures and uses them on his entire range. He would like the slight noise the caps make when they are twisted to be known as 'the click of quality'. Sounds good to me!

Current Release 2002 Steely-edged but pungent on the nose, clean, ripe-fruited and fresh on the palate, this is as good as Marlborough savvie gets. Pour a glass next time you're lucky enough to score some really fresh Bluff oysters, serve them with grainy bread and you'll see what all the fuss is about.

Johanneshof Marlborough Sauvignon Blanc

STYLE **dry**
QUALITY ♟♟♟♟
VALUE ☆☆☆
GRAPES
  Sauvignon Blanc
REGION **Marlborough**

CELLAR ▯ 1
PRICE **$18–20**

Warwick Foley and Edel Everling recently celebrated 10 years of running their tiny Marlborough winery. The property is situated on the Koromiko hillside, nine kilometres south of Picton, and features a wine cellar tunnelled into the hill.

Current Release 2002 The nose is pungent in the current hot-vintage style, but a touch of earthiness sets it a little apart from the bunch. It has nicely focused sweet-edged flavours and a good quota of zingy acids to keep things refreshing. Wait for the season to open and try it with whitebait fritters.

Kaikoura Marlborough Sauvignon Blanc

STYLE **dry**
QUALITY ♟♟♟♟
VALUE ☆☆☆⟨
GRAPES
  Sauvignon Blanc
REGION **Marlborough**

CELLAR ▯ 3
PRICE **$18–20**

The Kaikoura Wine Company was founded by direct descendants of Luke and Anne Abraham, the first European settlers on Kaikoura Flat. The winery is a pleasant place to visit and boasts an impressive cellar.

Current Release 2002 It doesn't sound pleasant, but many Marlborough savvies have aromas that can only be described as 'sweaty', and this is one of them. It's richly fruited on the palate, with guava and dried pineapple flavours edged by invigorating acids. It's good on its own, and goes well with lemon-drizzled chicken schnitzels.

Kaimira Estate Nelson Sauvignon Blanc

Kaimira Estate is one of the newest players on the Nelson wine scene, but its products have made quite a splash in a handful of vintages. Most of the fruit comes from the family's own vineyard, but some grapes are purchased from local growers.

Current Release 2002 Super-pungent on the nose, richly fruited on the palate, this is like Marlborough savvie on steroids. It's a wine with a sunny disposition, good balance and a fresh-faced finish. Enjoy it with crab cakes – made from Nelson crabs, naturally.

STYLE **dry**
QUALITY 🍷🍷🍷🍷🍷
VALUE ☆☆☆☆☆
GRAPES
  Sauvignon Blanc
REGION **Nelson**
CELLAR 1
PRICE **$16–18**

Kemblefield Hawke's Bay Sauvignon Blanc (Signature)

Winemaker and partner John Kemble personally signs the wines in his 'Signature' series. This member of the portfolio was made entirely from his own estate-grown grapes. Some earlier wines used fruit bought from local growers.

Current Release 2002 There's a savoury note in the bouquet behind passionfruit associations. It's smooth on the palate, thanks to the smartly integrated acids, with clean, melon-like flavours and a refreshing finish. Partner it with pork, cubed and casseroled with prunes.

STYLE **dry**
QUALITY 🍷🍷🍷
VALUE ☆☆☆
GRAPES
  Sauvignon Blanc 86%
  Sémillon 14%
REGION **Hawke's Bay**
CELLAR 1
PRICE **$16–18**

Kemblefield The Distinction Hawke's Bay Sauvignon Blanc

John fermented this top-shelf savvie in French oak barrels and left it there in contact with the yeast for five months. Part of the juice was encouraged to undergo a malolactic fermentation. That's common with chardonnay, but rare for sauvignon blanc.

Current Release 2002 There's a spicy edge on the more usual aromas of dried pineapple. It's broad and creamy on the palate, with flavours of ripe apples and tinned guavas. The finish is clean-cut and quite long. It makes a good partner for corn-fed chicken, roasted with a few sage leaves in its cavity.

STYLE **dry**
QUALITY 🍷🍷🍷🍷🍷
VALUE ☆☆☆☆
GRAPES
  Sauvignon Blanc
REGION **Hawke's Bay**
CELLAR 3
PRICE **$20–23**

Kennedy Point Vineyard Marlborough Sauvignon Blanc

STYLE **dry**
QUALITY ♟ ♟ ♟ ♟
VALUE ☆ ☆ ☆ ☆
GRAPES
  Sauvignon Blanc
REGION **Marlborough**

CELLAR 🍷 1
PRICE **$17–20**

The grapes come from Marlborough's pebble-scattered Berakah Estate, but the label owners have a vineyard on Auckland's Waiheke Island. Kennedy Point isn't the only island company to use Marlborough grapes – Goldwater Estate makes Marlborough sauvignon and chardonnay.
Current Release 2001 Suggestions of pineapple and passionfruit give it a classic South Island bouquet. It's fresh-faced and lively on the palate, with citric flavours and a refreshing finish. Partner it with a salad of penne pasta, grilled capsicums and thinly sliced fennel bulb.

Kim Crawford Hawke's Bay Sauvignon Blanc

STYLE **dry**
QUALITY ♟ ♟ ♟ ♟
VALUE ☆ ☆ ☆ ☆
GRAPES
  Sauvignon Blanc 75%
  Sémillon 25%
REGION **Hawke's Bay**

CELLAR 🍷 2
PRICE **$17–20**

Kim Crawford makes two variations on the savvie theme, this one and another using Marlborough fruit. Hawke's Bay savvie doesn't enjoy the international profile of its South Island cousin, but it has a keen following in this country.
Current Release 2002 Hawke's Bay? The bouquet is decidedly Marlborough-like, with grassy, pungent aromas aplenty – must be the sémillon component. It's equally lively and vibrant on the palate, with crisp acids and a super-refreshing finish. It makes a good aperitif, but you could try it with a leek and potato frittata.

Kim Crawford Marlborough Sauvignon Blanc

STYLE **dry**
QUALITY ♟ ♟ ♟ ♟
VALUE ☆ ☆ ☆
GRAPES
  Sauvignon Blanc
REGION **Marlborough**

CELLAR 🍷 2
PRICE **$20–23**

Kim Crawford has used a Stelvin screwcap for some of his wines, but this one is topped by a startlingly black synthetic 'cork'. The fruit came from the Brancott and Wairau Valleys, and five percent of the wine was fermented in new oak barrels.
Current Release 2001 Savoury and complex on the nose, lively and direct on the palate, this is a smartly made savvie with a point of difference from the small amount of oak, plus an acid-softening malolactic fermentation. It boasts loads of rich fruit and makes a good partner for pan-fried chicken pieces with a creamy sauce spiked with chopped fennel.

Konrad & Conrad Marlborough Sauvignon Blanc

STYLE **dry**
QUALITY ♟ ♟ ♟ ♟
VALUE ☆ ☆ ☆
GRAPES
  Sauvignon Blanc
REGION **Marlborough**

CELLAR 🍷 1
PRICE **$19–21**

Konrad & Conrad Hengstler are a father and son team with vineyards in two Marlborough sub-regions, Waihopai Valley (known locally as Spy Valley) and Rapaura. Dad does most of the work – Conrad is not yet into his teens.
Current Release 2001 The nose is pungent in the current Marlborough style, but it's not as over-the-top as some. Sweet fruit makes it a reasonably mouth-filling proposition and smartly integrated acids keep things lively through to the short but pretty finish. Greenshell mussels steamed open in a splash of this wine would do it proud.

Koura Bay Whalesback Awatere Valley Sauvignon Blanc

Geoff and Dianne Smith own the Koura Bay vineyard in Marlborough's Awatere Valley, and their daughters, Kate, Lisa and Megan all play a part in the business. That's the spirit of the New Zealand industry.

Current Release 2002 Sweaty on the nose, lean, clean and focused on the palate, this is a very direct example of the style for which Marlborough has become internationally famous. Place it alongside a plate of freshly shucked rock oysters and enjoy.

STYLE **dry**
QUALITY ▼ ▼ ▼
VALUE ☆ ☆ ⯪
GRAPES **Sauvignon Blanc**
REGION **Marlborough**
CELLAR 1
PRICE **$19–23**

Lake Chalice Sauvignon Blanc

This is one of the few wines on the market finished with a black plastic stopper – it certainly makes for a talking point at the dinner table! The grapes came from the company's own Falcon vineyard and a couple of other sites nearby.

Current Release 2002 Pungent and clean on the nose, straightforward and approachable on the palate, this is a very direct and pleasant example of the local style. It finishes a bit short, but that's no big deal with savvie. Partner it with pan-fried gurnard fillets and relax.

STYLE **dry**
QUALITY ▼ ▼ ▼ ⯑
VALUE ☆ ☆ ☆ ⯪
GRAPES **Sauvignon Blanc**
REGION **Marlborough**
CELLAR 1
PRICE **$16–19**

Lake Hayes Sauvignon Blanc

There aren't many blends of Marlborough and Central Otago wine, but this one works well, so perhaps other producers will try it. Just eight percent spent a bit of time in older oak barrels, but they had very little effect on the final flavour.

Current Release 2001 The nose is uncharacteristically subdued, at least by the standards of this exuberant variety. However, there's nothing subdued about the flavour. It's deliciously ripe-fruited and has acids that are perfectly in tune with the style. Penne pasta tossed with chopped garlic, blanched broccoli and 'melted' anchovies works well.

STYLE **dry**
QUALITY ▼ ▼ ▼ ▼
VALUE ☆ ☆ ☆
GRAPES **Sauvignon Blanc**
REGION **Marlborough Central Otago**
CELLAR 1
PRICE **$20–23**

Lawson's Dry Hills Marlborough Sauvignon Blanc

Mike Just fermented a small proportion of the juice for this upfront savvie in French oak barrels and allowed it to go through an acid-softening malolactic fermentation. US writer Dan Berger recently described it as 'superb'.

Current Release 2002 You want to know about Marlborough pungency? Smell this! The nose is absolutely classic, and the fruit characters are sweet-edged and rich. Focused in the middle and chunky on the finish, it makes a great match for potato gnocchi with asparagus spears and pine nuts.

STYLE **dry**
QUALITY ▼ ▼ ▼ ▼ ⯑
VALUE ☆ ☆ ☆ ⯪
GRAPES **Sauvignon Blanc**
REGION **Marlborough**
CELLAR 2
PRICE **$19–24**

Le Grys Marlborough Sauvignon Blanc

STYLE **dry**
QUALITY ♥ ♥ ♥
VALUE ★ ★ ★ ☆

GRAPES
  Sauvignon Blanc
REGION **Marlborough**

CELLAR 🍾 3
PRICE **$19–21**

About 15% of this wine was fermented in two-year-old French oak barrels, and 30% was encouraged to undergo an acid-softening malolactic fermentation. The fruit came from both the Awatere and Wairau Valleys.
Current Release 2001 The oak has added an attractively spicy edge to the perfumed bouquet. It's ripe, rich and smartly balanced on the palate, with typical passionfruit characters saving themselves for the finish. Enjoy it with penne pasta tossed while it's steaming hot with grated Parmesan, olive oil and a raw egg yolk.

Lincoln Heritage Collection Lukrica Marlborough Sauvignon Blanc

STYLE **dry**
QUALITY ♥ ♥ ♥ ♡
VALUE ★ ★ ★

GRAPES
  Sauvignon Blanc
REGION **Marlborough**

CELLAR 🍾 1
PRICE **$19–21**

This savvie is named for the founder's wife, Lukrica Fredatovich. Many Marlborough savvies carry just a wee bit of residual sugar to lift the fruit, but not this one – the winemaking team reckoned the fruit was so good it was made bone-dry.
Current Release 2002 There's a whack of old-style grassiness behind the melon aromas in the bouquet. It's reasonably rich on the palate, with vibrant acids and overall good balance. Partner it with zucchini, halved lengthwise, sprinkled with good Parmesan and grilled.

Lincoln Winemaker's Series Sauvignon Blanc

STYLE **dry**
QUALITY ♥ ♥ ♥ ♡
VALUE ★ ★ ★ ★

GRAPES
  Sauvignon Blanc
REGION **Waikato**

CELLAR 🍾
PRICE **$14–16**

Many savvie producers are turning to screwcap closures, but the Lincoln team used bright blue plastic stoppers for this member of their range. My advice? Drink up – plastic doesn't seem to keep the wine as well as corks or screwcaps.
Current Release 2002 I like the rich, grainy notes in the bouquet – this is savvie with a bit of grunt. It's a little creamier than most on the palate but remains pretty well focused through to the clean-cut finish. Smoked fish fritters should match it well.

Linden Estate Hawke's Bay Sauvignon Blanc

STYLE **dry**
QUALITY ♥ ♥ ♥ ♡
VALUE ★ ★ ★

GRAPES
  Sauvignon Blanc
REGION **Hawke's Bay**

CELLAR 🍾 1
PRICE **$18–20**

It's pretty hard to find because a big percentage is exported, but it's on sale at the cellar door and on a handful of restaurant wine lists. Linden Estate is currently going through some pretty major rebuilding.
Current Release 2000 Pineapple and dried pears sound more like Marlborough than Hawke's Bay, but there are plenty of both in the bouquet. It's soft-centred but nicely focused on the palate, and finishes cleanly. We discovered it goes well with lamb, but the trick is to cube the meat and cook it in a splash of the wine, then add the juice of half a lemon five minutes before it finishes cooking.

Lombardi Barrel Fermented Sauvignon Blanc

Fermenting savvie in oak has fallen from favour in recent years, but the Lombardi team believes it suits their fruit. Barrels played host to 40% of the juice for this model, but only a few of them were new.
Current Release 2000 The oak treatment has softened savvie's usual exuberance on the nose and left a decidedly citric impression. It's creamy on the palate, ripe-fruited and gentle but with crisp acids. Pork and fennel sausages arranged over a generous pile of mashed spuds would be the go here.

STYLE **dry**
QUALITY ▽▽▽▽
VALUE ☆☆☆☆
GRAPES **Sauvignon Blanc**
REGION **Hawke's Bay**
CELLAR 🍾 **2**
PRICE **$18–20**

Lombardi Hawke's Bay Sauvignon Blanc

Lombardi produces two savvies – this one, fermented in stainless steel, and another that spends some time in oak. Both are popular buys at good wine shops and in the Hawke's Bay restaurants that list them.
Current Release 2001 The pungent nose suggests Marlborough, but the sweet-edged, well-rounded fruit is pure Hawke's Bay. The winemaking team used quite a lot of skin contact to get all the flavour they could, and it worked well. Enjoy it alongside Chinese-style wok-fried fish with ginger and spring onions.

STYLE **dry**
QUALITY ▽▽▽▽
VALUE ☆☆☆
GRAPES **Sauvignon Blanc**
REGION **Hawke's Bay**
CELLAR 🍾 **1**
PRICE **$19–21**

Longridge Hawke's Bay Sauvignon Blanc

Longridge is a long-time Corbans brand, and rumours were rife that it would disappear once the company was absorbed by Montana. Not so – the label has been tidied up, and the wines are as popular as ever.
Current Release 2002 Wow – feijoas. That's the overriding impression on the nose, along with a bit of more traditional cut grass. It's sweet-fruited and smooth on the palate but with a keen edge to ensure a lively finish. Pull the cork next time you're pan-frying a tarakihi fillet or two.

STYLE **dry**
QUALITY ▽▽▽▽
VALUE ☆☆☆☆
GRAPES **Sauvignon Blanc**
REGION **Hawke's Bay**
CELLAR 🍾 **1**
PRICE **$15–17**

Lynskeys Wairau Peaks Marlborough Sauvignon Blanc

This was the first year of production for most of the grapes that went into this clean-cut savvie. The fruit was all harvested by hand, giving the pickers the opportunity to discard any bunches that weren't considered up to scratch.
Current Release 2001 The bouquet is savoury and faintly nutty, although the wine has seen no oak. There are certainly no distracting influences on the palate – it's clean, focused and very direct, with lively acids ensuring vibrancy right through to the finish. A sandwich made from chopped mussels and home-made mayonnaise would be good.

STYLE **dry**
QUALITY ▽▽▽▽
VALUE ☆☆☆
GRAPES **Sauvignon Blanc**
REGION **Marlborough**
CELLAR 🍾
PRICE **$18–20**

Main Divide Canterbury Sauvignon Blanc

STYLE **dry**

QUALITY ☐☐☐☐

VALUE ☆☆☆☆

GRAPES
Sauvignon Blanc

REGION **Canterbury**

CELLAR **1**

PRICE **$17–19**

Main Divide is the name used by many South Islanders for the Southern Alps, and favoured by Pegasus Bay's Donaldson family for a range of well-priced wines. Most people release sauvignon blanc early, but this one was held back.
Current Release 2001 The bouquet is savoury and funky, and evokes thoughts of crushed parsley and sage. It's lively on the palate, but a touch of creaminess through the middle gives it more depth than many of the genre. It's good with firm-fleshed fish fillets, pressed with chopped herbs and pan-fried.

Martinborough Vineyard Sauvignon Blanc

STYLE **dry**

QUALITY ☐☐☐☐

VALUE ☆☆☆☆

GRAPES
Sauvignon Blanc 97%
Sémillon 3%

REGION **Martinborough**

CELLAR **2**

PRICE **$20–23**

The 3% sémillon component was fermented in oak barrels. On the face of it, that would hardly seem enough to make a difference, but the winemaking team obviously thought it would. I won't argue – it's smart wine.
Current Release 2001 Fresh-faced in the bouquet, minerally and melon-like on the palate, this is a nicely balanced wine with very direct flavours. The variety's usual acids are certainly in evidence, but they are integrated well enough to act as background accessories to the ripe fruit. Enjoy it alongside traditional fish and chips from a serious retailer.

Matakana Estate Sémillon

STYLE **dry**

QUALITY ☐☐☐☐

VALUE ☆☆☆

GRAPES **Sémillon**

REGION **Matakana**

CELLAR **3**

PRICE **$22–24**

The sémillon grapes destined to be transformed into this classy white were left hanging longer than they were in '99, then picked in stages. The aim was to harvest only the ripest bunches each time.
Current Release 2000 Straw, green capsicums and a suggestion of ripe apples make for an appealing bouquet. It's nicely focused, with a smooth texture and quite rich flavours but enough acid lift to ensure it stays refreshing. The winemaking team suggests partnering it with seared crayfish tail and a mango/citrus salsa. Oh YES!

Matariki Reserve Sauvignon Blanc

STYLE **dry**

QUALITY ☐☐☐☐☐

VALUE ☆☆☆

GRAPES
Sauvignon Blanc 90%
Sémillon 10%

REGION **Hawke's Bay**

CELLAR **2**

PRICE **$25–28**

John O'Connor fermented just 30% of the juice for his top-shelf savvie in French oak barrels, leaving the rest in stainless steel. He also made an unoaked version, but it all went to the US.
Current Release 2000 The oak has added a savoury note to the aromas of ripe passionfruit and pineapple. It's nicely balanced, rich and quite complex, and boasts a long, savoury finish. It works well with slightly flattened and crumbed chicken breasts.

Matawhero Reserve Sauvignon Blanc

Conventional wisdom has it that sauvignon blanc is best enjoyed in its youth, but Denis Irwin has never been one to follow convention. This is his latest release, and he's proved his point – it's tasting pretty good.

Current Release 1999 I thought I detected a dash of dusty oak on the nose, but apparently it has seen only the inside of a stainless-steel tank. It's fresh despite its age, with clean fruit and a certain amount of elegance. It would be good with mushrooms, pan-fried with plenty of parsley and finished with a cream-based sauce.

STYLE **dry**
QUALITY ♟♟♟♟
VALUE ☆☆☆
GRAPES
  Sauvignon Blanc
REGION **Hawke's Bay**
CELLAR 2
PRICE **$20–23**

Matua Valley Hawke's Bay Sauvignon Blanc

Mark Robertson reports that 2002 was cooler and wetter than normal around the vineyards that gave him the grapes for this big-selling savvie. He compensated by leaving them on the vine longer once the sun finally came out.

Current Release 2002 There's a wee dash of spice behind the aromas of cape gooseberries and kiwifruit. It's quite broad on the palate, giving it a creamier texture than many of the genre. All in all, a very approachable wine with good balance between freshness and depth. Mark suggests cold or hot soup made from fresh green peas as a partner. Sounds good!

STYLE **dry**
QUALITY ♟♟♟♟
VALUE ☆☆☆☆
GRAPES
  Sauvignon Blanc
REGION **Hawke's Bay**
CELLAR 2
PRICE **$16–18**

Matua Valley Matheson Vineyard Hawke's Bay Sauvignon Blanc

Most sauvignon blanc in this country is pressed, fermented and bottled with as little fuss as possible, but this one gets all the drama. Mark Robertson ferments it in oak barrels and puts 20% through a malolactic fermentation.

Current Release 2002 There's a pleasantly savoury note on the nose – think muesli and you'll be close. Ripe fruit powers its way through the gentle oak characters on the palate, giving an overall impression of lusciousness bordered by crisp acids. Mark likes it with sashimi . . . what a wise lad!

STYLE **dry**
QUALITY ♟♟♟♟♟
VALUE ☆☆☆☆½
GRAPES
  Sauvignon Blanc
REGION **Hawke's Bay**
CELLAR 3
PRICE **$18–20**

Mebus Sauvignon Blanc

Michael and Hidde Mebus have one ambition – to produce a glass of wine that the customer wishes will never empty. They searched high and low for the perfect vineyard site, and believe they found it in Dakins Road, Wairarapa.

Current Release 2001 Fresh and fruity but a little softer than examples from further south, this savvie has its own appeal. The bouquet has suggestions of pineapple and melon, and the flavours are ripe and generous. It makes an excellent companion for greenshell mussels, simply steamed open and served 'as is'.

STYLE **dry**
QUALITY ♟♟♟♟
VALUE ☆☆☆
GRAPES
  Sauvignon Blanc
REGION **Wairarapa**
CELLAR 1
PRICE **$20–22**

Mills Reef Hawke's Bay Sauvignon Blanc

STYLE **dry**

QUALITY 🍷 🍷 🍷 🍷

VALUE ☆ ☆ ☆ ☆

GRAPES
Sauvignon Blanc

REGION Hawke's Bay

CELLAR 🍾 1

PRICE $15–18

Like many sauvignon blanc producers, Paddy and Tim Preston leave a wee bit of residual sugar in their savvies. It's not enough to kick it out of the dry category, but it gives the fruit a wee bit of a lift in the middle and on the finish.

Current Release 2002 It leans more to citric fruit on the nose than the passionfruit and pineapples often associated with the variety, but that's fine with me. It's lively, well focused and very refreshing, and makes a good partner for an omelette served alongside braised baby fennel.

Mills Reef Reserve Sauvignon Blanc

STYLE **dry**

QUALITY 🍷 🍷 🍷 🍷 🍷

VALUE ☆ ☆ ☆ ☆

GRAPES
Sauvignon Blanc

REGION Hawke's Bay

CELLAR 🍾 3

PRICE $19–22

The Mills Reef winery is in Katikati, near Tauranga, but Paddy Preston and his winemaking team draw all their grapes from Hawke's Bay. This savvie spent a few months in French oak barrels, so in the past it would have been called fumé blanc.

Current Release 2001 The oak hasn't done anything to subdue the pungent, tropical fruit aromas, but it has softened the texture a little. The overall effect is of richness and balance through the middle and on the refreshing finish. Tarakihi fillets, crumbed and shallow-fried, would suit it well.

Moana Park Sauvignon Blanc

STYLE **dry**

QUALITY 🍷 🍷 🍷 🍷

VALUE ☆ ☆ ☆ ☆

GRAPES
Sauvignon Blanc

REGION Hawke's Bay

CELLAR 🍾 1

PRICE $15–18

Ron Smith and Gay Robertson seem to have just about every grape variety known to mankind growing in their Dartmoor Valley property. No doubt they will eventually work out which styles do best in their particular part of the Bay.

Current Release 2001 The nose is subtle but pleasant enough, with a whisper of passionfruit behind impressions of straw. It's got a good quota of ripe fruit on the palate balanced by nicely integrated acids that add lift to the finish. Enjoy it with a salad based around sliced fennel bulb, cucumber and radishes.

Montana 'B' Brancott Estate Marlborough Sauvignon Blanc

STYLE **dry**

QUALITY 🍷 🍷 🍷 🍷 🍷

VALUE ☆ ☆ ☆

GRAPES
Sauvignon Blanc

REGION Marlborough

CELLAR 🍾 2

PRICE $26–28

This smartly packaged wine from Montana is proof in a bottle that sauvignon blanc can be serious. The fruit is picked super-ripe and the juice spends time in French oak barrels to add depth and complexity. The result is pure class.

Current Release 2001 The toasty, spicy notes behind the ripe fruit aromas give immediate notice that this is different from most Marlborough savvies. The oak has given it a creamy texture, but there are enough natural acids to ensure life and zing through to the lingering finish. Its perfect match would be half a grilled crayfish drizzled with lemon butter.

Montana Gisborne Sémillon

Some producers make sémillon like sauvignon blanc, with fermentation in stainless steel, but Brent Laidlaw likes to give his 'just a touch' of oak. The fruit came from the Patutahi district, which is also the source of Montana's super-flash 'P' gewürztraminer.
Current Release 2001 I get lime juice and honeydew melon on the nose – the oak is nowhere to be found. It's dry, crisp and very refreshing on the palate, with nicely balanced acids and a lively finish. It makes a good partner for rock oysters served straight from the shell and sprinkled with nothing but cracked pepper.

STYLE **dry**
QUALITY ♟ ♟ ♟ ♟
VALUE ☆ ☆ ☆ ☆ ⯪
GRAPES
   Sémillon 98%
   Sauvignon Blanc 2%
REGION **Gisborne**
CELLAR ▯ 3
PRICE **$14–16**

Montana Marlborough Sauvignon Blanc

Montana sells many container-loads of this sauvignon to the UK each year, but winemaker Jeff Clarke says they could always do with more – despite the company's huge vineyard holdings.
Current Release 2002 Boy – talk about grassy! Picking the grapes over a three-week period gave this big-selling savvie old-style cutting aromas and a high-acid, lively flavour profile in its extreme youth, but it should have settled down by now. Pull the cork next time you're having rock oysters.

STYLE **dry**
QUALITY ♟ ♟ ♟
VALUE ☆ ☆ ☆
GRAPES
   Sauvignon Blanc
REGION **Marlborough**
CELLAR ▯ 2
PRICE **$16–18**

Montana Reserve Marlborough Vineyard Selection Sauvignon Blanc

Patrick Materman sourced most of the fruit for this top-shelf savvie from the company's Brancott Estate vineyard, home to the Marlborough Food & Wine Festival each year, but some came from the nearby Squire vineyard.
Current Release 2002 Guavas, muesli, perhaps a suggestion of feijoa – it all happens in the bouquet. Creaminess isn't a character often associated with savvie, but that's definitely the texture of this fine example. It works because the fruit remains focused and the finish is delightfully fresh and clean. We enjoyed ours with a pâté made from salmon and scallops. Yum!

STYLE **dry**
QUALITY ♟ ♟ ♟ ♟ ♟
VALUE ☆ ☆ ☆ ☆
GRAPES
   Sauvignon Blanc
REGION **Marlborough**
CELLAR ▯ 2
PRICE **$20–23**

Morton Estate Hawke's Bay Sauvignon Blanc (White Label)

Morton Estate has done well with both the Hawke's Bay and Marlborough white label versions of sauvignon blanc over the last few vintages. They deserve their success – they're smartly made and very well priced.
Current Release 2002 The bouquet put me in mind of muesli, with a grainy edge, so the creamy, smooth-textured flavour profile was something of a surprise. It's a very approachable savvie, nicely balanced and easy to drink. It goes well with tuatua fritters drizzled with home-made mayonnaise.

STYLE **dry**
QUALITY ♟ ♟ ♟ ♟
VALUE ☆ ☆ ☆ ⯪
GRAPES
   Sauvignon Blanc
REGION **Hawke's Bay**
CELLAR ▯ 1
PRICE **$15–17**

Morton Estate Marlborough Sauvignon Blanc (White Label)

STYLE **dry**

QUALITY ▼ ▼ ▼

VALUE ☆ ☆ ☆

GRAPES
   Sauvignon Blanc

REGION **Marlborough**

CELLAR 1

PRICE **$16–18**

One of the better-priced Marlborough sauvignons on the market, this well-made white is a popular 'by the glass' choice for restaurants around the country. It has picked up a few awards in its various vintages.

Current Release 2002 It's got all the right kiwifruit and cape gooseberry aromas and lively, clean-cut flavours, with a dash of natural sweetness on the finish. It's a very refreshing wine that should find many friends. Try it with pan-fried gurnard fillets with the skin left on so it crisps up in the oil.

Mount Nelson Marlborough Sauvignon Blanc

STYLE **dry**

QUALITY ▼ ▼ ▼ ▼

VALUE ☆ ☆ ☆

GRAPES
   Sauvignon Blanc

REGION
   Marlborough 80%
   Waipara 20%

CELLAR 6

PRICE **$30–33**

Waipara wine magician Danny Schuster makes this wine for Marchese Antinori, an Italian wine producer, using classical European techniques. There's not a lot of it about, but it's well worth a serious search.

Current Release 2001 The pungent nose lets us know it's a New Zealand savvie, but the cracked wheat characters imparted from stirring the yeast lees left over from fermentation gives it a different twist. It's deliciously creamy on the palate, with ripe fruit flavours drifting onto a long finish. It's great with a pile of mussel fritters.

Mud House Wines Marlborough Sauvignon Blanc

STYLE **dry**

QUALITY ▼ ▼ ▼ ▼

VALUE ☆ ☆ ☆

GRAPES
   Sauvignon Blanc

REGION **Marlborough**

CELLAR 1

PRICE **$19–21**

With a residual sugar level of 4g/l, this savvie just squeezes into the 'dry' category. Leaving in a touch of sweetness is common practice with this variety. Proponents of the technique believe it gives the fruit a 'lift'.

Current Release 2002 The nose is perfumed and typically pungent, with suggestions of dried pineapple chunks and golden kiwifruit. The sweetness is quite evident on the palate, but lively acids do their best to keep things under control. Partner it with similarly sweet-edged food, like a Thai-style chicken salad.

Murdoch James Sauvignon Blanc

STYLE **dry**

QUALITY ▼ ▼ ▼ ▼

VALUE ☆ ☆ ☆

GRAPES
   Sauvignon Blanc

REGION **Martinborough**

CELLAR 2

PRICE **$22–24**

Martinborough is known as pinot country, but that's not to say white varieties don't perform well within its boundaries. Sauvignon blanc, in particular, seems to be very happy indeed with the local soil and climate. Watch out Marlborough!

Current Release 2002 This classy little number has savoury notes to go with the typical pungency on the bouquet and a flavour structure that luxuriates in sweet fruit. Typically varietal acids save themselves for a lively, refreshing finish. Classy stuff! It's the ultimate vegetable wine. Enjoy it with char-grilled courgettes, asparagus and eggplant.

Nautilus Marlborough Sauvignon Blanc

The Nautilus brand is owned by Yalumba of Australia, but operates as pretty much a stand-alone entity in this country. Twin Islands is a second label, but its wines occasionally do better in competitions.

Current Release 2002 Sweaty in the modern way, but with attractive passionfruit aromas filling in the gaps, this is typical of the region. It's clean and fresh in the flavour department and a little smoother than some as it drifts towards the finish. Try it with poached chicken breasts over couscous flavoured with preserved lemon.

STYLE **dry**
QUALITY ♟♟♟♟
VALUE ☆☆☆⯪
GRAPES **Sauvignon Blanc**
REGION **Marlborough**
CELLAR 🍶 **1**
PRICE **$19–21**

Neudorf Nelson Sauvignon Blanc

Past versions of Tim and Judy Finn's fresh-faced savvie have been made from Marlborough fruit, but in 2002 they used the first crop from their Brightwater vineyard and the second from another site in Motueka.

Current Release 2002 Think sliced mango, dried pineapple and a spoonful of passionfruit and you'll have the bouquet sussed. Lively but unassertive acids give it plenty of zing to go with the tropical fruit flavours and drift on to ensure a clean, lifted finish. It makes a great aperitif, but it's also good with salmon-based fish cakes.

STYLE **dry**
QUALITY ♟♟♟♟♟
VALUE ☆☆☆⯪
GRAPES **Sauvignon Blanc**
REGION **Nelson**
CELLAR 🍶 **2**
PRICE **$23–26**

Nga Waka Martinborough Sauvignon Blanc

When it comes to international press coverage of sauvignon blanc, Marlborough gets screeds more column centimetres than any other region. Fact is, the variety also does exceptionally well in Martinborough.

Current Release 2002 The bouquet is super-pungent, echoing the Marlborough style, but it has more mid-palate depth than many examples from further south. The fruit is fresh, the texture clean and lively and the finish invigorating. It goes really well with a salad of rocket leaves and just a few chunks of crayfish drizzled with really good olive oil.

STYLE **dry**
QUALITY ♟♟♟♟♟
VALUE ☆☆☆⯪
GRAPES **Sauvignon Blanc**
REGION **Martinborough**
CELLAR 🍶 **2**
PRICE **$25–27**

Ngatarawa Stables Hawke's Bay Sauvignon Blanc

Frost wiped out large parts of the Ngatarawa vineyard in November 2000, which meant there was no Stables savvie made in 2001. In 2002, things were looking good – but then the chardonnay was hit.

Current Release 2002 There's a wee touch of mealiness on the nose to go with the usual sauvignon raft of cape gooseberry and fiejoa aromas. It's decidedly sassy on the palate, with very direct flavours and a faintly grassy finish. Partner it with triangles of pita bread, crisped in the oven and served alongside smoked fish pâté.

STYLE **dry**
QUALITY ♟♟♟
VALUE ☆☆☆
GRAPES **Sauvignon Blanc**
REGION **Hawke's Bay**
CELLAR 🍶 **1**
PRICE **$15–17**

Nobilo Marlborough Sauvignon Blanc

STYLE off-dry
QUALITY 🍷 🍷 🍷 🍷 🍷
VALUE ☆ ☆ ☆ ☆ ☆
GRAPES
  Sauvignon Blanc
REGION Marlborough

CELLAR 🍾 2
PRICE $17—20

You want to know why the world is raving about sauvignon blanc from Marlborough? This one, the latest effort from the talented Darryl Woolley, is an absolutely classic example of the fresh-faced and lively local style.
Current Release 2002 It's got the oft-discussed 'sweat' on the nose, but it's not excessive and doesn't crowd out the passionfruit and dried pineapple aromas. It's the texture that makes it a winner in my book. It's undeniably smooth, but it has enough acid in reserve to keep it refreshing from go to whoa. Freshly steamed Marlborough Sounds mussels are perfect with it.

Okahu Estate Shipwreck Bay Sauvignon Blanc

STYLE dry
QUALITY 🍷 🍷 🍷
VALUE ☆ ☆ ☆ ☆
GRAPES
  Sauvignon Blanc
REGION Waikato

CELLAR 🍾 1
PRICE $16—18

Okahu Estate is in Northland, but Ben Morris used fruit from Te Kauwhata, in the Waikato, to craft the winery's first-ever sauvignon blanc. The plan is for it to replace sémillon, which has been part of the range in the past.
Current Release 2002 There's a touch of Marlborough-style 'sweat' on the nose, along with a pleasant graininess. It's lively and very direct on the palate, and boasts a reasonable quota of sweet fruit through to the short but pleasant finish. It would go well with Northland rock oysters, ideally freshly shucked.

Omaka Springs Marlborough Sauvignon Blanc

STYLE dry
QUALITY 🍷 🍷 🍷 🍷
VALUE ☆ ☆ ☆ ☆
GRAPES
  Sauvignon Blanc 90%
  Sémillon 10%
REGION Marlborough

CELLAR 🍾 1
PRICE $17—19

Adding a touch of sémillon to the blend isn't as popular with sauvignon blanc producers as it was a few years ago, but it paid off for the Omaka Springs team. The wine has won a couple of silver medals and quite a few multi-star recommendations.
Current Release 2001 The bouquet is spicy and complex, with suggestions of passionfruit and grapefruit juice. It's broadly focused but with a crisp, clean edge and boasts a long, smooth finish. It goes well with a goat cheese tart, served with a simple green salad.

Oyster Bay Marlborough Sauvignon Blanc

STYLE dry
QUALITY 🍷 🍷 🍷 🍷 🍷
VALUE ☆ ☆ ☆ ☆
GRAPES
  Sauvignon Blanc
REGION Marlborough

CELLAR 🍾 2
PRICE $17—19

The fruit for this big-selling savvie all came from the Wairau Valley, an area that is rapidly becoming wall-to-wall vineyards. It is a classic example of the regional style that sells like hot cakes in the UK.
Current Release 2001 Blimey – talk about passionfruit! There's a tonne of it on the nose, with no more than a suggestion of red capsicum to keep it company. The flavours are rich and ripe-fruited, and the acids know their place. Enjoy it with pan-fried flounder drizzled with just a little fresh lime juice and good olive oil.

Palliser Estate Sauvignon Blanc

This stylish savvie has done extremely well for Palliser, beating Marlborough wines in several competitive situations. The 2001 vintage was served to Business Class passengers on Cathay Pacific aircraft.
Current Release 2002 It's got a fair whack of Marlborough-style pungency on the nose, but it gives an impression of aromatic crispness. The flavour profile is fresh, lively and suggestive of tropical fruit like pineapple and melon. Keep that in mind and try it with Prince melon wedges wrapped in prosciutto ham.

STYLE **dry**
QUALITY ♔ ♔ ♔ ♔ ♔
VALUE ☆ ☆ ☆ ☆
GRAPES
  Sauvignon Blanc
REGION **Martinborough**
CELLAR ▯ **2**
PRICE **$22–24**

Pegasus Bay Sauvignon/Sémillon

The Donaldsons spent a lot of time on this blend. The juice stayed on the yeast lees left over from fermentation for nine months, with the sémillon component in used oak barrels during that time.
Current Release 2001 There's no more than a hint of oak spice in the bouquet – mostly, the wine speaks of passionfruit and cape gooseberries. The flavour is impressively rich and the balance near-perfect. The acids certainly make their presence felt, but that should help it to age. Put it away somewhere quiet, then try it with braised rabbit.

STYLE **dry**
QUALITY ♔ ♔ ♔ ♔
VALUE ☆ ☆ ☆
GRAPES
  **Sauvignon Blanc
  Sémillon**
REGION **Waipara**
CELLAR ▭ **1–7**
PRICE **$24–26**

Pencarrow Martinborough Sauvignon Blanc

The vines from which Palliser Estate's Alan Johnson and Sharon Goldsworthy get fruit for this second-label savvie are younger than those used for the top-shelf Palliser version, and they are usually allowed to give bigger crops.
Current Release 2002 It's pungent on the nose in the approved manner and refreshingly clean on the palate. You want flavour associations? Think rock melon and passionfruit. We enjoyed ours with a steaming bowl of freshly opened greenshell mussels, and were very pleased with ourselves.

STYLE **dry**
QUALITY ♔ ♔ ♔ ♔ ♔
VALUE ☆ ☆ ☆ ☆ ☆
GRAPES
  Sauvignon Blanc
REGION **Martinborough**
CELLAR ▯ **1**
PRICE **$19–21**

Peregrine Central Otago Sauvignon Blanc

The grapes for this wine came from a single site in Rafters Road, Gibbston. Central Otago isn't particularly well known for sauvignon blanc, but the grape obviously does well there. The style is popular with tourists visiting Queenstown.
Current Release 2001 Think freshly cut Pacific Rose apples with a spoonful of passionfruit pulp and you've got the bouquet. It's full-flavoured, with a creamy texture kept in check by lively acids, especially on the finish. Crumbed and shallow-fried Greenshell mussels suit it well.

STYLE **dry**
QUALITY ♔ ♔ ♔ ♔
VALUE ☆ ☆ ☆
GRAPES
  Sauvignon Blanc
REGION **Central Otago**
CELLAR ▯
PRICE **$19–22**

Ponder Estate Marlborough Chardonnay

STYLE dry

QUALITY ♟ ♟ ♟ ♟

VALUE ☆ ☆ ☆

GRAPES
Sauvignon Blanc

REGION Marlborough

CELLAR 2

PRICE $18–20

Lightly oaked but given a full acid-softening malolactic fermentation, this clean-cut Marlborough chardonnay was recently given a four-star rating by the *Wine Star* magazine tasting panel.

Current Release 2000 Oak spice sits behind the melon skin aromas on the bouquet. It leans more towards the stonefruit end of the spectrum on the palate, with keen but integrated acids putting an edge on the impression of ripe peaches. Use it as an accompaniment to crusty bread and a dipping bowl of Ponder Estate olive oil.

Quarry Road Sauvignon Blanc

STYLE dry

QUALITY ♟ ♟ ♟ ♟ ♟

VALUE ☆ ☆ ☆ ☆ ☆

GRAPES
Sauvignon Blanc

REGION Te Kauwhata

CELLAR 2

PRICE $16–18

Toby Cooper and Jenny Gander are determined to raise the profile of their winemaking region. It undoubtedly has the right history – grapes have been grown in and around Te Kauwhata for many years.

Current Release 2002 The bouquet is quite gentle, certainly compared to Marlborough examples, but there are some pleasant citrus and apple aromas in there. It's fresh, clean and lively on the palate and boasts immaculate balance. It would be perfect with pan-fried chicken breasts smeared with basil pesto just before they are served.

Rippon Sauvignon Blanc

STYLE dry

QUALITY ♟ ♟ ♟ ♟

VALUE ☆ ☆ ☆

GRAPES
Sauvignon Blanc

REGION Central Otago

CELLAR 3

PRICE $23–25

Lois and the late Rolfe Mills were Central Otago pioneers. Their son, Nick, has spent the last few years living in Burgundy and working with some of that region's great wine properties. Now, he's back at the family winery.

Current Release 2001 Citric and only faintly pungent, this savvie has more initial character than most. It's fresh, clean and crisp on the palate, but with a little more depth than many more northern examples. It works wonderfully well alongside a bowl of fettucine tossed with chopped spring vegetables.

Rippon Sauvignon Blanc/Sémillon

STYLE dry

QUALITY ♟ ♟ ♟ ♟

VALUE ☆ ☆ ☆

GRAPES
Sauvignon Blanc 74%
Sémillon 26%

REGION Central Otago

CELLAR 3

PRICE $22–24

In past vintages, Rippon has produced a straight sauvignon blanc, but in 2000 Russell Lake decided to add sémillon to the mix and to mature around 40% of the juice in oak barrels.

Current Release 2000 The nose has a Marlborough sort of pungency, but the texture on the palate is super-crisp in the best Central Otago style. It's a clean, well-focused wine that has to be one of the great partners for Bluff oysters, served with a hearty pile of grainy bread.

Robard & Butler Sauvignon Blanc

Corbans' Robard & Butler label used to be best known for port-style fortifieds, but since the company has been absorbed by Montana it is now worn by a bunch of cheap-and-cheerful table wines mostly seen gracing supermarket trolleys.

Current Release 2002 Think cape gooseberries marinated in lime juice and you've got close to the bouquet. It's simple, clean and very lively on the palate, with a refreshing finish. Use it as an easy-going hot-day sipper with a platter of summer nibbles.

STYLE **dry**
QUALITY ♟ ♟ ♟
VALUE ☆ ☆ ☆ ☆ ☆
GRAPES
   Sauvignon Blanc
REGION **Chile**
CELLAR 🍶
PRICE **$11–13**

Ruben Hall Sauvignon Blanc

The fruit is mostly from Gisborne, but a little bit of Hawke's Bay juice was blended in with the aim of fattening things out. It's one of very few savvies selling for $10, or even less at some outlets.

Current Release (non-vintage) The nose is grassy – just what we all used to love! There's some sweet fruit on the palate, but it smacks more of residual sugar than great grapes. Still, for the price, who's complaining? It makes a perfectly acceptable pre-barbie aperitif.

STYLE **dry**
QUALITY ♟ ♟ ♟
VALUE ☆ ☆ ☆ ☆
GRAPES
   Sauvignon Blanc
REGION **Gisborne**
      Hawke's Bay
CELLAR 🍶
PRICE **$10–12**

Sacred Hill Marlborough Sauvignon Blanc

Winemaker Tony Bish atrranged for his Marlborough savvie grapes to be picked at night because he wanted them to stay cool. The tank in which they were fermented was chilled for the same reason.

Current Release 2002 The nose has more complexity than is often evident with the upfront Marlborough style. Cut grass and cape gooseberry aromas mix with a touch of spice. There's plenty of rich fruit on the palate, but lively acids are on hand to keep things in proportion. It's smart wine that I like with a sliced chicken and fennel salad.

STYLE **dry**
QUALITY ♟ ♟ ♟ ♟
VALUE ☆ ☆ ☆
GRAPES
   Sauvignon Blanc
REGION **Marlborough**
CELLAR 🍶 2
PRICE **$20–22**

Sacred Hill Sauvage Sauvignon Blanc

The Sacred Hill team pioneered this savvie way back in 1992. Tony Bish arranges for the fruit to be hand-picked, presses it as whole bunches then ferments the juice in new and one-year-old French barrels, using wild yeasts rather than laboratory-bred models. It stays in oak for a year.

Current Release 2001 The bouquet is complex and savoury, with dried citrus fruits sitting at the back. It's smooth-centred and richly fruited on the palate, quite weighty through the middle but with a marmalade-like kick on the finish. I can't think of a better partner for pan-fried turkey breasts on wedges of grilled polenta.

STYLE **dry**
QUALITY ♟ ♟ ♟ ♟
VALUE ☆ ☆
GRAPES
   Sauvignon Blanc
REGION **Hawke's Bay**
CELLAR 🍶 3
PRICE **$30–33**

Sacred Hill Whitecliff Estate Sauvignon Blanc

STYLE **dry**

QUALITY ☆☆☆☆☆

VALUE ☆☆☆☆☆

GRAPES
Sauvignon Blanc

REGION
Hawke's Bay 85%
Marlborough 15%

CELLAR 2

PRICE $16–18

There have been a few changes made to the Whitecliff label in the last couple of vintages. Now, wines wearing it are more easily identified as Sacred Hill products, which saves confusion.

Current Release 2002 The aromatics combine pears, dried pineapple and a wee hint of lychees, and they manage to remain in good nick on the front palate. It's a sweet-fruited, clean and very approachable wine that is highly suited to equally focused foods. Try it alongside a plate of prawns that have been marinated in Chinese rice wine and lemongrass before being barbecued or grilled.

Saint Clair Marlborough Sauvignon Blanc

STYLE **dry**

QUALITY ☆☆☆☆

VALUE ☆☆☆

GRAPES
Sauvignon Blanc

REGION **Marlborough**

CELLAR 2

PRICE $17–19

Just over 90% of the fruit for this vivacious savvie came from vineyards in the Wairau Valley, with the rest sourced over the hills in the Awatere Valley. Winemaker Matt Thomson gave it minimal skin contact to retain its freshness.

Current Release 2002 The classic Marlborough bouquet is reminiscent of rock melon and mango, and the same characters drift onto the front palate. It's a full-flavoured, rich wine with plenty of sweet-fruited style. It's good on its own, but sits well alongside a whole baked snapper.

Saint Clair Marlborough Winemaker's Reserve Sauvignon Blanc

STYLE **dry**

QUALITY ☆☆☆☆☆

VALUE ☆☆☆☆

GRAPES
Sauvignon Blanc

REGION **Marlborough**

CELLAR 2

PRICE $22–24

The back label tells us that this wine from the highly regarded Saint Clair team is an overrun from an order for the company's Spanish distributor. The fruit came from the Rapaura and Fairhall sub-regions.

Current Release 2002 There's a savoury note on the nose that makes the wine smell vaguely like grilled pineapple, and that's fine by me. It's very focused on the palate, with good mid-palate richness complemented by the variety's usual zingy acids on the finish. Honour its heritage by partnering it with the Spanish seafood stew known as zarzuela.

Saint Clair Wairau Reserve Sauvignon Blanc

STYLE **dry**

QUALITY ☆☆☆☆☆

VALUE ☆☆☆☆

GRAPES
Sauvignon Blanc

REGION **Marlborough**

CELLAR 2

PRICE $23–25

Saint Clair draws its grapes from various parts of Marlborough, but this one came from the heart of the Wairau Valley, home to some of the best-known sauvignon blanc labels in the world. That's an amazing thought – a decade ago, few people overseas had heard of the area.

Current Release 2002 You want classic Marlborough savvie? This is it. The nose is decidedly pungent, and the flavour profile is all about rich, ripe fruit kept in place by well-focused acids. The finish is very refreshing and makes the wine good drinking on its own. Alternatively, try it with tuatua fritters and a mesclun salad.

Saints Vineyard Selection Marlborough Sauvignon Blanc

This wine was made from the first harvest from Montana's Awatere Valley vineyard, purchased a couple of years ago. Apparently, eight percent was fermented in oak, but it doesn't show – this is pure fruit!

Current Release 2002 Gosh – talk about pungent! This savvie really jumps out of the glass. After that upfront introduction it's clean and super-fresh on the palate, with vibrant acids keeping everything zingy through to the finish. It's good on its own, or with an Italian-style antipasto platter.

STYLE **dry**
QUALITY ♟ ♟ ♟ ♟ ♟
VALUE ☆ ☆ ☆ ☆ ☆
GRAPES **Sauvignon Blanc**
REGION **Marlborough**
CELLAR 1
PRICE **$17–19**

Sanctuary Marlborough Sauvignon Blanc

Sanctuary is a second label for Grove Mill, but its wines have been known to outperform their higher-priced cellarmates in competitions. This well-priced savvie is a hugely popular restaurant wine.

Current Release 2002 The bouquet is lively and clean and the flavour profile crisp, fruity and nicely balanced – what more could you ask for? Perhaps it doesn't have the palate depth of some local high-fliers, but it's thoroughly drinkable alongside dishes like seafood risotto or paella.

STYLE **dry**
QUALITY ♟ ♟ ♟ ♟
VALUE ☆ ☆ ☆ ☆ ☆
GRAPES **Sauvignon Blanc**
REGION **Marlborough**
CELLAR 2
PRICE **$15–17**

Seifried Sauvignon Blanc

Nelson and Marlborough share similar climates, but the Nelson sauvignon style is a little less pungent than most examples from over the hills. This is a good one.

Current Release 2002 The bouquet is stylish and leans towards the subtle, which is not a word often used to describe this enthusiastic variety. It's sweet-fruited and vibrant on the palate, boasts good sweet fruit through the middle and has a lean but well-focused finish. It's good with a mushroom and feta pie.

STYLE **dry**
QUALITY ♟ ♟ ♟ ♟
VALUE ☆ ☆ ☆
GRAPES **Sauvignon Blanc**
REGION **Nelson**
CELLAR 1
PRICE **$19–21**

Selaks Premium Selection Marlborough Sauvignon Blanc

With supplies of the 2001 model greatly reduced by Marlborough's worst drought on record, there was a big demand for this latest version of one of the country's most popular savvies. It's right up to its usual standard.

Current Release 2002 The nose is absolutely classic modern Marlborough – pungent with a dash of sweat. It's pleasantly creamy on the palate, which gives it more depth than many of the genre, but the integrated acids give it plenty of life on the finish. A perfect partner would be a pie filled with Marlborough Sounds mussels and chopped fennel.

STYLE **dry**
QUALITY ♟ ♟ ♟ ♟
VALUE ☆ ☆ ☆ ☆ ☆
GRAPES **Sauvignon Blanc**
REGION **Marlborough**
CELLAR 2
PRICE **$15–17**

Sherwood Estate Marlborough Sauvignon Blanc

STYLE dry
QUALITY ♟♟♟♟
VALUE ☆☆☆☆
GRAPES Sauvignon Blanc
REGION Marlborough
CELLAR 1
PRICE $14–16

The Sherwood Estate winery is in Canterbury, but the company owns vineyards not only in its home town, but also in Marlborough's Wairau Valley. This is one of the best-priced savvies on the market.

Current Release 2002 The nose is pungent in the approved manner, the flavours are sweet-edged and the acids fit nicely into place, adding lift without becoming too obtrusive. Partner it with a platter of freshly opened shellfish, raw or steamed as appropriate.

Shingle Peak Marlborough Sauvignon Blanc

STYLE dry
QUALITY ♟♟♟♟
VALUE ☆☆☆
GRAPES Sauvignon Blanc
REGION Marlborough
CELLAR 1
PRICE $16–18

After two light years in a row, Mark Robertson was pleased with both the quality and quantity of Marlborough fruit from the 2002 vintage. This mid-range savvie sells well, helped by the easily identifiable label featuruing a stylised mountain range.

Current Release 2002 The nose is super-pungent in classic hot-year Marlborough style. It's creamier than most on the palate, with rich, ripe fruit flavours edged by lively but integrated acids. Mark likes it with freshly shucked oysters — and why not!

Sileni Estate Selection Sémillon

STYLE dry
QUALITY ♟♟♟♟♟
VALUE ☆☆☆
GRAPES Sémillon
REGION Hawke's Bay
CELLAR 4
PRICE $25–27

Grant Edmonds arranged for his 2002 sémillon to be harvested by hand, pressed the grapes as whole bunches then fermented the resulting juice in stainless-steel tanks. About 20% finished its fermentation in oak barrels.

Current Release 2002 The bouquet is funky, citric and spicy – good stuff! There's a wealth of smart, sweet fruit on the front palate and good weight through the middle. It finishes with a dash of spicy sweetness and leaves you wanting more. Partner it with crumbed chicken breasts dabbed with wasabi mayonnaise and you'll be a happy wine lover.

Soljans Estate Lynham Vineyard Sauvignon Blanc

STYLE dry
QUALITY ♟♟♟
VALUE ☆☆☆
GRAPES Sauvignon Blanc
REGION Hawke's Bay
CELLAR
PRICE $15–17

The winemaking team at Soljans was understandably excited about moving to a new, purpose-built winery complex at Kumeu. After years of tripping over themselves at the unbelievably cramped Henderson headquarters it must have been bliss.

Current Release 2001 The nose is funky and savoury, and the flavour profile crisp-edged but creamy through the middle. The crispness returns to enliven the finish. It's a straightforward wine that suits simple fare like pan-fried snapper fillets with mashed potatoes and salad.

Solstone Sauvignon Blanc Wairarapa Valley

The Solstone vineyard boasts some of the oldest vines in the Wairarapa, and the owners believe their wines have extra intensity as a result. Vine age is certainly a factor in many of the great wines of Europe, so they've got a good argument.

Current Release 2001 There's a spicy note behind the kiwifruit aromas, and a reasonable amount of rich fruit on the palate, balanced by nicely integrated acids. The finish is clean and quite long. It makes a good partner for a salad based around Wairarapa goat cheese.

STYLE **dry**
QUALITY ♟ ♟ ♟ ⸸
VALUE ☆ ☆ ⸸
GRAPES
  Sauvignon Blanc
REGION **Wairarapa**

CELLAR 🍾 **2**
PRICE **$23–25**

Spy Valley Sauvignon Blanc

Spy Valley wines are gaining quite a reputation with overseas visitors to Marlborough, partly because they are featured on the wine list at the beautifully situated Timara Lodge, not far from the vineyards.

Current Release 2002 Pungent in the currently approved fashion, but with a dash of mealiness for extra interest, this is pretty classic stuff. It's smoother than many of the genre on the palate, but has an edge of crisp acids to keep things lively through to the finish. It's good with asparagus sandwiches made from fresh spears, not canned.

STYLE **dry**
QUALITY ♟ ♟ ♟ ⸸
VALUE ☆ ☆ ☆ ⸸
GRAPES
  Sauvignon Blanc
REGION **Marlborough**

CELLAR 🍾 **1**
PRICE **$17–19**

Staete Landt Marlborough Sauvignon Blanc

Consistency is a Staete Landt attribute. The company's sauvignon blanc differs little from year to year, always emphasising delightfully fresh fruit in crisp surroundings. This latest model is particularly smart.

Current Release 2002 It's classic Marlborough savvie but the nose seems a little more elegant than most of the genre. The flavour profile suggests passionfruit and ripe kiwifruit, and the finish is clean and refreshing. It makes a great aperitif, but works pretty well alongside a brace of char-grilled root vegetables.

STYLE **dry**
QUALITY ♟ ♟ ♟ ♟ ♟
VALUE ☆ ☆ ☆ ⸸
GRAPES
  Sauvignon Blanc
REGION **Marlborough**

CELLAR 🍾 **1**
PRICE **$22–24**

Stonecroft Sauvignon Blanc

Alan and Glen Limmer have talked about pulling out their sauvignon vines to make room for more syrah, the variety for which the label is best known. Trouble is, this savvie sells well – and deservedly so.

Current Release 2000 Sweet-fruited but with a mineral edge, this is smart wine. The aromas are beckoning, and the flavours are rich but not over the top. It's smartly balanced and perfectly focused, and goes brilliantly with an oyster and fennel pie, or a wedge of goat cheese.

STYLE **dry**
QUALITY ♟ ♟ ♟ ♟ ♟
VALUE ☆ ☆ ☆ ☆
GRAPES
  Sauvignon Blanc
REGION **Hawke's Bay**

CELLAR 🍾 **2**
PRICE **$19–22**

Stoneleigh Marlborough Sauvignon Blanc

STYLE **dry**
QUALITY � � � � �
VALUE ★ ★ ★ ★ ⯪
GRAPES
  Sauvignon Blanc
REGION **Marlborough**

CELLAR 🍾 2
PRICE **$17–19**

This zingy savvie is so ubiquitous it is often ignored by 'serious' wine enthusiasts. That's a shame. It's made from top-quality fruit, and in most years is one of the best interpretations of the style on the market.

Current Release 2002 It has typical hot-year Marlborough pungency on the nose, but it is subdued enough to allow the clean-edged fruit to shine through. It's superbly fresh on the palate, with nicely tuned acids and a suggestion of sweetness right at the finish. It's good with tuna hash cakes, ideally made from Italian tuna tinned in olive oil.

Stoneleigh Marlborough Sauvignon Blanc Rapaura Series

STYLE **dry**
QUALITY � � � � �
VALUE ★ ★ ★ ★
GRAPES
  Sauvignon Blanc
REGION **Marlborough**

CELLAR 🍾 3
PRICE **$21–24**

Fine-tuning sets this top-shelf savvie apart from its 'standard' cellarmate. Just six percent of the juice was fermented in new French oak barrels and left there for a few weeks to round out the flavour.

Current Release 2001 Golden kiwifruit backed by no more than a suggestion of spice provide the aromatic associations. It's deliciously sweet-fruited through the middle, with rich flavours tempered by sensibly integrated acids. It works perfectly alongside Japanese soba noodles topped by a piece of tarakihi that has had its skin rubbed with salt before being grilled.

Stony Batter Estate Road Works Sauvignon Blanc

STYLE **dry**
QUALITY � � � �
VALUE ★ ★⯪
GRAPES
  Sauvignon Blanc
REGION
  Waiheke Island

CELLAR 🍾 2
PRICE **$24–26**

Made from low-yielding vines and given a spell in oak barrels, this is a rare beast – Waiheke island is known for big-hearted reds, not sauvignon blanc. Luc Desbonnet's training was in France, which explains the Gallic approach to the variety.

Current Release 2001 Oak fermentation has added a smoky note to the ripe passionfruit and rock melon aromas. It's clean, lively and smartly balanced through the middle, and boasts a nicely refreshing finish. It goes well with home-made pasta strips drizzled with sage butter.

Te Awa Farm Longlands Sauvignon Blanc

STYLE **dry**
QUALITY � � � � �
VALUE ★ ★ ★ ★
GRAPES
  Sauvignon Blanc
REGION **Hawke's Bay**

CELLAR 🍾 3
PRICE **$18–20**

Winemaker Jenny Dobson and the Te Awa team purposefully chose a stony, arid site to grow sauvignon blanc. The vines don't give high yields, but the grapes have great intensity of flavour that transfers itself to the wine.

Current Release 2002 There's a spicy note behind the citrus and kiwifruit aromas, although the wine has seen no oak. It's impressively fresh and clean on the palate, with acids that provide good lift through the middle but know not to dominate proceedings. It's lively, but rich enough to suit chicken breasts in a mustard/cream sauce.

Te Mania Nelson Sauvignon Blanc

A silver medal at the Bragato awards was a thrill for the Te Mania team. Uniquely, the competition rewards growers rather than wine companies. In Te Mania's case, that covered both bases.

Current Release 2001 There's a good old whack of savvie's distinctive pungent passionfruit on the nose. It's sweet-fruited in front, rich in the middle and clean-cut on the finish, all of which adds up to a refreshing drop. Put it alongside a trayful of freshly shucked Nelson oysters adorned with nothing more distracting than cracked pepper and you'll be doing well.

STYLE **dry**
QUALITY ♟♟♟♟
VALUE ☆☆☆☆
GRAPES **Sauvignon Blanc**
REGION **Nelson**
CELLAR 1
PRICE **$17–19**

Te Mata Cape Crest Sauvignon Blanc

It's in the top price bracket for savvies, but it's very stylish. Part of the juice for this top-shelf member of the Te Mata portfolio is fermented and matured in French oak barrels. Unusually for the variety, it ages well.

Current Release 2001 Winemaker Peter Cowley says he aims for a 'feijoa' character in this savvie, and he's got it. It's a big, fruity wine with perfectly balanced acids through the middle and a long, well-focused finish. It sits perfectly alongside a shellfish pie, especially if it is flavoured with a touch of fennel.

STYLE **dry**
QUALITY ♟♟♟♟♟
VALUE ☆☆☆
GRAPES **Sauvignon Blanc**
REGION **Hawke's Bay**
CELLAR 3
PRICE **$23–26**

Te Mata Woodthorpe Sauvignon Blanc

Fans of Te Mata Castle Hill Sauvignon now have a new label to look out for – this is the new version. Woodthorpe Terraces is the name of the partnership's sprawling new vineyard in the Dartmoor Valley.

Current Release 2002 Clean and fresh with suggestions of kiwifruit and dried pineapple in the bouquet, this wine has instant appeal. It's fresh-faced and was obviously made from superbly ripe fruit. The finish is clean and satisfying. Partner it with squid, quickly pan-fried in olive oil with thinly sliced parboiled potatoes.

STYLE **dry**
QUALITY ♟♟♟♟♟
VALUE ☆☆☆☆
GRAPES **Sauvignon Blanc**
REGION **Hawke's Bay**
CELLAR 3
PRICE **$22–24**

Te Whare Ra Duke of Marlborough Sémillon

The sweetness level of this wine varies from year to year, but in 2001 it was decided to make it just off-dry. There's not a lot of it, so it is seldom seen away from the rustic winery just out of Blenheim.

Current Release 2001 The bouquet is shy, but there's a suggestion of citrus fruit and melon skin in there. It's sweet-fruited, straightforward and pleasant enough without encouraging heights of excitement. Try it with a platter of seafood-based nibbles like greenshell mussels with mayonnaise, grilled prawns and freshly shucked oysters.

STYLE **off-dry**
QUALITY ♟♟♟
VALUE ☆☆☆
GRAPES **Sémillon**
REGION **Marlborough**
CELLAR 2
PRICE **$16–18**

Terrace Road Marlborough Sauvignon Blanc

STYLE dry
QUALITY ♆♆♆♆
VALUE ☆☆☆
GRAPES
  Sauvignon Blanc
REGION Marlborough
CELLAR 2
PRICE $18–20

This lively savvie sells by the truck-load (well, almost) at the pleasant indoor/outdoor Cellier Le Brun Café in Marlborough. It goes well with the in-house antipasto platter.

Current Release 2001 Think passionfruit and pineapple chunks and you've got the aromatics sussed. It's vibrant, straightforward and very direct in its appeal, and sits happily with a wide range of food. If you don't fancy the antipasto, try it with Marlborough Sounds mussels.

Thornbury Marlborough Sauvignon Blanc

STYLE dry
QUALITY ♆♆♆♆♆
VALUE ☆☆☆☆⭒
GRAPES
  Sauvignon Blanc
REGION Marlborough
CELLAR 2
PRICE $18–20

Steve Bird is one of a handful of winemakers who use fruit from just two or three prime sites in different regions to craft a small portfolio of wines. It has worked well for him – his products have picked up several awards.

Current Release 2002 Perfumed on the nose with less 'sweat' than most '02 savvies and deliciously sweet-fruited on the palate, this is a very smart wine. The balance between grapiness and acid is spot-on and the finish immaculately clean. It's perfect with prawn-topped pizza.

Timara Sauvignon Blanc

STYLE dry
QUALITY ♆♆♆
VALUE ☆☆☆☆⭒
GRAPES
  Sauvignon Blanc
REGION Chile
CELLAR
PRICE $11–13

Montana uses a lot of Chilean juice for its bottom-end labels. Being a long, narrow country not unlike our own, it echoes our wide range of climatic conditions. Identifying this savvie's region of origin would be a challenge even for the experts.

Current Release 2001 Lime juice and cape gooseberries on the nose give it a bouquet like a more citric version of an early Marlborough model. It's keen-edged and vibrant on the palate and makes a perfectly acceptable summer afternoon pre-barbecue sipper, with or without nibbles.

Tohu Marlborough Sauvignon Blanc

STYLE dry
QUALITY ♆♆♆♆
VALUE ☆☆☆☆
GRAPES
  Sauvignon Blanc
REGION Marlborough
CELLAR 2
PRICE $16–19

This classically made savvie has picked up a few awards in the few vintages it has been available. Sales have no doubt been helped by the very smart packaging, and repeat purchases show that it lives up to expectations.

Current Release 2002 I get a suggestion of something like All-Bran on the nose. That's unusual for sauvignon, but it has a certain appeal. It's sweet-edged and chunky on the palate, with smartly balanced acids giving it plenty of lift through the middle and on the finish. It goes well with chicken pieces casseroled in good stock with a smidgen of preserved lemon.

Torlesse Waipara Sauvignon Blanc

Waipara savvie doesn't enjoy the huge reputation of its Marlborough cousin, but the grape grows well there. This one has been mistaken for a North Island version on more than one occasion.

Current Release 2002 The pungent nose is certainly very Marlborough-like, but a savoury edge gives it a point of difference. It's sweet-edged and lively on the palate, and makes a good partner for a brace of oysters, topped with grated Parmesan and lightly grilled for a change.

STYLE **dry**
QUALITY 🍷 🍷 🍷 🍷
VALUE ☆ ☆ ☆
GRAPES
  Sauvignon Blanc
REGION **Waipara**
CELLAR 🍾
PRICE **$18–20**

Twin Islands Sauvignon Blanc

Nautilus sources fruit from both the Awatere and Wairau Valleys, giving its winemaking team a wide range of flavours to work with. The name features regularly in wine competitions here and overseas.

Current Release 2002 Fresh and feisty on the nose, clean and frisky on the palate, this is a good-natured, straightforward savvie that couldn't possibly cause offence. Partner it with a stack of mini-sandwiches filled with ricotta, cucumber and sliced radishes, generously sprinkled with cracked black pepper.

STYLE **dry**
QUALITY 🍷 🍷 🍷
VALUE ☆ ☆ ☆
GRAPES
  Sauvignon Blanc
REGION **Marlborough**
CELLAR 🍾 1
PRICE **$15–17**

Vavasour Awatere Valley Marlborough Sauvignon Blanc

The vineyards near Vavasour's Awatere valley winery contributed 80% of the fruit for this savvie. The rest came from across the hills in the Wairau Valley. Glenn Thomas harvested both lots in the evening to retain the vibrant flavours.

Current Release 2002 I get passionfruit and dried apricots on the nose, with little sign of the variety's typical 'sweat'. It's creamy on the palate with clean, straightforward flavours edged by smartly integrated acids. It's good with seafood lasagne.

STYLE **dry**
QUALITY 🍷 🍷 🍷 🍷 🍷
VALUE ☆ ☆ ☆ ☆
GRAPES
  Sauvignon Blanc
REGION **Marlborough**
CELLAR 🍾 2
PRICE **$21–23**

Vidal Estate Sauvignon Blanc

Rod McDonald used fruit from six different vineyards to craft this wine. The various parcels were kept separate right through the fermentation process and pumped into different tanks. Blending took place just before the wine was bottled.

Current Release 2002 The nose is savoury and pungent, but gently so compared to Marlborough examples. It's a straightforward wine, with suggestions of dried pineapple and chopped red capsicums. Echo that character by partnering it with grilled capsicums on pita bread.

STYLE **dry**
QUALITY 🍷 🍷 🍷
VALUE ☆ ☆ ☆
GRAPES
  Sauvignon Blanc
REGION **Hawke's Bay**
CELLAR 🍾
PRICE **$16–18**

Villa Maria Cellar Selection Marlborough Sauvignon Blanc

STYLE **dry**
QUALITY ♟♟♟♟♟
VALUE ☆☆☆☆
GRAPES
  Sauvignon Blanc
REGION **Marlborough**

CELLAR **1**
PRICE **$20–23**

Vineyards in the Wairau and Awatere Valleys contributed fruit for this mid-range Villa savvie. The winemaking team aimed to make a wine with a little more restraint than the exuberant Reserve duo. It's a popular choice in restaurants around the country.

Current Release 2002 I get melon and limes on the nose – not particularly sauvignon-like but undeniably pleasant. The flavour, however, is classically sweet-edged, but with crisp acids ensuring plenty of life through to the finish. It's a good match for fettucine pasta tossed with nothing more distracting than garlic, parsley and seriously good olive oil.

Villa Maria Private Bin Marlborough Sauvignon Blanc

STYLE **dry**
QUALITY ♟♟♟♟
VALUE ☆☆☆☆
GRAPES
  Sauvignon Blanc
REGION **Marlborough**

CELLAR **1**
PRICE **$17–19**

The Marlborough region had less than 40mm of rain between January and April 2001, compared to the long-term average of 181mm. That was tough on farmers but good for grape growers. The fruit for this fresh-faced Savvie came from the Wairau and Awatere Valleys.

Current Release 2002 There's a subtle savoury note on the nose, with suggestions of passionfruit and dried apricots also evident. It's a very pretty wine on the palate, with rich flavours and a mouth-filling texture. Enjoy it with spaghetti tossed hot with freshly made pesto.

Villa Maria Reserve Clifford Bay Marlborough Sauvignon Blanc

STYLE **dry**
QUALITY ♟♟♟♟♟
VALUE ☆☆☆☆
GRAPES
  Sauvignon Blanc
REGION **Marlborough**

CELLAR **2**
PRICE **$25–27**

Taking the trophy for Best Sauvignon Blanc at the 2002 International Wine and Spirit Competition in London did wonders for local and international sales of this richly flavoured savvie. The grapes came from Villa's Awatere Valley vineyards.

Current Release 2001 The nose is pungent, but in a classy way, complex and inviting. It's creamy, richly fruited and full in the mouth, and simply screams of Marlborough sunshine. No wonder the Brits loved it! Partner it with a plate-load of tuatua fritters with home-made mayonnaise.

Villa Maria Reserve Wairau Valley Marlborough Sauvignon Blanc

Rave reviews in the UK and a gold medal in the 2002 Japan Wine Challenge are just some of the accolades that have been heaped upon this big-hearted savvie. It has done better overseas than here – local judges initially gave it only a bronze medal.

Current Release 2002 Pungent and chunky on the nose, big, bold and shouting of tropical fruit on the palate, this is quite a mouthful of wine. The texture is exemplary – smooth, but with a keen edge – and the finish long and refreshing. Partner it with prawn and mussel paella.

STYLE **dry**
QUALITY ♟ ♟ ♟ ♟ ♟
VALUE ☆ ☆ ☆
GRAPES
  Sauvignon Blanc
REGION **Marlborough**
CELLAR ▯ 2
PRICE **$25–27**

Vin Alto Sémillon

Enzo and Margaret Bettio are carving out a reputation for a range of unique (in New Zealand) Italian-style reds, but this stylish Sémillon shows that they are no slouches when it comes to whites. It's quite unlike any other local version.

Current Release 1998 This is a big, chunky wine that is just starting to hit its straps. The bouquet is savoury and complex, and the flavours are rich and sit in a delightfully smooth framework. Barbecued quail would make an ideal match.

STYLE **dry**
QUALITY ♟ ♟ ♟ ♟ ♟
VALUE ☆ ☆ ☆
GRAPES **Sémillon**
REGION **Clevedon**
CELLAR ▯ 4
PRICE **$30–32**

Waimea Estates Bolitho Sauvignon Blanc

Made from a small parcel of exceptional fruit, this top-shelf savvie isn't easy to find outside the Nelson region, but it's worth a search. Trevor Bolitho aged some of it on the yeast lees left over from fermentation and put 10% into oak barrels.

Current Release 2001 This is a mouth-filling wine that has all the usual sauvignon fruit richness, but with an added savoury dimension through the middle. Not everybody approves of oak-ageing the variety, but this one shows that a little timber character can really add something. It would make a good match for a seafood-topped pizza.

STYLE **dry**
QUALITY ♟ ♟ ♟ ♟ ♟
VALUE ☆ ☆ ☆ ☆
GRAPES
  Sauvignon Blanc
REGION **Nelson**
CELLAR ▯ 2
PRICE **$20–22**

Waimea Estates Sauvignon Blanc

Just eight percent of this wine was fermented in oak, which is an indication of the fine-tuning that goes into creating the exact flavour profile wanted by the winemaker. While it was chilling out in the barrels it sat on the yeast lees left over from fermentation.

Current Release 2001 All that fiddling about has created a very smart wine. It's got richness on the nose and front palate and more length than many of the genre. The texture is lively enough, but it's tempered by a classy amount of smoothness. Enjoy it with braised pork chops in a thyme-infused creamy sauce.

STYLE **dry**
QUALITY ♟ ♟ ♟ ♟ ♟
VALUE ☆ ☆ ☆ ☆ ☆
GRAPES
  Sauvignon Blanc
REGION **Nelson**
CELLAR ▯ 2
PRICE **$16–18**

Waipara Hills Sauvignon Blanc

STYLE dry

QUALITY ▼ ▼ ▼ ▽

VALUE ☆ ☆ ☆

GRAPES
Sauvignon Blanc

REGION Waipara

CELLAR 🍾 1

PRICE $19–21

Alan McCorkindale, once in charge of the Corbans winery in Marlborough, now makes wine for his own label as well as several others. Waipara Hills is a valued name on his client list.

Current Release 2002 The bouquet has a touch of spice to add interest to the usual passionfruit and ripe kiwifruit aromas. It's clean and well-focused on the palate, with well-balanced acids and a short but fresh-faced finish. Enjoy it with a bowl of Singapore-style prawn noodles.

Waipara Springs Sauvignon Blanc

STYLE dry

QUALITY ▼ ▼ ▼ ▼

VALUE ☆ ☆ ☆ ☆

GRAPES
Sauvignon Blanc

REGION
Waipara 90%
Marlborough 10%

CELLAR 🍾 2

PRICE $18–21

The Waipara climate has a sunny day/cold night pattern quite like Marlborough's, so it is logical that sauvignon blanc should perform well there. This one actually contains a little bit of Marlborough fruit.

Current Release 2002 Seriously pungent on the nose and boasting loads of super-fresh, ripe fruit flavours, this wine has instant appeal. The acids are in perfect tune, adding vivacity without making the texture too lean. It makes a good match for mussel fritters served on a rocket and feta cheese salad.

White Cloud Sauvignon Blanc

STYLE medium-dry

QUALITY ▼ ▼ ▽

VALUE ☆ ☆ ☆ ☆ ☆

GRAPES
Sauvignon Blanc

REGION Gisborne
Hawke's Bay

CELLAR 🍾

PRICE $9–11

The White Cloud range has been a huge success for The House of Nobilo. The wines all carry a recommended retail price of just under $10, and are often specialled to a dollar or two below that figure.

Current Release (non-vintage) There's a touch of fresh-bread yeast on the nose, but mostly the aromas are floral and citric. I find it too sweet in the flavour department, but I readily concede that a lot of people will love it. It's probably best on its own.

Wither Hills Sauvignon Blanc

STYLE dry

QUALITY ▼ ▼ ▼ ▼ ▼

VALUE ☆ ☆ ☆ ☆

GRAPES
Sauvignon Blanc

REGION Marlborough

CELLAR 🍾 2

PRICE $20–23

Just 5% of the juice for this savvie was fermented in new French barrels. That seems hardly enough to register, but Brent Marris reckons it's the details that make the difference between good and great wines.

Current Release 2002 Stylish. That's the word that springs to mind when you smell this immaculate Marlborough savvie. The aromas are inviting and the flavour profile fruity but crisp-edged. All in all, a very smart wine that goes perfectly with hot-smoked salmon hash cakes.

Unusual and Unspecified Whites

This chapter is where you will find wines labelled simply Dry White or something similar, but along with these 'cheap and cheerfuls' I have listed a few rather flasher bottles that don't specify the grape varieties from which they are made. Also in here are the unusual varieties such as breidecker, auxerrois and others, as well as unusual blends. Müller-thurgau, once the backbone of our industry, is now seen on so few labels that it qualifies for the same positioning. I have listed the grape varieties and their percentages if the makers were willing to divulge them, but in some cases the term 'others' has had to do.

Babich Winemaker's Reserve Hawke's Bay Viognier

There's not a lot of this little-known Babich wine about, but it's worth grabbing if you spot some. It was fermented in French oak barrels and left there for 10 months, but because they were older they have had a minimal effect on the flavour.

Current Release 2001 Ripe pears introduce things on the nose. It's sweet-fruited and quite rich on the palate, but with a rustic edge that rather appeals to the peasant in me. I imagine it would be perfect with crumbed pork schnitzels, served with rosemary and garlic potatoes and the youngest green beans you can find.

STYLE **dry**
QUALITY ♟ ♟ ♟ ♟
VALUE ☆ ☆ ☆
GRAPES **Viognier**
REGION **Hawke's Bay**
CELLAR **3**
PRICE **$30–33**

Collards Rothesay Viognier

Viognier, originally from France's Rhône Valley, is rare in this country, but many people believe it has a good future. This one was fermented in stainless steel, but the yeast lees were left in contact with the juice for 12 weeks.

Current Release 2002 I get pears and persimmon on the nose, and that suits me just fine. It's quite big on the palate, with a creamy texture and a long, smooth finish. It would be perfect alongside a brace of roasted quail on char-grilled grainy toast.

STYLE **dry**
QUALITY ♟ ♟ ♟ ♟
VALUE ☆ ☆ ☆ ⯪
GRAPES **Viognier**
REGION **West Auckland**
CELLAR **3**
PRICE **$25–28**

Corbans White Label Müller-Thurgau

STYLE off-dry
QUALITY ▽ ▽ ▽
VALUE ☆ ☆ ☆ ☆ ☆
GRAPES
   Müller-Thurgau
REGION Hawke's Bay

CELLAR 🍾 3
PRICE $9—11

The tasting notes accompanying this wine describe it as a 'medium' style, but it's closer to off-dry. It's sold as a 'cheap and cheerful', but I have a hunch that it might age surprisingly well. At this price, you can experiment.
Current Release 2002 There's a pleasant savoury note behind aromas reminiscent of spiced honey. The flavours are decidedly apple-like, with a sweet edge and assertive acids. It works pretty well with a mild chicken curry.

Glenmark Waipara Medium White

STYLE medium
QUALITY ▽ ▽ ▽
VALUE ☆ ☆ ☆
GRAPES
   Müller-Thurgau 70%
   Breidecker
   Pinot Gris
   Various
REGION Waipara

CELLAR 🍾 1
PRICE $12—14

John McCaskey was a Waipara pioneer, planting his first vines in 1981 and opening the district's first winery in 1986. His wines won some good awards in the early '90s, and he has plans to revitalise the image for the new millennium.
Current Release 1998 Impressions of comb honey and perfume give away the müller dominance. It's sweet, honeyish and easily quaffable on a hot day, and undoubtedly best on its own.

Herzog Marlborough Viognier

STYLE dry
QUALITY ▽ ▽ ▽ ▽ ▽
VALUE ☆ ☆ ☆
GRAPES Viognier
REGION Marlborough

CELLAR 🍾 5
PRICE $39—43

Hans Herzog uses techniques more usually associated with chardonnay to craft this big-hearted white. It spends a year in all-new French oak barrels and undergoes a full acid-softening malolactic fermentation.
Current Release 2002 Perfumed on the nose and big, rich and creamy on the palate, this is quite a mouthful of wine. I suspect some people might find it stylistically over the top, but it sure appeals to me. Try it with braised rabbit and you'll get the point.

Hyperion Selene Chardonnay/Pinot Gris

STYLE off-dry
QUALITY ▽ ▽ ▽
VALUE ☆ ☆ ☆
GRAPES
   Chardonnay 80%
   Pinot Gris 20%
REGION Matakana

CELLAR 🍾 3
PRICE $20—22

This is a pretty rare blend, but it works well. John Crone loves pinot gris, and figured it would add an extra dimension to chardonnay. He allowed it to retain a bit of residual sugar to lift the fruit.
Current Release 2000 'Pretty' seems the right description for this little smoothie. It starts dry, but the sweetness builds through the mid-palate so the impression on the finish is of medium-intense richness. Well chilled, it would make a good aperitif alongside simple summer nibbles.

Kim Crawford Pia Dry White

Pia means pious, and it is the name of Kim and Erica Crawford's daughter. Kim plans to make this wine only in exceptional vintages, and the make-up and grape source will vary from year to year.

Current Release 2000 The American oak barrels used for maturing this chunky white show themselves in the form of sweet vanilla notes in the bouquet. It's got plenty of stonefruit flavours in creamy surrounds, but integrated acids cut in to add zing on the finish. It's good with crusty bread dipped into extra virgin olive oil.

STYLE **dry**
QUALITY 🍷🍷🍷🍷
VALUE ☆☆
GRAPES **Chardonnay**
REGION **Hawke's Bay**
CELLAR 🍾 **3**
PRICE **$35–37**

Langdale of Canterbury Breidecker

Breidecker is a pretty rare variety, but it's popular enough in Canterbury to have earned a nickname – the Black & Decker wine. Carol Bunn and her team must have been thrilled to receive a silver medal with this one.

Current Release 2000 There's a spicy edge on the ripe mango aromas and a dash of riesling-like florals at the back. It's sweet, simple and immediately attractive and remains nicely balanced thanks to the smartly tuned acids. Enjoy it on its own some sunny afternoon.

STYLE **medium**
QUALITY 🍷🍷🍷🍷
VALUE ☆☆☆
GRAPES **Breidecker**
REGION **Canterbury**
CELLAR 🍾 **1**
PRICE **$12–14**

Langdale of Canterbury Pinot Blanc

Pinot blanc is not a grape we see a lot of in New Zealand, but it seems pretty happy on the Canterbury Plains. This one came from the Tuscany Downs vineyard, and the Langdale team put it into French oak barrels for five months.

Current Release 2001 Grainy, spicy and citric on the nose and displaying a reasonably complex collection of clean, focused flavours, this is an appealing wine with good balance between fruit and oak and an intriguing point of difference. Our bottle went well with a bowl of asparagus risotto topped with shavings of really good Parmigiano cheese.

STYLE **dry**
QUALITY 🍷🍷🍷🍷
VALUE ☆☆☆
GRAPES **Pinot Blanc**
REGION **Canterbury**
CELLAR 🍾 **3**
PRICE **$19–23**

Millton Gisborne Viognier Tietjen Vineyard

The front label tells us this is part of The Growers Series, and the back label explains that unlike the Millton's home-grown fruit, the grapes are not grown organically. Nevertheless, they have great respect for the Tietjen vineyard.

Current Release 2001 Ripe peaches and a dash of spice start things off well. It's smooth enough to be called creamy on the palate, but integrated acids lift the fruit nicely, particularly towards the finish. It's a good choice for Thai dishes, so try it with chicken pieces in a sauce based around coconut cream.

STYLE **dry**
QUALITY 🍷🍷🍷🍷🍷
VALUE ☆☆☆
GRAPES **Viognier**
REGION **Gisborne**
CELLAR 🍾 **3**
PRICE **$30–33**

Rippon Osteiner

STYLE off-dry
QUALITY ▽ ▽ ▽ ▽
VALUE ☆ ☆ ☆
GRAPES Osteiner
REGION Central Otago

CELLAR 3
PRICE $17–19

Is this the best osteiner in the country? Probably — it's almost certainly the only one. The grape originates in Germany, and it's a cross between riesling and the rather more austere sylvaner.
Current Release 2001 Citric and savoury on the nose, clean and fresh-faced on the palate, this is a straightforward wine with instant appeal. The acids are in good balance with the summery fruit and the finish is clean and direct. It's good with equally easy-going summer nibbles — vegetable sticks with olive oil for dipping, sun-dried tomatoes and the like.

Spencer Hill Grand Vendange

STYLE medium-dry
QUALITY ▽ ▽ ▽ ▽ ▽
VALUE ☆ ☆ ☆
GRAPES Sémillon
REGION Nelson

CELLAR 4
PRICE $24–26

This unusual wine is made from sémillon grapes, 30% of which were affected with botrytis. That usually adds up to a dessert style, but this one is medium-dry, carrying just 10 grammes of sugar per litre.
Current Release 1999 Botrytis is much in evidence in the form of spiced honey aromas. It is the balance that makes it so successful — it's spot-on. Sweet fruit dominates the mid-palate, but the finish is dry and refreshing. Clever stuff! It's probably best on its own, but you could try it with pan-fried duck liver.

St Aubyns Dry White

STYLE off-dry
QUALITY ▽ ▽ ▽
VALUE ☆ ☆ ☆ ☆ ☆
GRAPES
  Müller-Thurgau
  Sylvaner
  Riesling
REGION Gisborne

CELLAR
PRICE $6–8

St Aubyns wines are part of the Villa Maria portfolio, but they're better than many in this price range. The grapes used and the regions they come from vary from year to year — consistency is the aim.
Current Release (non-vintage) There's a grainy note on the nose, along with floral characters. It's a bit coarse in the middle and has a chunky finish, but heck — look at the price! Chill it well and partner it with summer nibbles.

St Aubyns Medium White

STYLE medium
QUALITY ▽ ▽ ▽
VALUE ☆ ☆ ☆
GRAPES
  Müller-Thurgau
REGION Gisborne

CELLAR
PRICE $6–8

Medium by name, medium by nature — this model is all müller, and comes solely from Gisborne. I've spotted it as the 'house white' in a couple of country cafés, and it's apparently popular at weddings.
Current Release (non-vintage) The nose is pure honeysuckle, which is certainly attractive enough. It's sweet-fruited, pleasant in the middle but rather clumsy on the finish. Use it to toast the bride and groom, then move on to something more serious.

St Helena Canterbury Pinot Blanc

St Helena has been making light-hearted wines from pinot blanc for a couple of decades, but new winemaker Alan McCorkindale is taking it pretty seriously, ageing some in oak and stirring the yeast lees.

Current Release 1999 Toasty oak backgrounds the ripe peach and pear aromas. It's got sweet fruit in nice balance with the oak, and flavours on the finish that reminded me of bananas. It goes well with a Malaysian chicken curry.

STYLE **dry**
QUALITY 🍷🍷🍷
VALUE ☆☆☆
GRAPES **Pinot Blanc**
REGION **Canterbury**
CELLAR 🍾 1
PRICE **$15–18**

Te Mata Woodthorpe Viognier

This classy white is one of the first products from the Woodthorpe Terraces vineyard, owned and operated by members of the Te Mata Estate team. This rare variety obviously performs well there – the 14% alcohol level means the grapes got very ripe indeed.

Current Release 2001 Dried figs and lemon rind, smoky oak and a dash of toasted nuts – that's the impression on the bouquet. It's a big, rich wine with an oily texture balanced by smartly integrated acids. The finish is long and spicy. We enjoyed ours with chicken breasts cooked with a generous amount of smoked paprika, and were well pleased.

STYLE **dry**
QUALITY 🍷🍷🍷🍷🍷
VALUE ☆☆☆☆
GRAPES **Viognier**
REGION **Hawke's Bay**
CELLAR 🍾 2
PRICE **$24–26**

Torlesse Chello

They're not specified on the label, but this wine is a 60/40 blend of müller-thurgau and riesling grown in the districts of Burnham and West Melton. It's certainly cheap enough, and is undeniably attractive.

Current Release (non-vintage) The bouquet is all about citric fruit, marmalade and honey. It's broadly focused in the flavour department, but there's enough zing in the middle to give it a refreshing finish. It was made for early drinking, but I've got a hunch it might cellar surprisingly well. Best on its own.

STYLE **medium**
QUALITY 🍷🍷🍷
VALUE ☆☆☆
GRAPES
  Müller-Thurgau 60%
  Riesling 40%
REGION **Canterbury**
CELLAR 🍾 3
PRICE **$10–12**

Villa Maria Private Bin Müller-Thurgau

There aren't many straight müllers on the market nowadays, but this one has done well for Villa, winning three bronze medals in 1999 and 2000. The small print on the label tells us it comes from Gisborne and Hawke's Bay.

Current Release 1999 Pears, pineapple and flowers combine to form an aromatic welcoming committee. It's clean, simple and pleasant on the palate, with sweet fruit and a short but rich finish. It's too sweet for food, so sip it solo (the wine, not you).

STYLE **medium**
QUALITY 🍷🍷🍷
VALUE ☆☆☆
GRAPES
  Müller-Thurgau
REGION **Gisborne**
  Hawke's Bay
CELLAR 🍾 2
PRICE **$8–10**

Wohnsiedler Müller-Thurgau

STYLE medium-sweet
QUALITY ♀ ♀
VALUE ☆ ☆
GRAPES
Müller-Thurgau
REGION Gisborne
CELLAR ▤
PRICE $7–9

Montana wasn't the first company to make a medium-sweet müller by blending unfermented grape juice into the almost finished wine, but the technocrats certainly fine-tuned the technique.
Current Release (non-vintage) It's citric, floral and pretty on the nose, but pretty thin in the flavour department. The label describes it as 'a fresh, German-style wine', and I guess that's reasonably accurate, if a little unfair on the Germans. If you get landed with a bottle, it's definitely best on its own.

White Cloud

STYLE medium
QUALITY ♀ ♀ ♀
VALUE ☆ ☆ ☆ ☆
GRAPES
Müller-Thurgau
Muscat
Sauvignon Blanc
REGION Gisborne
Hawke's Bay
Marlborough
Nelson
CELLAR ▤ 1
PRICE $8–10

White Cloud, not vintaged but wearing a frosted bottle for its sales around the world, is a huge success for the Nobilo group. If you can remember Blue Nun, you're on the right track – but our local hero has much brighter fruit.
Current Release (non-vintage) Müller and muscat dominate the bouquet, with floral and honey characters. It's straightforward, sweet-fruited and instantly appealing, which is exactly what its producers intended. Many buyers enjoy it with food, but it's really best on its own.

Red Wines

Cabernet Sauvignon, Merlot, Cabernet Franc and Malbec

Cabernet sauvignon, merlot, cabernet franc and malbec are often referred to as the Bordeaux varieties, because they are used in the great reds of that famous French region. Not all grapes travel well, but these four are happy in many parts of the world, and produce wines with strong family similarities. In New Zealand, merlot is becoming more dominant than cabernet in some parts of the country because it ripens up to three weeks earlier, avoiding grape-rotting autumn rain. Cabernet franc's con-tribution to a blend is warmth and floral charm, but when it is given star status it repays the compliment. Malbec is increasing in popularity with winemakers. It is a brash, earthy variety that adds grunt to any blend in which it is used.

AD (Alpha Domus) The Aviator

This is the top-of-the-heap red in the Alpha Domus collection. Evert Nijzink doesn't make a lot of it, but the price keeps the tyre-kickers away so supplies usually last for a fair while after its release.

Current Release 2000 Great balance is what this wine is all about. Spicy oak is perfectly aligned with cassis-like fruit on the nose, and firm tannins put just the right amount of an edge on the ripe berryish flavours. The finish is super-long and eye-closingly satisfying. There's nothing better with slices cut from a rare-cooked Denver leg of cervena.

STYLE dry

QUALITY 🍷🍷🍷🍷🍷

VALUE ★★☆

GRAPES
Cab Sauvignon 45%
Merlot 35%
Cabernet Franc 16%
Malbec 4%

REGION Hawke's Bay

CELLAR 6

PRICE $59–64

Alexander Martinborough Premium Cabernet Sauvignon/Franc

STYLE **dry**
QUALITY ♟♟♟♟♟
VALUE ☆ ☆ ☆ ☆

GRAPES
  Cab Sauvignon 90%
  Cabernet Franc 10%

REGION **Martinborough**

CELLAR ▭▭▭ **1–4**

PRICE **$28–32**

Most Martinborough producers concentrate on pinot noir, the variety with which the region has won an international reputation. Michael Finucane is determined to prove cabernet-based reds can perform just as well.
Current Release 1999 Berryish notes mingle with coffee aromas and sweet, savoury oak. It's smooth-textured, broadly focused but with enough tannic grip to provide plenty of mouth-feel in the middle and on the finish. It goes well with braised rump steak and onions.

Alexander Vineyard Cabernets/Merlot

STYLE **dry**
QUALITY ♟♟♟♟♟
VALUE ☆ ☆ ☆☆

GRAPES
  Cab Sauvignon 67%
  Cab Franc 16.5%
  Merlot 16%

REGION **Martinborough**

CELLAR ▭▭▭ **1–4**

PRICE **$32–34**

This is the 'biggie' of the Alexander red wine collection. The grapes were picked by hand and processed in an old-style basket press. The fledgling wine was matured in French oak barrels, 35% of which were new.
Current Release 2000 Smoky oak and plums get together on the nose. It's big, richly fruited and impressively balanced, thanks to tannins that know their place. It would make a great partner for saddle of hare, cooked rare, but an oxtail casserole would do just about as well.

Alexander Vineyard Martinborough Cabernet Franc

STYLE **dry**
QUALITY ♟♟♟♟
VALUE ☆ ☆ ☆☆

GRAPES
  Cabernet Franc 95%
  Cab Sauvignon 5%

REGION **Martinborough**

CELLAR ▯ **3**

PRICE **$23–25**

The fruit in this wine was originally destined for the company's premium red blend, but eventually the decision was made to bottle it virtually on its own. Michael Finucane describes it as a classic easy-drinking style.
Current Release 2000 Michael finds Christmas pudding on the nose, but I get a touch of the florals and a belt of oak spice. It's a pretty wine, with direct sweet-cherry flavours and drying tannins on the finish. It makes a good partner for an old-fashioned beef hash.

Alpha Domus Merlot/Cabernet Sauvignon

STYLE **dry**
QUALITY ♟♟♟
VALUE ☆ ☆ ☆☆

GRAPES **Merlot 55%**
  Cab Sauvignon 42%
  Cab Franc 2%
  Malbec 1%

REGION **Hawke's Bay**

CELLAR ▯ **2**

PRICE **$19–23**

This is the 'everyday' red in the Alpha Domus collection, and it's thoroughly drinkable. Evert Nijzink matured it in French oak barrels, but less than 20% of them were new because he didn't want the timber to bury the fruit.
Current Release 2001 The bouquet smells of pure, clean, uncomplicated fruit and the front palate gives much the same impression. As an approachable middleweight it doesn't expect to be taken too seriously, and it succeeds just fine on that level. Partner it with a bowl of beef meatballs, served as finger food with a few slices of buttered bread.

Alpha Domus The Navigator

This top-shelf red showcases the considerable skills of winemaker, Evert Nijzink. Evert had a stint working in Bordeaux and has a love of the grapes that have made that area world-famous. It shows.

Current Release 2000 There's some big oak in there, but the fruit's ripe and assertive enough to take it. The smooth texture makes it disturbingly easy to drink, and the plum and raspberry flavours fill the mouth with richness and linger long after the wine has been swallowed. Rare beef fillet would be the way to go.

STYLE **dry**
QUALITY ♟ ♟ ♟ ♟ ♟
VALUE ☆ ☆ ☆ ☆
GRAPES
  Merlot 50%
  Cab Sauvignon 20%
  Cab Franc 20%
  Malbec 10%
REGION **Hawke's Bay**
CELLAR 4
PRICE **$30–33**

Arahura Clevedon Merlot/Cabernet Sauvignon

Ken and Diane Mason were Clevedon pioneers, but their wines have never been easy to find. They've pinned their hopes on a series of reds made from the so-called Bordeaux varieties and have earned a good reputation.

Current Release 2000 There's some delightfully sweet fruit on the nose, reminiscent of blackcurrants and raspberries. The same sensations can be found on the palate. It's got good weight through the middle, but is faintly lean on the finish. Enjoy it with pork casseroled in red wine.

STYLE **dry**
QUALITY ♟ ♟ ♟ ♟
VALUE ☆ ☆ ☆ ☆
GRAPES
  Merlot 68%
  Cab Sauvignon 24%
  Cabernet Franc 8%
REGION **Clevedon**
CELLAR 1–3
PRICE **$23–26**

Arahura Merlot/Malbec

Blends of these two grapes without their usual barrelmates, cabernet sauvignon and cabernet franc, are pretty rare, but the Masons thought they tasted good together. Elegant oak completes the picture – it's smart wine.

Current Release 2000 Loads of sweet, berryish fruit fills the bouquet and front palate, and there's just enough gentle oak spice to fill in the gaps. It's a nicely textured wine with immediate appeal, but it should cellar well. It would make a great partner for a traditional English steak and kidney pie.

STYLE **dry**
QUALITY ♟ ♟ ♟ ♟ ♟
VALUE ☆ ☆ ☆ ½
GRAPES **Merlot**
  Malbec
REGION **Clevedon**
CELLAR 2–5
PRICE **$32–35**

Artisan Riverstone Vineyard Gimblett Gravels Merlot

This silver medal-winning merlot spent 10 months in oak barrels, 50% of them new. The fruit came from a 2.5-hectare site devoted entirely to merlot. It was planted in 1997.

Current Release 2000 There's some serious oak on the nose to back up the aromas of Black Doris plums. It's sweet-fruited, rich and ripe on the palate with smartly integrated tannins and a long finish. Hang the expense and match it with beef fillet, roasted rare as a whole piece and sliced a centimetre thick.

STYLE **dry**
QUALITY ♟ ♟ ♟ ♟ ♟
VALUE ☆ ☆ ☆ ☆ ½
GRAPES **Merlot**
REGION **Hawke's Bay**
CELLAR 2
PRICE **$24–26**

Askerne Hawke's Bay Young Vines Cabernet/Merlot/Malbec/Franc

STYLE dry

QUALITY ♟ ♟ ♟

VALUE ☆ ☆ ☆ ⟨

GRAPES
Cab Sauvignon 68%
Merlot 16%
Malbec 8%
Cabernet Franc 8%

REGION Hawke's Bay

CELLAR 🍾 2

PRICE $20–23

The grapes are the four 'biggies' of the red wine world, but the wine is priced to make it accessible to a wide audience. Oak maturation was kept to a minimum in keeping with the style.
Current Release 2001 The bouquet has a good quota of ripe berryfruit, but there's a suggestion of leafiness at the back. It's a smooth-centred middleweight on the palate, with a short but nicely fruited finish. Partner it with grilled sausages rolled into slices of lightly buttered bread.

Babich Hawke's Bay Cabernet/Merlot

STYLE dry

QUALITY ♟ ♟ ♟ ⟨

VALUE ☆ ☆ ☆ ☆

GRAPES
Cab Sauvignon 75%
Merlot 25%

REGION Hawke's Bay

CELLAR 🍾 3

PRICE $15–17

This blend spent a year in a mixture of French and American oak barrels. The grapes came from the Fernhill vineyard, which has produced some excellent fruit over the years for winemaker Adam Hazeldine.
Current Release 2000 Gentle oak spice sits behind aromas of blackberries and chocolate. It's a sweet-fruited middleweight, savoury-edged with integrated tannins adding grip to the finish. Try it alongside a marinated sirloin steak, briefly marinated in olive oil and rosemary before being barbecued rare.

Babich Irongate Cabernet/Merlot

STYLE dry

QUALITY ♟ ♟ ♟ ♟ ♟

VALUE ☆ ☆ ☆ ⟨

GRAPES
Cab Sauvignon 55%
Merlot 38%
Cabernet Franc 7%

REGION Hawke's Bay

CELLAR 🍾 2–6

PRICE $35–38

Hand-harvested fruit, fermentation in open vats, laboriously plunging the cap of skins back through the fermenting juice – this red has had the lot. After all that it was aged in French oak barrels, 25% of them new, for 16 months.
Current Release 2000 Merlot's distinctive leathery notes cut through on the berryish bouquet. It's sweet-fruited, rich and superbly ripe on the palate. Joe Babich suggests decanting it to help it open up – traditionally, it stays 'tight' for three or four years after being bottled. Roast saddle of hare would be perfect, but a rare sirloin steak would certainly do at a pinch.

Babich The Patriarch Cabernet Sauvignon

The Patriarch after whom this wine and its sister chardonnay were named was Josip Babich, who arrived from Dalmatia, worked in the kauri-gum swamps of the far north and saved enough to buy the land where the winery is still situated.

Current Release 2000 It's a biggie! Aromas of savoury oak and super-ripe blackcurrants lead to a flavour profile that is solid but rich, with open fruit ensuring richness through the middle. It makes a great partner for a salami-topped pizza.

STYLE **dry**
QUALITY ♟♟♟♟♟
VALUE ☆ ☆ ☆
GRAPES **Cab Sauvignon**
REGION **Hawke's Bay**
CELLAR 4
PRICE **$36–39**

Babich Winemakers Reserve Merlot

The fruit for this nicely balanced red came from the famed Gimblett Gravels region – in fact, the vineyard is in Gimblett Road itself. It spent a quiet few months in French oak barrels, 20% of which were new.

Current Release 1999 Black Doris plums with smoky oak on the side do it for me in the bouquet. There's an attractive savoury edge on the berryish fruit flavours, and a dash of typical merlot leather on the finish. Match the savouriness with a handful of chopped sage sprinkled over a plain tomato and cheese pizza.

STYLE **dry**
QUALITY ♟♟♟♟
VALUE ☆ ☆ ☆ ☆
GRAPES **Merlot**
REGION **Hawke's Bay**
CELLAR 3
PRICE **$22–24**

Benfield & Delamare
Cabernet Sauvignon/Cabernet Franc

Bill Benfield and Sue Delamare have been called fanatical in at least one wine shop's literature. That might be a bit over the top, but they are certainly fixated on the premise that great Bordeaux-style reds can be made from Martinborough grapes.

Current Release 2000 The bouquet is smoky and savoury and the flavour profile is broad at first, but perfectly focused on the finish. In between, there is a wealth of ripe fruit flavour given substance by nicely integrated tannins. It's a very classy red that goes well with pan-fried liver and bacon – in my view, a greatly underrated dish.

STYLE **dry**
QUALITY ♟♟♟♟♟
VALUE ☆ ☆ ☆
GRAPES
  Cab Sauvignon 85%
  Cabernet Franc 13%
  Merlot 2%
REGION **Martinborough**
CELLAR 6
PRICE **$53–56**

Bilancia Merlot

Lorraine Leheny and Warren Gibson used fruit from highly regarded Gimblett Road for this classy red, and they paid the grower for quality, not quantity. That's the best way to ensure really good grapes.

Current Release 2000 Smoky oak backs merlot's typical leather characters on the nose. It's nicely balanced, with rich, savoury characters ensuring plenty of flavour depth. The finish is lingering and gently spiced. It goes well with smoked beef, pot-roasted and served with young carrots, new potatoes and bok choy.

STYLE **dry**
QUALITY ♟♟♟♟
VALUE ☆ ☆ ☆
GRAPES **Merlot**
REGION **Hawke's Bay**
CELLAR 4
PRICE **$39–43**

Bilancia Merlot/Cabernet Sauvignon

STYLE dry
QUALITY 4 glasses
VALUE 3 stars
GRAPES
Merlot 60%
Cab Sauvignon 40%
REGION Hawke's Bay
CELLAR 1–5
PRICE $33–35

Lorraine Leheny got the grapes for this blend from the sought-after Gimblett Road area, where shingle on the soil reflects warmth onto the bunches. It spent 13 months in oak barrels.

Current Release 1999 Spicy oak mingles with the savoury notes of ripe merlot in the bouquet – the cabernet component seems content to take a back seat. It's broadly focused, with loads of ripe fruit and well-tuned tannins. It goes well with casseroled beef rump and parsnips.

Black Barn Vineyards Hawke's Bay Merlot/Cabernet Sauvignon/Cabernet Franc

STYLE dry
QUALITY 3½ glasses
VALUE 3½ stars
GRAPES
Merlot 54%
Cab Sauvignon 30%
Cabernet Franc 16%
REGION Hawke's Bay
CELLAR 3
PRICE $23–26

Only 15% of the French oak barrels in which this three-grape blend was matured were new, so they are in no danger of overpowering the fruit. Black Barn is the name adopted for wines from the Lombardi property, in Hawke's Bay.

Current Release 2001 Leather has got the gig on the nose, but there are also some pleasant plum aromas in there if you search. It's smooth on the front palate, builds a bit of tannic grip through the middle and finishes cleanly. It works well with all-beef chipolata sausages served with a pile of thickly sliced bread.

Black Barn Vineyards Hawke's Bay Reserve Merlot

STYLE dry
QUALITY 4 glasses
VALUE 2½ stars
GRAPES
Merlot 85%
Cab Sauvignon 10%
Cabernet Franc 4%
Malbec 1%
REGION Hawke's Bay
CELLAR 1–4
PRICE $36–39

It's labelled merlot, but as the table shows it's actually a blend of four varieties. All the reds in the Black Barn range are made from grapes processed in an old-style basket press. That means they really are hand-made.

Current Release 2001 Spicy oak sits happily behind the aromas of freshly polished leather and ripe blackberries. It's broadly textured on the front palate but has good focus through the middle. The spicy note returns to enliven the finish. If you can find a Hawke's Bay ostrich steak, cook it rare and try it with a glass of the wine.

Brajkovich Kumeu Merlot

STYLE dry
QUALITY 3 glasses
VALUE 4½ stars
GRAPES Merlot
REGION West Auckland
CELLAR 2
PRICE $15–17

Kumeu River winemaker, Master of Wine Michael Brajkovich, says sniffing merlot should be 'like climbing into an old Jaguar on a hot day'. It's a great analogy that describes the leather and tobacco aromas found in many examples.

Current Release 2000 I'm not sure about the old Jag, but there is certainly a touch of smokiness about the bouquet. It's a soft-centred, unassuming wine that wasn't designed to be cogitated over. Partner it with a ham and leek fritatta some hot summer's day and you'll be perfectly satisfied.

Breakaway Bay Cabernet Sauvignon/Malbec

Grapes for this Villa Maria red came from various sites in New Zealand and Argentina. The South American component was made into finished wine before being shipped out in pressurised containers.

Current Release (non-vintage) There's a light dash of spice on the nose to go with the blackberry and tar aromas. It's sweet-fruited on the palate, but suffers from leanness in the middle that drifts onto the finish. It works adequately with barbecued sausages, but it won't get you overly excited.

STYLE dry
QUALITY ♟♟♟
VALUE ☆☆☆☆☆
GRAPES Cab Sauvignon
Merlot
Syrah
Malbec
REGION Various
CELLAR 1
PRICE $12–14

Breakaway Bay Cabernet Sauvignon/Merlot

One of an increasing number of trans-country blends, this two-grape blend from Villa is better than most. The Argentinean component is shipped out in pressurised, chilled containers and blended in Auckland.

Current Release (non-vintage) There's a wee hint of leafiness on the nose, but mostly the aromas are of ripe plums and berryfruit. Gentle tannins ensure the fruit flavours dominate – oak plays only a minor part. It's an easy-going, pleasant wine that goes well with Italian-style steak, cut thin and served with a creamy sauce.

STYLE dry
QUALITY ♟♟♟
VALUE ☆☆☆☆☆
GRAPES Cab Sauvignon
Merlot
REGION Hawke's Bay
Argentina
CELLAR 2
PRICE $12–14

Brick Bay Matakana Pharos

Christine Didsbury's Brick Bay vineyard is best known for a delicious pinot gris, but it was between releases when this *Guide* went to press. This is the property's first red, and it has been highly praised. The grape varieties are on the back.

Current Release 2000 The oak was dominating the blackcurrant and plum aromas when I tried it, but that will have settled down by now. It's deliciously ripe-fruited on the palate, with tannins that add grip without making the wine too hard. It's excellent with penne pasta tossed with beef ragu.

STYLE dry
QUALITY ♟♟♟♟
VALUE ☆☆☆☆
GRAPES
Cab Sauvignon 60%
Cabernet Franc 30%
Merlot 10%
REGION Matakana
CELLAR 4
PRICE $27–31

Brightwater Vineyards Nelson Merlot

Most Nelsonian growers concentrate on pinot noir if they fancy growing a red grape, but a few enthusiasts believe cabernet sauvignon and merlot have a good future in the area. Good luck to them!

Current Release 1999 It's a middleweight, but it has some pleasantly smoky characters on the nose behind the usual aromas of ripe plums, and a reasonable quota of berry-like flavours. Gentle tannins leave the fruit to get on with the job, making it a good partner for roast duck in a berry-spiked sauce.

STYLE dry
QUALITY ♟♟♟♟
VALUE ☆☆☆☆
GRAPES Merlot
REGION Nelson
CELLAR 1
PRICE $20–23

Brookfields Otihi Estate Cabernet Sauvignon

STYLE **dry**
QUALITY 🍷🍷🍷🍷
VALUE ★★★★☆
GRAPES **Cab Sauvignon**
REGION **Hawke's Bay**
CELLAR 🍾 **3**
PRICE **$19–21**

The grapes for this straightforward cabernet were grown on shingle-covered flats adjoining the Ngaruroro River. Peter Robertson organised for them to be picked by hand, and matured the fledgling wine in mostly French oak.

Current Release 2001 There's a pleasant touch of smokiness behind the aromas of ripe blackcurrants, plus a suggestion of vanilla from the few American barrels in the mainly French line-up. It's clean and nicely focused on the palate, with sweet flavours through the middle and a moderately long finish. Ham and eggplant fritters would make a good match.

Brookfields Reserve Vintage Cabernet/Merlot

STYLE **dry**
QUALITY 🍷🍷🍷🍷🍷
VALUE ★★☆
GRAPES
  Cab Sauvignon 85%
  Merlot 10%
  Malbec 5%
REGION **Hawke's Bay**
CELLAR 🍾 **1–6**
PRICE **$50–55**

This three-grape blend, commonly known as 'Brookfield Gold Label', is made only in exceptional vintages. That means it's pretty hard to find, but it's worth a search. If all else fails, try calling the winery.

Current Release 2000 Big, ripe fruit aromas and flavours backed by sweet, spicy oak make this wine a winner from first sniff to last swallow. Good balance is its passport to success, and Peter Robertson has done well despite using all new barrels. Cleverly, they don't dominate the fruit. Partner it with a rare ostrich steak and drink a toast to Hawke's Bay.

C.J. Pask Hawke's Bay Reserve Merlot

STYLE **dry**
QUALITY 🍷🍷🍷🍷🍷
VALUE ★★☆
GRAPES **Merlot**
REGION **Hawke's Bay**
CELLAR 🍾 **3**
PRICE **$46–49**

Most people favour French oak for merlot, but Kate Radburnd included a few American barrels in the mix when she matured this one. Just as unusually, every one of them was new. She believed the fruit was big enough to take it.

Current Release 2000 This is one serious red! The bouquet is chock-full of ripe plum aromas, with the sweet, spicy oak sitting where it should, firmly in the background. It's rich, savoury and mouth-filling on the palate, and boasts a finish that goes on forever. Beef lasagne would match it well.

Camana Farm Forte

STYLE **dry**
QUALITY 🍷🍷🍷🍷
VALUE ★★★
GRAPES
  Cab Franc 50%
  Merlot 40%
  Cab Sauvignon 10%
REGION
  Waiheke Island
CELLAR 🍾 **1–3**
PRICE **$29–33**

The '99 version of this three-grape blend attracted a lot of attention, and this later model is at least as impressive. David and Veronika Evans-Gander are pioneering a new sub-region in the south-west of Waiheke Island, and early results look very promising.

Current Release 2000 Smoky oak backgrounds the aromas of ripe plums and blackberries. It's richly fruited on the palate, with the oak now serving to soften the texture and add an interesting touch of spice to the finish. It makes a good partner for an Italian-style beef and capsicum stew.

Canadoro Martinborough Cabernet Sauvignon

Who said you can't ripen cabernet in Martinborough – this local example has an alcohol level of 14.4%, and that means the grapes were very ripe indeed. Greg Robins matured it in a mixture of new and used French oak barrels for 10 months.
Current Release 2000 You want berries? This is like sniffing blackcurrant conserve! The lick of sweet oak in the background is a reminder that it's wine we're on about, and the same character drifts through to the palate. It's richly fruited and manages to stay nicely balanced despite all the alcohol. Enjoy it with pan-fried liver.

STYLE dry
QUALITY ▽▽▽▽▽
VALUE ☆☆☆☆
GRAPES Cab Sauvignon
REGION Martinborough
CELLAR 3
PRICE $28–30

Charles Wiffen Marlborough Merlot

Charles and Sandi Wiffen have made their name with whites, particularly sauvignon blanc and riesling, but this red is good enough to become a permanent member of their small portfolio.
Current Release 2001 Plummy fruit and spicy oak on the nose, ripe berries surrounded by smartly integrated tannins on the palate – this wine certainly showed promise when I tried it. It's a likeable middleweight that would go well with braised mutton chops in winter, or a pink lamb salad in summer.

STYLE dry
QUALITY ▽▽▽▽
VALUE ☆☆☆
GRAPES Merlot
REGION Marlborough
CELLAR 1–3
PRICE $35–38

Church Road Hawke's Bay Cabernet Sauvignon/Merlot

The Church Road winery boasts one of the most elegant interiors in the business. Functions are held on a raised area overlooking rows of barrels in which the latest vintage of this and other reds quietly build their flavours.
Current Release 2000 The bouquet is savoury and gently berryish. It's smooth on the palate, sweet-edged with well-directed flavours and a moderately long finish. Enjoy it with a 'sandwich' of thin slices of rare beef between two thicker slices of grilled eggplant.

STYLE dry
QUALITY ▽▽▽▽
VALUE ☆☆☆☆
GRAPES
  Cab Sauvignon 55%
  Merlot 40%
  Cabernet Franc 4%
  Malbec 1%
REGION Hawke's Bay
CELLAR 3
PRICE $21–24

Church Road Reserve Cabernet Sauvignon/Merlot

Montana is to be commended for keeping some wines back from sale until the winemaking team feels they're starting to really hit their straps. This one is still youthful, proving they knew what they were doing.
Current Release 1997 Merlot's earthy, leather characters dominate the bouquet, along with sweet, smoky oak. The youthful profile is still evident in the upfront ripe fruit flavours, given just enough grip by the restrained tannins. It makes a perfect partner for braised ox cheek.

STYLE dry
QUALITY ▽▽▽▽▽
VALUE ☆☆☆☆
GRAPES
  Cab Sauvignon 74%
  Merlot 20%
  Cabernet Franc 6%
REGION Hawke's Bay
CELLAR 3
PRICE $30–33

Clearview Estate Reserve Old Olive Block

STYLE **dry**

QUALITY ♟♟♟♟♟

VALUE ☆ ☆ ☆

GRAPES **Cab Sauvignon**
Cab Franc
Merlot
Malbec

REGION **Hawke's Bay**

CELLAR 🍶 **4**

PRICE **$35–38**

The winery is tiny, but Tim Turvey made enough of this big-hearted red to send a parcel to the UK – and the Brits loved it. It must have been quite a surprise. Overseas, most people think New Zealand vineyards are wall-to-wall sauvignon blanc.

Current Release 2000 There's a fair whack of oak spice on the nose, but the ripe berry and plum aromas can handle themselves. The flavours are rich, the texture impressively smooth and the finish grippy and long. Tim sometimes has ostrich steaks on his restaurant menu. Perfect!

Clearview Reserve Merlot/Malbec

STYLE **dry**

QUALITY ♟♟♟♟

VALUE ☆ ☆

GRAPES **Merlot**
Malbec

REGION **Hawke's Bay**

CELLAR 🍶 **3**

PRICE **$39–42**

Clearview wines have traditionally been hard to find, but they seem to be making it onto a few more retail shelves in recent vintages. The label is most famous for big, strapping chardonnays, but there are a number of reds in the portfolio.

Current Release 2000 Surprisingly for this label and these grapes, this is a middleweight red. It's got good sweet fruit aromas and a reasonable amount of mid-palate richness, but there's a suggestion of leafiness on the finish. It works okay with summer nibbles like salami and olives.

Collards Cabernet/Merlot

STYLE **dry**

QUALITY ♟♟♟

VALUE ☆ ☆ ☆ ☆ ☆

GRAPES
Cab Sauvignon
Merlot
Cabernet Franc

REGION **West Auckland**
Te Kauwhata
Hawke's Bay

CELLAR 🍶 **1**

PRICE **$11–13**

This three-grape blend (just – there's only a touch of cabernet franc) from the Collard family enjoys a steady following, and sells particularly well by mail order. The price makes it one of the least expensive reds in the country.

Current Release 2000 The smoky nose suggests good things to come, and indeed the clean, berryish flavours in smooth surroundings give this latest model a tad more character than the last couple were able to offer. It's a simply structured middleweight that makes an acceptable fun-time sipper.

Collards Hawke's Bay Merlot

STYLE **dry**

QUALITY ♟♟♟

VALUE ☆ ☆ ☆⸴

GRAPES **Merlot**

REGION **Hawke's Bay**

CELLAR 🍶 **2**

PRICE **$19–21**

This merlot doesn't have a high profile, despite being made from grapes grown on the famed shingle-covered soils of Hawke's Bay's Gimblett Gravels region. It spent a year in oak barrels.

Current Release 1999 Leather is a classic merlot aromatic association, and there's certainly plenty of it on the nose, along with a healthy dose of oak spice. It's a smooth-centred middleweight with some sweet fruit characters, a pleasant texture and a short but clean-cut finish. Try it with smoked beef sausages.

Collards Shanty Block Malbec

The Shanty Block was planted in Henderson by horticulturist J. W. Collard in 1910. That means the grapes used for this chunky red were from gnarled old vines that save their energy by giving low crops.

Current Release 2001 The bouquet is smoky and savoury, with oak spice filling in the gaps. It's broad and smooth on the palate, and would go well with non-assertive dishes like casseroled lamb, served on mashed potatoes.

STYLE **dry**
QUALITY ♟ ♟ ♟
VALUE ☆ ☆ ☆
GRAPES **Malbec**
REGION **West Auckland**
CELLAR **3**
PRICE **$25–27**

Coopers Creek
Cabernet Sauvignon/Cabernet Franc

These two varieties are cousins, and are seldom seen together without a bit of merlot. Simon Nunns kept them separate in a mixture of new and used American oak barrels, then blended them after eight months.

Current Release 2000 Cabernet franc has added a floral edge to the more overtly berryish aromas of its better-known cousin. It's a pleasant middleweight, sweet-fruited with a spicy edge from its time in oak, and works just fine alongside home-made pizza topped with salami, good mozzarella and pulped tomatoes.

STYLE **dry**
QUALITY ♟ ♟ ♟ ♟
VALUE ☆ ☆ ☆ ☆ ☆
GRAPES
  Cab Sauvignon 80%
  Cabernet Franc 20%
REGION **Hawke's Bay**
CELLAR **2**
PRICE **$16–18**

Coopers Creek Hawke's Bay Merlot

Simon Nunns matured this mid-range merlot in a mixture of French and American oak barrels. American oak is generally considered more outspoken than its European cousin, and often smells vaguely like coconut or vanilla.

Current Release 2000 I don't get any coconut in this wine, but there's a vanilla edge on the sweet, plummy aromas. The plum characters make it through pretty well unscathed to the palate, and the oak softens things out, especially on the finish. Enjoy it with a brace of lamb chops, grilled or pan-fried.

STYLE **dry**
QUALITY ♟ ♟ ♟ ♟
VALUE ☆ ☆ ☆ ☆ ☆
GRAPES **Merlot**
REGION **Hawke's Bay**
CELLAR **3**
PRICE **$16–18**

Coopers Creek The Gardener Reserve Huapai Merlot

The 'gardener' who has had this big-hearted red named after him is Cooper's Creek viticulturist, Wayne Morrow, who has looked after the gently sloping home vineyard for several years.

Current Release 1999 What a beauty! The suggestion of ripe plums on the nose leads to a flavour profile rich in sweet fruit and chocolate sensations. It's smooth-textured, but there's enough mid-palate grip to suggest it may well age longer than my cautious estimate. Enjoy it with liver, pan-fried with thinly sliced onions.

STYLE **dry**
QUALITY ♟ ♟ ♟ ♟ ♟
VALUE ☆ ☆ ☆ ☆
GRAPES **Merlot**
REGION **West Auckland**
CELLAR **2**
PRICE **$29–33**

Corbans Cottage Block
Cabernet Sauvignon/Cabernet Franc/Merlot

STYLE dry
QUALITY ▼▼▼▼▼
VALUE ★★★
GRAPES
  Cab Sauvignon 69%
  Cabernet Franc 18%
  Merlot 13%
REGION Hawke's Bay
CELLAR 4
PRICE $35–38

The Cottage Block series has been very successful for the Corbans/Montana group. The reds, particularly, have a keen following, and people seem relaxed about paying up to $75 for a bottle in restaurants.

Current Release 1998 It's a biggie! The bouquet represents the three varieties in equal measure, with blackcurrant, plum and faintly floral characters all making their presence felt. The flavours are rich and generous, and the tannins firm right through to the finish. Try it with casseroled beef and dumplings.

Corbans Estate Cabernet Sauvignon/Merlot

STYLE dry
QUALITY ▼▼
VALUE ★★★
GRAPES Cab Sauvignon
  Merlot
REGION
  north-west Victoria
CELLAR
PRICE $12–14

The fruit comes from north-west Victoria, but the wine is finished off in this country. Both Corbans and Montana (now under the same ownership) import overseas wine in bulk.

Current Release 2000 Gum leaves and leather occupy the bouquet. That sounds promising, but the flavour profile is thin and light, and the finish pretty unyielding. It might work okay with a beef sausage buttie, but don't leave it too long – it's not one for the long haul.

Corbans White Label Cabernet Sauvignon

STYLE dry
QUALITY ▼▼▼
VALUE ★★★
GRAPES Cab Sauvignon
REGION Australia
  Chile
CELLAR 1
PRICE $8–9

The fine print on the label tells us the fruit came from Australia and Chile, but nothing more specific. This simply structured red rockets out the doors of supermarkets around the country. At the price it is often discounted to, it's hardly surprising.

Current Release 2001 Raspberries and tomato leaf share the honours on the nose. It's clean and straightforward, with enough sweet fruit character to suggest it may have had a little residual sugar left in the mix. It makes a perfectly adequate accompaniment to a platter of easy-going nibbles like olives and sliced salami.

Corbans Winemaker's Cottage Block Marlborough
Cabernet Sauvignon/Merlot

STYLE dry
QUALITY ▼▼▼▼▼
VALUE ★★★★
GRAPES Cab Sauvignon
  Merlot
REGION Marlborough
CELLAR 3
PRICE $35–38

Yes, 1996 is the current release of this red – Montana must have found a few bottles under the sofa when they took over the Corbans brand. I'm delighted that they did. After nearly nine years in barrel and bottle, it's drinking splendidly.

Current Release 1996 Charred, smoky oak, ripe blackberries and plums, suggestions of leather and cassis – they're all there on the nose. It's so smooth on the palate that it merits the description 'velvety', which I don't get to use very often. Pay due homage to its seniority by partnering it with a really well-aged piece of beef sirloin, roasted.

Cornerstone Cabernet/Merlot/Malbec

Made as a joint effort by Bob Newton of Hawke's Bay and Dr John Forrest of Marlborough, this big-hearted red comes from the heart of the well-regarded Gimblett Gravels sub-region. *Cuisine* magazine recently gave it five stars.

Current Release 2000 Talk about Ribena for grown-ups – this wine smells like blackcurrant concentrate! It's full and rich on the palate, with perfect balance between fruit and oak and a long, sweet-edged finish. Partner all that opulence with casseroled venison, preferably wild.

STYLE **dry**
QUALITY ♟♟♟♟♟
VALUE ☆☆☆
GRAPES
  Cab Sauvignon 45%
  Merlot 35%
  Malbec 15%
  Cabernet Franc 5%
REGION **Hawke's Bay**
CELLAR ⬛▷ **1–5**
PRICE **$39–43**

Craggy Range Gimblett Gravels Merlot

This wine hadn't been bottled when I tried it, but potential as a barrel sample was enough for me to award it a top rating. Craggy Range boss Steve Smith is a huge fan of the Gimblett Gravels area.

Current Release 2001 Think ripe plums, recently polished leather and even sweet pipe tobacco and you'll have a handle on the bouquet. It's richly fruited, smartly balanced and mouth-fillingly smooth on the palate, and would go brilliantly with a rare-roasted saddle of hare. That's a hard meat to track down, but beef fillet would do at a pinch.

STYLE **dry**
QUALITY ♟♟♟♟♟
VALUE ☆☆☆☆⯪
GRAPES **Merlot**
REGION **Hawke's Bay**
CELLAR ⬛▷ **2–5**
PRICE **$25–28**

Craggy Range Winery Seven Poplars Vineyard Merlot

The debut 1999 version of this wine was voted one of the top 100 great wines of the world by the UK's respected *Decanter* magazine. This latest model spent a year in new French barrels and was then transferred to older models for another nine months.

Current Release 2000 Sweet plum aromas are joined by gentle spice on the nose, and they go together well. It's broadly textured on the palate with masses of ripe fruit giving it exceptional richness. The finish is long and satisfying. Viticulturist Steve Smith suggests partnering it with 'any meat dish that retains some juices'. Sounds like rare beef sirloin to me.

STYLE **dry**
QUALITY ♟♟♟♟♟
VALUE ☆☆⯪
GRAPES **Merlot**
REGION **Hawke's Bay**
CELLAR 🍾 **3**
PRICE **$40–43**

De Redcliffe Hawke's Bay Estates Cabernet/Merlot/Franc

STYLE **dry**

QUALITY ♟ ♟ ♟

VALUE ☆ ☆ ☆ ☆

GRAPES
Cab Sauvignon 51%
Merlot 35%
Cab Franc 14%

REGION Hawke's Bay

CELLAR 🍶 2

PRICE $15–17

De Redcliffe founder, Chris Canning, was the first person to blend cabernet sauvignon and merlot together in this country, at least in modern times. That was in 1983, and he has long since moved on from the wine business.

Current Release 1999 The bouquet is smoky and leathery, with cabernet's berry characters pushed to the back. It's on the light side, simply structured and undemanding, and makes a perfectly acceptable partner for simple fare like that favourite of the fund-raising cookbook, beef olives.

Delegat's Hawke's Bay Cabernet/Merlot

STYLE **dry**

QUALITY ♟ ♟ ♟ ♟

VALUE ☆ ☆ ☆ ☆ ☆

GRAPES
Cab Sauvignon 50%
Merlot 50%

REGION Hawke's Bay

CELLAR 🍶 2

PRICE $15–17

Winemakers Michael Ivicevich and Jamie Marfell aged the component parts of this mid-range blend in oak barrels for just six months. Most of them were French, but a few were American.

Current Release 2000 Smoky oak, blackcurrants and raspberries form the aromatic trio on the nose. It's a pleasant middleweight, with good texture and a ripe-fruited finish. It sits very happily indeed next to a home-made pizza with a simple topping of pulped tomatoes, good Parmigiano and torn basil leaves.

Delegat's Reserve Cabernet Sauvignon

STYLE **dry**

QUALITY ♟ ♟ ♟ ♟ ♟

VALUE ☆ ☆ ☆ ☆ ☆

GRAPES Cab Sauvignon

REGION Hawke's Bay

CELLAR 🍶 1–4

PRICE $20–23

The highly regarded Gimblett Road area, where shingle ensures good drainage and, as a bonus, reflects the sun's ripening rays onto the grapes, provided the fruit for this classy cabernet.

Current Release 2000 Ripe blackcurrants, blackberries and sweet, spicy oak form the welcoming committee. It's richly fruited, and achieves the difficult balancing act between power and elegance that is the aim of every winemaker. Enjoy it with a beef topside pot roast, sliced and draped over garlic-laced mashed potatoes.

Delegat's Reserve Merlot

STYLE **dry**

QUALITY ♟ ♟ ♟ ♟ ♟

VALUE ☆ ☆ ☆ ☆ ☆

GRAPES Merlot

REGION Hawke's Bay

CELLAR 🍶 4

PRICE $20–23

The grapes for this stylish red came from a vineyard with clayey soil, which seems to suit merlot. The winemaking team plunged the skins back through the juice during fermentation to increase the uptake of flavour and colour.

Current Release 2000 Newly polished leather and ripe plums are backed by sweet 'n' spicy oak in the bouquet. It's deliciously smooth on the palate, with the plum impressions joined by a suggestion of chocolate. Smart stuff! It goes really well with cervena back steaks, grilled blue – or rare, if you must.

Drylands Marlborough Winemaker's Reserve Merlot

Marlborough's well-publicised 2001 drought was tough for pastoralists, but winemakers were cautiously happy. Darryl Woolley picked a small crop of merlot, but the grapes had greatly intensified flavours.

Current Release 2001 It spent 10 months in French and American oak barrels, but they have added no more than a touch of spice to the primary aromas of ripe plums and sweet pipe tobacco. It's smooth, broadly focused and nicely balanced on the palate and makes a good partner for char-grilled pork chops topped with a garlicky tomato-based sauce.

STYLE **dry**
QUALITY ▽▽▽▽▽
VALUE ☆☆☆☆☆
GRAPES **Merlot**
REGION **Marlborough**
CELLAR **3**
PRICE **$20–23**

Dunleavy Waiheke Island Cabernet/Merlot

This is the second label to Te Motu, from the Dunleavy family's Waiheke Vineyards property. All the company's wines are held back until the team feels they're close to their best, so there's still some of the 1999 vintage about.

Current Release 2000 Gently berryish on the nose with no more than a dash of spice, this is a pleasant red with a soft texture courtesy of the nicely integrated oak. It has a good quota of sweet fruit and a reasonably long finish. It goes well with a sandwich of rare roast beef with chopped watercress.

STYLE **dry**
QUALITY ▽▽▽▽
VALUE ☆☆☆
GRAPES
  Cab Sauvignon 63%
  Merlot 18%
  Cab Franc 15%
  Malbec 4%
REGION
  Waiheke Island
CELLAR **3**
PRICE **$35–38**

Equinox Hawke's Bay Merlot/Cabernet Sauvignon

This nicely packaged red spent a year in oak barrels, mostly French but a few American. Because they were all at least a year old, they have had a relatively restrained effect on the flavour. That's good winemaking.

Current Release 2000 The oak has added quite gentle spicy, savoury characters to the predominant aromas of ripe plums. It's smooth on the palate, with broad flavours reminiscent of blackberries and currants. The finish is sweet-edged and quite long. It's good with home-made pizza topped with pulped tomatoes and discs of chorizo sausage.

STYLE **dry**
QUALITY ▽▽▽▽
VALUE ☆☆☆☆⯪
GRAPES
  Merlot 67%
  Cab Sauvignon 25%
  Malbec 8%
REGION **Hawke's Bay**
CELLAR **3**
PRICE **$20–23**

Esk Valley Hawke's Bay Merlot (Black Label)

Gordon Russell had pretty well given up on the 2000 vintage because of all the pre-Christmas rain. Then a long, dry February cheered him up immensely and he ended up with fruit he describes as 'excellent'.

Current Release 2000 Vanilla and smoky oak complement the ripe plum aromas. It's smooth and approachable on the palate, with middleweight fruit flavours bordered by gentle tannins. It would make a good partner for aubergine fritters smeared with a not-too-sweet fruit chutney.

STYLE **dry**
QUALITY ▽▽▽
VALUE ☆☆☆
GRAPES **Merlot**
REGION **Hawke's Bay**
CELLAR **2**
PRICE **$23–26**

Esk Valley Merlot/Cabernet Sauvignon (Black Label)

STYLE **dry**

QUALITY ▼▼▼▼

VALUE ☆ ☆ ☆ ☆

GRAPES
Merlot 59%
Cab Sauvignon 26%
Cabernet Franc 8%
Malbec 7%

REGION **Hawke's Bay**

CELLAR 🍾 2

PRICE **$23–26**

Winemaker Gordon Russell is a great fan of hand-plunging the juice for his red wines. It involves using a 'paddle' to push the cap of skins on top of the fermenting tank back through the juice, and it's very hard work.

Current Release 2000 Smoky oak sits behind the aromas of ripe blackberries. It's sweet-fruited, moderately rich through the middle and displays nicely balanced oak. It makes a good partner for Italian-style beef rissoles, made from minced beef, pine nuts, chopped onion and garlic.

Esk Valley Reserve Merlot/Cabernet Sauvignon/Malbec

STYLE **dry**

QUALITY ▼▼▼▼▼

VALUE ☆ ☆ ☆

GRAPES
Merlot 60%
Cab Sauvignon 21%
Malbec 19%

REGION **Hastings**

CELLAR 🍾 6

PRICE **$48–52**

The percentages change from year to year, but this is always one of the country's top reds. Gordon Russell also makes The Terraces from grapes grown behind the winery, but because it's exceedingly rare most people settle for this one.

Current Release 2000 Wow! Sweet, spicy oak, cassis, raspberries, blackberries, plums – name it, and you're likely to find it in the bouquet. It's equally complex and rich on the palate, but clever use of oak means the overall impression is of mouth-filling softness. There's nothing better with a cervena back steak topped with pan-fried mushrooms.

Esk Valley The Terraces

STYLE **dry**

QUALITY ▼▼▼▼▼

VALUE ☆ ☆ ☆

GRAPES
Merlot
Cabernet Franc
Malbec

REGION **Hawke's Bay**

CELLAR 🍾 8

PRICE **$75–79**

Gordon Russell makes this top-tier red solely from grapes gown on the steep terraced vineyard behind the winery. That means there's never much of it, but it's on sale briefly each year by mail order and from the cellar door.

Current Release 2000 Wow – it sure is a biggie! Blackcurrants, raspberries, smoky oak and a suggestion of coffee all contribute to the extraordinary bouquet. It's full, richly fruited and superbly smooth on the palate, with a finish that goes on for hours. Casseroled venison, ideally wild, would be perfect with it.

Fenton Cabernet Sauvignon/Merlot/Franc

There's not a lot of this top-shelf blend around, and none was made in 1999. The price was criticised at first, but other Waiheke producers have caught up. The Fenton crew says it is justified because it is made only in exceptional years.
Current Release 2000 'Big smoothie' pretty well sums up the flavour profile. Partly, that's because no new oak whatever was used in its maturation, but the texture is also the product of exceptionally ripe fruit, sensitively handled. It needs slow-cooked food to bring out its best — try it with braised beef shin.

STYLE **dry**
QUALITY ♟♟♟♟
VALUE ☆☆
GRAPES
  Cab Sauvignon 60%
  Merlot 30%
  Cab Franc 10%
REGION
  Waiheke Island
CELLAR ▭ 1–4
PRICE $45–48

Fenton The Red

The colourfully labelled 'red' is made in years when the fruit is considered not quite good enough for the top Fenton wine. That means the grapes used vary from year to year. Sometimes it is a blend, but in 2000 cabernet sauvignon got the gig to itself.
Current Release 2000 Cabernet's usual cassis and blackberry aromas are in good shape on the bouquet. It's not overly complex, but straightforward fruit flavours and good focus give it weight and warmth through the middle. Enjoy it with Italian-style meatballs in a tomato and basil sauce.

STYLE **dry**
QUALITY ♟♟♟
VALUE ☆☆⯪
GRAPES
  Cabernet Sauvignon
REGION
  Waiheke Island
CELLAR 🍾 2
PRICE $32–35

Firstland Hawke's Bay Cabernet Sauvignon/Merlot

Fruit for this two-grape blend came from two well-regarded vineyards, one in famed Gimblett Road, the other in Links Road. Mark Compton, whose winery is next to the plush Hotel du Vin, put them together and matured them in oak.
Current Release 1999 There's a good belt of plummy fruit on the nose and some pleasant ripe-fruit characters on the palate, but it is pretty basic in the middle and on the faintly leafy finish. Partner it with a platter of finger foods like salami and olives.

STYLE **dry**
QUALITY ♟♟♟
VALUE ☆☆☆⯪
GRAPES
  Cab Sauvignon 63%
  Merlot 31%
  Cabernet Franc 3%
  Syrah 3%
REGION Hawke's Bay
CELLAR 🍾 2
PRICE $20–22

Firstland Reserve Cabernet

The fruit came from the heart of the sought-after Gimblett Gravels area, and Mark Compton fermented and matured it for a year in a mixture of French and American oak barrels.
Current Release 1999 The nose is big, smoky and faintly tarry, presumably from the syrah. It's broadly textured with loads of ripe fruit in smooth surroundings. Restrained tannins provide about the right sort of edge, and make it a good partner for slow-cooked food like casseroled lamb shanks with sliced red onion.

STYLE **dry**
QUALITY ♟♟♟♟
VALUE ☆☆☆⯪
GRAPES
  Cab Sauvignon 78%
  Syrah 22%
REGION Hawke's Bay
CELLAR 🍾 3
PRICE $30–34

Forrest Marlborough Gibson's Creek Merlot

STYLE **dry**
QUALITY ▽ ▽ ▽ ▽
VALUE ☆ ☆ ☆ ☆
GRAPES **Merlot**
REGION **Marlborough**

CELLAR **2**
PRICE **$20–23**

This is one of two Forrest merlots on the market – the 2001 version, sourced from a different site, was supposed to replace this one, but there's still a bit to be found on retail shelves and restaurant wine lists around the country.
Current Release 2000 Leather and sweet pipe tobacco – yep, that's merlot alright! The fruit is sweet-edged with suggestions of mint and chocolate-coated cherries. Gentle oak adds just a wee bit of grip to the finish. Pull the cork and enjoy it with a brace of pork and fennel sausages, served with garlicky mashed potatoes.

Forrest Merlot

STYLE **dry**
QUALITY ▽ ▽ ▽ ▽ ▽
VALUE ☆ ☆ ☆ ☆ ☆
GRAPES **Merlot**
REGION **Marlborough**

CELLAR **3**
PRICE **$20–23**

One of a handful of reds topped with a screwcap closure, this wine always provokes comment. The fruit came from the Conders Bend vineyard, where the stony soil reflects the sun's ripening rays back up to the low-hanging bunches.
Current Release 2001 Sweet plums and cherries are in excellent shape on the nose and manage to travel pretty well unscathed onto the front palate. John Forrest matured it in American oak barrels, and they have added a suggestion of vanilla to the berryish flavours. Enjoy it alongside thinly sliced pan-fried beef with some sort of berry-based sauce.

Framingham Marlborough Merlot/Malbec

STYLE **dry**
QUALITY ▽ ▽ ▽
VALUE ☆ ☆ ☆
GRAPES
  Merlot 66%
  Malbec 30%
  Cab Sauvignon 4%
REGION **Marlborough**

CELLAR **2**
PRICE **$23–25**

Wines featuring merlot are reasonably common in Marlborough, but malbec is exceedingly rare. This one sells well at the Framingham cellar door. It was matured in French oak barrels.
Current Release 2001 Chunky on the nose, and showing a fair whack of malbec's typical stewed plum character, this gives the impression that it's going to be quite rustic. In fact, it's reasonably smooth through the middle, but a bit of leafiness on the finish mars the final impression. Partner it with kidneys on toast.

Gillan Marlborough Merlot

STYLE **dry**
QUALITY ▽ ▽ ▽
VALUE ☆ ☆ ☆
GRAPES **Merlot**
REGION **Marlborough**

CELLAR **3**
PRICE **$21–23**

The Gillan label is best-known for whites, specifically a reliably good sauvignon blanc and a big-selling bubbly, but this middleweight red has a keen following at the cellar door just out of Blenheim.
Current Release 2000 Leather and plums are in good shape on the nose, but the same characters on the palate are marred by a touch of leanness. It's not unpleasant, but it won't get you singing from the rooftops. It goes well with meat-leaning Spanish tapas, like smoked beef on wedges of grilled polenta.

Gladstone Cabernet Sauvignon/Merlot

When it comes to reds, the Wairarapa is better known for pinot than cabernet blends, but this member of Christine Kernohan's portfolio is a steady seller at the cellar door and in local shops.

Current Release 1999 Gosh – talk about berries! There's a rush of them on the nose, with sweet oak content to stay way out of the limelight. The flavour profile is smooth and classy in the middle, but faintly leafy on the finish. Partner it with tagliatelle pasta with a garlic and tomato topping and you should be happy enough.

STYLE **dry**
QUALITY ▯▯▯▯
VALUE ☆☆☆⯪
GRAPES
   Cab Sauvignon 85%
   Merlot 15%
REGION **Wairarapa**
CELLAR 3
PRICE **$27–29**

Gladstone Reserve Merlot

Christine Kernohan makes this red only when she considers the grapes are exceptional. At other times, the fruit is blended with cabernet. This is the first release since the 1998 version, so its many fans have had to hang out for quite a while.

Current Release 2001 Plums and leather, both classic merlot associations, are in good shape on the nose. It's a pleasant middleweight with nicely balanced fruit, gentle tannins and a clean-cut finish. It goes well with pan-fried lamb cutlets, especially if you splash a little into the pan and reduce it to make a quick sauce.

STYLE **dry**
QUALITY ▯▯▯▯
VALUE ☆☆⯪
GRAPES **Merlot**
REGION **Wairarapa**
CELLAR 3
PRICE **$30–33**

Glover's Crusader

This is probably the only wine in the country to combine cabernet sauvignon, pinot noir and shiraz, but Dave Glover has never been afraid to experiment. Against all the odds, it works.

Current Release 1998 Pinot wins out on the nose with suggestions of ripe cherries and strawberries. The flavours are more in the berryfruit mould, and shiraz (syrah) adds a spicy lick to the finish. It should work well with cubes of lamb, casseroled with chopped red onions and plenty of garlic.

STYLE **dry**
QUALITY ▯▯▯▯
VALUE ☆☆☆☆☆
GRAPES
   Cab Sauvignon 34%
   Pinot Noir 33%
   Shiraz 33%
REGION **Nelson**
CELLAR 2
PRICE **$18–20**

Glover's Moutere Cabernet Sauvignon

Dave Glover describes this as 'finer' than earlier vintages, and believes it will mature more rapidly. That's relative – 'more rapidly' still translates as several years. He believes wines go through a 'black hole' a year or so after being bottled.

Current Release 2000 Wow – cabernet on steroids! Cassis, timber, blackberries and vanilla can all be found in the bouquet. It's intensely sweet-fruited (although it is, of course, bone-dry) and boasts flavours reminiscent of bitter-sweet chocolate and strong coffee. An ideal food match? Shoot something large and spit-roast it.

STYLE **dry**
QUALITY ▯▯▯▯▯
VALUE ☆☆⯪
GRAPES
   Cab Sauvignon
REGION **Nelson**
CELLAR 2–9
PRICE **$34–37**

Glover's Nelson Cabernet Sauvignon

STYLE **dry**
QUALITY ▽▽▽▽
VALUE ☆ ☆ ☆ ☆
GRAPES
  Cab Sauvignon
REGION **Nelson**

CELLAR 🍾 3
PRICE **$20–23**

The 'Nelson' designation marks this as Glover's second-label cab. Pundits would have it that cabernet can't be grown in Nelson, but they forgot to tell Dave Glover. He's been turning the stuff into thoroughly drinkable wine for years.
Current Release 1999 Sweet oak and ripe berries kick things off nicely. It's rich, ripe and very approachable on the palate – quite different from the blockbuster reds we have become used to from this label. Partner it with lamb racks, ideally cooked on a barbecue.

Goldridge Estate Premium Reserve Hawke's Bay Merlot

STYLE **dry**
QUALITY ▽▽▽▽
VALUE ☆ ☆ ☆ ☆
GRAPES **Merlot**
REGION **Hawke's Bay**

CELLAR 🍾 2
PRICE **$20–23**

The fine print on the label tells us this red was 'barrique matured'. A barrique is a 225-litre oak barrel, considered the optimum size for absorption of oak character by the wine. It is also the best size for handling by one person.
Current Release 2000 Smoky, savoury oak mixes it up with the aromas of ripe berries in the bouquet. It's smooth but well-focused on the palate, certainly not a 'biggie', but pleasant enough by most measures. The back label suggests a very specific food match – rosemary-crusted, pink-cooked lamb racks on kumara mash with a plum berry sauce. Sounds good!

Goldwater Esslin Waiheke Island Merlot

STYLE **dry**
QUALITY ▽▽▽▽▽
VALUE ☆ ☆
GRAPES **Merlot**
REGION
  Waiheke Island

CELLAR 🍾 6
PRICE **$90–95**

This was one of the first local reds to sell for close to $100, but once people tasted it they found it hard to argue. Apart from anything else, it's pretty rare – only around 200 cases were made from the 2000 vintage.
Current Release 2000 Smoky tobacco backs the aromas of ripe plums in the bouquet. It's sweet-edged, rich and ripe-fruited on the palate, with a texture that can only be described as gloriously appealing. It makes a perfect partner for cervena steaks, simply grilled and served with young beans and baked potatoes.

Goldwater Waiheke Island Cabernet Sauvignon and Merlot

STYLE **dry**
QUALITY ▽▽▽▽▽
VALUE ☆ ☆ ☆
GRAPES
  Cab Sauvignon 50%
  Merlot 40%
  Cab Franc 10%
REGION
  Waiheke Island
CELLAR 🍾 1–6
PRICE **$69–75**

Kim and Jeanette Goldwater are dedicated Waihekeans, but they are happy to use grapes from other regions. This red is determinedly from the home site, but they recently planted a vineyard in Hawke's Bay's Gimblett Gravels region.
Current Release 2000 Yep, it's expensive – but boy, it's good! Sweet fruit is in perfect balance with savoury oak on the nose, and the same sensations drift onto the front palate. It's not a blockbuster in the 'Aussie red' sense, but it is beautifully elegant. Partner it with a piece of sensitively cooked beef eye fillet and you'll see the point.

Gunn Estate Cabernet/Malbec/Merlot

Most blends of these three varieties make malbec the small-percentage filler at the end, but the Gunn team decided to give it more of a chance to star. The three components spent 11 months in a mixture of French and American oak barrels. **Current Release 2001** Smoky and berryish on the nose, smooth and pleasant on the palate, this well-priced red fits into the 'easy-going' category. It won't get you shouting with glee, but partner it with a few grilled lamb chops and potato wedges and you'll be happy enough.

STYLE **dry**
QUALITY ♀ ♀ ♀
VALUE ☆ ☆ ☆ ☆
GRAPES
Cab Sauvignon 45%
Malbec 30%
Merlot 25%
REGION **Hawke's Bay**
CELLAR 2
PRICE **$16—18**

Gunn Estate Woolshed Merlot/Cabernet Sauvignon

The Gunns believe in holding some wines back until they consider them ready to drink, so this '99 model is the current release of this two-grape blend. It is named for a genuine woolshed on the property. **Current Release 1999** Smoky on the nose, with blackberries and currants also playing a role, and smooth on the palate, this is a highly approachable wine. The flavours are sweet-edged and the tannins nicely tuned to the style. It works well with a stew of cubed lamb, chopped ham and eggplant.

STYLE **dry**
QUALITY ♀ ♀ ♀ ♀
VALUE ☆ ☆ ☆ ☆
GRAPES
Merlot 75%
Cab Sauvignon 25%
REGION **Hawke's Bay**
CELLAR 3
PRICE **$20—23**

Harrier Rise Kumeu Monza Cabernets

The label carries a painting of a bright red 1930s model racing Alfa Romeo similar to the one driven by Italian ace, Tazio Nuvolari. Vineyard owner Tim Harris has had a couple of Alfas himself over the past few years, but they haven't been that old. **Current Release 1999** There's a trace of mint behind the plum and smoky oak aromas in the bouquet. It's smooth and sweet-edged on the palate, with restrained tannins adding just enough grip through the middle and on the moderately long finish. It goes well with cubes of eggplant stewed with fresh tomatoes, chopped garlic and red onion.

STYLE **dry**
QUALITY ♀ ♀ ♀ ♀
VALUE ☆ ☆ ☆
GRAPES
Cabernet Franc 95%
Merlot 5%
REGION **West Auckland**
CELLAR 3
PRICE **$28—32**

Harrier Rise Vineyards Bigny Coigne Kumeu Merlot

The name translates roughly as 'merlot corner', which is a way of explaining that owner Tim Harris has earmarked a corner of his site as being particularly well suited to the variety. Harrier Rise wines are seen mainly on restaurant wine lists. **Current Release 1999** Aromas reminiscent of ripe plums are backed by gentle, spicy oak. It's smooth, ripe-fruited and broad on the palate, with sweet-edged flavours through the middle leading to a firm finish. Enjoy it with a leg of lamb, wrapped in bacon and roasted pink.

STYLE **dry**
QUALITY ♀ ♀ ♀ ♀
VALUE ☆ ☆ ☆
GRAPES **Merlot**
REGION **West Auckland**
CELLAR 5
PRICE **$40—43**

Herzog Spirit of Marlborough Merlot/Cabernet Sauvignon

STYLE **dry**

QUALITY ♟ ♟ ♟ ♟ ♟

VALUE ☆ ☆

GRAPES
  Merlot 60%
  Cab Sauvignon 15%
  Cab Franc 15%
  Malbec 10%

REGION **Marlborough**

CELLAR ▭▭ **1–6**

PRICE **$65–68**

This wine presents a great argument for low cropping. Hans Herzog gets around a quarter of the national average in fruit from his cabernet vines, and it shows in greatly increased concentration.

Current Release 1999 Ripe currants and blackberries, chocolate, even a suggestion of coffee – they're all there in the bouquet. It's smooth, mouth-fillingly rich and incredibly opulent on the palate, and boasts a finish that goes on forever. A haunch of wild venison would seem appropriate, but it works well with a really good sirloin steak.

Highfield Marlborough Merlot

STYLE **dry**

QUALITY ♟ ♟ ♟ ♟

VALUE ☆ ☆ ☆ ☆

GRAPES **Merlot**

REGION **Marlborough**

CELLAR ▯ **3**

PRICE **$19–21**

Both French and American oak barrels were used for maturation of this wine, with the European models making up 80% of the mix. The various components stayed in them for 11 months before being bottled.

Current Release 1999 Plums and a suggestion of leather create a classic merlot bouquet. It's got a reasonable quota of sweet, open fruit on the palate, held in check by gentle tannins. It's good with a room-temperature salad based around pink-cooked lamb fillets and grilled vegetables.

House of Nobilo Merlot

STYLE **dry**

QUALITY ♟ ♟ ♟

VALUE ☆ ☆ ☆ ☆ ☆

GRAPES **Merlot**

REGION **Hawke's Bay**
  Gisborne

CELLAR ▯ **2**

PRICE **$15–17**

The grapes for this two-grape blend came from the Pikes Flat vineyard on the banks of the Mihaka River in Hawke's Bay, and a sheltered hillside site in Gisborne's Patutahi area. It was matured in a mixture of used French and American barrels.

Current Release 2001 Smoky oak, polished leather and Black Doris plums create a chunky bouquet. It's lighter than that rustic introduction suggests, with approachable berry flavours in gentle surrounds. Partner it with sliced beef and rocket leaves stuffed into a pita bread 'parcel'.

Huntaway Reserve Gisborne/Marlborough Merlot/Cabernet Sauvignon

STYLE **dry**

QUALITY ♟ ♟ ♟

VALUE ☆ ☆ ☆ ☆

GRAPES
  Merlot
  Cabernet Sauvignon

REGION **Gisborne**
  Marlborough

CELLAR ▯ **2**

PRICE **$20–23**

Neither Gisborne nor Marlborough are considered good bets for cabernet sauvignon, and merlot is generally marginal, so blending fruit from both regions is flying in the face of vinous fashion.

Current Release 1999 All the right leather and plum aromas are there on the nose. It's a nicely fruited middleweight that suffers from a trace of greenness in the middle, but gathers for a reasonably rich finish. It works okay alongside chicken thighs braised in red wine.

Huntaway Reserve Hawke's Bay Merlot/Cabernet Sauvignon

The Huntaway label, part of the Corbans/Montana portfolio, is one of the most ubiquitous on the market, and seems to be equally at home on the shelves of both supermarkets and upmarket retail outlets, as well as restaurant wine lists.

Current Release 2000 There's a fair whack of smoky oak on the nose, but the fruit is rich enough not to be intimidated. It's a very approachable wine with big, ripe berry flavors and a broad, mouth-filling texture. It goes well with a beef or cervena steak, ideally cooked no more than medium-rare. Partner the meat with rosemary-tossed potatoes and just-cooked broccoli.

STYLE **dry**
QUALITY ♟ ♟ ♟ ♟
VALUE ★ ★ ★ ★ ☆
GRAPES
  Merlot 54%
  Cab Sauvignon 46%
REGION **Hawke's Bay**
CELLAR 3
PRICE **$20–23**

Huntaway Reserve Hawke's Bay/Gisborne Cabernet Sauvignon/Merlot

Gisborne contributed the merlot to this three-grape blend; the other two varieties came from Hawke's Bay. The Corbans team said the hot vintage in both regions gave them exceptionally good fruit.

Current Release 1998 There's a whack of charred oak to go with the blackberry and leather aromas in the bouquet. It's generously fruited, with integrated tannins balancing the rich flavours and a touch of mint leaf on the finish. It works particularly well alongside a rare cervena steak.

STYLE **dry**
QUALITY ♟ ♟ ♟ ♟
VALUE ★ ★ ★ ★ ★
GRAPES
  Cab Sauvignon 44%
  Merlot 40%
  Cab Franc 16%
REGION
  Hawke's Bay 60%
  Gisborne 40%
CELLAR 3
PRICE **$20–22**

Huntaway Reserve Marlborough Malbec

Malbec is generally seen as a hot-climate variety, but it seems to grow well in Marlborough. It is being used increasingly in blends, but straight versions are still rare. This big-production line might change that.

Current Release 1999 Sweet prunes and savoury oak set the scene on the nose. Sweet fruit on the front palate carries on through, giving the wine a generous flavour profile. Gentle tannins add just the right amount of grip. It should work well with home-made pizza topped with tomato, bocconcini, garlic and mushrooms.

STYLE **dry**
QUALITY ♟ ♟ ♟ ♟ ♟
VALUE ★ ★ ★ ★ ★
GRAPES **Malbec**
REGION **Marlborough**
CELLAR 1–4
PRICE **$20–23**

Huthlee Estate Merlot/Cabernet Franc

STYLE **dry**

QUALITY ♟♟♟♟

VALUE ☆ ☆ ☆

GRAPES
Merlot 60%
Cab Franc 40%

REGION Hawke's Bay

CELLAR 2

PRICE $27–30

Merlot is calling the shots in an increasing number of Hawke's Bay reds. It ripens about three weeks earlier than cabernet sauvignon, and that means it misses the autumn rains that can sometimes dampen the berries. That's a big advantage.

Current Release 2000 It's not a big wine by any means, but it has a lot of ripe-fruited charm. The aromatic associations are of plums and blackberries, and the same characters drift onto the palate. Partner it with rissoles made from leftover roast beef and you'll be perfectly satisfied.

Hyperion Kronos Cabernet/Merlot

STYLE **dry**

QUALITY ♟♟♟♟

VALUE ☆ ☆ ☆ ☆

GRAPES
Cab Sauvignon 60%
Merlot 40%

REGION Matakana

CELLAR 3

PRICE $27–29

John Crone made seperate wines from his cabernet sauvignon and merlot grapes and matured them in oak barrels for a full year before blending them together. A good proportion of the oak was brand-new, so it has had quite an influence on the finished wine.

Current Release 1999 Despite the oak, it is ripe, plummy merlot fruit that dominates the bouquet, with cabernet's typical blackcurrant notes lagging behind. It's nicely balanced, grippy in the middle and boasts a reasonably long finish. It makes a good partner for a cervena steak, cooked rare or medium-rare at most.

Hyperion Millenios Cabernet Sauvignon

STYLE **dry**

QUALITY ♟♟♟♟

VALUE ☆ ☆ ☆ ☆

GRAPES Cab Sauvignon

REGION Matakana

CELLAR 3

PRICE $22–24

Winery owner John Crone describes this as his 'second label' cabernet, but he still lavishes lots of care and attention on it. The fruit was very ripe, and after crushing and pressing it spent a year in oak. It's a popular buy at the cellar shop.

Current Release 2000 Raspberries and chocolate – that's what I get on the nose of this nicely weighted red. It's sweet-fruited on the palate with gentle oak and a medium-length finish. Partner it with easy-going nibbles like salami, chunks of old cheddar and a few pieces of good, crusty bread and you should be well satisfied.

Kemblefield The Distinction Hawke's Bay Merlot

STYLE **dry**

QUALITY ♟♟♟♟

VALUE ☆ ☆ ☆

GRAPES Merlot 85%
Cab Sauvignon 8%
Cab Franc 7%

REGION Hawke's Bay

CELLAR 2

PRICE $22–24

John Kemble believes in holding some of his wines back until he feels they are ready to enjoy, so this '99 vintage is the current release. John is American, but that didn't prevent him from maturing it in French oak for 14 months.

Current Release 2000 There are some attractive smoky notes behind the ripe plum aromas in the bouquet. It's smooth, clean and smartly balanced on the palate – not a blockbuster, but that's not really the point. It's good with crumbed and shallow-fried beef schnitzels, served with baby new potatoes and green beans.

Kemblefield The Reserve Hawke's Bay Cabernet Sauvignon

Wines John Kemble labels 'The Reserve' are top of the heap. This big-hearted red was made from hand-harvested grapes which were plunged four times a day while they fermented. It's hard work, but it extracts every last bit of flavour.

Current Release 2000 There was a fair whack of smoky oak behind the blackberry and currant aromas in the bouquet when I tried the wine, but it should have settled down by now. It's smartly focused, with generous berry-like flavours and good grip through the middle and particularly on the lingering finish. Enjoy it with braised beef steak and onions.

STYLE **dry**
QUALITY ♟♟♟♟
VALUE ☆☆☆
GRAPES **Cab Sauvignon**
REGION **Hawke's Bay**
CELLAR 🍾 **3**
PRICE **$36–39**

Kemblefield Cabernet Sauvignon/Merlot (Signature)

Earlier versions of this wine had 'The signature' printed below the company name, but this current model carries partner and winemaker John Kemble's actual signature.

Current Release 2001 Funky seems the best word to describe the bouquet on this red – it's smoky and savoury, with chunky berry notes. It's a middleweight in the flavour department, with a touch of rusticity that rather appeals to my peasant's palate. Partner it with equally rustic food – braised ox tongue would be good.

STYLE **dry**
QUALITY ♟♟♟
VALUE ☆☆☆⚐
GRAPES
  Cab Sauvignon 59%
  Merlot 26%
  Cab Franc 15%
REGION **Hawke's Bay**
CELLAR 🍾 **2**
PRICE **$17–19**

Kennedy Point Vineyard Cabernet Sauvignon

With a 14% alcohol level, this is a big, solid red. Winemakers Neal Kunimara and Herb Friedli hid it away for 16 months in French oak barrels, 60% of them new. That's a long time by local standards, and a higher than usual percentage of new timber.

Current Release 2000 Despite all that oak, ripe blackcurrants are the dominant aromatic association. It's firm on the palate, but there's enough fruit richness to round things out. The finish is warm and pretty grippy, but should soften in a year or two. Then, match it with a beef pot roast accompanied by plenty of vegetables.

STYLE **dry**
QUALITY ♟♟♟♟
VALUE ☆☆⚐
GRAPES
  Cab Sauvignon 77%
  Merlot 15%
  Cabernet Franc 4%
  Malbec 4%
REGION
  Waiheke Island
CELLAR ▭ **1–4**
PRICE **$39–45**

Kerr Farm Kumeu Cabernet Sauvignon

STYLE **dry**

QUALITY ♟ ♟ ♟ ♟

VALUE ☆ ☆ ☆ ☆ ☆

GRAPES **Cab Sauvignon**

REGION **West Auckland**

CELLAR **2**

PRICE **$19–21**

This is a labour-intensive wine. The grapes were plunged by hand (and foot!) four times a day during fermentation, then the juice was transferred to French and American barrels for an 11-month stay.

Current Release 1999 Spicy oak and ripe blackberries form an appealing bouquet. It's nicely fruited, and boasts smartly controlled tannins to ensure there's just enough grip in the middle. Braised lamb shoulder chops with baby onions would be a good match.

Kim Crawford Tane

STYLE **dry**

QUALITY ♟ ♟ ♟ ♟ ♟

VALUE ☆ ☆ ☆

GRAPES
 Merlot 65%
 Cab Franc 35%

REGION **Hawke's Bay**

CELLAR **4**

PRICE **$39–43**

Kim Crawford joined the growing list of producers to reject cabernet sauvignon in favour of its cousin, cabernet franc, when he put the blend together for this red. Other wines are named for his children, but Tane is the Maori God of the forest.

Current Release 2000 Cabernet franc adds its faintly floral characters to the leather and ripe plum aromas of good merlot. It's nicely textured on the palate, with ripe fruit balanced by firm but integrated tannins. It makes a good partner for casseroled lamb and boiled new potatoes.

Kim Crawford Te Awanga Vineyard Merlot

STYLE **dry**

QUALITY ♟ ♟ ♟ ♟

VALUE ☆ ☆ ☆

GRAPES
 Merlot 86%
 Cab Franc 14%

REGION **Hawke's Bay**

CELLAR **2**

PRICE **$30–33**

The Te Awanga vineyard referred to in the name is near the Hawke's Bay coast, so maritime breezes keep the vines cool, especially overnight. Kim Crawford wines are seen on restaurant and wine bar lists from one end of the country to the other.

Current Release 2000 The bouquet is decidedly fruit-dominated, with raspberry and plum aromas to the fore. The spice normally found on the nose has migrated to the palate, where it puts a grippy edge on the ripe fruit flavours. Pink-roasted lamb makes a good partner.

Kim Crawford Wicken Vineyard Cabernet Franc

STYLE **dry**

QUALITY ♟ ♟ ♟

VALUE ☆ ☆ ☆

GRAPES **Cab Franc 86%**
 Merlot 14%

REGION **Hawke's Bay**

CELLAR **2**

PRICE **$29–32**

Reds that feature cabernet franc as the dominant grape are a rare commodity, but the grape performs pretty well when it is given a starring role. Kim Crawford has had a good response to this one, so he'll probably try the experiment again.

Current Release 2001 Toasty oak and raspberry-like fruit aromas set the scene. It's moderately rich on the palate, but leafy characters on the finish mar the good impression. Still, it goes perfectly well with a sandwich based around pink-cooked lamb.

Kingsley Estate Gimblett Road Cabernet Sauvignon

Kingsley Tobin makes just two wines from grapes grown on his small Hawke's Bay vineyard, but he has established a big reputation. This one recently scored a five-star rating from the respected *Cuisine* magazine tasting panel.

Current Release 2000 It's all there on the nose – coffee, ripe blackcurrants, seeet pipe tobacco and even a suggestion of chocolate. The same characters can be found on the palate, where they are held in place by firm but generous tannins. The finish lasts forever. It's good with Italian-style meatballs in a hearty garlic-laced tomato sauce.

STYLE **dry**
QUALITY ♟♟♟♟♟
VALUE ★★★☆
GRAPES **Cab Sauvignon**
REGION **Hawke's Bay**
CELLAR 🍾 6
PRICE **$37–41**

Konrad & Conrad Marlborough Merlot

This first-time red for the Hengstlers is hard to find away from the Marlborough region, but it's smartly made and pretty realistically priced. There's no Konrad & Conrad winery yet, so it was made by Graeme Paul at Marlborough Vintners.

Current Release 2000 The char that coats the inside of oak barrels is evident on the nose behind the ripe plum aromas. It's big-fruited and chunky with assertive tannins particularly obvious on the finish. Try it alongside lamb leg steaks, ideally cooked on a barbecue or char-grill to match that bouquet.

STYLE **dry**
QUALITY ♟♟♟♟
VALUE ★★★★
GRAPES **Merlot**
REGION **Marlborough**
CELLAR 🍾 3
PRICE **$23–25**

Kumeu River Melba

This red, named for company head Melba Brajkovich, used to fall happily into the 'cheap and cheerful' category, but it has become rather more serious in recent years. The blend changes from vintage to vintage.

Current Release 1999 Raspberries are the dominant aromatic association, which is all very pleasant. It's broadly textured through the middle thanks to the fully ripe fruit, but there's a belt of tannic firmness on the finish. It's smart wine that goes well with grilled Spanish chorizo sausages.

STYLE **dry**
QUALITY ♟♟♟♟♟
VALUE ★★★★
GRAPES **Merlot 70%**
Malbec 30%
REGION **West Auckland**
CELLAR 🍾 3
PRICE **$27–29**

Kumeu River Merlot

This is the first time the Brajkovich family has released a merlot wearing the top Kumeu River label since 1983. The fruit has gone into the company's blended red, Melba, in the interim, but in 2000 there was enough for both.

Current Release 2000 Smoky oak and a decidedly rakish dash of leather form a welcoming bouquet. Sweet fruit and smartly integrated tannins make it a success on the palate, and a lingering finish completes the picture. It works spendidly with barbecued sirloin, served medium-rare at most.

STYLE **dry**
QUALITY ♟♟♟♟
VALUE ★★★★
GRAPES **Merlot**
REGION **West Auckland**
CELLAR 🍾 3
PRICE **$22–26**

La Strada Cabernet Sauvignon

STYLE **dry**

QUALITY ▼▼▼▽

VALUE ☆☆☆☆

GRAPES
  Cab Sauvignon

REGION **Marlborough**

CELLAR 2

PRICE **$25–27**

Can't get cabernet ripe in Marlborough? Don't tell Hatsch Kalberer. His secret is very low cropping, forcing the vines to concentrate on ripening the grapes that are left behind.
Current Release 1997 My prejudices told me I should find some greenness in the bouquet, but there's not a trace of it. It's a fruit-led, berryish style with a big welcome in the middle, leading to a lingering finish. Partner it with pink-cooked lamb racks and you should be very happy indeed.

La Strada Merlot/Malbec

STYLE **dry**

QUALITY ▼▼▼▼

VALUE ☆☆☆☆

GRAPES
  Merlot 60%
  Malbec 30%
  Sangiovese,
  Cabernet Franc,
  Syrah 10%

REGION **Marlborough**

CELLAR 1–4

PRICE **$24–26**

Hatsch Kalberer makes several wines based on merlot, malbec and the cabernet cousins, sauvignon and franc. This time he combined three of the four, and added two rarer varieties for luck.
Current Release 1999 This is a very approachable wine with the label's trademark smoky oak on the nose, followed by a rush of ripe berry flavours on the front palate. The tannins know their place, so the structure is smooth and moreish. It's good with a lamb, potato and baby onion casserole.

La Strada Reserve Malbec

STYLE **dry**

QUALITY ▼▼▼▼▼

VALUE ☆☆☆

GRAPES **Malbec**

REGION **Marlborough**

CELLAR 8

PRICE **$48–52**

Malbec is a controversial variety. Those who don't like it call it 'the müller-thurgau of red grapes', but it's hard to think like that after tasting Hatsch Kalberer's big-hearted inter-pretation of the style.
Current Release 1999 Smoky, faintly tarry and just plain inviting in the bouquet, this is not a wine for wimps. It's got a bus-load of tannin, but there's enough ripe fruit in there to carry it off. The perfect food match? Wild venison would be great, but a serious piece of beef fillet would do.

La Strada Reserve Merlot

STYLE **dry**

QUALITY ▼▼▼▼▼

VALUE ☆☆☆

GRAPES **Merlot**

REGION **Marlborough**

CELLAR 1–4

PRICE **$43–45**

Hatsch Kalberer believes in releasing his wine when it's ready to drink, or at least getting close. That's why the La Strada wines you see on sale are usually a year or two older than most.
Current Release 1998 Smoky oak and a touch of leather – yep, that's merlot alright! This is a solid, chunky wine with lashings of plum-like fruit in a firm but mouth-filling framework. It's good with smoked beef, warmed through in a little gravy and served over a pile of mashed potatoes.

Lake Chalice Black Label Merlot

Matt Thomson and Chris Gambitsis got the fruit for this second-tier merlot from sites in Marlborough and Hawke's Bay, and matured the fledgling wine for eight months in a mixture of French and American oak barrels.

Current Release 2001 There's certainly a healthy amount of merlot's classic plum aromas on the nose, and the same character can be found on the front palate. It's smooth, comforting and approachable – not a big wine, but with a certain middleweight charm. Enjoy it alongside tagliatelle pasta tossed with nothing more distracting than chopped garlic, freshly grated Parmesan and top-quality olive oil.

STYLE **dry**
QUALITY ▾▾▾▾
VALUE ★★★★☆
GRAPES **Merlot**
REGION
  Marlborough
  Hawke's Bay
CELLAR 3
PRICE **$18–21**

Lake Chalice Platinum Cabernet Sauvignon

It's pretty difficult to get cabernet fully ripe in Marlborough, with the result that many local producers have abandoned the variety. Not the Lake Chalice team – this top-shelf version has won quite a few accolades.

Current Release 2001 The colour is intense and there's a good line-up of berry and cassis aromas in the bouquet. It's moderately rich on the palate, but despite the drought-like conditions in 2001 there's no mistaking the touch of cool-climate leaf on the finish. Overall though, it's a very drinkable wine that goes well with rissoles made from roast lamb leftovers.

STYLE **dry**
QUALITY ▾▾▾
VALUE ★★★
GRAPES
  Cab Sauvignon
REGION **Marlborough**
CELLAR 2
PRICE **$25–28**

Lake Chalice Platinum Merlot

Tasting this big-hearted red alongside the same company's Platinum cabernet is a reminder that merlot is far better suited to the Marlborough region. The grapes came from two sites and the wine was aged in French oak for a year.

Current Release 2001 Smoky oak and ripe plum and raspberry fruit aromas form an inviting bouquet. Nicely integrated tannins give it exceptional smoothness on the palate, forming highly suitable surroundings for the rich flavours. Partner it with braised beef with shiitake mushrooms and chopped celery.

STYLE **dry**
QUALITY ▾▾▾▾
VALUE ★★★★
GRAPES **Merlot**
REGION **Marlborough**
CELLAR 4
PRICE **$25–28**

Lincoln Heritage Collection Petar Hawke's Bay Cabernet/Merlot

This wine is named for Petar Fredatovich, who founded the label in 1937. The cabernet component came from the Gooding family in Te Kauwhata and the merlot from Chris and Ann Parker in Gisborne. It spent a year in French and American barrels.

Current Release 2000 Leather, tobacco and raspberries make up the bouquet. It's not a big wine, but it has its own straightforward appeal. The flavours are pleasantly sweet-edged and the finish moderately long. It makes a pretty good fist of things alongside Wiener schnitzels.

STYLE **dry**
QUALITY ▾▾▾
VALUE ★★★★
GRAPES
  Cab Sauvignon 60%
  Merlot 40%
REGION
  Te Kauwhata 60%
  Gisborne 40%
CELLAR 2
PRICE **$18–20**

Lincoln Winemaker's Series Gisborne Merlot

STYLE **dry**
QUALITY ♟ ♟ ♟
VALUE ☆ ☆ ☆ ☆ ☆
GRAPES **Merlot**
REGION **Gisborne**
CELLAR ▯ 3
PRICE **$15–18**

This merlot has previously appeared under the 'Parklands Estate' label. That's still where the grapes are sourced, but in 2001 it was decided to give the overall region the credit. It has been a big seller at the winery shop in West Auckland under both labels.

Current Release 2001 Tomato leaf and raspberries get it together in the bouquet – if there's any oak in there it's not noticeable. It's a friendly middleweight on the palate, with no sharp edges, reasonably ripe fruit flavours and a satisfying finish. Partner it with a rare roast beef sandwich and you should be a perfectly happy punter.

Lincoln Winemaker's Series Parklands Estate Merlot

STYLE **dry**
QUALITY ♟ ♟ ♟ ♟
VALUE ☆ ☆ ☆ ☆ ☆
GRAPES **Merlot**
REGION **Gisborne**
CELLAR ▯ 1
PRICE **$15–17**

Gisborne is known mostly for its white wines, but merlot is one red grape that seems to do well on the right sites. Justin Papesch made this one to drink young. 'Maximising flavour was my objective,' he says.

Current Release 2000 The wine saw no oak, but it still manages a faintly smoky edge on the major aromas of ripe plums. It's smooth on the palate, nicely fruited and very approachable. It would make a fine match for a summertime platter of mixed salamis and artisan breads.

Linden Estate Dam Block Cabernet/Malbec/Merlot

STYLE **dry**
QUALITY ♟ ♟ ♟ ♟ ♟
VALUE ☆ ☆ ☆ ☆
GRAPES
 Cab Sauvignon 65%
 Malbec 25%
 Merlot 10%
REGION **Hawke's Bay**
CELLAR ▭ 1–4
PRICE **$34–36**

This is the top red in the Linden Estate range. Nick Chan uses wild yeasts for the fermentation because he likes the vaguely feral character they impart. They're less predictable than laboratory-bred models, but that's part of the fun.

Current Release 2000 Cassis, ripe blackberries and loads of sweet, spicy oak. That's what I get in the bouquet, and I'm entirely happy to do so. It's richly fruited, ripe and warmly inviting on the palate with smartly balanced tannins and a long finish. Pull the cork next time you're having a good old-fashioned beef stew with dumplings.

Linden Estate Hawke's Bay Merlot

STYLE **dry**
QUALITY ♟ ♟ ♟ ♟
VALUE ☆ ☆ ☆ ☆
GRAPES **Merlot 95%**
 Malbec 5%
REGION **Hawke's Bay**
CELLAR ▯ 4
PRICE **$23–26**

Nick Chan had never had such a small crop of merlot – he was able to pick less than a tonne per acre. That might hurt financially, but the good news is that low-cropping vines give excellent fruit, and it shows.

Current Release 2001 Think ripe plums and leather and you've captured the bouquet. It's smart wine, with loads of ripe fruit flavours in an impressively smooth package. The finish is satisfying and hangs around for quite a while. Braised beef rump with carrots and baby onions would make a good fist of things.

Linden Estate Two Valleys Cabernet/Malbec/Merlot

Malbec is a controversial variety in this country – some producers love it, others reckon it's not worth planting. Nick Chan is keen enough on its distinctive flavour to have included 30% in this three-grape blend.

Current Release 2001 Spicy oak has got the gig on the nose, but there are some attractive ripe plum and blackberry notes peeking through the cracks. The flavour profile is smooth and smartly balanced, with a moderately long finish. It would make a good partner for pink-cooked double lamb cutlets with roasted red onion wedges and mashed kumara.

STYLE **dry**
QUALITY ▼▼▼▽
VALUE ☆☆☆☆
GRAPES
  Merlot 50%
  Malbec 30%
  Cab Sauvignon 20%
REGION **Hawke's Bay**
CELLAR **3**
PRICE **$19–22**

Lombardi Hawke's Bay Merlot/Cabernet Sauvignon

Andy Coltart and Kim Thorp are among many Hawke's Bay producers to put more emphasis on merlot than cabernet sauvignon in recent years. Both varieties ripen well on their small site, helped by their policy of crop-thinning.

Current Release 2000 The attractively spicy oak on the nose drifts onto the front palate. It's smooth, properly berryish and just plain enjoyable – not a 'biggie', but all the more approachable for that. Into offal? Braised ox tongue with baby vegetables would be perfect.

STYLE **dry**
QUALITY ▼▼▼▼
VALUE ☆☆☆☆
GRAPES
  Merlot 60%
  Cab Sauvignon 30%
  Cab Franc 10%
REGION **Hawke's Bay**
CELLAR **3**
PRICE **$22–24**

Longbush Gisborne Merlot

Gisborne is white wine country, but merlot can make a reasonable fist of things if the grower is willing to restrict the crop. This simple example from the Thorpe Brothers sells reasonably well in local cafés and bars.

Current Release 2000 Smoky oak and a suggestion of tobacco, typical of the variety, start things off. There are some pleasant plum notes on the front palate, but it's pretty lean through the middle and finishes short. Sip it quietly with casual nibbles, then move on.

STYLE **dry**
QUALITY ▼▼▽
VALUE ☆☆☆⋆
GRAPES **Merlot**
REGION **Gisborne**
CELLAR **1**
PRICE **$17–19**

Longridge Hawke's Bay Merlot/Cabernet

The Longridge range, once owned by Corbans and now part of the Montana portfolio, is popular in restaurants around the country. Nicely made and attractively packaged, the wines offer very good value.

Current Release 2000 There's a strong whiff of pencil shavings on the nose, along with a dash of ripe plums and polished leather. It's smooth on the palate, with pleasantly ripe fruit in a well-rounded framework. It goes well with tagliatelle pasta, tossed with chopped fresh tomatoes, good olive oil and torn basil.

STYLE **dry**
QUALITY ▼▼▼▽
VALUE ☆☆☆☆☆
GRAPES
  Merlot
  Cab Sauvignon
REGION **Hawke's Bay**
CELLAR **2**
PRICE **$15–17**

Longview Estate Gumdigger's Merlot/Cabernet Sauvignon/Cabernet Franc

STYLE **dry**
QUALITY ▽▽▽▽
VALUE ☆☆☆
GRAPES **Merlot**
REGION **Northland**
CELLAR 🇦 **3**
PRICE **$32–35**

The immaculately kept Longview Estate vineyard is a popular visiting place for travellers heading north. It's situated to the left of the main highway, and Mario and Barbara Vuletich always provide a warm welcome.

Current Release 2000 Spicy oak, blackcurrants and leather combine forces on the nose. It's rich, smooth and sweet-fruited with mouth-filling texture and a long finish. It makes a good partner for an open salad sandwich based around thick slices of rare roast beef.

Longview Estate Mario's Merlot

STYLE **dry**
QUALITY ▽▽▽▽
VALUE ☆☆☆
GRAPES **Merlot**
REGION **Northland**
CELLAR 🇦 **3**
PRICE **$27–29**

Mario Vuletich aged this home-grown merlot in French barrels for 15 months. That must mean he's got plenty of oak – many producers bottle the wine after a year because they need the barrels for the next vintage.

Current Release 2000 The oak has added a spicy note to the cherry and plum aromas in the bouquet. It's sweet-edged and smooth through the middle, but has enough tannic grip to firm up the finish. It works well with middle-loin lamb chops, trimmed of excess fat and pan-fried in good olive oil.

Longview Estate Scarecrow Cabernet Sauvignon

STYLE **dry**
QUALITY ▽▽▽▽
VALUE ☆☆☆☆
GRAPES
   Cab Sauvignon
REGION **Northland**
CELLAR 🇦 **2**
PRICE **$24–26**

This is one of only a handful of reds to be finished with a screwcap. It was a brave move for the Vuletiches, but they report favourable reaction from the public. The fledgling wine was aged for 14 months in French and American oak.

Current Release 2000 Dusty oak sits behind the blackcurrant aromas on the nose. It's sweet-fruited on the palate, with gentle tannins that help make it a pleasant middleweight. The finish is moderately long. Enjoy it with grilled beef sausages from a serious butcher.

Loopline Vineyard Wairarapa Cabernet Sauvignon/Franc

STYLE **dry**
QUALITY ▽▽▽▽
VALUE ☆☆☆☆
GRAPES
   Cab Sauvignon 50%
   Cab Franc 50%
REGION **Wairarapa**
CELLAR 🇦 **2**
PRICE **$20–23**

Only 1500 bottles were made of this blended red, so it might prove hard to find. The two varieties are relatively rare in the Wairarapa.

Current Release 2000 There's a touch of tomato leaf behind the blackberry aromas on the nose, but things are riper on the front palate. It's nicely fruited in the middle, a little lean on the finish but pleasant enough overall. Try it with Wiener schnitzel, new potatoes and broccoli.

Margrain Cabernet Sauvignon

There's quite a bit of history attached to this wine. The grapes came from a vineyard planted by the late Stan Chifney, one of the pioneers of the Martinborough region, and they were the last to be harvested. The vines have now been pulled out.

Current Release 2001 It's a tough call, ripening cabernet in Martinborough, which is why there's a touch of greenness on the nose. It's got a reasonable quota of berry flavours sitting in smooth surroundings, but the finish is lean and rather short. It works okay with beef chipolatas served with some sort of citric mustard.

STYLE **dry**
QUALITY ▼ ▼ ▽
VALUE ☆ ☆
GRAPES
  Cab Sauvignon
REGION **Martinborough**
CELLAR 🍾 2
PRICE **$28–32**

Matariki Quintology

John and Rosemary O'Connor's top-shelf red used to be labelled Anthology, but the name was changed for the 1999 and subsequent vintages. The grape varieties are listed on the back label, but not the front.

Current Release 2000 There's a pleasantly spicy edge on the aromas of ripe plums and blackberries, and I fancy there's something akin to sweet pipe tobacco in there as well. It's a big, broad red with an impressively smooth texture and a reasonably long finish. Enjoy it alongside a rare ostrich steak, ideally from a bird raised in Hawke's Bay.

STYLE **dry**
QUALITY ▼ ▼ ▼ ▼
VALUE ☆ ☆ ☆ ☆
GRAPES
  Cab Sauvignon 40%
  Merlot 24%
  Cab Franc 20%
  Syrah 10%
  Malbec 6%
REGION **Hawke's Bay**
CELLAR ▭▭ 1–4
PRICE **$29–33**

Matawhero Reserve Cabernet/Merlot

Denis Irwin has never been impressed by the argument that Gisborne is the wrong place to grow cabernet sauvignon. His vines are among the oldest in the district, giving him some advantages, but it's still a tough call.

Current Release 1999 The bouquet is savoury and more than a little dusty, with berryish fruit pushed to the back. It's very broad on the front palate, but big, solid tannins kick in through the middle and onto the finish. Partner it with smooth-textured food like slow-cooked beef.

STYLE **dry**
QUALITY ▼ ▼ ▼ ▽
VALUE ☆ ☆ ☆
GRAPES
  Cab Sauvignon 60%
  Merlot 40%
REGION **Gisborne**
CELLAR 🍾 2
PRICE **$32–35**

Matua Valley Ararimu Merlot/Cabernet Sauvignon

A gold medal at the New Zealand Wine Society Royal Easter Wine Show was a reward for all the effort that went into this three-grape blend. Mark Robertson selected only the best fruit from a handful of well-placed Hawke's Bay sites.

Current Release 2000 The bouquet is sweet and spicy, with suggestions of plums and blackcurrants behind the oak. It's richly fruited on the front palate, impressively smooth through the middle and spicy on the finish – a class act. Partner it with a rich beef and mushroom stew, served with thick slices of crusty bread to mop up the juices.

STYLE **dry**
QUALITY ▼ ▼ ▼ ▼ ▽
VALUE ☆ ☆ ☆
GRAPES
  Merlot 52%
  Cab Sauvignon 45%
  Malbec 3%
REGION **Hawke's Bay**
CELLAR 🍾 5
PRICE **$40–43**

Matua Valley Bullrush Vineyard Merlot

STYLE **dry**
QUALITY ▽ ▽ ▽ ▽
VALUE ☆ ☆ ☆ ⯪
GRAPES **Merlot**
REGION **Hawke's Bay**
CELLAR 🍾 3
PRICE **$27–29**

Winemaker Mark Robertson sourced his fruit from six-year-old vines grown on the Red Metal Triangle vineyard that also supplies fruit for the company's Matheson range. The crop was thinned to give greater concentration.

Current Release 2000 Spicy timber and just-polished leather get it together on the nose, along with a healthy amount of merlot's typical plum aromas. It's richly fruited on the palate. Gentle tannins add a healthy amount of grip to the middle and finish but it remains refreshingly direct in its appeal. It would work splendidly alongside a plate of pink-cooked liver and onions.

Matua Valley Hawke's Bay Cabernet Sauvignon/Merlot

STYLE **dry**
QUALITY ▽ ▽ ⯆
VALUE ☆ ☆ ☆ ☆
GRAPES
  Cab Sauvignon 70%
  Merlot 30%
REGION **Hawke's Bay**
CELLAR 🍾 2
PRICE **$16–18**

Mark Robertson has sometimes added malbec to this blend, but for 2000 he stuck with the two originals. It comes from a gravel-covered site in the Dartmoor Valley, where leaves are plucked away from the vines to expose the fruit.

Current Release 2000 Sweet raspberries dominate the bouquet – there's a dash of spice in there, but it's pretty subdued. It's soft, light and inoffensive in the mid-palate, but suffers from a faintly green finish. Try it with pink-roasted lamb fillets arranged over soft polenta.

Matua Valley Hawke's Bay Merlot

STYLE **dry**
QUALITY ▽ ▽ ▽ ⯆
VALUE ☆ ☆ ☆ ☆ ☆
GRAPES **Merlot**
REGION **Hawke's Bay**
CELLAR 🍾 2
PRICE **$16–19**

This mid-range red from the team at Matua is very well priced, and can sometimes be spotted on special for $15 or so. Winemaker Mark Robertson says he designed it to be enjoyed in its youth.

Current Release 2000 There's a spicy, savoury note backing the plum-like aromas. It's got good fruit with all the right flavour connections – berries, a dash of leather and more of the plum characters. The finish is reasonably long. It works well with beef schnitzels.

Matua Valley Matheson Vineyard Cabernet/Merlot

STYLE **dry**
QUALITY ▽ ▽ ▽ ▽ ▽
VALUE ☆ ☆ ☆ ☆ ☆
GRAPES
  Cab Sauvignon 85%
  Merlot 15%
REGION **Hawke's Bay**
CELLAR 🍾 3
PRICE **$20–23**

The Matheson vineyard is smack-dab in the middle of the Hawke's Bay sub-region known as the Red Metal Triangle, and winemaker Mark Robertson is rapt in the quality of the fruit it gives him.

Current Release 2001 This well-priced red seems very complete in the bouquet, with spicy oak and ripe, berryish fruit in perfect balance. It's a big smoothie on the palate, boasting super-ripe fruit in nicely textured surroundings. I can think of nothing better to partner a rare-cooked cervena back steak.

McCashin's Hawke's Bay Merlot

The winery is in Nelson, but Craig Gass liked the look of a parcel of Hawke's Bay fruit when he planned this wine. It had a nine-month's gestation period in American oak barrels before being born and bottled.

Current Release 2000 Plums and smoky oak trade blows on the nose. It's a nicely weighted wine, with loads of ripe fruit flavours edged by integrated but moderately grippy tannins. I like it with lamb rump, cooked pink and served with roast aubergine and zucchini.

STYLE **dry**
QUALITY ♟ ♟ ♟ ♟
VALUE ☆ ☆ ☆ ☆⸸
GRAPES **Merlot**
REGION **Hawke's Bay**
CELLAR ▯ 3
PRICE **$19–22**

Mebus Dakins Road Cabernet/Merlot/Malbec

Three varieties are listed on the label, but this big-hearted red also contains a percentage of cab sav's lighter cousin, cabernet franc. It spent its leisure time in oak barrels, mostly French but a few from the US, and all of them brand spanking new.

Current Release 2000 Berryish on the nose, fruity on the palate, this is pretty smart wine for a region where these varieties aren't supposed to do well. There's a dash of leafiness on the finish, but until then it performs well. Try it alongside casseroled lamb shanks with mashed potatoes and broccoli and you'll be happy enough.

STYLE **dry**
QUALITY ♟ ♟ ♟ ⸸
VALUE ☆ ☆ ☆
GRAPES
  Cab Sauvignon
  Merlot
  Malbec
  Cab Franc
REGION **Wairarapa**
CELLAR ▭ 1–4
PRICE **$30–33**

Mills Reef Elspeth Cabernet Sauvignon

Tim Preston has a lot of fun making various straight varietals and blends from the so-called Bordeaux varieties, cabernet sauvignon, merlot and cabernet franc. This one plays it straight, and is a popular buy at the pleasant winery shop.

Current Release 2000 Blackcurrants and other wild berries form the major aromatic impressions. Sweet, spicy oak sits at the back. It's very grippy on the palate at this stage of its life, but in a year or two the ripe fruit flavours will blossom and come alive. Then, partner it with beef osso buco.

STYLE **dry**
QUALITY ♟ ♟ ♟ ♟
VALUE ☆ ☆⸸
GRAPES
  Cab Sauvignon
REGION **Hawke's Bay**
CELLAR ▯ 3
PRICE **$40–43**

Mills Reef Elspeth Cabernet/Merlot

This is one of several reds in Paddy Preston's Mills Reef portfolio. The fruit is all sourced in Hawke's Bay and trucked across to the Bay of Plenty winery. It's a reasonably common practice in New Zealand – after all, we move houses on trucks!

Current Release 2000 Now this is a serious red. Blackcurrants and blackberries dominate the bouquet, with sweet, savoury oak content to sit in the background. It's chock-full of flavour, has firm tannins to keep things under control and boasts a long, rich finish. A good old-fashioned stew made from beef shin would be perfect with it.

STYLE **dry**
QUALITY ♟ ♟ ♟ ♟ ♟
VALUE ☆ ☆ ☆
GRAPES
  Cab Sauvignon
  Merlot
REGION **Hawke's Bay**
CELLAR ▯ 4
PRICE **$39–42**

Mills Reef Elspeth Cabernet/Syrah/Merlot

STYLE **dry**

QUALITY ♟ ♟ ♟ ♟

VALUE ☆ ☆ ☆

GRAPES
 Cab Sauvignon 30%
 Syrah 30%
 Merlot 25%
 Malbec 15%

REGION **Hawke's Bay**

CELLAR **5**

PRICE **$34–37**

Malbec is the mystery grape in this blend. The grapes all came from the Preston family's nicely situated vineyard in Mere Road, Hawke's Bay, but they were processed at the Bay of Plenty winery complex near Tauranga.

Current Release 1999 Sweet 'n' spicy sums up the bouquet – it's ripe-fruited and very inviting. It's a smooth, soft-centred luxuriously textured wine with integrated tannins, sweet fruit and a long finish. It needs slow-cooked food to be at its best – try it with an oxtail casserole.

Mills Reef Elspeth Malbec

STYLE **dry**

QUALITY ♟ ♟ ♟ ♟ ♟

VALUE ☆ ☆ ☆

GRAPES **Malbec**

REGION **Hawke's Bay**

CELLAR **4**

PRICE **$40–43**

What a beauty! I've been a little dubious about the use of malbec as a straight varietal, because the grape can go rather 'stewy' on its own. This big-hearted red has converted me. Tim Preston put it into French oak barrels for 18 months.

Current Release 2000 Prunes, dried raisins, ripe raspberries – they're all there on the nose. It's deliciously sweet-fruited on the palate, and that extended time in oak has softened the texture most satisfactorily. Enjoy it alongside the best piece of rare beef you can find.

Mills Reef Elspeth Merlot

STYLE **dry**

QUALITY ♟ ♟ ♟ ♟ ♟

VALUE ☆ ☆ ☆ ☆

GRAPES **Merlot**

REGION **Hawke's Bay**

CELLAR **1–5**

PRICE **$34–37**

The fine print on the label tells us this wine came from a single vineyard in Hawke's Bay, and the back label adds that it was in Mere Road. The soil around this part of the Bay is liberally scattered with heat-retaining shingle.

Current Release 1999 Smoky oak mixes it with spiced raspberries on the nose. It's a big smoothie on the palate, full of sweet fruit backed by firm tannins, and boasting a long, satisfying finish. It makes a fine partner for food with smoky flavours, so think beef or cervena cooked on the barbie.

Mills Reef Hawke's Bay Merlot/Cabernets

STYLE **dry**

QUALITY ♟ ♟ ♟

VALUE ☆ ☆ ☆ ☆ ☆

GRAPES
 Merlot 52%
 Cab Sauvignon 26%
 Cab Franc 22%

REGION **Hawke's Bay**

CELLAR **2**

PRICE **$12–16**

Paddy and Tim Preston lavished more care and attention on this red than its price tag would suggest. The three varieties were kept separate, but they were all aged in French oak for seven months. The blend was not filtered, but fined with egg whites.

Current Release 2000 Leather and charred oak make up quite a classic bouquet. It's a straightforward middleweight, with absolutely no sharp edges, a cruisy middle and a short but nicely fruited finish. Enjoy it alongside an old-fashioned steak and kidney pie.

Mills Reef Hawke's Bay Reserve Merlot

The Prestons sourced grapes from two sites in Hawke's Bay, then took them back to the family winery at Katikati, near Tauranga, for processing. It is one of several reds in the Mills Reef collection, all good sellers at the pleasant winery restaurant.

Current Release 2000 Leather and plum aromas make it easy to pick the grape variety. It's soft-centred on the palate, with oak adding the gentlest amount of tannic grip. That relaxed texture makes it a good match for slow-cooked dishes like casseroled beef and onions.

STYLE **dry**
QUALITY ♟ ♟ ♟ ♟
VALUE ☆ ☆ ☆
GRAPES **Merlot**
REGION **Hawke's Bay**
CELLAR 🍾 2
PRICE **$25–27**

Mills Reef Reserve Merlot/Cabernet

Most companies use the 'Reserve' designation for the top wines in their portfolio, but Mills Reef has a couple of wines that sit above theirs. Never mind – the wines are well put together and mostly pretty well priced.

Current Release 2000 Vanilla, leather and sweet pipe tobacco are typical merlot aromatic associations, and they're all in good shape on the nose. It's not a big wine, but it has some attractive ripe plum flavours and smartly integrated tannins. It would be good with lean mince pan-fried in olive oil with cubes of eggplant.

STYLE **dry**
QUALITY ♟ ♟ ♟ ♟
VALUE ☆ ☆ ☆ ☆
GRAPES **Merlot**
　　　　Cab Sauvignon
REGION **Hawke's Bay**
CELLAR 🍾 3
PRICE **$24–27**

Millton Gisborne Merlot/Cabernet Te Arai Vineyard

James and Annie Millton used a mixture of French and American oak barrels to mature this wine. They didn't filter it because they believed it would dilute the flavour, so it might throw a sediment in time.

Current Release 1999 The nose is smoky, with berry and plum aromas also part of the equation. It's sweet-fruited on the front palate and has good weight through the middle, but a lean finish mars the good impression. It works well with lamb and mint sausages served on creamy mashed potatoes.

STYLE **dry**
QUALITY ♟ ♟ ♟
VALUE ☆ ☆ ⯪
GRAPES
　　Merlot 74%
　　Cab Sauvignon 26%
REGION **Gisborne**
CELLAR 🍾 2
PRICE **$28–32**

Mission Gimblett Road Reserve Cabernet Sauvignon/Merlot

This big-hearted red had all the drama. Some of the fermenting grapes were plunged by hand to increase the uptake of colour and flavour, and the fledgling wine spent 22 months in new oak barrels.

Current Release 1998 Yeah! The nose is superbly berryish, with spicy oak acting as a seasoning at the back. It's a big smoothie in the flavour department and boasts a mouth-filling texture, good weight and a long, satisfying finish. Enjoy it alongside a loin of hare, if you can find one.

STYLE **dry**
QUALITY ♟ ♟ ♟ ♟ ♟
VALUE ☆ ☆ ☆ ☆ ☆
GRAPES
　　Cab Sauvignon 70%
　　Merlot 30%
REGION **Hawke's Bay**
CELLAR ⬳ 1–6
PRICE **$26–28**

Mission Hawke's Bay Cabernet Sauvignon

STYLE dry
QUALITY 🍷🍷🍷
VALUE ★★★★★
GRAPES
Cab Sauvignon 93%
Cabernet Franc 6%
Merlot 1%
REGION Hawke's Bay
CELLAR 1
PRICE $14–16

This is one of the least expensive blends of the three so-called Bordeaux varieties in the country, and it sells extremely well at the winery shop and in various retail outlets, restaurants and wine bars all over the country.

Current Release 2001 I can see why it's so popular – quite apart from the price. It's got the right sort of blackcurrant and raspberry aromas and a reasonable quota of ripe fruit flavours. Only a hint of leafiness on the finish mars the good impression. Partner it with beef minute steaks and relax.

Mission Hawke's Bay Cabernet/Merlot

STYLE dry
QUALITY 🍷🍷🍷
VALUE ★★★★★
GRAPES
Cab Sauvignon 55%
Merlot 25%
Cab Franc 20%
REGION Hawke's Bay
CELLAR 2
PRICE $12–15

Made in large quantities, this three-grape blend is hugely popular right around the country. It's no blockbuster, but it's very well priced. The grapes came from various sites around the Bay.

Current Release 1999 Spicy oak and a dash of blackberries start things off. It's smooth, nicely balanced and straightforward – just the thing when you're not in the mood for too much serious analysis. Enjoy it alongside a stack of grilled pure-beef chipolata sausages.

Mission Hawke's Bay Reserve Cabernet Franc

STYLE dry
QUALITY 🍷🍷🍷½
VALUE ★★★½
GRAPES
Cabernet Franc
REGION Hawke's Bay
CELLAR 1–4
PRICE $22–24

Cabernet franc is seldom seen without its mates, cabernet sauvignon and merlot, but in 1999 Paul Mooney decided one parcel of grapes was so good he couldn't bear to blend it. It was a good decision.

Current Release 1999 Physiologists say we can't smell sweetness, but this wine sure smells that way, with a rush of floral and redcurrant aromas. It's smooth, fairly light but undeniably classy on the palate, and should make a good partner for grilled lamb fillets, sliced on an angle and draped over mashed kumara.

Mission Hawke's Bay Reserve Cabernet Sauvignon

STYLE dry
QUALITY 🍷🍷🍷
VALUE ★★★½
GRAPES
Cab Sauvignon
REGION Hawke's Bay
CELLAR 2
PRICE $20–23

Paul Mooney has access to fruit from very old vines. After all, Mission is the oldest winery in the country still under its original ownership. Not that the vines date back to the 1800s, when the label was launched, but some are 20 years old.

Current Release 2000 Ripe plum and raspberry aromas are in good shape on the nose, but there's a suggestion of something rather more rustic in there that isn't so appealing. It disappears on the palate, where sweet fruit and well-tuned oak win the day. Partner it with beef stroganoff.

Moana Park Cabernet Franc

The Moana Park team has all the so-called Bordeaux varieties growing – cabernet sauvignon, merlot, malbec and cabernet franc – but seems more inclined to turn them into separate wines rather than blend them.

Current Release 2000 Putting half the juice into oak barrels has added a faintly dusty edge to the floral, fruity aromas on the nose. It's soft-centred and pretty on the palate, with gentle tannins that make it good with slow-cooked food like a casserole of cubed lamb with baby onions.

STYLE **dry**
QUALITY ▼▼▼
VALUE ☆☆☆☆
GRAPES **Cab Franc**
REGION **Hawke's Bay**
CELLAR 2
PRICE **$20–23**

Moana Park Cabernet Sauvignon/Merlot

The Moana Park label is worn by a number of single-variety reds, which makes this blend a bit of a rarity. It's seldom seen outside Hawke's Bay, but it has a loyal local following.

Current Release 2000 The nose is berryish in the approved fashion and the fruit on the front palate is smooth. A bit of grubbiness in the middle gives it a rather rustic flavour profile, but the finish is clean enough. Try it with a simple pizza of Parmigiano, mozzarella, pulped tomatoes and garlic.

STYLE **dry**
QUALITY ▼▼▼
VALUE ☆☆☆
GRAPES **Cab Sauvignon 65%**
Merlot 29%
Malbec 6%
REGION **Hawke's Bay**
CELLAR ▯
PRICE **$20–23**

Moana Park Malbec

One of very few 'straight' malbecs on the market, this one comes from the Dartmoor Valley. Local conditions seem to suit the variety, so we could well see more of it in the future.

Current Release 2000 Malbec is often thought of as a big, chunky grape, but this one is soft and openly fruity. It's approachably smooth on the palate, with sweet fruit in middleweight surroundings. The finish is clean and moderately long. It goes well with lamb racks, cooked no more than medium.

STYLE **dry**
QUALITY ▼▼▼▼
VALUE ☆☆☆
GRAPES **Malbec**
REGION **Hawke's Bay**
CELLAR 2
PRICE **$30–33**

Montana Cabernet Sauvignon/Merlot

This is one of several wines in the Montana portfolio to blend local juice with a shipment from overseas. They're all at the cheap-and-cheerful end of the market, and must help the company cash flow.

Current Release 2000 There's some pleasant spicy oak in the bouquet, along with at least a touch of sweet fruit. It's direct, light but okay – certainly better than some past vintages. Food? Well, it would be okay with sausage butties or something similar, but it won't make the earth move.

STYLE **dry**
QUALITY ▼▼▼
VALUE ☆☆☆☆
GRAPES **Cab Sauvignon**
Merlot
REGION **Hawke's Bay**
Marlborough
Chile
CELLAR 1
PRICE **$15–17**

Montana 'F' Fairhall Estate Cabernet Sauvignon/Merlot

STYLE **dry**
QUALITY ▼ ▼ ▼ ▼
VALUE ☆ ☆ ☆
GRAPES **Cab Sauvignon Merlot**
REGION **Marlborough**
CELLAR **3**
PRICE **$29–33**

The wine that wears the bold 'F' on the label has been made solely from cabernet sauvignon in the past, but in 1998 a measure of merlot was added to the mix. Conventional wisdom has it that the latter grape is better suited to Marlborough.

Current Release 1998 Charred oak characters seem happy to sit behind the raspberry notes that dominate the nose. It's broad on the front palate, boasts a fair quota of ripe fruit flavours through the middle but has a touch of leanness on the finish. Overall, a pleasant red that makes a perfectly acceptable match for roast lamb rumps with mint-flavoured gravy.

Montana Reserve Barrique Matured Merlot

STYLE **dry**
QUALITY ▼ ▼ ▼ ▼
VALUE ☆ ☆ ☆ ☆
GRAPES **Merlot**
REGION **Hawke's Bay Marlborough**
CELLAR **3**
PRICE **$20–23**

Montana has a huge collection of vineyards all over the country, and the facilities to make wine in any province its winemakers choose. This red is a blend of fruit from top sites in Hawke's Bay and Marlborough.

Current Release 2000 The bouquet is oaky, with merlot's typical plum aromas pushed to the back. It's a different story on the palate, however. The flavours are richly fruited and the texture smooth and relaxed. Partner it with a rare beef sandwich, but go easy on the mustard.

Morton Estate Hawke's Bay Merlot/Cabernet Sauvignon (Black Label)

STYLE **dry**
QUALITY ▼ ▼ ▼ ▼ ▼
VALUE ☆ ☆ ☆
GRAPES
Merlot 55%
Cab Sauvignon 45%
REGION **Hawke's Bay**
CELLAR **3**
PRICE **$55–58**

Yes, this is the current release of Morton's top-shelf merlot-dominant red. Evan Ward decided to hold some back to bring out when he felt it was drinking at its mature best. It spent its quiet time in a mixture of French and American oak barrels.

Current Release 1998 Coffee and a hint of bitter-sweet chocolate start things off in fine fashion. It's pleasantly soft on the palate after six years or so in barrel and bottle, but still boasts plenty of ripe blackcurrant and plum flavours and a big finish. It's good with well-aged beef fillet, cooked medium-rare at most.

Morton Estate Hawke's Bay The Mercure (White Label)

You have to read the back label to discover that this red is a blend of merlot and cabernet sauvignon. Previous vintages have favoured cabernet, but in 2000 Evan Ward and Chris Archer gave merlot the prime spot.

Current Release 2000 Charred oak and something reminiscent of blackcurrants get it together on the nose. It's a big, chunky wine with suggestions of coffee and chocolate to go with the more usual plums and cassis. At Coromandel's Puka Park lodge, it is served with rare lamb fillets over a tandoori chicken mousse.

STYLE **dry**
QUALITY ♟♟♟♟
VALUE ☆ ☆ ☆ ☆
GRAPES **Merlot**
       Cab Sauvignon
REGION **Hawke's Bay**
CELLAR **3**
PRICE **$19–22**

Mount Riley Cabernet/Merlot/Malbec

The cabernet came from the Wairau Valley and the other two varieties from Mount Riley's own Seventeen Valley property, a few kilometres away. This has to be one of the best-value reds on the market.

Current Release 2001 It's got all the right cassis and leather aromas, with a healthy dash of smoky oak at the back. It's been made in a very upfront style to show off the ripe fruit, and the tannins know well enough not to get too stroppy. It would suit a brace of grilled all-beef sausages served with potato wedges baked with rosemary and garlic.

STYLE **dry**
QUALITY ♟♟♟♟
VALUE ☆ ☆ ☆ ☆ ☆
GRAPES **Cab Sauvignon**
       Merlot
       Malbec
REGION **Marlborough**
CELLAR **2**
PRICE **$14–16**

Mud House Merlot

Most Marlborough producers concentrate on pinot noir if they want a red in their portolio. Mud House does have a pinot, but this merlot is exceedingly popular with the locals.
Current Release 2001 Leather and spicy oak form a classic varietal bouquet. It's sweet-edged on the front palate, delivers a good belt of plum-like fruit through the middle and finishes with about the right amount of grip for the style. Grilled lamb cutlets with green beans and rosemary-sprinkled potato wedges would be the way to go.

STYLE **dry**
QUALITY ♟♟♟♟
VALUE ☆ ☆☆
GRAPES **Merlot**
REGION **Marlborough**
CELLAR **3**
PRICE **$34–36**

Mudbrick Merlot

The Mudbrick fact sheet says the company was established with the aim of producing 'small amounts of intimately made wine'. This member of the range came from two different sites, and spent nine months in a mixture of new and used French oak barrels.

Current Release 2001 The nose is smoky and leathery in the approved merlot fashion. It's sweet-fruited on the front palate and boasts good richness through the middle, but shows a hint of greenness on the finish. It goes well with eggplant fritters with light chilli and tomato sauce.

STYLE **dry**
QUALITY ♟♟♟♟
VALUE ☆ ☆ ☆
GRAPES
  Merlot 88%
  Malbec 7%
  Cab Sauvignon 3.5%
  Syrah 1.5%
REGION
  Waiheke Island
CELLAR **3**
PRICE **$25–28**

Mudbrick Vineyard Cabernet Sauvignon/Franc

STYLE **dry**

QUALITY ▽ ▽ ▽ ▽

VALUE ☆ ☆ ☆

GRAPES
Cab Sauvignon 83%
Cab Franc 17%

REGION
Waiheke Island

CELLAR 🍾 2

PRICE $25–27

The fruit for this middleweight red was picked by hand and processed in a small basket press. The two varieties were kept separate, and spent 10 months in a mixture of new, one and two-year-old French and American oak barrels.

Current Release 2000 Blackcurrants and smoky oak share the honours on the nose. It's smooth, ripe-fruited and generous on the palate, with a short but satisfying finish. Try it alongside a brace of fritters based on chopped eggplant, zucchini and red capsicums.

Mudbrick Vineyard Reserve Merlot/Cabernets/Malbec

STYLE **dry**

QUALITY ▽ ▽ ▽ ▽

VALUE ☆ ☆ ☆

GRAPES
Merlot 53%
Cab Sauvignon 27%
Malbec 11%
Cabernet Franc 9%

REGION
Waiheke Island

CELLAR 🍾 4

PRICE $38–42

Two vineyards, in Church Bay and Onetangi, contributed fruit for this four-grape blend. The component parts were matured for 10 months in a mixture of new, one and two-year-old French oak barrels before being blended.

Current Release 2000 Sweet plums have got the gig on the nose. It's rich, ripe and moreish on the palate, with tannins that know their place. That adds up to approachability, and a wine that suits slow-cooked food like braised or casseroled lamb shanks, served with mashed potatoes.

Mudbrick Vineyard Shepherd's Point Cabernet Sauvignon/Merlot

STYLE **dry**

QUALITY ▽ ▽ ▽ ▽ ▽

VALUE ☆ ☆ ☆

GRAPES
Cab Sauvignon 60%
Merlot 40%

REGION
Waiheke Island

CELLAR 🍾 3

PRICE $38–42

A silver medal at the 2001 Air New Zealand Wine Awards and a five-star rating from *Winestate* magazine boosted this red's reputation. The fruit was picked by hand and processed in a small basket press. The fledgling wine then spent 10 months in French oak barrels.

Current Release 2000 The nose is all about ripe blackcurrants and blackberries, with spicy oak also making a contribution. It's sweet-fruited on the front palate and through the middle, and finishes with a healthy belt of tannic grip. It's good with Italian-style meatballs made with lean beef, chopped onion and pine nuts.

Murdoch James Cabernet Franc

Cabernet franc is commonly used to add 'charm' to its better-known cousin, cabernet sauvignon. Sraight versions are rare anywhere, but particularly in Martinborough. That didn't deter the Murdoch James team.

Current Release 2001 There's a fair whack of charred oak on the nose, with ripe berry aromas struggling to squeeze between the planks. Sweet fruit is the overriding impression on the front palate, but the oak tends to dry the middle. Give it time to settle down, then try it alongside a pot roast of fresh silverside with loads of veges.

STYLE **dry**
QUALITY ▼▼▼
VALUE ☆☆½
GRAPES **Cab Franc**
REGION **Martinborough**
CELLAR 🍷 **1–3**
PRICE **$28–32**

Murdoch James Cabernet Sauvignon

Martinborough has carved out an international reputation for pinot noir, but a handful of local producers also enjoy making wine from the so-called Bordeaux varieties. This one's 13.5% alcohol level shows that getting ripe grapes was not a problem.

Current Release 1999 Toast, blackberries and spice form a pretty typical cabernet bouquet. It's moderately big and chunky, with firm tannins adding plenty of grip to the middle and finish. It's good with char-grilled or barbecued (same thing really) beef, ideally served rare or close to it.

STYLE **dry**
QUALITY ▼▼▼▼
VALUE ☆☆☆☆
GRAPES **Cab Sauvignon**
REGION **Martinborough**
CELLAR 🍾 **22**
PRICE **$22–26**

Murdoch James Cabernets

This two-grape blend was made as two separate varietals and matured in barrels, mostly French but with a few American, for six months. The makers confidently suggest that it could be cellared for a decade and beyond, but I've been rather more cautious.

Current Release 2000 Smoky oak pairs up with ripe blackberry and blackcurrant aromas on the nose. The 14.5% alcohol level shows the grapes were very ripe, and they certainly taste like it. Some commentators have found greenness on the finish, but I just get more ripe fruit. Enjoy it alongside a cervena stew with plenty of garlic and baby onions.

STYLE **dry**
QUALITY ▼▼▼▼
VALUE ☆☆☆½
GRAPES
  Cab Franc 60%
  Cab Sauvignon 40%
REGION **Martinborough**
CELLAR 🍷 **1–3**
PRICE **$27–29**

Nautilus Marlborough Cabernet Sauvignon/Merlot

The shell depicted on all Nautilus bottles is that of the label's namesake – not a prawn, as a friend of mine once believed. Presuming it was a suggested food match, he couldn't understand why it appeared on the company's reds.

Current Release 1999 Smoky oak is in good form on the nose, along with a reasonable amount of berryishness. It's ripe-fruited and smooth through the middle but tends to be lean towards the finish. It goes well with rare lamb strips served over a salad of rocket leaves.

STYLE **dry**
QUALITY ▼▼▼▼
VALUE ☆☆☆
GRAPES **Cab Sauvignon**
  Merlot
REGION **Marlborough**
CELLAR 🍾 **3**
PRICE **$29–33**

Ngatarawa Alwyn Reserve Merlot/Cabernet

STYLE dry
QUALITY ▽▽▽▽▽
VALUE ☆☆�½

GRAPES
  Merlot 60%
  Cab Sauvignon 40%
REGION Hawke's Bay

CELLAR 4
PRICE $44–46

This top-shelf blend from Alwyn and Brian Corban sat quietly in French oak barrels for a full 18 months before being transferred to bottles. By New Zealand standards, that's a very long time – many producers settle for a year.
Current Release 2000 A spicy edge adds interest and complexity to the leather and berryfruit aromas. Rich fruit on the front palate is given extra smoothness by the nicely balanced oak. The finish is long and supremely satisfying. It makes a great partner for casseroled oxtail, served with creamy mashed potatoes.

Ngatarawa Glazebrook Merlot

STYLE dry
QUALITY ▽▽▽▽▽
VALUE ☆☆☆☆½

GRAPES
  Merlot 80%
  Cab Sauvignon 20%
REGION Hawke's Bay

CELLAR 3
PRICE $25–27

There's not a lot of this big-hearted red on retail shelves, but if you're visiting Hawke's Bay you should be able to buy it from the winery. It's labelled merlot but as the table shows, it contains a measure of cabernet.
Current Release 2000 Faintly smoky and reminiscent of ripe plums on the nose, superbly smooth and mouth-fillingly rich on the palate, this is very smart wine. I like it with that great French 'stew', cassoulet.

Ngatarawa Glazebrook Merlot/Cabernet

STYLE dry
QUALITY ▽▽▽▽▽
VALUE ☆☆☆☆

GRAPES
  Merlot 55%
  Cab Sauvignon 45%
REGION Hawke's Bay

CELLAR 3
PRICE $26–28

Gary Glazebrook helped found Ngatarawa, but now the company is run by cousins Alwyn and Brian Corban. The winery is housed in historic racing stables and the grounds boast a large ornamental pool filled with waterlilies.
Current Release 2000 There's some very stylish oak to go with the ripe plum and blackcurrant aromas. The smooth texture and rich berry flavours make it very approachable, and ensure it goes well with slow-cooked dishes like a pot-roasted leg of lamb, cooked for long enough in good stock for the meat to fall off the bone.

Ngatarawa Stables Hawke's Bay Cabernet/Merlot

STYLE dry
QUALITY ▽▽▽
VALUE ☆☆☆½

GRAPES
  Cab Sauvignon 80%
  Merlot 13%
  Cabernet Franc 7%
REGION
  Australia 55%
  Hawke's Bay 45%

CELLAR 2
PRICE $18–21

A Ngatarawa wine partly sourced in Australia? It's unusual, but it was necessary – the unseasonal frost that cut a swathe through Hawke's Bay in November 2000 wiped out a big percentage of Alwyn Corban's grapes.
Current Release 2001 Blackberries and plums are backed by gentle oak on the bouquet. It's light-hearted but pleasant on the palate, not an earth-mover but with a reasonable quota of ripe fruit and integrated tannins. Try it alongside cubes of skewered lamb and capsicum.

Nicks Head Gisborne Merlot

Nicks Head is a second label to Longbush, and as such part of the Thorpe brothers' portfolio. We suspect Young Nick would have been a rum drinker if he drank at all, but no doubt he'd be thrilled to have a wine named after him.
Current Release 2000 The nose is smoky and a bit leafy. It's a lightweight on the palate, with some berryish fruit in there but not a lot of depth. The finish is short and lean. Chill it slightly and use it to accompany a platter of summer nibbles.

STYLE **dry**
QUALITY ☗ ☗ ☖
VALUE ☆ ☆ ☆
GRAPES **Merlot 87%**
         Cab Franc 13%
REGION **Gisborne**
CELLAR **1**
PRICE **$14–16**

Nobilo Hawke's Bay/Marlborough Merlot

Nobilo produces quite a few trans-regional blends, and even a couple that use fruit from both sides of the Tasman. This one took advantage of the fact that merlot grows well in both the North and South Islands.
Current Release 2000 The bouquet is smoky and leathery, just as good merlot should be. The good impression continues on the palate, where sweet-edged fruit is balanced by gentle tannins. The finish is a wee bit lean, but overall it's an appealing drop. Enjoy it with a steak and kidney pie.

STYLE **dry**
QUALITY ☗ ☗ ☗ ☖
VALUE ☆ ☆ ☆ ☆ ☆
GRAPES **Merlot**
REGION **Hawke's Bay**
        Marlborough
CELLAR **2**
PRICE **$15–17**

Obsidian Cabernet/Merlot

Only two wines are made by this small but ambitious Waiheke property, and this is the 'biggie'. Its less expensive cellarmate is labelled Weeping Sands, and is sold mostly at restaurants on the island.
Current Release 2000 Coffee, toffee, spicy oak and blackcurrants – this big-hearted red has got the lot. Rich, mouth-filling fruit gives it good weight through the middle and a long finish. A saddle of rare-cooked hare would make a perfect accompaniment, but beef eye fillet should do almost as well.

STYLE **dry**
QUALITY ☗ ☗ ☗ ☗ ☗
VALUE ☆ ☆ ☆
GRAPES
  Cab Sauvignon 63%
  Merlot 30%
  Cab Franc 3.5%
  Malbec 3.5%
REGION
  Waiheke Island
CELLAR **1–4**
PRICE **$49–55**

Okahu Estate Ninety Mile Cabernet Sauvignon/Cabernet Franc/Merlot

STYLE dry
QUALITY ♟♟♟♟
VALUE ☆ ☆ ☆ ☆

GRAPES
Cab Sauvignon 36%
Cab Franc 32%
Merlot 22%
Shiraz 8%
Chambourcin 2%

REGION
Northland
South Auckland
Hawke's Bay

CELLAR 3
PRICE $24–27

It's labelled with the names of its three major grape varieties, but it contains two more. And that's not all. The fruit came not only from the home vineyard, but also from South Auckland and Hawke's Bay. It was matured in 53% French and 47% American oak barrels.

Current Release 2000 The bouquet conjures up images of charred oak and all sorts of berries. It's chunky and full-on in the flavour department, with a rich texture and a suggestion of chocolate on the finish. Vineyard owner Monty Knight suggests fillet steak smothered in mushrooms as a perfect partner. Sounds good!

Omaka Springs Merlot

STYLE dry
QUALITY ♟♟♟♟
VALUE ☆ ☆ ☆ ☆☆

GRAPES Merlot
REGION Marlborough

CELLAR 3
PRICE $17–19

Winemaker Ian Marchant left this merlot unfiltered because he wanted to retain every last flavour nuance. It will throw a bit of sediment in time, but as it's been made in an early-drinking style that shouldn't be a worry.

Current Release 2000 Leather, stewed plum and raspberry aromas get it together on the nose. It's very sweet-fruited on the front palate, settles down to present some pleasant middleweight berry flavours through the middle but suffers from slightly lean tannins on the finish. It works with braised pork belly in a soy-laced Asian-style broth.

Oneroa Bay Cabernet/Merlot

STYLE dry
QUALITY ♟♟♟
VALUE ☆ ☆☆

GRAPES
Cab Sauvignon 64%
Syrah 25%
Merlot 11%

REGION
Waiheke Island

CELLAR 3
PRICE $32–35

Oneroa Bay is an alternative label for Waiheke Island's Peninsula Estate. Past vintages of this red have been made from cabernet sauvignon and merlot, but in 1999 the syrah was looking pretty good, so in it went.

Current Release 1999 Smoky oak sits behind plum and blackcurrant aromas on the nose and drift onto the front palate. It's a smooth-centred middleweight with good integration of fruit and timber and a reasonably long finish. Pull the cork next time you're planning that old-time flatters' favourite, 'spag bol'.

Onetangi Road Merlot

This was the first wine from the tiny Onetangi Road vineyard, and it sold well throughout New Zealand and as far afield as the US. A bit was held back, so you might still find it at the cellar door.

Current Release 1998 Plums, raspberries and smoky oak get it together in the bouquet. It's nicely textured, with a reasonable quota of ripe fruit flavours aided and abetted by smartly balanced tannins. Enjoy it with penne pasta, quickly tossed with chopped piccolo tomatoes (skins and all), torn basil, olive oil and good Parmesan.

STYLE **dry**
QUALITY ♟♟♟♟
VALUE ☆☆
GRAPES **Merlot**
REGION
Waiheke Island
CELLAR 3
PRICE **$49–53**

Onetangi Road Merlot/Cabernet Sauvignon

Pretty well every New Zealand winemaker I've ever met enjoys a 'cleansing ale' after a day of working with grapes. With both a winery and a microbrewery on their tiny Waiheke Island property, John and Megan Wallace have got that scenario well covered.

Current Release 2000 Plums and blackberries get it together in the bouquet. Middleweight tannins give it good grip through the sweet-fruited middle and add firmness to the finish. It's a nicely textured wine, not a blockbuster but with its own appeal. Try it with a simple pizza, topped with nothing more distracting than mozzarella and Parmesan cheeses, garlic and pulped tomatoes.

STYLE **dry**
QUALITY ♟♟♟♟
VALUE ☆☆☆
GRAPES
Merlot 57%
Cab Sauvignon 43%
REGION
Waiheke Island
CELLAR 3
PRICE **$25–28**

Onetangi Road Reserve

This red is the 'biggie' of the small Onetangi Road portfolio. Production is tiny, so most of it is sold on the island. The '99 version, made from the same four grapes, is also on sale from the winery.

Current Release 2000 The sweet fruit aromas are backed by a suggestion of coffee in the bouquet. The rich fruit on the palate gets a helping hand from some seriously chunky tannins. It's a big wine, but sensitively used oak gives it firmness without dominating proceedings. It works well with a medium-rare sirloin steak served with garlic-spiked potato wedges.

STYLE **dry**
QUALITY ♟♟♟♟
VALUE ☆☆☆
GRAPES
Cab Sauvignon 48%
Merlot 33%
Malbec 10%
Cab Franc 9%
REGION
Waiheke Island
CELLAR 3
PRICE **$39–43**

C.J. Pask Declaration

The grape varieties are on the back label because European Union regulations don't allow three varieties to be used as the wine name. Kate Radburnd put the maturing wine into a mixture of French and American oak barrels for 19 months.

Current Release 1999 Smoky oak backs the aromas of ripe currants and blackberries. Rich fruit backed by serious but integrated tannins make it a 'big smoothie' on the palate. It's very smart wine that goes well with a rare ostrich steak, but if you're not into eating big birds a piece of beef fillet would do almost as well.

STYLE **dry**
QUALITY ♟♟♟♟
VALUE ☆☆☆
GRAPES
Cab Sauvignon 48%
Malbec 39%
Merlot 13%
REGION **Hawke's Bay**
CELLAR 1–5
PRICE **$50–54**

C.J. Pask Gimblett Road Cabernet Sauvignon

STYLE **dry**
QUALITY ♔ ♔ ♔ ♔
VALUE ☆ ☆ ☆ ☆
GRAPES **Cab Sauvignon**
REGION **Hawke's Bay**
CELLAR **3**
PRICE **$24–26**

This '98 red has been re-released, partly because frost that hit the Pask vineyards in 2001 meant very little wine was made from that vintage. It was matured in a mixture of French and American oak for 15 months.

Current Release 1998 Smoky oak and savoury, berryish fruit make a good combination on the nose. It's quite a big wine, but it has smoothed out nicely in the year since I last tasted it, and still boasts fruit and nicely tuned tannins. It's good with fettucine pasta tossed with rosemary, crushed garlic and cubes of pink-cooked lamb fillet.

C.J. Pask Gimblett Road Cabernet/Merlot

STYLE **dry**
QUALITY ♔ ♔ ♔ ♔ ♔
VALUE ☆ ☆ ☆ ☆ ☆
GRAPES
Cab Sauvignon 70%
Merlot 28%
Malbec 2%
REGION **Hawke's Bay**
CELLAR **3**
PRICE **$26–28**

Kate Radburnd matured this three-grape blend in a 50/50 mix of French and American oak barrels, 35% of which were new. Chris Pask was the first person to recognise the potential of the shingle-covered Gimblett Road area.

Current Release 2000 Smoky and chunky on the nose, smooth and smartly balanced on the palate, this is red that should appeal even to those who profess to prefer whites. Fruit and oak are in perfect balance, and both contribute to the long finish. It's good with simple but well-flavoured food – I'd go for a grilled T-bone steak.

C.J. Pask Gimblett Road Merlot

STYLE **dry**
QUALITY ♔ ♔ ♔ ♔
VALUE ☆ ☆ ☆⅓
GRAPES **Merlot**
REGION **Hawke's Bay**
CELLAR **3**
PRICE **$26–28**

Only 20% of the French and American oak barrels in which this red was matured were new, because Kate Radburnd didn't want to overpower the fruit. It did, after all, come from the sought-after Gimblett Gravels sub-region.

Current Release 2000 Smoky oak and chunky leather aromas form an appealing bouquet. It's classy stuff on the palate, with nicely focused ripe fruit flavours and a good quota of grippy but integrated tannins. Put it alongside a pile of Italian-style beef meatballs flavoured with chopped sage and relax.

C.J. Pask Hawke's Bay Reserve Cabernet Sauvignon

STYLE **dry**
QUALITY ♔ ♔ ♔ ♔ ♔
VALUE ☆ ☆ ☆⅓
GRAPES **Cab Sauvignon**
REGION **Hawke's Bay**
CELLAR **3**
PRICE **$35–42**

Most of the vines that gave Kate Radburnd the grapes for this straight cabernet are 13 years old, which makes them positively geriatric by New Zealand standards. Old vines give fruit with more flavour concentration.

Current Release 1998 This wine is getting better and better. There's a touch of tar on the nose, along with coffee and chocolate notes. It's big, rich and mouth-filling, with controlled tannins and a berryish finish. Enjoy it alongside grilled lamb chops with a sauce based around pulped tomatoes.

C.J. Pask Hawke's Bay Reserve Merlot

Most people favour French oak for merlot, but Kate Radburnd included a few American barrels in the mix when she matured this one. Just as unusually, every one of them was brand-new. She believed the fruit was big enough to take it.

Current Release 2000 This is one serious red! The bouquet is chock-full of ripe plum aromas, with the sweet, spicy oak sitting where it should, firmly in the background. It's rich, savoury and mouth-filling on the palate, and boasts a finish that goes on forever. Beef lasagne would match it well.

STYLE **dry**
QUALITY 🍷🍷🍷🍷🍷
VALUE ★★½
GRAPES **Merlot**
REGION **Hawke's Bay**
CELLAR **2**
PRICE **$46–49**

Passage Rock Forté

David and Veronika Evans-Gander matured this red in a combination of French and American oak barrels, 30% of them new. Their stated aim is to make wines that 'emphasise drinking pleasure'. Can't argue with that!

Current Release 2000 It's unusual to make cabernet franc the hero, but it works a treat. It has added a vaguely floral impression to the berryfruit and chocolate bouquet and smoothed out the texture through the middle. It's smartly balanced, mouth-fillingly rich and very satisfying. It's great with a Spanish-style 'stew' of black pudding and chorizo sausages.

STYLE **dry**
QUALITY 🍷🍷🍷🍷🍷
VALUE ★★★½
GRAPES
Cab Franc 50%
Merlot 30%
Cab Sauvignon 20%
REGION
Waiheke Island
CELLAR **3**
PRICE **$34–38**

Pegasus Bay Cabernet/Merlot

Waipara is pinot country, but the Donaldsons are keen on the so-called Bordeaux varieties. They believe pumping juice from the bottom of the fermenting tank over the cap of skins at the top increases the flavour intensity.

Current Release 2001 There are some attractive berry aromas on the nose and a fair belt of ripe fruit on the front palate. It's nicely balanced wine that suffers from a trace of greenness right on the finish, but that doesn't prevent it from being a satisfying mouthful. Partner it with a smoked beef salad.

STYLE **dry**
QUALITY 🍷🍷🍷
VALUE ★★★
GRAPES
Cab Sauvignon 45%
Merlot 30%
Malbec 15%
Cab Franc 10%
CELLAR **2**
REGION **Waipara**
PRICE **$27–29**

Peninsula Estate Cabernet Sauvignon/Merlot

STYLE dry
QUALITY 🍷🍷🍷🍷
VALUE ★★
GRAPES
Cab Sauvignon 62%
Merlot 20%
Cab Franc 14%
Malbec 4%
REGION
Waiheke Island
CELLAR 4
PRICE $45–48

This four-grape blend is described in winery literature as the label's 'flagship'. The name, and those of the other wines in the portfolio, was created after a session at the vineyard's raised lookout platform. Each label refers to an oceanic landmark.

Current Release 1998 I get a suggestion of greengage plums on the nose, which is unusual but perfectly acceptable. It's smooth-centred, richly fruited and nicely balanced on the palate, boasting good weight and flavours that keep the good news running right through to the reasonably long finish. Enjoy it alongside a wedge of seriously aged gouda cheese.

Pleasant Valley Signature Selection Hawke's Bay Cabernet/Malbec

STYLE dry
QUALITY 🍷🍷🍷
VALUE ★★★★
GRAPES
Cab Sauvignon 70%
Malbec 30%
REGION Hawke's Bay
CELLAR 2
PRICE $18–20

Stephan Yelas loved the fruit he sourced for this two-grape blend, and he didn't want to overpower it with oak. That's why only 20% of the barrels in which it was matured were new – the rest had already had a year or two's use.

Current Release 1999 There's a bucket-load of malbec's typical prune aromas in the bouquet – the cabernet is completely crowded out. It's big, tannic and grippy on the palate and was a little hard when I tried it, but should have softened by now. Try it with a classic corned beef dinner.

Ponder Estate Artist's Reserve Marlborough Merlot

STYLE dry
QUALITY 🍷🍷🍷🍷
VALUE ★★★
GRAPES Merlot
REGION Marlborough
CELLAR 2
PRICE $31–34

This recent addition to the Ponder Estate Artist's Reserve series spent nine months in a mixture of new and used French and American oak barrels. The painting on the label is by vineyard founder, Mike Ponder.

Current Release 2000 Sweet pipe tobacco and ripe raspberries share the honours on the nose. It's broadly textured, with ripe fruit flavours and gentle tannins leading to a clean, appealing finish. It works well with sheep kidneys and sliced onions on grainy toast.

Putiki Bay Waiheke Island Malbec

STYLE dry
QUALITY 🍷🍷🍷🍷
VALUE ★★★½
GRAPES Malbec
REGION
Waiheke Island
CELLAR 1–4
PRICE $26–29

Only 180 cases of this wine were made, and some of those were due to be sent overseas. Still, it's not a well-known label so you might still find a bottle or two around the traps, especially if you're visiting Waiheke some time in the next few months.

Current Release 2000 Maturation in French and American oak has added a savoury note to the blackcurrant-like bouquet. It's a weighty wine on the palate, with firm tannins giving a grippy edge to the sweet, plum-like fruit. Enjoy it with hearty fare like an oxtail casserole, served with mashed potatoes or 'wet' polenta.

Putiki Bay Waiheke Island Merlot

The fruit was picked by hand, the fermenting juice was plunged by the winemaker and a brawny helper or two (it's hard work), and the fledgling wine spent a year in French oak barrels. That all adds up to a serious attitude to making red wine.

Current Release 2000 The elegantly fruit-led nose leads to a palate that is rich in sweet fruit. Good balance between the fruit and oak equals tannins that add grip without hardening the flavour. There's a touch of leanness on the finish, but overall it's pleasant wine that would go well with a salad based on smoked beef.

STYLE **dry**
QUALITY ♟ ♟ ♟ ♟
VALUE ★★★
GRAPES **Merlot**
REGION **Waiheke Island**
CELLAR ▯ **3**
PRICE **$32–35**

Quarry Road Cabernet Sauvignon/Merlot

The fruit came from a mixture of young and old vines grown on two different Te Kauwhata sites, and after they had been crushed, pressed and fermented Toby Cooper put their juice into oak barrels for 10 months.

Current Release 2001 Leather and cassis aromas make all the right impressions in the bouquet, but the flavour profile is broad and a tad flabby. For all that, it's not unpleasant, and works okay with a rare beef, watercress and mustard sandwich.

STYLE **dry**
QUALITY ♟ ♟ ♟
VALUE ★★★★
GRAPES **Cab Sauvignon Merlot**
REGION **Te Kauwhata**
CELLAR ▯ **1**
PRICE **$16–18**

Ransom Dark Summit Cabernet Sauvignon & Merlot

Robin Ransom put this blend into a mixture of new and used French and American oak barrels and left it there for 21 months. The label has done well for him in the past, and helped put the name on the map.

Current Release 1998 Merlot's leather and plum aromas dominate the bouquet, even though it is the minor player. Sweet oak sits happily in the background. Rich, sweet fruit starts things off well on the palate, but the earthiness that was charming in its youth is beginning to dominate proceedings. Try it with lasagne, but don't wait too long.

STYLE **dry**
QUALITY ♟ ♟ ♟ ♟
VALUE ★★★★
GRAPES **Cab Sauvignon 67% Merlot 33%**
REGION **Matakana**
CELLAR ▯ **1**
PRICE **$20–26**

Ransom Mahurangi Cabernet/Merlot

Selling at most outlets for under $20, this two-grape blend makes a good companion to the top-shelf Dark Summit version. Robin Ransom reckons it spent two years in oak by accident. 'I fell behind,' he explains.

Current Release 1999 The long spell in barrels has added a smoky feel to the berryish aromas in the bouquet. It's a big, firm wine with good fruit and a certain rusticity. The finish is reasonably long and pleasantly sweet-fruited. It works well with serious beef sausages in a tomato-based sauce.

STYLE **dry**
QUALITY ♟ ♟ ♟
VALUE ★★★★
GRAPES **Cab Sauvignon Merlot**
REGION **Matakana**
CELLAR ▯ **2**
PRICE **$19–21**

Redmetal Vineyards Basket Press Merlot/Cabernet Franc

STYLE **dry**
QUALITY ♟♟♟♟
VALUE ☆☆
GRAPES **Merlot 68%**
Cab Franc 32%
REGION **Hawke's Bay**
CELLAR 🍾 **4**
PRICE **$43–46**

A basket press is a small, hand-operated device that is believed to extract maximum flavour from grapes. Obviously, it can't be used to make giant quantities of wine, but many winemakers favour it for small-production lines like this one. **Current Release 2000** Savoury oak, leather and Black Doris plums share the honours on the nose. It's deliciously ripe-fruited, with tannins that add plenty of grip through the middle but know not to dominate the overall mouth-filling richness. It makes a marvellous companion for cervena back steaks, cooked rare on a barbecue or indoor char-grill.

Redmetal Vineyards Merlot/Cabernet Franc/Cabernet Sauvignon

STYLE **dry**
QUALITY ♟♟♟♟♟
VALUE ☆☆☆☆
GRAPES
Merlot 52%
Cab Franc 35%
Cab Sauvignon 13%
REGION **Hawke's Bay**
CELLAR 🍾 **3**
PRICE **$25–27**

Grant Edmonds is on record as saying that he doesn't have much time for the cabernet sauvignon grape – merlot is his first love. Nevertheless, he concedes that the world's best-known red variety does have a place in a blend, albeit as a minor player. **Current Release 2000** There's a faintly floral edge on the predominant aromas of leather and charred oak. It's a smooth-centred middleweight on the palate, with a good quota of ripe berry flavours backed by gentle tannins. It works fine with pink-cooked lamb cutlets, but trim all the visible fat off before you pan-fry them.

Redmetal Vineyards The Merlot

STYLE **dry**
QUALITY ♟♟♟♟♟
VALUE ☆☆⚊
GRAPES **Merlot**
REGION **Hawke's Bay**
CELLAR ▭ **1–6**
PRICE **$89–94**

Red Metal label owner Grant Edmonds loves merlot, and he has made some stunning wines from it over the years. This is one of the most expensive examples of the variety in the country, but its price is justified by its rarity and its quality. **Current Release 2000** Oh boy! The smoke-tinged bouquet suggests sweet pipe tobacco, super-ripe plums and newly polished leather. It's seriously big on the palate, but perfect balance means it is still eminently approachable. The flavours put liquorice, coffee and dark chocolate in mind, but mostly it's just about great grapes, sensitively handled. A food match? It has to be casseroled venison.

Rippon Merlot/Syrah

STYLE **dry**
QUALITY ♟♟♟♟
VALUE ☆☆⚊
GRAPES **Merlot 60%**
Syrah 40%
REGION **Central Otago**
CELLAR 🍾 **3**
PRICE **$33–36**

These two grapes are seldom seen in one another's company, especially without friends like cabernet sauvignon in tow. On the face of it, neither grape would seem ideal for Central Otago conditions, but that didin't deter the Rippon team. **Current Release 1999** Think plum pudding and you've got a handle on the bouquet. Actually, you'll be pretty close if you think the same thing when you taste it. Not that's it's sweet, mind, but it does have that sort of roundness, spice and richness. Try it with casseroled lamb shanks and you'll be a happy punter.

Riverside Stirling Merlot/Cabernet

It's been around for a while, but the winery still holds a few cases of this two-grape blend and trickles them through the retail system from time to time. I don't believe they should hold onto it for much longer, but I'd be happy to be proved wrong.

Current Release 1998 The bouquet is still surprisingly fresh and youthful, but the bottle-aged characters are beginning to soften the flavour profile a bit too much. Nevertheless, it provides quite pleasant drinking at the moment, but serve it with not-too-heavy dishes like beef schnitzels.

STYLE **dry**
QUALITY ▽ ▽ ▽
VALUE ☆ ☆
GRAPES **Merlot**
Cab Sauvignon
REGION **Hawke's Bay**
CELLAR ▯ 1
PRICE **$34–36**

Robard & Butler Cabernet Sauvignon

It was made here, but the label tells us the fruit for this wine came from South East Australia, which is a legally defined grape-growing region taking in parts of South Australia, Victoria and New South Wales.

Current Release 2001 There's a fair whack of smoky, dusty oak on the nose but as it probably came from oak 'chips', not barrels, it will fade quite soon. The fruit is sweet and faintly jammy through the middle and edged by spice on the finish. It's a well-priced quaffer, and sits okay with easy-going nibbles.

STYLE **dry**
QUALITY ▽ ▽ ▽
VALUE ☆ ☆ ☆ ☆ ☆
GRAPES **Cab Sauvignon**
REGION
South East Australia
CELLAR ▯ 1
PRICE **$11–13**

Rongopai Vintage Reserve Cabernet Sauvignon/Merlot

Waikato growers reckon the 2000 vintage was the best they'd seen for 20 years. The weather stayed hot and dry, allowing grapes to be picked in peak condition. This red spent 10 months in oak.

Current Release 2000 The rich colour bodes well, and the touch of smokiness behind the ripe berry aromas continues the good impression. It doesn't quite live up to expectations on the palate, but it's a pleasant-enough middleweight that goes well with a plate of meatballs, tossed in home-made tomato sauce.

STYLE **dry**
QUALITY ▽ ▽ ▽
VALUE ☆ ☆ ☆
GRAPES
Cab Sauvignon 45%
Merlot 30%
Malbec 25%
REGION **Waikato**
CELLAR ▯ 2
PRICE **$25–27**

Rongopai Vintage Reserve Te Kauwhata Merlot/Malbec

Tom van Dam picked the fruit for this unusual two-grape blend by hand, then matured the fledgling wine in new French barrels for 13 months. He has since left the company, but the wine is still around.

Current Release 1999 I get coffee, vanilla and a touch of cinnamon on the nose, along with the smoky oak that dominated proceedings when it was younger. It's smooth and mouth-filling on the palate, and finishes cleanly. I like it with casseroled beef shin on the bone.

STYLE **dry**
QUALITY ▽ ▽ ▽ ▽
VALUE ☆ ☆ ☆ ☆
GRAPES **Merlot 50%**
Malbec 50%
REGION **Te Kauwhata**
CELLAR ▭▭ 1–4
PRICE **$23–25**

Ruben Hall Cabernet Sauvignon/Malbec

STYLE **dry**
QUALITY ♟ ♟ ♟
VALUE ☆ ☆ ☆ ☆ ☆
GRAPES **Cab Sauvignon**
Malbec
Syrah
Merlot
REGION **Various**
CELLAR 🍾 **1**
PRICE **$10–12**

Cabernet sauvignon and merlot from this country were blended with more cabernet, plus syrah and malbec, from a super-hot site in Argentina. It sounds complicated, but it is becoming more common as the price of some grape varieties goes up.

Current Release (non-vintage) Smoky oak and a touch of tar back ripe berry aromas. It's nicely put together, boasting good oak balance and a reasonable quota of sweet fruit, but a green finish spoils things at the last minute. Partner it with sausages served with a red capsicum salsa.

Sacred Hill Basket Press Merlot/Cabernet

STYLE **dry**
QUALITY ♟ ♟ ♟ ♟
VALUE ☆ ☆ ☆ ☆
GRAPES
Merlot 75%
Cab Sauvignon 11%
Malbec 9%
Cabernet Franc 5%
REGION **Hawke's Bay**
CELLAR 🍾 **3**
PRICE **$25–27**

Sacred Hill's basket press has been used to make various variations on the cabernet and merlot theme, so this merlot-dominant blend is a logical progression. Tony Bish says it all depends on the quality of the fruit.

Current Release 2000 Smoky oak and ripe plum aromas create a good impression on the nose. It's richly fruited, smartly balanced and finishes with a clean-cut flourish. It goes perfectly with lamb racks, brushed with olive oil, dusted with chopped rosemary and baked pink.

Sacred Hill Brokenstone Merlot

STYLE **dry**
QUALITY ♟ ♟ ♟ ♟ ♟
VALUE ☆ ☆ ☆
GRAPES **Merlot**
REGION **Hawke's Bay**
CELLAR 🍾 **5**
PRICE **$40–43**

This is Sacred Hill's top-tier merlot, and it spent 15 months in new French oak. It has won gold and silver medals, plus a couple of five-star ratings. The impressive '95 version, which includes 15% malbec, was recently re-released in small quantities.

Current Release 2000 The bouquet has an earthy edge on its typical leather notes, with smoky oak also playing a part. The flavours are soft, rich and smooth and the finish lingers most satisfactorily. It's a standout with pink-roasted duck breasts.

Sacred Hill Whitecliff Vineyards Merlot

STYLE **dry**
QUALITY ♟ ♟ ♟ ♟
VALUE ☆ ☆ ☆ ☆ ☆
GRAPES **Merlot**
REGION **Hawke's Bay**
CELLAR 🍾 **2**
PRICE **$16–18**

Winemaker Tony Bish says the 2000 vintage was perfect for merlot in the Bay. Lots of hot, dry days in February got the grapes fully ripe sooner than usual, bringing the harvest day forward by a week or so.

Current Release 2000 Sweet oak and aromas like plum conserve get things going in fine style. There's some nice, middleweight fruit in there, making this a very approachable package. A hint of chocolate is a bonus on the finish. It's perfect with a brace of roasted quail.

Saints Vineyard Selection Cabernet Sauvignon/Merlot

Past vintages of this wine have come solely from Hawke's Bay, but in 2000 and 2001 fruit was added from across the ditch. Trans-Tasman blending is still rare, but it's happening more than it used to.

Current Release 2001 Smoky oak has certainly got the gig on the nose – the fruit is quite subdued. It's pretty hard on the front palate, but sweet berry flavours build through the middle before drying tannins take over again on the finish. Give it a year, then try it with barbecued lamb chops.

STYLE **dry**
QUALITY ▾▾▾
VALUE ✩✩✩
GRAPES **Cab Sauvignon Merlot**
REGION **Hawke's Bay South East Australia**
CELLAR ▭ **1**
PRICE **$17–19**

Selaks Founder's Reserve Marlborough Merlot

Daryl Woolley and his team hand-plunged 20% of the juice for this tasty merlot. That's a process that pushes the floating cap of skins on top of the fermenting vat back into the bubbling juice. It's VERY hard work.

Current Release 2001 Leather and smoked cherries – that's my impression of the bouquet. It's a nicely focused wine with sweet-edged flavours ensuring plenty of richness through the middle. Integrated tannins give it just the right amount of grip. It's good with Italian-style baked beans, made with borlotti beans and imported canned tomatoes.

STYLE **dry**
QUALITY ▾▾▾▾▾
VALUE ✩✩✩✩✩
GRAPES **Merlot**
REGION **Marlborough**
CELLAR ▯ **5**
PRICE **$26–28**

Shepherd's Point Cabernet/Merlot/Syrah

Shepherd's Point is a relatively new vineyard planted in Waiheke's Onetangi Valley. The inaugural wines were made at the Mudbrick winery. Mudbrick owner, Nick Jones, is a 50% shareholder in the new venture.

Current Release 1999 There's a forest-floor aroma at the back of the ripe fruit in the bouquet, but get past that and you are rewarded with a broad-textured wine tasting of super-ripe berries and plums wrapped in sweet, spicy oak. It makes a good partner for braised tongue with red onion.

STYLE **dry**
QUALITY ▾▾▾▾
VALUE ✩✩✩
GRAPES **Cab Sauvignon 70% Merlot 15% Syrah 15%**
REGION **Waiheke Island**
CELLAR ▭ **1–4**
PRICE **$39–42**

Sileni Cellar Selection Merlot/Cabernet Franc

Given that the Sileni publicity material tells us the company's Cellar Selection wines are aimed at the 'everyday drinking' segment of the market, this is pretty smart wine that sells by the case-load at the cellar door.

Current Release 2002 The bouquet has charred oak behind the berries and there's a good quota of ripe, plummy fruit characters on the palate. The tannins know their place and the finish is satisfyingly long. Potato gnocchi with a lightly chilli-spiked chopped beef sauce would suit it well.

STYLE **dry**
QUALITY ▾▾▾▾
VALUE ✩✩✩
GRAPES **Merlot 60% Cab Franc 40%**
REGION **Hawke's Bay**
CELLAR ▯ **3**
PRICE **$25–27**

Sileni Merlot/Cabernets

STYLE **dry**

QUALITY ▽▽▽▽▽

VALUE ☆☆☆

GRAPES
Merlot 75%
Cab Franc 13%
Malbec 8%
Cab Sauvignon 4%

REGION Hawke's Bay

CELLAR 3

PRICE $35–37

Sileni has sorted its wines into three classes. The print under the name on this one reads 'Sileni Estates', which is the middle range. EV (Exceptional Vintage) wines sit above it, and Cellar Selection products are below.

Current Release 2000 Smoky oak and raspberry aromas set the scene. It seems very complete on the palate, with the oak settling happily into the background behind the primary flavours of ripe berries and plums. It's good with beef rump, braised with chopped carrot, onion and celery and sliced thickly for serving.

Soljans Barrique Reserve Hawke's Bay Merlot

STYLE **dry**

QUALITY ▽▽▽▽

VALUE ☆☆☆☆

GRAPES **Merlot**

REGION Hawke's Bay

CELLAR 3

PRICE $18–20

The barrels in which this straight merlot were matured were all French, but most of them had been used before. The winemaking team felt more new oak would have overshadowed the fruit.

Current Release 2000 Typical merlot leather is in good form on the nose. It's ripe-fruited and moderately rich on the palate, and boasts sensible tannins to add grip without drying the finish too much. Tony Soljan recommends it for lamb shanks – sounds good to me!

Solstone Cabernet Franc Reserve

STYLE **dry**

QUALITY ▽▽▽▽

VALUE ☆☆☆

GRAPES **Cab Franc**

REGION Wairarapa

CELLAR 4

PRICE $40–43

Wines made solely from cabernet sauvignon's more gentle cousin are rare anywhere in the country, but particularly in 'Pinot Paradise', the Wairarapa. The grapes for this example obviously got gloriously ripe – the alcohol level is a healthy 13.5%.

Current Release 2000 Cabernet franc is often described as smelling like violets, and there's certainly a floral note in the bouquet of this one. It's clean, fresh and sweet-fruited on the palate, with tannins that make their presence felt, but know their place. It is perfect alongside a rare cervena steak, served with a not-too-sweet berry-infused sauce.

Solstone Cabernet/Merlot Reserve

STYLE **dry**

QUALITY ▽▽▽▽

VALUE ☆☆☆

GRAPES
Cab Sauvignon 80%
Merlot 20%

REGION Wairarapa

CELLAR 3

PRICE $40–43

It's not easy to get cabernet sauvignon fully ripe in the Wairarapa, but pruning the vines in ways that encourage more sun onto the grapes helps. Leaves can also be plucked off to lessen shading, and the crop can be thinned to give the vine fewer bunches on which to concentrate.

Current Release 2000 Sweet oak is in good balance with the ripe raspberry and blackcurrant aromas on the nose. It's a generous wine with rich fruit flavours and quite solid tannins. The finish is long and satisfying. Try it with a café-style steak sandwich, ideally made with char-grilled focaccia.

Solstone Merlot Wairarapa Valley

The Wairarapa is best known for pinot noir, but this stylish red shows that merlot performs equally well on the right site. Because it ripens relatively early in the season it has a better chance of being picked before the autumn rains.

Current Release 2001 Leather and plums are classic merlot aromatic associations, and they're both in good shape on the nose. It's broadly textured, with gentle ripe-fruit flavours and a softly spoken finish. That makes it good with casseroles and braises. Cubed lamb, cooked long and slow, would be a good choice.

STYLE **dry**
QUALITY ▼▼▼▼
VALUE ☆ ☆ ☆ ☆
GRAPES
  Merlot 96%
  Malbec 4%
REGION **Wairarapa**
CELLAR 🍶 **3**
PRICE **$23–25**

Spy Valley Marlborough Merlot

Spy Valley wines have always been made at Framingham under the supervision of Alan McCorkindale. Now, Framingham's Ant Mackenzie has signed on as resident winemaker for Spy Valley – but Alan made this one.

Current Release 2001 I like the savoury notes behind the primary aromas of ripe plums and raspberries. It's smooth and richly fruited, with gentle tannins adding about the right amount of grip for the style. Enjoy it alongside the oldest wedge of gouda cheese you can find, and serve it with crusty bread rather than crackers.

STYLE **dry**
QUALITY ▼▼▼▼
VALUE ☆ ☆ ☆ ☆
GRAPES **Merlot**
REGION **Marlborough**
CELLAR 🍾 **3**
PRICE **$20–23**

Stonecroft Ruhanui

Stonecroft Syrah is decidedly in the hard-to-find bracket, so this three-grape blend is often called on to fly the company flag at regional tastings. If you meet up with its producer, Alan Limmer, ask him about his racing Torana.

Current Release 2000 Berryish fruit, smoky oak and a suggestion of newly polished leather – that's the bouquet sorted out. It's ripe-fruited and stylish on the palate, but with a touch of appealing rusticity towards the finish. An Auckland suburban restaurant named Café 98 has wild boar shanks on the menu. They would make a perfect match.

STYLE **dry**
QUALITY ▼▼▼▼
VALUE ☆ ☆ ☆
GRAPES
  Cab Sauvignon 39%
  Merlot 35%
  Syrah 26%
REGION **Hawke's Bay**
CELLAR 🍶 **4**
PRICE **$32–35**

Stonyridge Larose

It's pricier than ever, but no doubt proprietor/winemaker Stephen White, alias Serge Blanco, will get far more orders for this wine than he can ever hope to fill, and will end up having to send back thousands of dollars to its many slavering fans.

Current Release 2000 Coffee and spice (and all things nice!) make an immediately attractive introduction. It's certainly a biggie, but perfect balance between rich fruit and savoury oak give it a lot of elegance. Amazingly, it's drinking well now, but it will be much better for being put away in a quiet spot. Wild venison would make a good partner, so find a friendly hunter.

STYLE **dry**
QUALITY ▼▼▼▼▼
VALUE ☆ ☆ ☆
GRAPES
  Cab Sauvignon 55%
  Merlot 23%
  Malbec 10%
  Cabernet Franc 8%
  Petit Verdot 4%
REGION
  Waiheke Island
CELLAR 🍾 **2–8**
PRICE **$125–140**

Te Awa Farm Boundary

STYLE dry

QUALITY 🍷🍷🍷🍷🍷

VALUE ★★☆

GRAPES
Merlot 85%
Cab Sauvignon 10%
Cabernet Franc 5%

REGION Hawke's Bay

CELLAR 6

PRICE $50–54

Jenny Dobson and Gus Lawson's top red is made from parcels of fruit in parts of the vineyard that give smaller crops than other vines further along the rows. The smaller the crop, the more concentrated the fruit – and the better the wine.

Current Release 2000 Smoky oak, chunky berry-like fruit and loads of richness on the nose and through the palate make this wine an outstanding success. It's broad and superbly smooth from go to whoa. Actually, whoa is the hard bit, it's so frighteningly drinkable. Pull the cork next time you're roasting a decent-sized chunk of good beef.

Te Awa Farm Longlands Hawke's Bay Cabernet/Merlot

STYLE dry

QUALITY 🍷🍷🍷🍷

VALUE ★★★★

GRAPES
Cab Sauvignon 76%
Merlot 13%
Cab Franc 11%

REGION Hawke's Bay

CELLAR 3

PRICE $25–27

Te Awa is the shortened form of te awa o te atua, which translates as the river god. The name is a reference to the aquifer that trickles towards the sea, deep beneath the stone-covered soils of the home vineyard.

Current Release 2000 Smoke-edged blackcurrants – that's what I get on the nose. It's a chunky wine with firm tannins and broad flavours, yet it retains a measure of elegance because of the excellent balance between fruit and oak. It makes a great partner for a rare ostrich steak, using a bird raised in Hawke's Bay, of course.

Te Awa Farm Longlands Merlot

STYLE dry

QUALITY 🍷🍷🍷🍷

VALUE ★★★☆

GRAPES
Merlot 85%
Malbec 11%
Cabernet Franc 4%

REGION Hawke's Bay

CELLAR 4

PRICE $26–28

A lot of work went into making this wine. The fruit was picked by hand and the cap of skins was plunged back into the juice regularly during fermentation. Finally, it went into American and French oak barrels for 13 months.

Current Release 2000 There are plenty of the variety's trademark smoky, leather-like aromas on the nose, along with a dash of spicy oak. It's broadly textured in front, attractively chunky through the middle and has a ripe-fruited finish. Char-grilled foods suit it well, so try it with a pile of barbecued two-bone lamb chops.

Te Mania Three Brothers Nelson Merlot/Malbec/Cabernet Franc

Cabernet sauvigon and merlot are both quite rare in Nelson, and malbec decidedly so. This blend of the three varieties spent nine months in a mixture of French and American oak barrels. It sells well in the region, but only a few cases make it further afield.

Current Release 2001 There's a leafy edge at the start, but then the aromas of charred oak and leather take over. The flavour profile is leaner than that of past vintages, but it's pleasant enough in a straightforward way. Try it with lamb chops and mashed potatoes and whatever green vegetable you choose.

STYLE **dry**
QUALITY ♟ ♟ ♟
VALUE ☆ ☆ ☆
GRAPES **Merlot**
　　　　Malbec
　　　　Cab Sauvignon
REGION **Nelson**
CELLAR 🍾 **2**
PRICE **$20–23**

Te Mata Awatea Cabernet/Merlot

Named after a cargo ship that sailed the Auckland–Sydney–Wellington route in the 1930s, Awatea comes from a number of vineyards, mostly hosting younger vines than is the case with its big brother, Coleraine.

Current Release 2000 The nose is lightly smoky, but the predominant characters are reminiscent of currants and blackberries along with a healthy dose of leather. On the palate, it's focused and faintly earthy, which makes it a good partner for rustic fare like braised beef shin with mushrooms, or a good old-fashioned beef stew with dumplings.

STYLE **dry**
QUALITY ♟ ♟ ♟ ♟
VALUE ☆ ☆ ☆
GRAPES
　　Cab Sauvignon 52%
　　Merlot 31%
　　Cab Franc 16%
　　Petit Verdot 1%
REGION **Hawke's Bay**
CELLAR 🍾 **6**
PRICE **$35–38**

Te Mata Coleraine Cabernet/Merlot

Coleraine was our first icon red, and it is still widely regarded as the ultimate expression of the Hawke's Bay style. The grapes came from 12-year-old vines, and winemaker Peter Cowley handled their juice using what he calls 'classical' methods.

Current Release 2000 Smoky, spicy oak, generous but elegant fruit and an impressive dose of what can only be called style. This is a very impressive red, sweet-edged but with good grip, mouth-filling in the middle and boasting a finish that lasts until next week. There is nothing better next to a rare-roasted whole fillet of beef.

STYLE **dry**
QUALITY ♟ ♟ ♟ ♟
VALUE ☆ ☆ ☆
GRAPES
　　Cab Sauvignon 52%
　　Merlot 29%
　　Cab Franc 19%
REGION **Hawke's Bay**
CELLAR 🍾 **8**
PRICE **$54–58**

Te Mata Woodthorpe Cabernet/Merlot

STYLE **dry**

QUALITY ▾▾▾▾

VALUE ★ ★ ★ ★

GRAPES
Cab Sauvignon 44%
Merlot 42%
Cab Franc 14%

REGION Hawke's Bay

CELLAR 🍾 3

PRICE $21–23

This wine replaces the old Te Mata Estate Cabernet/Merlot, a long-time popular restaurant red. Original plans were to have no Te Mata identification on the Woodthorpe range, but now both names are featured on the label.

Current Release 2001 Smoky oak sits behind the plum and blackberry aromas in the bouquet. It's sweet-fruited and very approachable, with sensibly tuned tannins adding about the right amount of grip for its middleweight style. Enjoy it alongside stir-fried beef and mushrooms.

Te Motu Cabernet/Merlot

STYLE **dry**

QUALITY ▾▾▾▾▾

VALUE ★ ★

GRAPES
Cab Sauvignon 65%
Merlot 30%
Cabernet Franc 4%
Malbec 1%

REGION
Waiheke Island

CELLAR ▭▭▭▷ 2–6

PRICE $80–95

Terry Dunleavy, former executive officer of the Wine Institute of New Zealand, runs this Waiheke Island property with a couple of members of his large family. This red is sold in a couple of top restaurants in France.

Current Release 1999 Smoky, sweet oak sits happily behind the aromas of ripe blackcurrants and blackberries. It's an opulent wine on the palate, boasting loads of super-ripe fruit in velvety surroundings. The finish is long and very satisfying. In an ideal world, it should be partnered by rare-roasted saddle of hare . . . but cervena would do almost as well.

Te Whare Ra Sarah Jennings

STYLE **dry**

QUALITY ▾▾▾▾

VALUE ★ ★ ★ ★

GRAPES Cab Sauvignon
Merlot
Cab Franc
Malbec

REGION Marlborough

CELLAR 🍾 3

PRICE $22–25

Marlborough's cabernet producers can be counted on the fingers of one hand, but that doesn't deter the Te Whare Ra team. The winemaker who made this model didn't share the exact blend with anyone and has since left, but we know it's cabernet-dominant.

Current Release 2000 Big and berryish sums up the nose, and it's reasonably generous on the palate – certainly one of the better examples from this label. There's a typical touch of Marlborough greenness on the finish, but some would argue that we should accept that as simply part of the regional character. Whatever – try it with a pile of barbecued lamb chops and decide for yourself.

Te Whau The Point

The blend has varied slightly in its first couple of vintages, but both versions of this big-hearted red have put the emphasis on cabernet sauvignon, with a tiny bit of malbec to add grunt to the finish.

Current Release 2000 Malbec is there as only a tiny amount, but I reckon it still contributes an earthy note to the bouquet and firmness to the finish. In between, the wine is all about sweet fruit, smoky oak and lush berryfruit flavours. It's impressive stuff that suits slow-cooked food, like casseroled oxtail.

STYLE **dry**
QUALITY ▽▽▽▽▽
VALUE ☆☆☆☆
GRAPES
  Cab Sauvignon 58%
  Merlot 21%
  Cab Franc 18%
  Malbec 3%
REGION
  Waiheke Island
CELLAR 1–4
PRICE $38–42

Tom

It's named for Hawke's Bay and national industry icon, Tom McDonald, and it is Montana's flagship red. The lower price listed is ex-winery, and the upper depends on what any retailer wants to add. After all, it is one of the rarest reds around.

Current Release 1998 Merlot's ripe plum aromas are edged by suggestions of cherries and sweet, spicy oak. It's beautifully textured on the palate, smooth in front and superbly rich through the middle. Oak spice returns to add extra interest to the long finish. At its Hawke's Bay launch it was matched with roasted venison racks with truffled mushrooms. Oh yes!

STYLE **dry**
QUALITY ▽▽▽▽▽
VALUE ☆☆
GRAPES
  Merlot 50%
  Cab Sauvignon 28%
  Cab Franc 22%
REGION **Hawke's Bay**
CELLAR 6
PRICE $99–120

Torlesse Waipara Merlot

Straight merlot from Waipara is a rare commodity, so fans of the variety were cheering and marching in the streets when this one appeared on the market . . . well, almost. It was put together by Kym Rayner, and he's made a nice job of it.

Current Release 2001 Smoky oak backs the aromas of ripe plums on the nose. It's big-hearted but smooth, with smart balance between fruit and oak. The finish is spicy and long. It works really well with that old flatters' favourite, spag bol – especially if you add a few chopped chicken livers to the beef.

STYLE **dry**
QUALITY ▽▽▽▽▽
VALUE ☆☆☆☆
GRAPES **Merlot**
REGION **Waipara**
CELLAR 1–4
PRICE $30–33

Trinity Hill Gimblett Road Cabernet Sauvignon

John Hancock reckons this wine will peak in about five years, and will be still be drinking well in 10. He could well be right, but I've been rather more cautious with my cellaring recommendation. Time will tell!

Current Release 1998 Sweet, spicy oak backs the ripe berry aromas. It's soft on the palate, and very drinkable, but firm tannins cut in towards the lingering finish. Partner it with a simple pasta dish like fettucine tossed with chopped garlic, 'melted' anchovies and sage.

STYLE **dry**
QUALITY ▽▽▽▽▽
VALUE ☆☆☆
GRAPES
  Cabernet Sauvignon
REGION **Hawke's Bay**
CELLAR 4
PRICE $35–38

Trinity Hill Gimblett Road Cabernet Sauvignon/Merlot

STYLE **dry**

QUALITY ♀ ♀ ♀ ♀

VALUE ☆ ☆ ☆

GRAPES
Cab Sauvignon 45%
Merlot 45%
Cab Franc 10%

REGION **Hawke's Bay**

CELLAR 🍾 **2**

PRICE **$30–33**

The vineyard team picked the three varieties in this blend by hand and kept the juice separate in the winery. The components had a quiet time sitting around in French oak barrels for 20 months or so before they got together in the bottle.

Current Release 2000 Blackcurrants, cherries, raspberries – I fancy I can find them all in the bouquet. It's quite firm on the palate, but the rich fruit flavours win through and give it a pleasantly sweet-edged finish. There's nothing better with a rare sirloin steak.

Trinity Hill Gimblett Road Merlot

STYLE **dry**

QUALITY ♀ ♀ ♀ ♀

VALUE ☆ ☆ ☆

GRAPES **Merlot**

REGION **Hawke's Bay**

CELLAR 🍾 **3**

PRICE **$35–38**

Made from hand-picked grapes grown on exceptionally free-draining soil, this red was matured in French oak barrels, 75% of which were new, for 16 months. Because it was minimally filtered the back label warns that it may throw a sediment.

Current Release 2000 Smoky oak and a touch of sweet pipe tobacco start things off nicely. It's a smooth-centred middleweight on the palate, with ripe plum and wild berry flavours in well-rounded surroundings. It makes a splendid companion for lamb racks, cooked pink and served over mashed pumpkin.

Trinity Hill Shepherd's Croft Merlot/Cabernets/Syrah

STYLE **dry**

QUALITY ♀ ♀ ♀ ♀

VALUE ☆ ☆ ☆ ☆

GRAPES
Merlot 47%
Cab Franc 23%
Syrah 19%
Cab Sauvignon 11%

REGION **Hawke's Bay**

CELLAR 🍾 **2**

PRICE **$20–23**

The four varieties in this blend were made into separate wines and put into either French oak barrels or stainless-steel tanks for 16 months. Only then was the final combination decided. It has been filtered only lightly, so may throw a sediment.

Current Release 2000 Sweet, spicy oak was dominating the fruit when I tried this wine a few months ago, but the blackberry and plum aromas should have fought their way through the planks by now. It's smooth, sweet-edged and very approachable on the palate, and would make a good partner for Italian-style lamb and pork meatballs with fresh tomato sauce.

Twin Islands Cabernet Sauvignon/Merlot

The only successful cabernet-based wines from Marlborough are those made from vines forced to give exceptionally small crops. At the price of this one, we can presume that wasn't the case.
Current Release 2000 The bouquet is all oak – it smells like a pile of sawdust. The flavour profile has a few pleasant berry notes, but overall it's a pretty lean proposition. If you end up with a bottle, hide it on the BYO table at the next party you attend.

STYLE **dry**
QUALITY ▽ ▽ ▽
VALUE ☆ ☆ ☆
GRAPES **Cab Sauvignon
Merlot**
REGION **Marlborough**
CELLAR ▯ 2
PRICE **$20–23**

Twin Islands Marlborough Merlot/Cabernet Sauvignon/Cabernet Franc

The merlot and cabernet sauvignon for this blend came from Marlborough's Wairau Valley, but the cabernet franc was grown over the hills in the Awatere. The component parts were matured separately in French and American oak.
Current Release 1999 Leather and smoky oak get it together on the nose. It's a tad lean on the front palate but lifts itself pretty well through the middle. The finish is floral and leafy. It's no blockbuster, but at that price it's okay with a brace of barbecued bangers.

STYLE **dry**
QUALITY ▽ ▽ ▽
VALUE ☆ ☆ ☆ ☆
GRAPES
**Merlot 47%
Cab Sauvignon 35%
Cab Franc 18%**
REGION **Marlborough**
CELLAR ▯ 2
PRICE **$16–18**

Unison

Bruce and Anna-Barbara Helliwell grow merlot, cabernet sauvignon and syrah, and all three go into their two wines. The varieties are listed on the back label. This latest release was matured in French, American and, unusually, Slavonian oak.
Current Release 2001 Sweet plums and blackcurrants start things off well. It's smooth and rich on the palate, with good grip from the integrated tannins. The finish is sweet-edged and long. We were lucky enough to try it with wild boar shanks – now that was a GREAT combination!

STYLE **dry**
QUALITY ▽ ▽ ▽ ▽ ▽
VALUE ☆ ☆ ☆
GRAPES **Merlot
Cab Sauvignon
Syrah**
REGION **Hawke's Bay**
CELLAR ▯ 3
PRICE **$28–32**

Unison Selection

When world-renowned wine writer Jancis Robinson MW visited New Zealand a couple of years ago, she insisted on taking an earlier vintage of this red back to the UK with her. I wonder if she's pulled the cork yet?
Current Release 2000 Ripe plums, leather, smoky oak, super-ripe raspberries – they're all there in the bouquet. It's superbly rich and weighty on the palate, but the overall impression is of elegance. That's quite a balancing act. It makes a great partner for a traditional filet mignon with sauce Béarnaise.

STYLE **dry**
QUALITY ▽ ▽ ▽ ▽ ▽
VALUE ☆ ☆ ☆
GRAPES **Merlot
Cab Sauvignon
Syrah**
REGION **Hawke's Bay**
CELLAR ▯ 6
PRICE **$43–46**

Vidal Estate Cabernet Sauvignon/Merlot

STYLE **dry**

QUALITY 🍷 🍷 🍷

VALUE ☆ ☆ ☆ ☆

GRAPES
  Cab Sauvignon 61%
  Merlot 25%
  Cabernet Franc 8%
  Malbec 6%

REGION Hawke's Bay

CELLAR 🍾 2

PRICE $16–18

A year in a mixture of French and American oak barrels was the maturation regime favoured by Rod McDonald for the 2000 vintage. The four varieties were treated separately and blended just before being bottled.

Current Release 2000 Smoky, charred oak sits above the ripe berry aromas in the bouquet. It's clean and straightforward on the palate, with pleasant middleweight fruit and understated tannins. It's good with strips of rare beef over baby leaves, drizzled with mustard vinaigrette.

Vidal Estate Reserve Merlot/Cabernet Sauvignon

STYLE **dry**

QUALITY 🍷 🍷 🍷 🍷 🍷

VALUE ☆ ☆ ☆

GRAPES
  Merlot 54%
  Cab Sauvignon 37%
  Malbec 9%

REGION Hawke's Bay

CELLAR 🍾 4

PRICE $40–43

Vidal made a brave call by deciding to package this and other Reserve-status reds with a Stelvin screwcap. So far, the closure has been used almost exclusively for whites, despite reams of papers extolling its advantages over traditional cork.

Current Release 2000 Smoky oak, leather and blackcurrants – yep, that's merlot and cabernet alright! It's a chunky wine on the palate, which appeals to the peasant in me, with savoury red-berry flavours and a lingering, spice-edged finish. I enjoyed mine with a dish of oxtail that had been cooked long and slow, stripped off the bone and pressed like brawn, then crumbed and pan-fried.

Villa Maria Cellar Selection Merlot/Cabernet Sauvignon

STYLE **dry**

QUALITY 🍷 🍷 🍷 🍷 🍷

VALUE ☆ ☆ ☆ ☆

GRAPES Merlot
      Cab Sauvignon

REGION Hawke's Bay

CELLAR 🍾 2

PRICE $22–24

Three Hawke's Bay vineyards contributed grapes for this mid-range red. The grapes were treated separately in the winery, but all three parcels were plunged by hand and spent 16 months in oak barrels.

Current Release 2000 Smoky oak and blackcurrants form the major aromatic associations. It's smooth and sweet-edged on the palate, with smartly integrated tannins contributing just enough grip for the style. It's good with a wedge of well-aged gouda, served with crusty bread rather than crackers·

Villa Maria Reserve Hawke's Bay Merlot

STYLE **dry**

QUALITY 🍷 🍷 🍷 🍷 🍷

VALUE ☆ ☆ ☆

GRAPES Merlot

REGION Hawke's Bay

CELLAR 🍾 4

PRICE $39–43

The '99 version won two trophies, three gold medals and a list of five-star awards from prominent commentators and tasting panels, and this latest model has also done pretty well. It's not easy to find in some places, but well worth a search.

Current Release 2000 Smoky oak and ripe plum aromas are in perfect accord on the nose. It's rich, ripe-fruited and mouth-filling on the palate with firm but integrated tannins giving it grip that lasts right through to the impressively long finish. A rare cervena steak is perfect with it.

Villa Maria Reserve Hawke's Bay Merlot/Cabernet Sauvignon

This three-grape blend has done extraordinarily well for the Villa team in the last few vintages, taking trophies and a stack of top medals both in this country and overseas. It was made under the supervision of Michelle Richardson, who has since left.
Current Release 2000 Smoky, savoury oak sits behind the primary aromas of ripe blackcurrants and plums. There's a ton of berryish fruit on the front palate, and the smoothness through the middle makes it a mouth-filling success in the flavour department. It's perfect with a Hawke's Bay ostrich steak, cooked rare.

STYLE **dry**
QUALITY ♟♟♟♟♟
VALUE ☆ ☆☆
GRAPES
  Merlot 55%
  Cab Franc 38%
  Malbec 7%
REGION **Hawke's Bay**
CELLAR 🍾 **4**
PRICE **$39–42**

Vin Alto Ordinario

Asking $40-plus for a wine labelled Ordinario might seem like suicidal marketing, but that hasn't stopped Enzo and Margaret Bettio from building up a keen following for this red and the others in their Italian-styled portfolio.
Current Release 1996 Smoky, plum-like and faintly floral on the nose, this is a complex wine with a good depth of very ripe fruit flavours. The oak is nicely integrated into the overall effect, and smartly tuned tannins bring just enough grip to the finish. Enjoy it with a classic, simple pizza.

STYLE **dry**
QUALITY ♟♟♟♟♟
VALUE ☆ ☆☆
GRAPES **Cabernet Franc**
  Merlot
  Sangiovese
  Others
REGION **Clevedon**
CELLAR 🍾 **3**
PRICE **$40–45**

Vin Alto Retico

Made from grapes dried for up to two months in a specially constructed shed, this is New Zealand's only wine made in the style of the Italian classic, Amarone. It's a time-consuming and risky process, which is reflected in the price.
Current Release 1998 Floral-edged perfume, prunes, dried raspberries and sweet, spicy oak – they're all there on the nose. It's a huge wine on the palate with masses of rich, plum pudding-like fruit but a dry finish. Rare-roasted wild venison is its only possible partner.

STYLE **dry**
QUALITY ♟♟♟♟♟
VALUE ☆ ☆
GRAPES **Merlot**
  Cab Franc
  Others
REGION **Clevedon**
CELLAR 🍾 **10**
PRICE **$95–110**

Vin Alto Ritorno

I guess this could be described as a 'hand-me-down' wine. It is fermented on the air-dried grape skins left after Enzo and Margaret Bettio have made their $100-plus blockbuster, Retico.
Current Release 1998 Sweet-fruited, vaguely cherry-like on the nose and perfectly balanced on the palate, this is a very impressive wine. It's rich, but it manages to retain an impression of elegance. We enjoyed it with a casserole of cubed beef, tomatoes and baby onions, and were well pleased.

STYLE **dry**
QUALITY ♟♟♟♟♟
VALUE ☆☆
GRAPES
  Merlot
  Cabernet Franc
  Corvino
  Sangiovese Grosso
REGION **Clevedon**
CELLAR 🍾 **4**
PRICE **$65–75**

Waimarie Kumeu Testamant Cabernet Sauvignon/Cabernet Franc

STYLE **dry**

QUALITY ▼ ▼ ▼ ▼

VALUE ☆ ☆ ☆ ⯪

GRAPES **Cab Sauvignon Cab Franc**

REGION **West Auckland**

CELLAR ▭ **1–4**

PRICE **$27–30**

There's some serious oak in this two-grape blend. The winemaking team put the juice into a mixture of 50% French, 50% American barrels, all of which were brand-new. That's unusual, but they thought the fruit was big enough to take it.

Current Release 2000 Clever stuff! All that new timber should make tasting this wine something like chewing into a length of four-by-two, but in fact it is soft and generous, with lashings of sweet fruit and a lingering, chocolate-edged finish. Partner it with a pot-load of slow-braised lamb shanks and you should be very happy indeed.

Waipara Springs Cabernet Sauvignon

STYLE **dry**

QUALITY ▼ ▼ ▼

VALUE ☆ ☆ ☆ ⯪

GRAPES **Cab Sauvignon 90% Merlot 10%**

REGION **Waipara**

CELLAR ▯ **1**

PRICE **$21–23**

Waipara seems more suited to pinot noir than cabernet, but a few local producers have one or two of each in their portfolios. This one sells well at the cellar door, partly because it's reasonably well priced.

Current Release 2001 The bouquet was pretty solid timber when I tried it, but there were a few berry-like aromas trying to fight their way through the planks. The fruit is more obvious through the middle, but a suggestion of green leafiness mars the finish. Try it with stir-fried beef and spring onions.

Weeping Sands Waiheke Cabernet/Merlot

STYLE **dry**

QUALITY ▼ ▼ ▼ ▼

VALUE ☆ ☆ ☆

GRAPES **Cab Sauvignon 74% Merlot 26%**

REGION **Waiheke Island**

CELLAR ▯ **3**

PRICE **$29–32**

This is the second-label wine from Obsidian, an ambitious vineyard on Waiheke Island. It used to be called Island Red, but that proved too close to another local wine. In any case, Weeping Sands sounds considerably more romantic.

Current Release 2000 Maturing the wine in all-American oak barrels has added a vanilla-like note to the berryfruit aromas. It's a smooth-centred middleweight on the palate, with about the right amount of grip for the style. Partner it with chicken braised in red wine (this one, if you can spare it) and good stock.

West Brook Blue Ridge Merlot

STYLE **dry**

QUALITY ▼ ▼ ▼ ⯊

VALUE ☆ ☆ ☆ ⯪

GRAPES **Merlot**

REGION **Hawke's Bay**

CELLAR ▯ **2**

PRICE **$23–26**

West Brook is one of the famous historic names from West Auckland, where so many winemaking families began their dynasties. Today, grapes are sourced from various parts of the country. Blue Ridge wines sit at the top of the portfolio.

Current Release 2000 You want spicy oak and ripe berry aromas? They're there in good shape on the nose. It's not a big wine, but its quota of plum and raspberry flavours in reasonably grippy surrounds gives it plenty of appeal. Partner it with Italian-style meatballs with a rich tomato sauce.

Winslow Martinborough Turakirae Reserve Cabernet Sauvignon/Cabernet Franc

The grape proportions came from the back label, but they leave 4% unaccounted for. Either the writer can't add, or malbec makes up the balance. The '99 version of this big-hearted red scored silver at an international competition in London.

Current Release 2001 Spicy oak and ripe blackcurrants get it together in the bouquet. It's smooth, richly fruited and assertively tannic on the palate, and that means there's plenty of grip on the finish. Partner it with rissoles made from chopped corned beef, garlic and onions and topped with a hearty fresh tomato sauce.

STYLE **dry**
QUALITY ♟♟♟♟♟
VALUE ☆☆☆
GRAPES
  Cab Sauvignon 51%
  Cab Franc 36%
  Merlot 13%
REGION **Martinborough**
CELLAR ▭ **2–6**
PRICE **$45–48**

Winslow Petra Cabernet

Steve and Jennifer Tarring produced this red in 1997, but had to wait until 2000 for the next release. Now, they've had two in a row. This latest model spent a full year maturing in a mixture of new and old French and American oak barrels.

Current Release 2001 Charred oak and plums have a faintly floral edge on the bouquet. It's sweet-fruited and rich on the palate, with chunky tannins adding plenty of grip through the middle. The finish is firm and moderately long. It works well with char-grilled foods, particularly beef sirloin steak.

STYLE **dry**
QUALITY ♟♟♟♟
VALUE ☆☆☆
GRAPES
  Cab Sauvignon 88%
  Cab Franc 10%
  Malbec 2%
REGION **Martinborough**
CELLAR ▯ **3**
PRICE **$30–33**

Wishart Basket Press Merlot

The 'basket press' referred to in the name is a straight barrel-shaped object with semi-open slatted sides. A hand-operated screw forces the grapes downwards, and the juice runs through the gaps between the slats and is captured in a trough at the bottom.

Current Release 2001 Whatever oak was used in this wine's maturation, it doesn't show – the bouquet is all about ripe plum-like fruit. It's sweet-edged on the palate, with gentle tannins and good richness. The finish is quite long and very satisfying. It's great with a brace of grilled cervena sausages on mashed potatoes.

STYLE **dry**
QUALITY ♟♟♟♟
VALUE ☆☆☆☆
GRAPES **Merlot**
REGION **Hawke's Bay**
CELLAR ▯ **3**
PRICE **$23–26**

Wishart Hawke's Bay Merlot/Malbec/Cabernet

Don Bird is one of many Hawke's Bay producers to favour merlot over cabernet sauvignon, but in this blend even malbec, usually relegated to third slot, gets a higher priority. It was a bit of a gamble, but it paid off – it's very smart wine.

Current Release 2000 There's a fair whack of spicy oak in the bouquet, but the plummy, berryish fruit holds its own pretty well. It's the same story on the palate. The oak adds a savoury edge, but raspberry and plum characters predominate. Serious mince on toast (cook it with canned Italian tomatoes and use really good bread) suits it well.

STYLE **dry**
QUALITY ♟♟♟♟♟
VALUE ☆☆☆☆
GRAPES **Merlot**
  Malbec
  Cab Sauvignon
REGION **Hawke's Bay**
CELLAR ▯ **4**
PRICE **$28–32**

Pinot Noir

Pinot noir is regularly referred to as the world's most temperamental grape variety. British writer, Jancis Robinson, calls it a 'minx' of a grape – others are less poetic. Cabernet sauvignon, merlot and their mates perform in much the same way wherever in the world they are grown, but pinot noir is unpredictable. It can't even be relied on from year to year – one near-perfect harvest is no guarantee of a similar result for the following vintage, even if weather conditions are close to identical. But it is worth persisting, because overseas commentators are predicting that pinot noir is capable of doing for our red wine industry what sauvignon blanc did for our whites. Even the super-parochial Aussies admit pinot suits our climate better than theirs, and local examples are selling by the container-load across the Tasman. Pinot is expensive because it is hard to grow, or so the wine companies would have us believe – but increasing numbers of under-$20 examples are now hitting the shelves.

Akarua Pinot Noir

STYLE **dry**
QUALITY ♟♟♟♟♟
VALUE ☆ ☆ ☆ ☆⸱
GRAPES **Pinot Noir**
REGION **Central Otago**

CELLAR ⬜️ **1–4**
PRICE **$35–37**

The 2000 version of this wine scored gold at the 2002 International Wine and Spirit Competition. It was the first Akarua wine to be entered in an overseas competition, so the winemaking team was understandably ecstatic.
Current Release 2001 I'll be surprised if this later model doesn't echo its predecessor's success. Smoky oak and plummy fruit are in good shape on the nose, and the flavour profile boasts lashings of sweet, big-hearted fruit right through to the lingering finish. Partner it with a section of beef eye fillet, ideally cooked on the barbecue.

Akarua The Gulleys Pinot Noir

STYLE **dry**
QUALITY ♟♟♟⸱
VALUE ☆ ☆ ☆⸱
GRAPES **Pinot Noir**
REGION **Central Otago**

CELLAR 🍾 **3**
PRICE **$30–33**

Akarua winemaker Carol Bunn matured this second-label pinot in oak for 10 months, but only a quarter of the barrels were new because she didn't want to intimidate the fruit. Six different grape clones were used.
Current Release 2001 Cherries and plums form the major aromatic associations. It's sweet-fruited and smartly balanced on the palate, with gentle tannins giving it great approachability. It goes well with tagliatelle pasta tossed with a chunky tomato-based sauce.

Alana Estate Martinborough Pinot Noir

Alana Estate's winery became an instant landmark when it was opened in 1998. It is built into a terrace to allow for gravity-feeding of the juice, which winemaker John Kavanagh believes is a gentler technique than pumping.
Current Release 2000 Smoky oak sits behind the aromas of ripe Black Doris plums. It's not a big wine, but it's a very attractive one thanks to its quota of sweet-edged fruit and restrained tannins. Enjoy it with a seared ostrich steak, served with rosemary potatoes and blanched snow peas.

STYLE **dry**
QUALITY ♟ ♟ ♟ ♟
VALUE ☆ ☆ ☆
GRAPES **Pinot Noir**
REGION **Martinborough**
CELLAR 4
PRICE **$39–42**

Alexander Vineyard Martinborough Pinot Noir

The fruit was picked by hand and the juice extracted in an old-style basket press for this small-production pinot. It spent a year maturing quietly in French oak barrels before being bottled and released.
Current Release 2000 The chunky character behind the sweet fruit aromas gives the wine an Old World feeling on the nose. It's pretty solid on the palate, with firm tannins adding a definite edge to the ripe fruit flavours. It works well alongside a plate of liver and bacon topped by a garlicky tomato sauce.

STYLE **dry**
QUALITY ♟ ♟ ♟ ♟
VALUE ☆ ☆ ☆
GRAPES **Pinot Noir**
REGION **Martinborough**
CELLAR 3
PRICE **$32–35**

Alexandra Wine Company Davishon Pinot Noir

There's not a lot of this attractively packaged pinot about, but you'll certainly find it in the deep south. It spent 10 months maturing quietly in French oak barrels, 30% of which were new.
Current Release 2000 Spicy, savoury and faintly fungal, this is classic Central Otago pinot. It's smooth-centred on the palate, with ripe fruit flavours and a stylish finish. If you're a hunter, or are on bludging terms with one, try it with casseroled wild pork and add a few chopped mushrooms to the pot.

STYLE **dry**
QUALITY ♟ ♟ ♟ ♟ ♟
VALUE ☆ ☆ ☆ ☆ ☆
GRAPES **Pinot Noir**
REGION **Central Otago**
CELLAR 4
PRICE **$27–29**

Allan Scott Marlborough Pinot Noir

The grapes that went into this well-priced pinot were plunged by hand. That's hard work, but it's worth it because it extracts every last bit of colour and flavour out of the skins.
Current Release 2001 Smoky oak was dominating the cherry and raspberry aromas on the nose when I tried this wine. Grippy tannins give it solidity to go with the plum characters on the palate and dry out the finish. It works well with casseroled lamb.

STYLE **dry**
QUALITY ♟ ♟ ♟ ♟
VALUE ☆ ☆ ☆ ☆
GRAPES **Pinot Noir**
REGION **Marlborough**
CELLAR 3
PRICE **$25–28**

Artisan Fantail Island Auckland Pinot Noir

STYLE **dry**
QUALITY ♟♟♟♟
VALUE ☆☆☆☆☆
GRAPES **Pinot Noir**
REGION **West Auckland**
CELLAR 🍷 **2**
PRICE **$20–23**

Auckland pinot noir is as rare as a laughing economist, but viticulturist Rex Sunde has made a fair fist of this one. The Fantail Island site is in Oratia, which apparently translates as 'the place of persistent sun'.

Current Release 2000 Spiced cherries and strawberries say all the right things on the nose. It's ripe-fruited, fresh and clean, with no sharp edges and a moderately long finish. To sum up, a pleasant mouthful that goes particularly well with casseroled lamb spooned over a pile of 'wet' polenta (i.e. not grilled).

Ata Rangi Pinot Noir

STYLE **dry**
QUALITY ♟♟♟♟♟
VALUE ☆☆☆
GRAPES **Pinot Noir**
REGION **Martinborough**
CELLAR 🍷 **5**
PRICE **$60–65**

Lauded internationally, this splendid wine has won a heap of awards over the years. The 1993, 1994 and 1999 vintages each won the prestigious Bouchard-Finlayson trophy, beating wines from all over the world.

Current Release 2001 Smoky, spicy oak and aromas reminiscent of ripe plums and cherries set the scene. It's warm and generous on the palate, with a continuation of the cherry associations but the addition of a faintly fungal note. There is nothing better with pan-seared duck breast and mushrooms.

Ata Rangi Young Vines Pinot Noir

STYLE **dry**
QUALITY ♟♟♟♟
VALUE ☆☆☆☆
GRAPES **Pinot Noir**
REGION **Martinborough**
CELLAR 🍷 **2**
PRICE **$28–32**

Careful label-watching is required when ordering Ata Rangi pinot in restaurants. Not everyone lists this one as the Young Vines version, and although it's pleasant, it's in a very different league from its big-noting cellarmate.

Current Release 2002 Smoky oak sits behind the aromas of ripe plums and cherries. It's smooth and nicely fruited on the palate, has a suggestion of leafiness on the finish but presents as a pleasant middleweight despite of it. It makes a good companion for penne pasta with shredded duck and smoked bacon.

Babich Winemaker's Reserve Pinot Noir

STYLE **dry**
QUALITY ♟♟♟♟
VALUE ☆☆☆☆
GRAPES **Pinot Noir**
REGION **Marlborough**
CELLAR 🍷 **2**
PRICE **$25–28**

The fruit for this nicely focused pinot came from a sunny site in the heart of Marlborough's Wairau Valley. Future plans are to have it part-processed near the vineyard, but this one was fully produced in Auckland.

Current Release 2000 Pretty is the word that springs to mind when you sniff this wine – well, it was when I did. It's got all the required cherry/berry aromas and a smooth-centred flavour profile, and makes a perfect partner for a wedge or two of sun-dried tomato tart, served at room temperature rather than hot or chilled.

Black Ridge Pinot Noir

Pinot is the variety that most people associate with this tiny Central Otago vineyard. Verdun Burgess and Sue Edwards have produced some blockbuster examples over the years, using fruit from 17-year-old vines.
Current Release 2001 Strawberries get the gig on the nose of this super-concentrated cold-climate pinot. Picking lots of small grapes meant the ratio of skin to flesh was high, and that has translated to a grippy edge on the sweet-fruited flavours. I'd like to try it alongside a generous hunk of wild venison.

STYLE **dry**
QUALITY 🍷 🍷 🍷 🍷
VALUE ★ ★ ★
GRAPES **Pinot Noir**
REGION **Central Otago**
CELLAR 🍷 **1–6**
PRICE **$40–44**

Brajkovich Kumeu Pinot Noir

The Brajkovich family has made pinot noir its top red grape variety, so it makes sense to have a two-tier system. Nigel Tibbits made this in a middleweight style that is thoroughly enjoyable – and it's well priced.
Current Release 2000 Cherries and gentle oak have got the gig on the nose. It's appealingly sweet-fruited, with a pleasant texture and a charmingly open finish. It can't take strong flavours but it's good with mushrooms, either grilled or pan-fried and finished with a little chicken stock and cream, served on grainy toast.

STYLE **dry**
QUALITY 🍷 🍷 🍷 🍷
VALUE ★ ★ ★ ★ ★
GRAPES **Pinot Noir**
REGION **West Auckland**
CELLAR 🍷 **2**
PRICE **$20–23**

Cairnbrae Marlborough Pinot Noir

Cairnbrae has established its name with whites, particularly an impressively vivacious sauvignon blanc, but this red looks set to redress the balance. A fair bit heads off overseas, but it's still readily available.
Current Release 2000 Strawberry and cherry aromas are backed by gentle oak and a suggestion of mushrooms. It's mouth-fillingly soft on the palate, but a dash of spice towards the end has the effect of lengthening the finish. It's good with 'parcels' made by wrapping slices of pan-fried eggplant around mozzarella and baking them.

STYLE **dry**
QUALITY 🍷 🍷 🍷 🍷
VALUE ★ ★ ★⟨
GRAPES **Pinot Noir**
REGION **Marlborough**
CELLAR 🍷 **3**
PRICE **$34–37**

Carrick Central Otago Pinot Noir

Steve Davies matured this red in French oak barrels for 11 months, then let it settle for six months after bottling. He obviously got it right – it recently beat 130 New World pinots to first place in a London competition.
Current Release 2001 The nose has a feral edge that appeals to the peasant in me, but there is a good quota of ripe plum and cherry aromas in there as well. Sweet fruit and impeccable balance give it great palatory appeal, and make it an ideal partner for pink-cooked duck breasts with mushrooms and thinly sliced potatoes.

STYLE **dry**
QUALITY 🍷 🍷 🍷 🍷 🍷
VALUE ★ ★⟨
GRAPES **Pinot Noir**
REGION **Central Otago**
CELLAR 🍷 **1–4**
PRICE **$63–65**

Chancellor Estates Mt Cass Road Pinot Noir

STYLE **dry**
QUALITY ▽▽▽▽
VALUE ☆☆☆☆☆
GRAPES **Pinot Noir**
REGION **Waipara**
CELLAR ▬▭ **1–3**
PRICE **$26–28**

Winery owner Chris Parker arranged for this nicely fruited pinot to spend a year in French oak barrels. Chancellor wines sell well in Canterbury, and are reasonably easy to find around the country.

Current Release 2000 The oak has added a smoky character to the ripe plum and strawberry aromas. It's broadly textured thanks to smooth, integrated tannins, but the ripe fruit gathers itself for a big, rich finish. It's perfect alongside a salad topped with rare-roasted duck breast.

Chard Farm Finla Mor Pinot Noir

STYLE **dry**
QUALITY ▽▽▽▽▽
VALUE ☆☆☆☆
GRAPES **Pinot Noir**
REGION **Central Otago**
CELLAR ▯ **4**
PRICE **$38–41**

It can be hard to find away from the bottom of the South Island, but this smartly packaged Central Otago pinot has a legion of fans. It was matured in French oak barrels, but because only a few were new they haven't swamped the fruit.

Current Release 2001 I get suggestions of smoked cherries and dried Chinese mushrooms on the nose, along with just a hint of spicy oak. A certain leanness on the palate betrays its cold-climate origins, but rather than spoiling the flavour it fits with the style. Partner it with casseroled chicken and you'll get the point.

Chard Farm River Run Pinot Noir

STYLE **dry**
QUALITY ▽▽▽▽
VALUE ☆☆☆☆
GRAPES **Pinot Noir**
REGION **Central Otago**
CELLAR ▯ **2**
PRICE **$27–31**

This second-label pinot from the Chard Farm team is a popular buy at many of the dozens of cafés, bars and restaurants around the Queenstown region – especially in the tourist season. It recently scored four stars from *Cuisine* magazine.

Current Release 2001 It's not a biggie, but it's got all the right raspberry and cherry aromas in the bouquet and a reasonable quota of ripe fruit flavours. The tannins are nicely balanced for the style and the finish is fresh-faced and moderately long. It makes a good companion for a lamb and radish salad, made with grainy bread.

Cloudy Bay Pinot Noir

STYLE **dry**
QUALITY ▽▽▽▽
VALUE ☆☆☆
GRAPES **Pinot Noir**
REGION **Marlborough**
CELLAR ▯ **4**
PRICE **$38–41**

Pinot noir is the only red grape grown by the Cloudy Bay team. Some of it is blended with chardonnay to produce the big-selling bubbly, Pelorus, but there's enough left over each year to make this 'straight' version.

Current Release 2000 Spicy oak is in good balance with the ripe cherry and strawberry aromas. It's smooth-centred and ripe-fruited on the palate, with restrained tannins adding the right amount of grip for the style. Partner it with a plate of calf's liver and bacon.

Collards Queen Charlotte Pinot Noir

The 1997 version of this wine was scheduled to be the last, but the Collard family managed to source more fruit in 1999 so in the end they simply skipped a vintage. It's one of the best-priced pinots in the land.

Current Release 1999 Cherry aromas are backed by a touch of smokiness, and there's even a suggestion of chocolate. It's sweet-fruited and smartly balanced on the palate, with ripe flavours and a satisfying finish. Use a little to braise a pile of chicken thighs and drumsticks, and pour a glass as an accompaniment.

STYLE **dry**
QUALITY ♟ ♟ ♟ ♟
VALUE ☆ ☆ ☆ ☆ ☆
GRAPES **Pinot Noir**
REGION **Marlborough**
CELLAR 1
PRICE **$17–19**

Coney Pizzicato Pinot Noir

Martinborough is well known as pinot noir country, so it is only natural that Tim and Margaret Coney should want one in their portfolio. So far, their rieslings are better known, but it's early days yet.

Current Release 2000 The colour is light but attractive and the bouquet suggests cherries and mushrooms. There's some thoroughly pleasant fruit on the palate edged by quite grippy tannins, suggesting it might take kindly to short-term cellaring. It would make a good partner for a classic 'spag bol'.

STYLE **dry**
QUALITY ♟ ♟ ♟ ♟
VALUE ☆ ☆ ☆ ☆
GRAPES **Pinot Noir**
REGION **Martinborough**
CELLAR 1–3
PRICE **$34–38**

Coopers Creek Hawke's Bay Pinot Noir

There's not a lot of pinot noir grown in Hawke's Bay, but the team at Coopers Creek has been picking fruit from there for a few years. This is described as an 'early drinking' style by winemaker, Simon Nunns.

Current Release 1999 Strawberry and mushroom aromas dominate the bouquet, with a dash of dusty oak at the back. It's an open-fruited middleweight, with a pleasant texture and a short but clean finish. Try it with grilled mushrooms on grainy toast.

STYLE **dry**
QUALITY ♟ ♟ ♟
VALUE ☆ ☆ ☆ ☆ ☆
GRAPES **Pinot Noir**
REGION **Hawke's Bay**
CELLAR 2
PRICE **$16–18**

Covell Estate Pinot Noir

Bob and Des Covell hold all their wines back for a couple of years after bottling. Their style can best be described as idiosyncratic, but the label has a keen following around the Bay of Plenty, and the vineyard is a pleasant place to visit.

Current Release 1999 The colour leans towards the brown end of the spectrum, which is not a good sign. There's a sharp edge on the front palate, some reasonably pleasant fruit flavours through the middle but a hint of bitterness on the finish. Try it as a curiosity – it's quite different from the norm.

STYLE **dry**
QUALITY ♟ ♟
VALUE ☆ ☆ ☆
GRAPES **Pinot Noir**
REGION **Murupara**
CELLAR
PRICE **$20–23**

Daniel Schuster Omihi Hills Vineyard Selection Pinot Noir

STYLE **dry**
QUALITY ♟♟♟♟♟
VALUE ☆ ☆ ☆
GRAPES **Pinot Noir**
REGION **Waipara**
CELLAR ▭▭ **1–8**
PRICE **$50–55**

Danny Schuster's Omihi Hills vineyard is planted more densely than most, yet he still harvests only around 1.5 tonnes of grapes per acre, which equates to roughly one kilogram per vine. The result is great fruit intensity.
Current Release 2001 Sweet, spicy and deliciously opulent on the nose, this wine is impressive from the first sniff. It combines sweet and savoury flavours and boasts good weight and a superbly smooth texture that has the effect of lengthening the finish. Lamb rumps rubbed with dukkah before being roasted pink make a perfect accompaniment.

Daniel Schuster Twin Vineyards Pinot Noir

STYLE **dry**
QUALITY ♟♟♟
VALUE ☆ ☆ ☆ ☆
GRAPES **Pinot Noir**
REGION **Waipara**
CELLAR ▯ **2**
PRICE **$25–27**

This is Danny Schuster's second-label, 'early drinking' pinot and sells for around half the price of his impressive Selection model. The fruit came from the company's Petrie vineyard, and it was matured in French oak barrels for 14 months.
Current Release 2000 Savoury oak and sweet, cherry-like fruit populate the bouquet. It's got a pleasant texture and boasts good fruit through the middle, but things get a bit lean towards the finish. Partner it with a decent lamb and potato pie, served with the youngest green beans you can find.

Dashwood Marlborough Pinot Noir

STYLE **dry**
QUALITY ♟♟♟
VALUE ☆ ☆ ☆ ☆ ☆
GRAPES **Pinot Noir**
REGION **Marlborough**
CELLAR ▯ **2**
PRICE **$20–23**

Dashwood is a second label for Vavasour, the company that pioneered Marlborough's Awatere Valley. Winemaker Glenn Thomas has allowed the fruit to star by keeping the oak treatment to a minimum. It's one of very few pinots selling for under $25.
Current Release 2001 The nose is earthy and fungal – and yes, that is a good thing with pinot. Sweet fruit certainly has the gig on the palate. The flavours are upfront and welcoming and the tannins stay way in the background. It's a very approachable wine that suits chicken or rabbit casseroled with tinned Italian tomatoes.

Denton Reserve Pinot Noir

STYLE **dry**
QUALITY ♟♟♟
VALUE ☆ ☆ ☆
GRAPES **Pinot Noir**
REGION **Nelson**
CELLAR ▯ **3**
PRICE **$32–35**

Alex and Richard Denton had a good year in 2002. At the Nelson Tourism Awards function they were presented with awards for Best Tourism Experience and Best Winery Café, and went on to take the Supreme Award as the night's overall winner.
Current Release 1999 There's a touch of charred oak behind the aromas of smoky cherries. It's a tad lean on the front palate but fills out a little in the middle. Overall, a middleweight that has some appeal but doesn't seem to deserve its Reserve status. Mind you, it works pretty well with a corned beef and mustard sandwich.

Dry Gully Pinot Noir

This is the only wine Dry Gully produces, partly because the owners love the style, but largely because they feel their piece of land is perfect for pinot. A gold medal with their first release, 1997, boosted their confidence.
Current Release 1999 Mushrooms and plums get it together on the nose, and that's just fine with me. It's smooth-textured, boasts impressive fruit richness and finishes with gentle but grippy tannins. It's smart wine that suits well-flavoured dishes like a chicken and potato casserole.

STYLE **dry**
QUALITY ♟ ♟ ♟ ♟
VALUE ☆ ☆ ☆ ☆
GRAPES **Pinot Noir**
REGION **Central Otago**
CELLAR **3**
PRICE **$29–33**

Dry River Pinot Noir

It's not entered in competitions and seldom makes it to retail shelves or restaurant wine lists, but this immaculately made pinot is widely regarded as the country's best. Maker Neil McCallum believes it might last 10 years or more.
Current Release 2001 Smoked cherries and just a suggestion of mushrooms form a classic pinot bouquet. It's richly fruited, with a velvety texture courtesy of the perfectly integrated tannins. The finish is sweet-fruited, long and eminently satisfying. It's soft enough to accompany seared tuna, but I suspect it would be a standout with Peking duck.

STYLE **dry**
QUALITY ♟ ♟ ♟ ♟ ♟
VALUE ☆ ☆☆
GRAPES **Pinot Noir**
REGION **Martinborough**
CELLAR **1–6**
PRICE **$63–66**

Escarpment Martinborough Pinot Noir

Every pinot fan in the country has been waiting for the first release from Larry McKenna, the man many people call 'the Prince of Pinot'. It comes from 12-year-old vines grown on the Cleland vineyard. Larry says Burgundy was his inspiration.
Current Release 2001 Charred, smoky oak and suggestions of cloves and wild mushrooms form an appealingly feral bouquet. The flavour profile is all about sweet, rich fruit. The tannins are fully integrated, but still add grip and substance, especially on the finish. It was worth the wait. Roast duck would be perfect, but pink-roasted lamb racks would do.

STYLE **dry**
QUALITY ♟ ♟ ♟ ♟ ♟
VALUE ☆ ☆ ☆
GRAPES **Pinot Noir**
REGION **Martinborough**
CELLAR **8**
PRICE **$45–48**

Felton Road Block 3 Pinot Noir

This Bannockburn-grown red has been getting rave reviews from critics in the UK, the US and Australia, as well as this country, since its first vintage. It's exceedingly rare but very, very good.
Current Release 2001 Cherries, mushrooms and a touch of earthiness all play a part in the bouquet. It's a charming wine, but that tells only half the story, because there's a feeling of restrained power in the mouth-filling flavours. It goes wonderfully well with roast duck, served with kumara and young green beans.

STYLE **dry**
QUALITY ♟ ♟ ♟ ♟ ♟
VALUE ☆ ☆ ☆ ☆
GRAPES **Pinot Noir**
REGION **Central Otago**
CELLAR **1–4**
PRICE **$53–56**

Felton Road Pinot Noir

STYLE **dry**
QUALITY ▯▯▯▯▯
VALUE ☆☆☆☆
GRAPES **Pinot Noir**
REGION **Central Otago**
CELLAR **4**
PRICE **$40–43**

With supplies of the Block Three version severely restricted, this 'standard' model is the Felton Road pinot most people will be buying. Its slightly cheaper price indicates greater volume, not lesser quality – but it's still not exactly a bargain. **Current Release 2001** Smoky oak, dried mushrooms and cherries get it together on the nose. It's ripe, rich and nicely balanced on the palate, with oak that knows its place in the scheme of things. Enjoy it with lamb cutlets, cooked pink.

Fiddler's Green Waipara Pinot Noir

STYLE **dry**
QUALITY ▯▯▯▯▯
VALUE ☆☆☆☆
GRAPES **Pinot Noir**
REGION **Waipara**
CELLAR **4**
PRICE **$40–43**

Barry Johns has had some very favourable reviews for this nicely made pinot. Five different clones of the grape were used, and the fledgling wine spent 10 months in French oak barrels. Only 30% of them were new because he didn't want to overpower the fruit.
Current Release 2001 There's a fair whack of oak on the nose, despite the preponderance of used barrels, but the fruit is big enough to take it. It's directly flavoured, rich and mouth-fillingly generous on the palate, with loads of sweet fruit on the finish. There's nothing better with duck breasts cooked with star anise and Chinese Hoisin sauce.

Floating Mountain Waipara Pinot Noir

STYLE **dry**
QUALITY ▯▯▯▯
VALUE ☆☆☆☆
GRAPES **Pinot Noir**
REGION **Waipara**
CELLAR **3**
PRICE **$28–31**

This pinot is from long-time Canterbury winemaker, Mark Rattray. He suggests giving it time to breathe, and points out that the second glass reveals more than the first 'as air does its mystery work'. He encourages its enjoyment with food.
Current Release 2001 The bouquet is funky and reminiscent of ripe raspberries, and the flavour profile is ripe-fruited, smooth and classy. It's a big wine, but it boasts a measure of elegance that makes it a good partner for stylish food like a whole roasted fillet of beef.

Forrest Pinot Noir

STYLE **dry**
QUALITY ▯▯▯▯
VALUE ☆☆☆☆
GRAPES **Pinot Noir**
REGION **Marlborough**
CELLAR **3**
PRICE **$25–28**

Selling at 10 pounds rather than the 17 or 18 pounds asked for most Martinborough examples, this pinot is a big success in the UK. John Forrest kept his crop low, picking at around three tonnes to the acre.
Current Release 2001 Smoky oak had the gig on the nose when I tried this wine a few months ago, but there was some pleasant cherry-like fruit fighting its way through the timber. The soft-tannin texture makes it very approachable on the palate and the sweet fruit ensures a big finish. It works particularly well with pork loin chops topped with Italian-style fresh tomato sauce.

Foxes Island Pinot Noir

John Belsham produces just two wines, this softly spoken pinot and an elegant chardonnay. He made wine for a large number of Marlborough growers and wine companies before launching his own label.

Current Release 2000 The bouquet is savoury and spicy, with suggestions of mushrooms and cherries. It's a gentle wine on the palate, nicely fruited but quite understated. The finish is sweet-edged and moderately long. Don't overpower it with strong-flavoured food – it works well with casseroled chicken drumsticks.

STYLE **dry**
QUALITY ♚ ♚ ♚ ♚
VALUE ☆ ☆☆
GRAPES **Pinot Noir**
REGION **Marlborough**
CELLAR 🍾 **3**
PRICE **$39–41**

Framingham Marlborough Pinot Noir

Framingham is better known for white wines, particularly riesling, but this well-priced pinot has a keen following, especially around the Marlborough region.

Current Release 2001 Gentle oak adds a wee touch of spice to the aromas of mushrooms and smoked cherries (I've never smelled a smoked cherry, but I imagine this is what it would be like). It's a straightforward pinot with direct flavours and a clean, focused finish. It should go well with beef strips braised in Italian tomatoes from a tin.

STYLE **dry**
QUALITY ♚ ♚ ♚ ♚
VALUE ☆ ☆ ☆ ☆☆
GRAPES **Pinot Noir**
REGION **Marlborough**
CELLAR 🍾 **3**
PRICE **$22–24**

Fraser Murdoch James Estate Pinot Noir

Murdoch James produces two top-shelf pinots – this one, made with fruit from the Fraser Block vineyard on the Martinborough River Terraces, and another labelled 'Reserve'. One is not considered better than the other – 'they are simply different', says the team.

Current Release 2001 Smoky and earthy with a touch of chocolate on the nose and a mouthful of sweet fruit, this pinot is not for wimps. I imagine it's a 'love it or hate it' style – some would argue pinot should be more delicate – but it works pretty well for me. Partner it with braised beef shin pieces and you'll get the point.

STYLE **dry**
QUALITY ♚ ♚ ♚ ♚ ♚
VALUE ☆ ☆
GRAPES **Pinot Noir**
REGION **Martinborough**
CELLAR 🍾 **1–4**
PRICE **$55–60**

Gibbston Valley Pinot Noir

Grant Taylor uses only hand-picked fruit for his portfolio of wines. After fermentation, this one spent a quiet 11 months in French oak barrels. It's a popular choice at the winery's attractive indoor/outdoor restaurant.

Current Release 2001 Cherries and mushrooms get it together in the bouquet. It's broadly textured, which gives it smooth surroundings for the ripe fruit flavours. The finish is moderately long. Mushrooms on toast should suit it well.

STYLE **dry**
QUALITY ♚ ♚ ♚ ♚
VALUE ☆ ☆☆
GRAPES **Pinot Noir**
REGION **Marlborough**
CELLAR 🍾 **1–4**
PRICE **$45–48**

Gibbston Valley Reserve Pinot Noir

STYLE **dry**
QUALITY ▼ ▼ ▼ ▼ ▽
VALUE ☆ ☆
GRAPES **Pinot Noir**
REGION **Central Otago**
CELLAR **6**
PRICE **$65–68**

This wine has won a handful of medals and trophies through its various vintages, which I guess is why the price has suddenly rocketed up into the stratosphere. You want it, you'll pay for it!
Current Release 2000 I get a suggestion of stewed tamarillo behind the more usual aromas of ripe plums. It's big and sweet-fruited on the palate, with a smoky edge from its 11-month stint in French oak barrels. It would be good with pot-roasted wild duck but failing that, try it with a beef and baby onion casserole.

Gillan Marlborough Pinot Noir

STYLE **dry**
QUALITY ▼ ▼ ▼
VALUE ☆ ☆ ☆ ☆
GRAPES **Pinot Noir**
REGION **Marlborough**
CELLAR **2**
PRICE **$24–26**

Toni and Terry Gillan's pinot isn't one of the high-fliers, but it's priced considerably more reasonably than most. It's a good choice for many of the tapas served in the company's well-designed tasting room.
Current Release 2000 Mushrooms and smoked cherries are the aromatic associations I get on the nose. Big tannins threaten to swamp the middleweight fruit, but things settle down on the well-tuned finish. Try it with − what else − pan-fried mushrooms on grainy toast.

Gladstone Pinot Noir

STYLE **dry**
QUALITY ▼ ▼ ▼ ▽
VALUE ☆ ☆ ☆
GRAPES **Pinot Noir**
REGION **Wairarapa**
CELLAR **3**
PRICE **$32–35**

This is the first pinot noir produced under the Gladstone label, but there wasn't a lot of it made. Christine Kernohan's property is well worth a visit, and there are some pleasant cafés and an excellent wine shop in nearby Greytown.
Current Release 2001 The nose is savoury and spicy, with suggestions of typically varietal mushrooms and sweet loam. It's a pleasantly fruited middleweight on the palate, with gentle tannins and a clean finish. Try it with schnitzels, made from yearling beef and served with rosemary-flavoured potatoes.

Glover's Moutere Pinot Noir Front Block

STYLE **dry**
QUALITY ▼ ▼ ▼ ▽
VALUE ☆ ☆ ☆ ☆
GRAPES **Pinot Noir**
REGION **Nelson**
CELLAR **2–6**
PRICE **$32–36**

Dave Glover makes two pinots – this one, and another labelled 'Back Block' that sells mostly at the cellar door. The blocks are at the front and back of his hand-built winery and home, each of which he says gives him quite different fruit.
Current Release 1999 Think sweet cherry jam and spicy oak and you'll have an idea of the bouquet. It's quite approachable even in its youth, which is unusual for a Glover red, but could still do with a little quiet time. Grippy tannins and loads of super-ripe fruit make it a good partner for char-grilled sirloin steaks.

Glover's Nelson Pinot Noir

This is Dave Glover's 'second tier' pinot, simply because some of the fruit came from vineyards apart from those around his house. It sat in the cellar for a while in what he describes as 'a range' of French oak barrels before being bottled.
Current Release 2000 There's a fair old whack of smoky oak on the nose, but that will soften in time. The flavours are earthy but sweet-edged and the tannins are quite restrained – and that's something that can't often be said about Dave's wines! Enjoy it alongside a brace of garlic-spiked kidneys on thick slices of good, grainy toast.

STYLE **dry**
QUALITY ▼▼▼▽
VALUE ☆ ☆ ☆ ☆ ☆
GRAPES **Pinot Noir**
REGION **Nelson**
CELLAR ▭ **1–4**
PRICE **$20–23**

Glover's Pinot Noir Back Block

It's been called Dave Glover's best-ever pinot noir. Admittedly, the comment came from his son, but as winemaker for the Stonier vineyard in Victoria he should know what he's talking about. In 2000, there was no Front Block wine made.
Current Release 2000 The nose is absolutely chock-full of cherry, sweet loam and plum aromas. It's a big, mouth-filling wine with liquorice, mocha coffee and stewed plum flavours, all in a grippy but rounded package. It's not for wimps, but it looks splendid alongside a piece of rare-roasted cervena.

STYLE **dry**
QUALITY ▼▼▼▼
VALUE ☆ ☆ ☆☆
GRAPES **Pinot Noir**
REGION **Nelson**
CELLAR ▭ **2–8**
PRICE **$34–37**

Grove Mill Marlborough Pinot Noir

David Pearce used juice from four different clones to craft this middleweight pinot. The Burgundians, recognised as making the best examples of the style, firmly believe that using multiple clones produces better wine.
Current Release 2001 Smoky oak sits behind the aromas of ripe cherries, and I fancy there's a suggestion of plums in there as well. It's clean and fresh on the palate, not a big wine but nicely balanced with a clean finish. It works well with a platter of grilled vegetables like zucchini, eggplant and parsnips, scattered with the best Parmesan cheese you can find, freshly grated.

STYLE **dry**
QUALITY ▼▼▼▽
VALUE ☆ ☆ ☆
GRAPES **Pinot Noir**
REGION **Marlborough**
CELLAR ▯ **3**
PRICE **$34–36**

Hay's Lake Pinot Noir

It's not one of the Central Otago 'high-fliers', but this nicely balanced pinot is well worth searching out. It has a good following in the South Ialand, but is not seen so much in the North.
Current Release 2001 Sweet oak surrounds the generous aromas of cherries, plums and mushrooms. It's quite lush on the palate thanks to the integrated tannins, and boasts a long, fruit-filled finish. Partner it with pink-cooked lamb chops and you will be well pleased.

STYLE **dry**
QUALITY ▼▼▼▼
VALUE ☆ ☆ ☆☆
GRAPES **Pinot Noir**
REGION **Central Otago**
CELLAR ▯ **3**
PRICE **$36–39**

Herzog Pinot Noir

STYLE **dry**
QUALITY ♙♙♙♙♙
VALUE ☆ ☆ ☆
GRAPES **Pinot Noir**
REGION **Marlborough**

CELLAR ▯ **4**
PRICE **$48–52**

Hans Herzog uses the grapes' own wild yeasts to initiate the ferment of his big-hearted pinot, then leaves the skins sitting with the crushed berries for 18 days before pressing. The result is masses of character.
Current Release 2001 The oak spice on the nose is quite happy to sit behind the primary aromas of raspberries and porcini mushrooms. It's deliciously sweet-fruited on the palate, with nicely integrated tannins adding the right amount of grip. It makes a great partner for penne pasta tossed with sliced chorizo sausage and mushrooms in a tomato-based sauce.

Highfield Marlborough Pinot Noir

STYLE **dry**
QUALITY ♙♙♙♙
VALUE ☆ ☆ ☆
GRAPES **Pinot Noir**
REGION **Marlborough**

CELLAR ▯ **3**
PRICE **$42–46**

Using wooden 'paddles' to push the cap of skins back through the fermenting juice is hard work, but it pays off in flavour concentration. That was the routine with this one, and the winemaking team felt it was well worthwhile.
Current Release 2000 All the right pinot aromatic associations are there – strawberries, cherries and a touch of the funky fungals. It's not a big wine despite all that hand-plunging, but it has loads of sweet-fruited charm and an appealing rusticity on the finish. Steak and mushrooms would make an obvious accompaniment.

Huia Marlborough Pinot Noir

STYLE **dry**
QUALITY ♙♙♙♙
VALUE ☆ ☆ ☆ ⸮
GRAPES **Pinot Noir**
REGION **Marlborough**

CELLAR ▯ **3**
PRICE **$35–38**

Burgundy producers say the secret of making great pinot noir is to use as many clones of the grape as possible. Claire and Mike Allan used fruit from three sites, adding up to a total of eight clones.
Current Release 2001 The bouquet is earthy and decidedly fungal, which is all very European. Sweet fruit and oak that knows its place in the scheme of things give it a broad but fruity flavour profile, and make it a good partner for casseroled shanks of wild boar, which can be spotted on the occasional restaurant menu.

Hyperion Eos Pinot Noir

STYLE **dry**
QUALITY ♙♙♙♙♙
VALUE ☆ ☆ ☆ ☆ ☆
GRAPES **Pinot Noir**
REGION **Matakana**
CELLAR ▭ **1–3**
PRICE **$27–29**

There's a school of thought that pinot noir can't be grown successfully in the North Island, let alone in North Auckland, but John Crone is determined to prove the doubters wrong. This member of his small range spent a year in French oak barrels, 50% new.
Current Release 2000 Sweet, plummy fruit is backed by a faintly dungy note, the mark of some of the world's most interesting pinots. It's light in colour but has lashings of ripe, sweet fruit. There would be few better matches for a casserole full of beef shin pieces, cooked slowly with pulped tomatoes, carrots and baby onions.

Jackson Estate Pinot Noir

Jackson Estate is best known for whites, but this red has a loyal following. It's one of the best-priced examples on the market, and can sometimes be found for under $20 – an unheard-of price for pinot.
Current Release 2001 Cherries, strawberries and a wee hint of Chinese dried mushrooms form an interesting aromatic trio. It's sweet-fruited, light in texture but with plenty of clean, straightforward flavours. It's gentle enough to accompany red-fleshed fish, so try it alongside a seared kingfish steak.

STYLE **dry**
QUALITY ♟ ♟ ♟ ♟
VALUE ☆ ☆ ☆ ☆ ☆
GRAPES **Pinot Noir**
REGION **Marlborough**
CELLAR 🍾 **3**
PRICE **$20–23**

Johanneshof Marlborough Pinot Noir

There are very few pinots for sale at under $25, so this one is a popular purchase at the cellar door. Some Johanneshof wines are held to cellar before release, but this one is ready to go right now.
Current Release 2001 The nose is lightly fungal in typical pinot fashion, with cherry impressions taking a back seat. It's light and pleasantly sweet-fruited, but suffers from a lean finish. Partner it with lamb chops cooked with a little chopped sage.

STYLE **dry**
QUALITY ♟ ♟ ♟
VALUE ☆ ☆ ☆ ☆
GRAPES **Pinot Noir**
REGION **Marlborough**
CELLAR 🍾 **1**
PRICE **$21–23**

Kahurangi Estate Pinot Noir

The Day family spends a lot of time in the vineyard, plucking leaves away from the ripening grapes and even sorting through the bunches to throw away any individual berries that aren't ripening properly.
Current Release 1999 The aromas of cherries and mushrooms suit me just fine. Soft tannins make this wine very approachable, and good balance between fruit and oak give it a lot of easy-going appeal. The Days recommend it for lamb or an onion tart, so why not serve them together?

STYLE **dry**
QUALITY ♟ ♟ ♟ ♟
VALUE ☆ ☆ ☆ ☆ ☆
GRAPES **Pinot Noir**
REGION **Nelson**
CELLAR 🍾 **3**
PRICE **$19–22**

Kawarau Estate Reserve Pinot Noir

The Kawarau vineyard is situated at Lowburn, north of Cromwell, and it is managed organically. This member of the small portfolio was fermented in open-topped vats and spent 10 months in French oak barrels, 40% of which were new.
Current Release 2001 The bouquet is funky and feral in the best pinot style. It's a big smoothie on the palate, boasting sweet-edged flavours and a luxuriously soft texture courtesy of the fully integrated tannins. It makes a good partner for casseroled wild hare, but a pan-fried beef fillet steak would do at a pinch.

STYLE **dry**
QUALITY ♟ ♟ ♟ ♟
VALUE ☆ ☆ ☆ ☆
GRAPES **Pinot Noir**
REGION **Central Otago**
CELLAR 🍾 **4**
PRICE **$36–39**

Koura Bay Blue Duck Marlborough Pinot Noir

STYLE **dry**
QUALITY ♉ ♉ ♉ ♉
VALUE ☆ ☆ ☆ ⚝
GRAPES **Pinot Noir**
REGION **Marlborough**
CELLAR 🍾 3
PRICE **$35–37**

The Koura Bay winery comes up with great names for the wines in its collection. They work because they're so distinctive they are easy to remember. That's clever marketing.

Current Release 2001 Cherries, mushrooms and a smoky edge – yep, that's pinot alright! It's a broadly textured wine with a good quota of sweet fruit and a smooth finish. It makes a good partner for Chinese-style barbecued duck.

Kumeu River Pinot Noir

STYLE **dry**
QUALITY ♉ ♉ ♉ ♉ ♉
VALUE ☆ ☆ ☆ ☆
GRAPES **Pinot Noir**
REGION **West Auckland**
CELLAR ⬛▭ 2–6
PRICE **$35–38**

Winemakers Nigel Tibbits and Michael Brajkovich opted to age this top-shelf pinot in oak for a full year, but none of the barrels were new because they didn't want the raw flavours of unseasoned timber to dominate the fruit.

Current Release 2000 The nose is smoky, earthy and faintly fungal – all good signs for serious pinot. It's big-fruited and boasts solid tannins, but because the oak remains unobtrusive the overall impression is still elegant – clever stuff! Enjoy it with mushroom pie with a mesclun salad on the side.

La Strada Clayvin Vineyard Pinot Noir

STYLE **dry**
QUALITY ♉ ♉ ♉ ♉ ♉
VALUE ☆ ☆ ⚝
GRAPES **Pinot Noir**
REGION **Marlborough**
CELLAR 🍾 4
PRICE **$55–58**

It's not cheap, but it's very good. Hatsch Kalberer puts the emphasis on vineyard management rather than winery techniques, and it pays off in the flavour concentration of all the wines in his range.

Current Release 2001 It's rich, ripe and plummy on the nose and boasts a flavour profile that's sweet-edged, stylishly textured and put me in mind of raspberries. That all adds up to impressive drinkability right now, although it should also cellar well. Whenever you choose to pull the cork, try to track down a wild duck casserole to accompany it.

La Strada Pinot Noir

STYLE **dry**
QUALITY ♉ ♉ ♉ ♉ ⚆
VALUE ☆ ☆ ☆
GRAPES **Pinot Noir**
REGION **Marlborough**
CELLAR 🍾 3
PRICE **$35–38**

Hatsch Kalberer believes in forcing his vines into giving low crops, and his persistence pays off with intensity of flavour. La Strada wines are made by Fromm, but the vineyard name is in tiny print at the top of the label.

Current Release 2001 Smoky, charred oak and super-ripe cherries form the major aromatic associations. It's full-flavoured, smooth and impressively rich on the palate, with loads of ripeness through the middle and a long finish. It makes a good partner for lamb shanks, cooked in good stock and red wine for at least two hours.

La Strada Reserve Pinot Noir

Hatsch puts his top pinot into French oak for 18 months, an unusually long time by New Zealand standards — presumably because most producers need the barrels for the next vintage (well, they're expensive!).

Current Release 1998 Wow! Rich plum and raspberry aromas get their kicks from a dash of cracked pepper. It's positively unctuous on the palate, with mouth-filling richness that goes on long after it's been swallowed (no, I didn't spit it out!). For the ideal food match, shoot something large and spit-roast it.

STYLE **dry**
QUALITY ♟ ♟ ♟ ♟ ♟
VALUE ☆ ☆ ☆
GRAPES **Pinot Noir**
REGION **Marlborough**
CELLAR ▥ **2–6**
PRICE **$54–57**

Lake Hayes Central Otago Pinot Noir

The Lake Hayes team holds some of its wines back from release so they're ready to drink close to when they are bought. After all, something like 98% of all wine purchased in this country is consumed a few hours after it leaves the shop.

Current Release 1999 The oak is impressively gentle on the nose and sits politely behind the plum and strawberry aromas. This is the sort of wine non-red drinkers would pronounce as 'sweet', such is the ripeness of the fruit. It's deliciously balanced and still youthful, and would make a great partner for a rare-roasted saddle of hare.

STYLE **dry**
QUALITY ♟ ♟ ♟ ♟ ♟
VALUE ☆ ☆ ☆ ☆ ☆
GRAPES **Pinot Noir**
REGION **Central Otago**
CELLAR ▯ **4**
PRICE **$34–36**

Langdale of Canterbury Winemaker's Selection Pinot Noir

Carol Bunn made only 45 cases of this top-shelf pinot, so you'll have to hunt around for it. She took the hard decisions in the vineyard, restricting the crop to concentrate the flavour of the remaining bunches.

Current Release 1999 Smoky oak backs the ripe plum and cherry aromas on the nose, a combo that gives early notice this is a serious pinot. It's big, richly fruited and impressively well rounded on the palate, with a long finish. Carol recommends partnering it with lamb, either racks or shanks. Fair enough!

STYLE **dry**
QUALITY ♟ ♟ ♟ ♟ ♟
VALUE ☆ ☆ ☆ ☆ ☆
GRAPES **Pinot Noir**
REGION **Canterbury**
CELLAR ▥ **1–4**
PRICE **$28–33**

Lawson's Dry Hills Pinot Noir

Made from hand-picked fruit from two sites, this nicely balanced pinot was made using traditional techniques, including plunging the cap of skins into the juice. It's hard work, but winemaker Mike Just believes it's worth it.

Current Release 2001 Think mushrooms and cherries and you've got the bouquet sussed. It's a big smoothie on the palate, boasting loads of sweet fruit in faintly spicy surroundings. It would make a good partner for cubed lamb, casseroled with chopped red capsicums and tinned Italian tomatoes.

STYLE **dry**
QUALITY ♟ ♟ ♟ ♟
VALUE ☆ ☆ ☆ ☆ ☆
GRAPES **Pinot Noir**
REGION **Marlborough**
CELLAR ▯ **4**
PRICE **$26–29**

Le Grys Marlborough Adams Estate Pinot Noir

STYLE **dry**
QUALITY ▽ ▽ ▽ ▽ ▽
VALUE ★ ★ ★ ★ ☆
GRAPES **Pinot Noir**
REGION **Marlborough**
CELLAR **4**
PRICE **$31–33**

Le Grys is an alternative label for Mud House Wines, of Marlborough. This member of the range spent a year maturing quietly in French oak barrels, where it was regularly topped up.

Current Release 2000 There's a decidedly fungal note to the earthy bouquet, and that's just fine with me. It's a big smoothie on the palate, boasting rich fruit flavours in smooth surroundings. Duck is an ideal accompaniment, but a hearty chicken casserole would do at a pinch.

Loopline Vineyard Wairarapa Pinot Noir

STYLE **dry**
QUALITY ▽ ▽ ▽ ▽
VALUE ★ ★ ★ ☆
GRAPES **Pinot Noir**
REGION **Wairarapa**
CELLAR **2**
PRICE **$30–33**

Fruit for this well-priced pinot came from two Wairarapa vineyards, and is a blend of four clones. The fledgling wine spent nine months in a mixture of new and used French oak barrels.

Current Release 2001 This is best decribed as a 'fun' wine, boasting ripe cherry aromas and a wealth of bright, moderately rich flavours. The finish is clean, fresh-faced and moreish. It's good with light dishes like penne pasta tossed with fresh tomato sauce.

Lynskeys Wairau Peaks Marlborough Pinot Noir

STYLE **dry**
QUALITY ▽ ▽ ▽ ▽
VALUE ★ ★ ★ ☆
GRAPES **Pinot Noir**
REGION **Marlborough**
CELLAR **3**
PRICE **$35–37**

Kathy Lynskey grew up on a sheep farm, and has always wanted to make a living from the land. She bought her first vineyard in 1989, and launched the label in 1998. She has done well – her wines have scored some good ratings from magazines.

Current Release 2000 Cherries, Black Doris plums and a wee suggestion of mushrooms form an attractive aromatic trio. It's quite rich on the palate, with gentle tannins introducing the right amount of grip for the style. A seared tuna steak would make a perfect partner.

Main Divide Canterbury Pinot Noir

STYLE **dry**
QUALITY ▽ ▽ ▽ ▽
VALUE ★ ★ ★ ★ ☆
GRAPES **Pinot Noir**
REGION **Canterbury**
CELLAR **3**
PRICE **$23–25**

It's a second label to Pegasus Bay pinot, but it's pretty smart. Winemakers Lynnette Hudson and Matthew Donaldson put it in French oak barrels, 20% of which were new, for 18 months – a long time by local standards.

Current Release 2001 Sweet cherries are backed by a wee suggestion of leafiness on the nose, but they win the battle decisively. It's equally sweet-fruited and nicely balanced on the palate, with oak tannins that know their place in the scheme of things. It's gentle enough to accompany blue cod fillets cooked with tomatoes, chopped onions and garlic.

Margrain Pinot Noir

Strat Canning doesn't filter his pinot noir for fear of lessening its flavour, so if you plan to cellar it for a while it might be necessary to decant it before serving. He's not alone in his philosophy – many of the world's great reds are unfiltered.
Current Release 2001 Chunky and broadly appealing on the nose, richly fruited and smartly balanced on the palate – this is classy stuff. Nicely integrated oak allows the fruit to star, but adds just the right amount of grip to the finish. It works well with casseroled wild boar, but a chunky beef stew would certainly suffice.

STYLE **dry**
QUALITY ♀♀♀♀♀
VALUE ☆☆☆
GRAPES **Pinot Noir**
REGION **Martinborough**
CELLAR 1–3
PRICE **$40–42**

Martinborough Vineyard Pinot Noir

Martinborough Vineyards made its name with pinot noir and has produced some stunning examples over the years. Burgundy is the model, so the same techniques are employed as are the rule in this much-heralded part of France.
Current Release 2001 Cherries, chocolate, coffee and mushrooms. That might sound an unlikely combination, but it works. The flavours are closer to a ripe Black Doris plum, but there's a fair whack of sweet, vanilla-like oak in there as well. In an ideal world, it would be partnered by a brace of prosciutto-wrapped quail.

STYLE **dry**
QUALITY ♀♀♀♀
VALUE ☆☆
GRAPES **Pinot Noir**
REGION **Martinborough**
CELLAR 4
PRICE **$64–68**

Matariki Reserve Pinot Noir

John and Rosemary O'Connor are firm believers in the future of pinot noir in Hawke's Bay. They should be – their interpretation of the style has won a few top awards in its various vintages, and it's a popular choice in local restaurants.
Current Release 2000 Big, spicy oak characters dominate the plum aromas on the bouquet, but they should settle down in time. It's a solid, chunky wine on the palate, with flavours that lean towards ripe plums and charred timber. A rare kangaroo steak would be the way to go.

STYLE **dry**
QUALITY ♀♀♀♀
VALUE ☆☆☆
GRAPES **Pinot Noir**
REGION **Hawke's Bay**
CELLAR 4
PRICE **$46–49**

Matawhero Estate Pinot Noir

Denis Irwin once described his winemaking philosophy as 'doing Hemingway in a *Woman's Weekly* world'. Fair enough, but I think this one falls into the 'misprint' category. Sorry Denis – but don't stop experimenting!
Current Release 1999 The overall impression on the nose is of volatility, and things don't get any better on the palate. The texture is thin and quite reedy and the finish short and unsatisfying. One bottle opened out a little in 30 minutes or so, but the improvement could hardly be called dramatic. A food match? Forget it.

STYLE **dry**
QUALITY ♀♀
VALUE ☆☆
GRAPES **Pinot Noir**
REGION **Gisborne**
CELLAR
PRICE **$32–34**

Matua Valley Wairarapa Vineyard Pinot Noir

STYLE **dry**
QUALITY 🍷🍷🍷🍷🍷
VALUE ☆☆☆☆☆
GRAPES **Pinot Noir**
REGION **Wairarapa**
CELLAR **4**
PRICE **$27–29**

Mark Robertson got the grapes for this big, high-alcohol (14.5%) pinot from the Petrie vineyard, right in the heart of the Wairarapa. The fermenting juice was plunged by hand and spent 11 months maturing in 225-litre French oak barrels.

Current Release 2001 Mushrooms and ripe plums combine forces on the bouquet. It's a big, rich wine with lashings of ripe fruit flavour and an impressively smooth texture. It makes an awesome partner for duck, pricked all over and steamed, then roasted.

McCashin's Marlborough/Nelson Pinot Noir

STYLE **dry**
QUALITY 🍷🍷🍷🍷
VALUE ☆☆☆☆⯪
GRAPES **Pinot Noir**
REGION
Marlborough 67%
Nelson 33%
CELLAR **3**
PRICE **$24–26**

Both Marlborough and Nelson have good reputations for pinot noir, so combining fruit from the two regions makes perfect sense. Craig Gass matured the wine in French oak barrels for 11 months.

Current Release 2000 The nose is earthy and vaguely fungal, which is par for the course with good pinot. It's big and rich on the palate, soft in the middle but with chunky tannins cutting in to ensure a big finish. Enjoy it alongside a mushroom risotto, and include a few dried porcini.

Mills Reef Cooks Beach Pinot Noir

STYLE **dry**
QUALITY 🍷🍷🍷
VALUE ☆☆☆☆☆
GRAPES **Pinot Noir**
REGION **Coromandel**
CELLAR **2**
PRICE **$15–17**

Paddy Preston is excited about the potential of the site that supplied grapes for this red. The Shakespeare Cliff vineyard overlooks Mercury Bay and the Coromandel beaches. The soil is chalky clay, and he's very happy with that.

Current Release 2000 So what are the characters of Coromandel grapes? Dunno, but this one has cherries and mushrooms in abundance. It's spice-edged, quite chunky and generally appealing in a lightweight sort of way. It should work well with salami-topped pizza, ideally home-made.

Mills Reef Elspeth Pinot Noir

STYLE **dry**
QUALITY 🍷🍷🍷🍷
VALUE ☆☆☆⯪
GRAPES **Pinot Noir**
REGION **Te Horo**
CELLAR **1–4**
PRICE **$40–45**

Alistair Pain, of Te Horo Wines, pioneered winemaking in this tiny settlement an hour or so north of Wellington, and this one was made from local grapes by Paddy and Tim Preston at the swish Mills Reef winery in the Bay of Plenty.

Current Release 2000 I think they're on to something. Spicy oak sits behind a raft of savoury aromas to form an inviting bouquet. It's got loads of sweet fruit on the front palate and a luxurious texture in the middle – smart stuff! Use a glass to braise some chicken thighs and enjoy the rest as an accompaniment.

Montana Marlborough Pinot Noir

Much of the pinot noir grown on Montana's sprawling Marlborough vineyards ends up in the company's sparkling wines, but enough is harvested each year to support a small portfolio of straight varietals in various price brackets.
Current Release 2001 Savoury oak, mushrooms and cherries all play a part in the bouquet. It's a pleasant middleweight on the palate with good fruit flavours through the middle and no more than a trace of leanness on the finish. Partner it with lamb cutlets with beetroot chutney.

STYLE **dry**
QUALITY ☺ ☺ ☺
VALUE ☆ ☆ ☆ ☆ ☆
GRAPES **Pinot Noir**
REGION **Marlborough**
CELLAR **2**
PRICE **$16–18**

Montana Reserve Marlborough Pinot Noir

This big-hearted pinot from the Montana team at Marlborough is one of the few bargains in its category. The extra line on the label tells us it was 'Barrique Matured'. That means it spent a while in 225-litre French oak barrels.
Current Release 2000 It's appealingly smoky and quite chunky on the nose and big, smooth and richly fruited on the palate. The tannins are firm but integrated, and the fruit sweetness lasts right through to the finish – smart stuff! Enjoy it with twice-cooked duck (boiled in stock, dried then roasted).

STYLE **dry**
QUALITY ☺ ☺ ☺ ☺ ☺
VALUE ☆ ☆ ☆ ☆ ☆
GRAPES **Pinot Noir**
REGION **Marlborough**
CELLAR **4**
PRICE **$25–27**

Morton Estate Hawke's Bay Pinot Noir (White Label)

The fruit for this well-priced pinot came from Morton's Colefield and Riverview vineyards. Whether or not Hawke's Bay is suited to the pernickety pinot noir grape has been the subject of much local debate.
Current Release 2001 The bouquet is appropriately savoury and spicy and the flavour profile is clean and straightforward, with an attractive touch of rusticity towards the finish. All in all, a pleasant wine that sits well with a corned beef and mustard sandwich.

STYLE **dry**
QUALITY ☺ ☺ ☺
VALUE ☆ ☆ ☆ ☆ ☆
GRAPES **Pinot Noir**
REGION **Hawke's Bay**
CELLAR **2**
PRICE **$20–23**

Morton Estate Marlborough Pinot Noir (White Label)

Morton Estate is one of very few companies to produce pinots from two different regions. A bit of careful label-watching is necessary – this one is very nearly identical to the Hawke's Bay version reviewed above.
Current Release 2001 I get a suggestion of leafiness right in the front of the bouquet, but there are some pleasant cherry aromas in there as well. It's softly structured on the palate, with good fruit and gentle tannins. Its subtlety makes it good with chicken, cooked in stock and a little of the wine.

STYLE **dry**
QUALITY ☺ ☺ ☺
VALUE ☆ ☆ ☆
GRAPES **Pinot Noir**
REGION **Marlborough**
CELLAR **2**
PRICE **$18–21**

Morton Estate Stone Creek Marlborough Pinot Noir

STYLE **dry**
QUALITY 🍷 🍷 🍷 🍷
VALUE ☆ ☆ ☆ ☆
GRAPES **Pinot Noir**
REGION **Marlborough**
CELLAR 🍾 **1**
PRICE **$20–23**

Winemakers Evan Ward and Chris Archer reckon this is the best pinot Morton has made from Marlborough fruit since 1996. As the label tells us, it came from the Stone Creek vineyard, appropriately named because the surface is littered with river pebbles.
Current Release 2000 The bouquet is appealingly rustic, with mushrooms and sweet loam coming to mind. It's broadly textured, reasonably complex and appealingly sweet-fruited, and goes well with a chunky pork liver terrine, served with thick slices of grainy toast.

Mount Edward Central Otago Pinot Noir

STYLE **dry**
QUALITY 🍷 🍷 🍷 🍷 🍷
VALUE ☆ ☆ ☆ ☆
GRAPES **Pinot Noir**
REGION **Central Otago**
CELLAR 🍾 **1–4**
PRICE **$37–39**

The fruit came from three sites, one in Alexandra and two in the Gibbston Valley. The fledgling wine was matured in French oak barrels, 40% of them new, for 11 months before being bottled.
Current Release 2000 Savoury, vaguely fungal notes are backed by sweet, vanilla-like oak. It's superbly smooth and luxuriously fruited, with controlled tannins adding just the right amount of grip. Enjoy it with lamb and eggplant, both cubed and casseroled, served over polenta.

Mount Riley Marlborough Pinot Noir

STYLE **dry**
QUALITY 🍷 🍷 🍷 🍷
VALUE ☆ ☆ ☆ ☆ ☆
GRAPES **Pinot Noir**
REGION **Marlborough**
CELLAR 🍾 **2**
PRICE **$19–23**

Mount Riley produces two pinots, and although the Seventeen Valley version reviewed below has done best in competitions, both have enjoyed success. This 'standard' model was matured in a mixture of French and American oak.
Current Release 2001 Spicy oak and savoury mushrooms get it together in the bouquet. It's smooth-textured and nicely balanced on the palate, with a good quota of sweet fruit flavours in a middleweight package. Partner it with mahi-mahi steaks, just seared to retain all their juiciness.

Mount Riley Seventeen Valley Pinot Noir

STYLE **dry**
QUALITY 🍷 🍷 🍷 🍷 🍷
VALUE ☆ ☆ ☆ ☆
GRAPES **Pinot Noir**
REGION **Central Otago**
CELLAR 🍾 **4**
PRICE **$39–43**

Seventeen Valley is the top label for Marlborough-based Mount Riley wines. The name is that of a sub-region a little away from the bulk of Wairau Valley plantings. It has done exceptionally well for the company in the last few vintages.
Current Release 2000 There's a feral, rustic character about the bouquet that quite appeals to my peasant's palate. There's nothing rustic, however, about the flavour profile. It's sweet-fruited, rich and smooth from front to lingering finish. This is the wine to open when you've cooked a piece of beef shin really slowly in good stock.

Mountford Pinot Noir

Mountford owners Buffy and Michael Eaton give credit for the success of their wines to C. P. Lin, their winemaker, and Gerald Atkinson, who looks after the vineyard. They certainly seem to make a great team.

Current Release 2001 I've never smelled a smoked plum, but I imagine it would be rather like sniffing this wine – the bouquet is rich and savoury. Beautiful balance between ripe fruit and elegant tannins make it a major success in the flavour department and a long, sweet-edged finish completes the good impression. Duck breasts, lightly rubbed with Japanese mirin before being grilled, would be perfect.

STYLE **dry**
QUALITY ♟♟♟♟♟
VALUE ★★☆
GRAPES **Pinot Noir**
REGION **Waipara**
CELLAR 1–7
PRICE **$59–63**

Mud House Black Swan Pinot Noir

This top-of-the-line pinot isn't a common sight around the shops, but it has a keen and loyal following. The company produces two ranges of wine, Mud House and Le Grys. The latter sells well in the UK.

Current Release 2001 Smoky oak sits behind the fungal aromas that are a typical part of pinot's rustic charm. The flavours are all about sweet berries, with gentle oak providing grip through the middle. It's not a blockbuster, but it's pleasant enough alongside a salad of seared tuna with baby spinach leaves and garlic croutons.

STYLE **dry**
QUALITY ♟♟♟♟
VALUE ★★☆
GRAPES **Pinot Noir**
REGION **Marlborough**
CELLAR 1–3
PRICE **$40–43**

Muddy Water Waipara Pinot Noir

There's going to be a lot of Muddy Water pinot noir about in years to come – the vineyard owners have just top-grafted their sauvignon blanc with the variety. This one spent a year in French oak barrels.

Current Release 2000 Spicy, sweet oak meets the plummy fruit on pretty equal terms. It's an immensely appealing wine, with open fruit flavours in smooth surroundings. The finish is clean and refreshing. It makes a good partner for a room-temperature salad of grilled vegetables and sliced grilled sirloin.

STYLE **dry**
QUALITY ♟♟♟♟♟
VALUE ★★★☆
GRAPES **Pinot Noir**
REGION **Waipara**
CELLAR 4
PRICE **$38–42**

Murdoch James Estate Pinot Noir

This is one of two top-priced Murdoch James pinots. The fruit came from the Blue Rock vineyard, which was purchased and added to the the MJ fold a couple of years ago. Its cellarmate is labelled Fraser Pinot, so you'll find it under 'F'.

Current Release 2001 Smoky oak and mushroom characters backed by smartly integrated tannins make this a pleasant mouthful of wine. The grapes came from 15-year-old vines, and it shows in the impressive depth of flavour. It makes a great partner for rare-roasted saddle of hare, but should also work pretty well alongside an eye fillet steak.

STYLE **dry**
QUALITY ♟♟♟♟
VALUE ★★☆
GRAPES **Pinot Noir**
REGION **Martinborough**
CELLAR 1–4
PRICE **$45–48**

Nautilus Marlborough Pinot Noir

STYLE **dry**
QUALITY ▼ ▼ ▼ ▼ ▼
VALUE ☆ ☆ ☆ ☆
GRAPES **Pinot Noir**
REGION **Marlborough**
CELLAR 🍶 **4**
PRICE **$37–39**

Nautilus is the envy of other pinot producers for its purpose-built Marlborough winery, designed to produce nothing but that one variety. That means winemaker Clive Jones needs to make no compromises.
Current Release 2001 Smoky and sweet-edged in the bouquet, rich and opulent on the palate, this is a nicely balanced pinot with more substance than most. The oak is in good balance and the finish offers about the right amount of grip for the style. It works really well with chicken livers, pan-fried pink and served on a slice of thick, grainy toast.

Neudorf Moutere Home Block Pinot Noir

STYLE **dry**
QUALITY ▼ ▼ ▼ ▼ ▼
VALUE ☆ ☆ ☆
GRAPES **Pinot Noir**
REGION **Nelson**
CELLAR 🍶 **5**
PRICE **$48–52**

'Home Block' replaces the 'Reserve' designation used for earlier vintages of this top-shelf pinot. The Finns report that 2000 was a very ripe year for their fruit, which shows in the 14.5% alcohol level – grape sugars are converted to alcohol.
Current Release 2000 Spiced plums and cherries are joined by a dash of smokiness on the nose. It's richly fruited, sweet-edged and well-rounded on the palate, with flavours reminiscent of a range of different berries. The finish is long and eminently satisfying. Enjoy it alongside tagliatelle pasta with shredded duck and smoked bacon.

Nevis Bluff Pinot Noir

STYLE **dry**
QUALITY ▼ ▼ ▼ ▼
VALUE ☆ ☆ ☆ ☆
GRAPES **Pinot Noir**
REGION **Central Otago**
CELLAR ▤▻ **1–5**
PRICE **$28–35**

Nevis Bluff made quite a splash with its first wine, a big, chunky pinot gris. This red member of the two-wine portfolio was matured in oak barrels, 30% of which were new, the others one and two years old.
Current Release 1999 Sweet oak, a touch of earthiness and an impression of sweet plums combine to create a welcoming bouquet. It's smooth, nicely weighted and classy on the palate, with obviously ripe fruit shining through. It makes a good companion for a bowl of Chinese noodles topped with barbecued duck.

Nga Waka Martinborough Pinot Noir

STYLE **dry**
QUALITY ▼ ▼ ▼ ▼
VALUE ☆ ☆ ☆
GRAPES **Pinot Noir**
REGION **Martinborough**
CELLAR 🍶 **4**
PRICE **$42–45**

Roger Parkinson put this pinot into French oak barrels, 25% of them new, for 11 months. Be careful if you choose it as a lunchtime wine – it doesn't taste like it, but the alcohol is a massive 14%.
Current Release 2001 Think spiced cherries and sweet oak and you've got the bouquet sussed. It's deliciously sweet-fruited – the sort of wine that professed 'non-red' drinkers would find hugely appealing. The oak adds the right amount of grip and lengthens the finish. It goes brilliantly with mushroom and ham risotto.

Olssen's of Bannockburn Pinot Noir

Olssen's is one of very few wineries anywhere in the world to allow visitors to sample wine direct from the barrels, at an annual shindig a few weeks before each new harvest begins. **Current Release 2000** Charred oak puts an interesting edge on the primary aromas of ripe plums. It's broad, soft-profiled and smooth on the palate, with gentle tannins adding just the right amount of grip to the finish. It works well with a chunky rabbit casserole.

STYLE **dry**
QUALITY ♟♟♟♟
VALUE ☆ ☆ ☆ ☆
GRAPES **Pinot Noir**
REGION **Central Otago**
CELLAR **3**
PRICE **$35–37**

Omaka Springs Reserve Pinot Noir

Omaka Springs is as well known for olive oil as it is for wine. The property was one of the first in the country to combine the two enterprises, but they are kept determinedly separate. In Italy, grape vines are occasionally grown up the olive trees!
Current Release 2000 The bouquet is chunky and fungal, the latter a typical characteristic of the variety. It's sweet-fruited on the front palate, moderately rich through the middle and reasonably long-finishing. It's good with a roast vegetable platter – sprinkled with Omaka Springs olive oil, of course.

STYLE **dry**
QUALITY ♟♟♟♟
VALUE ☆ ☆ ☆ ☆
GRAPES **Pinot Noir**
REGION **Marlborough**
CELLAR **3**
PRICE **$25–27**

Palliser Estate Martinborough Pinot Noir

Alan Johnson sourced 10% of the fruit for this pinot from vines known as Dijon clone, after their usual home in France. It spent a year cooling its heels in French oak barrels, and was subjected to only minimal filtration.
Current Release 2001 Wow – talk about spicy! The savoury notes on the nose add extra interest to the sweet plum and cherry aromas, and a suggestion of mushrooms also plays a part. It's deliciously ripe-fruited, and the tannins add grip without dominating proceedings. All that adds up to a nicely balanced wine that goes well with a seared salmon steak.

STYLE **dry**
QUALITY ♟♟♟♟♟
VALUE ☆ ☆ ☆ ☆
GRAPES **Pinot Noir**
REGION **Martinborough**
CELLAR **1–4**
PRICE **$40–43**

C.J. Pask Gimblett Road Pinot Noir

There's not a lot of pinot noir grown in Hawke's Bay, but Kate Radburnd has made some good wines from it over the years. This one was matured in French and American oak, the latter very unusual for the variety.
Current Release 2000 Smoky oak sits behind pleasant aromas of strawberry and plums. It's a pleasant middleweight on the palate, not overly grippy and all the more successful for that. It works well with Wiener schnitzels – but buy beef, not veal.

STYLE **dry**
QUALITY ♟♟♟♟
VALUE ☆ ☆ ☆ ☆
GRAPES **Pinot Noir**
REGION **Hawke's Bay**
CELLAR **2**
PRICE **$28–32**

Pegasus Bay Pinot Noir

STYLE **dry**
QUALITY 🍷 🍷 🍷 🍷 🍷
VALUE ☆ ☆ ☆ ☆
GRAPES **Pinot Noir**
REGION **Waipara**

CELLAR **6**
PRICE **$40–43**

The Donaldsons plunge the fermenting juice for their pinot by hand. It's a laborious process that involves pushing the cap of skins back into the juice every four hours. The fledgling wine was then matured in French oak barrels.
Current Release 2001 Cherries and mushrooms get it together on the nose, but they are quite understated. It's a beautifully textured wine boasting sweet flavours, gentle tannins and a long, satisfying finish. There's nothing better with perfectly pink-cooked lamb racks.

Pegasus Bay Prima Donna Pinot Noir

STYLE **dry**
QUALITY 🍷 🍷 🍷 🍷 🍷
VALUE ☆ ☆ ☆
GRAPES **Pinot Noir**
REGION **Waipara**

CELLAR **6**
PRICE **$55–57**

You have to search to find the grape type – it's in fine print below the proprietary name. Winery owners the Donaldsons are great fans of opera, and hold functions featuring Canterbury performers and their operatically named wines.
Current Release 1999 The nose is smoky and carries a faint and attractive fungal whiff. It's deliciously fruited, with ripe plum flavours and a mouth-coating, super-smooth texture. There's nothing better with cubed lamb shoulder, cooked slowly for a couple of hours in good stock.

Pencarrow Martinborough Pinot Noir

STYLE **dry**
QUALITY 🍷 🍷 🍷 🍷
VALUE ☆ ☆ ☆ ☆
GRAPES **Pinot Noir**
REGION **Martinborough**

CELLAR **3**
PRICE **$29–33**

Pencarrow is a second label for Palliser Estate, but wines in the portfolio have been known to outpoint their big brothers in competitions. This one was obviously made from very ripe fruit – the alcohol level is a healthy 14.5%.
Current Release 2001 There's an attractive smoky note behind the clean-edged aromas of ripe plums and cherries. It's nicely fruited on the palate, not a 'biggie' despite the high alcohol, but a well-balanced middleweight with just enough grip to give it good mouth-feel. It works really well with kidneys on toast.

Pisa Range Estate Black Poplar Pinot Noir

STYLE **dry**
QUALITY 🍷 🍷 🍷 🍷
VALUE ☆ ☆ ☆ ☆
GRAPES **Pinot Noir**
REGION **Central Otago**

CELLAR **3**
PRICE **$34–36**

Warwick and Jenny Hawker have enlisted high-powered help for their new label. Rudi Bauer, one of the country's foremost pinot exponents, makes the wine. Viticultural consultant is Larry McKenna, the man they call 'the Prince of Pinot'.
Current Release 2000 Cherry and plum aromas sit in attractively rustic surrounds. It's pretty full-on in the flavour department, with rich flavours that put me in mind of chocolate-coated plums. The finish is long and nicely rounded. The ideal match would be casseroled duck, wild or domesticated, served on 'wet' polenta.

Ponder Estate Artist's Reserve Marlborough Pinot Noir

The grapes came from Mike Ponder's home vineyard and another one down the road owned by the Hilty family. The wine spent nine months in oak barrels, mostly French but some American.

Current Release 2000 The steely edge behind the faint earthiness on the nose is typical of the Ponder pinot style. It's directly fruited, with gentle tannins filling out the mid-palate and softening the finish. Try it with rare-roasted saddle of hare, if you're friendly with a hunter of small game.

STYLE **dry**
QUALITY ♟♟♟♟
VALUE ☆☆⟨
GRAPES **Pinot Noir**
REGION **Marlborough**
CELLAR 🍾 **3**
PRICE **$44–47**

Putiki Bay Waiheke Island Pinot Noir

In theory, notoriously difficult pinot noir is a strange choice for sunny Waiheke – conventional wisdom has it that it prefers a cooler climate. That hasn't deterred Detlev Danneman or his winemaker, Jamie Zapp. They like it, so they're making it.

Current Release 2000 A year in French oak barrels, 30% of them new, has added a savoury note to the predominant aromas of ripe cherries. Surprisingly given the climate, it is a pretty wine with classy balance between fruit and oak and a gentle but satisfying finish. It is soft enough to make a good partner for a pan-fried kingfish steak.

STYLE **dry**
QUALITY ♟♟♟♟
VALUE ☆☆☆⟨
GRAPES **Pinot Noir**
REGION
Waiheke Island
CELLAR 🍾 **3**
PRICE **$32–35**

Quartz Reef Pinot Noir

Rudi Bauer has made some splendid pinots under contract to various Central Otago companies over the years, and counts a 'Winemaker of the Year' trophy among his credits. Quartz Reef is his own label.

Current Release 2001 Sweet plums and cherries, spicy oak and a sort of 'forest floor' character add up to an appealing bouquet. The flavours are equally interesting, with the same suggestion of sweetness backed by gentle tannins. All in all, an enjoyable red that suits slow-cooked dishes like braised lamb shanks.

STYLE **dry**
QUALITY ♟♟♟♟⟨
VALUE ☆☆☆
GRAPES **Pinot Noir**
REGION **Central Otago**
CELLAR 🍾 **4**
PRICE **$42–45**

Rimu Grove Nelson Pinot Noir

The grapes were picked by hand and the cap of skins was plunged back through the juice three times each day during fermentation. The unfiltered wine was then aged in French oak barrels for nine montns.

Current Release 2001 There's a smoky edge behind the primary aromas of spiced plums and cherries. It's broad and smooth on the palate, pleasantly fruited through the middle but has a hint of leafiness right on the finish. It works pretty well with good old Kiwi-style corned beef.

STYLE **dry**
QUALITY ♟♟♟
VALUE ☆☆⟨
GRAPES **Pinot Noir**
REGION **Nelson**
CELLAR 🍾 **2**
PRICE **$38–40**

Rippon Jeunesse Pinot Noir

STYLE **dry**
QUALITY 🍷 🍷 🍷 🍷
VALUE ★ ★ ★ ☆
GRAPES **Pinot Noir**
REGION **Central Otago**
CELLAR 🍾 2
PRICE **$30–33**

This is a new line from the Rippon team, designed as a second label to their pinot noir 'biggie'. Jeunesse translates as youthfulness – an appropriate name which alludes not only to the vintage, but also to the age of the vines.
Current Release 2001 Cherry and strawberry aromas are backed by no more than a suggestion of spice. It's sweet-fruited and very approachable, with gentle tannins making it disturbingly easy to drink. Try it alongside a bowl of penne pasta tossed with chopped red onion, sage and the best olive oil and Parmesan cheese you can find.

Rippon Pinot Noir

STYLE **dry**
QUALITY 🍷 🍷 🍷 🍷 🍷
VALUE ★ ★ ★
GRAPES **Pinot Noir**
REGION **Central Otago**
CELLAR 🍾 5
PRICE **$47–52**

Rippon was producing classy pinot noir long before the whole Central Otago region gained an international reputation for the style. The variety is obviously very happy growing on the shores of Lake Wanaka.
Current Release 2000 Smoky, savoury oak is a pretty dominant force in the bouquet, but there's some seriously juicy fruit peering through the planks. It's a different story on the palate – ripe fruit rules the day, filling the mouth with flavour and creating a long finish. It's a big, generous wine that suits equally full-on food. Try braised beef shin pieces on the bone.

Rossendale Canterbury Pinot Noir

STYLE **dry**
QUALITY 🍷 🍷 🍷 🍷
VALUE ★ ★ ★ ★ ★
GRAPES **Pinot Noir**
REGION **Canterbury**
CELLAR 🍾 2
PRICE **$20–23**

The oak treatment given this well-priced pinot took two forms. A small amount went into barrels, in the traditional way, but another parcel had oak staves steeped in the tank. Good call – it scored silver at the Air New Zealand awards.
Current Release 2000 Ripe cherries and sweet oak kick things off. It's clean and straightforward, mouth-coatingly smooth right through the middle and finishes with a lick of spiced raspberries. It works well alongside beef schnitzels served with young green beans and garlicky mashed potato.

Saint Clair Doctor's Creek Pinot Noir

STYLE **dry**
QUALITY 🍷 🍷 🍷 🍷
VALUE ★ ★ ★ ★ ☆
GRAPES **Pinot Noir**
REGION **Marlborough**
CELLAR 🍾 2
PRICE **$23–25**

The Saint Clair winemaking team used both French and American oak for this red, but the US barrels were all older, so contributed very little to the final flavour. New American oak is quite aggressive – not at all what you want with pinot.
Current Release 2001 Gentle raspberry and strawberry aromas have a faintly spicy edge from the oak. It's a pretty wine on the palate, generous and approachable thanks to tannins that know their place in the scheme of things. It would go nicely with a pasta dish featuring smoked bacon and duck.

Saint Clair Omaka Reserve Pinot Noir

With a silver medal from the International Wine Challenge in London under its belt, this pinot should be feeling pretty smart – well, its producers should be. It was matured in French oak barrels, 35% of which were new.

Current Release 2000 Spiced cherries and mushrooms create a classic pinot bouquet. It's richly fruited, generously textured and perfectly balanced on the palate, all of which make it a splendid partner for braised pork chops, ideally served on puréed kumara.

STYLE **dry**
QUALITY ▼▼▼▼▼
VALUE ★★★★☆
GRAPES **Pinot Noir**
REGION **Marlborough**
CELLAR **4**
PRICE **$34–36**

Saints Vineyard Selection Marlborough Pinot Noir

Patrick Materman was rapt in the quality of his pinot noir fruit from the '99 vintage. The grapes came from Montana's Fairhall and Squire Estate vineyards, both in the sprawling Wairau Valley.

Current Release 1999 Cherries and mushrooms add up to a classic pinot bouquet. It's a middleweight, clean-cut but a touch leafy on the finish. It goes well enough with simple dishes like braised chicken drumsticks, especially if you use a glass or two as the braising liquid.

STYLE **dry**
QUALITY ▼▼▼
VALUE ★★★★☆
GRAPES **Pinot Noir**
REGION **Marlborough**
CELLAR **2**
PRICE **$20–23**

Seifried Pinot Noir

Hermann Seifried arranged for his pinot grapes to be picked at two and a half tonnes per acre, which is considerably lower than the national average. Restricted crops give more flavour.

Current Release 2001 The nose is mushroomy in the approved fashion for this variety. It's a little lean on the palate, but has good fruit and should soften and round out over the next year or two. Then, try it with a steak and mushroom pie, ideally home-made.

STYLE **dry**
QUALITY ▼▼▼
VALUE ★★★★
GRAPES **Pinot Noir**
REGION **Nelson**
CELLAR **3**
PRICE **$22–24**

Seifried Winemaker's Collection Pinot Noir

The debate over oak mostly concerns the relative merits of French or American barrels. Hermann Seifried avoided all that by maturing this top-shelf pinot in Hungarian oak. Apparently, it's rather like a cross between the two.

Current Release 2001 The nose is decidedly chocolatey. That's unusual for pinot, but I'm not complaining. It's richly fruited, with good texture and smartly balanced tannins through the middle. The finish is long and satisfying. Partner it with grilled lamb rumps with a not-too-sweet plum-based reduction sauce.

STYLE **dry**
QUALITY ▼▼▼▼
VALUE ★★★★
GRAPES **Pinot Noir**
REGION **Nelson**
CELLAR **4**
PRICE **$32–34**

Selaks Drylands Winemakers Reserve Pinot Noir

STYLE **dry**
QUALITY ♟ ♟ ♟
VALUE ☆ ☆ ☆ ☆ ☆
GRAPES **Pinot Noir**
REGION **Marlborough**
CELLAR 🍾 2
PRICE **$19–23**

The vines were bunch-thinned, which means grapes that didn't look as if they were ripening satisfactorily were cut off and discarded. That might seem like commercial suicide, but it usually pays off in flavour concentration in the finished wine.

Current Release 2001 There's a healthy whack of charred oak behind the ripe raspberry aromas. It's sweet-edged, smooth and pleasant on the palate but doesn't show anything to get really excited about. Still, it makes a perfectly acceptable partner for a salad of rocket leaves draped with thin slices of pink-roasted leg of lamb.

Sherwood Estate Canterbury/Marlborough Pinot Noir

STYLE **dry**
QUALITY ♟ ♟ ♟
VALUE ☆ ☆ ☆ ☆ ☆
GRAPES **Pinot Noir**
REGION
   Waipara 60%
   Marlborough 40%
CELLAR 🍾 1
PRICE **$15–17**

There are very few pinots from anywhere in the country that sell in the mid-teens, which makes this one a popular buy at the winery shop and on restaurant lists. It was matured in small oak barrels, but none of them were new.

Current Release 2001 There's a fungal note behind the primary aromas of cherries, which is all to the good. It's pretty lightweight in the flavour department, but there's a reasonable quota of sweet fruit – and at this price, who's quibbling? Try it with a home-made hamburger, and put in all the extras you want.

Sherwood Estate Marlborough Reserve Pinot Noir

STYLE **dry**
QUALITY ♟ ♟ ♟ ♟ ♟
VALUE ☆ ☆ ☆ ☆ ☆
GRAPES **Pinot Noir**
REGION **Marlborough**
CELLAR 🍾 1–4
PRICE **$28–30**

Dayne Sherwood and Andrew Meggitt are based in Canterbury, but they buy in some of their grapes from Marlborough. This member of the portfolio spent 14 months in French oak barrels. The big-fruited '99 version is also on sale around the country.

Current Release 2000 There's an earthy note behind the mushroom and smoky oak aromas. Ripe fruit in nicely textured surrounds make for an appealing package with a lingering finish. It makes a good partner for a char-grilled Scotch fillet steak topped with grilled flat mushrooms.

Shingle Peak Marlborough Pinot Noir

STYLE **dry**
QUALITY ♟ ♟ ♟ ♟
VALUE ☆ ☆ ☆ ☆ ☆
GRAPES **Pinot Noir**
REGION **Marlborough**
CELLAR 🍾 2
PRICE **$18–21**

The grapes were cropped low, and the fledgling wine spent its quiet time in a mixture of French and American oak barrels, 10% of which were new. American oak is seldom used for pinot, but it has done this one no harm.

Current Release 2000 The smoky oak sits behind the aromas of ripe plums and cherries. It's quite gentle on the palate, with the impression of smokiness continuing through the middle. The finish is nicely fruited and quite stylish. It works well with a rustic ratatouille.

Solstone Pinot Noir Wairarapa Valley

The tasting note sent out with this wine describes pinot as a 'ladylike' variety. We presume the writer means it is relatively delicate, but we can think of a few 'ladies' who would take umbrage at the suggested comparison.
Current Release 2001 A 10-month spell in oak barrels has added elegant spice to the cherry and mushroom-like primary aromas, and smoothed out the tannins on the palate. It's no blockbuster, but that's not what pinot is all about. Overall, a pleasant middleweight that goes perfectly well with Wiener schnitzels and pan-fried mushrooms.

STYLE **dry**
QUALITY ▓ ▓ ▓ ▐
VALUE ☆ ☆ ☆ ☆
GRAPES **Pinot Noir**
REGION **Wairarapa**
CELLAR 🍾 **3**
PRICE **$31–33**

Spy Valley Pinot Noir

The vineyard is large, the vines have a bit of age behind them and the marketing plan seems very well focused. No doubt we're going to hear a lot more of Bryan and Jan Johnson's Spy Valley label in the next few years.
Current Release 2001 I like the savoury notes on the nose – they put me in mind of smoked mushrooms. It's a broadly focused wine with ripe fruit flavours in smooth surroundings. It works well with a simple pizza – pulped tomatoes, fresh mozzarella, grated Parmesan and oreganum is all you need.

STYLE **dry**
QUALITY ▓ ▓ ▓ ▐
VALUE ☆ ☆ ☆ ☆
GRAPES **Pinot Noir**
REGION **Marlborough**
CELLAR 🍾 **2**
PRICE **$29–32**

Staete Landt Marlborough Pinot Noir

Staete Landt was the first name given to our country by Dutch explorer, Abel Tasman. The winery owners were born in the Netherlands, so there is an appropriate connection. Abel would have approved.
Current Release 2001 Spice-edged on the nose, sweet-fruited and stylish on the palate, this is a highly approachable pinot. Gentle tannins give it just the right amount of grip for the style, and make it a good partner for lamb chops, ideally cooked on a barbecue grill with olive oil-tossed potato wedges browned on the flatplate alongside.

STYLE **dry**
QUALITY ▓ ▓ ▓ ▓ ▐
VALUE ☆ ☆ ☆ ☆
GRAPES **Pinot Noir**
REGION **Marlborough**
CELLAR 🍾 **4**
PRICE **$37–39**

Stonecutter Martinborough Pinot Noir

Production is tiny at present and only three wines are produced, but we can expect steady growth from this relatively new name on the burgeoning Martinborough wine scene. The owners were once involved in environmental management.
Current Release 2000 Savoury and fungal on the nose, smooth, nicely fruited and smartly balanced on the palate, this is a thoroughly pleasant pinot that won't blow your socks off, but will fit into many occasions. Pull the cork next time you're having grilled lamb chops.

STYLE **dry**
QUALITY ▓ ▓ ▓ ▐
VALUE ☆ ☆ ☆ ☆
GRAPES **Pinot Noir**
REGION **Martinborough**
CELLAR ▭ **1–3**
PRICE **$28–32**

Stoneleigh Marlborough Pinot Noir Rapaura Series

STYLE **dry**
QUALITY ♟♟♟♟♟
VALUE ☆☆☆☆☆
GRAPES **Pinot Noir**
REGION **Marlborough**
CELLAR **4**
PRICE **$24–26**

A 12-month spell in new and used French oak barrels marks this as a serious pinot. The smartly packaged Rapaura Series wines, introduced after Corbans was absorbed by Montana, sell well here and overseas.
Current Release 2001 Elegant and gently spiced on the nose, smooth and richly fruited on the palate, this is a smart pinot with plenty of character despite its understated style. It makes an ideal partner for pork chops braised with chopped tomatoes, tinned Italian in winter or fresh Romas in summer, and dried porcini mushrooms.

Stoneleigh Vineyards Pinot Noir

STYLE **dry**
QUALITY ♟♟♟♟
VALUE ☆☆☆☆☆
GRAPES **Pinot Noir**
REGION **Marlborough**
CELLAR **2**
PRICE **$17–19**

One of very few pinots with an under-$20 recommended retail price, this big-production member of the Corbans portfolio still gets plunged by hand – although admittedly, a pneumatic plunger does the really hard work.
Current Release 2001 Oak spice is subtle on the nose, sitting contentedly behind the dominant aromas of ripe cherries and plums. It's sweet-edged and quite rich on the palate with tannins that add just enough grip for the middleweight style. Chinese-style barbecued duck, now available in most major centres, would suit it well.

Stratford Martinborough Pinot Noir

STYLE **dry**
QUALITY ♟♟♟♟
VALUE ☆☆☆
GRAPES **Pinot Noir**
REGION **Martinborough**
CELLAR **3**
PRICE **$41–45**

Strat Canning is a highly experienced winemaker who has worked with a handful of wineries around the Wairarapa region. His brother, Chris, established the Hotel du Vin in the Waikato, home to Firstland wines, but is no longer involved.
Current Release 2001 It's not a biggie, but it has a lot of gentle appeal. The aromas are reminiscent of cherries and plums and the flavours suggest ripe raspberries, with smoky oak contributing extra interest. Match that smokiness by partnering it with a smoked beef and potato salad.

Tasman Bay Nelson Pinot Noir

STYLE **dry**
QUALITY ♟♟♟♟
VALUE ☆☆☆☆☆
GRAPES **Pinot Noir**
REGION **Nelson**
CELLAR **3**
PRICE **$19–21**

Philip Jones and Mathew Rutherford used wild yeasts to ferment this pinot, then the embryonic wine was put into French oak barrels and left there for six months. They have been rewarded with a bronze medal.
Current Release 2000 Mushrooms and cherries are the classic pinot aromatic associations, and they're both in good form on the nose. It's a pretty wine on the palate, with attractively sweet fruit in middleweight surroundings. It goes well with pink-cooked lamb, either a roasted leg or pan-fried cutlets.

Te Kairanga Martinborough Pinot Noir

This is the 'standard' Te Kairanga pinot, but it's very smart. The grape bunches were thinned, the fruit was harvested by hand and the juice was plunged during fermentation. The wine then spent 10 months in French oak barrels, 30% of them new.

Current Release 2001 The bouquet is earthy, fungal and rustic – all characters that have been enhanced by plunging the cap of skins back into the fermenting juice. It's a big, sweet-fruited wine on the palate, but that appealing rusticity is much in evidence. Partner it with a dish that reflects it, like chicken pieces casseroled in red wine and good stock.

STYLE **dry**
QUALITY ♟♟♟♟
VALUE ☆☆☆☆
GRAPES **Pinot Noir**
REGION **Martinborough**
CELLAR **3**
PRICE **$35–38**

Te Kairanga Martinborough Reserve Pinot Noir

Te Kairanga's top-line pinot is made from fruit that shows exceptional potential in various parts of the vineyard. The vines are nurtured by removing leaves to expose the grapes to the sun, and the crop is thinned out to ensure concentration.

Current Release 2001 Smoky, charred oak sits alongside the aromas of mushrooms and ripe cherries – there's certainly no mistaking the variety. It's smooth, ripe-fruited and rich on the palate, with tannins adding good grip through the middle and on the long finish. The winemaking team suggests roast quail or pheasant as a partner. Yes!

STYLE **dry**
QUALITY ♟♟♟♟♟
VALUE ☆☆☆
GRAPES **Pinot Noir**
REGION **Martinborough**
CELLAR **6**
PRICE **$49–53**

Te Mania Nelson Barrique Selection Pinot Noir

This pleasant middleweight pinot spent nine months maturing in French oak barrels, but only 40% of them were new. The rest had been used for other wines over the past two vintages. The idea was to avoid overpowering the fruit.

Current Release 2000 Smoky oak sits behind the cherry/ berry aromas. It's certainly not a big wine, but it has some attractively ripe-fruit flavours in smooth surroundings, and may well develop more strength as it ages. It's restrained enough to go with a seared tuna steak.

STYLE **dry**
QUALITY ♟♟♟♟
VALUE ☆☆☆☆☆
GRAPES **Pinot Noir**
REGION **Nelson**
CELLAR **1–3**
PRICE **$24–26**

Te Mania Nelson Pinot Noir

Te Mania has established a good reputation with wines made from the pernickety pinot noir grape. This 'standard' model is one of the best-priced on the market, and sells well at the cellar door and at a number of cafés in Nelson and further afield.

Current Release 2001 There's a smoky note behind the primary aromas of ripe cherries. It's sweet-fruited and attractive on the palate, with gentle tannins adding about the right amount of grip for its middleweight style. Enjoy it alongside a home-made hamburger, using top-quality lean minced beef.

STYLE **dry**
QUALITY ♟♟♟
VALUE ☆☆☆☆
GRAPES **Pinot Noir**
REGION **Nelson**
CELLAR **2**
PRICE **$23–26**

Te Mania Nelson Pinot Noir Reserve

STYLE **dry**
QUALITY 🍷🍷🍷🍷
VALUE ★ ★ ★ ★
GRAPES **Pinot Noir**
REGION **Nelson**
CELLAR 🍶 **4**
PRICE **$30–33**

This is the first Reserve pinot from the Te Mania team. In the past, the top model was labelled 'Barrique Selection'. This one spent 10 months in French oak barrels, then sat quietly for six months in bottles before being released.
Current Release 2001 Smoky oak, plums and cherries – they're all there on the nose. It's deliciously sweet-fruited on the palate, and because the tannins know their place in the scheme of things it remains smooth right through to the lingering finish. Ours went well with a leg of lamb braised in stock with chopped carrots, onions and celery.

Terrace Downs Pinot Noir

STYLE **dry**
QUALITY 🍷🍷🍷
VALUE ★ ★★
GRAPES **Pinot Noir**
REGION **Central Otago**
CELLAR 🍶 **2**
PRICE **$35–37**

This Alexandra vineyard is managed by David Grant of William Hill Wines. The wine is made by Gerry Rowland, who is based in California but travels over at vintage each year. It's not the best-known Otago pinot, but it's seen on a few lists.
Current Release 2001 There's a smoky edge on the ripe cherry and plum aromas. It's simply structured and easy-going on the palate, not a 'biggie' but pleasant enough with simple but well-flavoured fare like mushroom risotto, made using dried porcini if possible.

Terrace Road Marlborough Pinot Noir

STYLE **dry**
QUALITY 🍷🍷🍷
VALUE ★ ★ ★ ★ ★
GRAPES **Pinot Noir**
REGION **Marlborough**
CELLAR 🍶 **2**
PRICE **$18–20**

The Terrace Road label is worn by the handful of still wines in the Cellier Le Brun portfolio. This well-priced pinot spent eight months sitting quietly in French oak barrels.
Current Release 2001 It's clean and fresh on the nose, with all the right suggestions of cherries and strawberries. The flavour profile is a little lean, but it's pleasant enough and sits well with a salad based around rocket leaves and cubes of just-seared tuna.

Thornbury Marlborough Pinot Noir

STYLE **dry**
QUALITY 🍷🍷🍷🍷
VALUE ★ ★ ★★
GRAPES **Pinot Noir**
REGION **Marlborough**
CELLAR 🍶 **3**
PRICE **$36–38**

The grapes were picked by hand and the juice pumped over the cap of skins to extract as much flavour and colour as possible when this nicely tuned pinot was put together. It spent 15 months in French oak barrels.
Current Release 2001 It's smoky and spicy on the nose, but those characters sit behind the upfront aromas of plums and cherries. The flavour profile is all about ripe fruit, aided and abetted by nicely tuned tannins. Overall, a smart wine that goes well with an all-vegetable moussaka.

Tohu Marlborough Pinot Noir

Grapes for this smartly labelled red were picked by hand, and after fermentation the juice spent a few months in French oak barrels. A big percentage of Tohu's production is sent overseas, but the wines are reasonably easy to find in this country.
Current Release 2001 Strawberry and cherry aromas are backed by a hint of smokiness. It's an approachable middleweight on the palate, with gentle tannins and a good quota of ripe fruit flavours. The finish is short but has no sharp edges. It's good with a sandwich made from pink-cooked lamb, chopped mint (not too much) and really ripe tomatoes.

STYLE **dry**
QUALITY ♗ ♗ ♗
VALUE ☆ ☆ ☆
GRAPES **Pinot Noir**
REGION **Marlborough**
CELLAR **2**
PRICE **$27–31**

Torlesse Pinot Noir

Torlesse is better known for whites than reds, but this well-priced pinot has a collection of loyal fans. It is occasionally sold for under $20, but a price tag a couple of dollars above the magic line is more common.
Current Release 2001 Suggestions of smoky oak and sweet cherries kick things off nicely. It's a middleweight in the flavour department – pleasant enough, but not one to get you excited. Partner it with veal schnitzels, draped over a pile of mashed potatoes and accompanied by young green beans.

STYLE **dry**
QUALITY ♗ ♗ ♗
VALUE ☆ ☆ ☆ ☆ ½
GRAPES **Pinot Noir**
REGION **Canterbury Waipara**
CELLAR **2**
PRICE **$20–23**

Trinity Hill Hawke's Bay Te Awanga Pinot Noir

Warren Gibson used fruit from five different clones to craft this pinot. Some of the juice was plunged by hand as it fermented, while another parcel was pumped over – a process that sprays juice from the bottom of the tank back over the skins at the top.
Current Release 2001 There's a dash of charred oak sitting behind the primary aromas of sweet plums. It's bigger on the palate than most examples from further south, with fully ripe flavours and grippy but integrated tannins. The finish is long and firm. Enjoy it with a beef and carrot casserole, served with mashed potatoes and Brussels sprouts.

STYLE **dry**
QUALITY ♗ ♗ ♗ ♗
VALUE ☆ ☆ ☆
GRAPES **Pinot Noir**
REGION **Hawke's Bay**
CELLAR **4**
PRICE **$39–43**

Twin Islands Marlborough Pinot Noir

Nautilus Estate is keen that Twin Islands is seen as simply an alternative range to the Nautilus collection, not a second label. Fair enough – but the wines are invariably less expensive.
Current Release 2001 Given that this is one of the least expensive pinots on the market there's some pretty smart fruit in the bouquet – think cherries and plums and you'll be close. It's not a big wine, but that's not the point. There's a moderate amount of richness on the palate and a clean, fresh finish. Enjoy it with chipolata sausages from a serious butcher.

STYLE **dry**
QUALITY ♗ ♗ ♗ ½
VALUE ☆ ☆ ☆ ☆ ☆
GRAPES **Pinot Noir**
REGION **Marlborough**
CELLAR **2**
PRICE **$20–23**

Two Paddocks Neill Pinot Noir

STYLE **dry**
QUALITY 🍷🍷🍷🍷🍷
VALUE ★ ★ ★ ☆
GRAPES **Pinot Noir**
REGION **Central Otago**
CELLAR 🍾 4
PRICE **$37–39**

Only 155 cases of this pinot were produced, which makes it pretty hard to find. Actor and Central Otago enthusiast Sam Neill owns the vineyard, Steve Moffit tends the vines and Dean Shaw makes the wine. They form a pretty formidable team.

Current Release 2000 There's an earthy, rustic note on the nose that rather appeals to the peasant in me, but the overriding impression is of good, sweet fruit. It's smartly balanced, with rich flavours suggestive of cherries and plums and a spicy, sweet-edged finish. It makes a great partner for pink-cooked roast lamb, spiked with rosemary and garlic before it hits the oven.

Valli Pinot Noir Colleen's Vineyard

STYLE **dry**
QUALITY 🍷🍷🍷🍷🍷
VALUE ★ ★ ★ ☆
GRAPES **Pinot Noir**
REGION **Central Otago**
CELLAR 🍾 3
PRICE **$39–41**

The grapes for this wine came from the Gibbston region. Grant Taylor, whose 'day job' is at Gibbston Valley Wines, matured it in French oak barrels, 40% of them new, for 11 months.

Current Release 2000 Cherries, sweet loam and a touch of smoky oak form a smartly aromatic trio. It's big, rich and ripe-fruited in the flavour department, and boasts a satisfyingly fresh-faced finish. Try it with slow-cooked lamb shanks with carrots and baby onions.

Vavasour Marlborough Pinot Noir

STYLE **dry**
QUALITY 🍷🍷🍷🍷
VALUE ★ ★ ★ ★
GRAPES **Pinot Noir**
REGION **Marlborough**
CELLAR 🍾 1–4
PRICE **$30–33**

The Awatere Valley designation on the label denotes the location of the winery, but this Marlborough sub-region contributed only 30% of the fruit for this pinot – the rest came from the Wairau Valley, across the hills. The wine spent 10 months in a mixture of new and used French oak barrels.

Current Release 2001 If you can imagine what smoked cherries would taste like, you've got the bouquet sussed. A backdrop of sweet oak completes the picture. It's smooth, pleasant and smartly balanced on the palate, with sweet flavours and nicely integrated tannins. We enjoyed ours with Peking-style slow-cooked lamb.

Vidal Estate Marlborough Pinot Noir

STYLE **dry**
QUALITY 🍷🍷🍷🍷
VALUE ★ ★ ★ ★ ☆
GRAPES **Pinot Noir**
REGION **Marlborough**
CELLAR 🍾 3
PRICE **$20–23**

Rod McDonald used fruit from several Marlborough vineyards to craft this well-priced pinot. Each parcel of juice was handled separately to give him more blending options when the time came.

Current Release 2001 The nose has smoky, plum-like characters sitting behind the ripe raspberry aromas. It's a middleweight on the palate, with mouth-drying tannins adding grip to the finish. Rod McDonald suggests it for game, so try it with wild duck if you're on bludging terms with a hunter.

Villa Maria Cellar Selection Marlborough Pinot Noir

With some good awards under its belt, this mid-priced pinot has beaten many brands costing half as much again. Good on ya, Villa! The grapes came from five different vineyards, and they were all picked by hand and processed separately.
Current Release 2001 Sweet plums and cherries create a most welcoming introduction. It's richly fruited, smooth-textured and just plain pleasant. The finish is moderately long and leaves you with a strong desire to have just one more sip. It works really well with fettucine pasta tossed with smoked bacon and shredded duck.

STYLE **dry**
QUALITY ♟ ♟ ♟ ♟
VALUE ☆ ☆ ☆
GRAPES **Pinot Noir**
REGION **Marlborough**
CELLAR **3**
PRICE **$30–33**

Villa Maria Reserve Marlborough Pinot Noir

Villa keeps its Reserve designation for wines that come from the best grapes the company's winemakers can find. This is a newcomer to the portfolio, but it was awarded the 'Wine of the Show' trophy at the 2002 Air New Zealand Wine Awards.
Current Release 2001 Charred oak and savoury cherry aromas are backed by a suggestion of field mushrooms. It's opulently textured and chock-full of ripe fruit flavours, and boasts an extraordinarily long finish. Try it alongside a layered beef and tomato pasta 'pie'.

STYLE **dry**
QUALITY ♟ ♟ ♟ ♟ ♟
VALUE ☆ ☆ ☆
GRAPES **Pinot Noir**
REGION **Marlborough**
CELLAR **6**
PRICE **$50–53**

Villa Maria Single Vineyard Lloyd Pinot Noir

The fruit for this member of Villa's 'Single Vineyard' range came from the Lloyd family's Te Rawatahi Vineyard, near Blenheim. The fruit was picked by hand and the cap of skins plunged through the juice four times a day during fermentation.
Current Release 2000 Cherries and mushrooms get together in the bouquet, and it works fine. It's a nicely textured wine, with fruit sweetness tempered by smartly integrated tannins. The finish is fresh and clean. It goes well with a chunky pork liver terrine served with hot buttered toast.

STYLE **dry**
QUALITY ♟ ♟ ♟ ♟
VALUE ☆ ☆ ☆
GRAPES **Pinot Noir**
REGION **Marlborough**
CELLAR **3**
PRICE **$40–43**

Voss Estate Pinot Noir

Martinborough is pinot country, and this one from Gary Voss and Annette Atkins does well on the show circuit – in the years they choose to enter it. It's not filtered, so may develop sediment in time.
Current Release 1999 Smoky, spicy oak sits behind the plum and strawberry aromas. It's a nicely textured wine, with smooth-edged tannins filling the mouth and ensuring a smooth finish. Try it with a wedge of well-aged tasty cheddar, served with bread rather than crackers.

STYLE **dry**
QUALITY ♟ ♟ ♟ ♟
VALUE ☆ ☆ ☆⯪
GRAPES **Pinot Noir**
REGION **Martinborough**
CELLAR **3**
PRICE **$35–38**

Waipara Hills Reserve Pinot Noir

STYLE dry
QUALITY ♟ ♟ ♟ ♟
VALUE ☆ ☆ ☆
GRAPES Pinot Noir
REGION Waipara

CELLAR 🍾 3
PRICE $37–41

Alan McCorkindale made this wine from fruit picked in the Garden Vineyard – appropriately named for its owners, D. and A. Garden. He reports that the vines were very low-yielding, and the fledgling wine spent a year in French oak barrels.

Current Release 2001 Spicy oak backs up the primary aromas of ripe plums and cherries, and I fancy I find a suggestion of mushrooms in there as well. Broad focus gives it a smooth flavour profile, and the middleweight fruit ensures a sweet-edged finish. All in all, a pleasant wine that suits mild-mannered dishes like casseroled lamb chops.

Waipara Springs Reserve Pinot Noir

STYLE dry
QUALITY ♟ ♟ ♟ ♟ ♟
VALUE ☆ ☆ ☆ ☆
GRAPES Pinot Noir
REGION Waipara
CELLAR 🍾 1–4
PRICE $38–42

Pressed in a traditional basket press, this big-hearted pinot was hand-plunged three times a day to extract as much flavour and colour from the skins as possible. After that, it spent nine months in French oak barrels.

Current Release 2001 Plums and cherries – the classic pinot associations – are in good shape on the nose. It's a big smoothie on the palate, with sweet fruit characters enhanced by the gentle tannins. The finish is long and memorable. It's good with beef and kumara kebabs.

Whitehaven Pinot Noir

STYLE dry
QUALITY ♟ ♟ ♟ ♟
VALUE ☆ ☆ ☆ ☆ ☆
GRAPES Pinot Noir
REGION Marlborough

CELLAR 🍾 3
PRICE $22–25

The fruit came from a range of vineyards in the Wairau, Awatere and Brancott Valleys, and it was all harvested by hand. After that, the winemaking team plunged the skins back into the fermenting juice at frequent intervals.

Current Release 2000 Cherries and a touch of mushroom set the scene in classic pinot style. It's a smooth-centred middleweight on the palate, instantly attractive and enjoyable with straightforward food like grilled chicken thighs arranged over a pile of puy lentils.

Winslow Colton Reserve Pinot Noir

STYLE dry
QUALITY ♟ ♟ ♟ ♟
VALUE ☆ ☆ ☆ ☆
GRAPES Pinot Noir
REGION Martinborough

CELLAR 🍾 2
PRICE $28–30

The vines were around six years old, but this was the first wine to be made from them. Winemaker Elise Montgomery fermented and matured the juice in a mixture of French and American oak barrels, about 25% of them new, for nine months.

Current Release 2001 Spicy oak behind the plum and cherry aromas give this wine a big bouquet. After that introduction the smooth, middleweight flavour profile is a bit of a surprise. It's pleasant, sweet-fruited and approachable, and goes well with that old flatting favourite, spaghetti Bolognese.

Wither Hills Pinot Noir

This stylish red is one of the most popular restaurant pinots on the market, despite the fact that it is often priced at $80-plus on the list, and sometimes considerably more. It deserves its success.

Current Release 2001 It's got all the right cherry and mushroom aromas on the nose, and a flavour profile that repeats those associations in approachably smooth surroundings. The finish is sweet-edged and satisfying. Enjoy it with seared kingfish steaks, served with a reduction of tomatoes and red onions.

STYLE **dry**
QUALITY ♟ ♟ ♟ ♟ ♟
VALUE ☆ ☆ ☆ ☆
GRAPES **Pinot Noir**
REGION **Marlborough**
CELLAR 🍾 **4**
PRICE **$40–44**

Pinotage and Blends

Wines made from pinotage, a cross between pinot noir and cinsault, used to be reasonably common in this country, but the variety fell from favour through the '80s and early '90s. There was a flurry of interest when sanctions were lifted on wines from South Africa, because this is the only other place in the world where it is grown, and some big, chunky examples came in and got people talking. That seems to have settled down, and pinotage has now regained its place in the scheme of things, as a grape that in most cases produces light to middleweight reds with a certain amount of peppery charm, but not a lot of depth or richness.

Babich East Coast Pinotage/Cabernet

STYLE **dry**
QUALITY ♟ ♟ ♟
VALUE ☆ ☆ ☆
GRAPES
　Pinotage 80%
　Cab Sauvignon 20%
REGION Gisborne
　　　Hawke's Bay
　　　Auckland
CELLAR 🍾 2
PRICE $13–15

The Babichs have been making wine from the pinotage grapes grown behind their winery for many years. The gnarled old vines contributed only a small part of this blend – as the label suggests, most of the fruit came from the East Coast.
Current Release 2000 Well, it's certainly berryish on the nose – think raspberries, blackberries and blackcurrants and you'll be close. It starts with a belt of fruit sweetness, but things get pretty lean in the middle and on the tomato-leaf finish. Match it with food that shares its touch of acid, like goat cheese or tomatoes.

Babich Winemakers Reserve Pinotage

STYLE **dry**
QUALITY ♟ ♟ ♟ ♟
VALUE ☆ ☆ ☆
GRAPES Pinotage
REGION Hawke's Bay
CELLAR 🍾 3
PRICE $22–24

Fruit for this big-hearted red came from Gimblett Road, Hawke's Bay, considered one of the premium red wine regions in the country. Adam Hazeldine put it into new American and used French oak barrels for a year.
Current Release 2000 Think junior syrah and you'll have a handle on this red. It's vaguely plummy, rustic and savoury, and there's a nice whiff of cracked pepper in there as well. Sweet-fruited and smooth on the palate, it makes a good partner for a pepper steak, pan-fried medium-rare and served with shoestring fries.

Kerr Farm Kumeu Pinotage

The fermenting juice for this red was plunged by hand four times a day to maximise the uptake of flavour and colour. It paid off – it has won both silver and bronze medals on the show circuit.

Current Release 1999 Chocolate and smoky oak combine well in the bouquet. It's a sweet-fruited, pleasant middleweight with soft, nicely balanced tannins and a medium-length finish. The back label suggests enjoying it with friends on the veranda 'some cruisy afternoon'. Fair enough!

STYLE **dry**
QUALITY ♉♉♉♉
VALUE ☆☆☆☆
GRAPES **Pinotage**
REGION **West Auckland**
CELLAR **2**
PRICE **$16–18**

Matua Valley Pinotage/Cabernet Sauvignon

Pinotage used to be reasonably common, fell from favour in the '80s and enjoyed a brief renaissance when big-hearted South African versions were allowed in following the collapse of apartheid. Matua is one of the few companies still using it.

Current Release 2000 I'm glad they are! The variety has added an earthy note to the primary aromas of raspberries and blackcurrants. It's a pleasant middleweight on the palate with good mouth feel and a short but sweet-fruited finish. I wouldn't place it with a haunch of venison, but it's perfectly okay with corned beef.

STYLE **dry**
QUALITY ♉♉♉
VALUE ☆☆☆☆☆
GRAPES **Pinotage**
　　　　Cab Sauvignon
REGION **Gisborne**
　　　　Hawke's Bay
CELLAR **2**
PRICE **$11–13**

Muddy Water Waipara Pinotage

This is the only pinotage we know of in the Waipara region, but it's a goodie. The Muddy Water team seems to have an affinity for the variety.

Current Release 2000 There's a pleasant peppery edge on the aromas of ripe blackberries. It's broad, sweet-fruited and appealing on the palate, with just enough grip on the lingering finish A piece of really old cheddar should suit it well, but serve it either solo or with crusty bread, not crackers.

STYLE **dry**
QUALITY ♉♉♉♉
VALUE ☆☆☆
GRAPES **Pinotage**
REGION **Waipara**
CELLAR **1–4**
PRICE **$26–30**

Okahu Estate Shipwreck Bay Pinotage/Chambourcin/Merlot

Monty Knight changes the percentages from vintage to vintage, but the three grapes stay the same. The wine spends its quiet time in a mixture of new and used oak barrels, mostly American but a few French.

Current Release 2001 Sweet-fruited with a spicy edge on the nose and smartly balanced on the palate, this is an approachable wine with ripe flavours and subdued tannins. Partner it with barbecued lamb chops and you should be a happy wine lover.

STYLE **dry**
QUALITY ♉♉♉
VALUE ☆☆☆
GRAPES
　Merlot 50%
　Chambourcin 25%
　Pinotage 25%
REGION **Northland**
CELLAR **1**
PRICE **$17–19**

Pleasant Valley Signature Selection Auckland Pinotage

STYLE **dry**
QUALITY ♟ ♟ ♟
VALUE ☆ ☆ ☆
GRAPES **Pinotage**
REGION **Auckland**

CELLAR 🍾 3
PRICE **$14–16**

The Yelas family has been making wine since the early 1900s, and today Stephan Yelas still produces quite a few different styles. This red spent six months in French oak barrels.
Current Release 1999 The nose is pretty stalky, but typical cracked pepper aromas are fighting to make their presence felt. It's soft-centred and pleasant enough on the palate, but don't expect the earth to move. Still, it should go okay with a rare pepper steak.

Riverside Stirling Pinotage

STYLE **dry**
QUALITY ♟ ♟ ♟ ♟
VALUE ☆ ☆ ☆ ☆
GRAPES **Pinotage**
REGION **Hawke's Bay**

CELLAR 🍾 3
PRICE **$20–23**

Pinotage is a rarity in Hawke's Bay, but Ian and Rachel Cadwallader and their winemaker, Russell Wiggins, had enough confidence in their fruit to give this one special marketing treatment – the name Stirling is used on only their best wines.
Current Release 2000 Plums and an impression of hot-climate dust set the scene. It's a smoothly balanced middleweight, with ripe fruit and about the right amount of tannin for the style. It would make a good partner for a pepperoni pizza, served with a simple green salad.

Saints Vineyard Selection Hawke's Bay Pinotage

STYLE **dry**
QUALITY ♟ ♟ ♟
VALUE ☆ ☆ ☆
GRAPES **Pinotage**
REGION **Hawke's Bay**

CELLAR 🍾 3
PRICE **$17–19**

Montana has a 23-acre pinotage block in Hawke's Bay, and all the fruit goes into this red. Steve Voysey and Brent Laidlaw matured it in a mixture of new and used French and American oak barrels.
Current Release 1999 Gentle spice backs the aromas of strawberries and raspberries in the bouquet, which is all highly acceptable. It's light and pleasant on the palate, with no sharp edges through the middle and a short but clean-cut finish. It goes well with peppered beef schnitzels.

Saints Vineyard Selection Marlborough Pinotage

STYLE **dry**
QUALITY ♟ ♟ ♟
VALUE ☆ ☆ ☆
GRAPES **Pinotage**
REGION **Marlborough**

CELLAR 🍾
PRICE **$17–19**

Past wines wearing this label have been made from Hawke's Bay grapes, but this one originated from Montana's giant Renwick Estate vineyard in Marlborough. I think they should have stuck with the Bay.
Current Release 2001 The bouquet has suggestions of charred oak behind aromas vaguely reminiscent of plums and cherries. It's rustic on the front palate and boasts some quite good fruit, but drifts into reediness in the middle and on the finish. It's acceptable with casual nibbles, but will never be an earth-mover.

Sanctuary Marlborough Pinotage/Pinot Noir

Why hasn't anyone else thought of this blend? It makes sense, given that pinotage is a cross of pinot noir and cinsault. The wine was fermented in tanks but put in a mixture of French and American barrels for a year to mature.

Current Release 2001 There's some attractively gentle spice on the nose to back the plum and strawberry aromas, but things get pretty lean in the flavour department. It's not without appeal, but I've preferred earlier vintages. Chill it slightly and use it as a light-hearted summer sipper.

STYLE **dry**
QUALITY ♟♟♟
VALUE ☆ ☆ ☆
GRAPES **Pinotage 90%**
Pinot Noir 10%
REGION **Marlborough**
CELLAR 🍾 **1**
PRICE **$15–17**

Soljans Estate Auckland Pinotage

Tony Soljan and the team stuck with pinotage when most producers abandoned it, but used Gisborne fruit for the '98 and '99 versions. They returned to West Auckland for the first example from the new millennium.

Current Release 2000 Sweet loam and cherries make a pleasant enough introduction. It's sweet-fruited, a little lean in the middle but with a suggestion of chocolate adding extra interest to the finish. It would be good with a platter of mixed salami and triangles of grilled pita bread

STYLE **dry**
QUALITY ♟♟♟
VALUE ☆ ☆ ☆ ☆
GRAPES **Pinotage**
REGION **Auckland**
CELLAR 🍾 **2**
PRICE **$15–17**

Te Awa Farm Longlands Pinotage

Pinotage is grown only in New Zealand and South Africa, and there's not a lot of it about. It seems an unusual variety to attract the interest of Te Awa Farm winemaker Jenny Dobson, given that she learned her skills in Bordeaux, France.

Current Release 2000 I get a dash of Aussie-style eucalyptus on the nose, along with aromas that remind me of greengage plums. It's a warm-hearted middleweight on the palate with reasonably ripe flavours backed by a dash of spice on the finish. It's good with a savoury lamb casserole, served with mashed potatoes.

STYLE **dry**
QUALITY ♟♟♟
VALUE ☆ ☆ ☆
GRAPES **Pinotage**
REGION **Hawke's Bay**
CELLAR 🍾 **2**
PRICE **$25–27**

Yelas Winemaker's Reserve Auckland Pinotage

This stylish red, from Stephan Yelas of the Pleasant Valley winery in West Auckland, spent nine months in brand-new French oak barrels. It is one of only a handful of premium pinotages on the market.

Current Release 1999 Smoky oak backs the ripe fruit aromas in the bouquet. It's soft, with a reasonable depth of ripe fruit flavour and a short but pleasantly peppery finish. If you can find a recipe for an Italian dish called eggplant timbale, it's a perfect partner.

STYLE **dry**
QUALITY ♟♟♟
VALUE ☆ ☆ ☆
GRAPES **Pinotage**
REGION **Auckland**
CELLAR 🍾 **1–4**
PRICE **$20–23**

Syrah (Shiraz)

Syrah, or shiraz if you prefer the Australian interpretation of the name, has been grown here for more than a century, but nobody did much with it until the mid '80s. Now, it is appearing everywhere from the far north to the deep south. It has a reputation for preferring a super-hot climate, so growing it in Canterbury or Marlborough would seem to be a lost cause — some commentators would argue that it definitely is. Nevertheless, eminently drinkable examples have been produced from grapes grown in what must be pretty inhospitable conditions, largely through the costly technique of cutting off half the bunches and discarding them, forcing the vines to concentrate their efforts into cramming flavour into the grapes that remain. Syrah is unlikely to ever become our greatest red, but it is certainly capable of playing a worthwhile part in our nationwide vinous tapestry.

Ata Rangi Syrah

STYLE dry
QUALITY ♟ ♟ ♟ ♟ ♟
VALUE ☆ ☆ ☆
GRAPES Syrah
REGION Martinborough
CELLAR ▯ 4
PRICE $40–43

New Zealand Syrah producers are still a rare commodity, but the numbers are slowly increasing. This is a new addition to the list, but it is already widely regarded as one of the best examples yet.
Current Release 2001 Cracked black pepper and ripe plums are joined by a suggestion of chocolate on the nose. It's smooth, lush and mysteriously complex on the palate, with a long, sweet-fruited finish. Enjoy it with liver and bacon in freshly made tomato sauce.

Babich Winemakers Reserve Syrah

STYLE dry
QUALITY ♟ ♟ ♟ ♟ ♟
VALUE ☆ ☆ ☆ ☆ ☆
GRAPES Syrah
REGION Hawke's Bay
CELLAR ▭ 1–3
PRICE $22–25

The fruit came from the heart of the Gimblett Gravels area and the wine spent time maturing in new American oak and used French barrels. That's an impressive heritage, and makes this one of the bargains in its class.
Current Release 2000 I like the faint impression of cracked pepper behind the upfront plumminess. Those plum characters cut in again on the finish, but between the first and last impressions there's a wealth of sweet fruit flavour edged by savoury oak. It makes a splendid companion for braised beef spooned over mashed potatoes.

Bilancia Syrah

Warren Gibson and Lorraine Leheney's Bilancia vineyard is called 'la collina', which is Italian for hillside. The vines grow at the base and up the side of a steep hill in the heart of the Gimblett Gravels sub-region. This is only their second syrah.
Current Release 2001 Cracked pepper and spice (and all things nice?) set the scene. It's a smartly fruited wine with plum and cherry flavours in a smooth-edged package. Partner it with casseroled duck legs and you should be very happy indeed.

STYLE **dry**
QUALITY ⚑ ⚑ ⚑ ⚑
VALUE ☆ ☆ ☆
GRAPES **Syrah**
REGION **Hawke's Bay**
CELLAR 🍷 3
PRICE **$34-36**

Brookfields Hillside Syrah

Peter Robertson has made his name with blends of the Bordeaux trio – cabernet sauvignon, merlot and cabernet franc. Now he's gone to France's Rhône Valley, the home of syrah, for his inspiration. The French would be impressed.
Current Release 2001 Cracked black pepper sits behind the primary aromas of ripe Black Doris plums. It's impressively sweet-fruited on the front palate, boasts a fabulously smooth texture through the middle and finishes with just the right amount of grip. Sorry vegetarians – it really needs a rare cervena steak to set it off.

STYLE **dry**
QUALITY ⚑ ⚑ ⚑ ⚑ ⚑
VALUE ☆ ☆ ☆
GRAPES **Syrah**
REGION **Hawke's Bay**
CELLAR 🍷 1-6
PRICE **$45-48**

Clevedon Hills Syrah

Made by Vin Alto's Margaret and Enzo Bettio from grapes nurtured by talkback supremo, Leighton Smith, this is an extremely impressive début. Leighton has long dreamed of producing a great syrah, and he has succeeded with his first vintage.
Current Release 2000 Delicious! That's the immediate impression from the smoky oak, ripe plum and clove aromas. The richly fruited flavour profile carries on the good impression. It's full, firm and boasts a lingering finish. Casseroled red meat is the ideal match – beef, cervena or even kangaroo (well, Leighton IS Australian!).

STYLE **dry**
QUALITY ⚑ ⚑ ⚑ ⚑
VALUE ☆ ☆ ⚑
GRAPES **Syrah**
REGION **Clevedon**
CELLAR 🍷 1-6
PRICE **$85-95**

Corbans Shiraz

The wine was made by Peter Hurlstone at Montana's Auckland winery, but the grapes came from a handful of sites in Victoria and South Australia. It spent six months gaining extra character from French and American oak.
Current Release 2001 There's a smoky character behind the aromas of ripe raspberries and plums. It's light and approachable on the palate, but lacks warmth. Take it to a crowded barbecue and forget it was once yours.

STYLE **dry**
QUALITY ⚑ ⚑ ⚑
VALUE ☆ ☆ ☆ ☆
GRAPES **Shiraz**
REGION
   NW Victoria
   South Australia
CELLAR 🍷
PRICE **$14-16**

Corbans White Label Shiraz

STYLE dry
QUALITY ▽ ▽ ▽
VALUE ★ ★ ★ ★
GRAPES Shiraz
REGION Australia
CELLAR 🍾
PRICE $8–10

You won't find any wines made from New Zealand-grown shiraz at this sort of price. The grape is not easy to grow on our side of the ditch, which is why this one is made in Australia and finished off here.

Current Release 2000 There's some good peppery spice on the nose, along with at least a dash of plum character. It's pretty lightweight on the palate, but the plum impressions carry through to give it a modicum of richness. Try it with Wiener schnitzels and fries.

Crossroads Classic Syrah

STYLE dry
QUALITY ▽ ▽ ▽ ▽
VALUE ★ ★ ★ ☆
GRAPES Syrah
REGION Hawke's Bay
CELLAR 🍾 3
PRICE $25–27

It's gone from Reserve to Classic in the transition from 1999 to 2001, but the price is the same. Whatever – it's nicely made wine that reinforces the future for this variety in the Bay. Local versions are more reminiscent of France than Australia.

Current Release 2001 There's a rustic character on the nose that I rather like, with ripe plum aromas content to take a back seat. The flavours are moderately rich and the oak spicy and appealingly textured. It's good with eggplant and zucchini fritters served with lightly spiced home-made tomato sauce.

Crossroads Reserve Syrah

STYLE dry
QUALITY ▽ ▽ ▽ ▽
VALUE ★ ★ ★ ☆
GRAPES Syrah
REGION Hawke's Bay
CELLAR ▤ 1–3
PRICE $25–27

Former partner and winemaker Malcolm Reeves says syrah seems pretty happy on the free-draining, shingle-covered soils around the Gimblett Road region, and that's where the grapes came from for this member of the Crossroads portfolio.

Current Release 1999 The bouquet is sweet-fruited, spicy and plummy, and the same description could be used for the flavour profile. It's not a big wine, but it has a pleasant texture courtesy of the well-integrated tannins. The finish is ripe and satisfying. It should work well with a seared ostrich steak.

Denton Syrah

STYLE dry
QUALITY ▽ ▽ ▽ ▽
VALUE ★ ★ ★ ★
GRAPES Syrah
REGION Nelson
CELLAR 🍾 2
PRICE $20–23

This is one of the least expensive wines in the Denton collection, but I think it's a little beauty. On the face of it, Nelson doesn't seem the obvious place to grow the heat-loving syrah grape, but it obviously likes the local clay soils.

Current Release 1999 There's a savoury edge on the cherry aromas and a dash of cracked black pepper at the back. It's not a big wine, but it boasts thoroughly pleasant sweet-edged fruit edged by gentle tannins. It's good with thin beef steak, pressed with cracked black pepper and quickly seared.

Dry River Arapoff Amaranth Syrah

Want to make a statement on the dinner table? This red is also available in 1500ml magnums, at a cost of $95. My good friend, Master of Wine Bob Campbell, says it's the best local syrah he's ever tasted.

Current Release 1998 A touch of charred oak sits behind a rush of cherry/berry aromas, and I fancy there's a dash of cracked pepper in there as well. The flavours are opulent, the texture impressively smooth and the finish long-lasting and supremely satisfying. Partner it with a classic filet mignon with mushrooms.

STYLE dry
QUALITY 🍷🍷🍷🍷🍷
VALUE ★★★
GRAPES Syrah
REGION Martinborough
CELLAR 2–6
PRICE $40–44

Glover's Spring Grove Shiraz

Most people label their syrah as just that, but Dave Glover prefers to use the Australian version of the name. He describes this member of his portfolio as 'rare and beautiful', but you might spot the odd bottle around the Nelson region.

Current Release 2000 Charred oak and attractive spice sit behind the Black Doris plum aromas. It's solid on the front palate but smooths out nicely through the middle before finishing with a whack of sweet fruit. It sits happily alongside a plate of mini-sandwiches made from rare beef and decent grainy mustard.

STYLE dry
QUALITY 🍷🍷🍷½
VALUE ★★½
GRAPES Shiraz
REGION Nelson
CELLAR 5
PRICE $30–33

Kennedy Point Vineyard Syrah

Adding a little bit of white juice to red wine is reasonably common in parts of France and Italy, so the Kennedy Point team thought they'd give it a go. The wine then spent 15 months in French oak barrels.

Current Release 2000 Sweet, plummy aromas introduce a smartly fruited palate structure. The tannins are nicely subdued, but add about the right amount of grip for the style. It's a well-balanced wine that should suit home-made pizza, simply topped with mozzarella, pulped tomatoes and basil.

STYLE dry
QUALITY 🍷🍷🍷🍷½
VALUE ★★★½
GRAPES Syrah 99%
Viognier 1%
REGION Waiheke Island
CELLAR 3
PRICE $34–38

La Strada Reserve Syrah

You'll need clairvoyant powers to track this wine down. Only 30 cases were sold in this country, but because a few were bought by dedicated retailers and restaurateurs, the odd bottle still surfaces.

Current Release 1999 It's more Rhône than Australia, and that's all to the good. The pepper and stewed plum aromas set a cracking pace, and the rich, mouth-filling flavours carry on the theme. It's a serious red that makes a great partner for cervena back steaks, cooked rare.

STYLE dry
QUALITY 🍷🍷🍷🍷🍷
VALUE ★★★
GRAPES Syrah
REGION Marlborough
CELLAR 5
PRICE $43–45

La Strada Syrah

STYLE dry
QUALITY 🍷 🍷 🍷 🍷
VALUE ☆ ☆ ☆ ☆
GRAPES Syrah
REGION Marlborough
CELLAR 🍾 1–3
PRICE $27–29

Syrah in Marlborough? On paper, it's a tough call. In our part of the world, the variety seems to like a bakingly hot climate, but Hatsch Kalberer is doing his best to prove otherwise.
Current Release 1997 Plums and cracked pepper make themselves equally at home in the bouquet. The flavours are more Rhône than Australia, but that's fine by me – think rich plum conserve and you'll get the picture. Only a hint of greenness on the finish mars the good impression. Enjoy it with a serious chunk of sirloin.

Langdale of Canterbury Winemaker's Selection Petit Syrah

STYLE dry
QUALITY 🍷 🍷 🍷 🍷
VALUE ☆ ☆ ☆ ☆
GRAPES Syrah
REGION Canterbury
CELLAR 🍾 1–4
PRICE $28–33

The wine is labelled petit syrah. It should probably be spelled petite syrah, but whatever name it goes by, it's the same grape others call syrah or shiraz. To confuse the issue, the Californians label a grape called durif as petite sirah (spelled with an 'i').
Current Release 1999 Cracked pepper with raspberries sounds an unlikely combination, but that's what I get on the nose. It's a soft-centred middleweight, smartly made and boasting nicely balanced tannins that add grip and length. Winemaker Carol Bunn says it's great alongside duck with a star anise and plum sauce.

Matariki Reserve Hawke's Bay Syrah

STYLE dry
QUALITY 🍷 🍷 🍷 🍷
VALUE ☆ ☆ ☆
GRAPES Syrah
REGION Hawke's Bay
CELLAR 🍾 4
PRICE $40–43

The fruit for John and Rosemary O'Connor's top-of-the-line syrah came from the heart of the Gimblett Gravels sub-region, and the juice was matured in French oak barrels, 39% of them new, the remainder between one and three years old.
Current Release 2000 Combine stewed plums and Chinese five-spice powder and you'll have something approximating the bouquet. It's a nicely balanced wine with plenty of sweet fruit flavours and a smooth texture through the middle. The finish is sweet-edged and long. I had a glass recently with a reasonably authentic haggis, and it worked well.

Matariki Syrah

STYLE dry
QUALITY 🍷 🍷 🍷 🍷
VALUE ☆ ☆ ☆
GRAPES Syrah
REGION Hawke's Bay
CELLAR 🍾 3
PRICE $40–43

This wine has proved a big success for John and Rosemary O'Connor in its various vintages. In '98 and '99 colours, it has twice picked up the 'Best Other Red' trophy at the New Zealand Wine Society Royal Easter Wine Show.
Current Release 2000 If you like reds with a bit of rustic 'grunt', this is for you. The aromas are decidedly earthy and the flavour profile firm and chunky. It certainly appeals to me, but I've got friends who have found it a bit over-the-top. It's great alongside a rare beef and rocket sandwich, made from the most rustic-looking bread you can find.

Mills Reef Elspeth Syrah

The 1999 version of this red was the only New Zealand wine served at a charity dinner in London organised for the Wine and Spirits Trades Benevolent Society. The others came from Australia, the US, Chile, South Africa and Italy.

Current Release 2001 It's a big, earthy wine but it boasts some delightfully ripe fruit characters. It smells of ripe plums and raspberries, with spicy oak also playing a part. The flavours are pretty full-on and the tannins add plenty of grip. It suits char-grilled food, so choose beef, ostrich or cervena steaks.

STYLE **dry**
QUALITY ♟♟♟♟♟
VALUE ★★☆
GRAPES **Syrah**
REGION **Hawke's Bay**
CELLAR 🍾 **5**
PRICE **$40–43**

Mission Gimblett Road Reserve Syrah

Fourteen months in a mixture of French and American oak – that's what winemaker Paul Mooney decided was about right for this classy red. He didn't filter it, so it might throw a bit of sediment.

Current Release 1998 Smoky oak and a dash of cracked pepper can both be found in the bouquet, but mostly it smells like plum conserve. It's smooth, broad and classy on the palate, with well-balanced tannins and a long finish. Pull the cork next time you're having a good old-fashioned beef stew with dumplings.

STYLE **dry**
QUALITY ♟♟♟♟♟
VALUE ★★★★☆
GRAPES **Syrah**
REGION **Hawke's Bay**
CELLAR ⬜▭ **1–4**
PRICE **$24–28**

Montana Shiraz

Montana now produces around half-a-dozen wines made here from Australian grapes, and intended for the New Zealand market. This one came from the Barossa Valley, McLaren Vale and Riverland, and spent six months in American oak barrels.

Current Release 2001 Berry and plum aromas are evident, but they're very gentle. It's light, smooth and acceptable on the palate, but doesn't ring any bells. Still, it would work quite well with beef sausages rolled into thin slices of lightly buttered bread.

STYLE **dry**
QUALITY ♟♟♟
VALUE ★★★★
GRAPES **Shiraz**
REGION
   South Australia
CELLAR 🍾
PRICE **$15–17**

Morton Estate Hawke's Bay Syrah (White Label)

Evan Ward enjoys working with the syrah grape, and this well-priced example of his skills is a big seller at the winery shop in Katikati. The shop is fronted by Brian Farmer, whose knowledge of wines from around the world is encyclopaedic.

Current Release 2000 Charred oak sits behind the aromas of ripe plums on the nose. It's a smooth-centred middleweight, with gentle tannins adding just enough grip to the ripe-fruited flavours. Evan recommends it for game, so if you can track down some wild venison, test his theory.

STYLE **dry**
QUALITY ♟♟♟
VALUE ★★★★
GRAPES **Syrah**
REGION **Hawke's Bay**
CELLAR 🍾 **2**
PRICE **$19–22**

Mudbrick Vineyard Syrah

STYLE dry
QUALITY ♟♟♟♟
VALUE ☆☆☆
GRAPES Syrah 91%
　　　　Malbec 9%
REGION
　Waiheke Island
CELLAR 4
PRICE $30–33

The views from the Mudbrick winery restaurant are spectacular, and make dining there a great fine-day experience. The wines are hard to find, but they're all available at the cellar door. This one is particularly rare – only 12 barrels were made.

Current Release 2001 Cracked pepper is a classic syrah association, and there's plenty of it on the nose, backed by smoky oak. It's quite plummy on the palate, with integrated tannins adding about the right amount of grip. The finish is reasonably long. It's not a big syrah, but it works well with casseroled lamb.

Murdoch James Shiraz

STYLE dry
QUALITY ♟♟♟♟♟
VALUE ☆☆☆
GRAPES Syrah
REGION Martinborough
CELLAR 1–4
PRICE $40–45

Temperature-controlled undergound cellars enabled the Fraser family to keep this wine cool for its 12-month sojourn in French oak barrels. The winery marketing sheet suggests cellaring for 8–10 years. I've been more cautious, but they could well be right.

Current Release 2000 There's some delightful spice on the nose to go with the ripe plum aromas. It's richly fruited and smartly balanced, with plenty of berry and plum flavours and a suggestion of bitter-sweet chocolate right on the finish. I can't imagine anything better with oxtail, cooked long and lovingly.

Okahu Estate Kaz Shiraz

STYLE dry
QUALITY ♟♟♟♟
VALUE ☆☆
GRAPES Syrah
REGION Northland
CELLAR 1–4
PRICE $50–55

Monty Knight was told he was crazy to grow syrah (shiraz is an alternative name for the same grape) in the far north, but he had the last laugh. This grunty evocation of the variety has been widely praised.

Current Release 2000 Sweet plummy fruit is supported by savoury oak in the bouquet, and the same characters transfer themselves pretty well intact to the front palate. It's a generous wine, with smartly integrated tannins and a wealth of ripe fruit. It makes a good partner for braised beef with baby carrots and onions.

C.J. Pask Reserve Syrah

STYLE dry
QUALITY ♟♟♟♟
VALUE ☆☆☆
GRAPES Syrah
REGION Hawke's Bay
CELLAR 3
PRICE $35–38

Kate Radburnd is enjoying working with a variety that has been touted as having a great future in the Bay. She certainly didn't hold back on the oak treatment – it spent 16 months in French oak casks, and they were all brand-new.

Current Release 2000 The new oak was dominating the plum aromas when I tried the wine, but it should have settled down by now. It's richly flavoured, with a fabulously smooth texture right through to the lingering finish. It makes a really good partner for corned beef with grainy mustard.

Passage Rock Oakura Bay Syrah

Most winemakers across the Tasman mature their syrah (which they call shiraz) in American oak, but French is the norm in New Zealand. David Evans-Gander split the difference. Half the maturation barrels were American, the rest were French.

Current Release 2000 Smoky oak is much in evidence in the bouquet, with aromas reminiscent of ripe plums lurking in the background. It's sweet-fruited and rich on the palate with nicely integrated tannins adding a reasonable amount of grip through the middle and on the finish. Try it alongside a medium-rare pepper steak.

STYLE **dry**
QUALITY ♟♟♟♟♟
VALUE ☆☆☆
GRAPES **Syrah**
REGION
Waiheke Island
CELLAR ⬛ **1—4**
PRICE **$36—39**

Peninsula Estate Anchorage Syrah

Peninsula's syrah has been labelled Gilmour in past vintages, but for 2000 it was given the name of the nearest charted rock to the vineyard. It must be quite a rock – it apparently forms part of the David and Maria Island group.

Current Release 2000 The bouquet carries all the right smoke and ripe plum associations, suggesting good things to come. It's pleasantly smooth on the palate, boasting obviously ripe fruit and smartly integrated tannins from its time in oak barrels. It goes well with a casserole of well-peppered beef, eggplant and zucchini.

STYLE **dry**
QUALITY ♟♟♟♟
VALUE ☆☆
GRAPES **Syrah**
REGION
Waiheke Island
CELLAR ⬛ **1—3**
PRICE **$40—44**

Saints Vineyard Selection Shiraz

Peter Hurlstone made this red at Montana's Auckland winery, but the grapes were grown in South Australia. It was fermented over a 10-day period to extract maximum skin colour, then spent nine months in a mixture of French and American oak barrels.

Current Release 2001 Charred oak is obvious on the nose, dominating the plum and raspberry aromas. It's light, smooth and approachable on the palate, with gentle tannins and a sweet-edged finish. Barbecued kangaroo steaks would be a geographically appropriate accompaniment.

STYLE **dry**
QUALITY ♟♟♟
VALUE ☆☆☆☆
GRAPES **Shiraz**
REGION
South Australia
CELLAR 🍾 **2**
PRICE **$16—18**

Stonecroft Crofters Syrah

Alan Limmer uses the Crofters label for wines made from grapes he feels are less than perfect. That gives the brand's many fans the opportunity to buy at a very good price. It's labelled 2000, but the cabernet and merlot are from 1999.

Current Release 2000 Charred, smoky oak sits behind the ripe plum aromas. It's light on the front palate and a little thin through the middle, but there are some pleasantly berryish fruit flavours in there. Enjoy it alongside a brace of barbecued spiced beef sausages.

STYLE **dry**
QUALITY ♟♟♟
VALUE ☆☆☆⯪
GRAPES
Syrah 90%
Cab Sauvignon 6%
Merlot 4%
REGION **Hawke's Bay**
CELLAR 🍾 **2**
PRICE **$20—23**

Stonecroft Syrah

STYLE dry
QUALITY ♟♟♟♟♟
VALUE ☆☆☆
GRAPES Syrah
REGION Hawke's Bay
CELLAR 5
PRICE $38–42

Alan and Glen Limmer are widely regarded as the best producers of syrah in the country, although Dry River's Neil and Dawn McCallum have given them a serious nudge a couple of times.
Current Release 1999 The spice – partly varietal, partly from oak – is pretty upfront, but mainly the aromas are reminiscent of ripe plums and raspberries. It's smooth-centred, immaculately balanced and thoroughly pleasant to drink. What more can I say? It's the perfect wine for roast duck.

Te Awa Farm Longlands Syrah

STYLE dry
QUALITY ♟♟♟♟
VALUE ☆☆☆
GRAPES Syrah
REGION Hawke's Bay
CELLAR 3
PRICE $35–38

Predictably, given that she completed her winemaking trraining in Bordeaux, Jenny Dobson favours the French style of syrah over the Aussie interpretation. This nicely balanced example of her skills sells well at the pleasant winery restaurant.
Current Release 2000 It's not a big wine – that was not Jenny's aim. The aromas are of ripe plums and the flavours lean towards raspberries, with a dash of spice from the oak for extra interest. Braised beef steak makes a pleasant accompaniment.

Te Mata Bullnose Syrah

STYLE dry
QUALITY ♟♟♟♟♟
VALUE ☆☆☆☆
GRAPES Syrah
REGION Hawke's Bay
CELLAR 3
PRICE $35–37

Why Bullnose? Vineyard owners Michael Morris and Peter Cowley are classic car fans, and named it for the 'bullnosed' Morris Cowley. The stylised bull on the label is taken from the car company logo – with appropriate permission, of course!
Current Release 2000 Plums, cloves, spice and leather. How's that for an aromatic quartet! It's smooth on the palate thanks to the restrained tannins, allowing the sweet fruit to dominate proceedings in a most satisfactory fashion. Food? It's got to be meat, and it's got to be wild. Hare, cooked rare, would do nicely.

Trinity Hill Hawke's Bay Syrah

STYLE dry
QUALITY ♟♟♟♟
VALUE ☆☆
GRAPES Syrah
REGION Hawke's Bay
CELLAR 3
PRICE $39–42

Winery manager John Hancock says this wine is a 'personal triumph'. The fruit was picked by hand, so only the best grapes were selected. He aimed to produce a wine in the style of France's Rhône Valley rather than Australia's Barossa Valley.
Current Release 2000 The bouquet is smoky and spicy, very much in a Rhône Valley style. It's sweet-edged and ripe on the palate, with suggestions of plums and cherries. It works really well alongside casseroled venison, ideally wild, although the farmed variety would certainly do.

Unusual and Unspecified Red Varieties and Blends

In this chapter, you will find not only 'drink now' wines labelled Dry Red and so on, but also multi-grape blends that carry only a proprietary name, without reference to the varieties from which they're made. Some specify the grapes on the back label, but as this *Guide* is designed to help you make a decision as you peruse the hundreds of labels on wine shop shelves, they have been listed here rather than in the chapters devoted to specific grapes.

Borthwick Estate Sangiovese

Paddy Borthwick has planted nearly half of his 14-hectare property in Dakins Road, Gladstone. Choosing sangiovese was a bit of a punt, but he has been pleased with his first efforts. Unfortunately, it's pretty hard to find.

Current Release 1999 Strawberry and plum aromas start things off nicely. It's certainly not big, but it has some pleasant berryish flavours in rather rustic surroundings. If you can get hold of some rabbit, use a little to bolster the stock in which you casserole it, then enjoy the rest as an accompaniment.

STYLE **dry**
QUALITY ♟ ♟ ♟ ♟
VALUE ☆ ☆ ☆
GRAPES
  Sangiovese Grosso
REGION **Wairarapa**

CELLAR **3**
PRICE **$22–24**

Artisan Fantail Island Vineyard Dominic

The Fantail Island vineyard at Oratia, West Auckland, is owned by Artisan founders Rex and Maria Sunde. They sourced some of their vines from Gerard Chave at Hermitage, in France. Only 60 cases were made of this three-grape blend.

Current Release 2001 There's a gentle savoury note on the bouquet, but mostly the aromas are of ripe berries. It's light and pleasant, and would make a good hot-day accompaniment for a platter of summertime nibbles like olives, various types of salami and the like.

STYLE **dry**
QUALITY ♟ ♟ ♟ ♟
VALUE ☆ ☆ ☆ ☆
GRAPES
  Gamay 60%
  Pinot Noir 30%
  Syrah 10%
REGION **West Auckland**

CELLAR **2**
PRICE **$17–19**

Ata Rangi Célèbre

STYLE dry
QUALITY ▽▽▽▽▽
VALUE ☆☆☆

GRAPES
Syrah 40%
Cab Sauvignon 40%
Merlot 20%

REGION Martinborough

CELLAR 4
PRICE $32–35

The blend for this big-hearted red varies quite drastically from year to year, but that hasn't prevented it from building up a huge following. It's particularly popular at restaurants around the country.

Current Release 2000 Cracked pepper and mocha coffee form an appealing introduction. It's deliciously sweet-fruited on the palate, with tannins that are more subdued than I remember from previous examples. It would make a perfect partner for casseroled cervena served with garlicky mashed potatoes.

Crossroads Hawke's Bay Talisman

STYLE dry
QUALITY ▽▽▽▽▽
VALUE ☆☆☆

GRAPES A winery secret
REGION Hawke's Bay

CELLAR 4
PRICE $38–42

The winery tells us that the six grape varieties in this blend were picked over a three-week period, but they won't say what they are. Merlot, syrah, cabernet franc, cabernet sauvignon, malbec and pinot noir are likely bets – see what you think.

Current Release 1999 Charred oak is in enthusiastic form on the berryish bouquet, but the fruit is big enough to take it. It's full, berryish and super-ripe on the palate, with the oak returning to give a tannic kick to the finish. Partner it with a serious rare beef sandwich, made with top-grade steak and grainy bread.

Heron's Flight Matakana Sangiovese

STYLE dry
QUALITY ▽▽▽▽▽
VALUE ☆☆

GRAPES
Sangiovese Grosso
REGION Matakana

CELLAR 5
PRICE $50–55

David Hoskins and Mary Evans love the way the sangiovese grape performs in Matakana, and are in the process of pulling other varieties out so they can plant more of it. Instead of a front label, the bottle has a pewter 'badge' of a flying heron.

Current Release 1999 The sweet, smoky oak on the nose is the result of a full year in new French barrels. The flavours are reminiscent of plums and blackberries, with a faintly liquorice edge. Obviously, it should accompany Italian food – try it with fettucine tossed with a spiced fresh tomato sauce.

Herzog Montepulciano

STYLE dry
QUALITY ▽▽▽▽▽
VALUE ☆☆☆

GRAPES
Montepulciano 85%
Cab Franc 15%

REGION Marlborough

CELLAR 5
PRICE $68–72

The tasting note put out by the Herzogs describes this wine as 'exotic and kinky', the latter word a first in wine-speak to the best of my knowledge. However you describe it, it's mightily impressive.

Current Release 2000 The bouquet is smooth and berryish and the flavour profile rich, full-on and so disturbingly addictive the label should carry a warning. I can think of no better match for an Italian-style wild boar casserole, but a good old Kiwi beef stew would do almost as well.

Hunter's Marlborough Sangiovese

It doesn't carry a vintage on the front, but the back label tells us Gary Duke blended wines from the 1996, 1998 and 1999 vintages to make this red, the first sangiovese from the Hunter's team. It's available mostly at the cellar door.

Current Release (non-vintage) The nose is berryish with a touch of crushed mint leaf and spice at the back. It's a clean, undemanding middleweight in the flavour department, and would make a good partner for a platter if summery nibbles – various salamis, olives and the like.

STYLE **dry**
QUALITY ♟ ♟ ♟
VALUE ☆ ☆ ☆
GRAPES
    Sangiovese Grosso
REGION **Marlborough**
CELLAR 🍾 2
PRICE **$19–21**

Kemblefield The Reserve Zinfandel

Making zinfandel has been a long-time dream for California-born John Kemble. He worked with the variety when he began his winemaking career at Ravenswood, in the Sonoma Valley, regarded as one of the top exponents of the style.

Current Release 2000 It's a good start, but I don't think it's the ultimate expression. The nose was oaky enough to bury the fruit when I tried it, and although the flavour profile was quite richly fruited, I detected a touch of leafiness towards the finish. It might settle down, so give it a year or two then try it with a genuine US-style hamburger.

STYLE **dry**
QUALITY ♟ ♟ ♟
VALUE ☆ ☆
GRAPES **Zinfandel**
REGION **Hawke's Bay**
CELLAR 🍾 3
PRICE **$51–53**

La Strada Sangiovese/Montepulciano

The two Italian grapes that make up this blend are often confused with one another in this country, but Hatsch Kalberer is convinced he's got the genuine article growing in his stone-covered Marlborough vineyard.

Current Release 1998 This is a pretty wine – berryish on the nose, charmingly sweet-fruited on the palate. That makes it sound light, but in fact it has some pretty serious tannins towards the back. It would make a good partner for fettucine with a classic Italian ragu sauce.

STYLE **dry**
QUALITY ♟ ♟ ♟ ♟ ♟
VALUE ☆ ☆ ☆ ☆
GRAPES
    Sangiovese Grosso 50%
    Montepulciano 50%
REGION **Marlborough**
CELLAR 🛏 1–4
PRICE **$46–49**

Lombardi Hawke's Bay Sangiovese/Cabernet Sauvignon

Lombardi's heritage is Italian and the portfolio includes an estate-grown olive oil, so making wine from Italian grape varieties was inevitable. This one puts Italy and France together – European unity in a bottle!

Current Release 2000 The nose is perfumed with a smoky edge, and there's a whack of sweet berry aromas in there as well. It's broad on the palate, impressively smooth and with a reasonably long finish. The food you enjoy with it has to be Italian, so try a classic osso buco.

STYLE **dry**
QUALITY ♟ ♟ ♟ ♟
VALUE ☆ ☆ ☆ ☆
GRAPES
    Sangiovese Grosso 50%
    Cab Sauvignon 50%
REGION **Hawke's Bay**
CELLAR 🍾 3
PRICE **$34–36**

Matua Valley Innovator Grenache

STYLE **dry**
QUALITY ♟♟♟♟♙
VALUE ☆ ☆ ☆⯪
GRAPES **Grenache**
REGION **Hawke's Bay**
CELLAR ▭ **1–3**
PRICE **$25–27**

There's not a lot of grenache grown in New Zealand. Mark Robertson got these grapes from a vineyard in the Ngatarawa region, where the soil is lean, red-tinged and scattered with river shingle that reflects sun back onto the ripening bunches.

Current Release 2000 Spicy and smoky on the nose, sweet-fruited and smartly balanced on the palate, this is nice wine. You want flavour associations? Try cherries and stewed plums. It's good with beef stew, but it's also rather good as a casual sipper, alongside a platter of savoury nibbles.

Mills Reef Elspeth One

STYLE **dry**
QUALITY ♟♟♟♟♟
VALUE ☆ ☆ ☆
GRAPES
  Merlot 45%
  Cab franc 15%
  Syrah 15%
  Malbec 15%
  Cab sauvignon 10%
REGION **Hawke's Bay**
CELLAR ▭ **1–4**
PRICE **$49-53**

Mills Reef has had a great deal of success with a series of outstanding Hawke's Bay reds. This one, the blend for which may change from year to year, is aimed right for the top – and deserves to reach it.

Current Release 2000 Charred oak, blackberries, red and black currants, plums – all the aromatic associations are there, and they're all in great shape. It's big and complex, but has a smooth heart. If you get the chance, partner it with casseroled wild venison.

Millton Gisborne Malbec Opou Vineyard

STYLE **dry**
QUALITY ♟♟♟
VALUE ☆ ☆ ☆
GRAPES **Malbec**
REGION **Gisborne**
CELLAR ▯ **2**
PRICE **$20-23**

Gisborne is known as white wine country, but quite a few red varieties have been trialled there over the years. The Milltons have been sensible with this one, not trying for a blockbuster and suggesting it should be enjoyed young.

Current Release 2000 The earthy bouquet suggests it is going to be a 'biggie', but in fact it is quite light in the flavour department. It has all the right plum and blackberry flavours and there's certainly nothing to object to, but it won't get you excited. Enjoy it with easy-going autumn nibbles.

Omaka Springs Marlborough Gamay

STYLE **dry**
QUALITY ♟♟♙
VALUE ☆ ☆ ☆
GRAPES **Gamay**
REGION **Marlborough**
CELLAR ▯
PRICE **$15-17**

Gamay is the grape used to produce Beaujolais Nouveau, the inoffensive red that is traditionally the first French wine on the market each year. New Zealand wines made from it are exceedingly rare.

Current Release 2000 The nose is chunky, with a smoky edge. So far, so good – but after that promising introduction it's lean and mean on the palate, with a leafy edge on the raspberry flavours. If you find yourself with a bottle, chill it lightly and share it with beer drinkers.

Solstone Quartet

Made from hand-picked fruit and matured in French oak barrels for a year, this four-grape blend is a popular buy at the many cafés and casual restaurants around the Wairarapa region. The makers suggest cellaring it for five or six years, but I've been a little more cautious.
Current Release 2001 Smoky oak and ripe blackberries get it together in the bouquet. It's a softly spoken red, and that makes it very approachable. Sweet fruit cruises through the middle, supported by gentle tannins. The finish is clean and pleasant. It goes well with dishes featuring grilled eggplant, either as part of a salad or atop a pizza.

STYLE **dry**
QUALITY ♟ ♟ ♟ ♟
VALUE ☆ ☆ ☆
GRAPES
  Cab Sauvignon 25%
  Cab Franc 25%
  Merlot 25%
  Malbec 25%
REGION Wairarapa
CELLAR 3
PRICE $25–28

Waiheke Vineyards Island Red

You won't see this two-grape red every year. It's a joint effort between the three Waiheke Island 'originals', Goldwater, Peninsula Estate and Stonyridge, and it is made from fruit considered not quite good enough for each property's top label.
Current Release 2000 Berryish and open-fruited in the bouquet, soft and non-frightening on the palate, this is an everyday red that should suit even those who profess to enjoy only white. Pull the cork next time you're planning to toss a tomato-dominant sauce through some good imported Italian penne pasta.

STYLE **dry**
QUALITY ♟ ♟ ♟
VALUE ☆ ☆ ☆
GRAPES
  Cab Sauvignon 50%
  Merlot 50%
REGION
  Waiheke Island
CELLAR 2
PRICE $25–28

Woodthorpe Gamay Noir

Te Mata Estate's owners, the Buck family, say they have a 'serious' clone of Gamay, not the light-hearted version that is used in France for Beaujolais Nouveau.
Current Release 2002 Now this is fun! The aromas are reminiscent of cherries and spice (and all things nice?), and the flavours are sweet-edged and moreish. That adds up to instant appeal. It's great with pink-cooked lamb cutlets.

STYLE **dry**
QUALITY ♟ ♟ ♟ ♟ ♟
VALUE ☆ ☆ ☆ ☆
GRAPES Gamay Noir
REGION Hawke's Bay
CELLAR 3
PRICE $19–22

Sparkling Wines, Rosé and Blush Wines, Dessert Wines

SPARKLING WINES

	QUALITY	VALUE	PRICE
Alan McCorkindale Brut	🍷🍷🍷½	★★½	$30-33
Allan Scott Méthode Traditionelle	🍷🍷🍷🍷	★★★½	$24-26
Aquila	🍷🍷½	★★★	$9-11
Arcadia Brut	🍷🍷🍷½	★★★	$21-23
Arcadia Lake Hayes Cuvée Brut 1998	🍷🍷🍷🍷	★★★	$30-33
Bernadino Spumante	🍷🍷🍷	★★★★	$7-9
Canterbury House Méthode Traditionelle	🍷🍷🍷½	★★★½	$24-27
Coopers Creek First Edition	🍷🍷🍷½	★★★½	$23-26
Corbans Winemakers Private Bin Marlborough Cuvée Riche 1997	🍷🍷🍷½	★★★	$25-27
Corbans Diva Brut Cuvée	🍷🍷	★★½	$9-12
Corbans Diva Cuvée	🍷🍷	★★½	$9-12
Cuvée Virginie Le Brun	🍷🍷🍷🍷🍷	★★½	$45-49
Daniel Le Brun Brut	🍷🍷🍷🍷	★★★½	$28-32
Daniel Le Brun Brut Taché	🍷🍷🍷½	★★½	$29-33
Daniel Le Brun Blanc de Blancs Vintage 1996	🍷🍷🍷🍷🍷	★★★½	$37-39
Daniel Le Brun Vintage 1996	🍷🍷🍷🍷½	★★★	$37-39

SPARKLING WINES

(continued)	QUALITY	VALUE	PRICE
Danie L Number One	🍷🍷🍷🍷	★★★	$35-38
Danie L Number Eight	🍷🍷🍷🍷½	★★★½	$27-29
Deutz Marlborough Cuvée	🍷🍷🍷🍷🍷	★★★	$29-33
Deutz Marlborough Cuvée Blanc de Blancs	🍷🍷🍷🍷🍷	★★★	$36-41
Elstree Cuvée Brut 1998	🍷🍷🍷🍷🍷	★★★	$29-33
Emmi 1995	🍷🍷🍷½	★★★½	$32-34
Fusion	🍷🍷🍷	★★★★	$11-13
Giesen Voyage	🍷🍷🍷½	★★★	$22-24
Gillan Brut	🍷🍷🍷	★★★	$23-26
Huia Marlborough Brut 1998	🍷🍷🍷🍷	★★½	$36-38
Hunter's Brut 1998	🍷🍷🍷½	★★★	$29-32
Jackson Vintage Brut 1994	🍷🍷🍷🍷½	★★★	$28-32
Johanneshof Emmi 1995	🍷🍷🍷	★★½	$32-35
Kaikoura Méthode Champenoise	🍷🍷🍷	★★½	$25-27
Kim Crawford Rory Brut 1996	🍷🍷🍷	★★★	$30-33
Lindauer Brut	🍷🍷🍷	★★★★★	$10-13
Lindauer Fraise	🍷🍷	★★★	$13-16
Lindauer Grandeur Cuvée	🍷🍷🍷🍷½	★½	$39-43
Lindauer Rosé	🍷🍷🍷	★★★½	$10-13
Lindauer Sec	🍷🍷½	★★½	$10-13
Lindauer Special Reserve	🍷🍷🍷🍷	★★★★½	$16-18
Matariki Blanc de Blanc 1997	🍷🍷🍷🍷	★★½	$38-43
Mills Reef Traditional Method	🍷🍷🍷	★★★★	$20-23

SPARKLING WINES

(continued)	QUALITY	VALUE	PRICE
Morton Brut	🍷🍷🍷🍷	★★★★	$18-21
Morton Méthode Champenoise 1995	🍷🍷🍷🍷½	★★★½	$32-26
Morton RD 1995	🍷🍷🍷🍷🍷	★★★	$25-27
Nautilus Cuvée Marlborough Brut	🍷🍷🍷🍷	★★★	$32-35
Nobilo Brut Pinot Noir Chardonnay	🍷🍷🍷½	★★★★	$14-16
Odyssey Blanc de Blancs Méthode Traditionelle 1999	🍷🍷🍷🍷	★★★½	$28-32
Palliser Estate Martinborough Méthode Traditionelle 1998	🍷🍷🍷🍷½	★★½	$35-38
Pelorus	🍷🍷🍷🍷½	★★★	$34-37
Pelorus Vintage 1998	🍷🍷🍷🍷🍷	★★½	$43-47
Perelle Lake Hayes Grande Cuvée Brut	🍷🍷🍷	★★½	$25-28
Quartz Reef Chauvet Brut	🍷🍷🍷🍷½	★★★★	$24-27
Saveé Sparkling Sauvignon Blanc	🍷🍷🍷½	★★★	$20-23
St Aubyns Dry	🍷🍷½	★★★½	$6-8
St Aubyns Medium	🍷🍷½	★★½	$6-8
Selaks Premium Selection Méthode Traditionelle	🍷🍷🍷	★★★	$23-27
Seresin Moana 1996	🍷🍷🍷🍷½	★★★	$40-43
Shingle Peak Marlborough Méthode Traditionelle	🍷🍷🍷½	★★★½	$18-21
Soljans Legacy	🍷🍷🍷	★★★½	$20-23
Terrace Road Classic Brut	🍷🍷🍷½	★★★	$19-21
Twin Islands Pinot Noir/Chardonnay Brut	🍷🍷🍷	★★★	$16-19
Verde	🍷🍷🍷½	★★★	$17-19
Vidal Brut 1994	🍷🍷🍷🍷	★★★½	$21-25

SPARKLING WINES

(continued)	QUALITY	VALUE	PRICE
White Cloud Sparkling	♟♟♟	★★★	$8-12
Woodbourne Estate Marlborough Blanc de Noir 1998	♟♟♟♟	★★★	$28-30

ROSÉ AND BLUSH WINES

	QUALITY	VALUE	PRICE
Alan Scott Marlborough Rosé 2002	♟♟♟♟	★★★★	$16-18
Ata Rangi Summer Rosé 2002	♟♟♟♟♟	★★★★	$17-19
Esk Valley Rosé 2002	♟♟♟♟♟	★★★	$17-19
Forrest Estate Marlborough Rosé 2002	♟♟♟♟	★★★	$16-18
Hunter's Marlborough Rosé 2002	♟♟♟	★★★★	$13-15
Linden Estate Merlot Rosé 2002	♟♟♟♟	★★★	$17-19
Margrain Pinot Rosé 2002	♟♟♟♟	★★★	$22-24
Martinborough Vineyard Rosé (500ml)	♟♟♟♟	★★★	$18-20
Mills Reef Rosé 2002	♟♟♟♟	★★★★	$14-16
Millton Merlot Rosé 2002	♟♟♟♟	★★★	$18-21
Okahu Estate Shpwreck Bay Rosé 2002	♟♟♟	★★★	$17-19
Onetangi Road Rosé 2001	♟♟♟♟	★★★★	$18-20
Redmetal Vineyards Rosé 2002	♟♟♟♟♟	★★★	$24-26
Riverside Dartmoor Rosé 2002	♟♟♟	★★★	$12-14
Rymer's Change Rosé 2002	♟♟♟♟	★★★★	$16-18
Sileni Cellar Selection Rosé 2002	♟♟♟♟♟	★★★★	$19-22
Unison Rosé 2002	♟♟♟♟♟	★★★★	$17-19
Winslow Rosetta Cabernet Rosé 2002	♟♟♟♟♟	★★★	$27-29

DESSERT WINES (375ml unless otherwise specified)

	QUALITY	VALUE	PRICE
AD Noble Selection 1998	♟♟♟♟♟	★★⯪	$40-43
Alpha Domus Leonardo Late Harvest Sémillon 2000	♟♟♟♟		$18-21
Ata Rangi Kahu Botrytised Riesling 2002	♟♟♟♟⯪	★★★	$28-32
Askerne Botrytised Sémillon 2000	♟♟♟	★★⯪	$25-27
Cainbrae Late Harvest Riesling 2001	♟♟♟	★★★	$20-23
Charles Wiffen Dessert Riesling 2000	♟♟♟♟♟	★★★	$28-34
Church Road Reserve Hawke's Bay Noble Sémillon 1997	♟♟♟♟⯪	★★⯪	$33-36
Clearview Estate Noble 51 2000	♟♟♟♟♟	★★	$65-70
Cloudy Bay Late Harvest Riesling 2000	♟♟♟♟♟	★★★⯪	$26-29
Collard Botrytis Riesling 1999	♟♟♟★★★★★		$20-23
Cooper's Creek Late Harvest Riesling 2000	♟♟♟⯪★★★★★		$19-23
Esk Valley Reserve Chenin Blanc Botrytis Selection 2000	♟♟♟♟	★★★	$40-43
Forrest Estate Marlborough Botrytised Chenin Blanc 2000	♟♟♟⯪	★★⯪	$27-29
Forrest Estate Marlborough Botrytised Riesling 2002	♟♟♟♟♟	★★★⯪	$27-29
Fromm La Strada Riesling Auslese (750mls)	♟♟♟♟⯪	★★★⯪	$42-46
Fromm La Strada Riesling Beerenauslese 2001	♟♟♟♟♟	★★	$90-95
Isabel Marlborough Noble Sauvage 1999	♟♟♟	★★	$49-53
Jackson Estate Botrytis Riesling 1999	♟♟♟♟⯪	★★★	$29-33
Johanneshof Marlborough Noble Late Harvest 1995	♟♟♟♟♟	★★★	$34-36

DESSERT WINES

(continued)

	QUALITY	VALUE	PRICE
Johanneshof Riesling Auslese 2001 (750ml)	♟♟♟♟	☆☆☆☆	$28-32
Lawsons Dry Hills Late Harvest 2001	♟♟♟♟♟	☆☆☆☆	$20-23
Margrain Riesling Botrytis Selection 2002	♟♟♟♟	☆☆☆	$30-33
Martinborough Vineyard Late Harvest Riesling 2002	♟♟♟♟♟	☆☆☆	$35-37
Matariki Late Harvest Riesling 2001	♟♟♟♟♟	☆☆☆	$29-32
Matus Valley Late Harvest Muscat 2002	♟♟♟♟	☆☆☆☆	$13-16
Mission Ice Wine 2002	♟♟♟	☆☆☆	$15-17
Mission Jewelstone Noble Riesling 1999	♟♟♟♟♟	☆☆☆	$30-33
Muddy Waters Sticky Fingers 1999	♟♟♟	☆☆☆☆	$14-19
Morton Estate Hawke's Bay Sémillon/Chardonnay 2000	♟♟♟♟	☆☆☆	$30-33
Ngatarawa Alwyn Reserve Late Harvest Riesling 2000	♟♟♟♟♟	☆☆☆	$60-63
Ngatarawa Glazebrook Noble Harvest Riesling 2000	♟♟♟♟♟	☆☆☆	$32-35
Olssen's of Bannockburn Desert Gold Late Harvest Riesling 2001	♟♟♟♟	☆☆☆	$35-37
Palliser Estate Martinborough Noble Chardonnay 2000	♟♟♟♟♟	☆☆☆☆	$23-27
Pegasus Bay Aria 2001 (750ml)	♟♟♟♟♟	☆☆☆☆	$28-32
Pegasus Bay Finale Noble Chardonnay 1999	♟♟♟♟♟	☆☆☆	$35-37
Reka 2000	♟♟♟♟	☆☆☆	$35-37
Rongopai Vintage Reserve Riesling Selection 2000	♟♟♟♟	☆☆☆	$25-27

DESSERT WINES

(continued)

	QUALITY	VALUE	PRICE
Sacred Hill h.a.l.o. Bortytis Sémillon 2000	🍷🍷🍷🍷 (4½)	★★★½	$25-27
Saints Gisborne Noble Sémillon 2000	🍷🍷🍷½	★★★★	$17-19
Seifried Riesling Ice Wine 2000	🍷🍷🍷🍷	★★★★	$21-23
Selaks Marlborough Ice Wine 2000	🍷🍷🍷½	★★★★	$14-17
Sileni Estate Selection Late Harvest Sémillon 2002	🍷🍷🍷½	★★★½	$22-24
Sileni Estates Pourriture Noble 2001	🍷🍷🍷🍷½	★★★	$32-35
Stables Late Harvest 2000	🍷🍷🍷½	★★½	$17-19
Te Mania Nelson Late Harvest Botrytis Riesling 2000	🍷🍷🍷½	★★½	$27-29
Villa Maria Noble Riesling Botrytis Selection 2001	🍷🍷🍷🍷🍷	★★★	$48-52
Virtu Noble Semillon 1996	🍷🍷🍷🍷🍷	★★★	$40-43
Waimea Estates Late Harvest Riesling 2001	🍷🍷🍷½	★★★½	$16-18
Waipara Springs Botrytised Riesling 2000	🍷🍷🍷	★★½	$28-32
Wairau River Botrytised Riesling Reserve 1999	🍷🍷🍷🍷	★★★	$35-40
West Brook Blue Ridge Late Harvest Riesling 2000	🍷🍷🍷🍷	★★★	$27-29
Whitehaven Single Vineyard Reserve Noble Riesling 2000	🍷🍷🍷🍷	★★★½	$19-21

Glossary

Acid More obvious in white wine than red, acid is the upfront crispness that gives a wine 'zing' in the mouth. Think about biting into a chilled gala apple and you'll be close.

Aftertaste The taste sensation that lingers after the wine has been swallowed. Sometimes described as 'finish'.

Alcohol A by-product of the fermentation process. Wines with a lot of alcohol often feel warm in the mouth.

Alcohol by volume The amount of alcohol expressed as a percentage of the contents of the bottle. Must be printed on the label by law.

Aperitif A drink taken before a meal with the purpose of stimulating the appetite.

Aroma A grapey odour most often detected in young wine. Strictly speaking, it's not the same as a wine's bouquet, but the two are often used interchangeably.

Aromatic A quality that makes a wine's characters seem to jump out of the glass. Obvious in most Marlborough sauvignon blanc.

Astringent Extremely dry and often tannic, causing puckering of the cheeks. Can mean the wine will age well.

Auslese German term, sometimes used by New Zealand winemakers to describe a wine that is sweet.

Autolysis Usually called yeast autolysis, and used to describe the fresh-baked bread character found in the bouquet of some sparkling wines.

Back-blending The process of adding unfermented grape juice to finished wine to add sweetness and body.

Balance Harmony between the wine's various flavour components. Think of an orchestra where no one player dominates.

Barnyard A not-unpleasant character often found in wines that have been matured in used barrels.

Barrel An oak container in which some wines are fermented and/or aged. French oak is spicier and more subtle than American.

Barrel fermentation The process of fermenting the infant wine in oak barrels rather than stainless steel tanks. Particularly popular for chardonnay, and detected by mealy, nutty aromas.

Barrique The most common size of barrel, holding 225 litres. Considered the optimum size to give just enough oak character to the wine.

Bead The bubbles in sparkling wine.

Beerenauslese German term, used occasionally in New Zealand to describe a sweet dessert wine.

Bitterness Desirable in beer, but not in wine. Picked up most readily at the back of the mouth, and showing that the wine has been over-enthusiastically pressed, or is suffering from spoilage.

Blend A mixture of two or more components, usually either different grape varieties or grapes from different regions.

Body Mouth-filling substance – the opposite of thin.

Botrytis Full name *Botrytis cinerea*. A mould that forms on the surface of some grapes and sucks out the water. Not always desirable, but when the skin doesn't split, grapes infected with it can make some of the most glorious sweet wines in the world.

Bouquet The jigsaw of interesting and, hopefully, pleasant aromas given off by the wine. Some come from the grapes, forming part of the aroma, but most are created during the winemaking process. More important than the taste when determining quality and origin.

Breathing The process of allowing air into the wine by removing the cork and (sometimes) decanting. To some extent, it compresses the ageing process, and is therefore useful in allowing fiercely tannic young reds to be enjoyed long before their prime.

Broad A wine that is soft and sometimes flabby.

Brut The lowest level of sweetness in sparkling wine. Only *brut natur* or similarly labelled wines are drier.

Carbonic maceration The technique of fermenting whole, uncrushed bunches of grapes. It makes red wines that are chock-full of flavour when they are young, but which usually fade after a couple of years.

Cassis An aroma often found in cabernet sauvignon, named after a blackcurrant liqueur originally from Dijon, in France.

Chalky A dry, dusty character sometimes found in very young wine.

Cheesy A sour-milk character that suggests carelessness with the wine's malolactic fermentation.

Cigar box The smell of wood and tobacco often found in young cabernet sauvignon and, especially, merlot.

Cloudy Tiny particles suspended in the wine, causing it to lose its sheen. A cause for concern.

Cloying Sweet and out of balance, so that the palate is overpowered by sugar without redeeming acid.

Corked Tainted by a faulty cork. Often detected by a smell like the inside of an old wardrobe, or damp cardboard. Corked bottles should always be rejected in restaurants, or returned to suppliers.

Creamy Smooth and viscous – a textural term usually applied to white wine.

Crisp As refreshing as biting into a chilled, tree-ripened apple. Usually applied to white wine.

Cuvée French term for a blend of varieties or vintages.

Depth Richness and generosity of flavour.

Doughnut A wine that starts and finishes well, but lacks flavour in the middle.

Dry A wine with no apparent sweetness.

Dull Unexciting. Can be used to describe the colour, the bouquet or the taste.

Dumb Lacking bouquet and, to some extent, taste. May be simply the product of excessive youth or over-chilling.

Dusty A mouth-feel caused by the presence of oak components in the wine, particularly obvious in hot-climate reds.

Earthy A loamy, barnyard character, often adding character and interest.

Esters Volatile compounds that sometimes occur during maturation. They can be detected by a medicinal character in the bouquet.

Extractive A very tannic wine that has spent considerable time fermenting on the grape skins, extracting maximum flavour. Acceptable if it's not overdone.

Finesse Delicacy and elegance.

Fining The process of floating a substance (classically, beaten egg whites) on top of unfiltered wine to force solid particles to the bottom of the tank or barrel. The wine is then siphoned into another container.

Finish See aftertaste.

Firm The opposite of flabby. Wine that seems complete and well-controlled.

Flabby Lacking acid 'zing' (whites) or tannic firmness (reds).

Fleshy A grapey character often found in young wines.

Flinty A dry, stony odour like a newly struck flint.

Flowery (floral) Aromatic and highly perfumed.

Fortified Wine strengthened by the addition of brandy or grape spirit, e.g. port and sherry.

Freeze concentration The process of freezing the water content of grape juice to allow the remaining syrup to be pumped off. Used to make sweet wine.

Fresh Full of youthful exuberance.

Furry A tooth-coating sensation caused by tannin.

Garlic A highly undesirable odour that indicates the presence of sorbic acid.

Generic In this country, usually means a wine labelled simply 'New Zealand', rather than according to the region where the grapes were grown.

Grassy A herbaceous character sometimes found in young sauvignon blanc, particularly from Marlborough. Not desirable in reds.

Grip The feeling that the wine has got hold of the inside of your mouth. The opposite of flabby.

Hard Ungiving, lacking warmth.

Hollow A wine with no middle. See doughnut.

Hot A warm sensation in the mouth, usually caused by high alcohol.

Implicit sweetness The sensation of sweetness in a dry wine, usually caused by glycerol or a high alcohol level, and sometimes simply by very ripe fruit.

Inky Once used to describe a metallic taste caused by contact with iron fittings. Since most iron in wineries has been replaced by stainless steel, the term is now used to describe the colour of a red wine so dark it's opaque.

Integrated The marriage of wine's various components. See balance.

Jammy Obvious, unsubtle aromas and flavours sometimes found in young reds.

Late harvest Wine made from grapes that have been left to hang on the vine for days or weeks after the normal harvest time, causing them to shrivel like raisins and concentrate their sugars. Usually used to make sweet wines.

Leathery An earthy aroma often associated with merlot.

Lifted Desirable aromas that help give the wine a distinctive bouquet.

Limpid Very clean and bright. Used to describe the colour.

Long A lingering finish. Sign of a very good wine.

Malic acid The sharp, fruit acid found in grapes. Think Granny Smith apples.

Malolactic fermentation The natural process that converts malic (fruit) acids into lactic (milk) acids, and therefore softens the wine. Happens in all red wines, but not all whites. Can be controlled by the winemaker, and is often used for 20–30% of chardonnay juice.

Meaty Commonly, a wine with lots of body, but occasionally used as a criticism, to describe a raw beef character.

Mercaptans Unpleasant odours variously reminiscent of stale cabbage, burned rubber, old garlic or dirty socks.

Méthode Champenoise and **Méthode Traditionelle** The process of putting wine through a second fermentation in the actual bottle in which it will eventually be sold. Used to create the world's best sparkling wines.

Mouldy An unpleasant smell that can come from the use of a faulty cork or grubby old barrels.

Mousse The bubbly head on sparkling wine.

Mousy A grubby aroma or taste caused by bacterial spoilage. Like the bottom of a pet mouse's cage.

Mouth feel The feeling in the mouth, such as viscosity, as opposed to the flavour.

Must The mixture of skins, pips and odd leaves and stalks left after the juice has been extracted from the grapes.

Musty A stale odour, caused by a faulty cork or old barrels.

Nose The wine's smell or bouquet.

Nutty A pleasant odour and taste sometimes found in oak-aged whites.

Oxidation Excessive exposure to air, causing a browned colour and flat taste.

Peppery A flavour usually found in Australian shiraz, but also associated with New Zealand syrah and pinotage.

Phenolics Resin-like substances produced by the presence of solids in the fermenting wine.

Preservative Substance, usually sulphur, added to wine in minute quantities to guard against spoilage.

Pressings The mixture of skins and pips left after the weight of grapes has extracted the first 'free-run' juice. Sometimes added back to increase the uptake of colour and flavour.

Pricked A smell like glue or floor polish. Betrays the undesirable presence of ethyl acetate.

Prickly Slightly effervescent. Usually found in young whites, sometimes by design.

Puncheon A barrel holding 500 litres. Less desirable than a barrique because there is a greater wine-to-wood ratio.

Pungent A wine with a glass-leaping bouquet.

Rancio A nutty character often found in old fortified wines.

Residual sugar Unfermented, naturally occurring fructose and/or glucose remaining in the wine after fermentation is complete.

Rough Out of balance; unrefined.

Round Smooth, velvety and generous in the mouth.

Rubbery Betrays the presence of mercaptans. A fault.

Sappy A stalky character sometimes found in wines made from unripe grapes. Early Marlborough cabernets were notorious for it.

Sec French term for dry, but sometimes used here to denote slightly sweet.

Soft A wine with a smooth, unctuous structure.

Solera A series of barrels containing wine from various vintages. The newest is topped up from the next in line, and so on until the oldest wine is used. Common in the production of sherry.

Solids Suspended particles of skin and flesh. Removed by cold-settling, filtration or fining.

Spicy Spice-like character, most often associated with gewürztraminer but also found in some oak-aged wines.

Stalky Green, bitter character caused by having too many stalks in with the grape juice, or by picking immature grapes.

Tannin A character most often associated with wood, but also found in the skins, pips and stalks of grapes. Gives grip to red wine and helps it age with character.

Tart Suggests a temporary excess of acid. Should soften with age.

Toasty A desirable well-done toast character usually caused by using barrels with heavily charred interiors.

Trockenbeerenauslese A term used in Germany and occasionally New Zealand to describe a super-sweet dessert wine.

Vanillan A vanilla-bean character often found in wine that has been aged in American oak barrels.

Varietal Wine that strongly reflects the character of the grape variety used to make it.

Volatile Spoiled by an excess of undesirable components such as acetic and formic acids.

Volatile acidity (VA) See volatile.

Wood ageing The process of ageing wine in oak barrels, to add complexity and flavour.

Yeast autolysis See autolysis.

Notes